The Art of Digital Video

The Art of Digital Video

Fourth Edition

John Watkinson

AMSTERDAM • BOSTON • HEIDELBERG • LONDON • NEW YORK • OXFORD
PARIS • SAN DIEGO • SAN FRANCISCO • SINGAPORE • SYDNEY • TOKYO

Focal Press is an imprint of Elsevier

Senior Acquisitions Editor: Angelina Ward
Publishing Services Manager: George Morrison
Project Manager: Lianne Hong
Assistant Editor: Kathryn Spencer
Marketing Manager: Christine Degon, Marcel Koppes
Cover Design: Eric DeCicco
Cover Images: iStockphoto

Focal Press is an imprint of Elsevier
30 Corporate Drive, Suite 400, Burlington, MA 01803, USA
Linacre House, Jordan Hill, Oxford OX2 8DP, UK

 Recognizing the importance of preserving what has been written, Elsevier prints its
books on acid-free paper whenever possible.

Library of Congress Cataloging-in-Publication Data
Watkinson, John, 1950-
The art of digital video / by John Watkinson. — 4th ed.
   p. cm.
Includes bibliographical references and index.
ISBN-13: 978-0-240-52005-6 (hardcover : alk. paper) 1. Digital video. I. Title.
TK6680.5.W383 2008
778.59—dc22

                                                     2007047332

British Library Cataloguing-in-Publication Data
A catalogue record for this book is available from the British Library.

ISBN: 978-0-240-52005-6

For information on all Focal Press publications
visit our website at www.books.elsevier.com

08 09 10 11 5 4 3 2 1

Typeset by Charon Tec Ltd (A Macmillan Company), Chennai, India
www.charontec.com

Printed in the United States of America

Working together to grow
libraries in developing countries

www.elsevier.com | www.bookaid.org | www.sabre.org

ELSEVIER   BOOK AID International   Sabre Foundation

For Liza

Contents

CHAPTER 5   Digital Video Processing

Preface to Fourth Edition

Since the first edition of this book was published in 1990, digital technology has caused some far-reaching changes in the way television programs are produced and broadcast. Early digital video equipment was large, expensive, and unusual, whereas today it is the norm. This author argued long ago that once it became possible to digitize video then digital video would be indistinguishable from other types of data. This has certainly been borne out. Increasingly television systems are adopting information technology (IT) solutions instead of dedicated equipment. The maintenance requirement has fallen dramatically as equipment becomes more reliable. The tremendous rate of development of flat screens has meant that the cathode ray tube has practically died out.

Techniques such as MPEG compression, along with the ever-falling cost of hard disk storage, have had a considerable impact and will continue to do so. Increasingly production is performed, at least in standard definition, on workstations connected to file servers by IT-based networks, meaning that traditional solutions such as digital video recorders and digital video interfaces are in decline. That change of emphasis is reflected in this book. Whilst IT has been used in television production to lower costs and increase flexibility, it also must change television out of recognition. The widespread availability of Internet access provides competition that must erode traditional television viewing. The availability of random-access technology at consumer prices means that commercial breaks can be edited out by the viewer, and this destroys the business model of commercial television.

Not surprisingly this book has also changed out of recognition. At one time the readers of this book might well have been specialists, but that is no longer the case, and this book must be suitable for a wider audience. Naturally all of the new technologies are included here, but there is one thing that is not new, and that is the approach that this book has always taken, which is to approach complex subjects a step at a time from straightforward beginnings. To suit a wide range of readers, some of the more complex subjects have been separated out into essays, and some of the key topics have been highlighted.

Earlier editions argued the quality advantages of digital video, whereas this now seems superfluous. With the widespread use of heavy compression to deliver an unparalleled number of television channels, the technical quality has fallen to match the thinly spread program-making talent.

Digital technology is also allowing the cinema to compete more strongly, whereas television fights back with high definition. It remains to be seen what will happen in the long term.

John Watkinson
Burghfield Common, April 2008

Acknowledgments

I must first thank David Kirk, who invited me to write a series on digital video for Broadcast Systems Engineering, the magazine which he then edited, and Ron Godwyn, who succeeded him. The response to that series provided the impetus to turn it into a book.

Earlier editions of this book owe much to the support of Margaret Riley of Focal Press who is now enjoying well-earned retirement.

The publications of the Society of Motion Picture and Television Engineers, the European Broadcasting Union and the Audio Engineering Society have been extremely useful.

I am indebted to the many people who have found time to discuss complex subjects and to suggest reference works. Particular thanks go to David Lyon, Roderick Snell, Tim Borer, Bruce Devlin, Takeo Eguchi, Jim Wilkinson, David Huckfield and John Ive, Steve Owen, Yoshinobu Oba, Mark Schubin, Luigi Gallo, Mikael Reichel, Graham Roe, David Stone, Robin Caine, Dave Trytko, Joe Attard, John Watney, Fraser Morrison, Roger Wood, Tom Cavanagh, Steve Lyman, Kees Schouhamer Immink, Peter de With, Gerard de Haan, Ab Weber, Tom MacMahon, Dave Marsh, John Mallinson and Peter Kraniauskas.

This edition could not have reached the present high standard without the professionalism of Amorette Pedersen of Elsevier Burlington.

John Watkinson
Burghfield Common, England

xv

CHAPTER 1
Introducing Digital Video

Digital video is a large subject that draws upon an equally large number of technologies. Fortunately, every process can be broken down into smaller steps, each of which is relatively easy to follow. The main difficulty in the study is to appreciate where the small steps fit into the overall picture. The purpose of this chapter is to summarise the subject and to point out how those technologies are used, without attempting any explanations beyond basics. More comprehensive explanations can be found in the later chapters that are identified here.

TELEVISION SYSTEMS

Ultimately, the purpose of television is to amuse human eyes and ears. Without an understanding of the human visual system (HVS) and the human auditory system (HAS) little progress is to be expected. This book will have something to say about those systems and their expectations in Chapters 2 and 7. Whatever the technology used, television systems all have the same basic requirements. As a minimum, equipment is needed to *acquire* moving images and associated sounds and to broadcast them. Whilst this would be sufficient for a live event, many programs are prepared in advance and this requires storage devices. Cameras may have a built-in storage device or send the acquired images to a separate device by cable or radio link. The acquired information may be transferred to an intermediate storage device for editing and other production steps in a process called *ingestion,* and the completed program may be transferred again to another storage device for *playout* to air.

1

Thus television systems need equipment that can acquire, store, edit, and manipulate video signals as well as being able to send them from one place to another. In addition to the traditional terrestrial and satellite broadcasting channels, images may also be distributed by networks, including the Internet, and by media such as DVDs (digital video disc or digital versatile disc).

The first methods used in television transmission and storage were understandably analog, and the signal formats essentially were determined by requirements of the cathode ray tube (CRT) as a display, so that the receiver might be as simple as possible and be constructed with a minimum number of vacuum tubes. Following the development of magnetic audio recording during World War II, a need for television recording was perceived. This was initially due to the various time zones across the United States. Without recording, popular television programs had to be performed live several times so they could be seen at the peak viewing time in each time zone. Ampex eventually succeeded in recording monochrome video in the 1950s, and the fundamentals of the Quadruplex machine were so soundly based that subsequent analog video recorders only refined the process.[1] Digital technology took over not because these devices did not work, but because it required less maintenance and worked more quickly and at lower cost, whilst allowing new freedoms.

There are two powerful factors that influence television equipment and it is vital to understand them. The first is that there is a large installed base of receivers and it is unpopular and unwise to adopt new techniques that make them obsolete overnight. Thus television standards move rather slowly, and new ones tend to be compatible with previous ones. The introduction of colour television was done in such a way that existing sets would still display the monochrome part of the signal. Digital video signals tend to be compatible with existing analog signals so that, for example, a digital editing device can be used in an analog TV station, or a traditional TV can display signals from a digital set top box or integrated receiver-decoder (IRD).

The second factor is the steady progress of microelectronics and data storage, whereby the cost of performing a given process or of storing a given quantity of information continues to fall. Thus equipment becomes widely available when it is economical, and not necessarily when it is invented.

VIDEO SIGNALS

Video signals are electrical waveforms that allow moving pictures to be conveyed from one place to another. Observing the real world with the human eye results in a two-dimensional image on the retina. This image changes with time and so the basic information is three-dimensional. With two eyes a stereoscopic view can be obtained and stereoscopic television is possible with suitable equipment. The experimental demonstrations the author has seen were breathtaking, but use is restricted to specialist applications and has yet to be exploited in broadcasting.

An electrical waveform is two-dimensional in that it carries a voltage changing with respect to time. To convey three-dimensional picture information down a two-dimensional cable it is necessary to resort to scanning. Instead of attempting to convey the brightness of all parts of a picture at once, scanning conveys the brightness of a single point that moves with time, typically along a series of near-horizontal lines known as a *raster*. After the image is scanned once, the process repeats at the *frame rate*. If the frame rate is high enough, the HVS believes that it is most likely to be seeing moving objects instead of a rapid series of still images. The layman may go to the movies, but the pictures do not actually move.

One of the vital concepts to grasp is that digital video is simply an alternative means of carrying a video signal. Although there are a number of ways in which this can be done, there is one system, known as pulse code modulation (PCM), that is in virtually universal use.[2] Figure 1.1 shows how PCM works. Instead of being continuous, the distance across the image is represented in a discrete, or stepwise, manner. The image is not carried by continuous representation, but by measurement at regular intervals. This process is called *sampling* and the frequency with which samples are taken is called the sampling rate or sampling frequency, F_s. The sampling frequency may be measured in samples per second or samples per millimetre. The former is a temporal sampling frequency, whereas the latter is a spatial sampling frequency. The temporal sampling frequency is obtained by multiplying the spatial sampling frequency by the scanning speed.

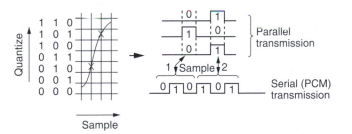

FIGURE 1.1
When a signal is carried in numerical form, either parallel or serial, the mechanisms of Figure 1.4 ensure that the only degradation is in the conversion process.

It should be stressed that sampling is an analog process. Each sample still varies infinitely as the original waveform did. To complete the conversion to PCM, the magnitude of each sample is then represented to finite accuracy by a discrete number in a process known as *quantizing*.

DIGITAL VIDEO

In television systems the input image that falls on the camera sensor will be continuous in time and continuous in two spatial dimensions corresponding to the height and width of the sensor. In analog video systems, the time axis is sampled into frames, and the vertical axis is sampled into scanned lines. Digital video uses a third sampling process whereby a continuous line is replaced by a row of picture elements or *pixels*. Such a system was first proposed by Ayrton and Perry as early as 1880, a century before it could widely be adopted.

The number of pixels in an image is very large, so it is clearly impractical to send each one down its own wires. Instead, the pixels are sent sequentially. It is common for the pixel rate to be an integer multiple of the line scanning rate. Pixels then appear in the same place on every line, and a monochrome digital image is a rectangular array of pixels at which the brightness is stored as a number. As shown in Figure 1.2a, the array will generally be arranged with an even spacing between pixels, which are in rows and columns. By placing the pixels close together, it is hoped that the observer will perceive a continuous image.

In a completely digital system, the number of pixels and the aspect ratio of the image may be chosen with considerable freedom. However, where compatibility with an existing analog standard is needed, the digital version may be no more than the result of passing the analog video signal into an analog-to-digital convertor (ADC) having a suitable sampling rate.

Those who are not familiar with digital principles often worry that sampling takes away something from a signal because it does not take notice of what happened between the samples. This would be true in a system having infinite bandwidth, but no signal can have infinite bandwidth. All analog signal sources from cameras, VTRs, and so on have a resolution or frequency response limit, as indeed do devices such as CRTs and human vision. When a signal has finite bandwidth, the rate at which it can change is limited, and the way in which it changes becomes predictable. When a waveform can change between samples in only one way, it is then necessary to convey only the samples, and the original

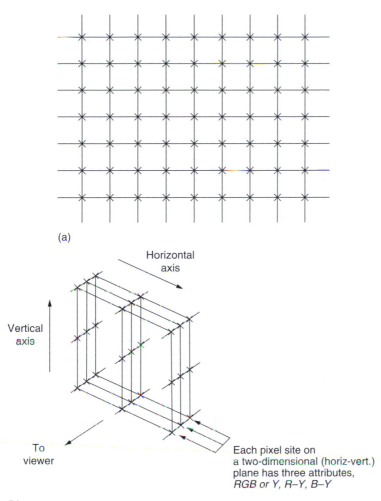

(a)

(b)

FIGURE 1.2
(a) A picture can be stored digitally by representing the brightness at each of the points shown by a binary number. For a colour picture each point becomes a vector and has to describe the brightness, hue, and saturation of that part of the picture. Samples are usually but not always formed into regular arrays of rows and columns, and it is most efficient if the horizontal spacing and vertical spacing are the same. (b) In the case of component video, each pixel site is described by three values and so the pixel becomes a vector quantity.

waveform can unambiguously be reconstructed from them. A more detailed treatment of the principle will be given in Chapter 4.

As stated, each sample is also discrete, or represented in a stepwise manner. The magnitude of the sample, which will be proportional to the voltage of the video

BINARY CODING

Humans prefer to use numbers expressed to the base of 10, having evolved with that number of digits. Other number bases exist; most people are familiar with the duodecimal system, which uses the dozen and the gross. The most minimal system is binary, which has only two digits, 0 and 1. *Bi*nary dig*its* are universally contracted to *bits.* These are readily conveyed in switching circuits by an "on" state and an "off" state. With only two states, there is little chance of error.

In decimal systems, the digits in a number (counting from the right, or least significant, end) represent 1's, 10's, 100's, 1000's, etc. Figure 1.3 shows that in binary, the bits represent 1, 2, 4, 8, 16, etc. A multidigit binary number is commonly called a word, and the number of bits in the word is called the word length. The righthand bit is called the least significant bit (LSB), whereas the bit on the lefthand end of the word is called the most significant bit (MSB). Clearly more digits are required in binary than in decimal, but they are more easily handled. A word of 8 bits is called a byte, which is a contraction of "by eight." The capacity of memories and storage media is measured in bytes, but to avoid large numbers, kilobytes, megabytes, and gigabytes are often used. As memory addresses are themselves binary numbers, the word length limits the address range. The range is found by raising 2 to the power of the word length. Thus a 4-bit word has 16 combinations and could address a memory having 16 locations. A 10-bit word has 1024 combinations, which is close to 1000. In digital terminology, 1 K = 1024, so a kilobyte of memory contains 1024 bytes. A megabyte (1 MB) contains 1024 kilobytes and a gigabyte contains 1024 megabytes.

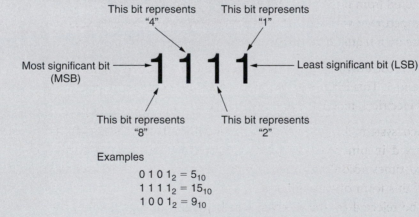

Examples
$$0\ 1\ 0\ 1_2 = 5_{10}$$
$$1\ 1\ 1\ 1_2 = 15_{10}$$
$$1\ 0\ 0\ 1_2 = 9_{10}$$

FIGURE 1.3
In a binary number, the digits represent increasing powers of 2 starting from the LSB. Also defined here are MSB and word length. When the word length is 8 bits, the word is a byte. Binary numbers are used as memory addresses, and the range is defined by the address word length. Some examples are shown here.

signal, is represented by a whole number. This quantizing results in an approximation, but the size of the error can be controlled until it is negligible. If, for example, we were to measure the height of humans to the nearest metre, virtually all adults would register 2 metres high and obvious difficulties would result.

These are generally overcome by measuring height to the nearest centimetre. Clearly there is no advantage in going further and expressing our height in a whole number of millimetres or even micrometres. The point is that an appropriate resolution can also be found for video signals, and a higher figure is not beneficial. The link between video quality and sample resolution is explored in Chapter 4. The advantage of using whole numbers is that they are not prone to drift. If a whole number can be carried from one place to another without numerical error, it has not changed at all. By describing video waveforms numerically, the original information has been expressed in a way that is better able to resist unwanted changes.

Essentially, digital video carries the original image numerically. The number of the pixel is an analog of its location on the screen, and the magnitude of the sample is (in the case of luminance) an analog of the brightness at the appropriate point in the image. In fact the series of pixels along a line in a digital system is only a sampled version of the waveform that an analog system would have produced.

As both axes of the digitally represented waveform are discrete, that waveform can accurately be restored from numbers as if it were being drawn on graph paper. If we require greater accuracy, we simply choose paper with smaller squares. Clearly more numbers are then required and each one could change over a larger range.

Digital systems almost universally use binary coding in which there are only two symbols, 0 and 1. This is because binary is easiest to represent by real phenomena such as electrical, magnetic, or optical signals.

In a digital video system, the whole number representing the value of the sample is expressed in binary. The signals sent have two states and change at predetermined times according to some stable clock. Figure 1.4 shows the consequences of this form of transmission. If the binary signal is degraded by noise, this will be rejected by the receiver, which judges the signal solely by whether it is above or below the halfway threshold, a process known as slicing. The signal will be carried in a channel with finite bandwidth, and this limits the slew rate of the signal; an ideally upright edge is made to slope. Noise added to a sloping signal can change the time at which the slicer judges that the level passed through the threshold. This effect is also eliminated when the output of the slicer is reclocked. However many stages the binary signal passes through, it still comes out the same, only later.

Video samples represented by whole numbers can reliably be carried from one place to another by such a scheme, and if the number is correctly received, there has been no loss of information en route.

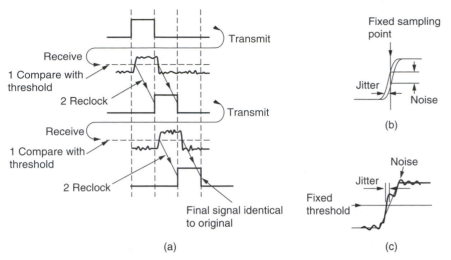

FIGURE 1.4

(a) A binary signal is compared with a threshold and reclocked on receipt; thus the meaning will be unchanged. (b) Jitter on a signal can appear as noise with respect to fixed timing. (c) Noise on a signal can appear as jitter when compared with a fixed threshold.

There are two ways in which binary signals can be used to carry samples and these are also shown in Figure 1.1. When each digit of the binary number is carried on a separate wire this is called parallel transmission. The state of the wires changes at the sampling rate. Using multiple wires is cumbersome and it is preferable to use a single wire in which successive digits from each sample are sent serially. This is the definition of pulse code modulation. Clearly the bit clock frequency must now be higher than the sampling rate.

STANDARD AND HIGH-DEFINITION VIDEO

Alice in Wonderland said "When I use a word, it means exactly what I want it to mean." The same principle will be found in television. It should be appreciated that when the 405-line monochrome TV service was initiated in the UK, it was referred to as high definition. Today, the term "standard definition" (SD) refers to the TV scanning standards that were used in broadcasting over the last third of the 20th century. These have 500 or 600 lines per frame, but use interlaced scanning, which means that their effective definition on moving pictures is considerably less than the number of lines would suggest.

When the term "high definition" (HD) is encountered, one has to be aware that the writer may be using his own definition. It is this author's opinion that "high definition" is a poor term because it implies that the only attribute a moving picture can have is static definition and that all that is necessary is to increase it.

Nothing could be further from the truth. Instead the recent progress that has been made in understanding the HVS should be respected. This work suggests that there is a set of parameters that require attention to improve television picture quality and that static definition is only one of them. Clearly if the static definition alone is improved, the system may simply be better able to reveal other shortcomings to the viewer. The author has seen plenty of systems like that, which do not seem to be a real advance.

In general all one can assume from the term "high definition" is that the picture has more lines in it than the SD systems have. Comparisons of system performance based on the number of lines alone give misleading results. This is because some HD systems use interlaced scanning and some do not. The reader will find a comprehensive essay comparing interlaced with progressive scanning in Chapter 2, which will conclude that it is unsuitable for systems with a large number of lines, to the extent that "interlaced HD" is virtually an oxymoron.

The European Broadcast Union (EBU) recommended in 2004 that European HD services should use progressive scan.

It should be noted that the way the line count is measured has changed. For example, in 625-line SDTV, there are 625 lines in the entire frame period, but some of these are lost to CRT retrace or flyback and do not appear on the screen. In modern systems only the number of lines actually visible is quoted. This makes sense because only visible lines need to be transmitted in digital systems and in many modern displays there is no flyback mechanism.

Obviously the finer the pixel spacing, the greater the resolution of the picture will be, but the amount of data needed to store one picture, and the cost, will increase as the square of the resolution. A further complication is that HDTV pictures have a wider aspect ratio, increasing the pixel count further.

Without the use of compression, high-quality SDTV requires around 200 million bits per second, whereas HDTV requires more like a gigabit per second. Clearly digital video production could become commonplace only when such data rates could be handled economically. Consumer applications and broadcasting could become possible only when compression technology became available to reduce the data rate. Chapter 6 deals with video compression.

COLOUR

Colorimetry will be treated in depth in Chapter 2 and only the basics will be introduced here. Colour is created in television by the additive mixing in the display of three primary colours: red, green, and blue (RGB). Effectively, the display needs to be supplied with three video signals, each representing a primary colour. Because practical colour cameras generally also have three separate sensors, one for each primary colour, a camera and a display can be directly connected. RGB consists of three parallel signals, each requiring the same bandwidth, and is used where the highest accuracy is needed. RGB is not used for broadcast applications because of the high cost.

If RGB is used in the digital domain, it will be seen from Figure 1.2b that each image consists of three superimposed layers of samples, one for each primary colour. The pixel is no longer a single number representing a scalar brightness value, but a vector that describes in some way the brightness, hue, and saturation of that point in the picture. In RGB, the pixels contain three unipolar numbers representing the proportion of each of the three primary colours at that point in the picture.

Some saving of bandwidth can be obtained by using colour difference working. The HVS relies on brightness to convey detail, and much less resolution is needed in the colour information. Accordingly R, G, and B are matrixed together to form a luma (and monochrome-compatible) signal Y, which alone needs full bandwidth. The eye is not equally sensitive to the three primary colours, as can be seen in Figure 1.5, and so the luma signal is a weighted sum.

The matrix also produces two colour difference signals, R–Y and B–Y. Colour difference signals do not need the same bandwidth as Y, because the eye's acuity does not extend to colour vision. One-half or one-quarter of the bandwidth will do, depending on the application.

In the digital domain, each pixel again contains three numbers, but one of these is a unipolar number representing the luma and the other two are bipolar numbers

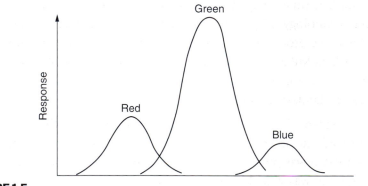

FIGURE 1.5
The response of the human eye to colour is not uniform.

representing the colour difference values. As the colour difference signals need less bandwidth, in the digital domain this translates to the use of a lower sampling rate, typically between one-half and one-sixteenth the bit rate of the luma.

For monochrome-compatible analog colour television broadcasting, the NTSC, PAL, and SECAM systems interleave into the spectrum of a monochrome signal a subcarrier that carries two colour difference signals of restricted bandwidth. The subcarrier is intended to be invisible on the screen of a monochrome television set. A subcarrier-based colour system is generally referred to as composite video, and the modulated subcarrier is called chroma. Composite video is classified as a compression technique because it allows colour pictures in the same bandwidth as monochrome.

In the digital domain the use of composite video is not appropriate for broadcasting and the most common equivalent process is the use of an MPEG compression scheme. From a broadcasting standpoint MPEG is simply a more efficient digital replacement for composite video.

CONVERGENCE OF VIDEO AND INFORMATION TECHNOLOGY

When professional digital video equipment first became available in the 1980s, it was very expensive and was attractive only to those who needed the benefits that it offered. At that time compression was little used and most equipment operated with the full PCM bit rate, offering exceptional picture quality. The generation loss of analog videotape was eliminated, as PCM digital copies are indistinguishable from the original.

However, once video has been digitized, it differs from generic data only by having an implicit time base. Thus, in principle, computers, now known as information technology (IT), could handle video. The cost of computing devices fell and the processing power and storage capacity rose. Compression algorithms such as MPEG were developed. It became first possible, then easy, then trivial to use IT not just for video production but also for consumer equipment, at least in standard definition.

Whilst digital video allows extremely high picture quality, this was rarely explored. Instead the freedom of information technology transformed the way in which video was produced, distributed, and viewed, and in most cases the picture quality was actually worse than that of an analog off-air picture, with the possible exception of well-made DVDs.

TWO'S COMPLEMENT

In the two's complement system, the upper half of the pure binary number range has been redefined to represent negative quantities. This allows digital codes to represent bipolar values found in audio and colour difference signals. If a pure binary counter is constantly incremented and allowed to overflow, it will produce all the numbers in the range permitted by the number of available bits, and these are shown for a 4-bit example drawn around the circle in Figure 1.6. As a circle has no real beginning, it is possible to consider it as starting wherever it is convenient. In two's complement, the quantizing range represented by the circle of numbers does not start at 0, but starts on the diametrically opposite side of the circle. Zero is midrange, and all numbers with the MSB set are considered negative. The MSB is thus the equivalent of a sign bit, where 1 = minus. Two's complement notation differs from pure binary in that the most significant bit is inverted to achieve the half-circle rotation.

Figure 1.7 shows how a real ADC is configured to produce two's complement output. At (a) an analog offset voltage equal to one-half the quantizing range is added to the bipolar analog signal to make it unipolar as at (b).

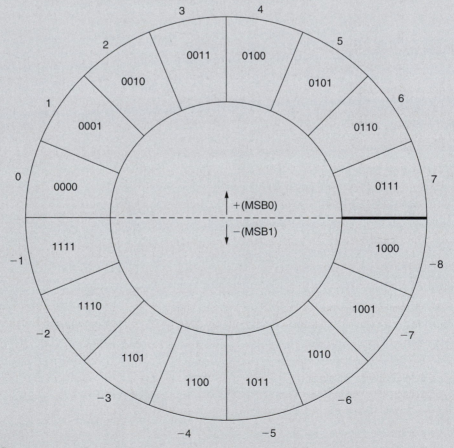

FIGURE 1.6
In this example of a 4-bit two's complement code, the number range is from −8 to +7. Note that the MSB determines polarity.

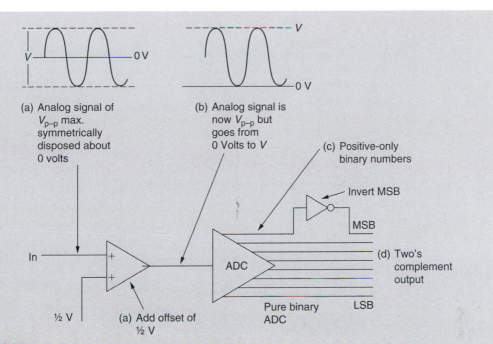

FIGURE 1.7

A two's complement ADC. In (a) an analog offset voltage equal to one-half the quantizing range is added to the bipolar analog signal to make it unipolar as in (b). The ADC produces positive-only numbers (c), but the MSB is then inverted (d) to give a two's complement output.

The ADC produces positive-only numbers at (c), which are proportional to the input voltage. The MSB is then inverted at (d) so that the all-0's code moves to the centre of the quantizing range. The analog offset is often incorporated into the ADC as is the MSB inversion. Some convertors are designed to be used in either pure binary or two's complement mode. In this case the designer must arrange the appropriate digital convertor conditions at the input. The MSB inversion may be selectable by an external logic level. In the digital video interface standards the colour difference signals use offset binary because the codes of all 0's and all 1's are at the end of the range and can be reserved for synchronising. A digital vision mixer simply inverts the MSB of each colour difference sample to convert it to two's complement.

The two's complement system allows two sample values to be added, or "mixed," in video parlance, and the result will be referred to the system midrange; this is analogous to adding analog signals in an operational amplifier.

Figure 1.8 illustrates how adding two's complement samples simulates a bipolar mixing process. The waveform of input A is depicted by solid black samples and that of B by samples with a solid outline. The result of mixing is the linear sum of the two waveforms obtained by adding pairs of sample values. The dashed lines depict the output values. Beneath each set of samples is the calculation, which will be seen to give the correct result. Note that the calculations are pure binary. No special arithmetic is needed to handle two's complement numbers.

It is sometimes necessary to phase reverse or invert a digital signal. The process of inversion in two's complement is simple. All bits of the sample value are inverted to form the one's complement, and 1 is added. This can be checked by mentally inverting some of the values in Figure 1.6. The inversion is transparent, and performing a second inversion gives the original sample values.

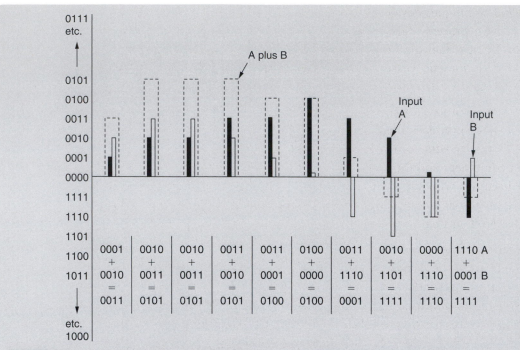

FIGURE 1.8
Using two's complement arithmetic, single values from two waveforms are added together with respect to midrange to give a correct mixing function.

Using inversion, signal subtraction can be performed using only adding logic. The inverted input is added to perform a subtraction, just as in the analog domain. This permits a significant saving in hardware complexity, because only carry logic is necessary and no borrow mechanism need be supported.

In summary, two's complement notation is the most appropriate scheme for bipolar signals and allows simple mixing in conventional binary adders. It is in virtually universal use in digital video and audio processing.

Two's complement numbers can have a radix point and bits below it, just as pure binary numbers can. It should, however, be noted that in two's complement, if a radix point exists, numbers to the right of it are added. For example, 1100.1 is not -4.5, it is $-4 + 0.5 = 3.5$.

Thus a mere comparison of digital and analog video is missing the point. Its most exciting aspects are the tremendous possibilities that are denied to analog technology. Networks, error correction, random access, compression, motion estimation, and interpolation are difficult or impossible in the analog domain, but are straightforward in the digital domain.

Systems and techniques developed in other industries for other purposes can be used to store, process, and transmit video. Computer equipment is available at low cost because the volume of production is far greater than that of professional video equipment. Disk drives and memories developed for computers can be put to use in video products.

As the power of processors increases, it becomes possible to perform under software control processes that previously required dedicated hardware. This causes a dramatic reduction in hardware cost. Inevitably the very nature of broadcast equipment and the ways in which it is used are changing along with the manufacturers who supply it. The computer industry is taking over from traditional broadcast manufacturers, because they have the economics of mass production on their side.

Whereas tape is a linear medium and it is necessary to wait for the tape to wind to a desired part of the recording, the head of a hard disk drive can access any stored data in milliseconds. This is known in computers as direct access and in broadcasting as nonlinear access. As a result the nonlinear editing workstation based on hard drives has eclipsed the use of videotape for editing.

Communications networks developed to handle data can happily carry digital video and accompanying audio over indefinite distances without quality loss. Techniques such as ADSL allow compressed digital video to travel over a conventional telephone line to the consumer.

Digital TV broadcasting uses coding techniques to eliminate the interference, fading, and multipath reception problems of analog broadcasting. At the same time, more efficient use is made of available bandwidth.

One of the fundamental requirements of computer communication is that it is bi-directional. When this technology becomes available to the consumer, services such as video-on-demand and interactive video become possible. Television programs may contain metadata that allows the viewer rapidly to access web sites relating to items mentioned in the program. When the TV set is a computer there is no difficulty in displaying both on the same screen.

Increasingly the viewer will be deciding what and when to watch instead of passively accepting the broadcaster's output. With a tape-based VCR, the consumer was limited to time-shifting broadcast programs that could not be viewed until recording was over. Now that the hard drive-based consumer VCR, or personal video recorder (PVR), is available, the consumer has more power. For example, he or she may never watch another TV commercial again. The consequences of this technology are far-reaching.

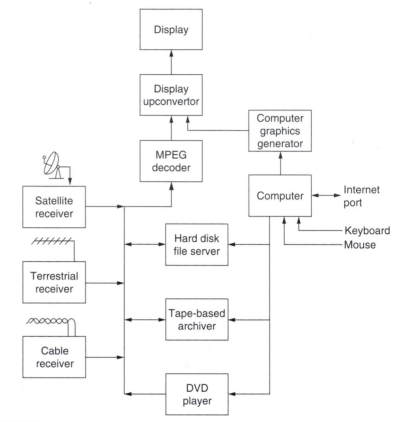

FIGURE 1.9
The TV set of the future may look something like this.

Figure 1.9 shows what the television set of the future may look like. MPEG compressed signals may arrive in real time by terrestrial or satellite broadcast, via a cable, or on media such as DVD. The TV set is simply a display, and the heart of the system is a hard drive-based server. This can be used to time-shift broadcast programs, to skip commercial breaks, or to assemble requested movies transmitted in non-real time. If equipped with a web browser, the server may explore the web looking for material of the same kind the viewer normally watches. As the cost of storage falls, the server may download this material speculatively.

Note that when the hard drive is used to time-shift or record, it simply stores the MPEG bitstream. On playback the bitstream is decoded and the picture quality will be as good as the original MPEG coder allowed. The generation loss due to using an analog VCR is eliminated.

The worlds of digital video, digital audio, film, communication, and computation are now closely related, and that is where the real potential lies. The time when television was a specialist subject that could evolve in isolation from other disciplines is long gone; digital technology has made sure of that. Video has now become a branch of IT. Importantly, the use of digital technology in filmmaking, if it can still be called that, is also widespread and it too is now a branch of IT, especially electronic cinema in which the "film" arrives as a data file over a secure network.

Ultimately digital technology will change the nature of television broadcasting out of recognition. Once the viewer has nonlinear storage technology and electronic program guides, the broadcaster's transmitted schedule is irrelevant. Increasingly viewers will be able to choose what is watched and when, rather than the broadcaster deciding for them. The broadcasting of conventional commercials will cease to be effective when viewers have the technology to skip them. Viewers can also download video over the Internet.

Anyone with a web site and a suitable file server can become a "broadcaster." Given that the majority of TV sets and computers are and will remain powered by house current, and that an Internet or broadband connection will soon be as ubiquitous as a power socket, it seems difficult to justify using radio signals to communicate with fixed receiving devices. The development of digital video broadcasting to handheld devices (DVB-H) may be an indicator of what will happen.

BASICS: TRANSMISSION, STORAGE, AND COMPRESSION

These three technologies are strongly related. Transmission of digital video, or of any type of data, requires that the value of the bits results in discrete changes of state of some parameter in the transmission channel. This may be the voltage in a cable, the intensity of light in an optical fibre, or the amplitude or phase of a radio signal. The receiving device must be able to decode the original data bits from the signal that may have suffered various forms of degradation on the way. It is practically impossible to modulate a transmission directly with the state of the bits. A run of identical bits would cause a constant signal and the receiver would lose count. Instead a modulation scheme or channel code is used at the transmitter, with a matching decoding scheme at the receiver.

If the output waveform of a channel coder is recorded, the result is a storage device. Channel codes can be optimized for the characteristics of magnetic or optical disks, magnetic tapes, and so on. Chapter 8 considers channel coding.

The rate of transmission is always limited by the available bandwidth. This limitation is the most serious in terrestrial broadcasting, in which the radio spectrum must be shared with other services. Storage devices are limited by their capacity. In both cases an apparent improvement can be had using compression. A compressor produces an impression of the image that uses fewer bits and thus allows an extension of playing time in storage devices or a reduction of bandwidth in transmission. Chapter 6 discusses video compression techniques.

As an alternative to compression, where a transmission bandwidth limit exists, data may be sent at a lower than normal bit rate, instead of in real time, and stored at the receiver. When the entire message has been received, the storage device can then replay in real time. Clearly the transmission does not need to be at a fixed bit rate, or even continuous, provided all of the data are received. Such a mechanism is ideally suited to networks, where a short interruption of delivery due to congestion does not affect a message that is only being stored.

There is no such thing as an ideal channel, either transmitted or recorded. Real channels cause some degree of timing error and some proportion of data bits may be incorrect. These deficiencies are addressed by time base correction and error correction. Time base correction requires temporary storage in memory that is then read with a stable clock. Error correction is achieved by adding check bits at the encoder and by comparing them with the data at the decoder. Paradoxically, compressed data are more sensitive to error and need more check bits.

TIME COMPRESSION AND PACKETISING

When real-time signals such as audio and video are converted, the ADC must run at a constant and correct clock rate and it outputs an unbroken stream of samples during the active line. Following a break during blanking, the sample stream resumes. Time compression allows the sample stream to be broken into blocks for convenient handling.

Figure 1.10 shows an ADC feeding a pair of RAMs (random access memories). When one is being written by the ADC, the other can be read, and vice versa. As soon as the first RAM is full, the ADC output switches to the input of the other RAM so that there is no loss of samples. The first RAM can then be read at a higher clock rate than the sampling rate. As a result the RAM is read in less time than it took to write it, and the output from the system then pauses until the second RAM is full. The samples are now time compressed. Instead of being an unbroken stream that is difficult to handle, the samples are now subdivided into smaller groups with convenient pauses in between them. In network transmission, these groups are referred to as packets, whereas in recording, they are commonly

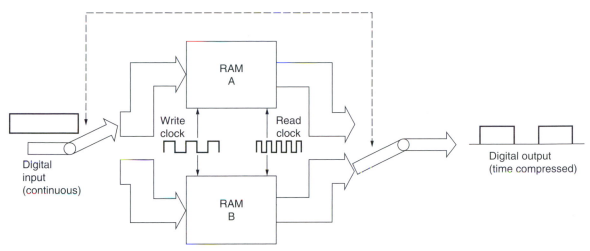

FIGURE 1.10
In time compression, the unbroken real-time stream of samples from an ADC is broken up into discrete blocks. This is accomplished by the configuration shown here. Samples are written into one RAM at the sampling rate by the write clock. When the first RAM is full, the switches change over, and writing continues into the second RAM whilst the first is read using a higher-frequency clock. The RAM is read faster than it was written and so all of the data will be output before the other RAM is full. This opens spaces in the data flow, which are used as described in the text.

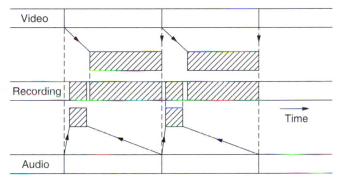

FIGURE 1.11
Time compression is used to shorten the length of track needed by the video. Heavily time-compressed audio samples can then be recorded on the same track using common circuitry.

known as blocks. The pauses allow numerous processes to take place. A rotary head recorder might spread the data from a frame over several tape tracks; a hard disk might move its heads to another track. In all types of recording and transmission, the time compression of the samples allows time for synchronising patterns, subcode, and error-correction check words to be inserted.

In digital VTRs, the video data are time compressed so that part of the track is left for audio data. Figure 1.11 shows that heavy time compression of the audio

MULTIPLEXING PRINCIPLES

Multiplexing is used where several signals are to be transmitted down the same channel. The channel bit rate must be the same as or greater than the sum of the source bit rates. Figure 1.12 shows that when multiplexing is used, the data from each source has to be time compressed. This is done by buffering source data in a memory at the multiplexer. It is written into the memory in real time as it arrives, but will be read from the memory with a clock that has a much higher rate. This means that the readout occurs in a shorter time span. If, for example, the clock frequency is raised by a factor of 10, the data for a given signal will be transmitted in a tenth of the normal time, leaving time in the multiplex for nine more such signals.

In the demultiplexer another buffer memory will be required. Only the data for the selected signal will be written into this memory at the bit rate of the multiplex. When the memory is read at the correct speed, the data will emerge with their original time base.

In practice it is essential to have mechanisms to identify the separate signals to prevent them being mixed up and to convey the original signal clock frequency to the demultiplexer. In time-division multiplexing the time base of the transmission is broken into equal slots, one for each signal. This makes it easy for the demultiplexer, but forces a rigid structure on all the signals such that they must all be locked to one another and have an unchanging bit rate. Packet multiplexing overcomes these limitations. The multiplexer must switch between different time-compressed signals to create the bitstream and this is much easier to organize if each signal is in the form of data packets of constant size. Figure 1.13 shows a packet multiplexing system.

Each packet consists of two components: the header, which identifies the packet, and the payload, which is the data to be transmitted. The header will contain at least an identification code (ID), which is unique for each signal in the multiplex. The demultiplexer checks the ID codes of all incoming packets and discards those that do not have the wanted ID.

In complex systems it is common to have a mechanism to check that packets are not lost or repeated. This is the purpose of the packet continuity count, which is carried in the header. For packets carrying the same ID, the count should increase by 1 from one packet to the next. Upon reaching the maximum binary value, the count overflows and recommences.

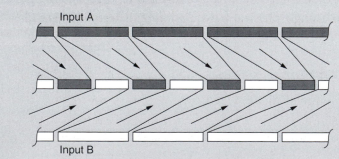

FIGURE 1.12
Multiplexing requires time compression on each input.

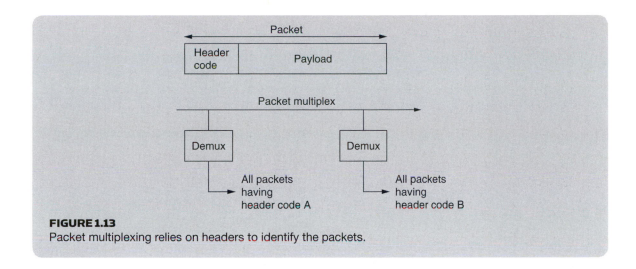

FIGURE 1.13
Packet multiplexing relies on headers to identify the packets.

data raises the data rate up to that of the video data so that the same tracks, same heads, and much common circuitry can be used to record both.

Subsequently, any time compression can be reversed by time expansion. Samples are written into a RAM at the incoming clock rate, but read out at the standard sampling rate. Unless there is a design fault, time compression is totally undetectable. In a recorder, the time expansion stage can be combined with the time base correction stage so that speed variations in the medium can be eliminated at the same time. The use of time compression is universal in digital recording and widely used in transmission. In general the instantaneous data rate at the medium is not the same as the rate at the convertors, although clearly the average rate must be the same.

Another application of time compression is to allow several channels of information to be carried in a single physical transmission. This technique is called multiplexing.

SYNCHRONISATION AND TIME BASE CORRECTION

Figure 1.14a shows a minimal digital video system. This is no more than a point-to-point link that conveys analog video from one place to another. It consists of a pair of convertors and hardware to serialize and de-serialize the samples. There is a need for standardisation in serial transmission so that various devices can be connected together. These standards for digital interfaces are described in Chapter 10.

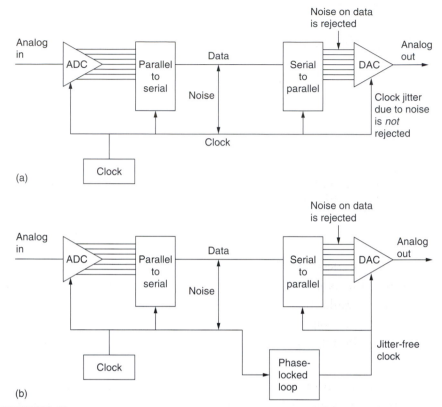

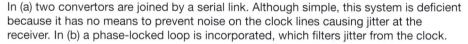

FIGURE 1.14
In (a) two convertors are joined by a serial link. Although simple, this system is deficient because it has no means to prevent noise on the clock lines causing jitter at the receiver. In (b) a phase-locked loop is incorporated, which filters jitter from the clock.

Analog video entering the system is converted in the ADC to samples that are expressed as binary numbers. A typical sample would have a word length of 8 bits. The sample is connected in parallel into an output register, which controls the cable drivers. The cable also carries the sampling rate clock. The data are sent to the other end of the line where a slicer selects noise picked up on each signal. Sliced data are then loaded into a receiving register by the clock and sent to the digital-to-analog convertor (DAC), which converts the sample back to an analog voltage.

Following a casual study one might conclude that if the convertors were of transparent quality, the system must be ideal. Unfortunately this is incorrect. As Figure 1.4 showed, noise can change the timing of a sliced signal. Whilst this system rejects noise that threatens to change the numerical value of the

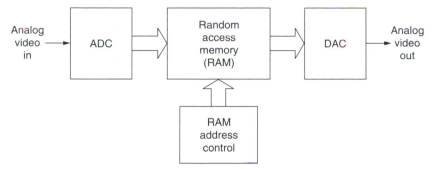

FIGURE 1.15

In the frame store, the recording medium is a RAM. Recording time available is short compared with other media, but access to the recording is immediate and flexible, as it is controlled by addressing the RAM.

samples, it is powerless to prevent noise from causing jitter in the receipt of the word clock. Noise on the word clock means that samples are not converted with a regular time base, and the impairment caused can be noticeable. Stated another way, analog characteristics of the interconnect are not prevented from affecting the reproduced waveform and so the system is not truly digital.

The jitter problem is overcome in Figure 1.14b by the inclusion of a phase-locked loop, which is an oscillator that synchronises itself to the average frequency of the clock but which filters out the instantaneous jitter. The operation of a phase-locked loop is analogous to the function of the flywheel on a piston engine. The samples are then fed to the convertor with a regular spacing and the impairment is no longer audible. Chapter 4 shows why the effect occurs and deduces the clock accuracy needed for accurate conversion.

The system of Figure 1.14 is extended in Figure 1.15 by the addition of some RAM. What the device does is determined by the way in which the RAM address is controlled. If the RAM address increases by one every time a sample from the ADC is stored in the RAM, a recording can be made for a short period until the RAM is full. The recording can be played back by repeating the address sequence at the same clock rate but reading the memory into the DAC. The result is generally called a frame store.[3]

If the memory capacity is increased, the device can be used for recording. At a rate of 200 million bits per second, each frame of SDTV needs a megabyte of memory and so the RAM recorder will be restricted to a fairly short playing time.

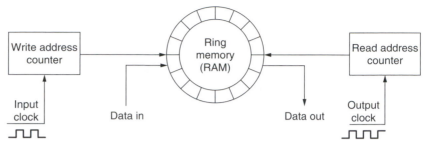

FIGURE 1.16
If the memory address is arranged to come from a counter that overflows, the memory
can be made to appear circular. The write address then rotates endlessly, overwriting
previous data once per revolution. The read address can follow the write address by
a variable distance (not exceeding one revolution) and so a variable delay takes place
between reading and writing.

Using compression, the playing time of a RAM-based recorder can be extended.
For some applications, a camcorder that stores images in a Flash memory
card rather than on disk or tape has advantages. For predetermined images
such as test patterns and station IDs, read-only memory (ROM) can be used
instead.

If the RAM is used in a different way, it can be written and read at the same
time. The device then becomes a synchroniser, which allows video interchange
between two systems that are not genlocked. Controlling the relationship
between the addresses makes the RAM a variable delay. The addresses are generated by counters that overflow to zero after they have reached a maximum
count at the end of a frame. As a result the memory space appears to be circular as shown in Figure 1.16. The read and write addresses chase one another
around the circle. If the read address follows close behind the write address,
the delay is short. If it stays just ahead of the write address, the maximum
delay is reached. If the input and output have identical frame rates, the address
relationship will be constant, but if there is a drift, then the address relationship will change slowly. Eventually the addresses will coincide and then cross.
Properly handled, this results in the omission or repetition of a frame.

The issue of signal timing has always been critical in analog video, but the
adoption of digital routing relaxes the requirements considerably. Analog vision
mixers need to be fed by equal-length cables from the router to prevent propagation delay variation. In the digital domain this is no longer an issue as delay
is easily obtained and each input of a digital vision mixer can have its own

local synchroniser. A synchroniser with less than a frame of RAM can be used to remove static timing errors due, for example, to propagation delays in large systems. The finite RAM capacity gives a finite range of timing error that can be accommodated. This is known as the window. Provided signals are received having timing within the window of the inputs, all inputs are retimed to the same phase within the mixer. Chapter 10 deals with synchronising large systems.

ERROR CORRECTION AND CONCEALMENT

All practical recording and transmission media are imperfect. Magnetic media, for example, suffer from noise and dropouts. In a digital recording of binary data, a bit is either correct or incorrect, with no intermediate stage. Small amounts of noise are rejected, but inevitably, infrequent noise impulses cause some individual bits to be in error. Dropouts cause a larger number of bits in one place to be in error. An error of this kind is called a burst error. Whatever the medium and whatever the nature of the mechanism responsible, data either are recovered correctly or suffer some combination of bit errors and burst errors. In optical disks, random errors can be caused by imperfections in the moulding process, whereas burst errors are due to contamination or scratching of the disk surface.

The visibility of a bit error depends upon which bit of the sample is involved. If the LSB of one sample were in error in a detailed, contrasty picture, the effect would be totally masked and no one could detect it. Conversely, if the MSB of one sample were in error in a flat field, no one could fail to notice the resulting spot. Clearly a means is needed to render errors from the medium inaudible. This is the purpose of error correction. In compression systems, bit errors cause greater difficulty as the result in a variable-length coding scheme may be loss of synchronisation and damage to a significant picture area.

In binary, a bit has only two states. If it is wrong, it is necessary only to reverse the state and it must be right. Thus the correction process is trivial and perfect. The main difficulty is in identifying the bits that are in error. This is done by coding the data; adding redundant bits. Adding redundancy is not confined to digital technology; airliners have several engines and cars have twin braking systems. Clearly the more failures that have to be handled, the more redundancy is needed. If a four-engine airliner is designed to fly normally with one engine failed, three of the engines have enough power to reach cruise speed, and the fourth one is redundant. The amount of redundancy is equal to the amount of failure that can be handled. In the case of the failure of two engines, the plane can still fly, but it must slow down; this is graceful degradation. Clearly the chances of a two-engine failure on the same flight are remote.

In digital recording, the amount of error that can be corrected is proportional to the amount of redundancy, and it will be shown in Chapter 8 that within this limit, the samples are returned to exactly their original value. Consequently corrected samples are undetectable. If the amount of error exceeds the amount of redundancy, correction is not possible, and, to allow graceful degradation, concealment will be used. Concealment is a process in which the value of a missing sample is estimated from those nearby. The estimated sample value is not necessarily exactly the same as the original, and so under some circumstances concealment can be audible, especially if it is frequent. However, in a well-designed system, concealments occur with negligible frequency unless there is an actual fault or problem.

Concealment is made possible by rearranging the sample sequence prior to recording. This is shown in Figure 1.17, where odd-numbered samples

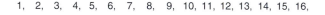

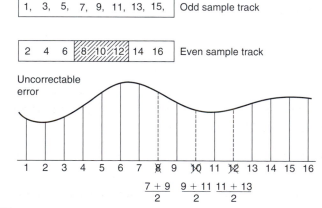

FIGURE 1.17

In cases in which the error correction is inadequate, concealment can be used provided that the samples have been ordered appropriately during recording. Odd and even samples are recorded in different places as shown here. As a result an uncorrectable error causes incorrect samples to occur singly, between correct samples. In the example shown, sample 8 is incorrect, but samples 7 and 9 are unaffected and an approximation of the value of sample 8 can be had by taking the average value of the other two. This interpolated value is substituted for the incorrect value.

are separated from even-numbered samples prior to recording. The odd and even sets of samples may be recorded in different places on the medium, so that an uncorrectable burst error affects only one set. On replay, the samples are recombined into their natural sequence, and the error is now split up so that it results in every other sample being lost in a two-dimensional structure. The picture is now described half as often, but can still be reproduced with some loss of accuracy. This is better than not being reproduced at all, even if it is not perfect. Many digital video recorders use such an odd/even distribution for concealment. Clearly if any errors are fully correctable, the distribution is a waste of time; it is needed only if correction is not possible.

The presence of an error-correction system means that the video (and audio) quality is independent of the medium/head quality within limits. There is no point in trying to assess the health of a machine by watching a monitor or listening to the audio, as this will not reveal whether the error rate is normal or within a whisker of failure. The only useful procedure is to monitor the frequency with which errors are being corrected and to compare it with normal figures. Professional DVTRs have an error rate display for this purpose and in addition most allow the error-correction system to be disabled for testing.

TRANSMISSION

Transmission is only moving data from one place to another. It can be subdivided in different ways, according, for example, to the purpose to which it is put or the distance involved. In digital video production, transmission over short distances will use standardised interfaces that are unidirectional, real time, and uncompressed. The SDI standard (serial digital interface) and its HD equivalent will be covered in Chapter 10.

Networking is also a form of transmission. Networks can be private and local, or worldwide. In general networks will not work in real time and will use some form of compression, although there are exceptions when only short distances are involved.

Transmission also includes what was traditionally called broadcasting, by which signals are radiated from terrestrial or satellite-based transmitters over a wide area. In genuine broadcasting, everyone with a receiver may view the signal. In some cases payment is required and the transmission may be encrypted to

PRODUCT CODES

Digital systems such as broadcasting, optical disks, and magnetic recorders are prone to burst errors. Adding redundancy equal to the size of expected bursts to every code is inefficient. Figure 1.18a shows that the efficiency

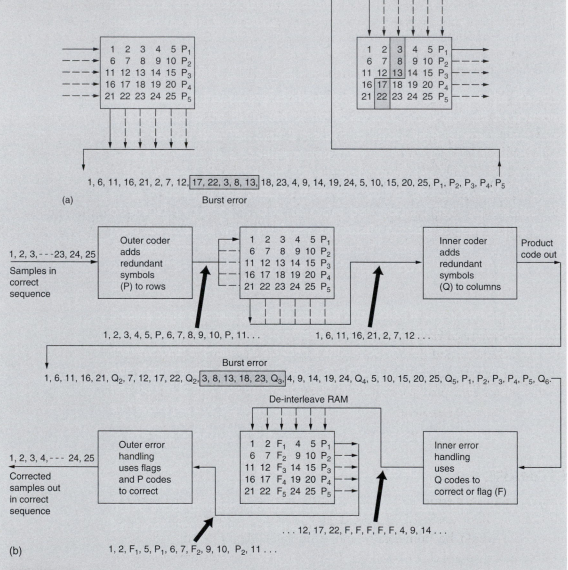

FIGURE 1.18

(a) Interleaving is essential to make error-correction schemes more efficient. Samples written sequentially in rows into a memory have redundancy *P* added to each row. The memory is then read in columns and the data are sent to the recording medium. On replay the nonsequential samples from the medium are de-interleaved to return them to their normal sequence. This breaks up the burst error (outlined) into one error symbol per row in the memory, which can be corrected by the redundancy *P*.

of the system can be raised using interleaving. Sequential samples from the ADC are assembled into codes, but these are not recorded/transmitted in their natural sequence. A number of sequential codes are assembled along rows in a memory. When the memory is full, it is copied to the medium by reading down columns. Subsequently, the samples need to be de-interleaved to return them to their natural sequence. This is done by writing samples from tape into a memory in columns, and when it is full, the memory is read in rows. Samples read from the memory are now in their original sequence so there is no effect on the information. However, if a burst error occurs, as is shown outlined on the diagram, it will damage sequential samples in a vertical direction in the de-interleave memory. When the memory is read, a single large error is broken down into a number of small errors whose size is exactly equal to the correcting power of the codes and the correction is performed with maximum efficiency.

An extension of the process of interleaving is one in which the memory array has not only rows made into code words, but also columns made into code words by the addition of vertical redundancy. This is known as a product code. Figure 1.18b shows that in a product code the redundancy calculated first and checked last is called the outer code, and the redundancy calculated second and checked first is called the inner code. The inner code is formed along tracks on the medium. Random errors due to noise are corrected by the inner code and do not impair the burst-correcting power of the outer code. Burst errors are declared uncorrectable by the inner code, which flags the bad samples on the way into the de-interleave memory. The outer code reads the error flags to locate the erroneous data. As it does not have to compute the error locations, the outer code can correct more errors.

prevent unauthorised viewing. In the case of networks, data are delivered only to specified addresses, and in the case of a service for which payment is required, data would be sent only to addresses known to have paid. This has a security advantage over encrypted services, because the encryption is often bypassed by those with the necessary skills.

STORAGE

Given a competent error- and time base-correction system, it is impossible to tell what medium was used to store digital video, as in each case the reproduced data would be numerically and temporally identical. Thus the traditional analog approach of choosing the medium for its picture quality no longer applies, as the quality is determined elsewhere. Instead, storage media are selected using other attributes, including cost per bit and access time. Subsidiary attributes include ruggedness, behaviour during power loss, and whether the medium is interchangeable.

NOISE AND PROBABILITY

Probability is a useful concept when dealing with processes that are not completely predictable. Thermal noise in electronic components is random, and although under given conditions the noise power in a system may be constant, this value determines only the heat that would be developed in a resistive load. In digital systems, it is the instantaneous voltage of noise that is of interest, because it is a form of interference that could alter the state of a bit if it were large enough. Unfortunately the instantaneous voltage cannot be predicted; indeed if it could the interference could not be called noise. Noise can be quantified statistically only by measuring or predicting the likelihood of a given noise amplitude.

Figure 1.19 shows a graph relating the probability of occurrence to the amplitude of noise. The noise amplitude increases away from the origin along the horizontal axis, and for any amplitude of interest, the probability of that noise amplitude occurring can be read from the curve. The shape of the curve is known as a Gaussian distribution, which crops up whenever the overall effect of a large number of independent phenomena is considered. Thermal noise is due to the contributions from countless molecules in the component concerned. Magnetic recording depends on superimposing some average magnetism on vast numbers of magnetic particles.

If it were possible to isolate an individual noise-generating microcosm of a tape or a head on the molecular scale, the noise it could generate would have physical limits because of the finite energy present. The noise distribution might then be rectangular as shown in Figure 1.20a, where all amplitudes below the physical limit are equally likely. The output of a random number generator can have a uniform probability if each possible value occurs once per sequence. If the combined effect of two of these uniform probability processes is considered, clearly the maximum amplitude is now doubled, because the two effects can add; but provided the two effects are uncorrelated, they may also subtract, so the probability is no longer rectangular, but becomes triangular as in Figure 1.20b. The probability falls to 0 at peak amplitude because the chances of two independent mechanisms reaching their peak value with the same polarity at the same time are understandably small.

If the number of mechanisms summed together is now allowed to increase without limit, the result is the Gaussian curve shown in Figure 1.20c, in which it will be seen that the curve has no amplitude limit, because it is just possible that all mechanisms will simultaneously reach their peak value together, although the chances of this happening are incredibly remote. Thus the Gaussian curve is the overall probability of a large number of uncorrelated uniform processes.

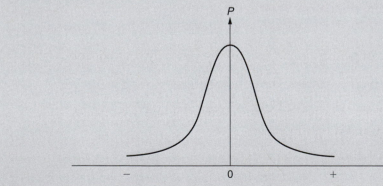

FIGURE 1.19
White noise in analog circuits generally has the Gaussian amplitude distribution shown.

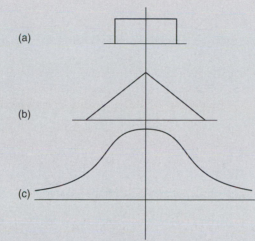

FIGURE 1.20
(a) A rectangular probability function; all values are equally likely but fall between physical limits. (b) The sum of two rectangular probability functions, which is triangular. (c) The Gaussian curve, which is the sum of an infinite number of rectangular probability functions.

Winchester disk	Tape	Optical disk
Fast access speed High cost per bit Non-exchangeable	Slow access speed Low cost per bit Exchangeable	Medium access speed Low cost per bit Exchangeable

FIGURE 1.21
Different storage media have different combinations of attributes and no one technology is superior in all respects.

Figure 1.21 shows that cost per bit and access time are generally contradictory. The fastest devices are solid state, including RAM and Flash memory; next comes the hard disk, followed by tape, hampered by the need to wind to the correct spot. However, if the cost per bit is considered, the order is reversed. Tape is a very inexpensive and simple medium.

The fastest and largest capacity disks are magnetic and these generally are not interchangeable. However, optical disks generally do allow interchange. Some of these are intended for mass replication and cannot be recorded (ROM or read only memory disks), some can be recorded once only (R, or recordable),

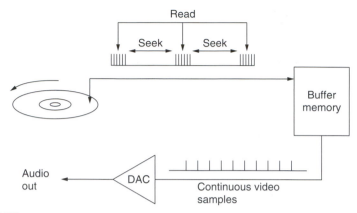

FIGURE 1.22
In a hard disk recorder, a large-capacity memory is used as a buffer or time base corrector between the convertors and the disk. The memory allows the convertors to run constantly despite the interruptions in disk transfer caused by the head moving between tracks.

and some can be rerecorded indefinitely (RW, or read–write). These will be contrasted in Chapter 9.

The magnetic disk drive was perfected by the computer industry to allow rapid random access to data, and so it makes an ideal medium for editing. As will be seen in Chapter 9, the heads do not touch the disk, but are supported on a thin air film, which gives them a long life. The rapid access of disks has made them extremely popular and accordingly a great deal of development has taken place resulting in storage capacities that stretch the imagination. Unfortunately the same research funds have not been available for tape, whose potential is also massive but underexplored.

The economics of computers cannot be ignored and instead of constructing large-capacity disks for special purposes, the economic solution is to use arrays of mass-produced disk drives in devices known as file servers.

The disk drive suffers from intermittent data transfer owing to the need to reposition the heads. Figure 1.22 shows that disk-based devices rely on a quantity of RAM acting as a buffer between the real-time video environment and the intermittent data environment.

Figure 1.23 shows the block diagram of a camcorder based on hard disks and compression. The recording time and picture quality may not compete with full-bandwidth tape-based devices, but following acquisition the disks can be used directly in an edit system, allowing a useful time saving in ENG (Electronic News Gathering) applications.

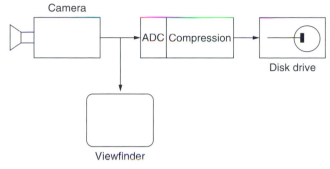

FIGURE 1.23

In a disk-based camcorder, the PCM data rate from the camera may be too high for direct recording on disk. Compression is used to cut the bit rate and extend playing time. If a standard file structure is used, disks may physically be transferred to an edit system after recording.

The rotary head recorder has the advantage that the spinning heads create a high head-to-tape speed, offering a high bit rate recording without high tape speed. Whilst mechanically complex, the rotary head transport has been raised to a high degree of refinement and offers the lowest cost per bit of all digital record-ers.[4] Digital VTRs segment incoming fields into several tape tracks and invisibly reassemble them in memory on replay to keep the tracks reasonably short.

Figure 1.19 shows a representative block diagram of a DVTR. Following the con-vertors, a compression process may be found. In an uncompressed recorder, there will be a distribution of odd and even samples and a shuffle process for concealment purposes. An interleaved product code will be formed prior to the channel coding stage, which produces the recorded waveform. On replay the data separator decodes the channel code and the inner and outer codes perform correction. Following the deshuffle the data channels are recombined and any necessary concealment will take place. Any compression will be decoded prior to the output convertors. Chapter 9 considers rotary head recorders.

VIDEO COMPRESSION AND MPEG

In its native form, digital video suffers from an extremely high data rate, par-ticularly in high definition. One approach to the problem is to use compression that reduces the bit rate significantly with a moderate loss of subjective quality of the picture. The human eye is not equally sensitive to all spatial frequencies, so some coding gain can be obtained by using fewer bits to describe the less visible frequencies. Video images typically contain a great deal of redundancy in that flat areas contain the same pixel value repeated many times. Further-more, in many cases there is little difference between one picture and the next, and compression can be achieved by sending only the differences.

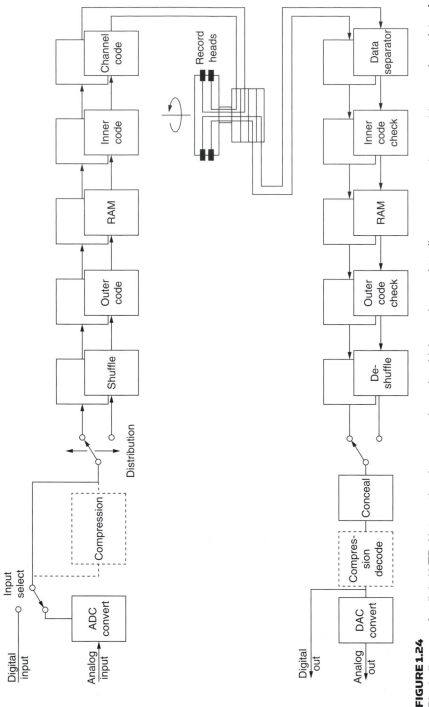

FIGURE 1.24

Block diagram of a digital VTR. Note optional compression unit, which may be used to allow a common transport to record a variety of formats.

Whilst these techniques may achieve considerable reduction in bit rate, it must be appreciated that compression systems reintroduce the generation loss of the analog domain to digital systems. As a result high compression factors are suitable only for final delivery of fully produced material to the viewer.

For editing purposes, compression must be restricted to exploiting the redundancy within each picture individually. If a mild compression factor is used, multiple generation work is possible without artifacts becoming visible. Where offline or remote editing is used (see Chapter 5), higher compression factors may be used as the impaired pictures are not seen by the viewer.

Clearly a consumer DVTR or PVR needs only single-generation operation and has simple editing requirements. A much greater degree of compression can then be used, which may take advantage of redundancy between fields. The same is true for broadcasting, in which bandwidth is at a premium. A similar approach may be used in disk-based camcorders that are intended for ENG purposes.

The future of television broadcasting (and of any high-definition television) lies completely in compression technology. Compression requires an encoder prior to the medium and a compatible decoder after it. Extensive consumer use of compression could not occur without suitable standards. The ISO-MPEG

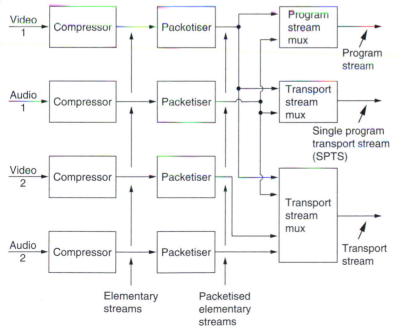

FIGURE 1.25
The bitstream types of MPEG-2. See text for details.

STATISTICAL MULTIPLEXING

Packet multiplexing has advantages over time-division multiplexing because it does not set the bit rate of each signal. A demultiplexer simply checks packet IDs and selects all packets with the wanted code. It will do this however frequently such packets arrive. Consequently it is practicable to have variable bit rate signals in a packet multiplex. The multiplexer has to ensure that the total bit rate does not exceed the rate of the channel, but that rate can be allocated arbitrarily between the various signals.

As a practical matter it is usually necessary to keep the bit rate of the multiplex constant. With variable rate inputs this is done by creating null packets that are generally called stuffing or padding. The headers of these packets contain a unique ID that the demultiplexer does not recognize and so these packets are discarded on arrival.

In an MPEG environment, statistical multiplexing can be extremely useful because it allows for the varying difficulty of real program material. In a multiplex of several television program, it is unlikely that all the programs will encounter difficult material simultaneously. When one program encounters a detailed scene or frequent cuts that are hard to compress, more data rate can be allocated at the allowable expense of the remaining programs that are handling easy material.

coding standards were specifically designed to allow wide interchange of compressed video data. Digital television broadcasting and the digital video disc both use MPEG standard bitstreams that are detailed in Chapter 6.

Figure 1.20 shows that the output of a single compressor is called an elementary stream. In practice audio and video streams of this type can be combined using multiplexing. The program stream is optimized for recording and the multiplexing is based on blocks of arbitrary size. The transport stream is optimized for transmission and is based on blocks of constant size. In production equipment such as disk-based workstations and VTRs that are designed for editing, the MPEG standard is less useful and many successful products use non-MPEG compression.

Compression and the corresponding decoding are complex processes and take time, adding to existing delays in signal paths. Concealment of uncorrectable errors is also more difficult on compressed data.

REAL TIME?

Analog television causes such a small delay to the signals that pictures seen in the home from a live broadcast are substantially instantaneous. With the advent of digital technology innumerable sources of delay have crept in. Techniques such as multiplexing, error correction, and particularly compression all cause delay, as does the subsequent time base correction. Consequently with digital television there is no longer any real-time television in a strict

ASYNCHRONOUS, SYNCHRONOUS, AND ISOCHRONOUS SYSTEMS

In generic data transmission, the data do not have an implied time base and simply need to be received correctly. In this case it does not matter if the transmission is intermittent or has a variable bit rate. This type of transmission is asynchronous; the date rate has no fixed relation to any timing reference.

Digital interfaces used in TV production are intended to work in real time and thus use dedicated cables that run at a fixed bit rate that has some predetermined relationship with the picture scanning frequencies. This is a synchronous transmission.

Compression and networking, alone or together, are fundamentally incompatible with synchronous systems. Compressors produce a bit rate that varies with picture complexity and networks have to share a single resource between a multitude of unpredictable demands.

The solution is the isochronous system. The receiver has a system that accurately reconstructs the original time base of the signal from specially transmitted codes. The encoder and decoder both have a significant quantity of buffer memory so that the transmission between them can be intermittent, typically using packets. Provided enough packets are sent that the receiver buffer is never empty, a continuously decoded video signal can be output. It does not matter exactly when the packets are sent. In some networks it is possible to prioritise isochronous data so that if a receiver buffer is in danger of becoming empty, transmission of packets to replenish the buffer take priority over generic data. Digital television broadcasts are generally isochronous. Clearly the buffering memories add further delay to that already due to error correction and compression.

interpretation. This can easily be verified by visiting a retailer demonstrating analog and digital televisions on the same broadcast channel, where the digital channel will be seen to be obviously behind the analog channel.

A further issue is that the digital production process also causes significant delay, especially where special effects are introduced. The result all too often is that the timing of the sound with respect to the picture slips, leading to obvious loss of "lip-sync." Lip sync loss is often blamed on digital transmission, but in fact MPEG transport streams have extremely accurate time base reconstruction. Generally loss of lip sync on a television is seen because that is the way the broadcaster is presenting it.

DIGITAL AUDIO

Audio was traditionally the poor relation in television, with the poor technical quality of analog TV sound compounded by the miserable loudspeaker fitted in many TV sets. The introduction of the Compact Disc served to raise the consumer's expectations in audio and this was shortly followed in many countries by the introduction of the NICAM 728 system, which added stereo digital audio to analog broadcast TV.

With the advent of digital television broadcasting, the audio is naturally digital, but also compressed, with the choice of format divided between the ISO-MPEG audio coding standards and the Dolby AC-3 system. These are compared in Chapter 7. In the digital domain, where multiplexing is easy, any number of audio channels can be combined in one channel. HDTV broadcasting also offers "surround sound." The form of surround sound appears to have been taken directly from cinema practice and may not be optimal for the domestic environment or even give the best possible quality.

DIGITAL CINEMA

Digital cinema is a good example of how digital technology solves a number of problems at once. The traditional cinema relies on the physical distribution of release prints. These are heavy and expensive. The number of release prints is limited and so is the number of cinemas that can simultaneously show the same title. A further concern is that unauthorised copies of movies can be made onto videotape or recordable DVDs and these can then be duplicated and sold.

In digital cinema, there is no film. The projector is a data projector and requires a suitable data input. This will typically be provided from a file server based on hard disks, which in turn obtain the data over a network. If suitably robust encryption is used, the transmitted data are essentially meaningless to unauthorised people. Generally the data remain in the encrypted state on the file server and the decryption takes place in the projector itself so that the opportunities for unauthorised copying are severely limited.

The file server does not need to download in real time and there is no limit to the number of cinemas that can show the same title. Naturally, without film there is no possibility of film damage and the picture quality will not deteriorate over time.

References

1. Ginsburg, C.P. Comprehensive description of the Ampex video tape recorder. SMPTE J., 66, 177–182 (1957).
2. Devereux, V.G. Pulse code modulation of video signals: 8 bit coder and decoder. BBC Res. Dept. Rept., EL-42 No. 25 (1970).
3. Pursell, S., and Newby, H. Digital frame store for television video. SMPTE J., 82, 402–403 (1973).
4. Baldwin, J.L.E. Digital television recording history and background. SMPTE J., 95, 1206–1214 (1986).

CHAPTER 2

Optical and Video Principles

INTRODUCTION

Light is a form of radiation and physical laws have been constructed to explain its behaviour. The general science of radiation is called *radiometry*. However, physical laws cannot explain the sense we call vision or the impression of colour. For applications of imaging technology such as television and cinema, light is what can be seen by a human being and this is the subject of *photometry*. In that context, any discussion must include the characteristics of the eye in all the relevant domains. Once the operation of the human visual system (HVS) is understood, it will be clear that, to obtain realism, imaging quality has to meet adequate criteria in a number of domains. These include at least contrast, noise level, colour accuracy, static and dynamic resolution, flicker, and motion portrayal. Once these topics are appreciated, it then becomes possible to analyse today's popular imaging technologies to see why they all look different and to suggest a way forward to a new level of realism that will be expected in applications such as simulators and electronic cinema. Figure 2.1 shows some of the interactions between domains that complicate matters. Technically, contrast exists only in the brightness domain and is independent of resolution, which exists in the image plane. In the HVS, the subjective parameter of sharpness is affected by both and so these cannot be treated separately. Sharpness is also affected by the accuracy of motion portrayal. It would appear that colour vision evolved later as an enhancement to monochrome vision. The resolution of the eye to colour changes is very poor.

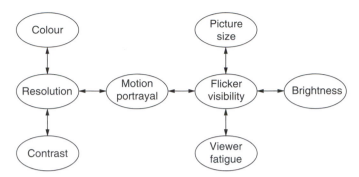

FIGURE 2.1
The various domains in which images can be analysed are not independent in the human visual system. Some of the interactions are shown here.

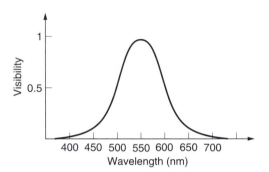

FIGURE 2.2
The luminous efficiency function shows the response of the HVS to light of different wavelengths.

WHAT IS LIGHT?

Electromagnetic radiation exists over a fantastic range of frequencies, f, and corresponding wavelengths, λ, connected to the speed of light, c, by the equation

$$c = f \times \lambda.$$

The HVS has evolved to be sensitive to a certain range of frequencies, which we call light. The frequencies are extremely high and it is the convention in optics to describe the wavelength instead.

Figure 2.2 shows that the HVS responds to radiation in the range of 400 to 700 nanometres (nm = m $\times$ 10^{-9}) according to a curve known as a *luminous efficiency function* having a value defined as unity at the peak that occurs at a wavelength of 555 nm under bright light conditions. Within that range different distributions of intensity with respect to wavelength exist, which are called *spectral power distributions* or SPDs. The variations in SPD give rise to the sensation that

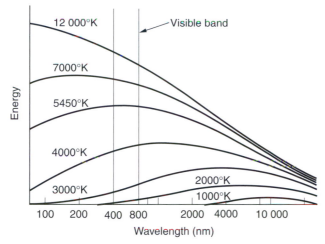

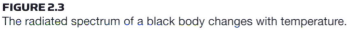

FIGURE 2.3
The radiated spectrum of a black body changes with temperature.

we call colour. A narrowband light source with a wavelength of 400 nm appears violet, and shorter wavelengths are called ultraviolet. Similarly light with a wavelength of 700 nm appears red and longer wavelengths are called infrared. Although we cannot see infrared radiation, we can feel it as the sensation of heat.

SOURCES OF LIGHT

Light sources include a wide variety of heated bodies, from the glowing particles of carbon in candle flames to the sun. Radiation from a heated body covers a wide range of wavelengths. In physics, light and radiant heat are the same thing, differing only in wavelength, and it is vital to an understanding of colour to see how they relate. This was first explained by Max Planck, who proposed the concept of a *black body*. Being perfectly nonreflective, the only radiation that could come from it would be due to its temperature. Figure 2.3 shows that the intensity and spectrum of radiation from a body are a function of the temperature. The peak of the distribution at each temperature is found on a straight line according to Wien's law.

Radiation from the sun contains ultraviolet radiation, but this is (or was) strongly scattered by the earth's atmosphere and is accordingly weak. Incidentally this scattering of short wavelengths is why the sky appears blue. As temperature falls, the intensity of the radiation becomes too low to be useful. The wavelength range of human vision evolved to sense a reasonable dynamic range of black-body radiation between practical limits.

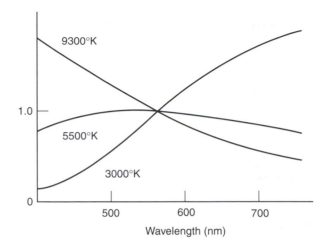

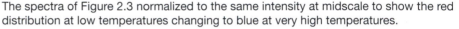

FIGURE 2.4
The spectra of Figure 2.3 normalized to the same intensity at midscale to show the red distribution at low temperatures changing to blue at very high temperatures.

The concept of *colour temperature* follows from Planck's work. Figure 2.4 shows a different version of Figure 6.3 in which the SPDs have been scaled so they all have the same level at one wavelength near the centre of the range of the HVS. A body at a temperature of around 3000° Kelvin (K) radiates an SPD centred in the infrared, and the HVS perceives only the lefthand end of the distribution as the colour red, hence the term "red hot." As the temperature increases, at about 5000°K the peak of the SPD aligns with the peak of the sensitivity of the HVS and we see white, hence the term "white hot." Red hot and white hot are a layman's colour temperature terms. A temperature of 9000°K takes the peak of the SPD into the ultraviolet and we see the righthand end of the distribution as blue. The term "blue hot" is not found because such a temperature is not commonly reached on Earth.

It is possible to characterize a thermal *illuminant* or source of light simply by specifying the temperature in degrees K of a black body that appears to be the same colour to a human observer. Non-thermal illuminants such as discharge lamps may be given an equivalent colour temperature, but their SPD may be quite different from that of a heated body. Although the radiation leaving the sun is relatively constant, the radiation arriving on earth varies throughout the day. Figure 2.5a shows that at midday, the sun is high and the path through the atmosphere is short. The amount of scattering at the blue end of the spectrum is minimal and the light has a bluish quality. However, at the end of the day, the sun is low and the path through the atmosphere is much longer, as Figure 2.5b shows. The extent of blue scattering is much greater and the remaining

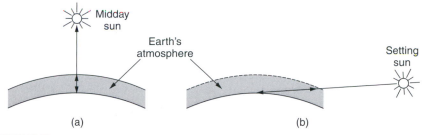

FIGURE 2.5
(a) At midday the path of sunlight through the atmosphere is short. (b) When the sun is low the path through the atmosphere is longer, making the effect of blue scattering more obvious.

radiation reaching the observer becomes first orange as the sun gets low and finally red as it sets. Thus the colour temperature of sunlight is not constant. In addition to the factors mentioned, clouds will also change the colour temperature. Light can also be emitted by atoms in which electrons have been raised from their normal, stable, orbit to one of higher energy by some form of external stimulus other than heat, which could be ultraviolet light or electrical.

Electrons that fall back to the valence band emit a quantum of energy as a photon whose frequency is proportional to the energy difference between the bands. The process is described by Planck's law,

$$\text{energy difference } E = H \times f,$$

where H is Planck's constant, 6.6262×10^{-34} Joules/Hertz.

The wavelength of the light emitted is a function of the characteristics of a particular atom, and a great variety exists. The SPD of light sources of this kind is very narrow, appearing as a *line* in the spectrum. Some materials are monochromatic, whereas some have two or more lines. Useful and efficient illuminants can be made using mixtures of materials to increase the number of lines, although the spectrum may be far from white in some cases. Such illuminants can be given an effective colour temperature, even though there is nothing in the light source at that temperature. The colour temperature is that at which a black body and the illuminant concerned give the same perceived result to the HVS. This type of light generation is the basis of mercury and sodium lights, fluorescent lights, Day-Glo paint, the aurora borealis, whiteners in washing powder, phosphors in CRT and plasma displays, lasers, and LEDs. It should be noted that although these devices have colour temperatures as far as the HVS is concerned, their line spectrum structure may cause them to have unnatural effects on other colour-sensitive devices such as film and TV cameras.

OPTICAL PRINCIPLES

The wave theory of light suggests that a wavefront advances because an infinite number of point sources can be considered to emit spherical waves, which will add only when they are all in the same phase. This can occur only in the plane of the wavefront. Figure 2.6 shows that at all other angles, interference between spherical waves is destructive. Note the similarity with sound propagation described in Chapter 5. When such a wavefront arrives at an interface with a denser medium, such as the surface of a lens, the velocity of propagation is reduced; therefore the wavelength in the medium becomes shorter, causing the wavefront to leave the interface at a different angle (Figure 2.7). This is known as refraction. The ratio of velocity *in vacuo* to velocity in the medium is known as the refractive index of that medium; it determines the relationship between the angles of the incident and the refracted wavefronts. Reflected light, however, leaves at the same angle to the normal as the incident light. If the speed of light in the medium varies with wavelength, dispersion takes place, in which incident white light will be split into a rainbow-like spectrum, leaving the interface at

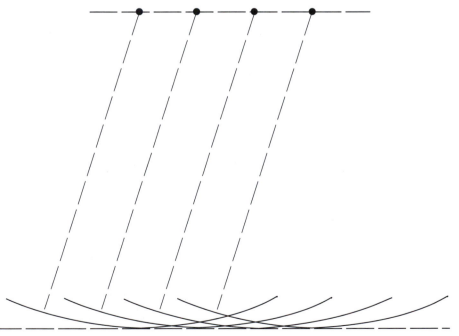

FIGURE 2.6
Plane-wave propagation considered as infinite numbers of spherical waves.

different angles. Glass used for chandeliers and cut glass is chosen to be highly dispersive, whereas glass for lenses in cameras and projectors will be chosen to have a refractive index that is as constant as possible with changing wavelength. The use of monochromatic light allows low-cost optics to be used as they need to be corrected for only a single wavelength. This is done in optical disk pickups and in colour projectors that use one optical system for each colour.

In natural light, the electric-field component will be in many planes. Light is said to be polarized when the electric field direction is constrained. The wave can be considered as made up of two orthogonal components. When these are in phase, the polarization is said to be linear. When there is a phase shift between the components, the polarization is said to be elliptical, with a special case at 90° called circular polarization. These types of polarization are contrasted in Figure 2.8. To create polarized light, anisotropic materials are necessary. Polaroid material, invented by Edwin Land, is vinyl that is made anisotropic by stretching it whilst hot. This causes the long polymer molecules to line up

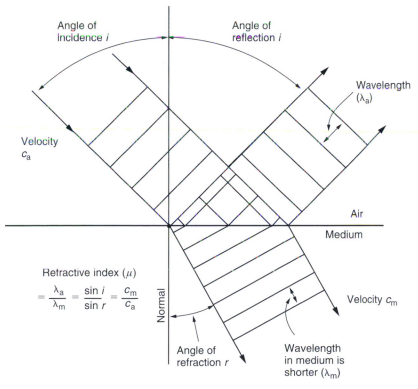

FIGURE 2.7
Reflection and refraction, showing the effect of the velocity of light in a medium.

Polarisation

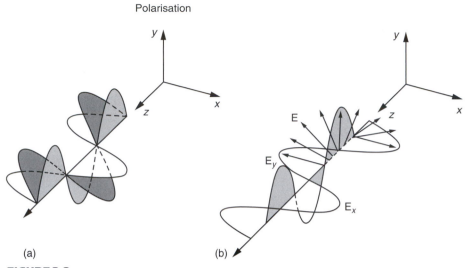

(a)   (b)

FIGURE 2.8
(a) Linear polarization: orthogonal components are in phase. (b) Circular polarization: orthogonal components are in phase quadrature.

along the axis of stretching. If the material is soaked in iodine, the molecules are rendered conductive and short out any electric-field component along themselves. Electric fields at right angles are unaffected; thus the transmission plane is at right angles to the stretching axis.

Stretching plastics can also result in anisotropy of the refractive index; this effect is known as birefringence. If a linearly polarized wavefront enters such a medium, the two orthogonal components propagate at different velocities, causing a relative phase difference proportional to the distance travelled. The plane of polarization of the light is rotated. Where the thickness of the material is such that a 90° phase change is caused, the device is known as a quarter-wave plate. The action of such a device is shown in Figure 2.9. If the plane of polarization of the incident light is at 45° to the planes of greatest and least refractive index, the two orthogonal components of the light will be of equal magnitude, and this results in circular polarization. Similarly, circular-polarized light can be returned to the linear-polarized state by a further quarter-wave plate. Rotation of the plane of polarization is a useful method of separating incident and reflected light in a laser disk pickup. Using a quarter-wave plate, the plane of polarization of light leaving the pickup will have been turned 45°, and on return it will be rotated a further 45°, so that it is now at right angles to the plane of polarization of light from the source. The two can easily be separated by a polarizing prism, which

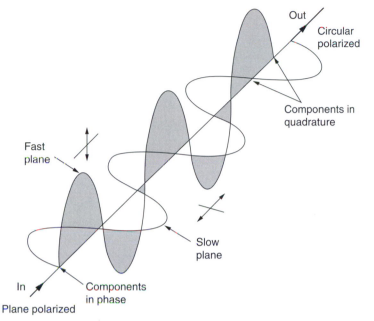

FIGURE 2.9
Different speeds of light in different planes rotate the plane of polarization in a quarter-wave plate to give a circularly polarized output.

acts as a transparent block to light in one plane, but as a prism to light in the other plane, such that reflected light is directed toward the sensor.

PHOTOMETRIC UNITS

Radiometric and photometric units are different because the latter are affected by the luminous efficiency function of the eye. Figure 2.10 shows the two sets of units for comparison. Figure 2.11 shows an imaginary point light source radiating equally in all directions. An imaginary sphere surrounds the source. The source itself has a power output, measured in Watts, and this power uniformly passes through the area of the sphere, so the power per unit area will follow an inverse square law. Power per unit area is known as intensity, with units of Watts per square metre. Given a surface radiating with a certain intensity, viewed at right angles to the surface the maximum *brightness* would be measured. Viewed from any other angle the brightness would fall off as a cosine function. The above units are indifferent to wavelength and whether the HVS can see the radiation concerned. In photometry, the equivalent of power is *luminous flux*, whose unit is the lumen, the equivalent of intensity is *luminous intensity* measured in candela, and the equivalent of brightness is *luminance*, measured in nits.

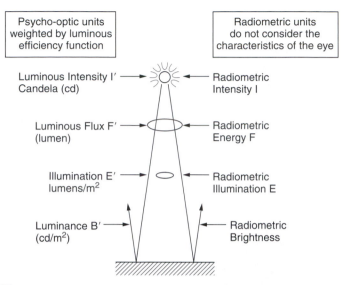

FIGURE 2.10
Radiometric and photometric units compared.

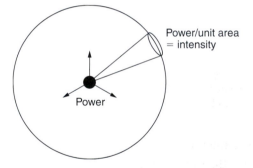

FIGURE 2.11
An imaginary point source radiating through a spherical area is helpful to visualize the units used to measure light.

It is difficult to maintain a standard of luminous flux, so instead the candela (cd) is defined. The candela replaced the earlier unit of candle power and is defined in such a way as to make the two units approximately the same. One square centimetre of platinum at its freezing point of 2042°K radiates 60 cd. The lumen is defined as the luminous flux radiated over a unit solid angle by a source whose intensity is one candela. The nit is defined as one candela per square metre. As an example, a CRT may reach 200–300 nits.

In an optical system, the power of the source is often concentrated in a certain direction and so for a fixed number of candela the brightness in that direction would rise. This is the optical equivalent of forward gain in an antenna.

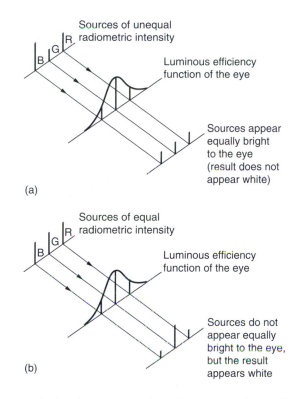

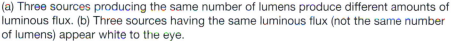

FIGURE 2.12
(a) Three sources producing the same number of lumens produce different amounts of luminous flux. (b) Three sources having the same luminous flux (not the same number of lumens) appear white to the eye.

The lumen (lm) is a weighted value based on the luminous efficiency function of the HVS. Thus the same numerical value in lumens will appear equally bright to the HVS whatever the colour. If three sources of light, red, green, and blue, each of one lumen, are added, the total luminous flux will be three lumen but the result will not appear white. It is worthwhile discussing this in some detail. Figure 2.12a shows three monochromatic light sources of variable intensity that are weighted by the luminous efficiency function of the HVS to measure the luminous flux correctly. To obtain one lumen from each source, the red and blue sources must be set to produce more luminous flux than the green source. This means that the spectral distribution of the source is no longer uniform and so it will not appear white. In contrast, Figure 2.12b shows three sources that have the same luminous flux. After being weighted by the luminous efficiency function, each source produces a different number of lumens, but the eye perceives the effect as white. Essentially the eye has a non-uniform response, but in judging colour it appears to compensate for that so

MTF, CONTRAST, AND SHARPNESS

All imaging devices, including the eye, have finite performance, and the modulation transfer function (MTF) is a way of describing the ability of an imaging system to carry detail. The MTF is essentially an optical frequency response and is a function of depth of contrast with respect to spatial frequency. Prior to describing the MTF it is necessary to define some terms used in assessing image quality.

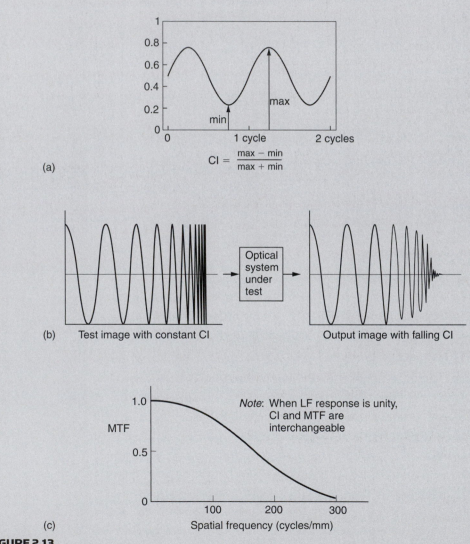

(a)

$$CI = \frac{max - min}{max + min}$$

(b) Test image with constant CI

Output image with falling CI

Note: When LF response is unity, CI and MTF are interchangeable

(c)

FIGURE 2.13
(a) The definition of contrast index (CI). (b) Frequency sweep test image having constant CI. (c) MTF is the ratio of output and input CIs.

Spatial frequency is measured in cycles per millimetre (mm^{-1}). Contrast index (CI) is shown in Figure 2.13a. The luminance variation across an image has peaks and troughs and the relative size of these is used to calculate the contrast index as shown. A test image can be made having the same contrast index over a range of spatial frequencies as shown in Figure 2.13b. If a non-ideal optical system is used to examine the test image, the output will have a contrast index that falls with rising spatial frequency.

The ratio of the output CI to the input CI is the MTF as shown in Figure 2.13c. In the special case in which the input CI is unity, the output CI is identical to the output MTF. It is common to measure resolution by quoting the frequency at which the MTF has fallen to one-half. This is known as the 50 percent MTF frequency. The limiting resolution is defined as the point at which the MTF has fallen to 10 percent.

Whilst MTF resolution testing is objective, human vision is subjective and gives an impression we call sharpness. However, the assessment of sharpness is affected by contrast. Increasing the contrast of an image will result in an increased sensation of sharpness even though the MTF is unchanged. When CRTs having black areas between the phosphors were introduced, it was found that the improved contrast resulted in subjectively improved sharpness even though the MTF was unchanged.

Similar results are obtained with CRTs having non-reflective coatings. The perceived contrast of a display is also a function of the surroundings. Displays viewed in dark surroundings, such as cinema film and transparencies, appear to lack contrast, whereas when the same technical contrast is displayed with light surroundings, the contrast appears correct. This is known as the *surround effect*. It can be overcome by artificially expanding the contrast prior to the display. This will be considered later when the subject of gamma is treated.

that a spectrum that is physically white, i.e., having equal luminous flux at all visible wavelengths, also appears white to the eye. As a consequence it is more convenient to have a set of units in which equal values result in white. These are known as *tristimulus units* and are obtained by weighting the value in lumens by a factor that depends on the response of the eye to each of the three wavelengths. The weighting factors add up to unity so that three tristimulus units, one of each colour, when added together produce one lumen.

THE HUMAN VISUAL SYSTEM

The HVS evolved as a survival tool. A species that could use vision to sense an impending threat or to locate food or a mate would have an obvious advantage. From an evolutionary standpoint, using the visual system to appreciate art or entertainment media is very recent.

The HVS has two obvious transducers, namely the eyes, coupled to a series of less obvious but extremely sophisticated processes, which take place in the brain. The result of these processes is what we call sight, a phenomenon that is difficult to describe. At an average reading distance of 350 mm, the letters in this book subtend an angle to the eye of about a third of a degree. The lines from which the letters are formed are about one-tenth of a millimetre across and subtend an angle of about one minute (one-sixtieth of a degree). The field of view of the HVS is nearly a hemisphere. A short calculation will reveal how many pixels would be needed to convey that degree of resolution over such a wide field of view. The result is simply staggering. If we add colour and we also wish to update all those pixels to allow motion, it is possible to estimate what bandwidth would be needed. The result is so large that it is utterly inconceivable that the nerves from the eye to the brain could carry so much data, or that the brain could handle it. Clearly the HVS does not work in this way. Instead the HVS does what the species finds most useful. It helps create a model in the mind of the reality around it.

Figure 2.14 shows the concept. The model can be considered like a kind of three-dimensional frame store in which objects are stored as the HVS identifies them. Inanimate objects are so-called because they do not move. They can be modelled once and left in the model until there is evidence to suggest that there has been a change. In contrast, animate objects need more attention, because they could be bringing benefit or detriment. The HVS solves both of these requirements with the same mechanism. The eyes can swivel to scan the environment and their owner can move within it. This scanning process allows the model to be built using eyes with a relatively narrow field of view. Within this narrow field of view, the provision of high resolution and colour vision does not require an absurd bandwidth, although it does require good lighting. Although the pixels are close together, the total number is fairly small.

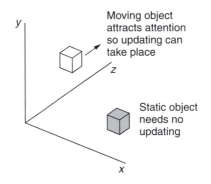

FIGURE 2.14
The human concept of reality can be likened to a three-dimensional store in the mind in which objects are placed as they are recognized. Moving objects attract the attention because they need to be updated in the model.

Such narrow vision alone is not useful because events outside the field of vision do not alert the HVS to the need for an update of the model. Thus in addition there is a wider field of view, which has relatively poor resolution and is colourblind, but which works at low light levels and responds primarily to small changes or movements. Sitting at a laptop computer writing these words, I can see only a small part of the screen in detail. The rest of the study is known only from the model. On my right is a mahogany bracket clock, but in peripheral vision it appears as a grey lump. However, in my mind the wood and the brass are still the right colour. The ticking of the clock is coming from the same place in the model as the remembered object, reinforcing the illusion.

If I were to be replaced with a camera and a stereo microphone, and the two then turned to the right toward the clock, the visual image and the sound image would both move left. However, if I myself turn right this doesn't happen. The signals from the balance organs in the ear, the sound image model, and the visual model produce data consistent with the fact that it was I that moved and the result is that the model doesn't move. Instead I have become another object in the model and am moving within it. The advantage of this detached approach is that my limbs are included in the model so that I can see an object and pick it up.

This interaction between the senses is very strong and disparities between the senses are a powerful clue that one is being shown an illusion. In advanced systems for use in electronic cinema or flight simulators, it is vital to maintain accurate tracking between the visual image, the sound image, and the sense of balance. Disparities that are not obvious may result in fatigue or nausea.

One consequence of seeing via a model is that we often see what we expect to see rather than what is before us. Optical illusions demonstrate this, and Maurits Escher turned it into an art form. The technique of camouflage destroys familiar shapes and confuses the modelling process. Animals and birds may freeze when predators approach because their lack of motion doesn't trigger peripheral vision.

THE EYE

All television signals ultimately excite some response in the eye and the viewer can describe the result only subjectively. Familiarity with the operation and limitations of the eye is essential to an understanding of television principles.

The simple representation of Figure 2.15 shows that the eyeball is nearly spherical and is swivelled by muscles so that it can track movement. This has a large bearing on the way moving pictures are reproduced. The space

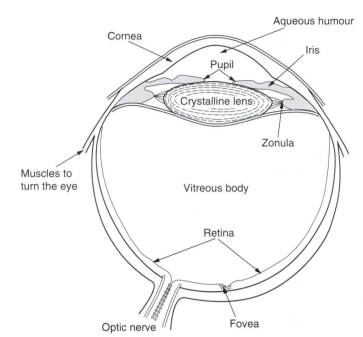

FIGURE 2.15
A simple representation of an eyeball. See text for details.

between the cornea and the lens is filled with transparent fluid known as aqueous humour. The remainder of the eyeball is filled with a transparent jelly known as vitreous humour. Light enters the cornea, and the amount of light admitted is controlled by the pupil in the iris. Light entering is involuntarily focused on the retina by the lens in a process called visual accommodation. The lens is the only part of the eye that is not nourished by the bloodstream and its centre is technically dead. In a young person the lens is flexible and muscles distort it to perform the focusing action. In old age the lens loses some flexibility and causes presbyopia or limited accommodation. In some people the length of the eyeball is incorrect, resulting in myopia (shortsightedness) or hypermetropia (longsightedness). The cornea should have the same curvature in all meridia, and if this is not the case, astigmatism results.

The retina is responsible for light sensing and contains a number of layers. The surface of the retina is covered with arteries, veins, and nerve fibres and light has to penetrate these to reach the sensitive layer. This contains two types of discrete receptors known as rods and cones from their shape. The distribution and characteristics of these two receptors are quite different. Rods dominate the periphery of the retina, whereas cones dominate a central area known as the fovea, outside which their density drops off. Vision using the rods is monochromatic

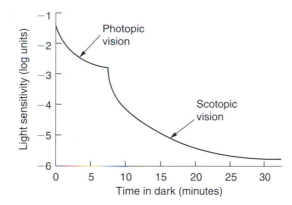

FIGURE 2.16
Retinal sensitivity changes after sudden darkness. The initial curve is due to adaptation of cones. At very low light levels cones are blind and monochrome rod vision takes over.

and has poor resolution but remains effective at very low light levels, whereas the cones provide high resolution and colour vision but require more light. Figure 2.16 shows how the sensitivity of the retina slowly increases in response to entering darkness. The first part of the curve is the adaptation of cone or photopic vision. This is followed by the greater adaptation of the rods in scotopic vision. At such low light levels the fovea is essentially blind and small objects that can be seen in the peripheral rod vision disappear when stared at.

The cones in the fovea are densely packed and directly connected to the nervous system, allowing the highest resolution. Resolution then falls off away from the fovea. As a result the eye must move to scan large areas of detail. The image perceived is not just a function of the retinal response, but is also affected by processing of the nerve signals. The overall acuity of the eye can be displayed as a graph of the response plotted against the degree of detail being viewed. Image detail is generally measured in lines per millimetre or cycles per picture height, but this takes no account of the distance from the image to the eye. A better unit for eye resolution is one based upon the subtended angle of detail, as this will be independent of distance. Units of cycles per degree are then appropriate. Figure 2.17 shows the response of the eye to static detail. Note that the response to very low frequencies is also attenuated. An extension of this characteristic allows the vision system to ignore the fixed pattern of shadow on the retina due to the nerves and arteries.

The retina does not respond instantly to light, but requires between 0.15 and 0.3 second before the brain perceives an image. The resolution of the eye is primarily a spatio-temporal compromise. The eye is a spatial sampling device; the spacing of the rods and cones on the retina represents a spatial sampling

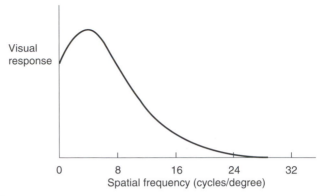

FIGURE 2.17
Response of the eye to different degrees of detail.

frequency. The measured acuity of the eye exceeds the value calculated from the sample site spacing because a form of oversampling is used.

The eye is in a continuous state of unconscious vibration called saccadic motion. This causes the sampling sites to exist in more than one location, effectively increasing the spatial sampling rate provided there is a temporal filter that is able to integrate the information from the various positions of the retina.

This temporal filtering is responsible for "persistence of vision." Flashing lights are perceived to flicker until the critical flicker frequency (CFF) is reached; the light appears continuous for higher frequencies. The CFF is not constant but varies with brightness. Note that the field rate of European television at 50 fields per second is marginal with bright images. Film projected at 48 Hz works because cinemas are darkened and the screen brightness is actually quite low. Figure 2.18 shows the two-dimensional or spatiotemporal response of the eye.

If the eye were static, a detailed object moving past it would give rise to temporal frequencies, as Figure 2.19a shows. The temporal frequency is given by the detail in the object, in lines per millimetre, multiplied by the speed. Clearly a highly detailed object can reach high temporal frequencies even at slow speeds, yet Figure 2.18 shows that the eye cannot respond to high temporal frequencies.

However, the human viewer has an interactive visual system, which causes the eyes to track the movement of any object of interest. Figure 2.19b shows that when eye tracking is considered, a moving object is rendered stationary with respect to the retina so that temporal frequencies fall to zero and much the same acuity to detail is available despite motion. This is known as dynamic resolution and it is how humans judge the detail in real moving pictures. Dynamic resolution will be considered in the next section.

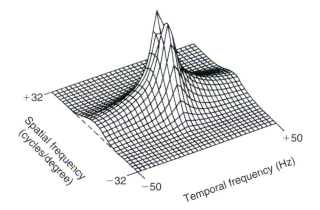

FIGURE 2.18

The response of the eye shown with respect to temporal and spatial frequencies. Note that even slow relative movement causes a serious loss of resolution. The eye tracks moving objects to prevent this loss.

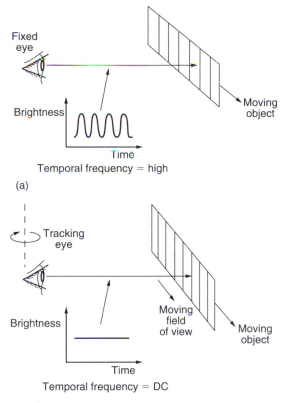

FIGURE 2.19

In (a) a detailed object moves past a fixed eye, causing temporal frequencies beyond the response of the eye. This is the cause of motion blur. In (b) the eye tracks the motion and the temporal frequency becomes zero. Motion blur cannot then occur.

GAMMA

The true brightness of a television picture can be affected by electrical noise on the video signal. As contrast sensitivity is proportional to brightness, noise is more visible in dark picture areas than in bright areas. For economic reasons, video signals have to be made nonlinear to render noise less visible. An inverse gamma function takes place at the camera so that the video signal is nonlinear for most of its journey. Figure 2.20 shows a reverse gamma function. As a true power function requires infinite gain near black, a linear segment is substituted. It will be seen that contrast variations near black result in larger signal amplitude than variations near white. The result is that noise picked up by the video signal has less effect on dark areas than on bright areas. After a gamma function at the display, noise at near-black levels is compressed with respect to noise at near-white levels. Thus a video transmission system using gamma has a lower perceived noise level than one without. Without gamma, vision signals would need around 30 dB better signal-to-noise ratio for the same perceived quality and digital video samples would need 5 or 6 extra bits.

In practice the system is not rendered perfectly linear by gamma correction and a slight overall exponential effect is usually retained to reduce further the effect of noise in the darker parts of the picture. A gamma correction factor of 0.45 may be used to achieve this effect.

Clearly image data that are intended for display on a video system must have the correct gamma characteristic or the grey scale will not be correctly reproduced. Image data from computer systems often have gamma characteristics that are incompatible with the standards adopted in video and a gamma conversion process will be required to obtain a correct display. This may take the form of a lookup table.

Electrical noise has no DC component and so cannot shift the average video voltage. However, on extremely noisy signals, the nonlinear effect of gamma is to exaggerate the white-going noise spikes more than the black-going spikes. The result is that the black level appears to rise and the picture loses contrast.

There is a strong argument to retain gamma in the digital domain for analog compatibility. In the digital domain transmission noise is eliminated, but instead the conversion process introduces quantizing noise. Consequently gamma is retained in the digital domain.

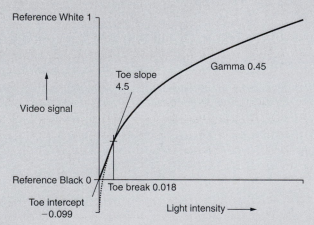

FIGURE 2.20
CCIR Rec. 709 inverse gamma function used at camera has a straight line approximation at the lower part of the curve to avoid boosting camera noise. Note that the output amplitude is greater for modulation near black.

Figure 2.21 shows that digital luma can be considered in several equivalent ways. In Figure 2.21a a linear analog luminance signal is passed through a gamma corrector to create luma and this is then quantized uniformly. In (b) the linear analog luminance signal is fed directly to a nonuniform quantizer. In (c) the linear analog luminance signal is uniformly quantized to produce digital luminance. This is converted to digital luma by a digital process having a nonlinear transfer function.

Whilst the three techniques shown give the same result, (a) is the simplest, (b) requires a special ADC with gamma-spaced quantizing steps, and (c) requires a high-resolution ADC of perhaps 14 or 16 bits because it works in the linear luminance domain where noise is highly visible. Technique (c) is used in digital processing cameras, in which long word length is common practice.

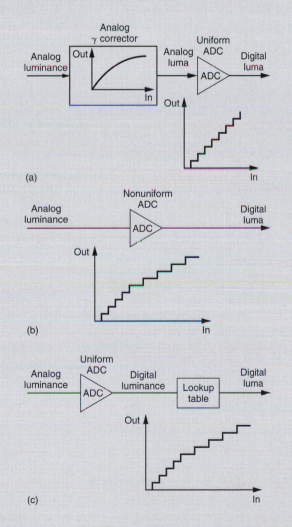

FIGURE 2.21
(a) Analog gamma correction prior to ADC. (b) Non-uniform quantizer gives direct gamma conversion.
(c) Digital gamma correction using lookup table.

As digital luma with 8-bit resolution gives the same subjective performance as digital luminance with 14-bit resolution it will be seen that gamma can also be considered an effective perceptive compression technique.

As all television signals, analog and digital, are subject to gamma correction, it is technically incorrect to refer to the Y signal as luminance, because this parameter is defined as linear in colorimetry. Charles Poynton proposed that the term luma should be used to describe luminance that has been gamma corrected.

The contrast sensitivity of the eye is defined as the smallest brightness difference that is visible. In fact the contrast sensitivity is not constant, but increases in proportion to brightness. Thus whatever the brightness of an object, if that brightness changes by about 1 percent it will be equally detectable.

MOTION PORTRAYAL AND DYNAMIC RESOLUTION

As the eye uses involuntary tracking at all times, the criterion for measuring the definition of moving image portrayal systems has to be dynamic resolution, defined as the apparent resolution perceived by the viewer in an object moving within the limits of accurate eye tracking. The traditional metric of static resolution in film and television has to be abandoned as unrepresentative.

Figure 2.22a shows that when the moving eye tracks an object on the screen, the viewer is watching with respect to the optic flow axis, not the time axis, and these are not parallel when there is motion. The optic flow axis is defined as an imaginary axis in the spatio-temporal volume that joins the same points on objects in successive frames. When many objects move independently each will have its own optic flow axis.

The optic flow axis is identified by motion-compensated standards convertors to eliminate judder and also by MPEG compressors because the greatest similarity from one picture to the next is along that axis. The success of these devices is testimony to the importance of the theory.

Figure 2.22b shows that when the eye is tracking, successive pictures appear in different places with respect to the retina. In other words if an object is moving down the screen and followed by the eye, the raster is actually moving up with respect to the retina. Although the tracked object is stationary with respect to the retina and temporal frequencies are zero, the object is moving with respect to the sensor and the display and in those units high temporal frequencies will exist. If the motion of the object on the sensor is not correctly portrayed, dynamic resolution will suffer.

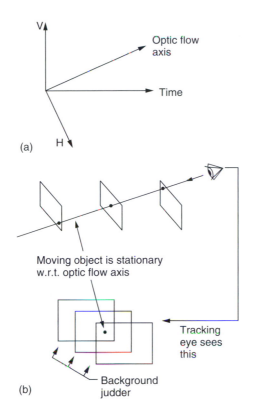

FIGURE 2.22
(a) The optic flow axis joins points on a moving object in successive pictures.
(b) When a tracking eye follows a moving object on a screen, that screen will be seen
in a different place at each picture. This is the origin of background strobing.

In real-life eye tracking, the motion of the background will be smooth, but in
an image-portrayal system based on periodic presentation of frames, the background will be presented to the retina in a different position in each frame. The
retina separately perceives each impression of the background, leading to an
effect called background strobing.

The criterion for the selection of a display frame rate in an imaging system is sufficient reduction of background strobing. It is a complete myth that the display
rate simply needs to exceed the critical flicker frequency. Manufacturers of graphics displays that use frame rates well in excess of those used in film and television are doing so for a valid reason: it gives better results! Note that the display
rate and the transmission rate need not be the same in an advanced system.

Dynamic resolution analysis confirms that both interlaced television and conventionally projected cinema film are both seriously sub-optimal. In contrast,
progressively scanned television systems have no such defects.

SCANNING

It is difficult to convey two-dimensional images from one place to another directly, whereas electrical and radio signals are easily carried. The problem is how to convert a two-dimensional image into a single voltage changing with time. The solution is to use the principle of scanning. Figure 2.23a shows that the monochrome camera produces a video signal whose voltage is a function of the image brightness at a single point on the sensor. This voltage is converted back to the brightness of the same point on the display. The points on the sensor and display must be scanned synchronously if the picture is to be re-created properly. If this is done rapidly enough it is largely invisible to the eye. Figure 2.23b shows that the scanning is controlled by a triangular or sawtooth waveform in each dimension, which causes a constant-speed forward scan followed by a rapid return or flyback. As the horizontal scan is much more

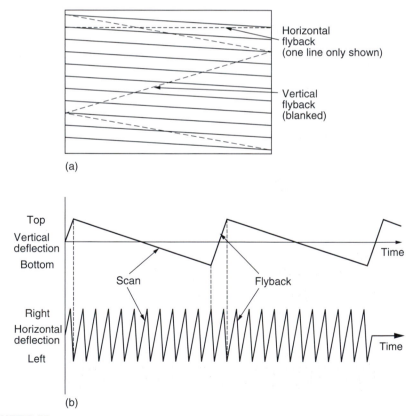

FIGURE 2.23
Scanning converts two-dimensional images into a signal that can be sent electrically. In (a) the scanning of camera and display must be identical. (b) The scanning is controlled by horizontal and vertical sawtooth waveforms.

rapid than the vertical scan the image is broken up into lines that are not quite horizontal.

In the example of Figure 2.23b, the horizontal scanning frequency or line rate, F_h, is an integer multiple of the vertical scanning frequency, or frame rate, and a progressive scan system results in which every frame is identical. Figure 2.23c shows an interlaced scan system in which there is an integer number of lines in two vertical scans or fields. The first field begins with a full line and ends on a half line and the second field begins with a half line and ends with a full line. The lines from the two fields interlace or mesh on the screen. Current analog broadcast systems such as PAL (Phase Alternate Line) and NTSC (National Television Systems Committee) use interlace, although in MPEG systems it is not necessary.

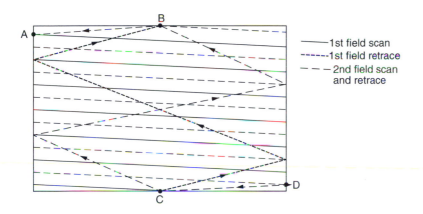

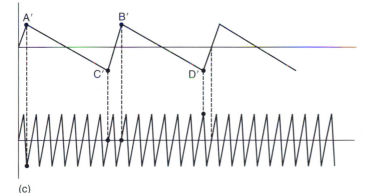

(c)

FIGURE 2.23
(Continued) (c) Where two vertical scans are needed to complete a whole number of lines, the scan is interlaced. The frame is now split into two fields.

PROGRESSIVE OR INTERLACED SCAN?

Interlaced scanning is a crude compression technique, which was developed empirically in the 1930s as a way of increasing the picture rate to reduce flicker without a matching increase in the video bandwidth. Instead of transmitting entire frames, the lines of the frame are sorted into odd lines and even lines. Odd lines are transmitted in one field, even lines in the next. A pair of fields is supposed to interlace to produce a frame, but it will be seen that this frequently does not happen. Figure 2.24a shows that the vertical/temporal arrangement of lines in an interlaced system forms a quincunx pattern (somewhat like the five of dice). Not surprisingly the vertical/temporal spectrum of an interlaced signal shows the same pattern.

Study of the vertical/temporal spectrum allows many of the characteristics of interlace to be deduced. Like quincunxial spatial sampling, interlace has a triangular passband, as Figure 2.24b shows. The highest vertical

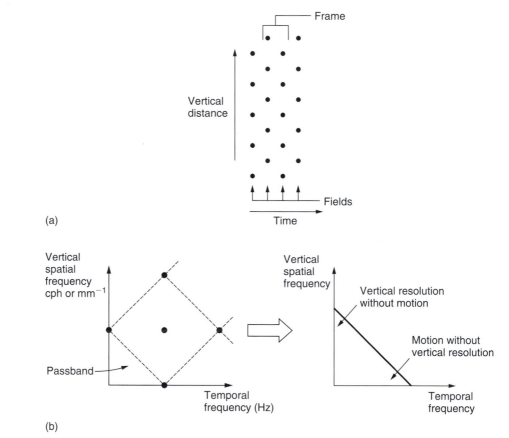

(a)

(b)

FIGURE 2.24
(a) Interlaced systems shift the lines in between pictures. Two pictures, or fields, make a frame. (b) The vertical temporal spectrum of an interlaced system and its triangular passband, allowing motion or vertical resolution but not both.

resolution is obtained at the point shown, and this is obtained only with a temporal frequency of zero, i.e., when there is no motion. This suggests that interlaced systems have poor dynamic resolution, which is what is found in practice.

Although the passband is triangular, a suitable reconstruction filter cannot be implemented in any known display. Figure 2.24c shows that in, for example, a CRT display, there is no temporal filter, only a vertical filter due to the aperture effect of the electron beam. There are two problems: First, fine vertical detail will be displayed at the frame rate. The result is that although the field rate is above the CFF, a significant amount of frame rate energy is still present to cause flicker. Second, in the presence of motion there will be vertical aliasing. Transform duality holds that any phenomenon can be described in both domains. Figure 2.24d shows that vertical detail such as an edge may be present in only one field of the pair and this results in frame rate flicker called "interlace twitter."

Figure 2.25a shows a dynamic resolution analysis of interlaced scanning. When there is no motion, the optic flow axis and the time axis are parallel and the apparent vertical sampling rate is the number of lines in a frame. However, when there is vertical motion (Figure 2.25b), the optic flow axis turns. In the case shown, the sampling structure due to interlace results in the vertical sampling rate falling to one-half its stationary value. Consequently interlace does exactly what would be expected from a half-bandwidth filter. It halves the vertical resolution when

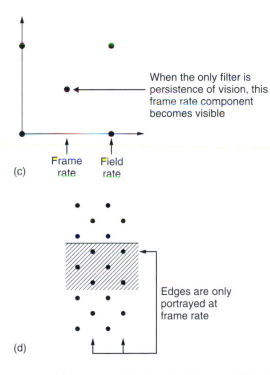

(c)

Frame rate   Field rate

When the only filter is persistence of vision, this frame rate component becomes visible

(d)

Edges are only portrayed at frame rate

FIGURE 2.24
(Continued) (c) With the spectrum of (b) on a real display, the triangular filter is absent, allowing energy at the frame rate to be visible as flicker. (d) The flicker originates on horizontal edges, which appear in only one field.

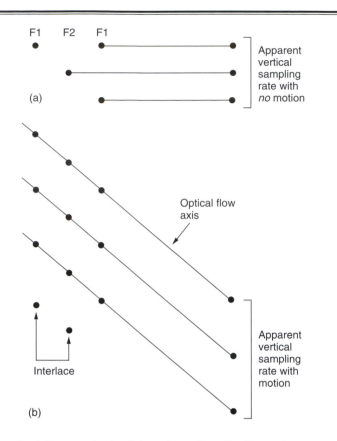

F1   F2   F1

Apparent
vertical
sampling
rate with
(a)   *no* motion

Optical flow
axis

Interlace

Apparent
vertical
sampling
rate with
motion

(b)

FIGURE 2.25
When an interlaced picture is stationary, viewing takes place along the time axis.

any motion with a vertical component occurs. In a practical television system, there is no anti-aliasing filter in the vertical axis and so when the vertical sampling rate of an interlaced system is halved by motion, high spatial frequencies will alias or heterodyne, causing annoying artifacts in the picture. This is easily demonstrated.

Figure 2.26a shows how a vertical spatial frequency well within the static resolution of the system aliases when motion occurs. In a progressive scan system this effect is absent and the dynamic resolution due to scanning can be the same as the static case. Interlaced systems handle motion transverse to the scanning lines very poorly by aliasing, whereas motion parallel to the scanning lines results in a strange artifact. If the eye is tracking a horizontally moving object, the object itself will be portrayed quite well because the interlace mechanism will work. However, Figure 2.26b shows that the background strobing will appear *feathered* because only half of the lines are present in each version of the background. Vertical edges in the background appear as shown in the figure.

Feathering is less noticeable than vertical aliasing and for this reason interlaced television systems always have horizontal raster lines. In real life, horizontal motion is more common than vertical.

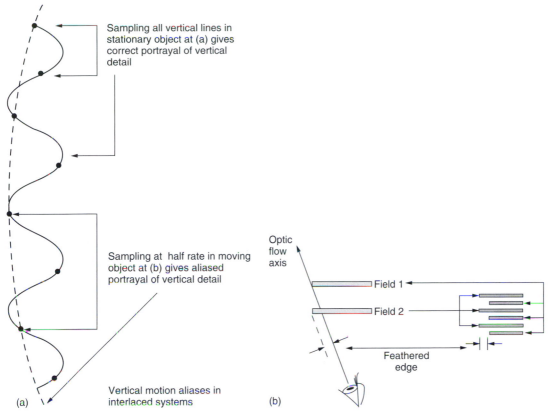

Sampling all vertical lines in stationary object at (a) gives correct portrayal of vertical detail

Sampling at half rate in moving object at (b) gives aliased portrayal of vertical detail

Optic flow axis

Field 1

Field 2

Feathered edge

Vertical motion aliases in interlaced systems

(a)

(b)

FIGURE 2.26
(a) The halving in sampling rate causes high spatial frequencies to alias. (b) To an eye following a horizontally moving object, vertical lines in the background will appear feathered because each field appears at a different place on the retina.

It is easy to calculate the vertical image motion velocity needed to obtain the half-bandwidth speed of interlace, because it amounts to one raster line per field. In 525/60 (NTSC) there are about 500 active lines, so motion as slow as one picture height in 8 seconds will halve the dynamic resolution. In 625/50 (PAL) there are about 600 lines, so the half-bandwidth speed falls to one picture height in 12 seconds. This is why NTSC, with fewer lines and lower bandwidth, doesn't look soft, as might be expected compared to PAL, because it actually has better dynamic resolution. Figure 2.27 shows that the situation deteriorates rapidly if an attempt is made to use interlaced scanning in systems with a lot of lines. In 1250/50, the resolution is halved at a vertical speed of just one picture height in 24 seconds. In other words on real moving video a 1250/50 interlaced system has the same dynamic resolution as a 625/50 progressive system. By the same argument a 1080 I system has the same performance as a 480 P system.

Now that techniques such as digital compression and spatial oversampling are available, the format used for display need not be the same as the transmission format. Thus it is difficult to justify the use of interlace in a

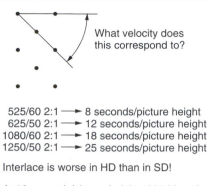

What velocity does this correspond to?

525/60 2:1 ⟶ 8 seconds/picture height
625/50 2:1 ⟶ 12 seconds/picture height
1080/60 2:1 ⟶ 18 seconds/picture height
1250/50 2:1 ⟶ 25 seconds/picture height

Interlace is worse in HD than in SD!

At 18 seconds/picture height 1080 I has the same vertical resolution as static NTSC

FIGURE 2.27
Interlace works best in systems with few lines, e.g., NTSC. Increasing the number of lines reduces performance if the frame rate is not also raised. Here are shown the vertical velocities at which various interlace standards fail.

transmission format. In fact interlace causes difficulties that are absent in progressive systems. Progressive systems are separable. Vertical filtering need not affect the time axis and vice versa. Interlaced systems are not separable, and two-dimensional filtering is mandatory. A vertical process requires motion compensation in an interlaced system, whereas in a progressive system it does not. Interlace, however, makes motion estimation more difficult. When compression is used, compression systems should not be cascaded. As digital compression techniques based on transforms are now available, it makes no sense to use an interlaced, i.e., compressed, video signal as an input. Better results will be obtained if a progressive scan signal is used.

Computer-generated images and film are not interlaced, but consist of discrete frames spaced on a time axis. As digital technology is bringing computers and television closer the use of interlaced transmission is an embarrassing source of incompatibility. The future will bring image delivery systems based on computer technology and oversampling cameras and displays that can operate at resolutions much closer to the theoretical limits. Given the level of technology at the time of its introduction, interlace was an appropriate solution, whereas it now impedes progress. Interlace causes difficulty in any process that requires image manipulation. This includes DVE (digital video effects) generators, standards convertors, and display convertors/scalers. All these devices give better results when working with progressively scanned data and if the source material is interlaced, a de-interlacing process will be necessary and will be considered in Chapter 5.

SYNCHRONISING

It is vital that the horizontal and the vertical scanning at the camera are simultaneously replicated at the display. This is the job of the synchronising or sync system, which must send timing information to the display alongside the video signal. In very early television equipment this was achieved using two quite separate or noncomposite signals. Figure 2.28a shows one of the first (U.S.) television signal standards in which the video waveform had an amplitude of 1 Volt peak to peak (pk–pk) and the sync signal had an amplitude of 4 Volts pk–pk. In practice, it was more convenient to combine both into a single electrical waveform, called at the time composite video, which carries the synchronising information as well as the scanned brightness signal. The single signal is effectively shared by using some of the flyback period for synchronising.

The 4 Volt sync signal was attenuated by a factor of 10 and added to the video to produce a 1.4-Volt pk–pk signal. This was the origin of the 10:4 video: sync relationship of U.S. analog television practice. Later the amplitude was reduced to 1 Volt pk–pk so that the signal had the same range as the original noncomposite video. The 10:4 ratio was retained. As Figure 2.28b shows, this ratio results in some rather odd voltages, and to simplify matters, a new unit called the IRE unit (after the Institute of Radio Engineers) was devised. Originally this was defined as 1 percent of the video voltage swing, independent of the actual amplitude in use, but it came in practice to mean 1 percent of 0.714 Volt. In European analog systems shown in Figure 2.28c the messy numbers were avoided by using a 7:3 ratio and the waveforms are always measured in milli-Volts. Whilst such a signal was originally called composite video, today it would be referred to as monochrome video or Ys, meaning "luma carrying syncs," although in practice the "s" is often omitted.

Figure 2.28d shows how the two signals are separated. The voltage swing needed to go from black to peak white is less than the total swing available. In a standard analog video signal the maximum amplitude is 1 Volt pk–pk. The upper part of the voltage range represents the variations in brightness of the image from black to white. Signals below that range are "blacker than black" and cannot be seen on the display. These signals are used for synchronising.

Figure 2.29a shows the line synchronising system partway through a field or frame. The part of the waveform that corresponds to the forward scan is called

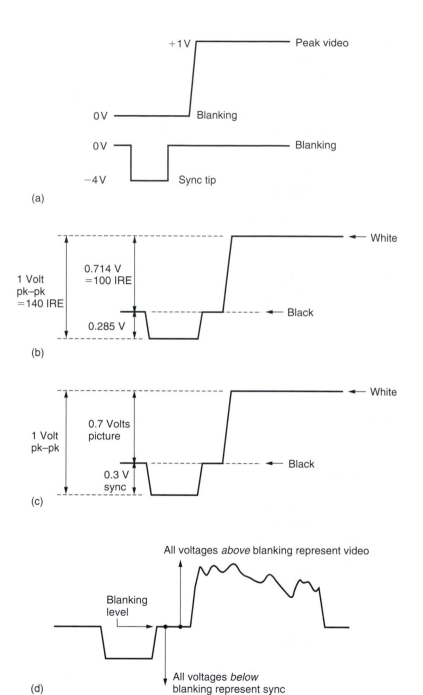

FIGURE 2.28

(a) Early video used separate vision and sync signals. The U.S. one-Volt video waveform in (b) has a 10:4 video:sync ratio. (c) European systems use a 7:3 ratio to avoid odd voltages. (d) Sync separation relies on two voltage ranges in the signal.

the active line and during the active line the voltage represents the brightness of the image. In between the active line periods are horizontal blanking intervals in which the signal voltage will be at or below black. Figure 2.29b shows that in some systems the active line voltage is superimposed on a pedestal or black level setup voltage of 7.5 IRE. The purpose of this setup is to ensure that the blanking interval signal is below black on simple displays so that it is guaranteed to be invisible on the screen. When setup is used, black level and blanking level differ by the pedestal height. When setup is not used, black level and blanking level are one and the same.

The blanking period immediately after the active line is known as the front porch, which is followed by the leading edge of sync. When the leading edge of sync passes through 50 percent of its own amplitude, the horizontal retrace pulse is considered to have occurred. The flat part at the bottom of the horizontal sync pulse is known as sync tip and this is followed by the trailing edge of sync,

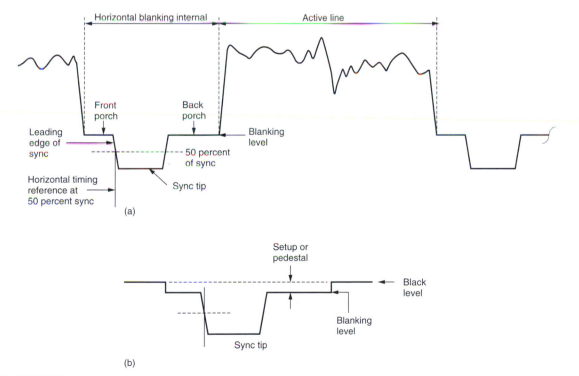

FIGURE 2.29
(a) Part of a video waveform with important features named. (b) Use of pedestal or setup.

which returns the waveform to blanking level. The signal remains at blanking level during the back porch, during which the display completes the horizontal flyback. The sync pulses have sloping edges because if they were square they would contain high frequencies, which would go outside the allowable channel bandwidth on being broadcast.

The vertical synchronising system is more complex because the vertical flyback period is much longer than the horizontal line period and horizontal synchronisation must be maintained throughout it. The vertical synchronising pulses

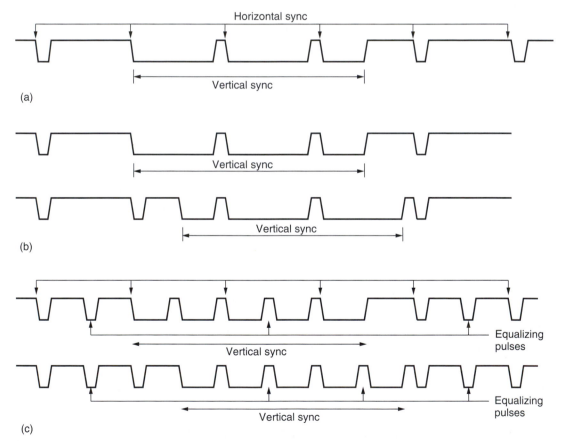

FIGURE 2.30
(a) A simple vertical pulse is longer than a horizontal pulse. (b) In an interlaced system there are two relationships between *H* and *V.* (c) The use of equalizing pulses to balance the DC component of the signal.

are much longer than horizontal pulses so that they are readily distinguishable. Figure 2.30a shows a simple approach to vertical synchronising. The signal remains predominantly at sync tip for several lines to indicate the vertical retrace, but returns to blanking level briefly immediately prior to the leading edges of the horizontal sync, which continues throughout. Figure 2.30b shows that the presence of interlace complicates matters, as in one vertical interval the vertical sync pulse coincides with a horizontal sync pulse, whereas in the next the vertical sync pulse occurs halfway down a line.

In practice the long vertical sync pulses were found to disturb the average signal voltage too much, and to reduce the effect extra equalizing pulses were put in, halfway between the horizontal sync pulses. The horizontal time base system can ignore the equalizing pulses because it contains a flywheel circuit, which expects pulses only roughly one line period apart. Figure 2.30c shows the final result of an interlaced system with equalizing pulses. The vertical blanking interval can be seen, with the vertical pulse itself toward the beginning.

In digital video signals it is possible to synchronise simply by digitizing the analog sync pulses. However, this is inefficient because many samples are needed to describe them. In practice the analog sync pulses are used to generate timing reference signals (TRS), which are special codes inserted into the video data that indicate the picture timing. In a manner analogous to the analog approach of dividing the video voltage range into two, one for syncs, the solution in the digital domain is the same: certain bit combinations are reserved for TRS codes and these cannot occur in legal video. TRS codes are detailed in Chapter 10.

It is essential to extract the timing or synchronising information from a sync or Ys signal accurately to control some processes such as the generation of a digital sampling clock. Figure 2.32a shows a block diagram of a simple sync separator. The first stage will generally consist of a black-level clamp, which stabilizes the DC conditions in the separator. Figure 2.32b shows that if this is not done the presence of a DC shift on a sync edge can cause a timing error.

The sync time is defined as the instant when the leading edge passes through the 50 percent level. The incoming signal should ideally have a sync amplitude of either 0.3 Volt pk–pk or 40 IRE, in which case it can be sliced or converted to a binary waveform by using a comparator with a reference of either 0.15 Volt

BLACK-LEVEL CLAMPING

As the synchronising and picture content of the video waveform are separated purely by the voltage range in which they lie, it is clear that if any accidental drift or offset of the signal voltage takes place it will cause difficulty. Unwanted offsets may result from low-frequency interference such as power line hum picked up by cabling. The video content of the signal also varies in amplitude with scene brightness, changing the average voltage of the signal. When such a signal passes down a channel not having a response down to DC, the baseline of the signal can wander. Such offsets can be overcome using a black-level clamp, which is shown in Figure 2.31. The video signal passes through an operational amplifier, which can add a correction voltage or DC offset to the waveform. At the output of the amplifier the video waveform is sampled by a switch, which closes briefly during the back porch when the signal should be at blanking level. The sample is compared with a locally generated reference blanking level and any discrepancy is used to generate an error signal, which drives the integrator producing the correction voltage. The correction voltage integrator will adjust itself until the error becomes zero.

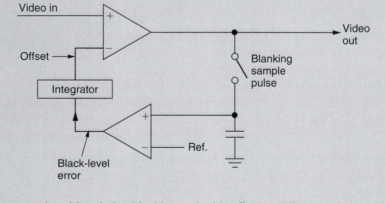

FIGURE 2.31
Black-level clamp samples video during blanking and adds offset until the sample is at black level.

or 20 IRE. However, if the sync amplitude is for any reason incorrect, the slicing level will be wrong. Figure 2.32a shows that the solution is to measure both blanking and sync tip voltages and to derive the slicing level from them with a potential divider. In this way the slicing level will always be 50 percent of the input amplitude. To measure the sync tip and blanking levels, a coarse sync separator is required, which is accurate enough to generate sampling pulses for the voltage measurement system. Figure 2.32c shows the timing of the sampling process.

Once a binary signal has been extracted from the analog input, the horizontal and vertical synchronising information can be separated. All falling edges are

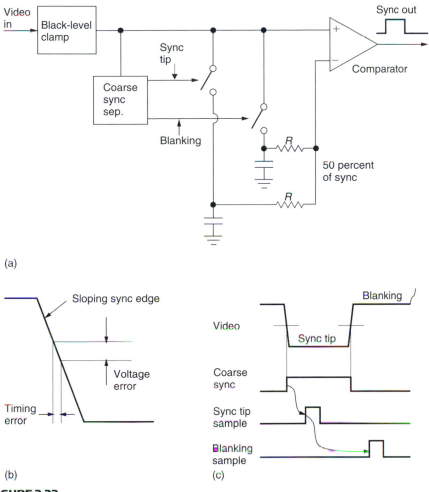

(a)

(b)   (c)

FIGURE 2.32
(a) Sync separator block diagram; see text for details. (b) Slicing at the wrong level introduces a timing error. (c) The timing of the sync separation process.

potential horizontal sync leading edges, but some are due to equalizing pulses and these must be rejected. This is easily done because equalizing pulses occur partway down the line. A flywheel oscillator or phase-locked loop will lock to genuine horizontal sync pulses because they always occur exactly one line period apart. Edges at other spacings are eliminated. Vertical sync is detected with a timer whose period exceeds that of a normal horizontal sync pulse. If the sync waveform is still low when the timer expires, there must be a vertical pulse present. Once again a phase-locked loop may be used, which will continue to run if the input is noisy or disturbed. This may take the form of a counter, which counts the number of lines in a frame before resetting.

The sync separator can determine which type of field is beginning because in one the vertical and horizontal pulses coincide, whereas in the other the vertical pulse begins in the middle of a line.

BANDWIDTH AND DEFINITION

As the conventional analog television picture is made up of lines, the line structure determines the definition or the fineness of detail that can be portrayed in the vertical axis. The limit is reached in theory when alternate lines show black and white. In a 625-line picture there are roughly 600 unblanked lines. If 300 of these are white and 300 are black then there will be 300 complete cycles of detail in one picture height. One unit of resolution, which is a unit of spatial frequency, is c/ph or cycles per picture height. In practical displays the contrast will have fallen to virtually nothing at this ideal limit and the resolution actually achieved is around 70 percent of the ideal, or about 210 c/ph. The degree to which the ideal is met is known as the Kell factor of the display.

Definition in one axis is wasted unless it is matched in the other and so the horizontal axis should be able to offer the same performance. As the aspect ratio of conventional television is 4:3 then it should be possible to display 400 cycles in one picture width, reduced to about 300 cycles by the Kell factor. As part of the line period is lost due to flyback, 300 cycles per picture width becomes about 360 cycles per line period.

In 625-line television, the frame rate is 25 Hz and so the line rate F_h will be

$$F_h = 625 \times 25 = 15,625 \, \text{Hz}.$$

If 360 cycles of video waveform must be carried in each line period, then the bandwidth required will be given by

$$15,625 \times 360 = 5.625 \, \text{MHz}.$$

In the 525-line system, there are roughly 500 unblanked lines allowing 250 c/ph theoretical definition, or 175 lines allowing for the Kell factor. Allowing for the aspect ratio, equal horizontal definition requires about 230 cycles per picture width. Allowing for horizontal blanking this requires about 280 cycles per line period.

In 525-line video, $F_h = 525 \times 30 = 15{,}750\,Hz$. Thus the bandwidth required is

$$15{,}750 \times 280 = 4.4\,MHz.$$

If it is proposed to build a high-definition television system, one might start by doubling the number of lines and hence double the definition. Thus in a 1250-line format about 420 c/ph might be obtained. To achieve equal horizontal definition, bearing in mind the aspect ratio is now 16:9, then nearly 750 cycles per picture width will be needed. Allowing for horizontal blanking, then around 890 cycles per line period will be needed. The line frequency is now given by

$$F_h = 1250 \times 25 = 31{,}250\,Hz$$

and the bandwidth required is given by

$$31{,}250 \times 890 = 28\,MHz.$$

Note the dramatic increase in bandwidth. In general the bandwidth rises as the square of the resolution because there are more lines and more cycles needed in each line. It should be clear that, except for research purposes, high-definition television will never be broadcast as a conventional analog signal because the bandwidth required is simply uneconomic. If and when high-definition broadcasting becomes common, digital compression techniques will make it economical.

APERTURE EFFECT

The aperture effect will show up in many aspects of television in both the sampled and the continuous domains. The image sensor has a finite aperture function. In tube cameras and in CRTs, the beam will have a finite radius with a Gaussian distribution of energy across its diameter. This results in a Gaussian spatial frequency response. Tube cameras often contain an aperture corrector, which is a filter designed to boost the higher spatial frequencies that are attenuated by the Gaussian response. The horizontal filter is simple enough, but the vertical filter will require line delays to produce points above and below the line

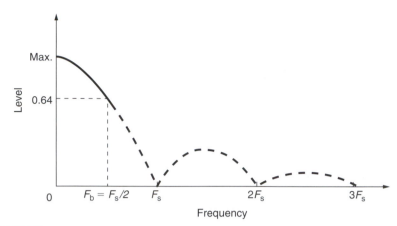

FIGURE 2.33
Frequency response with 100 percent aperture nulls at multiples of sampling rate. The area of interest is up to half the sampling rate.

to be corrected. Aperture correctors also amplify aliasing products and an over-corrected signal may contain more vertical aliasing than resolution.

Some digital-to-analog convertors keep the signal constant for a substantial part of or even the whole sample period. In CCD cameras, the sensor is split into elements that may almost touch in some cases. The element integrates light falling on its surface. In both cases the aperture will be rectangular. The case in which the pulses have been extended in width to become equal to the sample period is known as a zero-order hold system and has a 100 percent aperture ratio.

Rectangular apertures have a sin x/x spectrum, which is shown in Figure 2.33. With a 100 percent aperture ratio, the frequency response falls to a null at the sampling rate and as a result is about 4 dB down at the edge of the baseband.

The temporal aperture effect varies according to the equipment used. Tube cameras have a long integration time and thus a wide temporal aperture. Whilst this reduces temporal aliasing, it causes smear on moving objects. CCD cameras do not suffer from lag and as a result their temporal response is better. Some CCD cameras deliberately have a short temporal aperture as the time axis is resampled by a shutter. The intention is to reduce smear, hence the popularity of such devices for sporting events, but there will be more aliasing on certain subjects.

The eye has a temporal aperture effect, which is known as persistence of vision, and the phosphors of CRTs continue to emit light after the electron beam has passed. These produce further temporal aperture effects in series with those in the camera.

SCANNING FORMATS FOR SD AND HDTV

The scanning format is defined as the parameters by which time and the image plane are divided up by the scanning process. The parameters were originally the frame rate, the number of line periods in the frame period, and whether the scanning was interlaced or progressive. The number of line periods in the frame periods includes those lines in which flyback takes place in a CRT and which are blanked.

Now that the majority of cameras and displays use pixel-based structures, having no tangible flyback mechanism, the definition has changed. Recent scanning formats are defined by the number of active lines. This makes more sense as these are the lines that are actually visible and correspond to the vertical pixel count.

It might be thought that the scanning parameters of television would be based on psycho-optics, but this has yet to happen. The 525/60 scanning of U.S. SDTV, having 2:1 interlace, chose a field rate identical to the local power frequency. The power frequency of 50 Hz was chosen as the basis for the European SDTV scanning formats. For economy of scale, the line frequency was chosen to be close to that of the U.S. system so that the same CRT scanning transformers could be used. This led to 625 lines being specified, as 625×50 is close to 525×60.

COLOUR VISION

Colour vision is made possible by the cones on the retina, which occur in three different types, responding to different colours. Figure 2.20 showed that human vision is restricted to a range of light wavelengths from 400 to 700 nm. Shorter wavelengths are called ultraviolet and longer wavelengths are called infrared. Note that the response is not uniform, but peaks in the area of green. The response to blue is very poor and makes a nonsense of the traditional use of blue lights on emergency vehicles.

Figure 2.34 shows an approximate response for each of the three types of cone. If light of a single wavelength is observed, the relative responses of the three sensors allow us to discern what we call the colour of the light. Note that at both ends of the visible spectrum there are areas in which only one receptor responds; all colours in those areas look the same. There is a great deal of variation in receptor response from one individual to the next and the curves used in television are the average of a great many tests. In a surprising number of

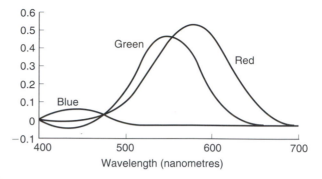

FIGURE 2.34
All human vision takes place over this range of wavelengths. The response is not uniform, but has a central peak. The three types of cone approximate to the three responses shown to give colour vision.

people the single receptor zones are extended and discrimination between, for example, red and orange is difficult.

The full resolution of human vision is restricted to brightness variations. Our ability to resolve colour details is only about a quarter of that.

COLORIMETRY

The triple-receptor characteristic of the eye is extremely fortunate as it means that we can generate a range of colours by adding together light sources having just three different wavelengths in various proportions. This process is known as additive colour matching, which should be clearly distinguished from the subtractive colour matching that occurs with paints and inks. Subtractive matching begins with white light and selectively removes parts of the spectrum by filtering. Additive matching uses coloured light sources that are combined.

An effective colour television system can be made in which only three pure or single wavelength colours or primaries can be generated. The primaries need to be similar in wavelength to the peaks of the three receptor responses, but need not be identical. Figure 2.35 shows a rudimentary colour television system. Note that the colour camera is in fact three cameras in one, of which each is fitted with a different coloured filter. Three signals, R, G, and B, must be transmitted to the display, which produces three images that must be superimposed to obtain a colour picture.

In practice the primaries must be selected from available phosphor compounds. Once the primaries have been selected, the proportions needed to reproduce a

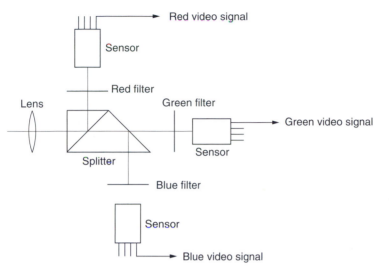

FIGURE 2.35
Simple colour television system. Camera image is split by three filters. Red, green, and blue video signals are sent to three primary-coloured displays whose images are combined.

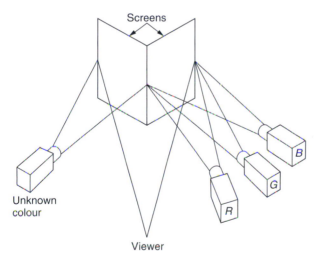

FIGURE 2.36
Simple colorimeter. Intensities of primaries on the right screen are adjusted to match the test colour on the left screen.

given colour can be found using a colorimeter. Figure 2.36 shows a colorimeter that consists of two adjacent white screens. One screen is illuminated by three light sources, one of each of the selected primary colours. Initially, the second screen is illuminated with white light and the three sources are adjusted until

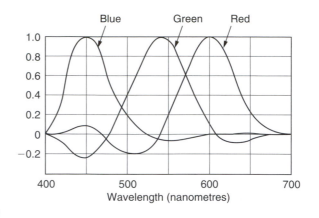

FIGURE 2.37
Colour mixture curves show how to mix primaries to obtain any spectral colour.

the first screen displays the same white. The sources are then calibrated. Light of a single wavelength is then projected onto the second screen. The primaries are once more adjusted until both screens appear to have the same colour. The proportions of the primaries are noted. This process is repeated for the whole visible spectrum, resulting in the colour mixture curves shown in Figure 2.37. In some cases it will not be possible to find a match because an impossible negative contribution is needed. In this case we can simulate a negative contribution by shining some primary colour onto the test screen until a match is obtained. If the primaries were ideal monochromatic (single-wavelength) sources, it would be possible to find three wavelengths at which two of the primaries were completely absent. However, practical phosphors are not monochromatic, but produce a distribution of wavelengths around the nominal value, and to make them spectrally pure other wavelengths have to be subtracted.

The colour mixture curves dictate what the response of the three sensors in the colour camera must be. The primaries are determined in this way because it is easier to make camera filters to suit available CRT phosphors than the other way round.

As there are three signals in a colour television system, they can be simultaneously depicted only in three dimensions. Figure 2.38 shows the RGB colour space, which is basically a cube with black at the origin and white at the diagonally opposite corner. Figure 2.39 shows the colour mixture curves plotted in RGB space. For each visible wavelength a vector exists whose direction is determined by the proportions of the three primaries. If the brightness is allowed to vary it will affect all three primaries, and thus the length of the vector, in the same proportion.

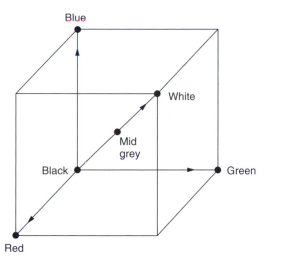

FIGURE 2.38
RGB colour space is three-dimensional and not easy to draw.

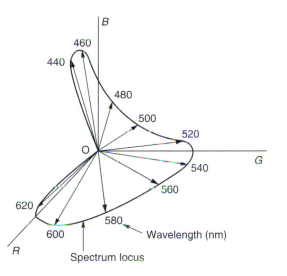

FIGURE 2.39
Colour mixture curves plotted in RGB space result in a vector whose locus moves with wavelength in three dimensions.

Depicting and visualizing the RGB colour space are not easy, and it is also difficult to take objective measurements from it. The solution is to modify the diagram to allow it to be rendered in two dimensions on flat paper. This is done by eliminating luminance (brightness) changes and depicting only the colour at constant brightness. Figure 2.40a shows how a constant luminance unit plane intersects the RGB space at unity on each axis. At any point on the plane the three components add up to 1. A two-dimensional plot results when

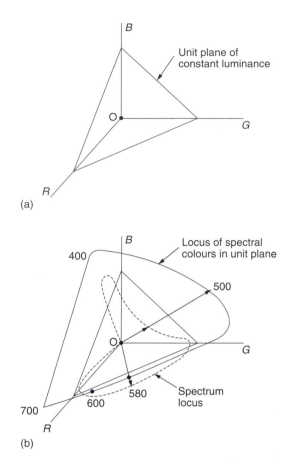

FIGURE 2.40
(a) A constant luminance plane intersects *RGB* space, allowing colours to be studied in two dimensions only. (b) The intersection of the unit plane by vectors joining the origin and the spectrum locus produces the locus of spectral colours, which requires negative values of *R*, *G*, and *B* to describe it.

vectors representing all colours intersect the plane. Vectors may be extended if necessary to allow intersection. Figure 2.40b shows that the 500 nm vector has to be produced (extended) to meet the unit plane, whereas the 580 nm vector naturally intersects. Any colour can now be specified uniquely in two dimensions.

The points at which the unit plane intersects the axes of RGB space form a triangle on the plot. The horseshoe-shaped locus of pure spectral colours goes outside this triangle because, as was seen above, the colour mixture curves require negative contributions for certain colours.

Having the spectral locus outside the triangle is a nuisance, and a larger triangle can be created by postulating new coordinates called *X, Y,* and *Z* representing

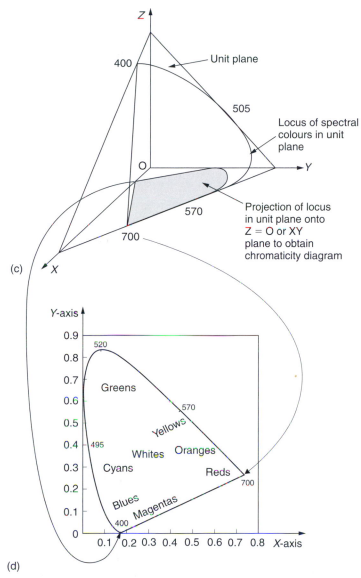

FIGURE 2.40
(Continued) In (c) a new coordinate system, X, Y, and Z, is used so that only positive values are required. The spectrum locus now fits entirely in the triangular space where the unit plane intersects these axes. To obtain the CIE chromaticity diagram (d), the locus is projected onto the XY plane.

hypothetical primaries that cannot exist. This representation is shown in Figure 2.40c.

The Commission Internationale d'Eclairage (CIE) standard chromaticity diagram shown in Figure 2.40d is obtained in this way by projecting the unity

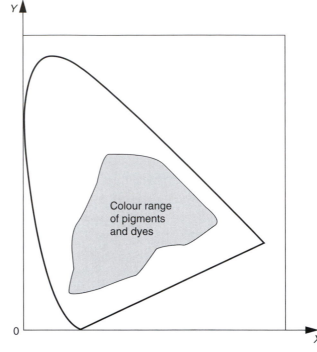

FIGURE 2.41
The colour range of television compares well with printing and photography.

luminance plane onto the *XY* plane. This projection has the effect of bringing the red and blue primaries closer together. Note that the curved part of the locus is due to spectral or single-wavelength colours. The straight base is due to nonspectral colours obtained by additively mixing red and blue.

As negative light is impossible, only colours within the triangle joining the primaries can be reproduced and so practical television systems cannot reproduce all possible colours. Clearly efforts should be made to obtain primaries that embrace as large an area as possible. Figure 2.41 shows how the colour range or gamut of television compares with paint and printing inks and illustrates that the comparison is favourable. Most everyday scenes fall within the colour gamut of television. Exceptions include saturated turquoise and spectrally pure iridescent colours formed by interference in a duck's feathers or reflections in a Compact Disc. For special purposes displays have been made having four primaries to give a wider colour range, but these are uncommon.

Figure 2.42 shows the primaries initially selected for NTSC. However, manufacturers looking for brighter displays substituted more efficient phosphors having

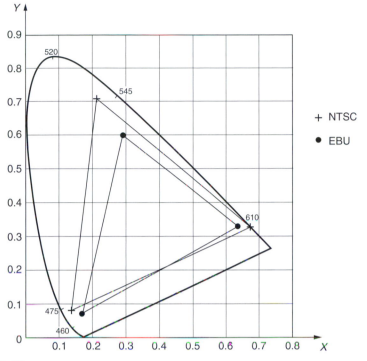

FIGURE 2.42
The primary colours for NTSC were initially as shown. These were later changed to more efficient phosphors, which were also adopted for PAL. See text.

a smaller colour range. This was later standardised as the SMPTE C phosphors, which were also adopted for PAL.

Whites appear in the centre of the chromaticity diagram, corresponding to roughly equal amounts of primary colour. Two terms are used to describe colours: hue and saturation. Colours having the same hue lie on a straight line between the white point and the perimeter of the primary triangle. The saturation of the colour increases with distance from the white point. As an example, pink is a desaturated red.

The apparent colour of an object is also a function of the illumination. The "true colour" will be revealed only under ideal white light, which in practice is uncommon. An ideal white object reflects all wavelengths equally and simply takes on the colour of the ambient illumination. Figure 2.43 shows the locations of three "white" sources or illuminants on the chromaticity diagram. Illuminant A corresponds to a tungsten filament lamp, illuminant B corresponds

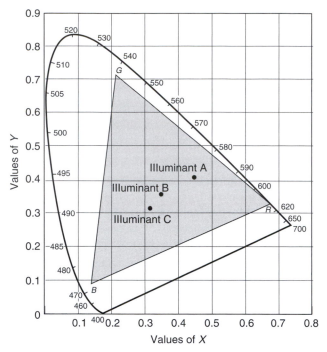

FIGURE 2.43
Positions of three common illuminants on chromaticity diagram.

to midday sunlight, and illuminant C corresponds to typical daylight, which is bluer because it consists of a mixture of sunlight and light scattered by the atmosphere. In everyday life we accommodate automatically to the change in apparent colour of objects as the sun's position or the amount of cloud changes and as we enter artificially lit buildings, but colour cameras accurately reproduce these colour changes. Attempting to edit a television program from recordings made at different times of day or indoors and outdoors would result in obvious and irritating colour changes unless some steps are taken to keep the white balance reasonably constant.

COLOUR DIFFERENCE SIGNALS

There are many different ways in which television signals can be carried and these will be considered here. A monochrome camera produces a single luma signal, Y or Ys, whereas a colour camera produces three signals, or components, R, G, and B, which are essentially monochrome video signals representing an image in each primary colour. In some systems sync is present on a separate signal (RGBs), rarely it is present on all three components, whereas most commonly it is present only on the green component, leading to the term RGsB. The use of the green component for sync has led to suggestions that the components should be called GBR. As the original and long-standing term RGB or RGsB correctly reflects the sequence of the colours in the spectrum it remains to be seen whether GBR will achieve common usage. Like luma, RGsB signals may use 0.7- or 0.714-Volt signals, with or without setup.

RGB and Y signals are incompatible, yet when colour television was introduced it was a practical necessity that it should be possible to display colour signals on a monochrome display and vice versa.

Creating or transcoding a luma signal from R, Gs, and B is relatively easy. Figure 2.34 showed the spectral response of the eye, which has a peak in the green region. Green objects will produce a larger stimulus than red objects of the same brightness, with blue objects producing the least stimulus. A luma signal can be obtained by adding R, G, and B together, not in equal amounts, but in a sum that is weighted by the relative response of the eye. Thus:

$$Y = 0.299R + 0.587G + 0.114B.$$

Syncs may be regenerated, but will be identical to those on the Gs input and when added to Y result in Ys as required.

If Ys is derived in this way, a monochrome display will show nearly the same result as if a monochrome camera had been used in the first place. The results are not identical because of the nonlinearities introduced by gamma correction.

As colour pictures require three signals, it should be possible to send Ys and two other signals, which a colour display could arithmetically convert back to R, G, and B. There are two important factors that restrict the form the other two signals may take. One is to achieve reverse compatibility. If the source is a monochrome camera, it can produce only Ys and the other two signals will be completely absent. A colour display should be able to operate on the Ys signal only and show a monochrome picture. The other is the requirement to conserve bandwidth for economic reasons.

These requirements are met by sending two colour difference signals along with Ys. There are three possible colour difference signals, R−Y, B−Y, and G−Y. As the green signal makes the greatest contribution to Y, then the amplitude of G−Y would be the smallest and would be most susceptible to noise. Thus R−Y and B−Y are used in practice, as Figure 2.44 shows.

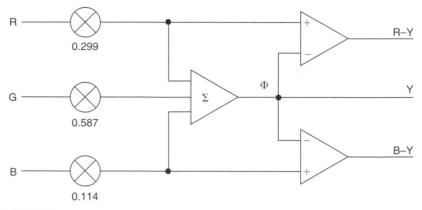

FIGURE 2.44
Colour components are converted to colour difference signals by the transcoding shown here.

R and B are readily obtained by adding Y to the two colour difference signals. G is obtained by rearranging the expression for Y above such that

$$G = \frac{Y - 0.3R - 0.11B}{0.59}$$

If a colour CRT is being driven, it is possible to apply inverted luma to the cathodes and the R−Y and B−Y signals directly to two of the grids so that the tube performs some of the matrixing. It is then necessary only to obtain G−Y for the third grid, using the expression

$$G-Y = -0.51(R-Y) - 0.186(B-Y).$$

If a monochrome source having only a Ys output is supplied to a colour display, R−Y and B−Y will be zero. It is reasonably obvious that if there are no colour difference signals the colour signals cannot be different from one another and R = G = B. As a result the colour display can produce only a neutral picture.

The use of colour difference signals is essential for compatibility in both directions between colour and monochrome, but it has a further advantage, which follows from the way in which the eye works. To produce the highest resolution in the fovea, the eye will use signals from all types of cone, regardless of colour. To determine colour the stimuli from three cones must be compared. There is evidence that the nervous system uses some form of colour difference processing to make this possible. As a result the acuity of the human eye is available only in monochrome. Differences in colour cannot be resolved so well. A further factor is that the lens in the human eye is not achromatic and this means that the ends of the spectrum are not well focused. This is particularly notice-able on blue.

If the eye cannot resolve colour very well there is no point is expending valuable bandwidth sending high-resolution colour signals. Colour difference working allows the luma to be sent separately at full bandwidth. This deter-mines the subjective sharpness of the picture. The colour difference signals can be sent with considerably reduced bandwidth, as little as one-quarter that of luma, and the human eye is unable to tell.

In practice analog component signals are never received perfectly, but suffer from slight differences in relative gain. In the case of RGB a gain error in one signal will cause a colour cast on the received picture. A gain error in Y causes no colour cast and gain errors in R−Y or B−Y cause much smaller perceived colour casts. Thus colour difference working is also more robust than RGB working.

The overwhelming advantages obtained by using colour difference signals mean that in broadcast and production facilities RGB is seldom used. The outputs from the RGB sensors in the camera are converted directly to Y, R−Y, and B−Y in the camera control unit and output in that form. Standards exist for both analog and digital colour difference signals to ensure compatibility between equipment from various manufacturers. The M-II and Betacam for-mats record analog colour difference signals, and there are a number of colour difference digital formats.

Whilst signals such as Y, R, G, and B are unipolar or positive only, it should be stressed that colour difference signals are bipolar and may meaningfully take on levels below 0 Volts.

The wide use of colour difference signals has led to the development of test signals and equipment to display them. The most important of the test signals is the ubiquitous colour bars. Colour bars are used to set the gains and tim-ing of signal components and to check that matrix operations are performed using the correct weighting factors. Further details will be found in Chapter 4. The origin of the colour bar test signal is shown in Figure 2.45. In 100 per-cent amplitude bars, peak amplitude binary RGB signals are produced, having one, two, and four cycles per screen width. When these are added together in a weighted sum, an eight-level luma staircase results because of the unequal weighting. The matrix also produces two colour difference signals, R−Y and B−Y, as shown. Sometimes 75 percent amplitude bars are generated by suitably

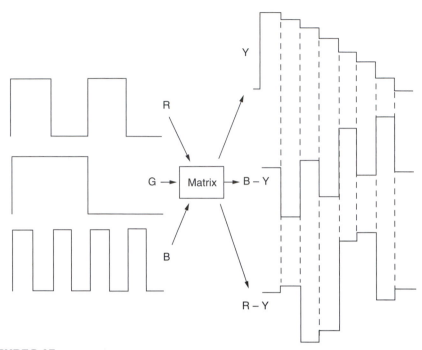

FIGURE 2.45

Origin of colour difference signals representing colour bars. Adding R, G, and B according to the weighting factors produces an irregular luminance staircase.

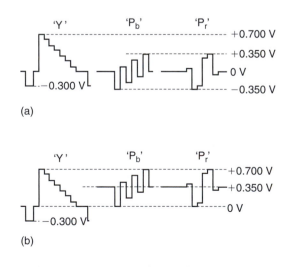

(a)

(b)

FIGURE 2.46

(a) 100 percent colour bars represented by SMPTE/EBU standard colour difference signals. (b) Level comparison is easier in waveform monitors if the B−Y and R−Y signals are offset upward.

reducing the RGB signal amplitude. Note that in both cases the colours are fully saturated; it is only the brightness that is reduced to 75 percent. Sometimes the white bar of a 75 percent bar signal is increased to 100 percent to make calibration easier. Such a signal is sometimes erroneously called a 100 percent bar signal.

Figure 2.46a shows a SMPTE/EBU standard colour difference signal set in which the signals are called Ys, P_b, and P_r. Syncs of 0.3 Volt are on luma only and all three video signals have a 0.7-Volt pk–pk swing with 100 percent bars. To obtain these voltage swings, the following gain corrections are made to the components:

$$P_r = 0.71327(R-Y) \quad \text{and} \quad P_b = 0.56433(B-Y).$$

Within waveform monitors, the colour difference signals may be offset by 350 mV as in Figure 2.46b to match the luma range for display purposes.

CHAPTER 3
Digital Principles

INTRODUCTION

Starting with binary data, one can define a process to manipulate those data entirely mathematically. It is important to understand the process before considering the implementation. A large number of choices of processing mechanisms exist today, all of which must give the same result if properly engineered. A fixed set of gates may be hardwired to implement a process in which the highest speed is required, whereas a general purpose processor can implement a process under software control at lower speed but with greater flexibility. Somewhere between those extremes, a field programmable gate array (FPGA) is a set of logic gates whose configuration can be externally programmed.

There will be a fixed number of bits in a PCM (Pulse Code Modulation) video sample, and this number determines the size of the quantizing range. In the 8-bit samples used in much digital video equipment, there are 256 different numbers. Each number represents a different analog signal voltage, and care must be taken during conversion to ensure that the signal does not go outside the convertor range, or it will be clipped. In Figure 3.2a it can be seen that in an 8-bit pure binary system, the number range goes from 00hex, which represents the smallest voltage, through to FFhex, which represents the largest positive voltage. The video waveform must be accommodated within this voltage range, and Figure 3.2b shows how this can be done for a PAL composite signal. A luminance signal is shown in Figure 3.2c. As component digital systems handle only the active line, the quantizing range is optimized to suit the gamut of the unblanked luminance. There is a small offset to handle slightly misadjusted inputs.

PURE BINARY CODE

For digital video use, the prime purpose of binary numbers is to express the values of the samples that represent the original analog video waveform. Figure 3.1 shows some binary numbers and their equivalent in decimal. The radix point has the same significance in binary: symbols to the right of it represent one-half, one-quarter, and so on. Binary is convenient for electronic circuits, which do not get tired, but numbers expressed in binary become very long, and writing them is tedious and error-prone. The octal and hexadecimal notations are both used for writing binary because conversion is so simple. Figure 3.1 also shows that a binary number is split into groups of three or four digits starting at the least significant end, and the groups are individually converted to octal or hexadecimal digits. Because 16 different symbols are required in hex, the letters A–F are used for the numbers above 9.

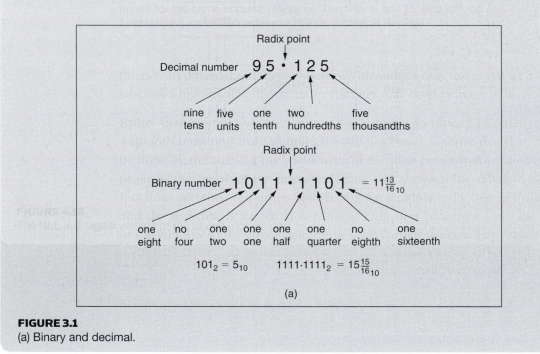

FIGURE 3.1
(a) Binary and decimal.

Binary	Hex	Decimal
0000	0	0
0001	1	1
0010	2	2
0011	3	3
0100	4	4
0101	5	5
0110	6	6
0111	7	7
1000	8	8
1001	9	9
1010	A	10
1011	B	11
1100	C	12
1101	D	13
1110	E	14
1111	F	15

Binary	Octal
000000	00
000001	01
000010	02
000011	03
000100	04
000101	05
000110	06
000111	07 ← Overflow
001000	10
001001	11
etc.	etc.

10101 011 · 011   Binary
2 5   3 · 3   Octal
× ×   ×   ×
64 8   1 $\frac{1}{8}$
$= 171\frac{3}{8}_{10}$

There is no 8 or 9 in Octal

(b)

1100 0000 1111 1111 1110 1110   Binary
C   0   F   F   E   E   Hex

0   15   15   14   14
×   ×   ×   ×
65 536 4096 256 16

12
×
1,048,576   = 12,648,430$_{10}$

(c)

FIGURE 3.1
(b) In octal, groups of 3 bits make one symbol, 0–7. (c) In hex, groups of 4 bits make one symbol, 0–F. Note how much shorter the number is in hex.

Colour difference signals are bipolar and so blanking is in the centre of the signal range. To accommodate colour difference signals in the quantizing range, the blanking voltage level of the analog waveform has been shifted as in Figure 3.2d so that the positive and negative voltages in a real signal can be expressed by binary numbers that are only positive. This approach is called offset binary. Strictly speaking both the composite and the luminance signals are also offset binary, because the blanking level is partway up the quantizing scale.

Offset binary is perfectly acceptable where the signal has been digitized only for recording or transmission from one place to another, after which it will be converted directly back to analog. Under these conditions it is not necessary for the quantizing steps to be uniform, provided both the ADC (analog-to-digital)

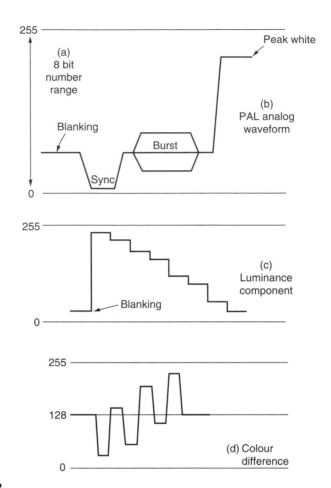

FIGURE 3.2
(a) The unipolar quantizing range of an 8-bit pure binary system. (b) The analog input must be shifted to fit into the quantizing range, as shown for PAL. (c) In component, sync pulses are not digitized, so the quantizing intervals can be smaller. (d) An offset of half-scale is used for colour difference signals.

and the DAC (digital-to-analog convertors) are constructed to the same standard. In practice, it is the requirements of signal processing in the digital domain that make both nonuniform quantizing and offset binary unsuitable.

Figure 3.3 shows that analog video signal voltages are referred to blanking. The level of the signal is measured by how far the waveform deviates from blanking, and attenuation, gain, and mixing all take place around blanking level. Digital vision mixing is achieved by adding sample values from two or more different sources, but unless all the quantizing intervals are of the same size and there is no offset, the sum of two sample values will not represent the sum of the two original analog voltages. Thus sample values that have been obtained

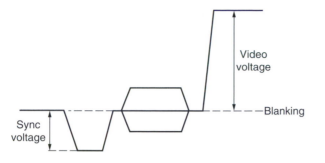

FIGURE 3.3
All video signal voltages are referred to blanking and must be added with respect to that level.

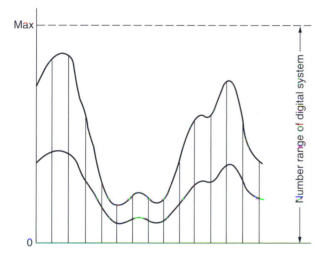

FIGURE 3.4
The result of an attempted attenuation in pure binary code is an offset. Pure binary cannot be used for digital video processing.

by nonuniform or offset quantizing cannot readily be processed because the binary numbers are not proportional to the signal voltage.

If two offset binary sample streams are added together in an attempt to perform digital mixing, the result will be that the offsets are also added and this may lead to an overflow. Similarly, if an attempt is made to attenuate by, say, 6.02 dB by dividing all the sample values by 2, Figure 3.4 shows that the offset is also divided and the waveform suffers a shifted baseline. This problem can be overcome with digital luminance signals simply by subtracting the offset from each sample before processing to obtain numbers truly proportional to the luminance voltage. This approach is not suitable for colour difference or composite signals because negative numbers would result when the analog voltage goes below blanking and pure binary coding cannot handle them. The problem with offset binary is that it works with reference to one end of the range. Chapter 1 introduced the two's complement numbering scheme, which operates symmetrically with reference to the centre of the range.

DIGITAL PROCESSING

However complex a digital process, it can be broken down into smaller stages until finally one finds that there are really only two basic types of element in use, and these can be combined in some way and supplied with a clock to implement virtually any process. Figure 3.5 shows that the first type is a logic element. This produces an output that is a logical function of the input with minimal delay. The second type is a storage element that samples the state

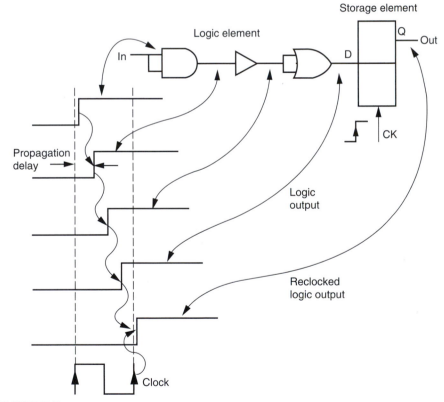

FIGURE 3.5
Logic elements have a finite propagation delay between input and output and cascading them delays the signal an arbitrary amount. Storage elements sample the input on a clock edge and can return a signal to near coincidence with the system clock. This is known as reclocking. Reclocking eliminates variations in propagation delay in logic elements.

of the input(s) when clocked and holds or delays that state. The strength of binary logic is that the signal has only two states, and considerable noise and distortion of the binary waveform can be tolerated before the state becomes uncertain. At every logic element, the signal is compared with a threshold and can thus pass through any number of stages without being degraded. In addition, the use of a storage element at regular locations throughout logic circuits eliminates time variations or jitter. Figure 3.5 shows that if the inputs to a logic element change, the output will not change until the propagation delay of the element has elapsed. However, if the output of the logic element forms the

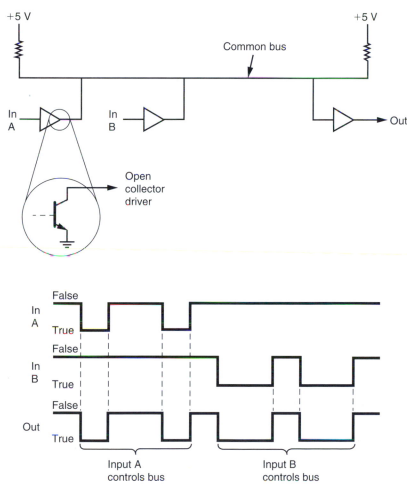

FIGURE 3.6
Using an open-collector drive, several signal sources can share one common bus. If negative logic is used, the bus drivers turn off their output transistors with a false input, allowing another driver to control the bus. This will not happen with positive logic.

LOGIC ELEMENTS

In logic systems, all logical functions, however complex, can be configured from combinations of a few fundamental logic elements or gates. It is not profitable to spend too much time debating which are the truly fundamental ones, because most can be made from combinations of others. Figure 3.7 shows the important simple gates and their derivatives and introduces the logical expressions to describe them, which can be compared with the truth table notation. The figure also shows the important fact that when negative logic is used, the OR gate function interchanges with that of the AND gate. Sometimes schematics are drawn to reflect which voltage state represents the true condition. In the so-called intentional logic scheme, a negative logic signal always starts and ends at an inverting "bubble." If an AND function is required between two negative logic signals, it will be drawn as an AND symbol with bubbles on all the terminals, even though the component used will be a positive logic OR gate. Opinions vary on the merits of intentional logic.

Positive logic name	Boolean expression	Positive logic symbol	Positive logic truth table			Plain English
Inverter or NOT gate	$Q = \overline{A}$	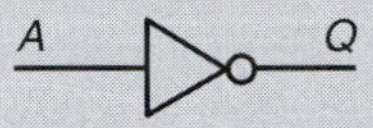	A $\mid$ Q 0 $\mid$ 1 1 $\mid$ 0			Output is opposite of input
AND gate	$Q = A \cdot B$	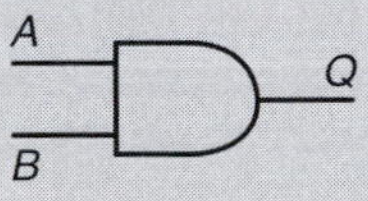	A B $\mid$ Q 0 0 $\mid$ 0 0 1 $\mid$ 0 1 0 $\mid$ 0 1 1 $\mid$ 1			Output true when both inputs are true only
NAND (Not AND) gate	$Q = \overline{A \cdot B}$ $= \overline{A} + \overline{B}$	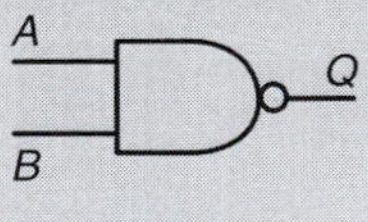	A B $\mid$ Q 0 0 $\mid$ 1 0 1 $\mid$ 1 1 0 $\mid$ 1 1 1 $\mid$ 0			Output false when both inputs are true only
OR gate	$Q = A + B$	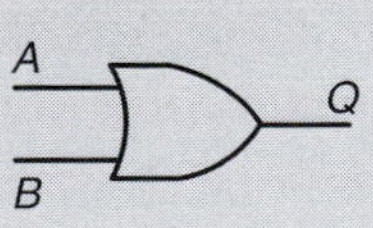	A B $\mid$ Q 0 0 $\mid$ 0 0 1 $\mid$ 1 1 0 $\mid$ 1 1 1 $\mid$ 1			Output true if either or both inputs true
NOR (Not OR) gate	$Q = \overline{A + B}$ $= \overline{A} \cdot \overline{B}$	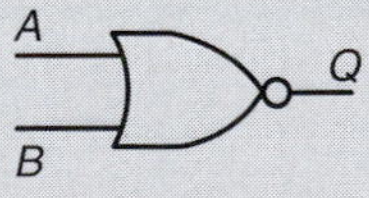	A B $\mid$ Q 0 0 $\mid$ 1 0 1 $\mid$ 0 1 0 $\mid$ 0 1 1 $\mid$ 0			Output false if either or both inputs true
Exclusive OR (XOR) gate	$Q = A \oplus B$	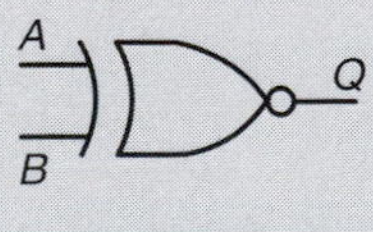	A B $\mid$ Q 0 0 $\mid$ 0 0 1 $\mid$ 1 1 0 $\mid$ 1 1 1 $\mid$ 0			Output true if inputs are different

FIGURE 3.7
The basic logic gates compared.

input to a storage element, the output of that element will not change until the input is sampled at the next clock edge. In this way the signal edge is aligned to the system clock and the propagation delay of the logic becomes irrelevant. The process is known as reclocking.

The two states of the signal when measured with an oscilloscope are simply two voltages, usually referred to as high and low. The actual voltage levels will depend on the type of logic family in use and on the supply voltage used. Within logic, these levels are not of much consequence, and it is necessary to know them only when interfacing between different logic families or when driving external devices. The pure logic designer is not interested at all in these voltages, only in their meaning. Just as the electrical waveform from a microphone represents sound velocity, so the waveform in a logic circuit represents the truth of some statement. As there are only two states, there can only be true or false meanings. The true state of the signal can be assigned by the designer to either voltage state. When a high voltage represents a true logic condition and a low voltage represents a false condition, the system is known as positive, or high, true logic. This is the usual system, but sometimes the low voltage represents the true condition and the high voltage represents the false condition. This is known as negative or low true logic. Provided that everyone is aware of the logic convention in use, both work equally well.

Negative logic is often found in the TTL (transistor transistor logic) family, because in this technology it is easier to sink current to ground than to source it from the power supply. Figure 3.6 shows that if it is necessary to connect several logic elements to a common bus so that any one can communicate with any other, an open collector system is used, in which high levels are provided by pull-up resistors and the logic elements pull only the common line down. If positive logic were used, when no device was operating the pull-up resistors would cause the common line to take on an absurd true state, whereas if negative logic were used, the common line would pull up to a sensible false condition when there was no device using the bus. Whilst the open collector is a simple way of obtaining a shared bus system, it is limited in frequency of operation due to the time constant of the pull-up resistors charging the bus capacitance. In the so-called tristate bus systems, there are both active pull-up and active pull-down devices connected in the so-called totem-pole output configuration. Both devices can be disabled to a third state, in which the output assumes a high impedance, allowing some other driver to determine the bus state.

If numerical quantities need to be conveyed down the two-state signal paths described here, then the only appropriate numbering system is binary, which

STORAGE ELEMENTS

The basic memory element in logic circuits is the latch, which is constructed from two gates as shown in Figure 3.8a and which can be set or reset. A more useful variant is the D-type latch shown in Figure 3.8b, which remembers the state of the input either at the time a separate clock changes state for an edge-triggered device or after it goes false for a level-triggered device. D-type latches are commonly available with four or eight latches to the chip. A shift register can be made from a series of latches by connecting the Q output of one latch to the D input of the next and connecting all the clock inputs in parallel. Data are delayed by the number of stages in the register. Shift registers are also useful for converting between serial and parallel data transmissions.

Where large numbers of bits are to be stored, cross-coupled latches are less suitable because they are more complicated to fabricate inside integrated circuits than dynamic memory and consume more current.

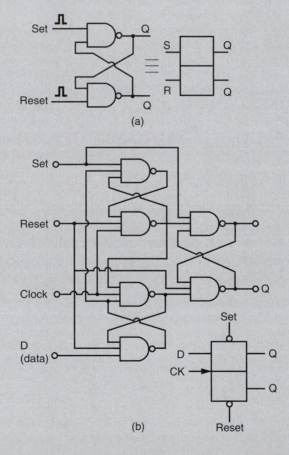

FIGURE 3.8

Digital semiconductor memory types. In (a), one data bit can be stored in a simple set–reset latch, which has little application because the D-type latch in (b) can store the state of the single data input when the clock occurs. These devices can be implemented with bipolar transistors or FETs and are called static memories because they can store indefinitely. They consume a lot of power.

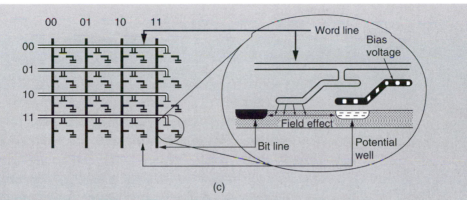

(c)

FIGURE 3.8

(Continued) In (c), a bit is stored as the charge in a potential well in the substrate of a chip. It is accessed by connecting the bit line with the field effect from the word line. The single well where the two lines cross can then be written or read. These devices are called dynamic RAMs because the charge decays, and they must be read and rewritten (refreshed) periodically.

In large random access memories (RAMs), the data bits are stored as the presence or absence of charge in a tiny capacitor as shown in Figure 3.8c. The capacitor is formed by a metal electrode, insulated by a layer of silicon dioxide from a semiconductor substrate; hence the term MOS (metal oxide semiconductor). The charge will suffer leakage, and the value would become indeterminate after a few milliseconds. Where the delay needed is less than this, decay is of no consequence, as data will be read out before they have had a chance to decay. Where longer delays are necessary, such memories must be refreshed periodically by reading the bit value and writing it back to the same place. Most modern MOS RAM chips have suitable circuitry built in. Large RAMs store thousands of bits, and it is clearly impractical to have a connection to each one. Instead, the desired bit has to be addressed before it can be read or written. The size of the chip package restricts the number of pins available, so that large memories use the same address pins more than once. The bits are arranged internally as rows and columns, and the row address and the column address are specified sequentially on the same pins.

has only two symbols, 0 and 1. Just as positive or negative logic could represent the truth of a logical binary signal, the same choice is available to a numerical binary signal. Normally, a high voltage level will represent a binary 1 and a low voltage will represent a binary 0, described as a "high for a 1" system. Clearly a "low for a 1" system is just as feasible. Decimal numbers have several columns, each of which represents a different power of 10; in binary the column position specifies the power of 2.

Several binary digits or bits are needed to express the value of a binary video sample. These bits can be conveyed at the same time by several signals to form a parallel system, which is most convenient inside equipment or for short distances because it is inexpensive, or one at a time down a single signal path, which is more complex, but convenient for cables between pieces of equipment because the connectors require fewer pins. When a binary system is used to convey numbers in this way, it can be called a digital system.

BINARY ADDITION

The circuitry necessary for adding pure binary or two's complement numbers is shown in Figure 3.9. Addition in binary requires 2 bits to be taken at a time from the same position in each word, starting at the least significant bit. Should both be 1's, the output is 0, and there is a carry-out generated. Such a circuit is called a half-adder, shown in Figure 3.9a, and is suitable for the least-significant bit of the calculation. All higher stages will require a circuit that can accept a carry input as well as two data inputs. This is known as a full adder (Figure 3.9b). Multibit full adders are available in chip form and have carry-in and carry-out terminals to allow them to be cascaded to operate on long word lengths. Such a device is also convenient for inverting a two's complement number, in conjunction with a set of inverters. The adder chip has one set of inputs grounded, and the carry-in permanently held true, such that it adds 1 to the one's complement number from the inverter.

When mixing by adding sample values, care has to be taken to ensure that if the sum of the two sample values exceeds the number range the result will be clipping rather than wraparound. In two's complement, the action necessary depends on the polarities of the two signals. Clearly if one positive and one negative number are added, the result cannot exceed the number range. If two positive numbers are added, the symptom of positive overflow is that the most significant bit sets, causing an erroneous negative result, whereas a negative overflow results in the most significant bit clearing. The overflow control circuit will be designed to detect these two conditions and override the adder output. If the MSB (most significant bit) of both inputs is 0, the numbers are both positive, thus if the sum has the MSB set, the output is replaced with the maximum positive code (0111…). If the MSB of both inputs is set, the numbers are both negative, and if the sum has no MSB set, the output is replaced with the maximum negative code (1000…). These conditions can also be connected to warning indicators. Figure 3.9c shows this system in hardware. The resultant clipping on overload is sudden, and sometimes a PROM is included, which translates values around and beyond maximum to soft-clipped values below or equal to maximum.

A storage element can be combined with an adder to obtain a number of useful functional blocks, which will crop up frequently in audio equipment.

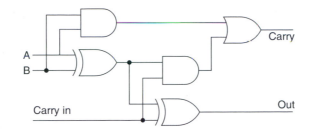

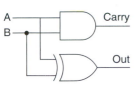

(a)

Data A	Bits B	Carry in	Out	Carry out
0	0	0	0	0
0	0	1	1	0
0	1	0	1	0
0	1	1	0	1
1	0	0	1	0
1	0	1	0	1
1	1	0	0	1
1	1	1	1	1

(b)

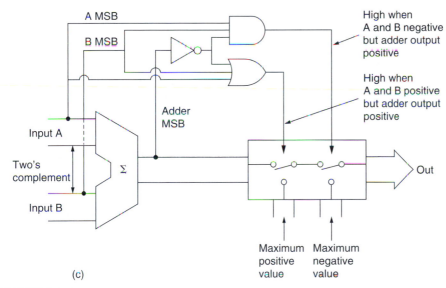

(c)

FIGURE 3.9

(a) Half adder. (b) Full-adder circuit and truth table. (c) Comparison of sign bits prevents wraparound on adder overflow by substituting clipping level.

Figure 3.10a shows that a latch is connected in a feedback loop around an adder. The latch contents are added to the input each time it is clocked. The configuration is known as an accumulator in computation because it adds up or accumulates values fed into it. In filtering, it is known as a discrete time integrator. If the input is held at some constant value, the output increases by that amount on each clock. The output is thus a sampled ramp.

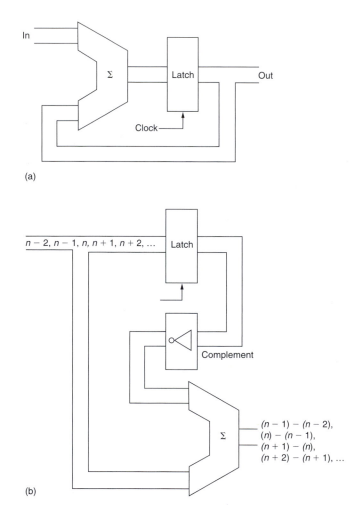

(a)

(b)

FIGURE 3.10
Two configurations common in processing. In (a) the feedback around the adder adds the previous sum to each input to perform accumulation or digital integration. In (b) an inverter allows the difference between successive inputs to be computed. This is differentiation.

MODULO-*N* ARITHMETIC

Conventional arithmetic that is in everyday use relates to the real world of counting actual objects, and to obtain correct answers the concepts of borrow and carry are necessary in the calculations. There is an alternative type of arithmetic that has no borrow or carry, which is known as modulo arithmetic. In modulo-*N* no number can exceed *N*. If it does, *N* or whole multiples of *N* are subtracted until it does not. Thus 25 modulo-16 is 9 and 12 modulo-5 is 2. The count shown in Figure 3.11 is from a 4-bit device that overflows when it reaches 1111 because the carry-out is ignored. If a number of clock pulses *M* are applied from the zero state, the state of the counter will be given by *M* Mod.16. Thus modulo arithmetic is appropriate to systems in which there is a fixed word length and this means that the range of values the system can have is restricted by that word length. A number range that is restricted in this way is called a finite field.

Modulo-2 is a numbering scheme that is used frequently in digital processes. Figure 3.12 shows that in modulo-2 the conventional addition and subtraction are replaced by the XOR function such that

$$A + B \text{ Mod.2} = A \text{ XOR } B.$$

When multibit values are added Mod.2, each column is computed quite independent of any other. This makes Mod.2 circuitry very fast in operation as it is not necessary to wait for the carries from lower-order bits to ripple up to the higher-order bits. Modulo-2 arithmetic is not the same as conventional arithmetic and takes some getting used to. For example, adding something to itself in Mod.2 always gives the answer 0.

| 1 | 1 | 1 | 1 |

$1111 = 8 + 4 + 2 + 1 = 15_{10}$

$\downarrow + 1$ $\downarrow + 1$

| 1 | 0 | 0 | 0 | 0 |

$1\ 0000 = 16 + 0 + 0 + 0 + 0 = 16_{10}$

This '1' cannot be handled

| 0 | 0 | 0 | 0 | $\leftarrow 15_{10} + 1_{10} = 0$ mod-16

FIGURE 3.11
As a fixed-word-length counter cannot hold the carry-out bit, it will resume at 0. Thus a 4-bit counter expresses every count as a modulo-16 number.

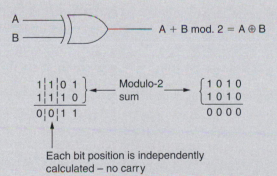

$A + B \text{ mod. 2} = A \oplus B$

$$
\begin{array}{l}
1\ 1\ 0\ 1 \\
1\ 1\ 1\ 0 \\
\hline
0\ 0\ 1\ 1
\end{array}
\leftarrow
\begin{array}{c}
\text{Modulo-2} \\
\text{sum}
\end{array}
\rightarrow
\begin{array}{l}
1\ 0\ 1\ 0 \\
1\ 0\ 1\ 0 \\
\hline
0\ 0\ 0\ 0
\end{array}
$$

Each bit position is independently calculated – no carry

FIGURE 3.12
In modulo-2 calculations, there can be no carry or borrow operations and conventional addition and subtraction become identical. The XOR gate is a modulo-2 adder.

Figure 3.10b shows that the addition of an inverter allows the difference between successive inputs to be obtained. This is digital differentiation. The output is proportional to the slope of the input.

GAIN CONTROL BY MULTIPLICATION

When a digital recording is made, the gain of the analog input will usually be adjusted so that the quantizing range is fully exercised to make a recording of maximum signal-to-noise ratio. During postproduction, the recording may be played back and mixed with other signals, and the desired effect can be achieved only if the level of each can be controlled independently. Gain is controlled in the digital domain by multiplying each sample value by a coefficient. If that coefficient is less than 1, attenuation will result; if it is greater than 1, amplification can be obtained.

Multiplication in binary circuits is difficult. It can be performed by repeated adding, but this is too slow to be of any use. In fast multiplication, one of the inputs will simultaneously be multiplied by 1, 2, 4, etc., by hardwired bit shifting. Figure 3.13 shows that the other input bits will determine which of these powers will be added to produce the final sum and which will be neglected. If multiplying by 5, the process is the same as multiplying by 4, multiplying by 1, and adding the two products. This is achieved by adding the input to itself shifted two places. As the word length of such a device increases, the complexity increases exponentially, so this is a natural application for an integrated circuit. It is probably true that digital video would not have been viable without such chips.

THE COMPUTER

The computer is now a vital part of digital video systems, being used both for control purposes and to process video signals as data. In control, the computer finds applications in database management, automation, editing, and electromechanical systems such as tape drives and robotic cassette handling. Now that processing speeds have advanced sufficiently, computers are able to manipulate certain types of digital video in real time. Where very complex calculations are needed, real-time operation may not be possible and instead the computation proceeds as fast as it can in a process called rendering. The rendered data are stored so that they can be viewed in real time from a storage medium when the rendering is complete.

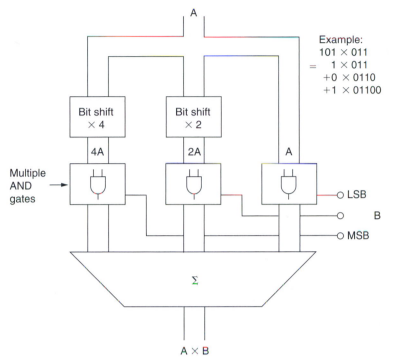

A

Example:
101 × 011
=   1 × 011
    +0 × 0110
    +1 × 01100

FIGURE 3.13

Structure of the fast multiplier: the input A is multiplied by 1, 2, 4, 8, etc., by bit shifting. The digits of the B input then determine which multiples of A should be added together by enabling AND gates between the shifters and the adder. For long word lengths, the number of gates required becomes enormous, and the device is best implemented in a chip.

The computer is a programmable device in that its operation is not determined by its construction alone, but instead by a series of instructions forming a program. The program is supplied to the computer one instruction at a time so that the desired sequence of events takes place.

Programming of this kind has been used for over a century in electromechanical devices, including automated knitting machines and street organs that are programmed by punched cards. However, the computer differs from these devices in that the program is not fixed, but can be modified by the computer itself. This possibility led to the creation of the term software to suggest a contrast to the constancy of hardware.

Computer instructions are binary numbers, each of which is interpreted in a specific way. As these instructions do not differ from any other kind of data, they can be stored in RAM. The computer can change its own instructions by accessing the RAM. Most types of RAM are volatile, in that they lose data when power is removed. Clearly if a program is stored entirely in this way, the computer will not be able to recover from a power failure. The solution is that a very simple starting or bootstrap program is stored in nonvolatile ROM, which will contain instructions to bring in the main program from a storage system such as a disk drive after power is applied. As programs in ROM cannot be altered, they are sometimes referred to as firmware to indicate that they are classified between hardware and software.

Making a computer do useful work requires more than simply a program that performs the required computation. There is also a lot of mundane activity that does not differ significantly from one program to the next. This includes deciding which part of the RAM will be occupied by the program and which by the data, producing commands to the storage disk drive to read the input data from a file and write back the results. It would be very inefficient if all programs had to handle these processes themselves. Consequently the concept of an operating system was developed. This manages all the mundane decisions and creates an environment in which useful programs or applications can execute.

The ability of the computer to change its own instructions makes it very powerful, but it also makes it vulnerable to abuse. Programs exist that are deliberately written to do damage. These viruses are generally attached to plausible messages or data files and enter computers through storage media or communications paths.

There is also the possibility that programs contain logical errors such that in certain combinations of circumstances the wrong result is obtained. If this results in the unwitting modification of an instruction, the next time that instruction is accessed the computer will crash. In consumer-grade software, written for the vast personal computer market, this kind of thing is unfortunately accepted.

For critical applications, software must be verified. This is a process that can prove that a program can recover from absolutely every combination of circumstances and keep running properly. This is a nontrivial process, because the number of combinations of states a computer can get into is staggering. As a result most software is unverified.

It is of the utmost importance that networked computers that can suffer virus infection or computers running unverified software are never used in a life-support or critical application.

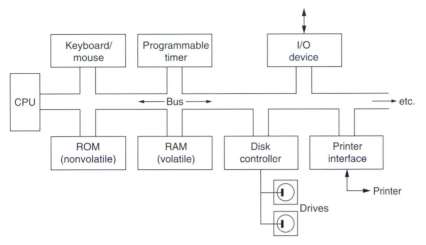

FIGURE 3.14
A simple computer system. All components are linked by a single data/address/control bus. Although cheap and flexible, such a bus can make only one connection at a time, so it is slow.

Figure 3.14 shows a simple computer system. The various parts are linked by a bus, which allows binary numbers to be transferred from one place to another. This will generally use tristate logic (see Digital Processing) so that when one device is sending to another, all other devices present a high impedance to the bus.

The ROM stores the start-up program; the RAM stores the operating system, applications programs, and the data to be processed. The disk drive stores large quantities of data in a nonvolatile form. The RAM needs only to be able to hold part of one program as other parts can be brought from the disk as required. A program executes by fetching one instruction at a time from the RAM to the processor along the bus.

The bus also allows keyboard/mouse inputs and outputs to the display and printer. Inputs and outputs are generally abbreviated to I/O. Finally a programmable timer will be present, which acts as a kind of alarm clock for the processor.

INTERRUPTS

Ordinarily instructions are executed in the order that they are stored in RAM. However, some instructions direct the processor to jump to a new memory location. If this is a jump to an earlier instruction, the program will enter a loop. The loop must increment a count in a register each time, and contain a conditional instruction called a branch, which allows the processor to jump out of the loop when a predetermined count is reached.

THE CPU

The processor or CPU (central processing unit) is the heart of the system. Figure 3.15 shows a simple example of a CPU. The CPU has a bus interface, which allows it to generate bus addresses and input or output data. Sequential instructions are stored in RAM at contiguously increasing locations so that a program can be executed by fetching instructions from a RAM address specified by the program counter (PC) to the instruction register in the CPU. As each instruction is completed, the PC is incremented so that it points to the next instruction. In this way the time taken to execute the instruction can vary.

The processor is notionally divided into data paths and control paths. Figure 3.15 shows the data path. The CPU contains a number of general-purpose registers or scratchpads, which can be used to store partial results in complex calculations. Pairs of these registers can be addressed so that their contents go to the ALU (arithmetic logic unit). This performs various arithmetic (add, subtract, etc.) or logical (and, or, etc.) functions on the input data. The output of the ALU may be routed back to a register or output. By reversing this process it is possible to get data into the registers from the RAM. The ALU also outputs the conditions resulting from the calculation, which can control conditional instructions.

Which function the ALU performs and which registers are involved are determined by the instruction currently in the instruction register that is decoded in the control path. One pass through the ALU can be completed in one cycle of the processor's clock. Instructions vary in complexity as do the number of clock cycles needed to complete them. Incoming instructions are decoded and used to access a lookup table, which converts them into microinstructions, one of which controls the CPU at each clock cycle.

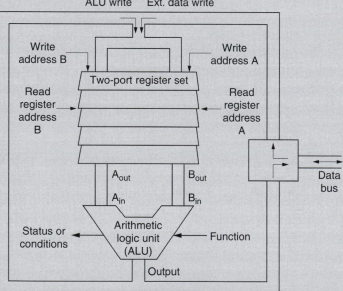

FIGURE 3.15
The data path of a simple CPU. Under the control of an instruction, the ALU will perform some function on a pair of input values from the registers and store or output the result.

However, it is often required that the sequence of execution should be change-able by some external event. This might be the changing of some value due to a keyboard input. Events of this kind are handled by interrupts, which are created by devices needing attention. Figure 3.16 shows that in addition to the PC, the CPU contains another dedicated register called the stack pointer. Figure 3.17 shows how this is used. At the end of every instruction the CPU checks to see if an interrupt is asserted on the bus.

If it is, a different set of microinstructions is executed. The PC is incremented as usual, but the next instruction is not executed. Instead, the contents of the PC are stored so that the CPU can resume execution when it has handled the current event. The PC state is stored in a reserved area of RAM known as the stack, at an address determined by the stack pointer.

Once the PC is stacked, the processor can handle the interrupt. It issues a bus interrupt acknowledge, and the interrupting device replies with a unique code identifying itself. This is known as a vector, which steers the processor to a RAM address containing a new program counter. This is the RAM address of the first instruction of the subroutine that is the program that will handle the interrupt. The CPU loads this address into the PC and begins execution of the subroutine.

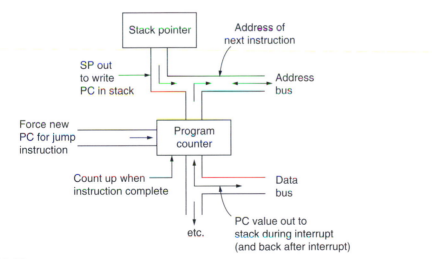

FIGURE 3.16
Normally the program counter (PC) increments each time an instruction is completed in order to select the next instruction. However, an interrupt may cause the PC state to be stored in the stack area of RAM prior to the PC being forced to the start address of the interrupt subroutine. Afterward the PC can get its original value back by reading the stack.

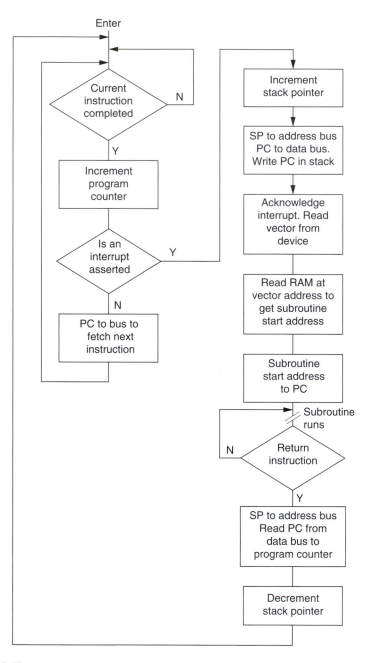

FIGURE 3.17
How an interrupt is handled. See text for details.

At the end of the subroutine there will be a return instruction. This causes the CPU to use the stack pointer as a memory address to read the return PC state from the stack. With this value loaded into the PC, the CPU resumes execution where it left off.

The stack exists so that subroutines can themselves be interrupted. If a subroutine is executing when a higher-priority interrupt occurs, the subroutine can be suspended by incrementing the stack pointer and by storing the current PC in the next location in the stack.

When the second interrupt has been serviced, the stack pointer allows the PC of the first subroutine to be retrieved. Whenever a stack PC is retrieved, the stack pointer decrements and thereby points to the PC of the next item of unfinished business.

DIGITAL SIGNAL PROCESSORS

Although general-purpose computers can be programmed to process digital audio or image data, they are not ideal for the following reasons:

1. The number of arithmetic operations, particularly multiplications, is far higher than for data processing.
2. Processing is required in real time; data processors do not generally work in real time.
3. The program needed generally remains constant for the duration of a session, or changes slowly, whereas a data processor rapidly jumps between many programs.
4. Data processors can suspend a program on receipt of an interrupt; audio and image processors must work continuously for long periods.
5. Data processors tend to be I/O (input–output) limited, in that their operating speed is constrained by the problems of moving large quantities of data and instructions into the CPU.

Audio processors in contrast have a relatively small input and output rate, but compute intensively, whereas image processors also compute intensively but tend to outstrip the I/O capabilities of conventional computer architectures. A common video process is spatial interpolation used for resizing or oversampling. Spatial filters compute each output pixel value as a function of all input pixel values over a finite-sized window. The windows for the output pixels have extensive overlap. In a conventional CPU, shortage of internal registers means that a filter algorithm would have to fetch the input pixel values within the window from memory for every output pixel to be calculated. With an 8 × 8 window size, 1 input pixel falls within 64 different windows, with the result that the

THE PROGRAMMABLE TIMER

Ordinarily processors have no concept of time and simply execute instructions as fast as their clock allows. This is fine for general-purpose processing, but not for time-critical processes such as video. One way in which the processor can be made time conscious is to use programmable timers. These are devices that reside on the computer bus and run from a clock. The CPU can set up a timer by loading it with a count. When the count is reached, the timer will interrupt. To give an example, if the count were to be equal to one frame period, there would be one interrupt per frame, and this would result in the execution of a subroutine once per frame, provided, of course, that all the instructions could be executed in one frame period.

conventional processor would have to fetch the same value from the same location 64 times, whereas in principle it needs to be fetched only once.

This is sufficient justification for the development of specialized digital signal processors (DSPs). These units are equipped with more internal registers than data processors to facilitate implementation of, for example, multipoint filter algorithms. The arithmetic unit will be designed to multiply/accumulate rapidly using techniques such as pipelining, which allows operations to overlap. The functions of the register set and the arithmetic unit are controlled by a micro-sequencer, which interprets the instructions in the program. Figure 3.18 shows the interior structure of a DSP chip.

Where a DSP is designed specifically for image processing, it is possible to incorporate one CPU per pixel. With a massively parallel approach such as this, the speed of each CPU can be very slow and it can be implemented serially, making it trivially easy to optimize the word length of the calculation to the accuracy requirement. DSPs are used in many other industries in which waveforms that were originally analog need to be manipulated in the digital domain. In fact this is probably the best definition of DSP, which distinguishes it from computation in general. Equipment intended for convergent audio/video systems can take advantage of DSP devices designed for applications such as synthetic aperture radar and pattern recognition.

Figure 3.19a shows a simple digital mixer that accepts two PCM inputs, sets the gain of each, and then mixes (adds) the two together. The sum will have increased in word length and must be digitally dithered prior to rounding to the required output word length. Figure 3.19b shows a simple DSP system that is designed to do the same job. The hardware is trivial: a few ports and a DSP chip (known colloquially as an "engine"). The program needed to operate the DSP is shown in (c). This has been written in English rather than in DSP

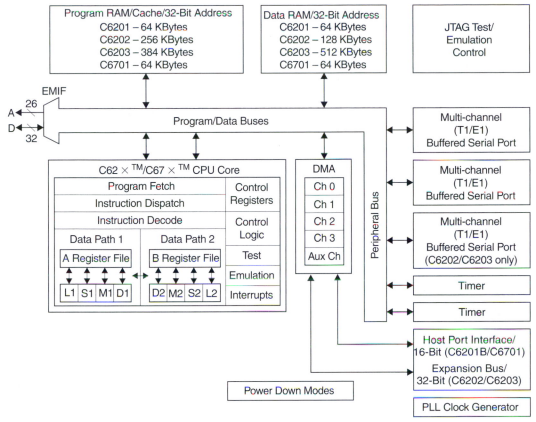

FIGURE 3.18
A DSP is a specialized form of computer (courtesy of Texas Instruments).

language, which is incomprehensible to most humans. If all the steps in the program are executed in turn, the output value ought to be the same as if the hardware of Figure 3.19a had been used.

One problem is that the DSP engine is designed to run as fast as its technology allows, whereas in PCM results are required at the signal sampling rate. This is solved by using interrupts. The interrupt signal can occur at any time with respect to the processor clock without causing difficulty as it will be examined only when an instruction has been completed, prior to executing another one. The normal program is suspended, and a different program, known as a subroutine, is executed instead. When the subroutine is completed, the normal program resumes.

In a PCM DSP application, the normal program may be an idling program; i.e., it doesn't do anything useful or it may rotate the lights on the front

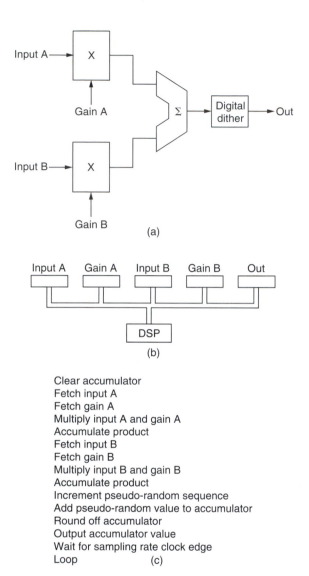

FIGURE 3.19
(a) A simple mixer built conventionally. (b) The same mixer implemented with DSP. The instructions in (c) operate the DSP.

panel. The sample calculation is contained in the subroutine. The master sampling rate clock from a phase-locked loop is then used to generate interrupts to the DSP just after input samples have been made available. Figure 3.20 shows that if this is done the subroutine is executed at the sampling rate with idling periods between. In practice this is true only if the subroutine is short enough to be executed within the sample period. If it cannot, a more elegant program or a more powerful "engine" must be sought.

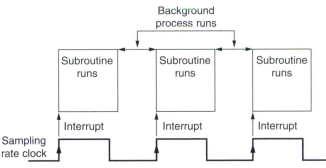

FIGURE 3.20
Synchronising a signal processor with real time using interrupts. The processing is carried out by a subroutine.

TIME BASE CORRECTION

In Chapter 1 it was stated that a strength of digital technology is the ease with which delay can be provided. Accurate control of delay is the essence of time base correction, necessary whenever the instantaneous time of arrival or rate from a data source does not match the destination. In digital video, the destination will almost always have perfectly regular timing, namely the sampling rate clock of the final DAC. Time base correction consists of aligning jittery signals from storage media or transmission channels with that stable reference.

A further function of time base correction is to reverse the time compression applied prior to recording or transmission. As was shown in Chapter 1 under Time Compression and Packetising, digital recorders compress data into blocks to facilitate editing and error correction as well as to permit head switching between blocks in rotary-head machines. Owing to the spaces between blocks, data arrive in bursts on replay, but must be fed to the output convertors in an unbroken stream at the sampling rate.

In computer hard-disk drives, which are used in digital video workstations, time compression is also used, but a converse problem arises. Data from the disk blocks arrive at a reasonably constant rate, but cannot necessarily be accepted at a steady rate by the logic because of contention for the use of buses and memory by the different parts of the system. In this case the data must be buffered by a relative of the time base corrector, which is usually referred to as a silo.

Although delay is easily implemented, it is not possible to advance a data stream. Most real machines cause instabilities balanced about the correct timing: the output jitters between too early and too late. Because the information

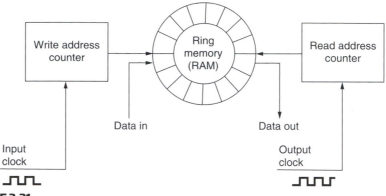

Data in   Data out

Input   Output
clock   clock

FIGURE 3.21
Most TBCs are implemented as a memory addressed by a counter, which periodically
overflows to give a ring structure. The memory allows the read and write timing to be
asynchronous.

cannot be advanced in the corrector, only delayed, the solution is to run the
machine in advance of real time. In this case, correctly timed output signals
will need a nominal delay to align them with reference timing. Early output
signals will receive more delay, and late output signals will receive less delay.

Under Digital Processing the principles of digital storage elements, which can
be used for delay purposes, were presented. The shift-register approach and the
RAM approach to delay are very similar, as a shift register can be thought of as
a memory whose address increases automatically when clocked. The data rate
and the maximum delay determine the capacity of the RAM required. Figure
3.21 shows that the addressing of the RAM is done by a counter that overflows
endlessly from the end of the memory back to the beginning, giving the memory a ring-like structure. The write address is determined by the incoming data,
and the read address is determined by the outgoing data. This means that the
RAM has to be able to read and write at the same time. The switching between
read and write involves not only a data multiplexer but also an address multiplexer. In general, the arbitration between read and write will be done by signals from the stable side of the TBC as Figure 3.22 shows. In the replay case
the stable clock will be on the read side. The stable side of the RAM will read
a sample when it demands, and the writing will be locked out for that period.
However, the input data cannot be interrupted in many applications, so a small
buffer silo is installed before the memory, which fills up as the writing is locked
out and empties again as writing is permitted. Alternatively, the memory will
be split into blocks as was shown in Chapter 1, such that when one block is
reading, a different block will be writing, and the problem does not arise.

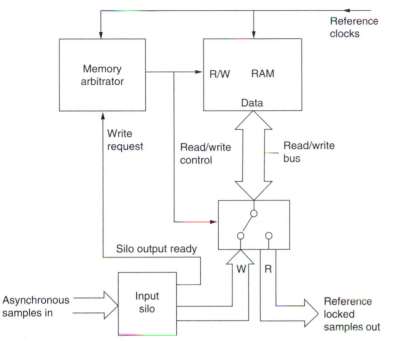

FIGURE 3.22
In a RAM-based TBC, the RAM is reference synchronous, and an arbitrator decides when it will read and when it will write. During reading, asynchronous input data back up in the input silo, asserting a write request to the arbitrator. The arbitrator will then cause a write cycle between read cycles.

In most digital video applications, the sampling rate exceeds the rate at which economically available RAM chips can operate. The solution is to arrange several video samples into one longer word, known as a superword, and to construct the memory so that it stores superwords in parallel.

When used in a hard-disk system, a silo will allow data to and from the disk, which is turning at constant speed. When the disk is being read, Figure 3.23a shows that the silo starts empty, and if there is bus contention, the silo will start to fill. When the bus is free, the disk controller will attempt to empty the silo into the memory. The system can take advantage of the interblock gaps on the disk, containing headers, preambles, and redundancy, for in these areas there are no data to transfer, and there is some breathing space to empty the silo before the next block. In practice the silo need not be empty at the start of every block, provided it never becomes full before the end of the transfer. If this happens some data are lost and the function must be aborted. The block containing the silo overflow will generally be reread on the next revolution. In sophisticated systems, the silo has a kind of dipstick and can interrupt the CPU if the data get too

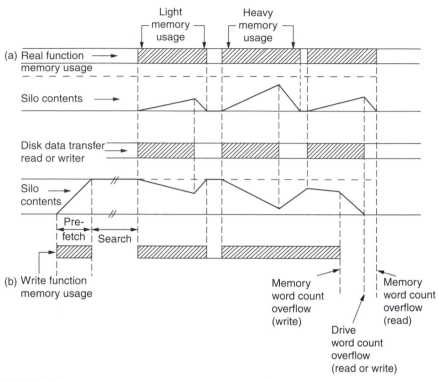

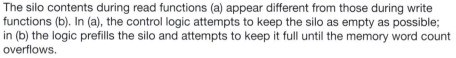

FIGURE 3.23
The silo contents during read functions (a) appear different from those during write functions (b). In (a), the control logic attempts to keep the silo as empty as possible; in (b) the logic prefills the silo and attempts to keep it full until the memory word count overflows.

deep. The CPU can then suspend some bus activity to allow the disk controller more time to empty the silo.

When the disk is to be written, as in Figure 3.23b, a continuous data stream must be provided during each block, as the disk cannot stop. The silo will be prefilled before the disk attempts to write, and the disk controller attempts to keep it full. In this case all will be well if the silo does not become empty before the end of the transfer. Figure 3.24 shows the silo of a typical disk controller with the multiplexers necessary to put it in the read data stream or the write data stream.

MULTIPLEXING PRINCIPLES

Multiplexing is used where several signals are to be transmitted down the same channel. The channel bit rate must be the same as or greater than the sum of the source bit rates. Figure 3.25 shows that when multiplexing is used, the data from

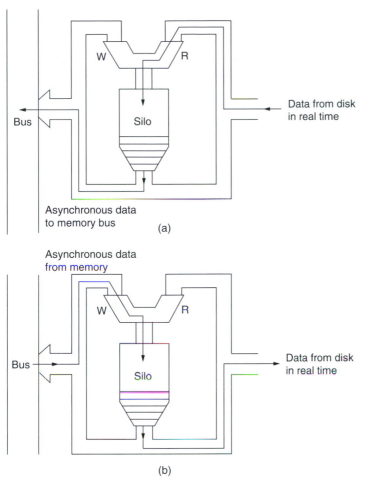

FIGURE 3.24
To guarantee that the drive can transfer data in real time at regular intervals (determined by disk speed and density) the silo provides buffering to the asynchronous operation of the memory access process. In (a) the silo is configured for a disk read. The same silo is used in (b) for a disk write.

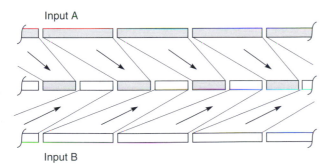

FIGURE 3.25
Multiplexing requires time compression on each input.

PACKETS

The multiplexer must switch between different time-compressed signals to create the bitstream and this is much easier to organize if each signal is in the form of data packets of constant size. Figure 3.26 shows a packet multiplexing system.

Each packet consists of two components: the header, which identifies the packet, and the payload, which is the data to be transmitted. The header will contain at least an identification code (ID), which is unique for each signal in the multiplex. The demultiplexer checks the ID codes of all incoming packets and discards those that do not have the wanted ID.

In complex systems it is common to have a mechanism to check that packets are not lost or repeated. This is the purpose of the packet continuity count, which is carried in the header. For packets carrying the same ID, the count should increase by one from one packet to the next. Upon reaching the maximum binary value, the count overflows and recommences.

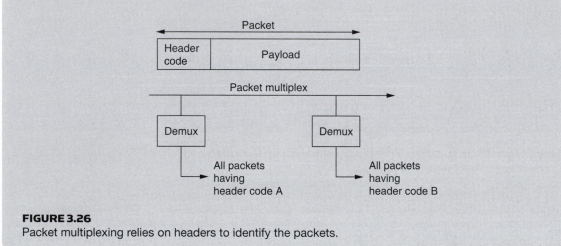

FIGURE 3.26
Packet multiplexing relies on headers to identify the packets.

each source has to be time compressed. This is done by buffering source data in a memory at the multiplexer. It is written into the memory in real time as it arrives, but will be read from the memory with a clock that has a much higher rate. This means that the readout occurs in a smaller time span. If, for example, the clock frequency is raised by a factor of 10, the data for a given signal will be transmitted in a tenth of the normal time, leaving time in the multiplex for nine more such signals.

In the demultiplexer another buffer memory will be required. Only the data for the selected signal will be written into this memory at the bit rate of the multiplex. When the memory is read at the correct speed, the data will emerge with their original time base.

In practice it is essential to have mechanisms to identify the separate signals to prevent them being mixed up and to convey the original signal clock frequency to the demultiplexer. In time-division multiplexing the time base of the transmission is broken into equal slots, one for each signal. This makes it easy for the demultiplexer, but forces a rigid structure on all the signals such that they must all be locked to one another and have an unchanging bit rate. Packet multiplexing overcomes these limitations.

STATISTICAL MULTIPLEXING

Packet multiplexing has advantages over time-division multiplexing because it does not set the bit rate of each signal. A demultiplexer simply checks packet IDs and selects all packets with the wanted code. It will do this however frequently such packets arrive. Consequently it is practicable to have variable bit rate signals in a packet multiplex. The multiplexer has to ensure that the total bit rate does not exceed the rate of the channel, but that rate can be allocated arbitrarily between the various signals.

As a practical matter it is usually necessary to keep the bit rate of the multiplex constant. With variable rate inputs this is done by creating null packets, which are generally called stuffing or packing. The headers of these packets contain a unique ID, which the demultiplexer does not recognize, and so these packets are discarded on arrival.

In an MPEG environment, statistical multiplexing can be extremely useful because it allows for the varying difficulty of real program material. In a multiplex of several television programs, it is unlikely that all the programs will encounter difficult material simultaneously. When one program encounters a detailed scene or frequent cuts that are hard to compress, more data rate can be allocated at the allowable expense of the remaining programs that are handling easy material.

DIGITAL FADERS AND CONTROLS

In a digital mixer, the gain coefficients will originate in hand-operated faders, just as in analog. Analog faders may be retained and used to produce a varying voltage, which is converted to a digital code or gain coefficient in an ADC, but it is also possible to obtain coefficients directly in digital faders. Digital faders are a form of displacement transducer in which the mechanical

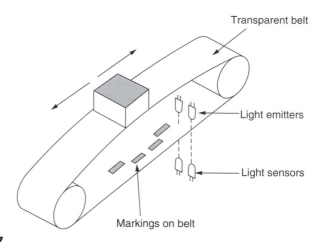

Transparent belt

Light emitters

Light sensors

Markings on belt

FIGURE 3.27

An absolute linear fader uses a number of light beams, which are interrupted in various combinations according to the position of a grating. A Gray code shown in Figure 3.28 must be used to prevent false codes.

position of the control is converted directly to a digital code. The positions of other controls, such as jog wheels on VTRs or editors, will also need to be digitized. Controls can be linear or rotary, and absolute or relative. In an absolute control, the position of the knob determines the output directly. In a relative control, the knob can be moved to increase or decrease the output, but its absolute position is meaningless.

Figure 3.27 shows an absolute linear fader. A grating is moved with respect to several light beams, one for each bit of the coefficient required. The interruption of the beams by the grating determines which photocells are illuminated. It is not possible to use a pure binary pattern on the grating because this results in transient false codes due to mechanical tolerances. Figure 3.28 shows some examples of these false codes. For example, on moving the fader from 3 to 4, the MSB goes true slightly before the middle bit goes false. This results in a momentary value of $4 + 2 = 6$ between 3 and 4. The solution is to use a code in which only 1 bit ever changes in going from one value to the next. One such code is the Gray code, which was devised to overcome timing hazards in relay logic but is now used extensively in position encoders. Gray code can be converted to binary in software or in a suitable PROM or gate array.

Figure 3.29 shows a rotary incremental encoder. This produces a sequence of pulses whose number is proportional to the angle through which it has been turned. The rotor carries a radial grating over its entire perimeter. This turns over a second fixed radial grating whose bars are not parallel to those of the first grating.

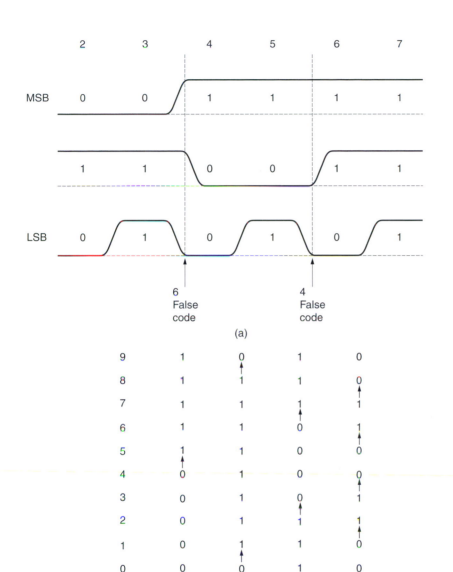

FIGURE 3.28
(a) Binary cannot be used for position encoders because mechanical tolerances cause false codes to be produced. (b) In Gray code, only 1 bit (arrowed) changes in between positions, so no false codes can be generated.

The resultant moiré fringes travel inward or outward depending on the direction of rotation. Two suitably positioned light beams falling on photocells will produce outputs in quadrature. The relative phase determines the direction, and the frequency is proportional to speed. The encoder outputs can be connected to a

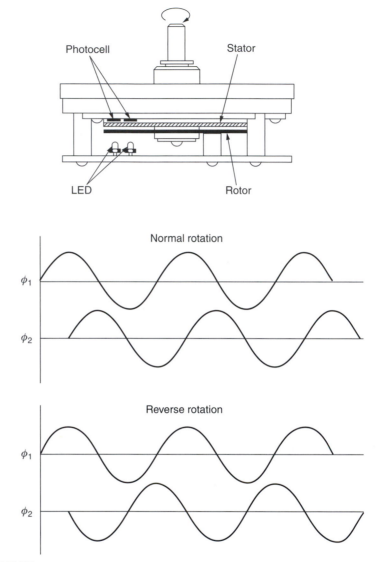

FIGURE 3.29
The fixed and rotating gratings produce moiré fringes, which are detected by two light paths as quadrature sinusoids. The relative phase determines the direction, and the frequency is proportional to speed of rotation.

counter whose contents will increase or decrease according to the direction in which the rotor is turned. The counter provides the coefficient output.

The word length of the gain coefficients requires some thought, as they determine the number of discrete gains available. If the coefficient word length is inadequate,

THE GALOIS FIELD

Figure 3.30 shows a simple circuit consisting of three D-type latches, which are clocked simultaneously. They are connected in series to form a shift register. At Figure 3.30a a feedback connection has been taken from the output to the input and the result is a ring counter in which the bits contained will recirculate endlessly. At (b) one XOR gate is added so that the output is fed back to more than one stage. The result is known as a twisted-ring counter and it has some interesting properties. Whenever the circuit is clocked, the lefthand bit moves to the righthand latch, the centre bit moves to the lefthand latch, and the centre latch becomes the XOR of the two outer latches. The figure shows that whatever the starting condition of the 3 bits in the latches, the same state will always be reached again after seven clocks, except if zero is used. The states of the latches form an endless ring of nonsequential numbers called a Galois field, after the French mathematical prodigy Evariste Galois, who discovered them. The states of the circuit form a maximum length sequence (prs) because there are as many states as are permitted by the word length. As the states of the sequence have many of the characteristics of random numbers, yet are repeatable, the result can also be called a pseudo-random sequence. As the all-zeros case is disallowed, the maximum length of a sequence generated by a register of m bits cannot exceed $(2^m - 1)$ states. The Galois field, however, includes the zero term. It is useful to explore the bizarre mathematics of Galois fields, which use modulo-2 arithmetic. Familiarity with such manipulations is helpful when studying error correction, particularly the Reed–Solomon codes used in recorders and treated in Chapter 8. They will also be found in processes that require pseudo-random numbers, such as digital dither, treated in Chapter 4, and randomized channel codes used in, for example, DVB and discussed in Chapter 10.

The circuit of Figure 3.30 can be considered as a counter and the four points shown will then be representing different powers of 2 from the MSB on the left to the LSB on the right. The feedback connection from the MSB

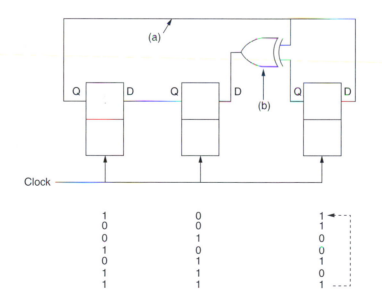

FIGURE 3.30
The circuit shown is a twisted-ring counter, which has an unusual feedback arrangement. Clocking the counter causes it to pass through a series of nonsequential values. See text for details.

to the other stages means that whenever the MSB becomes 1, two other powers are also forced to 1 so that the code of 1011 is generated.

Each state of the circuit can be described by combinations of powers of x, such as

$$x^2 = 100,$$

$$x = 010,$$

$$x^2 + x = 110, \text{ etc.}$$

The fact that 3 bits have the same state because they are connected together is represented by the Mod.2 equation

$$x^3 + x + 1 = 0.$$

Let $x = a$, which is a primitive element.

Now

$$a^3 + a + 1 = 0. \tag{3.1}$$

In modulo-2,

$$a + a = a^2 + a^2 = 0,$$

$$a = x = 010,$$

$$a^2 = x^2 = 100,$$

$$a^3 = a + 1 = 011 \text{ from (3.1),}$$

$$a^4 = a \times a^3 = a(a + 1) = a^2 + a = 110,$$

$$a^5 = a \times a^4 = a(a^2 + a) = a^3 + a^2 = 111,$$

$$a^6 = a^3 \times a^3 = (a + 1)^2 = a^2 + a + a + 1 = a^2 + 1 = 101,$$

$$a^7 = a(a^2 + 1) = a^3 + a = a + 1 + a = 1 = 001.$$

In this way it can be seen that the complete set of elements of the Galois field can be expressed by successive powers of the primitive element. Note that the twisted-ring circuit of Figure 3.30 simply raises a to higher and higher powers as it is clocked. Thus the seemingly complex multibit changes caused by a single clock of the register become simple to calculate using the correct primitive and the appropriate power.

The numbers produced by the twisted-ring counter are not random; they are completely predictable if the equation is known. However, the sequences produced are sufficiently similar to random numbers that in many cases they will be useful. They are thus referred to as pseudo-random sequences. The feedback connection is chosen such that the expression it implements will not factorize. Otherwise a maximum-length sequence could not be generated because the circuit might sequence around one or other of the factors depending on the initial condition. A useful analogy is to compare the operation of a pair of meshed gears. If the gears have a number

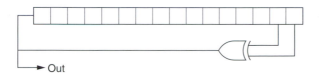

FIGURE 3.31
The PRS generator of DVB.

of teeth that is relatively prime, many revolutions are necessary to make the same pair of teeth touch again. If the number of teeth have a common multiple, far fewer turns are needed.

Figure 3.31 shows the pseudo-random sequence generator used in DVB. Its purpose is to modify the transmitted spectrum so that the amount of energy transmitted is as uniform as possible across the channel.

the gain control becomes "steppy," particularly toward the end of a fadeout. A compromise between performance and the expense of high-resolution faders is to insert a digital interpolator having a low-pass characteristic between the fader and the gain control stage. This will compute intermediate gains to higher resolution than the coarse fader scale so that the steps cannot be discerned.

FILTERS

Figure 3.32 shows an optical system of finite resolution. If an object containing an infinitely sharp line is presented to this system, the image will be an intensity function known in optics as a *point spread function*. Such functions are almost invariably symmetrical in optics. There is no movement or change here, the phenomenon is purely spatial. A point spread function is a spatial impulse response. All images passing through the optical system are convolved with it. Figure 3.32b shows that the object may be scanned by an analog system to produce a waveform. The image may also be scanned in this way. These waveforms are now temporal. However, the second waveform may be obtained in another way, using an analog filter in series with the first scanned waveform that has an equivalent impulse response. This filter must have linear phase, i.e., its impulse response must be symmetrical.

Figure 3.32c shows that the object may also be sampled, in which case all samples but one will have a value of zero. The image may also be sampled, and owing to the point spread function, there will now be a number of nonzero sample values. However, the image samples may also be obtained by passing the input sample into a digital filter having the appropriate impulse response. Note that it is possible to obtain the same result as in Figure 3.32c by passing the scanned waveform of (b) into an ADC and storing the samples in a memory. Clearly there are a number of equivalent routes leading to the same result. One result of this is that optical systems and sampled systems can simulate one another. This gives us considerable freedom to perform processing in the most advantageous domain that gives the required result. There are many parallels between analog, digital, and optical filters, which this chapter treats as a common subject.

It should be clear from Figure 3.32 why video signal paths need to have linear phase. In general, analog circuitry and filters tend not to have linear phase because they must be *causal*, which means that the output can occur only after the input. Figure 3.33a shows a simple RC network and its impulse response. This is the familiar exponential decay due to the capacitor discharging through

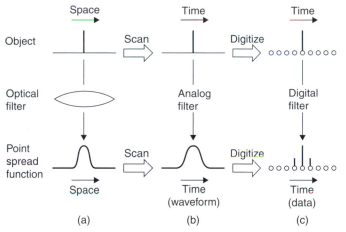

(a)   (b)   (c)

FIGURE 3.32

(a) In optical systems an infinitely sharp line is reproduced as a point spread function, which is the impulse response of the optical path. (b) Scanning either object or image produces an analog time-variant waveform. The scanned object waveform can be converted to the scanned image waveform with an electrical filter having an impulse response, which is an analog of the point spread function. (c) The object and image may also be sampled or the object samples can be converted to the image samples by a filter with an analogous discrete impulse response.

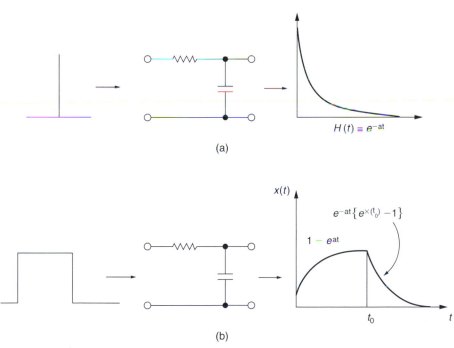

$$H(t) = e^{-at}$$

(a)

$x(t)$

$e^{-at}\{e^{\times(t_o)} - 1\}$

$1 - e^{at}$

t_0 t

(b)

FIGURE 3.33

(a) The impulse response of a simple RC network is an exponential decay. This can be used to calculate the response to a square wave, as in (b).

the resistor (in series with the source impedance, which is assumed here to be negligible). The figure also shows the response to a square wave at (b). With other waveforms the process is inevitably more complex.

Filtering is unavoidable. Sometimes a process has a filtering effect that is undesirable, for example, the limited frequency response of a video amplifier or loss of resolution in a lens, and we try to minimize it. On other occasions a filtering effect is specifically required. Analog or digital filters, and sometimes both, are required in DACs, in ADCs, in the data channels of digital recorders and transmission systems, and in DSP. Optical filters may also be necessary in imaging systems to convert between sampled and continuous images. Optical systems used in displays and in laser recorders also act as spatial filters.[1]

Figure 3.34 shows that impulse response testing tells a great deal about a filter. With a perfect filter, all frequencies should experience the same time delay. If some groups of frequencies experience a delay different from the others, there is a group-delay error. As an impulse has an infinite spectrum, a filter suffering from group-delay error will separate the different frequencies of an impulse along the time axis. A pure delay will cause a phase shift proportional to frequency, and a filter with this characteristic is said to be phase-linear. The impulse response of a phase-linear filter is symmetrical. If a filter suffers from group-delay error it cannot be phase-linear. It is almost impossible to make a perfectly phase-linear analog filter, and many filters have a group-delay equalization stage following them, which is often as complex as the filter itself. In the digital domain it is straightforward to make a phase-linear filter, and phase equalization becomes unnecessary.

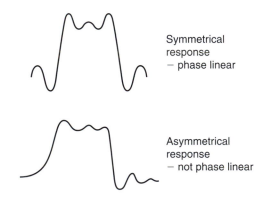

Symmetrical
response
— phase linear

Asymmetrical
response
— not phase linear

FIGURE 3.34
If a filter is not phase-linear, different frequencies will emerge at different times if an impulse is input. This is undesirable in video circuitry.

Because of the sampled nature of the signal, whatever the response at low frequencies may be, all PCM channels (and sampled analog channels) act as low-pass filters because they cannot contain frequencies above the Nyquist limit of half the sampling frequency.

TRANSFORMS

Transforms are a useful subject because they can help to understand processes that cause undesirable filtering or to design filters. The information itself may be subject to a transform. Transforming converts the information into another analog. The information is still there, but expressed with respect to temporal or spatial frequency rather than time or space. Instead of binary numbers representing the magnitude of samples, there are binary numbers representing the magnitude of frequency coefficients. The close relationship of transforms to convergent technologies makes any description somewhat circular, as Figure 3.35 shows. The solution adopted in this chapter is to introduce a number of filtering-related topics and to return to the subject of transforms whenever a point can be illustrated.

Transforms are only a different representation of the same information. As a result, what happens in the frequency domain must always be consistent with what happens in the time or space domains. A filter may modify the frequency response of a system, and/or the phase response, but every combination of frequency and phase response has a corresponding impulse response in the time domain. Figure 3.36 shows the relationship between the domains. On the left is the frequency domain. Here an input signal having a given spectrum is input to a filter having a given frequency response. The output spectrum will

DVB			
Image sampling	DCT-based compression	Randomizing	OFDM modulation
Transforms help explain Nyquist rate and resolution	Transform makes video data easier to compress	Transforms explain why randomizing optimizes transmitter spectrum	Modulator performs an inverse transform

FIGURE 3.35
Transforms are extensively found in convergent systems. They may be used to explain the operation of a process, or a process may actually create a transform. Here the relationship between transforms and DVB is shown.

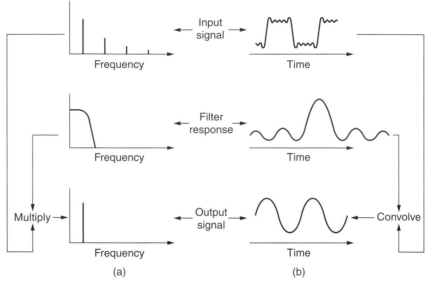

FIGURE 3.36
(a) If a signal having a given spectrum is passed into a filter, multiplying the two spectra will give the output spectrum. Equally transforming the filter frequency response will yield the impulse response of the filter. (b) If this is convolved with the time-domain waveform, the result will be the output waveform, whose transform is the output spectrum.

be the product of the two functions. If the functions are expressed logarithmically in decibels, the product can be obtained by simple addition. On the right, the time-domain output waveform represents the convolution of the impulse response with the input waveform. However, if the frequency transform of the output waveform is taken, it must be the same as the result obtained from the frequency response and the input spectrum. This is a useful result because it means that when image sampling is considered, it will be possible to explain the process in both domains.

CONVOLUTION

When a waveform is input to a system, the output waveform will be the convolution of the input waveform and the impulse response of the system. Convolution can be followed by reference to the graphic example in Figure 3.37. Where the impulse response is asymmetrical, the decaying tail occurs *after* the input. As a result it is necessary to reverse the impulse response in time so that it is mirrored prior to sweeping it through the input waveform. The output voltage is proportional to the shaded area shown where the two impulses overlap. If the impulse response is symmetrical, as would be the case with a linear phase filter, or in an optical system, the mirroring process is superfluous.

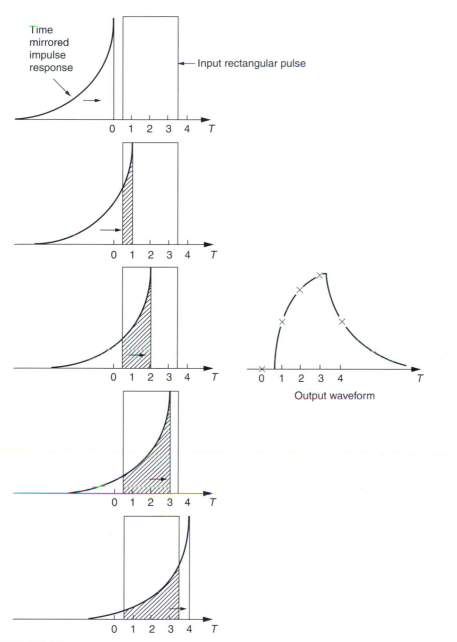

FIGURE 3.37

In the convolution of two continuous signals (the impulse response with the input), the impulse must be time reversed or mirrored. This is necessary because the impulse will be moved from left to right, and mirroring gives the impulse the correct time-domain response when it is moved past a fixed point. As the impulse response slides continuously through the input waveform, the area where the two overlap determines the instantaneous output amplitude. This is shown for five different times by the crosses on the output waveform.

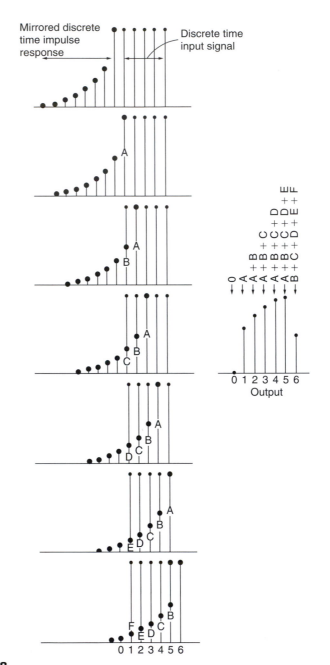

FIGURE 3.38

In discrete time convolution, the mirrored impulse response is stepped through the input one sample period at a time. At each step, the sum of the cross-products is used to form an output value. As the input in this example is a constant height pulse, the output is simply proportional to the sum of the coincident impulse response samples. This figure should be compared with Figure 3.37, filters used for image processing, sampling rate conversion, and oversampling.

The same process can be performed in the sampled, or discrete, time domain as shown in Figure 3.38. The impulse and the input are now a set of discrete samples, which clearly must have the same sample spacing. The impulse response has value only where impulses coincide. Elsewhere it is zero. The impulse response is therefore stepped through the input one sample period at a time. At each step, the area is still proportional to the output, but as the time steps are of uniform width, the area is proportional to the impulse height and so the output is obtained by adding up the lengths of overlap. In mathematical terms, the output samples represent the convolution of the input and the impulse response by summing the coincident cross-products.

FIR AND IIR FILTERS

Filters can be described in two main classes, as shown in Figure 3.39, according to the nature of the impulse response. Finite-impulse response (FIR) filters are always stable and, as their name suggests, respond to an impulse once, as they have only a forward path. In the temporal domain, the time for which the filter responds to an input is finite, fixed, and readily established. The same is therefore true about the distance over which an FIR filter responds in the spatial domain. FIR filters can be made perfectly phase-linear if required. Most filters used for sampling rate conversion and oversampling fall into this category.

Infinite-impulse response (IIR) filters respond to an impulse indefinitely and are not necessarily stable, as they have a return path from the output to the input. For this reason they are also called recursive filters. As the impulse

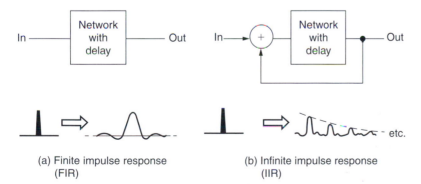

(a) Finite impulse response (FIR)

(b) Infinite impulse response (IIR)

FIGURE 3.39
An FIR filter (a) responds only once to an input, whereas the output of an IIR filter (b) continues indefinitely, rather like a decaying echo.

response is not symmetrical, IIR filters are not phase-linear. Noise reduction units may employ recursive filters and will be treated in Chapter 5.

FIR FILTERS

An FIR filter works by graphically constructing the impulse response for every input sample. It is first necessary to establish the correct impulse response. Figure 3.40a shows an example of a low-pass filter that cuts off at 1/4 of the sampling rate. The impulse response of a perfect low-pass filter is a sin x/x curve, where the time between the two central zero crossings is the reciprocal of the cutoff frequency. According to the mathematics, the waveform has always existed and carries on forever. The peak value of the output coincides with the input impulse. This means that the filter is not causal, because the output has changed before the input is known. Thus in all practical applications it is necessary to truncate the extreme ends of the impulse response, which causes an aperture effect, and to introduce a time delay in the filter equal to half the duration of the truncated impulse to make the filter causal. As an input impulse is shifted through the series of registers in Figure 3.40b, the impulse response is created, because at each point it is multiplied by a coefficient as in Figure 3.40c. These coefficients are simply the result of sampling and quantizing the desired impulse response. Clearly the sampling rate used to sample the impulse must be the same as the sampling rate for which the filter is being designed. In practice the coefficients are calculated, rather than attempting to sample an actual impulse response. The coefficient word length will be a compromise between cost and performance. Because the input sample shifts across the system registers to create the shape of the impulse response, the configuration is also known as a transversal filter. In operation with real sample streams, there will be several consecutive sample values in the filter registers at any time to convolve the input with the impulse response.

Simply truncating the impulse response causes an abrupt transition from input samples that matter and those that do not. Truncating the filter superimposes a rectangular shape on the time-domain impulse response. In the frequency domain the rectangular shape transforms to a $\sin x/x$ characteristic, which is superimposed on the desired frequency response as a ripple. One consequence of this is known as Gibb's phenomenon, a tendency for the response to peak just before the cutoff frequency.[2,3] As a result, the length of the impulse that must be considered will depend not only on the frequency response, but also on the amount of ripple that can be tolerated. If the relevant period of the impulse is measured in sample periods, the result will be the number of points or multiplications needed in the filter. Figure 3.41 compares the performance of

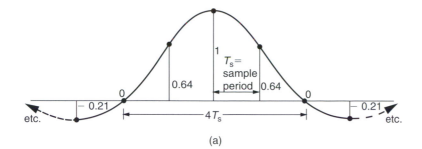

(a)

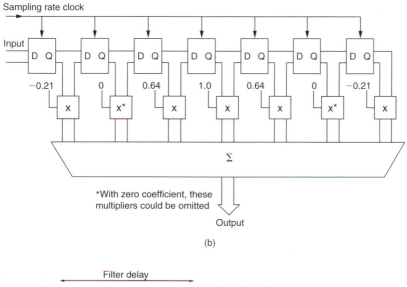

*With zero coefficient, these multipliers could be omitted

Output

(b)

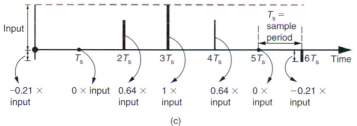

(c)

FIGURE 3.40

(a) The impulse response of a low-pass filter (LPF) is a sin x/x curve, which stretches from $-\infty$ to $+\infty$ in time. The ends of the response must be neglected and a delay introduced to make the filter causal. (b) The structure of an FIR LPF. Input samples shift across the register and at each point are multiplied by different coefficients. (c) When a single unit sample shifts across the circuit of Figure 3.43b, the impulse response is created at the output as the impulse is multiplied by each coefficient in turn.

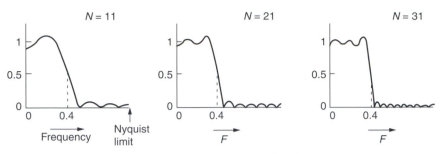

FIGURE 3.41
The truncation of the impulse in an FIR filter caused by the use of a finite number of points (N) results in ripple in the response. Shown here are three different numbers of points for the same impulse response. The filter is an LPF that rolls off at 0.4 of the fundamental interval (courtesy of Philips Technical Review).

filters with different numbers of points. Video filters may use as few as 8 points, whereas a high-quality digital audio FIR filter may need as many as 96 points.

Rather than simply truncate the impulse response in time, it is better to make a smooth transition from samples that do not count to those that do. This can be done by multiplying the coefficients in the filter by a window function that peaks in the centre of the impulse. Figure 3.42 shows some different window functions and their responses. The rectangular window is the case of truncation, and the response is shown at I. A linear reduction in weight from the centre of the window to the edges characterizes the Bartlett window (II), which trades ripple for an increase in transition-region width. At III is shown the Hamming window, which is essentially a raised cosine shape. Not shown is the similar Hamming window, which offers a slightly different trade-off between ripple and the width of the main lobe. The Blackman window introduces an extra cosine term into the Hamming window at half the period of the main cosine period, reducing Gibb's phenomenon and ripple level, but increasing the width of the transition region. The Kaiser window is a family of windows based on the Bessel function, allowing various trade-offs between ripple ratio and main lobe width. Two of these are shown in IV and V. The drawback of the Kaiser windows is that they are complex to implement.

Filter coefficients can be optimized by computer simulation. One of the best-known techniques used is the Remez exchange algorithm, which converges on the optimum coefficients after a number of iterations.

In the example of Figure 3.43, the low-pass filter of Figure 3.40 is shown with a Bartlett window. Acceptable ripple determines the number of significant sample

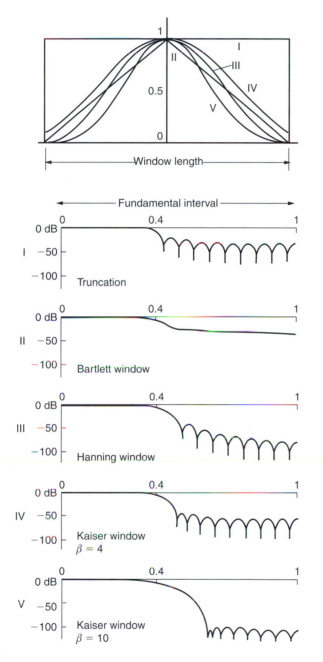

FIGURE 3.42

The effects of window functions. At top, various window functions are shown in continuous form. Once the number of samples in the window is established, the continuous functions shown here are sampled at the appropriate spacing to obtain window coefficients. These are multiplied by the truncated impulse response coefficients to obtain the actual coefficients used by the filter. The amplitude responses (I–V) correspond to the window functions illustrated (responses courtesy of Philips Technical Review).

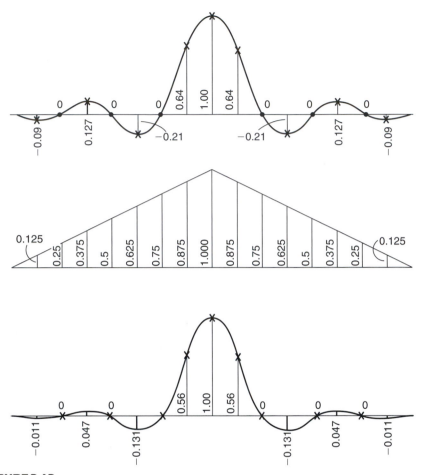

FIGURE 3.43
A truncated sin x/x impulse (top) is multiplied by a Bartlett window function (centre) to produce the actual coefficients used (bottom).

periods embraced by the impulse. This determines in turn both the number of points in the filter and the filter delay. As the impulse is symmetrical, the delay will be half the impulse period. The impulse response is a sin x/x function, and this has been calculated in the figure. The sin x/x response is next multiplied by the window function to give the windowed impulse response.

If the coefficients are not quantized finely enough, it will be as if they had been calculated inaccurately, and the performance of the filter will be less than expected. Figure 3.44 shows an example of quantizing coefficients. Conversely, raising the word length of the coefficients increases cost.

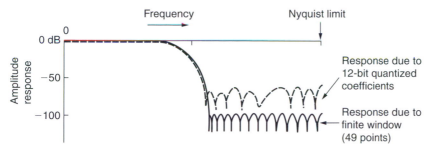

FIGURE 3.44
Frequency response of a 49-point transversal filter with infinite precision (solid line) shows ripple due to finite window size. Quantizing coefficients to 12 bits reduces attenuation in the stop band (responses courtesy of Philips Technical Review).

The FIR structure is inherently phase-linear because it is easy to make the impulse response absolutely symmetrical. The individual samples in a digital system do not know in isolation what frequency they represent, and they can pass through the filter only at a rate determined by the clock. Because of this inherent phase-linearity, an FIR filter can be designed for a specific impulse response, and the frequency response will follow.

The frequency response of the filter can be changed at will by changing the coefficients. A programmable filter need have only several sets of coefficients in a memory; the address supplied to the memory will select the response. The frequency response of a digital filter will also change if the clock rate is changed, so it is often less ambiguous to specify a frequency of interest in a digital filter in terms of a fraction of the fundamental interval rather than in absolute terms. The configuration shown in Figure 3.40 serves to illustrate the principle. The units used on the diagrams are sample periods and the response is proportional to these periods or spacings, and so it is not necessary to use actual figures.

Where the impulse response is symmetrical, it is often possible to reduce the number of multiplications, because the same product can be used twice, at equal distances before and after the centre of the window. This is known as folding the filter. A folded filter is shown in Figure 3.45.

SAMPLING-RATE CONVERSION

Sampling-rate conversion or interpolation is an important enabling technology on which a large number of practical digital video devices are based. In digital video, the sampling rate takes on many guises. When analog video is sampled

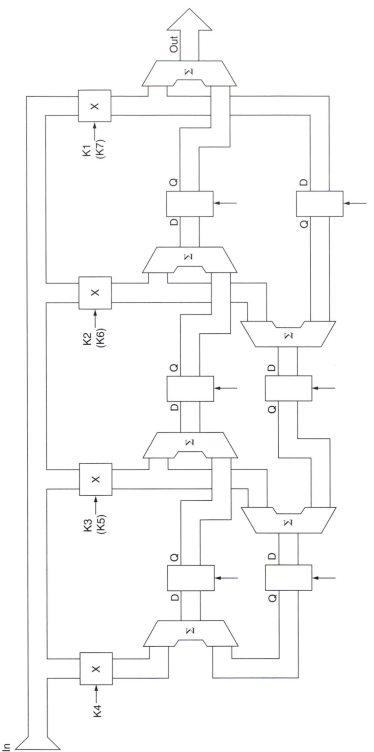

FIGURE 3.45

A seven-point folded filter for a symmetrical impulse response. In this case K1 and K7 will be identical, and so the input sample can be multiplied once and the product fed into the output shift system in two different places. The centre coefficient K4 appears once. In an even-numbered filter the centre coefficient would be used twice.

in real time, the sampling rate is temporal, but where pixels form a static array, the sampling rate is a spatial frequency.

Some of the applications of interpolation are set out here:

1. Standards convertors need to change two of the sampling rates of the video they handle, namely the temporal frame rate and the vertical line spacing, which is in fact a spatial sampling frequency. Standards convertors working with composite digital signals will also need to change the sampling rate along the line because it will be a multiple of the appropriate subcarrier frequency.

2. Different sampling rates exist today for different purposes. Most component digital devices sample at 13.5 MHz, using the 4:2:2 format, but other variations are possible, such as 3:1:1. Composite machines sample at a multiple of the subcarrier frequency of their line standard. Rate conversion allows material to be exchanged freely between such formats. For example, the output of a 4:2:2 paint system at 13.5 MHz may be digitally converted to 4Fsc for use as input to a composite digital recorder.

3. To take advantage of oversampling convertors, an increase in sampling rate is necessary for DACs and a reduction in sampling rate is necessary for ADCs. In oversampling the factors by which the rates are changed are simpler than in other applications.

4. In effects machines, the size of the picture may be changed without the pixel spacing being changed. This is exactly the converse of the standards convertor, which leaves the picture size unchanged and changes the pixel spacing. Alternatively the picture may be shifted with respect to the sampling matrix by any required distance to subpixel accuracy. Similar processes are necessary in motion estimation for standards convertors and data reduction.

5. When a digital VTR is played back at other than the correct speed to achieve some effect or to correct pitch, the sampling rate of the reproduced audio signal changes in proportion. If the playback samples are to be fed to a digital mixing console that works at some standard frequency, audio sampling-rate conversion will be necessary. Whilst DVTRs universally use an audio sampling rate of 48 kHz, Compact Disc uses 44.1 kHz, and 32 kHz is common for broadcast use (e.g. DVB).

6. When digital audio is used in conjunction with film or video, difficulties arise because it is not always possible to synchronise the sampling rate with the frame rate. An example of this is where the digital audio

recorder uses its internally generated sampling rate, but also records studio timecode. On playback, the timecode can be made the same as on other units, or the sampling rate can be locked, but not both. Sampling-rate conversion allows a recorder to play back an asynchronous recording locked to timecode.

There are three basic but related categories of rate conversion, as shown in Figure 3.46. The most straightforward (Figure 3.46a) changes the rate by an integer ratio, up or down. The timing of the system is thus simplified because all samples (input and output) are present on edges of the higher-rate sampling clock. Such a system is generally adopted for oversampling convertors; the exact sampling rate immediately adjacent to the analog domain is not critical and will be chosen to make the filters easier to implement.

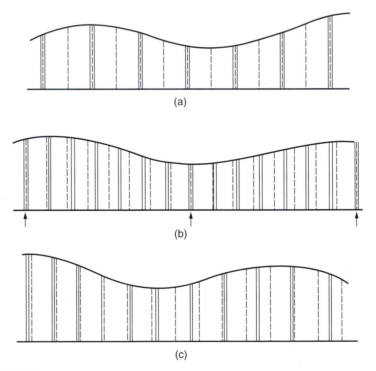

FIGURE 3.46
Categories of rate conversion. (a) Integer-ratio conversion, in which the lower-rate samples are always coincident with those of the higher rate. There are a small number of phases needed. (b) Fractional-ratio conversion, in which sample coincidence is periodic. A larger number of phases is required. The example here is conversion from 50.4 to 44.1 kHz (8/7). (c) Variable-ratio conversion, in which there is no fixed relationship, and a large number of phases are required.

Next in order of difficulty is the category shown at Figure 3.46b, in which the rate is changed by the ratio of two small integers. Samples in the input periodically time-align with the output. Such devices can be used for converting from $4 \times F_{sc}$ to $3 \times F_{sc}$, in the vertical processing of standards convertors, or between the various rates of CCIR-601.

The most complex rate-conversion category is that in which there is no simple relationship between input and output sampling rates, and in fact they may vary. This situation, shown in Figure 3.46c, is known as variable-ratio conversion. The temporal or spatial relationship of input and output samples is arbitrary. This problem will be met in effects machines that zoom or rotate images.

The technique of integer-ratio conversion is used in conjunction with oversampling convertors in digital video and audio and in motion estimation and compression systems in which subsampled or reduced resolution versions of an input image are required. These applications will be detailed in Chapter 5. Sampling-rate reduction by an integer factor is dealt with first.

Figure 3.47a shows the spectrum of a typical sampled system in which the sampling rate is a little more than twice the analog bandwidth. Attempts to reduce the sampling rate simply by omitting samples, a process known as decimation, will result in aliasing, as shown in Figure 3.47b. Intuitively it is obvious that omitting samples is the same as if the original sampling rate was lower. To prevent aliasing, it is necessary to incorporate low-pass filtering into the system, by which the cutoff frequency reflects the new, lower, sampling rate. An FIR-type low-pass filter could be installed, as described earlier in this chapter, immediately prior to the stage at which samples are omitted, but this would be wasteful, because for much of its time the FIR filter would be calculating sample values that are to be discarded. The more effective method is to combine the low-pass filter with the decimator so that the filter calculates only values to be retained in the output sample stream. Figure 3.47c shows how this is done. The filter makes one accumulation for every output sample, but that accumulation is the result of multiplying all relevant input samples in the filter window by an appropriate coefficient. The number of points in the filter is determined by the number of input samples in the period of the filter window, but the number of multiplications per second is obtained by multiplying that figure by the output rate. If the filter is not integrated with the decimator, the number of points has to be multiplied by the input rate. The larger the rate-reduction factor, the more advantageous the decimating filter ought to be, but this is not quite the case, as

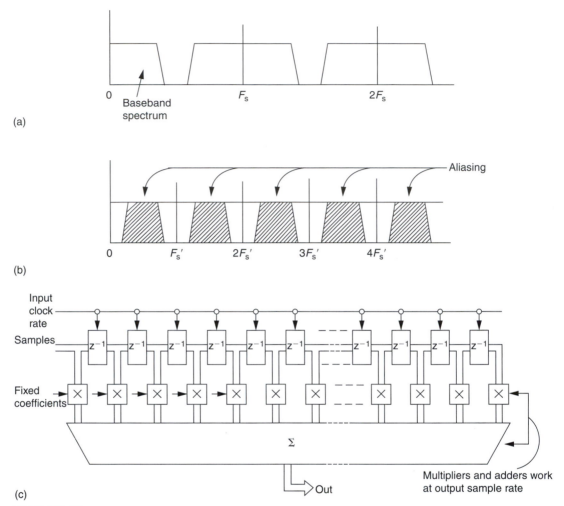

(a)

(b)

(c)

FIGURE 3.47
The spectrum of a typical digital sample stream in (a) will be subject to aliasing as in (b) if the baseband width is not reduced by an LPF. (c) An FIR low-pass filter prevents aliasing. Samples are clocked transversely across the filter at the input rate, but the filter computes only at the output sample rate. Clearly this will work only if the two are related by an integer factor.

the greater the reduction in rate, the longer the filter window will need to be to accommodate the broader impulse response.

When the sampling rate is to be increased by an integer factor, additional samples must be created at even spacing between the existing ones. There is no need for the bandwidth of the input samples to be reduced because, if the original sampling rate was adequate, a higher one must also be adequate.

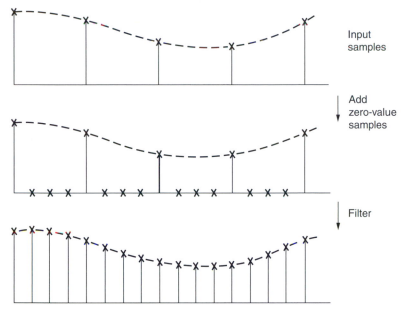

FIGURE 3.48
In integer-ratio sampling, rate increase can be obtained in two stages. First, zero-value samples are inserted to increase the rate, and then filtering is used to give the extra samples real values. The filter necessary will be an LPF with a response that cuts off at the Nyquist frequency of the input samples.

Figure 3.48 shows that the process of sampling-rate increase can be thought of in two stages. First, the correct rate is achieved by inserting samples of zero value at the correct instant, and then the additional samples are given meaningful values by passing the sample stream through a low-pass filter that cuts off at the Nyquist frequency of the original sampling rate. This filter is known as an interpolator, and one of its tasks is to prevent images of the input spectrum from appearing in the extended baseband of the output spectrum.

How do interpolators work? Remember that, according to sampling theory, all sampled systems have finite bandwidth. An individual digital sample value is obtained by sampling the instantaneous voltage of the original analog waveform, and because it has zero duration, it must contain an infinite spectrum. However, such a sample can never be observed in that form because of the reconstruction process, which limits the spectrum of the impulse to the Nyquist limit. After reconstruction, one infinitely short digital sample ideally represents a sin x/x pulse whose central peak width is determined by the response of the reconstruction filter, and whose amplitude is proportional to the sample value. This implies that, in reality, one sample value has meaning over a considerable

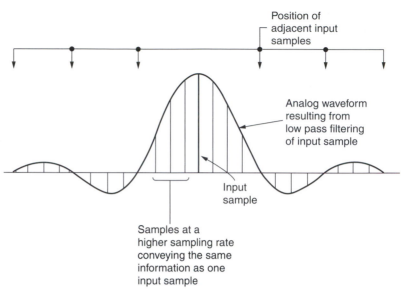

Position of adjacent input samples

Analog waveform resulting from low pass filtering of input sample

Input sample

Samples at a higher sampling rate conveying the same information as one input sample

FIGURE 3.49
A single sample results in a sin x/x waveform after filtering in the analog domain. At a new, higher, sampling rate, the same waveform after filtering will be obtained if the numerous samples of differing size shown here are used. It follows that the values of these new samples can be calculated from the input samples in the digital domain in an FIR filter.

time span, rather than just at the sample instant. If this were not true, it would be impossible to build an interpolator.

As in rate reduction, performing the steps separately is inefficient. The bandwidth of the information is unchanged when the sampling rate is increased; therefore the original input samples will pass through the filter unchanged, and it is superfluous to compute them. The combination of the two processes into an interpolating filter minimizes the amount of computation.

As the purpose of the system is purely to increase the sampling rate, the filter must be as transparent as possible, and this implies that a linear-phase configuration is mandatory, suggesting the use of an FIR structure. Figure 3.49 shows that the theoretical impulse response of such a filter is a sin x/x curve that has zero value at the position of adjacent input samples. In practice this impulse cannot be implemented because it is infinite. The impulse response used will be truncated and windowed as described earlier. To simplify this discussion, assume that a sin x/x impulse is to be used. There is a strong parallel with the operation of a DAC in which the analog voltage is returned to the time-continuous state by summing the analog impulses due to each sample. In a digital interpolating filter, this process is duplicated.[4]

If the sampling rate is to be doubled, new samples must be interpolated exactly halfway between existing samples. The necessary impulse response is shown in Figure 3.50; it can be sampled at the output sample period and quantized to form coefficients. If a single input sample is multiplied by each of these coefficients in turn, the impulse response of that sample at the new sampling rate will be obtained. Note that every other coefficient is zero, which confirms that no computation is necessary on the existing samples; they are just transferred to the output. The intermediate sample is computed by adding together the impulse responses of every input sample in the window. The figure shows how this mechanism operates. If the sampling rate is to be increased by a factor of 4, three sample values must be interpolated between existing input samples. Figure 3.51 shows that it is necessary to sample only the impulse response at one-quarter the period of input samples to obtain three sets of coefficients, which will be used in turn. In hardware-implemented filters, the input sample, which is passed straight to the output, is transferred by using a fourth filter phase in which all coefficients are 0 except the central one, which is unity.

Fractional-ratio conversion allows interchange between different CCIR-601 rates, such as 4:2:2 and 4:2:0. Fractional ratios also occur in the vertical axis of standards convertors. Figure 3.46 showed that when the two sampling rates have a simple fractional relationship m/n, there is a periodicity in the relationship between samples in the two streams. It is possible to have a system clock running at the least-common multiple frequency, which will divide by different integers to give each sampling rate.[5]

The existence of a common clock frequency means that a fractional-ratio convertor could be made by arranging two integer-ratio convertors in series. This configuration is shown in Figure 3.52a. The input-sampling rate is multiplied by m in an interpolator, and the result is divided by n in a decimator. Although this system would work, it would be grossly inefficient, because only one in n of the interpolator's outputs would be used. A decimator followed by an interpolator would also offer the correct sampling rate at the output, but the intermediate sampling rate would be so low that the system bandwidth would be quite unacceptable.

As has been seen, a more efficient structure results from combining the processes. The result is exactly the same structure as an integer-ratio interpolator

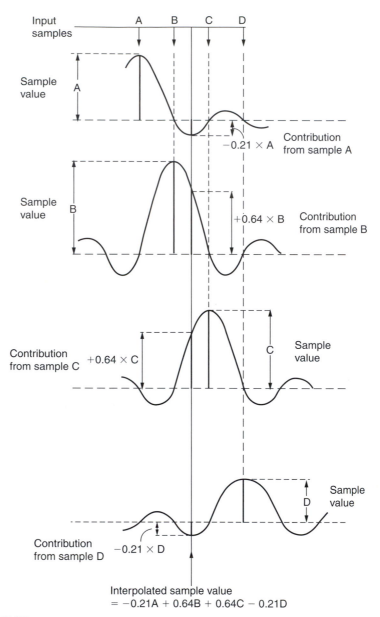

FIGURE 3.50

A 2× oversampling interpolator. To compute an intermediate sample, the input samples are imagined to be sin x/x impulses, and the contributions from each at the point of interest can be calculated. In practice, rather more samples on either side need to be taken into account.

157

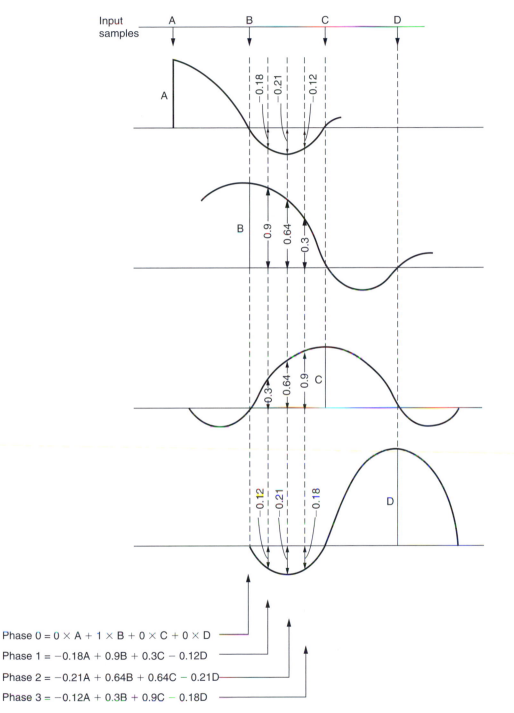

Input samples

A B C D

−0.18
−0.21
−0.12

A

B

0.9
0.64
0.3

0.3
0.64
0.9

C

−0.12
−0.21
−0.18

D

Phase 0 = 0 × A + 1 × B + 0 × C + 0 × D

Phase 1 = −0.18A + 0.9B + 0.3C − 0.12D

Phase 2 = −0.21A + 0.64B + 0.64C − 0.21D

Phase 3 = −0.12A + 0.3B + 0.9C − 0.18D

FIGURE 3.51

In 4× oversampling, for each set of input samples, four phases of coefficients are necessary, each of which produces one of the oversampled values.

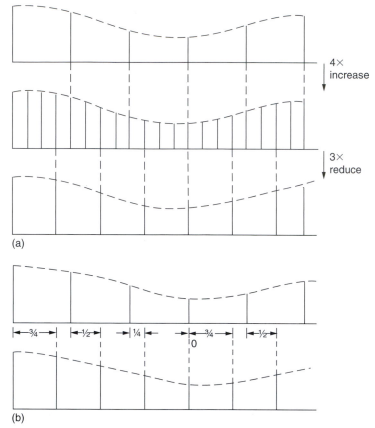

FIGURE 3.52
(a) Fractional-ratio conversion of 3/4 in this sample is by increasing to 4× input prior to reducing by 3×. The inefficiency due to discarding previously computed values is clear. In (b), efficiency is raised because only needed values will be computed. Note how the interpolation phase changes for each output. Fixed coefficients can no longer be used.

and requires an FIR filter. The impulse response of the filter is determined by the lower of the two sampling rates, and as before it prevents aliasing when the rate is being reduced and prevents images when the rate is being increased. The interpolator has sufficient coefficient phases to interpolate m output samples for every input sample, but not all these values are computed; only interpolations that coincide with an output sample are performed. It can be seen in Figure 3.52b that input samples shift across the transversal filter at the input sampling rate, but interpolations are performed only at the output sample rate. This is possible because a different filter phase will be used at each interpolation.

In the previous examples, the sample rate or spacing of the filter output had a constant relationship to the input, which meant that the two rates had to be phase-locked. This is an undesirable constraint in some applications, including image manipulators. In a variable-ratio interpolator, values will exist for the points at which input samples were made, but it is necessary to compute what the sample values would have been at absolutely any point between available samples. The general concept of the interpolator is the same as for the fractional-ratio convertor, except that an infinite number of filter phases is ideally necessary. Because a realizable filter will have a finite number of phases, it is necessary to study the degradation this causes. The desired continuous temporal or spatial axis of the interpolator is quantized by the phase spacing, and a sample value needed at a particular point will be replaced by a value for the nearest available filter phase. The number of phases in the filter therefore determines the accuracy of the interpolation. The effects of calculating a value for the wrong point are identical to those of sampling with clock jitter, in that an error occurs proportional to the slope of the signal. The result is program-modulated noise. The higher the noise specification, the greater the desired time accuracy and the greater the number of phases required. The number of phases is equal to the number of sets of coefficients available and should not be confused with the number of points in the filter, which is equal to the number of coefficients in a set (and the number of multiplications needed to calculate one output value).

The sampling jitter accuracy necessary for 8-bit working is measured in picoseconds. This implies that something like 32 filter phases will be required for adequate performance in an 8-bit sampling-rate convertor.

TRANSFORMS AND DUALITY

The duality of transforms provides an interesting insight into what is happening in common processes. Fourier analysis holds that any periodic waveform can be reproduced by adding together an arbitrary number of harmonically related sinusoids of various amplitudes and phases. Figure 3.53 shows how a square wave can be built up of harmonics. The spectrum can be drawn by plotting the amplitude of the harmonics against frequency. It will be seen that this gives a spectrum that is a decaying wave. It passes through 0 at all even multiples of the fundamental. The shape of the spectrum is a $\sin x/x$ curve. If a square wave has a $\sin x/x$ spectrum, it follows that a filter with a rectangular impulse response will have a $\sin x/x$ spectrum.

A low-pass filter has a rectangular spectrum, and this has a $\sin x/x$ impulse response. These characteristics are known as a transform pair. In transform pairs,

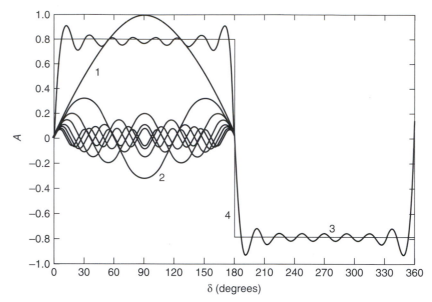

FIGURE 3.53
Fourier analysis of a square wave into fundamental and harmonics. *A*, amplitude;
δ, phase of fundamental wave in degrees; 1, first harmonic (fundamental); 2, odd
harmonics 3–15; 3, sum of harmonics 1–15; 4, ideal square wave.

if one domain has one shape of the pair, the other domain will have the other
shape. Figure 3.54 shows a number of transform pairs. At Figure 3.54a a square
wave has a sin x/x spectrum and a sin x/x impulse has a square spectrum. In general the product of equivalent parameters on either side of a transform remains
constant, so that if one increases, the other must fall. If (a) shows a filter with a
wider bandwidth, having a narrow impulse response, then (b) shows a filter of
narrower bandwidth that has a wide impulse response. This is duality in action.
The limiting case of this behaviour is that in which one parameter becomes
zero, and the other goes to infinity. At (c) a time-domain pulse of infinitely short
duration has a flat spectrum. Thus a flat waveform, i.e., DC, has only zero in its
spectrum. The impulse response of the optics of a laser disk (d) has a sin^2 x/x^2
intensity function, and this is responsible for the triangular falling frequency
response of the pickup. The lens is a rectangular aperture, but as there is no such
thing as negative light, a sin x/x impulse response is impossible. The squaring
process is consistent with a positive-only impulse response. Interestingly, the
transform of a Gaussian response in still Gaussian.

Duality also holds for sampled systems. A sampling process is periodic in
the time domain. This results in a spectrum that is periodic in the frequency

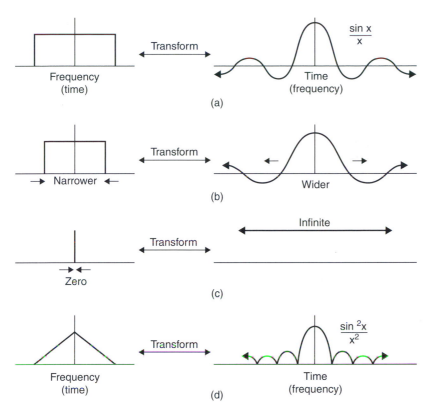

FIGURE 3.54
Transform pairs. (a) The dual of a rectangle is a sin x/x function. If one is time domain, the other is frequency domain. (b) Narrowing one domain widens the other. The limiting case of this is (c). (d) The transform of the sin x/x squared function is triangular.

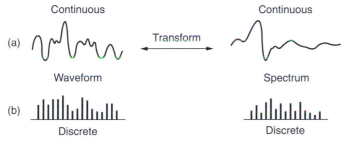

FIGURE 3.55
(a) A continuous time signal has continuous spectrum. (b) A discrete time signal has discrete spectrum.

domain. If the time between the samples is reduced, the bandwidth of the system rises. Figure 3.55a shows that a continuous time signal has a continuous spectrum, whereas in Figure 3.55b the frequency transform of a sampled signal is also discrete. In other words sampled signals can be analysed into only a finite number of frequencies. The more accurate the frequency analysis has to be, the more samples are needed in the block. Making the block longer reduces the ability to locate a transient in time. This is the Heisenberg inequality, which is the limiting case of duality, because when infinite accuracy is achieved in one domain, there is no accuracy at all in the other.

THE FOURIER TRANSFORM

If the amplitude and phase of each frequency component are known, linearly adding the resultant components in an inverse transform results in the original waveform. In digital systems the waveform is expressed as a number of discrete samples. As a result the Fourier transform analyses the signal into an equal number of discrete frequencies. This is known as a discrete Fourier transform, or DFT, in which the number of frequency coefficients is equal to the number of input samples. The FFT (fast Fourier transform) is no more than an efficient way of computing the DFT.[6] As was seen in the previous section, practical systems must use windowing to create short-term transforms.

It will be evident from Figure 3.56 that the knowledge of the phase of the frequency component is vital, as changing the phase of any component will seriously alter the reconstructed waveform. Thus the DFT must accurately analyse the phase of the signal components.

There are a number of ways of expressing phase. Figure 3.57 shows a point that is rotating about a fixed axis at constant speed. Looked at from the side, the point oscillates up and down at constant frequency. The waveform of that motion is a sine wave, and that is what we would see if the rotating point were to translate along its axis whilst we continued to look from the side.

One way of defining the phase of a waveform is to specify the angle through which the point has rotated at time zero ($T = 0$). If a second point is made to revolve at 90° to the first, it would produce a cosine wave when translated. It is possible to produce a waveform having arbitrary phase by adding together the sine and the cosine wave in various proportions and polarities. For example, adding the sine and cosine waves in equal proportion results in a waveform lagging the sine wave by 45°.

Figure 3.57 shows that the proportions necessary are respectively the sine and the cosine of the phase angle. Thus the two methods of describing phase can be readily interchanged.

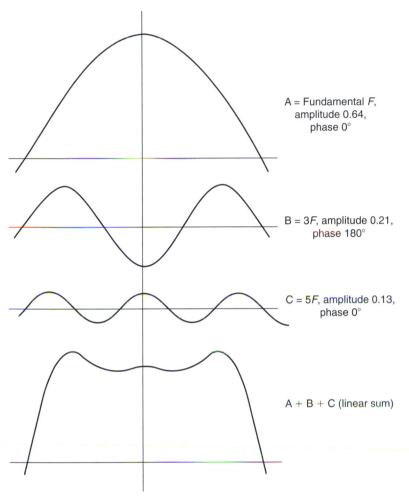

A = Fundamental F, amplitude 0.64, phase 0°

B = 3F, amplitude 0.21, phase 180°

C = 5F, amplitude 0.13, phase 0°

A + B + C (linear sum)

FIGURE 3.56
Fourier analysis allows the synthesis of any waveform by the addition of discrete frequencies of appropriate amplitude and phase.

The discrete Fourier transform spectrum analyses a string of samples by searching separately for each discrete target frequency. It does this by multiplying the input waveform by a sine wave, known as the basis function, having the target frequency and adding up or integrating the products. Figure 3.58a shows that multiplying by basis functions gives a nonzero integral when the input frequency is the same, whereas Figure 3.58b shows that with a different input frequency (in fact all other different frequencies) the integral is zero, showing that no component of the target frequency exists. Thus from a real waveform containing many frequencies all frequencies except the target frequency are excluded. The magnitude of the integral is proportional to the amplitude of the target component.

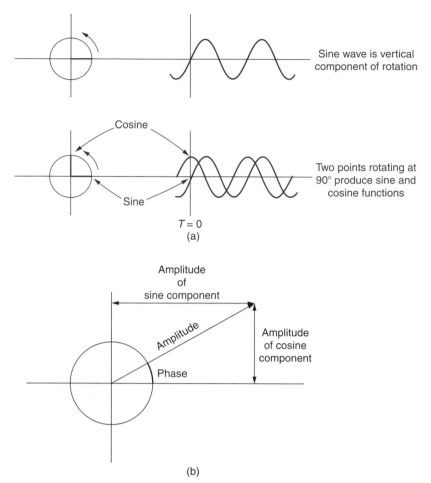

Sine wave is vertical component of rotation

Cosine

Two points rotating at 90° produce sine and cosine functions

Sine

$T = 0$

(a)

Amplitude of sine component

Amplitude

Amplitude of cosine component

Phase

(b)

FIGURE 3.57
The origin of sine and cosine waves is to take a particular viewpoint of a rotation. Any phase can be synthesized by adding proportions of sine and cosine waves.

Figure 3.58c shows that the target frequency will not be detected if it is phase-shifted 90° as the product of quadrature waveforms is always 0. Thus the discrete Fourier transform must make a further search for the target frequency using a cosine basis function. It follows from the arguments above that the relative proportions of the sine and cosine integrals reveal the phase of the input component. Thus each discrete frequency in the spectrum must be the result of a pair of quadrature searches.

Searching for one frequency at a time as above will result in a DFT, but only after considerable computation. However, a lot of the calculations are repeated

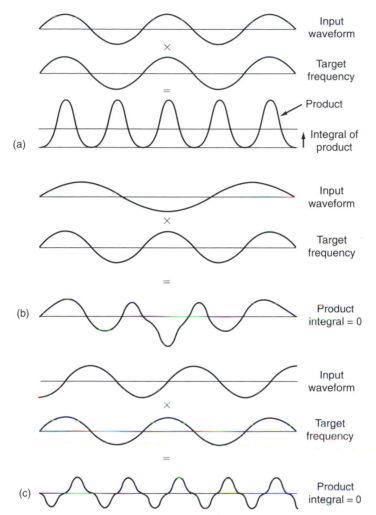

FIGURE 3.58
The input waveform is multiplied by the target frequency and the result is averaged
or integrated. In (a) the target frequency is present and a large integral results. With
another input frequency the integral is 0 as in (b). The correct frequency will also result
in a 0 integral shown in (c) if it is at 90° to the phase of the search frequency. This is
overcome by making two searches in quadrature.

many times over in different searches. The FFT gives the same result with less
computation by logically gathering together all the places where the same calculation is needed and making the calculation once.

The amount of computation can be reduced by performing the sine and cosine
component searches together. Another saving is obtained by noting that every
180° the sine and cosine have the same magnitude but are simply inverted in

sign. Instead of performing four multiplications on two samples 180° apart and adding the pairs of products it is more economical to subtract the sample values and multiply twice, once by a sine value and once by a cosine value.

The first coefficient is the arithmetic mean, which is the sum of all the sample values in the block divided by the number of samples. Figure 3.59 shows how

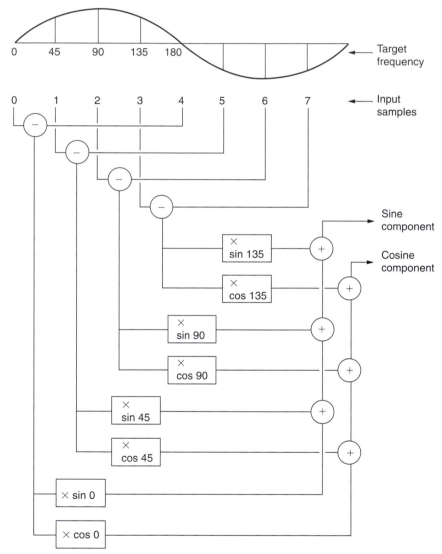

FIGURE 3.59
An example of a filtering search. Pairs of samples are subtracted and multiplied by sampled sine and cosine waves. The products are added to give the sine and cosine components of the search frequency.

the search for the lowest frequency in a block is performed. Pairs of samples are subtracted as shown, and each difference is then multiplied by the sine and the cosine of the search frequency. The process shifts one sample period, and a new sample pair is subtracted and multiplied by new sine and cosine factors. This is repeated until all the sample pairs have been multiplied. The sine and cosine products are then added to give the value of the sine and cosine coefficients respectively.

It is possible to combine the calculation of the DC component, which requires the sum of samples, and the calculation of the fundamental, which requires sample differences, by combining stages shown in Figure 3.60a, which take a

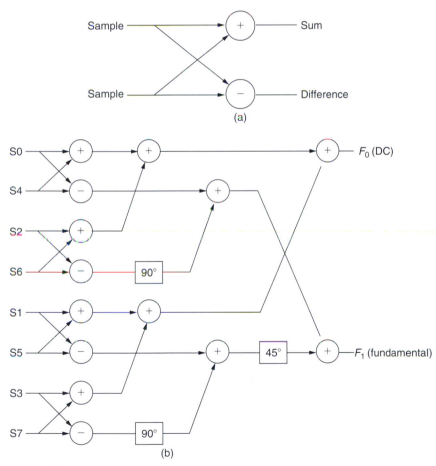

FIGURE 3.60
The basic element of an FFT is known as a butterfly (a) because of the shape of the signal paths in a sum and difference system. Butterflies are used to compute the first two coefficients as shown in (b).

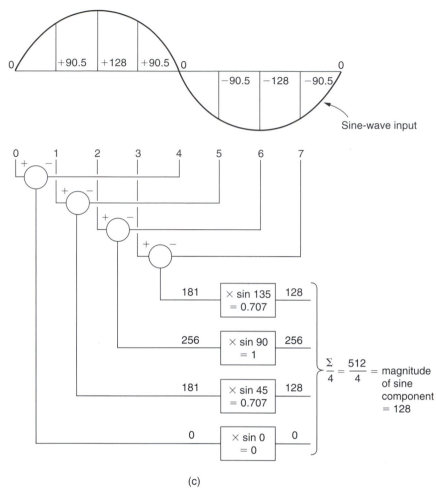

FIGURE 3.60
(Continued) (c) An actual calculation of a sine coefficient. This should be compared with the result shown in (d).

pair of samples and add and subtract them. Such a stage is called a butterfly because of the shape of the schematic. Figure 3.60b shows how the first two components are calculated. The phase rotation boxes attribute the input to the sine or cosine component outputs according to the phase angle. As shown, the box labelled 90° attributes nothing to the sine output, but unity gain to the cosine output. The 45° box attributes the input equally to both components.

Figure 3.60c shows a numerical example. If a sine-wave input is considered where 0° coincides with the first sample, this will produce a zero sine coefficient and non-0 cosine coefficient, whereas (d) shows the same input waveform shifted by 90°. Note how the coefficients change over.

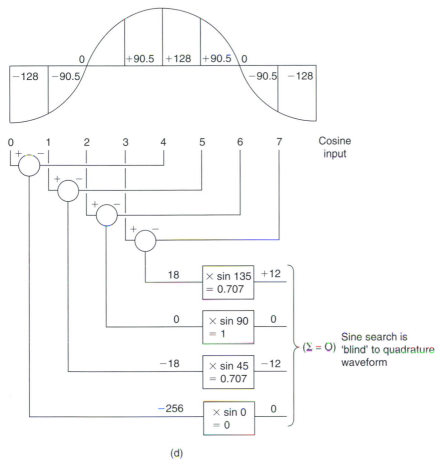

FIGURE 3.60
(Continued) (d) With a quadrature input the frequency is not seen.

Figure 3.60e shows how the next frequency coefficient is computed. Note that exactly the same first-stage butterfly outputs are used, reducing the computation needed.

A similar process may be followed to obtain the sine and cosine coefficients of the remaining frequencies. The full FFT diagram for eight samples is shown in Figure 3.61a. The spectrum this calculates is shown in Figure 3.61b. Note that only half of the coefficients are useful in a real band-limited system because the remaining coefficients represent frequencies above one-half of the sampling rate.

In STFTs the overlapping input sample blocks must be multiplied by window functions. The principle is the same as for the application in FIR filters shown under FIR Filters. Figure 3.62 shows that multiplying the search frequency by

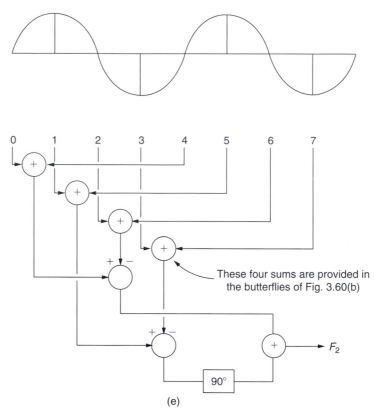

FIGURE 3.60
(Continued) (e) The butterflies used for the first coefficients form the basis of the computation of the next coefficient.

the window has exactly the same result except that this need be done only once and much computation is saved. Thus in the STFT the basis function is a windowed sine or cosine wave.

The FFT is used extensively in such applications as phase correlation, in which the accuracy with which the phase of signal components can be analysed is essential. It also forms the foundation of the discrete cosine transform.

THE DISCRETE COSINE TRANSFORM (DCT)

The DCT is a special case of a discrete Fourier transform in which the sine components of the coefficients have been eliminated leaving a single number. This is actually quite easy. Figure 3.63a shows a block of input samples to a transform process. By repeating the samples in a time-reversed order and performing a discrete Fourier transform on the double-length sample set a DCT

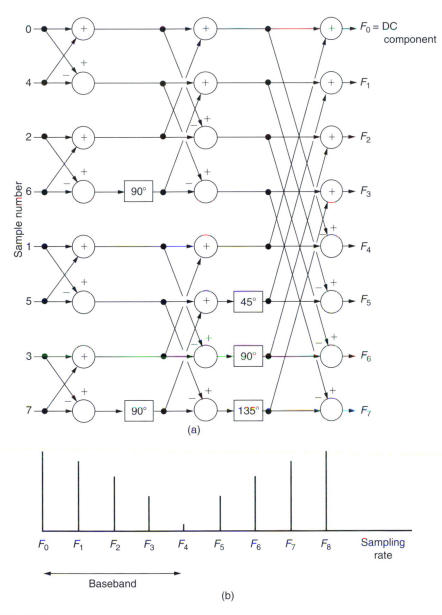

FIGURE 3.61
(a) The full butterfly diagram for an FFT. The spectrum this computes is shown in (b).

is obtained. The effect of mirroring the input waveform is to turn it into an even function whose sine coefficients are all 0. The result can be understood by considering the effect of individually transforming the input block and the reversed block.

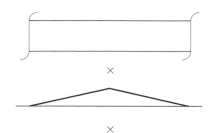

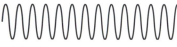

FIGURE 3.62
Multiplication of a windowed block by a sine-wave basis function is the same as multiplying the raw data by a windowed basis function but requires less multiplication as the basis function is constant and can be precomputed.

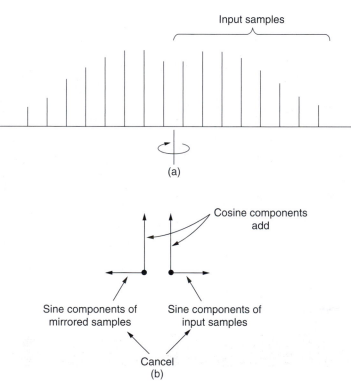

FIGURE 3.63
The DCT is obtained by mirroring the input block, as shown in (a), prior to an FFT. The mirroring cancels out the sine components, as in (b), leaving only cosine coefficients.

Figure 3.63b shows that the phase of all the components of one block are in the sense opposite to those in the other. This means that when the components are added to give the transform of the double-length block all the sine components cancel out, leaving only the cosine coefficients, hence the name of the transform.[7] In practice the sine component calculation is eliminated. Another advantage is that doubling the block length by mirroring doubles the frequency resolution, so that twice as many useful coefficients are produced. In fact a DCT produces as many useful coefficients as input samples.

For image processing two-dimensional transforms are needed. In this case for every horizontal frequency, a search is made for all possible vertical frequencies. A two-dimensional DCT is shown in Figure 3.64. The DCT is separable in that the two-dimensional DCT can be obtained by computing in each dimension separately. Fast DCT algorithms are available.[8]

Figure 3.65 shows how a two-dimensional DCT is calculated by multiplying each pixel in the input block by terms that represent sampled cosine waves of various spatial frequencies. A given DCT coefficient is obtained when the result

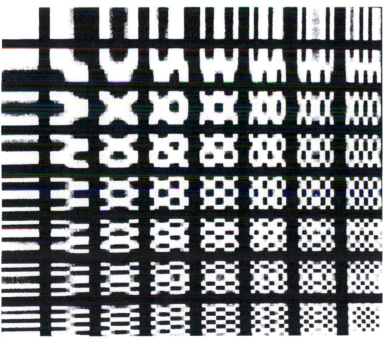

FIGURE 3.64
The discrete cosine transform breaks up an image area into discrete frequencies in two dimensions. The lowest frequency can be seen here at the top-left corner. Horizontal frequency increases to the right and vertical frequency increases downward.

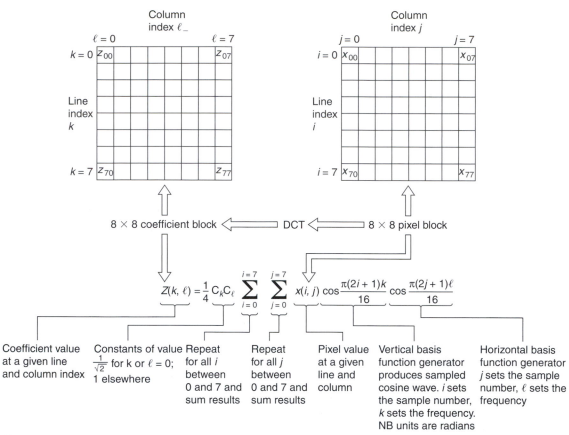

FIGURE 3.65
A two-dimensional DCT is calculated as shown here. Starting with an input pixel block one calculation is necessary to find a value for each coefficient. After 64 calculations using different basis functions the coefficient block is complete.

of multiplying every input pixel in the block is summed. Although most compression systems, including JPEG and MPEG, use square DCT blocks, this is not a necessity and rectangular DCT blocks are possible and are used in, for example, Digital Betacam, SX, and DVC.

The DCT is primarily used in MPEG-2 because it converts the input waveform into a form in which redundancy can be easily detected and removed. More details of the DCT can be found in Chapter 6.

THE WAVELET TRANSFORM

The wavelet transform was not discovered by any one individual, but has evolved via a number of similar ideas and was given a strong mathematical

Fourier transform   Wavelet transform

FIGURE 3.66
Unlike discrete Fourier transforms, wavelet basis functions are scaled so that they contain the same number of cycles irrespective of frequency. As a result their frequency discrimination ability is a constant proportion of the centre frequency.

foundation only relatively recently.[9–12] The wavelet transform is similar to the Fourier transform in that it has basis functions of various frequencies that are multiplied by the input waveform to identify the frequencies it contains. However, the Fourier transform is based on periodic signals and endless basis functions and requires windowing. The wavelet transform is fundamentally windowed, as the basis functions employed are not endless sine waves, but are finite on the time axis; hence the name. Wavelet transforms do not use a fixed window, but instead the window period is inversely proportional to the frequency being analysed. As a result a useful combination of time and frequency resolutions is obtained. High frequencies corresponding to transients in audio or edges in video are transformed with short basis functions and therefore are accurately located. Low frequencies are transformed with long basis functions that have good frequency resolution.

Figure 3.66 shows that a set of wavelets or basis functions can be obtained simply by scaling (stretching or shrinking) a single wavelet on the time axis. Each wavelet contains the same number of cycles such that as the frequency reduces, the wavelet gets longer. Thus the frequency discrimination of the wavelet transform is a constant fraction of the signal frequency. In a filter bank such a characteristic would be described as "constant Q." Figure 3.67 shows that the division of the frequency domain by a wavelet transform is logarithmic, whereas in the Fourier transform the division is uniform. The logarithmic coverage is effectively dividing the frequency domain into octaves and as such parallels the frequency discrimination of human hearing.

As it is relatively recent, the wavelet transform has yet to be widely used although it shows great promise. It has successfully been used in audio and in commercially available nonlinear video editors and in other fields such as radiology and geology.

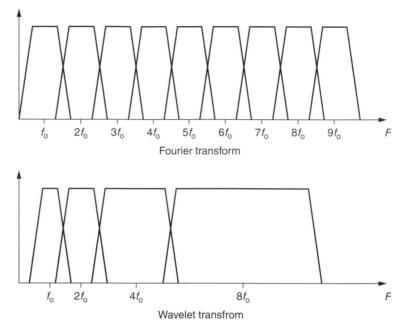

Fourier transform

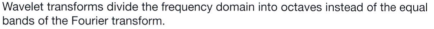

Wavelet transfrom

FIGURE 3.67
Wavelet transforms divide the frequency domain into octaves instead of the equal bands of the Fourier transform.

In video, wavelet compression does not display the "blocking" of DCT-based coders at high compression factors; instead compression error is spread over the spectrum and appears as white noise.[13] It is naturally a multiresolution transform allowing scalable decoding.

References

1. Ray, S.F. *Applied Photographic Optics,* Chap. 17, Oxford: Focal Press (1988).
2. van den Enden, A.W.M., and Verhoeckx, N.A.M. Digital signal processing: theoretical background. Philips Tech. Rev., 42, 110–144 (1985).
3. McClellan, J.H., Parks, T.W., and Rabiner, L.R. A computer program for designing optimum FIR linear-phase digital filters. IEEE Trans. Audio and Electroacoustics, AU-21, 506–526 (1973).
4. Crochiere, R.E., and Rabiner, L.R. Interpolation and decimation of digital signals: a tutorial review. Proc. IEEE, 69, 300–331 (1981).
5. Rabiner, L.R. Digital techniques for changing the sampling rate of a signal. In B. Blesser, B. Locanthi, and T.G. Stockham Jr. (eds.), *Digital Audio,* pp. 79–89, New York: Audio Engineering Society (1982).

6. Kraniauskas, P. *Transforms in Signals and Systems,* Chap. 6, Wokingham: Addison Wesley (1992).

7. Ahmed, N., Natarajan, T., and Rao, K. Discrete cosine transform. IEEE Trans. Computers, C-23, 90–93 (1974).

8. De With, P.H.N. *Data Compression Techniques for Digital Video Recording,* Delft, The Netherlands: Technical University of Delft (1992) (Ph.D. thesis).

9. Goupillaud, P., Grossman, A., and Morlet, J. Cycle-octave and related transforms in seismic signal analysis. Geoexploration, 23, 85–102 (1984/5).

10. Daubechies, I. The wavelet transform, time-frequency localisation and signal analysis. IEEE Trans. Information Theory, 36, 961–1005 (1990).

11. Rioul, O., and Vetterli, M. Wavelets and signal processing. IEEE Signal Process. Mag., October, 14–38 (1991).

12. Strang, G., and Nguyen, T. *Wavelets and Filter Banks,* Wellesley, MA: Wellesley–Cambridge Press (1996).

13. Huffman, J. Wavelets and image compression. Presented at the 135th SMPTE Tech. Conf. (Los Angeles), Preprint No. 135198 (1993).

CHAPTER 4
Conversion

INTRODUCTION TO CONVERSION

There are a number of ways in which a video waveform can digitally be represented, but the most useful and therefore common is pulse code modulation, or PCM, which was introduced in Chapter 1. The input is a continuous-time, continuous-voltage video waveform, and this is converted into a discrete-time, discrete-voltage format by a combination of sampling and quantizing. As these two processes are orthogonal (a $64,000 word for at right angles to one another) they are totally independent and can be performed in either order. Figure 4.1a shows an analog sampler preceding a quantizer, whereas Figure 4.1b shows an asynchronous quantizer preceding a digital sampler. Ideally, both will give the same results; in practice each has different advantages and suffers from different deficiencies. Both approaches will be found in real equipment.

The independence of sampling and quantizing allows each to be discussed quite separately in some detail, prior to combining the processes for a full understanding of conversion.

Whilst sampling an analog video waveform takes place in the time domain in an electrical ADC (analog-to-digital convertor), this is because the analog waveform is the result of scanning an image. In reality the image has been spatially sampled in two dimensions (lines and pixels) and temporally sampled into pictures along a third dimension. Sampling in a single dimension will be considered before moving on to more dimensions.

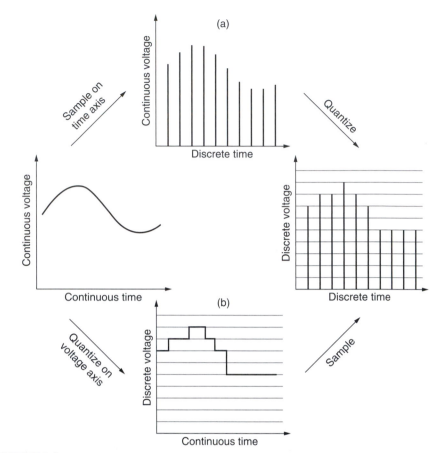

FIGURE 4.1
Because sampling and quantizing are orthogonal, the order in which they are
performed is not important. In (a) sampling is performed first and the samples are
quantized. This is common in audio convertors. In (b) the analog input is quantized
into an asynchronous binary code. Sampling takes place when this code is latched on
sampling clock edges. This approach is universal in video convertors.

SAMPLING AND ALIASING

Sampling is no more than periodic measurement, and it will be shown here
that there is no theoretical need for sampling to be detectable. Practical television equipment is, of course, less than ideal, particularly in the case of temporal sampling.

Video sampling must be regular, because the process of time base correction
prior to conversion back to a conventional analog waveform assumes a regular

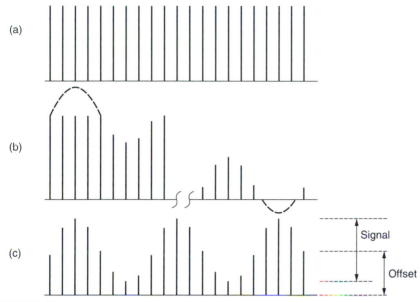

FIGURE 4.2
(a) The sampling process requires a constant-amplitude pulse train. This is amplitude modulated by the waveform to be sampled. (b) If the input waveform has excessive amplitude or incorrect level, the pulse train clips. (c) For a bipolar waveform, the greatest signal level is possible when an offset of half the pulse amplitude is used to centre the waveform.

original process as was shown in Chapter 1. The sampling process originates with a pulse train, which is shown in Figure 4.2a to be of constant amplitude and period. The video waveform amplitude-modulates the pulse train in much the same way as the carrier is modulated in an AM radio transmitter. One must be careful to avoid overmodulating the pulse train, as shown in Figure 4.2b, and this is achieved by applying a DC offset to the analog waveform so that blanking corresponds to a level partway up the pulses as in Figure 4.2c.

In the same way that AM radio produces sidebands or images above and below the carrier, sampling also produces sidebands, although the carrier is now a pulse train and has an infinite series of harmonics as shown in Figure 4.3a. The sidebands repeat above and below each harmonic of the sampling rate as shown in Figure 4.3b.

The sampled signal can be returned to the continuous-time domain simply by passing it into a low-pass filter. This filter has a frequency response that prevents the images from passing, and only the baseband signal emerges, completely

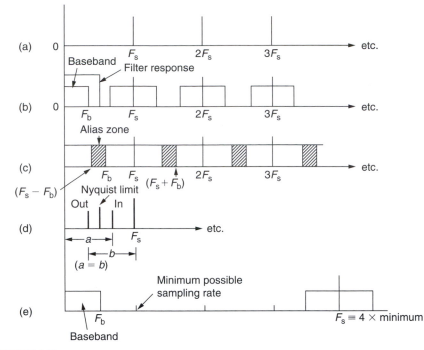

FIGURE 4.3
(a) Spectrum of sampling pulses. (b) Spectrum of samples. (c) Aliasing due to sideband overlap. (d) Beat-frequency production. (e) 4× oversampling.

unchanged. If considered in the frequency domain, this filter can be called an anti-image filter; if considered in the time domain it can be called a reconstruction filter. It can also be considered as a spatial filter if a sampled still image is being returned to a continuous image. Such a filter will be two-dimensional.

If an input is supplied having an excessive bandwidth for the sampling rate in use, the sidebands will overlap (Figure 4.3c) and the result is aliasing, in which certain output frequencies are not the same as their input frequencies but instead become difference frequencies (Figure 4.3d). It will be seen from Figure 4.3 that aliasing does not occur when the input frequency is equal to or less than half the sampling rate, and this derives the most fundamental rule of sampling, which is that the sampling rate must be at least twice the input bandwidth. Sampling theory is usually attributed to Shannon,[1,2] who applied it to information theory at around the same time as Kotelnikov in Russia. These applications were pre-dated by Whittaker. Despite that it is often referred to as Nyquist's theorem.

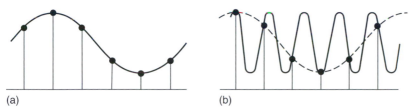

(a)   (b)

FIGURE 4.4
In (a), the sampling is adequate to reconstruct the original signal. In (b) the sampling rate is inadequate, and reconstruction produces the wrong waveform (detailed). Aliasing has taken place.

Whilst aliasing has been described above in the frequency domain, it can be described equally well in the time domain. In Figure 4.4a the sampling rate is obviously adequate to describe the waveform, but in Figure 4.4b it is inadequate and aliasing has occurred.

One often has no control over the spectrum of input signals and in practice it is necessary also to have a low-pass filter at the input to prevent aliasing. This anti-aliasing filter prevents frequencies of more than half the sampling rate from reaching the sampling stage. The requirement for an anti-aliasing filter extends to the spatial domain in devices such as CCD sensors.

Whilst electrical or optical anti-aliasing filters are quite feasible, there is no corresponding device that can precede the image sampling at frame or field rate in film or TV cameras and as a result aliasing is commonly seen on television and in the cinema, owing to the relatively low frame rates used.

With a frame rate of 24 Hz, a film camera will alias on any object changing at more than 12 Hz. Such objects include the spokes of stagecoach wheels. When the spoke-passing frequency reaches 24 Hz the wheels appear to stop. Temporal aliasing in television is less visible than might be thought because of the way in which the eye perceives motion. This was discussed in Chapter 2.

RECONSTRUCTION

If ideal low-pass anti-aliasing and anti-image filters are assumed, having a vertical cutoff slope at half the sampling rate, an ideal spectrum shown in Figure 4.5a is obtained. It was shown in Chapter 3 that the impulse response of a phase-linear ideal low-pass filter is a $\sin x/x$ waveform in the time domain, and this is repeated

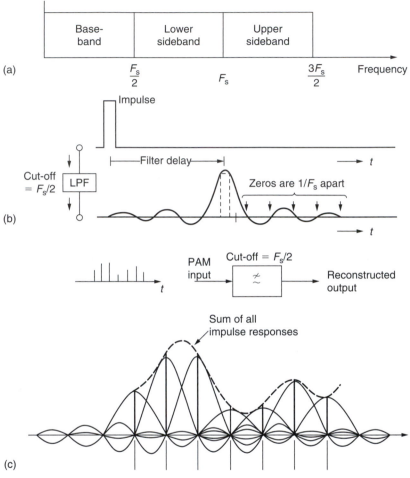

FIGURE 4.5
If ideal "brick wall" filters are assumed, the efficient spectrum of (a) results. An ideal low-pass filter has an impulse response shown in (b). The impulse passes through zero at intervals equal to the sampling period. When convolved with a pulse train at the sampling rate, as shown in (c), the voltage at each sample instant is due to that sample alone as the impulses from all other samples pass through zero there.

in Figure 4.5b. Such a waveform passes through zero Volts periodically. If the cutoff frequency of the filter is one-half of the sampling rate, the impulse passes through zero at the sites of all other samples. It can be seen from Figure 4.5c that at the output of such a filter, the voltage at the centre of a sample is due to that sample alone, because the value of all other samples is zero at that instant. In other words the continuous time output waveform must join up the tops of the input samples.

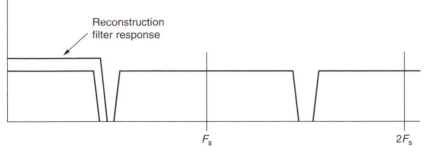

Reconstruction
filter response

F_s $2F_s$

FIGURE 4.6
As filters with finite slope are needed in practical systems, the sampling rate is raised slightly beyond twice the highest frequency in the baseband.

In between the sample instants, the output of the filter is the sum of the contributions from many impulses, and the waveform smoothly joins the tops of the samples. If the time domain is being considered, the anti-image filter of the frequency domain can equally well be called the reconstruction filter. It is a consequence of the band-limiting of the original anti-aliasing filter that the filtered analog waveform could travel between the sample points in only one way. As the reconstruction filter has the same frequency response, the reconstructed output waveform must be identical to the original band-limited waveform prior to sampling. A rigorous mathematical proof of reconstruction can be found in Betts.[3]

The ideal filter with a vertical "brick-wall" cutoff slope is difficult to implement. As the slope tends to vertical, the delay caused by the filter goes to infinity. In practice, a filter with a finite slope has to be accepted as shown in Figure 4.6. The cutoff slope begins at the edge of the required band, and consequently the sampling rate has to be raised a little to drive aliasing products to an acceptably low level. There is no absolute factor by which the sampling rate must be raised; it depends upon the filters that are available and the level of aliasing products that are acceptable. The latter will depend upon the word length to which the signal will be quantized.

FILTER DESIGN

It is not easy to specify anti-aliasing and reconstruction filters, particularly the amount of stop band rejection needed. The resulting aliasing would depend on, among other things, the amount of out-of-band energy in the input signal. As a further complication, an out-of-band signal will be attenuated by the response of

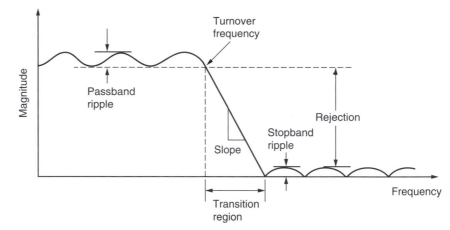

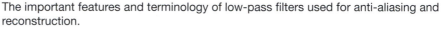

FIGURE 4.7
The important features and terminology of low-pass filters used for anti-aliasing and reconstruction.

the anti-aliasing filter to that frequency, but the residual signal will then alias, and the reconstruction filter will reject it according to its attenuation at the new frequency to which it has aliased. To take the opposite extreme, if a camera that had no response at all above the video band were used, no anti-aliasing filter would be needed.

It would also be acceptable to bypass one of the filters involved in a copy from one digital machine to another via the analog domain, although a digital transfer is, of course, to be preferred.

The nature of the filters used has a great bearing on the subjective quality of the system. Entire books have been written about analog filters, and they will be treated only briefly here.

Figure 4.7 shows the terminology used to describe the common elliptic low-pass filter. These are popular because they can be realized with fewer components than other filters of similar response. It is a characteristic of these elliptic filters that there are ripples in the passband and stop band. In much equipment the anti-aliasing filter and the reconstruction filter will have the same specification, so that the passband ripple is doubled. Sometimes slightly different filters are used to reduce the effect.

Active filters can simulate inductors using op–amp techniques, but they tend to suffer non-linearity at high frequencies at which the falling open-loop gain reduces the effect of feedback. Active filters also can contribute noise, but this is not necessarily a bad thing in controlled amounts, because it can act as a dither source.

For video applications, the phase response of such filters must be linear (see Chapter 2). Because a sharp cutoff is generally achieved by cascading many filter sections that cut at a similar frequency, the phase responses of these sections will accumulate. The phase may start to leave linearity at only a half of the passband frequency, and near the cutoff frequency the phase error may be severe. Effective group delay equalization is necessary.

It is possible to construct a ripple-free phase-linear filter with the required stopband rejection, but it may be expensive due to the amount of design effort needed and the component complexity, and it might drift out of specification as components age. The money may be better spent in avoiding the need for such a filter. Much effort can be saved in analog filter design by using oversampling. Chapter 3 showed that digital filters are inherently phase-linear and, using LSIs, can be inexpensive to construct. The technical superiority of oversampling convertors along with economics means that they are increasingly used, which is why the subject is more prominent in this book than the treatment of filter design.

TWO-DIMENSIONAL SAMPLING SPECTRA

Analog video is sampled in the time domain and vertically, whereas a two-dimensional still image such as a photograph must be sampled horizontally and vertically. In both cases a two-dimensional spectrum will result, one vertical/temporal and one vertical/horizontal.

Figure 4.8a shows a square matrix of sampling sites that has an identical spatial sampling frequency both vertically and horizontally. The corresponding spectrum is shown in Figure 4.8b. The baseband spectrum is in the centre of the diagram, and the repeating sampling sideband spectrum extends vertically and horizontally. The star-shaped spectrum results from viewing an image of a man-made object, such as a building, containing primarily horizontal and vertical elements. A more natural scene such as foliage would result in a more circular or elliptical spectrum. To return to the baseband image, the sidebands must be filtered out with a two-dimensional spatial filter. The shape of the two-dimensional frequency response shown in Figure 4.8c is known as a Brillouin zone.

Figure 4.8d shows an alternative sampling-site matrix known as quincunx sampling because of the similarity to the pattern of five dots on a die. The resultant

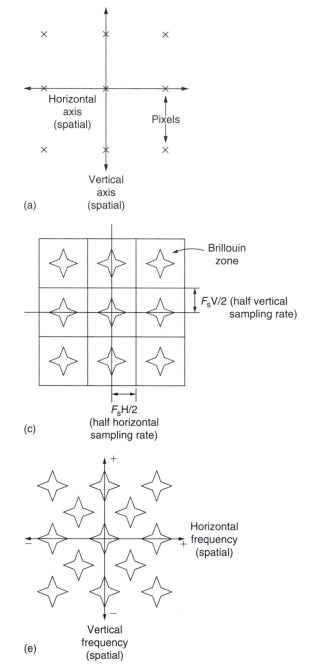

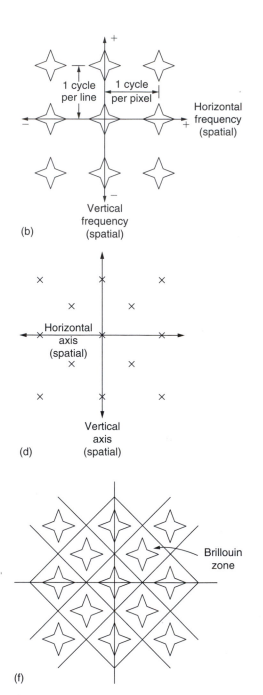

FIGURE 4.8
Image sampling spectra. The rectangular array of (a) has a spectrum, shown in (b), having a rectangular repeating structure. Filtering to return to the baseband requires a two-dimensional filter whose response lies within the Brillouin zone shown in (c). Quincunx sampling is shown in (d) to have a similar spectral structure (e). An appropriate Brillouin zone is required as in (f).

spectrum has the same characteristic pattern as shown in Figure 4.8e. The corresponding Brillouin zones are shown in (f). Quincunx sampling offers a better compromise between diagonal and horizontal/vertical resolution but is complex to implement.

It is highly desirable to prevent spatial aliasing, because the result is visually irritating. In tube cameras the spatial aliasing will be in the vertical dimension only, because the horizontal dimension is continuously scanned. Such cameras seldom attempt to prevent vertical aliasing. CCD sensors can, however, alias in both horizontal and vertical dimensions, and so an anti-aliasing optical filter is generally fitted between the lens and the sensor. This takes the form of a plate, which diffuses the image formed by the lens. Such a device can never have a sharp cutoff nor will the aperture be rectangular. The aperture of the anti-aliasing plate is in series with the aperture effect of the CCD elements, and the combination of the two effectively prevents spatial aliasing and generally gives a good balance between horizontal and vertical resolution, allowing the picture a natural appearance.

With a conventional approach, there are effectively two choices. If aliasing is permitted, the theoretical information rate of the system can be approached. If aliasing is prevented, realizable anti-aliasing filters cannot sharp cut, and the information conveyed is below system capacity.

These considerations also apply at the television display. The display must filter out spatial frequencies above one-half the sampling rate. In a conventional CRT this means that a vertical optical filter should be fitted in front of the screen to render the raster invisible. Again the aperture of a simply realizable filter would attenuate too much of the wanted spectrum, and so the technique is not used.

Figure 4.9 shows the spectrum of analog monochrome video (or of an analog component). The use of interlace has an effect on the vertical/temporal spectrum that is similar to the use of quincunx sampling on the vertical/horizontal spectrum. The concept of the Brillouin zone cannot really be applied to reconstruction in the spatial/temporal domains. This is partly due to there being two different units in which the sampling rates are measured and partly because the temporal sampling process cannot prevent aliasing in real systems.

Sampling conventional video along the line to create pixels makes the horizontal axis of the three-dimensional spectrum repeat at multiples of the sampling rate. Thus combining the three-dimensional spectrum of analog luminance

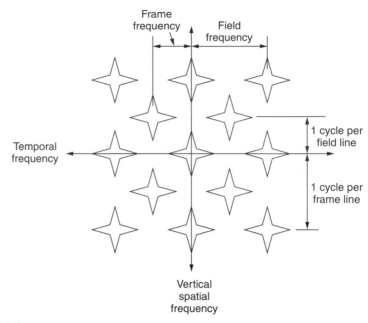

FIGURE 4.9
The vertical/temporal spectrum of monochrome video due to interlace.

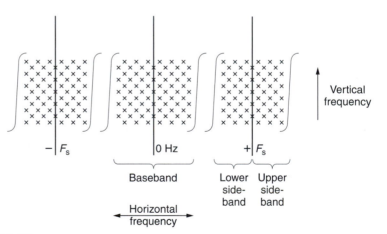

FIGURE 4.10
The spectrum of digital luminance is the baseband spectrum repeating around multiples of the sampling rate.

shown in Figure 4.9 with the sampling spectrum of Figure 4.3b gives the final spectrum shown in Figure 4.10. Colour difference signals will have a similar structure but often use a lower sampling rate and thereby have less horizontal resolution or bandwidth.

THE PHASE-LOCKED LOOP

All digital video systems need to be clocked at the appropriate rate to function properly. Whilst a clock may be obtained from a fixed frequency oscillator such as a crystal, many operations in video require genlocking or synchronising the clock to an external source. The phase-locked loop excels at this job, and many others, particularly in connection with recording and transmission.

In phase-locked loops, the oscillator can run at a range of frequencies according to the voltage applied to a control terminal. This is called a voltage-controlled oscillator or VCO. Figure 4.11 shows that the VCO is driven by a phase error measured between the output and some reference. The error changes the control voltage in such a way that the error is reduced, such that the output eventually has the same frequency as the reference. A low-pass filter is fitted in the control voltage path to prevent the loop becoming unstable. If a divider is placed between the VCO and the phase comparator, as in the figure, the VCO frequency can be made to be a multiple of the reference. This also has the effect of making the loop more heavily damped, so that it is less likely to change frequency if the input is irregular.

In digital video, the frequency multiplication of a phase-locked loop is extremely useful. Figure 4.12 shows how the 13.5 MHz clock of component digital video is obtained from the sync pulses of an analog reference by such a multiplication process.

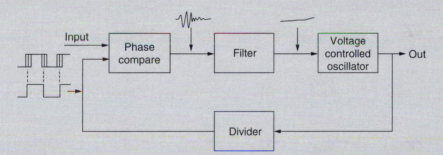

FIGURE 4.11
A phase-locked loop requires these components as a minimum. The filter in the control voltage serves to reduce clock jitter.

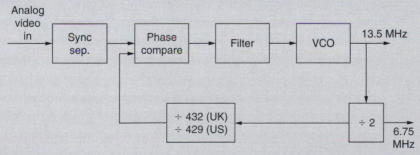

FIGURE 4.12
To obtain 13.5 MHz from input syncs, a phase-locked loop with an appropriate division ratio is required.

Figure 4.13 shows the NLL, or numerically locked loop. This is similar to a phase-locked loop, except that the two phases concerned are represented by the state of a binary number. The NLL is useful to generate a remote clock from a master. The state of a clock count in the master is periodically transmitted to the NLL, which will re-create the same clock frequency. The technique is used in MPEG transport streams.

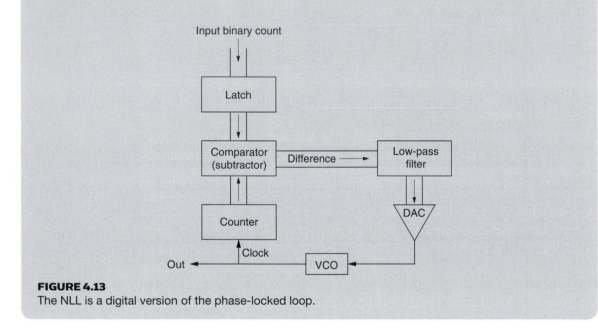

FIGURE 4.13
The NLL is a digital version of the phase-locked loop.

SAMPLING CLOCK JITTER

The instants at which samples are taken in an ADC and the instants at which DACs (digital-to-analog convertors) make conversions must be evenly spaced, otherwise unwanted signals can be added to the video. Figure 4.14 shows the effect of sampling clock jitter on a sloping waveform. Samples are taken at the wrong times. When these samples have passed through a system, the time base correction stage prior to the DAC will remove the jitter, and the result is shown in Figure 4.15. The magnitude of the unwanted signal is proportional to the slope of the audio waveform and so the amount of jitter that can be tolerated falls at 6dB per octave. As the resolution of the system is increased by the use of longer sample word length, tolerance to jitter is further reduced. The nature of the unwanted signal depends on the spectrum of the jitter. If the jitter is random, the effect is noise-like and relatively benign unless the amplitude is

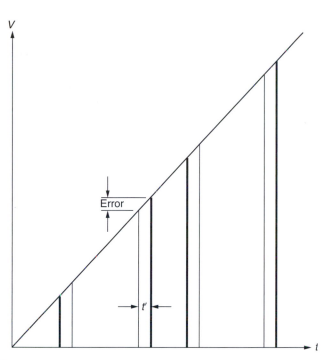

FIGURE 4.14
The effect of sampling timing jitter on noise. A sloping signal sampled with jitter
has error proportional to the slope.

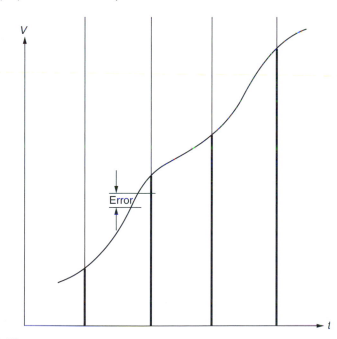

FIGURE 4.15
The effect of sampling timing jitter on noise. When jitter is removed by reclocking, the
result is noise.

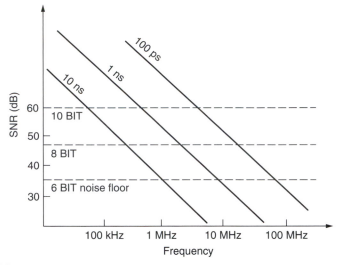

FIGURE 4.16

The effects of sampling clock jitter on signal-to-noise ratio at various frequencies, compared with the theoretical noise floors with different word lengths.

excessive. Figure 4.16 shows the effects of differing amounts of random jitter with respect to the noise floor of various word lengths. Note that even small amounts of jitter can degrade a 10-bit convertor to the performance of a good 8-bit unit. There is thus no point in upgrading to higher-resolution convertors if the clock stability of the system is insufficient to allow their performance to be realized.

Clock jitter is not necessarily random. Figure 4.17 shows that one source of clock jitter is cross talk or interference on the clock signal, although a balanced clock line will be more immune to such cross talk. The unwanted additional signal changes the time at which the sloping clock signal appears to cross the threshold voltage of the clock receiver. This is simply the same phenomenon as that of Figure 4.14 but in reverse. The threshold itself may be changed by ripple on the clock receiver power supply. There is no reason these effects should be random; they may be periodic and potentially visible.[4]

The allowable jitter is measured in picoseconds and clearly steps must be taken to eliminate it by design. Convertor clocks must be generated from clean power supplies that are well decoupled from the power used by the logic because a convertor clock must have a signal-to-noise ratio on the same order as that of the signal. Otherwise noise on the clock causes jitter, which in turn causes noise in the video. The same effect will be found in digital audio signals, which are perhaps more critical.

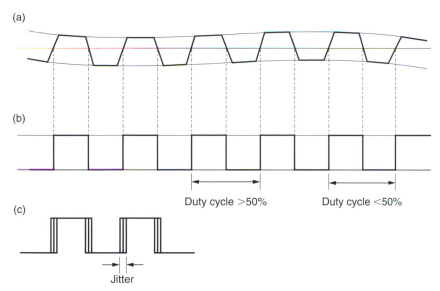

(a)

(b)

Duty cycle >50%   Duty cycle <50%

(c)

Jitter

FIGURE 4.17
Cross talk in transmission can result in unwanted signals being added to the clock
waveform. It can be seen here that a low-frequency interference signal affects the
slicing of the clock and causes a periodic jitter.

QUANTIZING

Quantizing is the process of expressing some infinitely variable quantity by discrete or stepped values. Quantizing turns up in a remarkable number of everyday guises. Figure 4.18 shows that an inclined ramp enables infinitely variable
height to be achieved, whereas a stepladder allows only discrete heights to
be had. A stepladder quantizes height. When accountants round off sums of
money to the nearest pound or dollar they are quantizing. Time passes continuously, but the display on a digital clock changes suddenly every minute because
the clock is quantizing time.

In video and audio the values to be quantized are infinitely variable voltages from an analog source. Strict quantizing is a process that operates in the
voltage domain only. For the purpose of studying the quantizing of a single
sample, time is assumed to stand still. This is achieved in practice either by the
use of a track-hold circuit or the adoption of a quantizer technology such as a
flash convertor, which operates before the sampling stage.

Figure 4.20 shows that the process of quantizing divides the input voltage
range up into quantizing intervals Q, also referred to as steps S. In applications
such as telephony these may advantageously be of differing size, but for digital
video the quantizing intervals are made as identical as possible. If this is done,

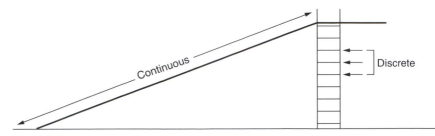
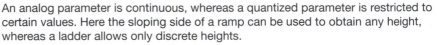

FIGURE 4.18
An analog parameter is continuous, whereas a quantized parameter is restricted to certain values. Here the sloping side of a ramp can be used to obtain any height, whereas a ladder allows only discrete heights.

the binary numbers that result are truly proportional to the original analog voltage, and the digital equivalents of mixing and gain changing can be performed by adding and multiplying sample values. If the quantizing intervals are unequal this cannot be done. When all quantizing intervals are the same, the term "uniform quantizing" is used. The term "linear quantizing" will be found, but this is, like military intelligence, a contradiction in terms.

The term LSB (least significant bit) will also be found in place of quantizing interval in some treatments, but this is a poor term because quantizing works in the voltage domain. A bit is not a unit of voltage and can have only two values. In studying quantizing, voltages within a quantizing interval will be discussed, but there is no such thing as a fraction of a bit.

Whatever the exact voltage of the input signal, the quantizer will locate the quantizing interval in which it lies. In what may be considered a separate step, the quantizing interval is then allocated a code value, which is typically some form of binary number. The information sent is the number of the quantizing interval in which the input voltage lies. Whereabouts that voltage lies within the interval is not conveyed, and this mechanism puts a limit on the accuracy of the quantizer. When the number of the quantizing interval is converted back to the analog domain, it will result in a voltage at the centre of the quantizing interval, as this minimizes the magnitude of the error between input and output. The number range is limited by the word length of the binary numbers used. In an 8-bit system, 256 different quantizing intervals exist, although in digital video those at the extreme ends of the range are reserved for synchronising.

QUANTIZING ERROR

It is possible to draw a transfer function for such an ideal quantizer followed by an ideal DAC, and this is also shown in Figure 4.19. A transfer function is

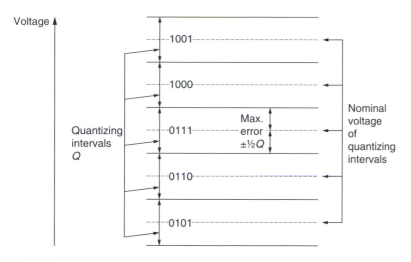

FIGURE 4.19
Quantizing assigns discrete numbers to variable voltages. All voltages within the same quantizing interval are assigned the same number, which causes a DAC to produce the voltage at the centre of the intervals shown by the dashed lines.

simply a graph of the output with respect to the input. In audio, when the term linearity is used, this generally means the overall straightness of the transfer function. Linearity is a goal in video and audio, yet it will be seen that an ideal quantizer is anything but linear.

Figure 4.20a shows that the transfer function is somewhat like a staircase, and the blanking level is halfway up a quantizing interval, or on the centre of a tread. This is the so-called mid-tread quantizer, which is universally used in video and audio. Figure 4.20b shows the alternative midriser transfer function, which causes difficulty because it does not have a code value at blanking level and as a result the numerical code value is not proportional to the analog signal voltage.

Quantizing causes a voltage error in the sample, which is given by the difference between the actual staircase transfer function and the ideal straight line. This is shown in Figure 4.20c to be a sawtooth-like function, which is periodic in Q. The amplitude cannot exceed $\pm\frac{1}{2}Q$ peak-to-peak unless the input is so large that clipping occurs.

Quantizing error can also be studied in the time domain where it is better to avoid complicating matters with the aperture effect of the DAC. For this reason it is assumed here that output samples are of negligible duration. Then impulses from the DAC can be compared with the original analog waveform and the difference will be impulses representing the quantizing error waveform.

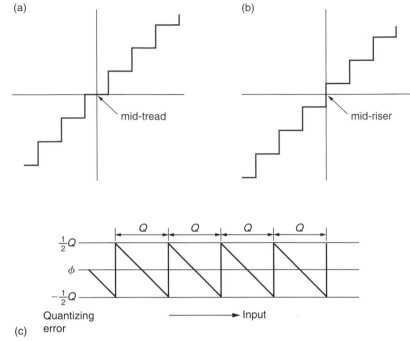

FIGURE 4.20
Quantizing assigns discrete numbers to variable voltages. This is the characteristic of the mid-tread quantizer shown in (a). An alternative system is the midriser system shown in (b). Here zero Volts analog falls between two codes and there is no code for zero. Such quantizing cannot be used prior to signal processing because the number is no longer proportional to the voltage. Quantizing error cannot exceed $\pm \frac{1}{2}Q$ as shown in (c).

This has been done in Figure 4.21. The horizontal lines in the drawing are the boundaries between the quantizing intervals, and the curve is the input waveform. The vertical bars are the quantized samples, which reach to the centre of the quantizing interval. The quantizing error waveform shown in Figure 4.21b can be thought of as an unwanted signal, which the quantizing process adds to the perfect original. If a very small input signal remains within one quantizing interval, the quantizing error is the signal.

As the transfer function is nonlinear, ideal quantizing can cause distortion. As a result practical digital video equipment deliberately uses non-ideal quantizers to achieve linearity. The quantizing error of an ideal quantizer is a complex function, and it has been researched in great depth.[5-8] It is not intended to go into such depth here. The characteristics of an ideal quantizer will be pursued only far enough to convince the reader that such a device cannot be used in quality video or audio applications.

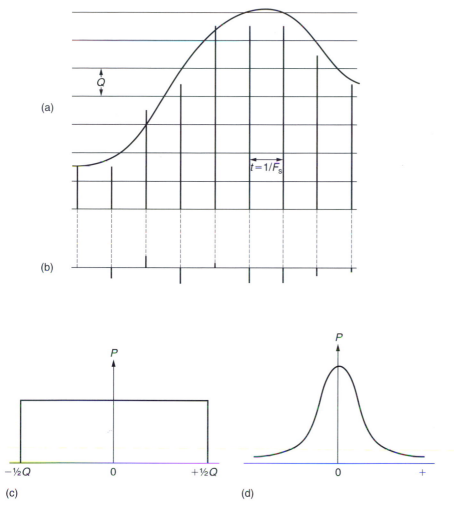

FIGURE 4.21
In (a) an arbitrary signal is represented to finite accuracy by PAM needles, whose peaks
are at the centre of the quantizing intervals. The errors caused can be thought of as
an unwanted signal (b) added to the original. In (c) the amplitude of a quantizing error
needle will be from $-\frac{1}{2}Q$ to $+\frac{1}{2}Q$ with equal probability. Note, however, that white
noise in analog circuits generally has Gaussian amplitude distribution, shown in (d).

As the magnitude of the quantizing error is limited, its effect can be minimized
by making the signal larger. This will require more quantizing intervals and
more bits to express them. The number of quantizing intervals multiplied by
their size gives the quantizing range of the convertor. A signal outside the range
will be clipped. Provided that clipping is avoided, the larger the signal, the less
will be the effect of the quantizing error.

Where the input signal exercises the whole quantizing range and has a complex waveform (such as from a contrasty, detailed scene), successive samples will have widely varying numerical values and the quantizing error on a given sample will be independent of that on others. In this case the size of the quantizing error will be distributed with equal probability between the limits. Figure 4.21c shows the resultant uniform probability density. In this case the unwanted signal added by quantizing is an additive broadband noise uncorrelated with the signal, and it is appropriate in this case to call it quantizing noise. This is not quite the same as thermal noise, which has a Gaussian probability shown in Figure 4.21d (see Chapter 1, Transmission, for a treatment of statistics). The difference is of no consequence as in the large-signal case the noise is masked by the signal. Under these conditions, a meaningful signal-to-noise ratio (SNR) can be calculated as follows.

In a system using n-bit words, there will be 2^n quantizing intervals. The largest sinusoid that can fit without clipping will have this peak-to-peak amplitude. The peak amplitude will be half as great, i.e., $2^{n-1}Q$, and the rms amplitude will be this value divided by $\sqrt{2}$. The quantizing error has an amplitude of $\frac{1}{2}Q$ peak, which is the equivalent of $Q\sqrt{12}$ rms. The signal-to-noise ratio for the large signal case is then given by:

$$20 \log_{10} \frac{\sqrt{12} \times 2^{n-1}}{\sqrt{2}} \, \mathrm{db} = 20 \log_{10} (\sqrt{6} \times 2^{n-1}) \, \mathrm{dB}$$

$$= 20 \log 2^n \times \frac{\sqrt{6}}{2} \, \mathrm{dB}$$

$$= 20n \, \log 2 + 20 \log \frac{\sqrt{6}}{2} \, \mathrm{dB} \tag{4.1}$$

$$= 6.02n + 1.76 \, \mathrm{dB}$$

By way of example, an 8-bit system will offer very nearly 50 dB SNR.

Whilst the above result is true for a large complex input waveform, treatments that then assume that quantizing error is always noise give results that are at variance with reality. The expression above is valid only if the probability density of the quantizing error is uniform. Unfortunately at low depths of modulations, and particularly with flat fields or simple pictures, this is not the case.

At low modulation depth, quantizing error ceases to be random and becomes a function of the input waveform and the quantizing structure as Figure 4.21 shows. Once an unwanted signal becomes a deterministic function of the wanted signal, it has to be classed as a distortion rather than a noise. Distortion can also be predicted from the nonlinearity, or staircase nature, of the transfer function. With a large signal, there are so many steps involved that we must stand well back, and a staircase with 256 steps appears to be a slope. With a small signal there are few steps and they can no longer be ignored.

The effect can be visualized readily by considering a television camera viewing a uniformly painted wall. The geometry of the lighting and the coverage of the lens mean that the brightness is not absolutely uniform, but falls slightly at the ends of the TV lines. After quantizing, the gently sloping waveform is replaced by one that stays at a constant quantizing level for many sampling periods and then suddenly jumps to the next quantizing level. The picture then consists of areas of constant brightness with steps between, resembling nothing more than a contour map, hence the use of the term contouring to describe the effect.

Needless to say, the occurrence of contouring precludes the use of an ideal quantizer for high-quality work. There is little point in studying the adverse effects further as they should be and can be eliminated completely in practical equipment by the use of dither. The importance of correctly dithering a quantizer cannot be emphasized enough, because failure to dither irrevocably distorts the converted signal: there can be no process that will subsequently remove that distortion. The signal-to-noise ratio derived above has no relevance to practical applications as it will be modified by the dither.

INTRODUCTION TO DITHER

At high signal levels, quantizing error is effectively noise. As the depth of modulation falls, the quantizing error of an ideal quantizer becomes more strongly correlated with the signal and the result is distortion, visible as contouring. If the quantizing error can be decorrelated from the input in some way, the system can remain linear but noisy. Dither performs the job of decorrelation by making the action of the quantizer unpredictable and gives the system a noise floor like an analog system.[9,10]

In one approach, pseudo-random noise (see Chapter 3) with rectangular probability and a peak-to-peak amplitude of Q was added to the input signal prior to quantizing, but was subtracted after reconversion to analog. This is known as subtractive dither and was investigated by Schuchman[11] and much later by Sherwood.[12] Subtractive dither has the advantages that the dither amplitude is non-critical, the noise has full statistical independence from the signal[7] and has the same level as the quantizing error in the large-signal undithered case.[13] Unfortunately, it suffers from practical drawbacks, because the original noise waveform must accompany the samples or must be synchronously re-created at the DAC. This is virtually impossible in a system in which the signal may have been edited or where its level has been changed by processing, as the noise needs to remain synchronous and be processed in the same way. All practical digital video systems use non-subtractive dither, where the dither signal is added prior to quantization and no attempt is made to remove it at the DAC.[14] The introduction of dither prior to a conventional quantizer inevitably causes a slight reduction in the signal-to-noise ratio attainable, but this reduction is a small price to pay for the elimination of nonlinearities.

The ideal (noiseless) quantizer of Figure 4.20 has fixed quantizing intervals and must always produce the same quantizing error from the same signal. In Figure 4.22 it can be seen that an ideal quantizer can be dithered by linearly adding a controlled level of noise, either to the input signal or to the reference voltage, which is used to derive the quantizing intervals. There are several ways of considering how dither works, all of which are equally valid.

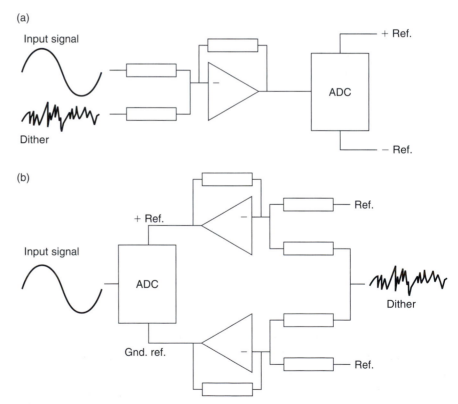

FIGURE 4.22
Dither can be applied to a quantizer in one of two ways. In (a) the dither is linearly added to the analog input signal, whereas in (b) it is added to the reference voltages of the quantizer.

The addition of dither means that successive samples effectively find the quantizing intervals in different places on the voltage scale. The quantizing error becomes a function of the dither, rather than a predictable function of the input signal. The quantizing error is not eliminated, but the subjectively unacceptable distortion is converted into a broadband noise, which is more benign.

Some alternative ways of looking at dither are shown in Figure 4.23. Consider the situation in which a low-level input signal is changing slowly within a quantizing interval. Without dither, the same numerical code is output for a number of sample periods, and the variations within the interval are lost. Dither has the effect of forcing the quantizer to switch between two or more states. The higher the voltage of the input signal within a given interval, the more probable it becomes that the output code will take on the next higher value. The lower the input voltage within the interval, the more probable it is that the output code will take the next lower value. The dither has resulted in a form of duty cycle modulation, and the resolution of the system has been extended indefinitely instead of being limited by the size of the steps.

Dither can also be understood by considering what it does to the transfer function of the quantizer. This is normally a perfect staircase, but in the presence of dither it is smeared horizontally until with dither of a certain amplitude the average transfer function becomes straight.

REQUANTIZING AND DIGITAL DITHER

Recent ADC technology allows the resolution of video samples to be raised from 8 bits to 10 or even 12 bits. The situation then arises that an existing 8-bit device such as a digital VTR needs to be connected to the output of an ADC with greater word length. The words need to be shortened in some way.

It will be seen in Chapter 5 that when a sample value is attenuated, the extra low-order bits that come into existence below the radix point preserve the resolution of the signal and the dither in the least significant bit(s), which linearizes the system. The same word extension will occur in any process involving multiplication, such as digital filtering. It will subsequently be necessary to shorten the word length. Low-order bits must be removed to reduce the resolution whilst keeping the signal magnitude the same. Even if the original conversion was correctly dithered, the random element in the low-order bits will now be some way below the end of the intended word. If the word is simply truncated by discarding the unwanted low-order bits, or rounded to the nearest integer, the linearizing effect of the original dither will be lost.

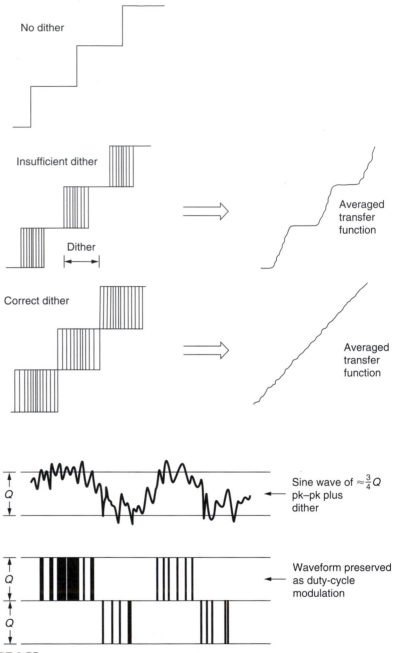

FIGURE 4.23
Wideband dither of the appropriate level linearizes the transfer function to produce noise instead of distortion. This can be confirmed by spectral analysis. In the voltage domain, dither causes frequent switching between codes and preserves resolution in the duty cycle of the switching.

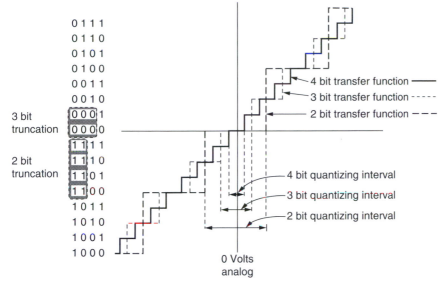

0 1 1 1
0 1 1 0
0 1 0 1
0 1 0 0
0 0 1 1
0 0 1 0

3 bit
truncation [0 0 0] 1
[0 0 0] 0

2 bit
truncation [1 1] 1 1
[1 1] 1 0
[1 1] 0 1
[1 1] 0 0
1 0 1 1
1 0 1 0
1 0 0 1
1 0 0 0

4 bit transfer function ——
3 bit transfer function - - - - -
2 bit transfer function – – –

4 bit quantizing interval
3 bit quantizing interval
2 bit quantizing interval

0 Volts
analog

FIGURE 4.24
Shortening the word length of a sample reduces the number of codes that can describe
the voltage of the waveform. This makes the quantizing steps bigger, hence the term
"requantizing." It can be seen that simple truncation or omission of the bits does not
give analogous behaviour. Rounding is necessary to give the same result as if the larger
steps had been used in the original conversion.

Shortening the word length of a sample reduces the number of quantizing intervals available without changing the signal amplitude. As Figure 4.24 shows, the
quantizing intervals become larger and the original signal is requantized with
the new interval structure. This will introduce requantizing distortion having the
same characteristics as quantizing distortion in an ADC. It then is obvious that
when shortening the word length of a 10-bit convertor to 8 bits, the 2 low-order
bits must be removed in a way that displays the same overall quantizing structure as if the original convertor had been only of 8-bit word length. It will be
seen from Figure 4.24 that truncation cannot be used because it does not meet
the above requirement, but results in signal-dependent offsets because it always
rounds in the same direction. Proper numerical rounding is essential in video
applications because it accurately simulates analog quantizing to the new interval size. Unfortunately the 10-bit convertor will have a dither amplitude appropriate to quantizing intervals one-quarter the size of an 8-bit unit and the result
will be highly nonlinear.

In practice, the word length of samples must be shortened in such a way that
the requantizing error is converted to noise rather than distortion. One technique that meets this requirement is to use digital dithering[15] prior to rounding.
This is directly equivalent to the analog dithering in an ADC.

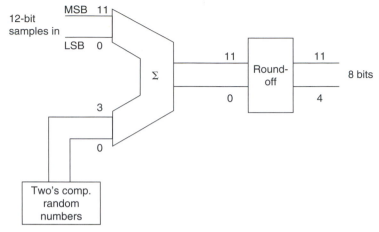

FIGURE 4.25
In a simple digital dithering system, two's complement values from a random-number generator are added to low-order bits of the input. The dithered values are then rounded up or down according to the value of the bits to be removed. The dither linearizes the requantizing.

Digital dither is a pseudo-random sequence of numbers. If it is required to simulate the analog dither signal of Figures 4.20 and 4.21, then it is obvious that the noise must be bipolar so that it can have an average voltage of zero. Two's complement coding must be used for the dither values.

Figure 4.25 shows a simple digital dithering system (i.e., one without noise shaping) for shortening sample word length. The output of a two's complement pseudo-random sequence generator (see Chapter 3) of appropriate word length is added to input samples prior to rounding. The most significant of the bits to be discarded is examined to determine whether the bits to be removed sum to more or less than half a quantizing interval. The dithered sample is either rounded down, i.e., the unwanted bits are simply discarded, or rounded up, i.e., the unwanted bits are discarded but 1 is added to the value of the new short word. The rounding process is no longer deterministic because of the added dither, which provides a linearizing random component.

If this process is compared with that of Figure 4.22 it will be seen that the principles of analog and digital dither are identical; the processes simply take place in different domains using two's complement numbers, which are rounded, or voltages, which are quantized, as appropriate. In fact quantization of an analog-dithered waveform is identical to the hypothetical case of rounding after bipolar digital dither in which the number of bits to be removed is

DITHER TECHNIQUES

The intention here is to treat the processes of analog and digital dither as identical except where differences need to be noted. The characteristics of the noise used are rather important for optimal performance, although many suboptimal but nevertheless effective systems are in use. The main parameters of interest are the peak-to-peak amplitude, the amplitude probability distribution function (PDF), and the spectral content.

The most comprehensive ongoing study of nonsubtractive dither has been that of Vanderkooy and Lipshitz[14,16] and the treatment here is based largely upon their work.

RECTANGULAR PDF DITHER

Chapter 3 showed that the simplest form of dither (and therefore the easiest to generate) is a single sequence of random numbers that have uniform or rectangular probability. The amplitude of the dither is critical. Figure 4.26a shows the time-averaged transfer function of one quantizing interval in the presence of various amplitudes of rectangular dither. The linearity is perfect at an amplitude of 1Q peak-to-peak and then deteriorates for larger or smaller amplitudes. The same will be true of all levels that are an integer multiple of Q. Thus there is no freedom in the choice of amplitude.

With the use of such dither, the quantizing noise is not constant. Figure 4.26b shows that when the analog input is exactly centred in a quantizing interval (such that there is no quantizing error), the dither has no effect and the output code is steady. There is no switching between codes and thus no noise. On the other hand, when the analog input is exactly at a riser or boundary between intervals, there is the greatest switching between codes and the greatest noise is produced. Mathematically speaking, the first moment or mean error is zero but the second moment, which in this case is equal to the variance, is not constant. From an engineering standpoint, the system is linear but suffers noise modulation: the noise floor rises and falls with the signal content and this is audible in the presence of low-frequency signals. The dither adds an average noise amplitude of $Q\sqrt{12}$ rms to the quantizing noise of the same level. To find the resultant noise level it is necessary to add the powers as the signals are uncorrelated. The total power is given by

$$2 \times \frac{Q^2}{12} = \frac{Q^2}{6},$$

and the rms voltage is $Q\sqrt{6}$. Another way of looking at the situation is to consider that the noise power doubles and so the rms noise voltage has increased by 3 dB in comparison with the undithered case. Thus for an n-bit word length, using the same derivation as Eq. (4.1) above, the signal-to-noise ratio for Q pk–pk rectangular dither will be given by

$$6.02n - 1.24 \text{ dB}. \tag{4.2}$$

Unlike the undithered case, this is a true signal-to-noise ratio and linearity is maintained at all signal levels. By way of example, for a 10-bit system nearly 59 dB SNR is achieved. The 3 dB loss compared to the undithered case is a small price to pay for linearity.

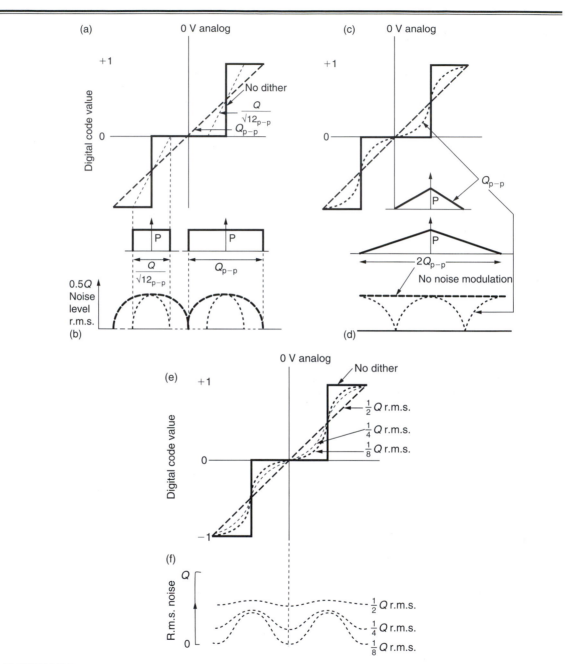

FIGURE 4.26
(a) Use of rectangular probability dither can linearize, but noise modulation (b) results. Triangular PDF dither (c) linearizes, and noise modulation is eliminated as in (d). Gaussian dither (e) can also be used, almost eliminating noise modulation (f).

TRIANGULAR PDF DITHER

The noise modulation due to the use of rectangular-probability dither is undesirable. It comes about because the process is too simple. The undithered quantizing error is signal dependent and the dither represents a single uniform-probability random process. This is capable of decorrelating the quantizing error only to the extent that its mean value is zero, rendering the system linear. The signal dependence is not eliminated, but is displaced to the next statistical moment. This is the variance and the result is noise modulation. If a further uniform-probability random process is introduced into the system, the signal dependence is displaced to the next moment and the second moment or variance becomes constant.

Adding together two statistically independent rectangular probability functions produces a triangular probability function. A signal having this characteristic can be used as the dither source.

Figure 4.26c shows the averaged transfer function for a number of dither amplitudes. Linearity is reached with a pk–pk amplitude of 2Q and at this level there is no noise modulation. The lack of noise modulation is another way of stating that the noise is constant. The triangular PDF of the dither matches the triangular shape of the quantizing error function.

The dither adds two noise signals having an amplitude of $Q/12$rms to the quantizing noise of the same level. To find the resultant noise level it is necessary to add the powers as the signals are uncorrelated. The total power is given by

$$3 \times \frac{Q^2}{12} = \frac{Q^2}{4},$$

and the rms voltage is $Q/4$. Another way of looking at the situation is to consider that the noise power is increased by 50 percent in comparison to the rectangular dithered case and so the rms noise voltage has increased by 1.76 dB. Thus for an n-bit word length, using the same derivation as Eqs. (4.1) and (4.2) above, the signal-to-noise ratio for Q pk–pk rectangular dither will be given by

$$6.02n - 3\,\text{dB}. \tag{4.3}$$

Continuing the use of a 10-bit example, a SNR of 57.2 dB is available, which is 4.8 dB worse than the SNR of an undithered quantizer in the large-signal case. It is a small price to pay for perfect linearity and an unchanging noise floor.

GAUSSIAN PDF DITHER

Adding more uniform probability sources to the dither makes the overall probability function progressively more like the Gaussian distribution of analog noise. Figure 4.26d shows the averaged transfer function of a quantizer with various levels of Gaussian dither applied. Linearity is reached with ½Qrms and at this level noise modulation is negligible. The total noise power is given by

$$Q^2/4 + Q^2/12 = 3 \times Q^2/12 + Q^2/12 = Q^2/3,$$

and so the noise level will be $Q/3$rms. The noise level of an undithered quantizer in the large signal case is $Q/12$ and so the noise is higher by a factor of

$$\frac{Q}{\sqrt{3}} \times \frac{\sqrt{12}}{Q} = \frac{Q}{\sqrt{3}} \times \frac{2\sqrt{3}}{Q} = 2 = 6.02 \text{ dB}. \tag{4.4}$$

Thus the SNR is given by $6.02(n-1) + 1.76$ dB. A 10-bit system with correct Gaussian dither has a SNR of 56 dB.

This is inferior to the figure in Eq. (4.3) by 1.1 dB. In digital dither applications, triangular probability dither of 2Q pk–pk is optimum because it gives the best possible combination of nil distortion, freedom from noise modulation, and SNR. Using dither with more than two rectangular processes added is detrimental. Whilst this result is also true for analog dither, it is not practicable to apply it to a real ADC as all real analog signals contain thermal noise that is Gaussian. If triangular dither is used on a signal containing Gaussian noise, the results derived above are not obtained. ADCs should therefore use Gaussian dither of Q/2rms and performance will be given by Eq. (4.4).

infinite, and remains identical for practical purposes when as few as 8 bits are to be removed. Analog dither may actually be generated from bipolar digital dither (which is no more than random numbers with certain properties) using a DAC.

BASIC DIGITAL-TO-ANALOG CONVERSION

This direction of conversion will be discussed first, because ADCs often use embedded DACs in feedback loops. The purpose of a digital-to-analog convertor is to take numerical values and reproduce the continuous waveform that they represent. Figure 4.27 shows the major elements of a conventional conversion subsystem, i.e., one in which oversampling is not employed. The jitter in the clock needs to be removed with a VCO or VCXO. Sample values are buffered in a latch and fed to the convertor element, which operates on each cycle of the clean clock. The output is then a voltage proportional to the number for at least a part of the sample period. A resampling stage may be found next, to remove switching transients, reduce the aperture ratio, or allow the use of a convertor, which takes a substantial part of the sample period to operate. The resampled waveform is then presented to a reconstruction filter, which rejects frequencies above the video band.

This section is primarily concerned with the implementation of the convertor element. The most common way of achieving this conversion is to control binary-weighted currents and sum them in a virtual earth. Figure 4.28 shows the classical R–2R DAC structure. This is relatively simple to construct, but the

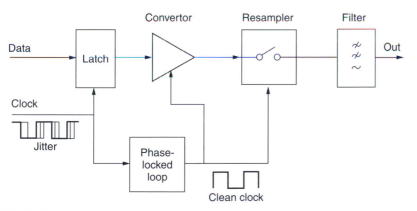

FIGURE 4.27
The components of a conventional convertor. A jitter-free clock drives the voltage conversion, whose output may be resampled prior to reconstruction.

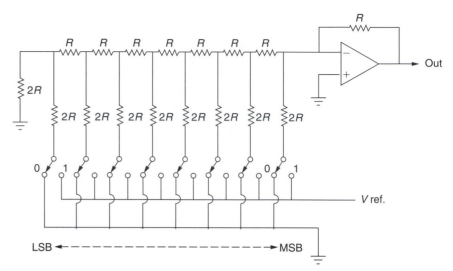

FIGURE 4.28
The classical R–2R DAC requires precise resistance values and "perfect" switches.

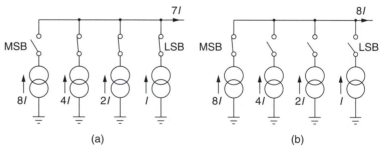

FIGURE 4.29
(a) Current flow with an input of 0111 is shown. (b) Current flow with an input code 1 greater.

resistors have to be extremely accurate. To see why this is so, consider the example of Figure 4.29. In (a) the binary code is about to have a major overflow, and all the low-order currents are flowing. In (b), the binary input has increased by one, and only the most significant current flows. This current must equal the sum of all the others plus one. The accuracy must be such that the step size is within the required limits. In this 8-bit example, if the step size needs to be a rather casual 10 percent accurate, the necessary accuracy is only one part in 2560, but for a 10-bit system it would become one part in 10,240. This degree of accuracy is difficult to achieve and maintain in the presence of ageing and temperature change.

BASIC ANALOG-TO-DIGITAL CONVERSION

The general principle of a quantizer is that different quantized voltages are compared with the unknown analog input until the closest quantized voltage is found. The code corresponding to this becomes the output. The comparisons can be made in turn with the minimal amount of hardware or simultaneously with more hardware.

The flash convertor is probably the simplest technique available for PCM video conversion. The principle is shown in Figure 4.30. The threshold voltage of every quantizing interval is provided by a resistor chain, which is fed by a reference voltage. This reference voltage can be varied to determine the sensitivity of the input. There is one voltage comparator connected to every reference voltage, and the other input of all the comparators is connected to the analog input. A comparator can be considered to be a one-bit ADC. The input voltage determines how many of the comparators will have a true output. As one comparator is necessary for each quantizing interval, then, for example, in an 8-bit system there will be 255 binary comparator outputs, and it is necessary to use a priority encoder to convert these to a binary code. Note that the quantizing stage is asynchronous; comparators change state as and when the variations in the input waveform result in a reference voltage being crossed. Sampling takes place when the comparator outputs are clocked into a subsequent latch. This is an example of quantizing before sampling, as was illustrated in Figure 4.1. Although the device is simple in principle, it contains a lot of circuitry and can be practicably implemented only on a chip. The analog signal has to drive many inputs, which results in a significant parallel capacitance, and a low-impedance driver is essential to avoid restricting the slewing rate of the input. The extreme speed of a flash convertor is a distinct advantage in oversampling. Because computation of all bits is performed simultaneously, no track/hold circuit is required, and droop is eliminated. Figure 4.30c shows a flash convertor chip. Note the resistor ladder and the comparators followed by the priority encoder. The MSB can be selectively inverted so that the device can be used either in offset binary or in two's complement mode.

The flash convertor is ubiquitous in digital video because of the high speed necessary. For audio purposes, many more conversion techniques are available and these are considered in Chapter 7.

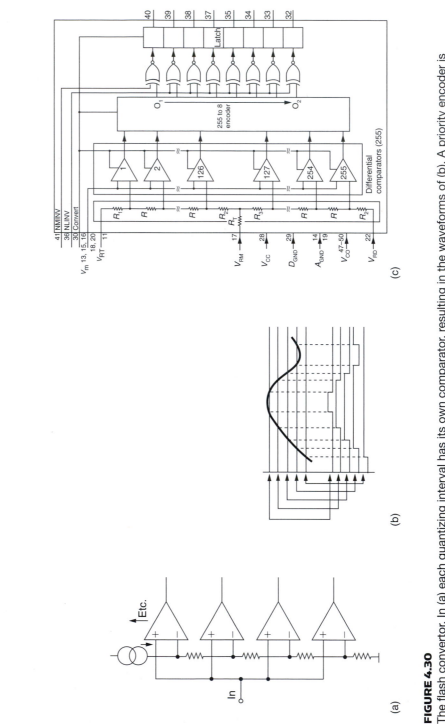

FIGURE 4.30

The flash convertor. In (a) each quantizing interval has its own comparator, resulting in the waveforms of (b). A priority encoder is necessary to convert the comparator outputs to a binary code. Shown in (c) is a typical 8-bit flash convertor primarily intended for video applications (courtesy of TRW).

OVERSAMPLING

Oversampling means using a sampling rate that is greater (generally substantially greater) than the Nyquist rate. Neither sampling theory nor quantizing theory requires oversampling to be used to obtain a given signal quality, but Nyquist rate conversion places extremely high demands on component accuracy when a convertor is implemented. Oversampling allows a given signal quality to be reached without requiring very close tolerance, and therefore expensive, components.

Figure 4.31 shows the main advantages of oversampling. In Figure 4.31a it will be seen that the use of a sampling rate considerably above the Nyquist rate allows the anti-aliasing and reconstruction filters to be realized with a much more gentle cutoff slope. There is then less likelihood of phase linearity and ripple problems in the passband. Figure 4.31b shows that information in an analog signal is two-dimensional and can be depicted as an area that is the product of bandwidth and the linearly expressed signal-to-noise ratio. The figure also shows that the same amount of information can be conveyed down a channel with a SNR of half as much (6 dB less) if the bandwidth used is doubled, with 12 dB less SNR if bandwidth is quadrupled, and so on, provided that the modulation scheme used is perfect.

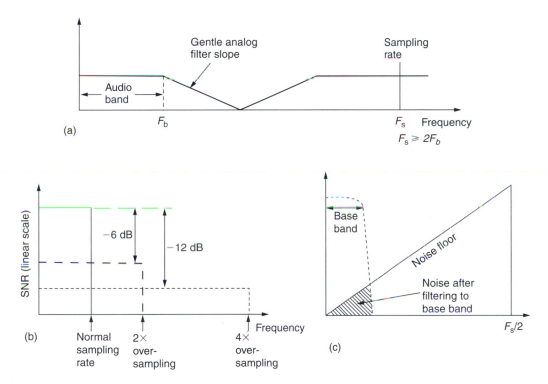

FIGURE 4.31
Oversampling has a number of advantages. In (a) it allows the slope of analog filters to be relaxed. In (b) it allows the resolution of convertors to be extended. In (c) a noise-shaped convertor allows a disproportionate improvement in resolution.

The information in an analog signal can be conveyed using some analog modulation scheme in any combination of bandwidth and SNR that yields the appropriate channel capacity. If bandwidth is replaced by sampling rate and SNR is replaced by a function of word length, the same must be true for a digital signal as it is no more than a numerical analog. Thus raising the sampling rate potentially allows the word length of each sample to be reduced without information loss.

Information theory predicts that if a signal is spread over a much wider bandwidth by some modulation technique, the SNR of the demodulated signal can be higher than that of the channel it passes through, and this is also the case in digital systems. The concept is illustrated in Figure 4.32. In Figure 4.32a 4-bit samples are delivered at sampling rate F. As 4 bits have 16 combinations, the information rate is $16F$. In (b) the same information rate is obtained with 3-bit samples by raising the sampling rate to $2F$ and in (c) 2-bit samples having four combinations must be delivered at a rate of $4F$. Whilst the information rate has been maintained, it will be noticed that the bit rate of (c) is twice that of (a). The reason for this is shown in Figure 4.33. A single binary digit can have only two states; thus it can convey only two pieces of information, perhaps "yes" or "no." Two binary digits together can have four states and can thus convey four pieces of information, perhaps "spring, summer, autumn, or winter," which is two pieces of information per bit. Three binary digits grouped together can have eight combinations and convey eight pieces of information, perhaps "doh, re, mi, fah, so, lah, te, or doh," which is nearly three pieces of information per digit. Clearly the further this principle is taken, the greater the benefit. In a 16-bit system, each bit is worth 4 K pieces of information. It is always more efficient, in information-capacity terms, to use the combinations of long binary words than to send single bits for every piece of information. The greatest efficiency is reached when the longest words are sent at the slowest rate, which must be the Nyquist rate. This is one reason PCM recording is more common than delta modulation, despite the simplicity of implementation of the latter type of convertor. PCM simply makes more efficient use of the capacity of the binary channel.

As a result, oversampling is confined to convertor technology, in which it gives specific advantages in implementation. The storage or transmission system will usually employ PCM, in which the sampling rate is a little more than twice the input bandwidth. Figure 4.34 shows a digital VTR using oversampling convertors.

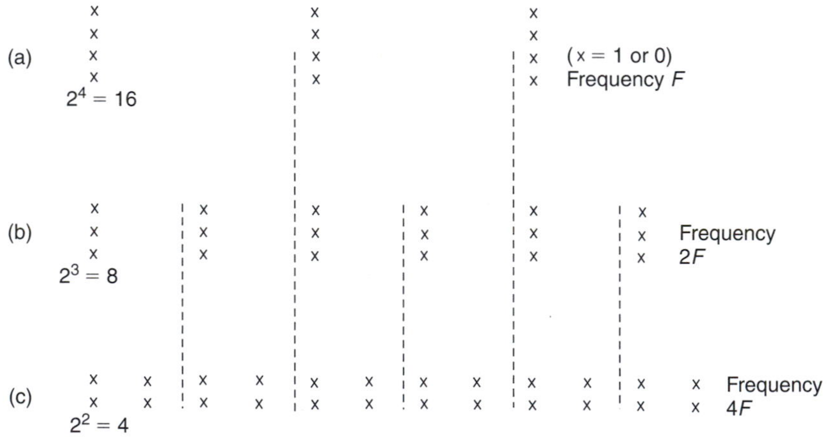

FIGURE 4.32
Information rate can be held constant when frequency doubles by removing 1 bit from each word. In all cases here it is $16F$. Note that the bit rate of (c) is double that of (a). Data storage in oversampled form is inefficient.

1-bit	2-bit	3-bit	4-bit	16-bit
			0000 0	0000
			0001 1	
			0010 2	
			0011 3	
			0100 4	
			0101 5	
			0110 6	Digital
			0111 7	audio
		000 doh	1000 8	sample
		001 re	1001 9	values
		010 mi	1010 A	
		011 fah	1011 B	
	00 = Spring	100 so	1100 C	
	01 = Summer	101 lah	1101 D	
0 = No	10 = Autumn	110 te	1110 E	
1 = Yes	11 = Winter	111 doh	1111 F	FFFF

	1-bit	2-bit	3-bit	4-bit	16-bit
No of bits	1	2	3	4	16
Information per word	2	4	8	16	65 536
Information per bit	2	2	≈3	4	4096

FIGURE 4.33
The amount of information per bit increases disproportionately as word length increases. It is always more efficient to use the longest words possible at the lowest word rate. It will be evident that 16-bit PCM is 2048 times as efficient as delta modulation. Oversampled data are also inefficient for storage.

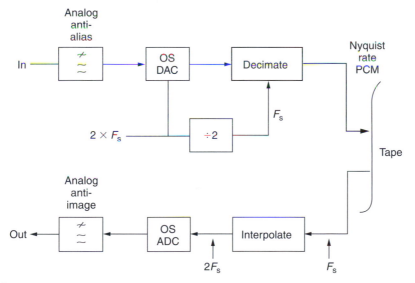

FIGURE 4.34
An oversampling digital VTR. The convertors run faster than sampling theory suggests to ease analog filter design. Sampling-rate reduction allows efficient PCM recording on tape.

The ADC runs at n times the Nyquist rate, but once in the digital domain the rate needs to be reduced in a type of digital filter called a decimator. The output of this is conventional Nyquist-rate PCM, according to the tape format, which is then recorded. On replay the sampling rate is raised once more in a further type of digital filter called an interpolator. The system now has the best of both worlds: using oversampling in the convertors overcomes the shortcomings of analog anti-aliasing and reconstruction filters and the word length of the convertor elements is reduced, making them easier to construct; the recording is made with Nyquist-rate PCM, which minimizes tape consumption.

Oversampling is a method of overcoming practical implementation problems by replacing a single critical element or bottleneck with a number of elements whose overall performance is what counts. As Hauser[17] properly observed, oversampling tends to overlap the operations that are quite distinct in a conventional convertor. In earlier sections of this chapter, the vital subjects of filtering, sampling, quantizing, and dither have been treated almost independently. Figure 4.35a shows that it is possible to construct an ADC of predictable performance by taking a suitable anti-aliasing filter, a sampler, a dither source, and a quantizer and assembling them like building bricks. The bricks are effectively in series and so the performance of each stage can limit only the overall performance. In contrast Figure 4.35b shows that with oversampling the overlap of operations allows different processes to augment one another, allowing a synergy that is absent in the conventional approach.

If the oversampling factor is n, the analog input must be bandwidth limited to $n \times F_s/2$ by the analog anti-aliasing filter. This unit need only have flat frequency response and phase linearity within the audio band. Analog dither of an amplitude compatible with the quantizing interval size is added prior to sampling at $n \times F_s$ and quantizing.

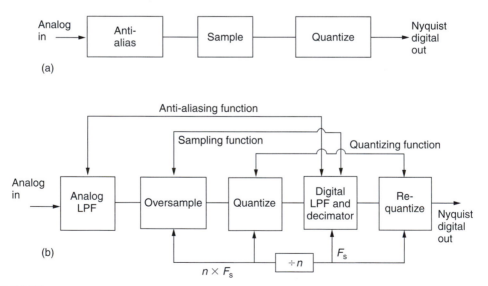

FIGURE 4.35
A conventional ADC performs each step in an identifiable location as in (a). With oversampling, many of the steps are distributed as shown in (b).

Next, the anti-aliasing function is completed in the digital domain by a low-pass filter that cuts off at $F_s/2$. Using an appropriate architecture this filter can be absolutely phase-linear and implemented to arbitrary accuracy. Such filters were discussed in Chapter 3. The filter can be considered to be the demodulator of Figure 4.31, in which the SNR improves as the bandwidth is reduced. The word length can be expected to increase. The multiplications taking place within the filter extend the word length considerably more than the bandwidth reduction alone would indicate. The analog filter serves only to prevent aliasing into the baseband at the oversampling rate; the signal spectrum is determined with greater precision by the digital filter.

With the information spectrum now Nyquist limited, the sampling process is completed when the rate is reduced in the decimator. One sample in n is retained.

The excess word-length extension due to the anti-aliasing filter arithmetic must then be removed. Digital dither is added, completing the dither process, and the quantizing process is completed by requantizing the dithered samples to the appropriate word length, which will be greater than the word length of the first quantizer. Noise shaping may also be employed.

Figure 4.36a shows the building-brick approach of a conventional DAC. The Nyquist rate samples are converted to analog voltages and then a steep-cut analog low-pass filter is needed to reject the sidebands of the sampled spectrum.

Figure 4.36b shows the oversampling approach. The sampling rate is raised in an interpolator, which contains a low-pass filter that restricts the baseband spectrum to the audio bandwidth shown. A large frequency gap now exists between the baseband and the lower sideband. The multiplications in the interpolator extend the word length considerably and this must be reduced within the capacity of the DAC element by the addition of digital dither prior to requantizing.

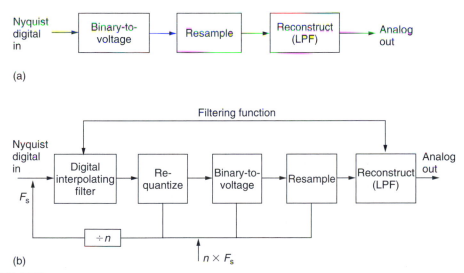

FIGURE 4.36
A conventional DAC in (a) is compared with the oversampling implementation in (b).

Oversampling may also be used to considerable benefit in other dimensions. Figure 4.37 shows how vertical oversampling can be used to increase the resolution of a TV system. A 1250-line camera, for example, is used as the input device, but the 1250-line signal is fed to a standards convertor, which reduces the number of lines to 625. The standards convertor must incorporate a vertical low-pass spatial filter to prevent aliasing when the vertical sampling rate is effectively halved. Such a filter was described in Chapter 3. As it is a digital filter, it can have arbitrarily accurate performance, including a flat passband and steep cutoff slope. The combination of the vertical aperture effect of the 1250-line camera and the vertical LPF in the standards convertor gives a better spatial frequency response than could be achieved with a 625-line camera. The improvement in subjective quality is quite noticeable in practice.

In the case of display technology, oversampling can also be used, this time to render the raster invisible and to improve the vertical aperture of the display. Once more a standards convertor is required, but this now doubles the number of input lines using interpolation. Again the filter can have arbitrary accuracy. The vertical aperture of the 1250-line display does not affect the passband of the input signal because of the use of oversampling.

Oversampling can also be used in the time domain to reduce or eliminate display flicker. A different type of standards convertor that doubles the input field rate by interpolation is necessary. The standards convertor must use motion compensation, otherwise moving objects will not be correctly positioned in intermediate fields and will suffer from judder. Motion compensation is considered in Chapter 5.

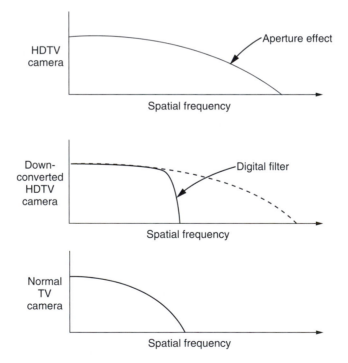

FIGURE 4.37
Using an HDTV camera with down-conversion is a form of oversampling and gives better results than a normal camera because the aperture effect is overcome.

FACTORS AFFECTING CONVERTOR QUALITY

In theory the quality of a digital audio system comprising an ideal ADC followed by an ideal DAC is determined at the ADC. The ADC parameters such as the sampling rate, the word length, and any noise shaping used put limits on the quality that can be achieved. Conversely the DAC itself may be transparent, because it converts only data whose quality is already determined back to the analog domain. In other words, the ADC determines the system quality and the DAC does not make things any worse.

In practice both ADCs and DACs can fall short of the ideal, but with modern convertor components and attention to detail the theoretical limits can be approached very closely and at reasonable cost. Shortcomings may be the result of an inadequacy in an individual component, such as a convertor chip, or due to incorporating a high-quality component in a poorly thought-out system. Poor system design can destroy the performance of a convertor. Whilst oversampling is a powerful technique for realizing high-quality convertors, its use depends on digital interpolators and decimators, whose quality affects the overall conversion quality.

ADCs and DACs have the same transfer function; they are distinguished only by the direction of operation, and therefore the same terminology can be used to classify the possible shortcomings of both. Figure 4.38 shows the transfer functions resulting from the main types of convertor error:

- **(a)** Offset error: A constant appears to have been added to the digital signal. This has a serious effect in video systems because it alters the black level. Offset error is sometimes cancelled by digitally sampling the convertor output during blanking and feeding it back to the analog input as a small control voltage.
- **(b)** Gain error: The slope of the transfer function is incorrect. Because convertors are often referred to one end of the range, gain error causes an offset error. Severe gain error causes clipping.
- **(c)** Integral linearity: This is the deviation of the dithered transfer function from a straight line. It has exactly the same significance and consequences as linearity in analog circuits, because if it is inadequate, harmonic distortion will be caused.
- **(d)** Differential nonlinearity: This is the amount by which adjacent quantizing intervals differ in size. It is usually expressed as a fraction of a quantizing interval.

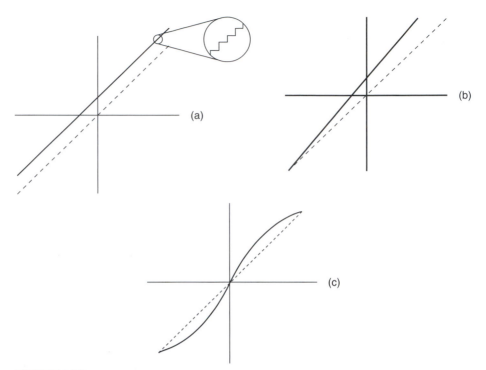

FIGURE 4.38
Main convertor errors (solid line) compared with perfect transfer function (dotted line).
These graphs hold for ADCs and DACs, and the axes are interchangeable; if one is
chosen to be analog, the other will be digital.

(e) Monotonicity: Monotonicity is a special case of differential nonlinearity. Non-monotonicity means that the output does not increase
for an increase in input. Figure 4.29 showed how this can happen in a
DAC. With a convertor input code of 01111111 (127 decimal), the seven
low-order current sources of the convertor will be on. The next code is
10000000 (128 decimal), where only the eighth current source is operating. If the current it supplies is in error on the low side, the analog
output for 128 may be less than that for 127. In an ADC non-monotonicity
can result in missing codes. This means that certain binary combinations
within the range cannot be generated by any analog voltage. If a device
has better than 12Q linearity it must be monotonic. It is not possible for
a 1-bit convertor to be non-monotonic.

(f) Absolute accuracy: This is the difference between actual and ideal output for a given input. For video and audio it is rather less important
than linearity. For example, if all the current sources in a convertor have
good thermal tracking, linearity will be maintained, even though the
absolute accuracy drifts.

DIGITIZING COMPONENT VIDEO

It is not necessary to digitize analog sync pulses in component systems, because the only useful video data are those sampled during the active line. As the sampling rate is derived from sync, it is necessary only to standardise the size and position of a digital active line and all other parts of the video waveform can be re-created at a later time. The position is specified as a given number of sampling clock periods from the leading edge of sync, and the length is simply a standardised number of samples. The digital active line is typically somewhat longer than the analog active line to allow for some drift in the line position of the analog input and to place edge effects in digital filters outside the screen area. Some of the first and last samples of the digital active line will represent blanking level, thereby avoiding abrupt signal transitions caused by a change from blanking level to active signal. When converting analog signals to digital it is important that the analog unblanked picture should be correctly positioned within the line. In this way the analog line will be symmetrically disposed within the digital active line. If this is the case, when converting the data back to the analog domain, no additional blanking will be necessary, as the blanking at the ends of the original analog line will be re-created from the data. The DAC can pass the whole of the digital active line for conversion and the result will be a correctly timed analog line with blanking edges in the right position.

However, if the original analog timing was incorrect, the unblanked analog line may be too long or off-centre in the digital active line. In this case a DAC may apply digital blanking to the line data prior to conversion. Some equipment gives the user the choice of using blanking in the data or locally applied blanking prior to conversion.

In addition to specifying the location of the samples, it is also necessary to standardise the relationship between the absolute analog voltage of the waveform and the digital code value used to express it so that all machines will interpret the numerical data in the same way. These relationships are in the voltage domain and are independent of the scanning standard used. Thus the same relationships will be found in both SD and HD component formats. Clearly digital interfaces assume the same standards for gamma and colour primaries as the original analog system.[18]

Figure 4.39 shows how the luminance signal fits into the quantizing range of a digital system. Numbering for 10-bit systems is shown on the right with figures for 8 bits on the left. Black is at a level of 64_{10} (16_{10}) and peak white is at 940_{10} (235_{10}) so that there is some tolerance of imperfect analog signals and overshoots caused by filter ringing. The sync pulse will clearly go outside the quantizing range, but this is of no consequence as

FIGURE 4.39
The standard luminance signal fits into 8- or 10-bit quantizing structures as shown here.

conventional syncs are not transmitted. The visible voltage range fills the quantizing range and this gives the best possible resolution.

The colour difference signals use offset binary, in which 512_{10} (128_{10}) is the equivalent of blanking voltage. The peak analog limits are reached at 64_{10} (16_{10}) and 960_{10} (240_{10}), respectively, allowing once more some latitude for maladjusted analog inputs and filter ringing.

Note that the code values corresponding to all 1's or all 0's (i.e., the two extreme ends of the quantizing range) are not allowed to occur in the active line as they are reserved for synchronising. ADCs must be followed by circuitry that detects these values and forces the code to the nearest legal value if out-of-range analog inputs are applied. Processing circuits that can generate these values must employ digital clamp circuits to remove the values from the signal. Fortunately this is a trivial operation.

The peak-to-peak amplitude of Y is 880 (220) quantizing intervals, whereas for the colour difference signals it is 900 (225) intervals. There is thus a small gain difference between the signals. This will be cancelled out by the opposing gain difference at any future DAC, but must be borne in mind when digitally converting to IT standards.

The sampling rate used in SD was easily obtained as only two scanning standards had to be accommodated. It will be seen that in HD there are further constraints. In principle, the sampling rate of a system need satisfy only the requirements of sampling theory and filter design. Any rate that does so can be used to convey a video signal from one place to another. In practice, however, there are a number of factors that limit the choice of sampling rate considerably.

It should be borne in mind that a video signal represents a series of two-dimensional images. If a video signal is sampled at an arbitrary frequency, samples in successive lines and pictures could be in different places. If, however, the video signal is sampled at a rate that is a multiple of line rate the result will be that samples on successive lines will be in the same place and the picture will be converted to a neat array having vertical columns of samples that are in the same place in all pictures. This allows for the spatial and temporal processing needed in, for example, standards convertors and MPEG coders. A line-locked sampling rate can conveniently be obtained by multiplication of the H-sync frequency in a phase-locked loop. The position of samples along the line is then determined by the leading edge of sync.

Considering SD sampling rates first, whilst the bandwidth required by 525/59.94 is less than that required by 625/50, and a lower sampling rate might have been used, practicality suggested a common sampling rate. The benefit of a standard H-locked sampling rate for component video is that the design of standards convertors is simplified and DVTRs have a constant data rate independent of standard. This was the goal of CCIR (now ITU) Recommendation 601, which combined the 625/50 input of EBU Doc. Tech. 3246 and 3247 with the 525/59.94 input of SMPTE RP 125.

ITU-601 recommends the use of certain sampling rates, which are based on integer multiples of the carefully chosen fundamental frequency of 3.375 MHz. This frequency is normalized to 1 in the document.

To sample 625/50 luminance signals without quality loss, the lowest multiple possible is 4, which represents a sampling rate of 13.5 MHz. This frequency permits exactly 858 sample periods per line in 525/59.94 and 864 sample periods per line in 625/50.

In the component analog domain, the colour difference signals typically have one-half the bandwidth of the luminance signal. Thus a sampling rate multiple of 2 is used and results in 6.75 MHz. This sampling rate allows respectively 429 and 432 sample periods per line. The use of interlace makes vertical interpolation of down-sampled colour difference data difficult. As a result, interlaced production formats down sample the colour difference data only horizontally.

Component video sampled in this way has a 4:2:2 format. Whilst other combinations are possible, 4:2:2 is the format for which the majority of production equipment is constructed and is the only SD component format for which parallel and serial interface standards exist (see Chapter 10). Figure 4.40 shows the spatial arrangement given by 4:2:2 sampling. Luminance samples appear at half the spacing of colour difference samples, and every other luminance sample is co-sited with a pair of colour difference samples. Co-siting is important because it allows all attributes of one picture point to be conveyed with a three-sample vector quantity. Modification of the three samples allows such techniques as colour correction to be performed. This would be difficult without co-sited information. Co-siting is achieved by clocking the three ADCs simultaneously. In some equipment one ADC is multiplexed between the two colour difference signals. To obtain co-sited data it will then be necessary to have an analog delay in one of the signals.

For full bandwidth RGB working, 4:4:4 can be used with a possible 4:4:4:4 use if a key signal is included. For lower bandwidths, multiples of 1 and 3 can also be used for colour difference and luminance, respectively. The 4:1:1 format delivers colour bandwidth in excess of that required by the composite formats. It is used in the 525-line version of the DVC quarter-inch digital video format. The 3:1:1 format meets 525-line bandwidth requirements. The factors of 3 and 1 do not, however, offer a columnar structure and are inappropriate for quality postproduction.

In 4:2:2 the colour difference signals are sampled horizontally at half the luminance sampling rate, yet the vertical colour difference sampling rates are the same as for luminance. Progressively scanned formats have no difficulty with vertical interpolation and down sampling should be employed in both axes. Figure 4.41 shows that in 4:2:0

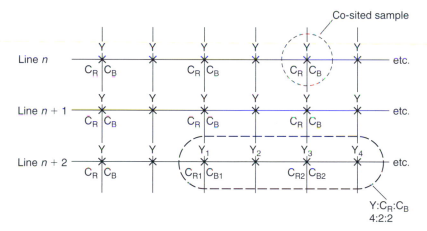

FIGURE 4.40
In CCIR-601 sampling mode 4:2:2, the line synchronous sampling rate of 13.5 MHz results in samples having the same position in successive lines, so that vertical columns are generated. The sampling rates of the colour difference signals C_R and C_B are one-half that of luminance, i.e., 6.75 MHz, so that there are alternate Y-only samples and co-sited samples that describe Y, C_R, and C_B. In a run of four samples, there will be four Y samples, two C_R samples, and two C_B samples, hence 4:2:2.

sampling, the colour difference samples exist only on alternate lines so that the same vertical and horizontal resolution is obtained. The 4:2:0 format is used in the 625-line version of the DVC format and in the MPEG "Main Level Main Profile" format for multimedia communications and, in particular, DVB.

Figure 4.42 shows that in 4:2:2 there is one luminance signal sampled at 13.5 MHz and two colour difference signals sampled at 6.75 MHz. Three separate signals with different clock rates are inconvenient and so

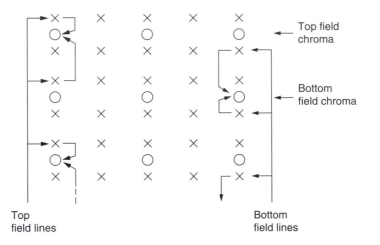

FIGURE 4.41
In 4:2:0 coding the colour difference pixels are down sampled vertically as well as horizontally. Note that the sample sites need to be vertically interpolated so that when two interlaced fields are combined the spacing is even.

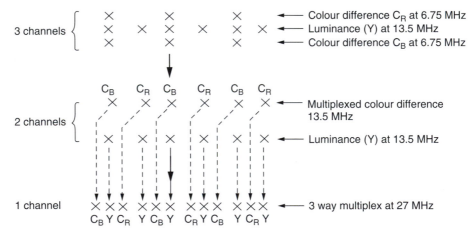

FIGURE 4.42
The colour difference sampling rate is one-half that of luminance, but there are two colour difference signals, C_R and C_B, hence the colour difference data rate is equal to the luminance data rate, and a 27 MHz interleaved format is possible in a single channel.

multiplexing can be used. If the colour difference signals are multiplexed into one channel, then two 13.5 MHz channels will be required. Such an approach is commonly found within digital component processing equipment, with which the colour difference processing can take place in a single multiplexed channel.

If the colour difference and luminance channels are multiplexed into one, a 27 MHz clock will be required. The word order is standardised to be C_B, Y, C_R, Y, etc.

To demultiplex the samples unambiguously, the first sample in the line is defined as C_B and a unique sync pattern is required to identify the beginning of the multiplex sequence. HD adopts the same principle, although the frequencies are higher.

There are two ways of handling 16:9 aspect ratio video in SD. In the anamorphic approach both the camera and the display scan wider but there is no change to the sampling rates employed and the same 27 MHz data stream can be employed unchanged. Compared with 4:3, the horizontal spacing of the pixels in 16:9 must be greater as they are spread across a wider picture. This must result in a reduction of horizontal resolution, but standard 4:3 production equipment can be used subject to some modifications to the shape of pattern wipes in vision mixers. When viewed on a 4:3 monitor anamorphic signals appear squeezed horizontally.

In the second approach, the pixel spacing is kept the same as in 4:3 and the number of samples per active line must then be increased by 16:12. The luminance sampling rate becomes 18 MHz and the colour difference sampling rate becomes 9 MHz. Strictly speaking the format no longer adheres to ITU-601 because the sampling rates are no longer integer multiples of 3.375 MHz. If, however, 18 MHz is considered to be covered by Rec. 601, then it must be described as 5.333 … : 2.666 … : 2.666 ….

If the sampling rate is chosen to be a common multiple of the U.S. and European line rates, the resultant spacing between the pixels has to be accepted. In computer graphics, pixels are always square, which means the horizontal and vertical spacing is the same. In 601 sampling, the pixels are not square and their aspect ratio differs between the U.S. and the European standards. This is because the horizontal sampling rate is the same but the number of lines in the picture is different.

When ITU-601 was being formulated, the computer and television industries were still substantially separate and the lack of square pixels was not seen as an issue. In 1990 CCIR-709 recommended that HD formats should be based on 1920 pixels per active line and use sampling rates based on 2.25 MHz (6.75/3), again making it unlikely that square pixels would result at all frame rates.

Subsequently, the convergence of computer, film, and television technology has led to square pixels being adopted in HD formats at all frame rates, a common sampling rate having necessarily been abandoned. Another change is in the way of counting lines. In traditional analog video formats, the number of lines was the total number, including blanking, whereas in computers the number of lines has always been the number visible on the screen, i.e., the height of the pixel array. HD video standards adopted the same approach, Thus in the 625-line standard, there will be 625 line periods per frame, whereas in the 1080-line HD standard there are 1080 unblanked lines but 1125 line periods per frame.

In 4:2:2 the sampling rate for luma is H-synchronous 13.5 MHz. This is divided by 2 to obtain the colour difference sampling rate. Figure 4.43 shows that in 625-line systems the control system[19] waits for 132 luma sample periods after an analog sync edge before commencing sampling the line. Then 720 luma samples and 360 of each type of colour difference sample are taken, 1440 samples in all. A further 12 sample periods will

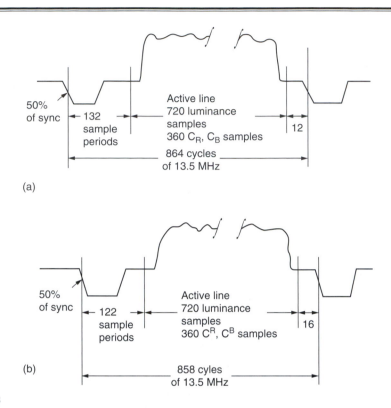

(a)

(b)

FIGURE 4.43
(a) In 625-line systems to CCIR-601, with 4:2:2 sampling, the sampling rate is exactly 864 times the line rate, but only the active line is sampled, 132 sample periods after sync. (b) In 525-line systems to CCIR-601, with 4:2:2 sampling, the sampling rate is exactly 858 times the line rate, but only the active line is sampled, 122 sample periods after sync. Note that the active line contains exactly the same quantity of data as for 50 Hz systems.

elapse before the next sync edge, making 132 + 720 + 12 = 864 sample periods. In 525-line systems,[20] the analog active line is in a slightly different place and so the controller waits 122 sample periods before taking the same digital active line samples as before. There will then be 16 sample periods before the next sync edge, making 122 + 720 + 16 = 858 sample periods.

For 16:9 aspect ratio working, the line and field rate remain the same, but the luminance sampling rate may be raised to 18 MHz and the colour difference sampling rates are raised to 9 MHz. This results in the sampling structure shown for 625 lines in Figure 4.43a and for 525 lines in Figure 4.43b. There are now 960 luminance pixels and 2 × 480 colour difference pixels per active line.

Given the large number of HD scanning standards, it is possible only to outline the common principles here. Specific standards will differ in line and sample counts. Those who are accustomed to analog SD will note that in HD the analog sync pulses are different. In HD, the picture quality is more sensitive to horizontal scanning jitter and so the signal-to-noise ratio of the analog sync edge is improved by doubling the amplitude. Thus the sync edge starts at the most negative part of the waveform, but continues rising until it is as far above blanking as it was below. As a result 50% of sync, the level at which slicing of the sync pulse is defined to take place, is actually at blanking level. All other voltages and gamuts remain the same as for SD.

The treatment of SD formats introduced the concept of the digital active line being longer than the analog line. Some HD formats have formalized this by describing the total active pixel array as the production aperture and the slightly smaller area within that, corresponding to the unblanked area of the analog format, as the clean aperture. The quantizing standards of HD are the same as for SD, except that the option of 12-bit resolution is added.

SMPTE 274M[21] describes 1125 lines per frame 16:9 aspect ratio HD standards having a production aperture of 1920×1080 pixels and a clean aperture of 1888×1062 pixels. The standard uses square pixels, thus $1080 \times 16 = 1920 \times 9$. Both interlaced and progressive scanning is supported, at a wide variety of frame rates, basically 24, 25, 30, 50, and 60 Hz with the option of incorporating the reduction in frequency of 0.1% for synchronisation to the traditional NTSC timing.

As with SD, the sampling clock is line locked. However, there are some significant differences between the SD and the HD approaches. In SD, a common sampling rate is used for both line standards and results in pixels that are not square. In HD, the pixels are square and the sampling rate changes with the format.

It is slowly being understood that improved picture quality comes not from putting more pixels into the image but from eliminating interlace and increasing the frame rate. Unfortunately there are still those who believe that data describing digital television images somehow differ from computer data. The bizarre adherence to the obsolete principle of interlacing seems increasingly to be based on maintaining an artificial difference between computers and television for marketing purposes rather than on any physics or psycho-optics. The failure of the ATSC and FCC to understand these principles has led to a damaging proliferation of HD television standards in the United States. The retention of 24 Hz frame rate in digital cinema is equally difficult to comprehend. At least in Europe the recommendation has been made that HD television services will use progressive scanning.

SMPTE 296M describes the 720P standard,[22] which uses frames containing 750 lines of which 30 correspond to the vertical interval. Note that as interlace is not used, the number of lines per frame does not need to be odd. The 720P standard has square pixels and so must have $720 \times 16/9 = 1280$ pixels per line. The production aperture is thus 1280×720 pixels. A clean aperture is not defined.

The 1280×720 frame can be repeated at 60, 50, 30, 25, or 24 Hz. The same interface symbol rate as in 274M is used, so clearly this must also be a common multiple of 24, 25, 30, 50, and 60 times 750 Hz.

720/60 has a line rate of 45 kHz and has 1650 sample periods per line, corresponding to a luma sampling rate of 74.25 MHz. The colour difference sampling rate is half of that, but as there are two colour difference signals, the overall symbol rate becomes 148.5 MHz, which is at the capacity limit of the original HD digital interface. Unfortunately the 720P format retains 4:2:2 sampling. Had it used 4:2:0 sampling, the beneficial option of a 75 Hz frame rate could have been added with no increase in bit rate.

To support a higher bit rate, a new interface standard running at twice the original HD rate has been introduced. This allows delivery of 1920×1080 progressively scanned formats as well as 2048-pixel-wide images used in digital cinema.

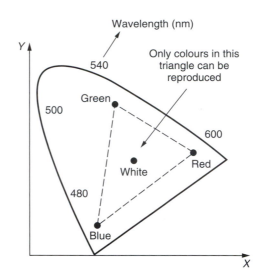

FIGURE 4.44
Additive mixing colour systems can reproduce colours only within a triangle in which the primaries lie on each vertex.

COLOUR IN THE DIGITAL DOMAIN

Colour cameras and most graphics computers produce three signals, or components, R, G, and B, which are essentially monochrome video signals representing an image in each primary colour. Figure 4.44 shows that the three primaries are spaced apart in the chromaticity diagram and the only colours that can be generated fall within the resultant triangle.

RGB signals are strictly compatible only if the colour primaries assumed in the source are present in the display. If there is a primary difference the reproduced colours are different. Clearly broadcast television must have a standard set of primaries. The EBU television systems have only ever had one set of primaries. NTSC started off with one set and then adopted another because the phosphors were brighter. Computer displays have any number of standards because initially all computer colour was false, i.e., synthetic, and the concept of accurate reproduction did not arise. Now that computer displays are going to be used for television it will be necessary for them to adopt standard phosphors or to use colorimetric transcoding on the signals.

Fortunately the human visual system is quite accommodating. The colour of daylight changes throughout the day, so everything changes colour with it. Humans, however, accommodate to that. We tend to see the colour we expect rather than the actual colour. The colour reproduction of printing and photographic media is pretty appalling, but so is human colour memory, and so it is acceptable.

On the other hand, our ability to discriminate between colours presented simultaneously is remarkably good, hence the difficulty car repairers have in getting paint to match.

RGB and Y signals are incompatible, yet when colour television was introduced it was a practical necessity that it should be possible to display colour signals on a monochrome display and vice versa.

Creating or transcoding a luminance signal from RGB is relatively easy. The spectral response of the eye has a peak in the green region. Green objects will produce a larger stimulus than red objects of the same brightness, with blue objects producing the least stimulus. A luminance signal can be obtained by adding R, G, and B together, not in equal amounts, but in a sum that is weighted by the relative response of the human visual system. Thus:

$$Y = 0.299R + 0.587G + 0.114B.$$

Note that the factors add up to 1. If Y is derived in this way, a monochrome display will show nearly the same result as if a monochrome camera had been used in the first place. The results are not identical because of the nonlinearities introduced by gamma correction and by imperfect colour filters.

As colour pictures require three signals, it should be possible to send Y and two other signals, which a colour display could arithmetically convert back to RGB. There are two important factors that restrict the form that the other two signals may take. One is to achieve reverse compatibility. If the source is a monochrome camera, it can produce only Y and the other two signals will be completely absent. A colour display should be able to operate on the Y signal only and show a monochrome picture. The other is the requirement to conserve bandwidth for economic reasons.

These requirements are met in the analog domain by creating two colour difference signals, R−Y and B−Y. In the digital domain the equivalents are C_R and C_B.

Whilst signals such as Y, R, G, and B are unipolar or positive only, colour difference signals are bipolar and may meaningfully take on negative values. Figure 4.45a shows the colour space available in 8-bit RGB. In computers, 8-bit RGB

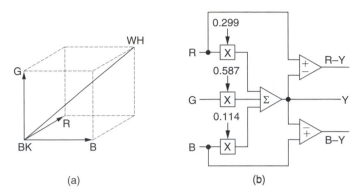

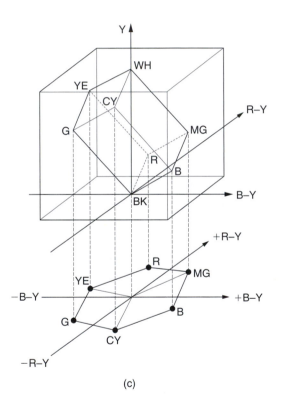

FIGURE 4.45
RGB transformed to colour difference space. This is done because R−Y (C$_R$) and
B−Y (C$_B$) can be sent with reduced bandwidth. (a) RGB cube. The white/black axis
is diagonal and all locations within the cube are legal. (b) RGB to colour difference
transform. (c) RGB cube mapped into colour difference space is no longer a cube.
Only combinations of Y, C$_R$, and C$_B$ that fall within the three-dimensional space
shown are legal. Projection of the space downward creates the familiar vectorscope
display.

is common and we often see claims that 16 million different colours are possible. This is utter nonsense.

A colour is a given combination of hue and saturation and is independent of brightness. Consequently all sets of RGB values having the same ratios produce the same colour. For example, R = G = B always gives the same colour whether the pixel value is 0 or 255. Thus there are 256 brightnesses that have the same colour, allowing a more believable 65,000 different colours.

Figure 4.45(c) shows the RGB cube mapped into 8-bit colour difference space so that it is no longer a cube. Now the grey axis goes straight up the middle because greys correspond to both C_R and C_B being zero. To visualize colour difference space, imagine looking down along the grey axis. This makes the black and white corners coincide in the centre. The remaining six corners of the legal colour difference space now correspond to the six boxes on a component vectorscope. Although there are still 16 million combinations, many of these are now illegal. For example, as black or white is approached, the colour differences must fall to zero.

From an information theory standpoint, colour difference space is redundant. With some tedious geometry, it can be shown that fewer than a quarter of the codes are legal. The luminance resolution remains the same, but there is about half as much information in each colour axis. This is because the colour difference signals are bipolar. If the signal resolution has to be maintained, 8-bit RGB should be transformed to a longer word length in the colour difference domain, 9 bits being adequate. At this stage the colour difference transform doesn't seem efficient because 24-bit RGB converts to 26-bit Y, C_R, C_B.

In most cases the loss of colour resolution is invisible to the eye, and 8-bit resolution is retained. The results of the transform computation must be digitally dithered to avoid posterizing.

The inverse transform to obtain RGB again at the display is straightforward. R and B are readily obtained by adding Y to the two colour difference signals. G is obtained by rearranging the expression for Y above such that

$$G = \frac{Y - 0.3R - 0.11B}{0.59}$$

If a monochrome source having only a Y output is supplied to a colour display, CR and CB will be zero. It is reasonably obvious that if there are no colour

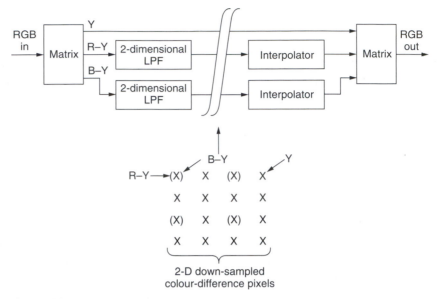

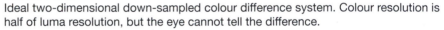

FIGURE 4.46
Ideal two-dimensional down-sampled colour difference system. Colour resolution is half of luma resolution, but the eye cannot tell the difference.

difference signals the colour signals cannot be different from one another and R = G = B. As a result the colour display can produce only a neutral picture.

The use of colour difference signals is essential for compatibility in both directions between colour and monochrome, but it has a further advantage, which follows from the way in which the eye works. To produce the highest resolution in the fovea, the eye will use signals from all types of cone, regardless of colour. To determine colour the stimuli from three cones must be compared.

There is evidence that the nervous system uses some form of colour difference processing to make this possible. As a result the full acuity of the human eye is available only in monochrome. Detail in colour changes cannot be resolved so well. A further factor is that the lens in the human eye is not achromatic and this means that the ends of the spectrum are not well focused. This is particularly noticeable on blue.

In this case there is no point is expending valuable bandwidth sending high-resolution colour signals. Colour difference working allows the luminance to be sent separately at full bandwidth. This determines the subjective sharpness of the picture. The colour difference information can be sent with considerably reduced resolution, as little as one-quarter that of luma, and the human eye is unable to tell.

The acuity of human vision is axisymmetric. In other words, detail can be resolved equally at all angles. When the human visual system assesses the sharpness of a TV picture, it will measure the quality of the worst axis and the extra information on the better axis is wasted. Consequently the most efficient row-and-column image sampling arrangement is the so-called "square pixel." Now pixels are dimensionless and so this is meaningless. However, it is understood to mean that the horizontal and vertical spacing between pixels is the same. Thus it is the sampling grid that is square, rather than the pixel.

The square pixel is optimal for luminance and also for colour difference signals. Figure 4.46a shows the ideal. The colour sampling is co-sited with the luminance sampling but the colour sample spacing is twice that of luminance. The colour difference signals after matrixing from RGB have to be low-pass filtered in two dimensions prior to down sampling to prevent aliasing of HF detail. At the display, the down-sampled colour data have to be interpolated in two dimensions to produce colour information in every pixel. In an oversampling display the colour interpolation can be combined with the display up-sampling stage.

Co-siting the colour and luminance pixels means that the transmitted colour values are displayed unchanged. Only the interpolated values need to be calculated. This minimizes generation loss in the filtering. Down sampling the colour by a factor of 2 in both axes means that the colour data are reduced to one-quarter of their original amount. When viewed by a human this is essentially a lossless process.

References

1. Shannon, C.E. A mathematical theory of communication. Bell Syst. Tech. J., 27, 379 (1948).
2. Jerri, A.J. The Shannon sampling theorem—its various extensions and applications: a tutorial review. Proc. IEEE, 65, 1565–1596 (1977).
3. Betts, J.A. *Signal Processing Modulation and Noise*, Chap. 6, Sevenoaks: Hodder & Stoughton (1970).
4. Harris, S. The effects of sampling clock jitter on Nyquist sampling analog to digital convertors and on oversampling delta-sigma ADCs. J. Audio Eng. Soc., 38, 537–542 (1990).

5. Bennett, W.R. Spectra of quantized signals. Bell Syst. Tech. J., 27, 446–472 (1948).

6. Widrow, B. Statistical analysis of amplitude quantized sampled-data systems. Trans. AIEE, Part II, 79, 555–568 (1961).

7. Lipshitz, S.P., Wannamaker, R.A., and Vanderkooy, J. Quantization and dither: a theoretical survey. J. Audio Eng. Soc., 40, 355–375 (1992).

8. Maher, R.C. On the nature of granulation noise in uniform quantization systems. J. Audio Eng. Soc., 40, 12–20 (1992).

9. Goodall, W.M. Television by pulse code modulation. Bell Syst. Tech. J., 30, 33–49 (1951).

10. Roberts, L.G. Picture coding using pseudo-random noise. IRE Trans. Inform. Theory, IT-8, 145–154 (1962).

11. Schuchman, L. Dither signals and their effect on quantizing noise. Trans. Commun. Technol., COM-12, 162–165 (1964).

12. Sherwood, Some theorems on quantization and an example using dither. In Conf. Rec., 19th Asilomar Conference on Circuits, Systems, and Computers (Pacific Grove, CA) (1985).

13. Gerzon, M., and Craven, P.G. Optimal noise shaping and dither of digital signals. Presented at the 87th Audio Engineers Society Convention (New York) Preprint No. 2822 (J-1) (1989).

14. Vanderkooy, J., and Lipshitz, S.P. Resolution below the least significant bit in digital systems with dither. J. Audio Eng. Soc., 32, 106–113 (1984).

15. Vanderkooy, J., and Lipshitz, S.P., Digital dither. Presented at the 81st Audio Engineers Society Convention (Los Angeles) Preprint 2412 (C-8) (1986).

16. Vanderkooy, J., and Lipshitz, S.P. Digital dither. In *Audio in Digital Times*, New York: AES (1989).

17. Hauser, M.W., Principles of oversampling A/D conversion. J. Audio Eng. Soc., 39, 326 (1991).

18. CCIR Recommendation 601–1, Encoding parameters for digital television for studios.

19. EBU Doc. Tech. 3246.

20. SMPTE 125 M, Television bit parallel digital interface component video signal 4:2:2.

21. SMPTE 274 M Proposed standard—1920 × 1080 image sample structure digital representation and digital timing reference sequences for multiple picture rates.

22. SMPTE 296 M 1280 × 720 progressive image sample structure—analog and digital representation and analog interface (2001).

CHAPTER 5

Digital Video Processing

INTRODUCTION

As the power of digital processing devices continues to rise without a corresponding increase in price, this subject has seen and will continue to see dramatic changes. Increasingly processes that required dedicated hardware are carried out in general-purpose processors. Gate arrays grow ever more capable. Although the hardware changes, nevertheless the principles explained here remain the same.

A SIMPLE DIGITAL VISION MIXER

The luminance path of a simple SD component digital mixer is shown in Figure 5.1. The CCIR-601 digital input is offset binary in that it has a nominal black level of 16_{10} in an 8-bit system (64 in a 10-bit system), and a subtraction has to be made in order that fading will take place with respect to black. On a perfect signal, subtracting 16 (or 64) would achieve this, but on a slightly out-of-range signal, it would not. Because the digital active line is slightly longer than the analog active line, the first sample should be blanking level, and this will be the value to subtract to obtain pure binary luminance with respect to black. This is the digital equivalent of black-level clamping. The two inputs are then multiplied by their respective coefficients and added together to achieve the mix. Peak limiting will be required as in Chapter 3, under Binary Addition, and then, if the output is to be to CCIR-601, 16_{10} (or 64) must be added to each sample value to establish the correct offset. In some video applications, a cross-fade will be needed, and a rearrangement of the cross-fading equation allows one multiplier to be used instead of two, as shown in Figure 5.2.

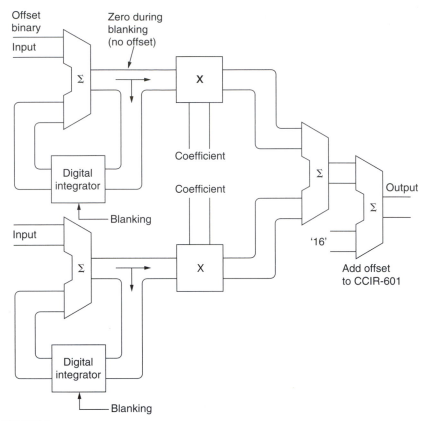

FIGURE 5.1
A simple digital mixer. Offset binary inputs must have the offset removed. A digital integrator will produce a counter-offset, which is subtracted from every input sample. This will increase or reduce until the output of the subtractor is zero during blanking. The offset must be added back after processing if a CCIR-601 output is required.

The colour difference signals are offset binary with an offset of 128_{10} in 8-bit systems (512 in 10-bit systems), and again it is necessary to normalize these with respect to blanking level so that proper fading can be carried out. Because colour difference signals can be positive or negative, this process results in two's complement samples. Figure 5.3 shows some examples. In this form, the samples can be added with respect to blanking level.

Following addition, a limiting stage is used as before, and then, if it is desired to return to CCIR-601 standard, the MSB must be inverted once more to convert from two's complement to offset binary.

In practice the same multiplier can be used to process luminance and colour difference signals. Because these will be arriving time multiplexed at 27 MHz,

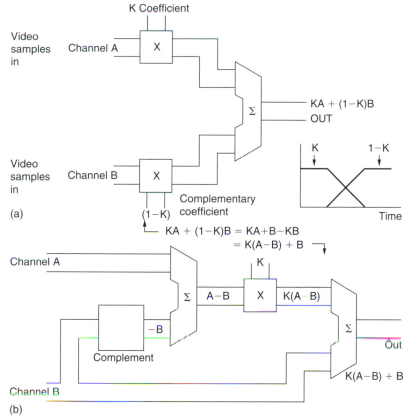

FIGURE 5.2
(a) Cross-fade requires two multipliers. (b) Reconfiguration requires only one multiplier.

it is necessary only to ensure that the correct coefficients are provided at the right time. Figure 5.4 shows an example of part of a slow fade. As the co-sited samples C_B, Y, and C_R enter, all are multiplied by the same coefficient K_n, but the next sample will be luminance only, so this will be multiplied by $K_n + 1$. The next set of co-sited samples will be multiplied by $K_n + 2$ and so on. Clearly coefficients that change at 13.5 MHz must be provided. The sampling rate of the two inputs must be exactly the same, and in the same phase, or the circuit will not be able to add on a sample-by-sample basis. If the two inputs have come from different sources, they must be synchronised by the same master clock and/or time base correction must be provided on the inputs.

Some thought must be given to the word length of the system. If a sample is attenuated, it will develop bits that are below the radix point. For example, if an

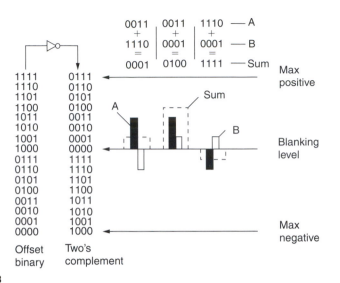

FIGURE 5.3
Offset binary colour difference values are converted to two's complement by reversing the state of the first bit. Two's complement values *A* and *B* will then add around blanking level.

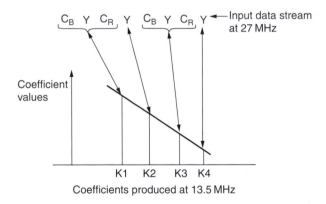

FIGURE 5.4
When using one multiplier to fade both luminance and colour difference in a 27 MHz multiplex 4:2:2 system, one coefficient will be used three times on the co-sited samples, whereas the next coefficient will be used for only a single luminance sample.

8-bit sample is attenuated by 24 dB, the sample value will be shifted four places down. Extra bits must be available within the mixer to accommodate this shift. Digital vision mixers may have an internal word length of 16 bits or more. When several attenuated sources are added together to produce the final mix, the result will be a 16-bit sample stream. As the output will generally need to be of the same format as the input, the word length must be shortened. Shortening the word length of samples effectively makes the quantizing intervals larger and can thus be called requantizing. This must be done very carefully to avoid artifacts

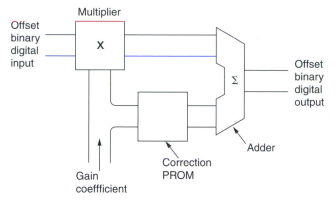
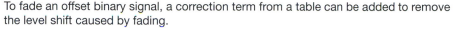

FIGURE 5.5
To fade an offset binary signal, a correction term from a table can be added to remove the level shift caused by fading.

and the necessary processes were shown in Chapter 4 under Requantizing and Digital Dither.

BLANKING

It is often necessary to blank the ends of active lines smoothly to prevent out-of-band signals being generated. This is usually the case when an effects machine has cropped the picture to fit inside a coloured border. The border will be generated by supplying constant luminance and colour difference values to the data stream. Blanking consists of sloping-off the active line by multiplying the sample values by successively smaller coefficients until blanking is reached. This is easy when the sample values have been normalized so that zero represents black, but when the usual offset of 16_{10} is present, multiplication by descending coefficients will cause a black-level shift. The solution is to use a correction table, which can be seen in Figure 5.5. This is addressed by the multiplier coefficient and adds a suitable constant to the multiplier output. If the multiplier were to have a gain of one-half, this would shift the black level by eight quantizing intervals, and so the correction table would add eight to the output. When the multiplier has fully blanked, the output will be zero, and the correction table has to add 16_{10} to the output.

KEYING

Keying is the process in which one video signal can be cut into another to replace part of the picture with a different image. One application of keying is where a switcher can wipe from one input to another using one of a variety of different patterns. Figure 5.6 shows that an analog switcher performs such an

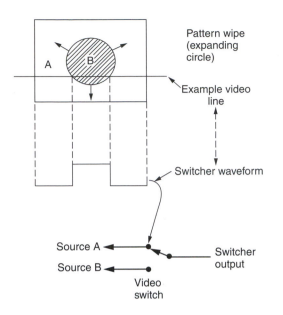

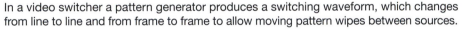

FIGURE 5.6
In a video switcher a pattern generator produces a switching waveform, which changes from line to line and from frame to frame to allow moving pattern wipes between sources.

effect by generating a binary switching waveform in a pattern generator. Video switching between inputs actually takes place during the active line. In most analog switchers, the switching waveform is digitally generated and then fed to a DAC, whereas in a digital switcher, the pattern generator outputs become the coefficients supplied to the cross-fader, which is sometimes referred to as a cutter. The switching edge must be positioned to an accuracy of a few nanoseconds, much less than the spacing of the pixels, otherwise slow wipes will not appear to move smoothly, and diagonal wipes will have stepped edges, a phenomenon known as ratcheting.

Positioning the switch point to subpixel accuracy is not particularly difficult, as Figure 5.7 shows. A suitable series of coefficients can position the effective cross-over point anywhere. The finite slope of the coefficients results in a brief cross-fade from one video signal to the other. This soft keying gives a much more realistic effect than binary switchers, which often give a "cut out with scissors" appearance. In some machines the slope of the cross-fade can be adjusted to achieve the desired degree of softness.

CHROMA KEYING

Another application of keying is to derive the switching signal by processing video from a camera in some way. By analysing colour difference signals, it is

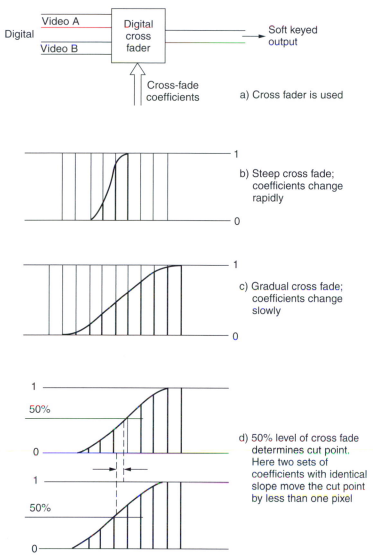

FIGURE 5.7
Soft keying. See text for details.

possible to determine where in a picture a particular colour occurs. When a key signal is generated in this way, the process is known as chroma keying, which is the electronic equivalent of matting in film.

In a 4:2:2 component system, it will be necessary to provide coefficients to the luminance cross-fader at 13.5 MHz. Chroma samples occur at only half this frequency, so it is necessary to provide a chroma interpolator artificially to raise the chroma sampling rate. For chroma keying a simple linear interpolator is

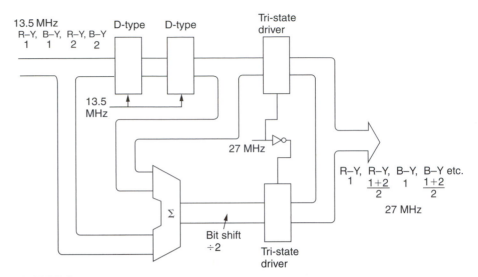

FIGURE 5.8

Alternate C_R and C_B samples may be averaged by a two-sample delay and an adder. Output will then alternate between sample values and averaged sample values at 27 MHz. Demultiplexing the output will give two colour difference signals each at 13.5 MHz so that they can be used to produce coefficients at that rate to key luminance.

perfectly adequate. Intermediate chroma samples are simply the average of two adjacent samples. Figure 5.8 shows how a multiplexed C_R, C_B signal can be averaged using a delay of two clocks.

As with analog switchers, chroma keying is also possible with composite digital inputs, but decoding must take place before it is possible to obtain the key signals. The video signals that are being keyed may, however, remain in the composite digital format.

In switcher/keyers, it is necessary to obtain a switching signal, which ramps between two states from an input signal, which can be any allowable video waveform. Manual controls are provided so that the operator can set thresholds and gains to obtain the desired effect. In the analog domain, these controls distort the transfer function of a video amplifier so that it is no longer linear. A digital keyer will perform the same functions using logic circuits.

Figure 5.9a shows that the effect of a non-linear transfer function is to switch when the input signal passes through a particular level. The transfer function is implemented in a memory in digital systems. The incoming video sample value acts as the memory address, so that the selected memory location is proportional to the video level. At each memory location, the appropriate output level code is stored. If, for example, each memory location stored its own address, the output would equal the input, and the device would be transparent. In practice,

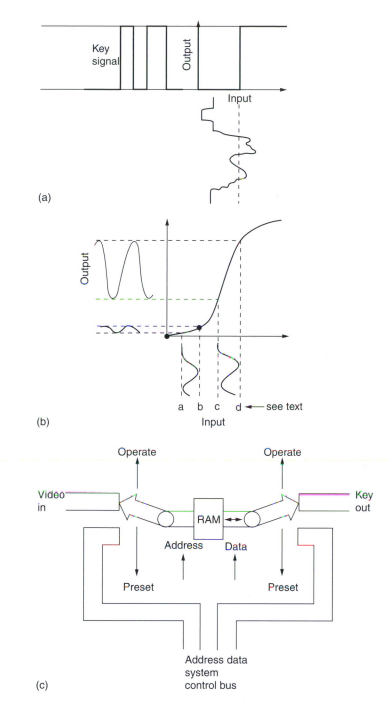

FIGURE 5.9
(a) A non-linear transfer function can be used to produce a keying signal. (b) The non-linear transfer function emphasizes contrast in part of the range but reduces it at other parts. (c) If a RAM is used as a flexible transfer function, it will be necessary to provide multiplexers so that the RAM can be preset with the desired values from the control system.

switching is obtained by distorting the transfer function to obtain more gain in one particular range of input levels at the expense of less gain at other input levels. With the transfer function shown in Figure 5.9b, an input level change from a to b causes a smaller output change, whereas the same level change between c and d causes a considerable output change. If the memory is RAM, different transfer functions can be loaded in by the control system, and this requires multiplexers in both data and address lines as shown in Figure 5.9c. In practice such a RAM will be installed in Y, C_R, and C_B channels, and the results will be combined to obtain the final switching coefficients.

SIMPLE EFFECTS

If a RAM of the type shown in Figure 5.9 is inserted in a digital luminance path, the result will be solarizing, which is a form of contrast enhancement. Figure 5.10 shows that a family of transfer functions that control the degree of contrast enhancement can be implemented. When the transfer function becomes so distorted that the slope reverses, the result is luminance reversal, in which black and white are effectively interchanged. Solarizing can also be implemented in colour difference channels to obtain chroma solarizing. In effects machines, the degree of solarizing may need to change smoothly so that the effect can be gradually introduced. In this case the various transfer functions will be kept in different pages of a table, so that the degree of solarization can be selected immediately by changing the page address of the table. One page will have a straight transfer function, so the effect can be turned off by selecting that page.

In the digital domain it is easy to introduce various forms of quantizing distortion to obtain special effects. Figure 5.11 shows that eight-bit luminance allows 256 different brightnesses, which to the naked eye appears to be a continuous range. If some of the low-order bits of the samples are disabled, then a smaller number of brightness values describes the range from black to white. For example, if six bits are disabled, only two bits remain, and so only four possible brightness levels can be output. This gives an effect known as contouring because the visual effect somewhat resembles a relief map.

When the same process is performed with colour difference signals, the result is to limit the number of possible colours in the picture, which gives an effect known as posterizing, because the picture appears to have been coloured by paint from pots. Solarizing, contouring, and posterizing cannot be performed in the composite digital domain, due to the presence of the subcarrier in the sample values.

Figure 5.12 shows a latch in the luminance data that is being clocked at the sampling rate. It is transparent to the signal, but if the clock to the latch is divided down by some factor n, the result will be that the same sample value will be

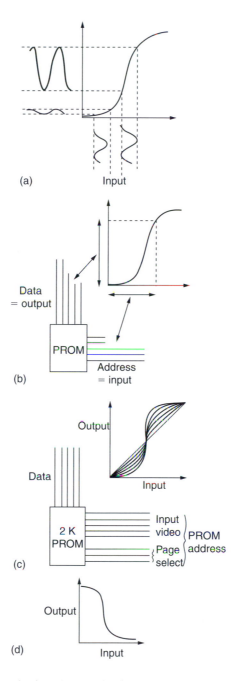

(a)

Input

Data
= output

PROM

Address
= input

(b)

Output

Data

Input

2 K
PROM

Input
video ⎫ PROM
⎬
Page ⎭ address
select

(c)

Output

Input

(d)

FIGURE 5.10
Solarization. (a) The non-linear transfer function emphasizes contrast in part of the range but reduces it in other parts. (b) The desired transfer function is implemented in a table. Each input sample value is used as the address to select a corresponding output value stored in the table. (c) A family of transfer functions can be accommodated in a larger table. Page select affects the high-order address bits of the table. (d) Transfer function for luminance reversal.

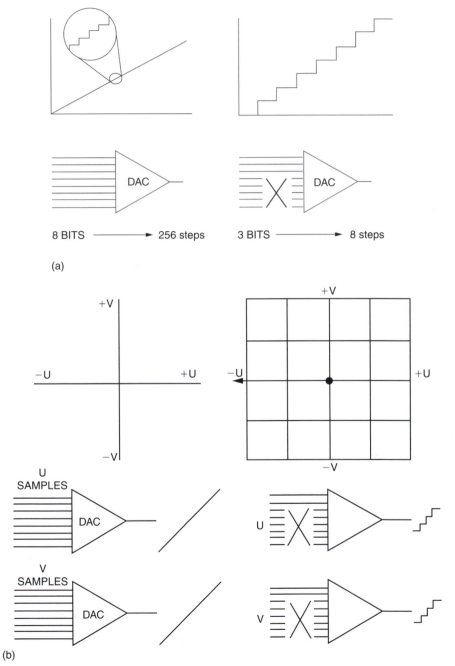

FIGURE 5.11
(a) In contouring, the least significant bits of the luminance samples are discarded, which reduces the number of possible output levels. (b) At left, the 8-bit colour difference signals allow 2^{16} different colours. At right, eliminating all but 2 bits of each colour difference signal allows only 2^4 different colours.

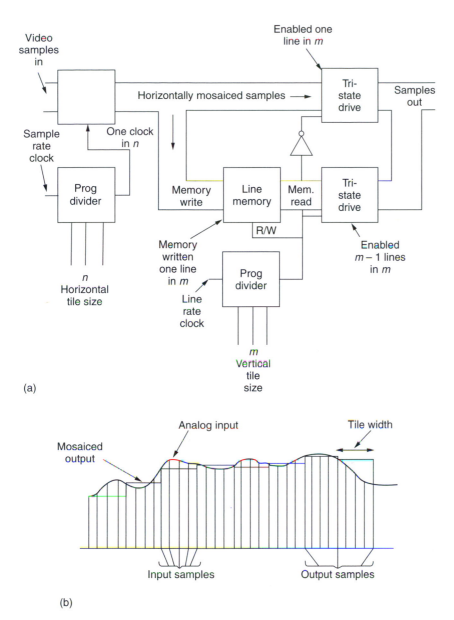

(a)

(b)

FIGURE 5.12

(a) Simplified diagram of mosaicing system. At the left-hand side, horizontal mosaicing is done by intercepting sample clocks. On one line in *m*, the horizontally mosaiced line becomes the output and is simultaneously written into a one-line memory. On the remaining (*m* – 1) lines the memory is read to produce several identical successive lines to give the vertical dimensions of the tile. (b) In mosaicing, input samples are neglected, and the output is held constant by failing to clock a latch in the data stream for several sample periods. Heavy vertical lines here correspond to the clock signal occurring. Heavy horizontal line is the resultant waveform.

MAPPING

The principle of all video manipulators is the same as the technique used by cartographers for centuries. Cartographers are faced with a continual problem in that the earth is round and paper is flat. To produce flat maps, it is necessary to project the features of the round original onto a flat surface. Figure 5.13 shows an example of this. There are a number of different ways of projecting maps, and all of them must, by definition, produce distortion. The effect of this distortion is that distances measured near the extremities of the map appear farther than they actually are. Another effect is that great circle routes (the shortest or longest path between two places on a planet) may appear curved on a projected map. The type of projection used is usually printed somewhere on the map, a very common system being that due to Mercator. Clearly the process of mapping involves some three-dimensional geometry to simulate the paths of light rays from the map so that they appear to have come from the curved surface. Video effects machines work in exactly the same way.

The distortion of maps means that things are not where they seem. In time-sharing computers, every user appears to have his own identical address space in which his program resides, despite the fact that many different programs are simultaneously in the memory. To resolve this contradiction, memory management units are constructed that add a constant value to the address the user thinks he has (the virtual address) in order to produce the physical address. As long as the unit gives each user a different constant, they can all program in the same virtual address space without one corrupting another's programs. Because the program is no longer where it seems to be, the term of mapping was introduced. The address space of a computer is one dimensional, but a video frame expressed as rows and columns of pixels can be considered to have a two-dimensional address, as in Figure 5.14. Video manipulators work by mapping the pixel addresses in two dimensions.

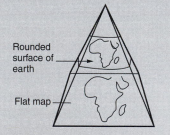

FIGURE 5.13
Map projection is a close relative of video effects units, which manipulate the shape of pictures.

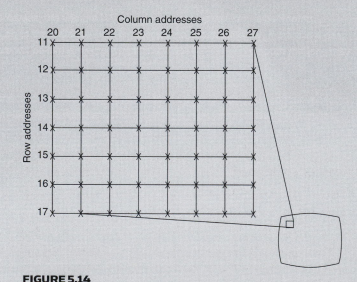

FIGURE 5.14
The entire TV picture can be broken down into uniquely addressable pixels.

held on the output for *n* clock periods, giving the video waveform a staircase characteristic. This is the horizontal component of the effect known as mosaicing. The vertical component is obtained by feeding the output of the latch into a line memory, which stores one horizontally mosaiced line and then repeats that line *m* times. As *n* and *m* can be independently controlled, the mosaic tiles can be made to be of any size and rectangular or square at will. Clearly the mosaic circuitry must be implemented simultaneously in luminance and colour difference signal paths. It is not possible to perform mosaicing on a composite digital signal, because it will destroy the chroma. It is common to provide a bypass route, which allows mosaiced and unmosaiced video to be simultaneously available. Dynamic switching between the two sources controlled by a separate key signal then allows mosaicing to be restricted to certain parts of the picture.

PLANAR DIGITAL VIDEO EFFECTS

One can scarcely watch television nowadays without becoming aware of picture manipulation. Flips, tumbles, spins, and page-turn effects; perspective rotation; and rolling the picture onto the surface of a solid are all commonly seen. In all but the last mentioned, the picture remains flat, hence the title of this section. Non-planar manipulation requires further complexity, which will be treated in due course.

Effects machines that manipulate video pictures are close relatives of the machines that produce computer-generated images.[1] Such images require an enormous number of computations per frame processing power, yet must work in real time, unlike computer rendering that may work offline.

ADDRESS GENERATION AND INTERPOLATION

There are many different manipulations possible, and the approach here will be to begin with the simplest, which require the least processing, and to graduate to the most complex, introducing the necessary processes at each stage.

It has been stated that address mapping is used to perform transforms. Now that rows and columns are processed individually, the mapping process becomes much easier to understand. Figure 5.15 shows a single row of pixels, which are held in a buffer in which each can be addressed individually and transferred to another. If a constant is added to the read address, the selected pixel will be to the right of the place where it will be put. This has the effect of moving the picture to the left. If the buffer represented a column of pixels, the picture would be moved vertically. As these two transforms can be controlled independently, the picture could be moved diagonally.

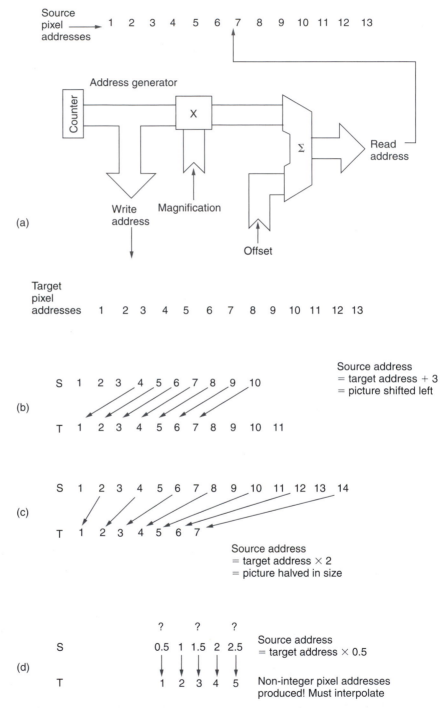

FIGURE 5.15
Address generation is the fundamental process behind transforms.

If the read address is multiplied by a constant, say two, the effect is to bring samples from the input closer together on the output, so that the picture size is reduced. Again independent control of the horizontal and vertical transforms is possible, so that the aspect ratio of the picture can be modified. This is very useful for telecine work when CinemaScope films are to be broadcast. Clearly the secret of these manipulations is in the constants fed to the address generators. The added constant represents displacement, and the multiplied constant represents magnification. A multiplier constant of less than 1 will result in the picture getting larger. Figure 5.15 also shows, however, that there is a problem. If a constant of 0.5 is used, to make the picture twice as big, half of the addresses generated are not integers. A memory does not understand an address of 2.5! If an arbitrary magnification is used, nearly all the addresses generated are noninteger. A similar problem crops up if a constant of less than one is added to the address in an attempt to move the picture less than the pixel spacing. The solution to the problem is interpolation. Because the input image is spatially sampled, those samples contain enough information to represent the brightness and colour all over the screen. When the address generator comes up with an address of 2.5, it actually means that what is wanted is the value of the signal interpolated halfway between pixel 2 and pixel 3. The output of the address generator will thus be split into two parts. The integer part will become the memory address, and the fractional part is the phase of the necessary interpolation. To interpolate pixel values a digital filter is necessary.

Figure 5.16 shows that the input and output of an effects machine must be at standard sampling rates to allow digital interchange with other equipment. When the size of a picture is changed, this causes the pixels in the picture to fail to register with output pixel spacing. The problem is exactly the same as sampling-rate conversion, which produces a differently spaced set of samples that still represent the original waveform. One pixel value actually represents the peak brightness of a two-dimensional intensity function, which is the effect of the modulation transfer function of the system on an infinitely small point. As each dimension can be treated separately, the equivalent in one axis is that the pixel value represents the peak value of an infinitely short impulse that has been low-pass filtered to the system bandwidth. The waveform is that of a $\sin x/x$ curve, which has value everywhere except at the centre of other pixels. To compute an interpolated value, it is necessary to add together the contribution from all relevant samples, at the point of interest. Each contribution can be obtained by looking up the value of a unity $\sin x/x$ curve at the distance from the input pixel to the output pixel to

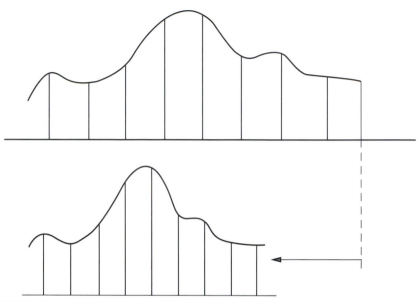

FIGURE 5.16

It is easy, almost trivial, to reduce the size of a picture by pushing the samples closer together, but this is not often of use, because it changes the sampling rate in proportion to the compression. When a standard sampling-rate output is needed, interpolation must be used.

obtain a coefficient and multiplying the input pixel value by that coefficient. The process of taking several pixel values, multiplying each by a different coefficient, and summing the products can be performed by the FIR (finite-impulse response) configuration described earlier. The impulse response of the filter necessary depends on the magnification. When the picture is being enlarged, the impulse response can be the same as at normal size, but as the size is reduced, the impulse response has to become broader (corresponding to a reduced spatial frequency response) so that more input samples are averaged together to prevent aliasing. The coefficient store will need a two-dimensional structure, such that the magnification and the interpolation phase must both be supplied to obtain a set of coefficients. The magnification can easily be obtained by comparing successive outputs from the address generator.

As was seen in Chapter 3, the number of points in the filter is a compromise between cost and performance, 8 being a typical number for high quality. As there are two transform processes in series, every output pixel will be the result of 16 multiplications, so there will be 216 million multiplications per second taking place in the luminance channel alone for a 13.5 MHz sampling rate unit. The quality of the output video also depends on the number of different interpolation phases available between pixels. The address generator may compute fractional addresses to any accuracy, but these will be rounded off to the nearest available phase in the digital filter. The effect is that the output pixel value provided is actually the value a tiny distance away and has the same result as sampling clock jitter, which is to produce program-modulated noise. The greater the number of phases provided, the larger will be the size of the coefficient store needed. As the coefficient store is two-dimensional, an increase in the number of filter points and phases causes an exponential growth in size and cost. The filter itself can be implemented readily with fast multiplier chips, but one problem is accessing the memory to provide input samples. What the memory must do is take the integer part of the address generator output and provide simultaneously as many adjacent pixels as there are points in the filter. This problem may be solved by making the memory from several smaller memories with an interleaved address structure, so that several pixel values can be provided simultaneously.

SKEW AND ROTATION

It has been seen that adding a constant to the source address produces a displacement. It is not necessary for the displacement constant to be the same throughout the frame. If the horizontal transform is considered, as in Figure 5.17a, the effect of making the displacement a function of line address is to cause a skew. Essentially each line is displaced by a different amount. The necessary function generator is shown in simplified form in Figure 5.17b, although it could equally be realized in a fast CPU with appropriate software.

It will be seen that the address generator is really two accumulators in series, of which the first operates once per line to calculate a new offset, which grows linearly from line to line, and the second operates at pixel rate to calculate source addresses from the required magnification. The initial state of the second accumulator is the offset from the first accumulator.

If two skews, one vertical and one horizontal, are performed in turn on the same frame, the result is a rotation as shown in Figure 5.17c. Clearly the skew angle parameters for the two transforms must be in the correct relationship to obtain pure rotation. Additionally the magnification needs to be modified by a cosine function of the rotation angle to counteract the stretching effect of the skews.

In the horizontal process, the offset will change once per line, whereas in the vertical process, the offset will change once per column. For simplicity, the offset generators are referred to as the slow address generators, whereas the accumulators, which operate at pixel rate, are called the fast address generators.

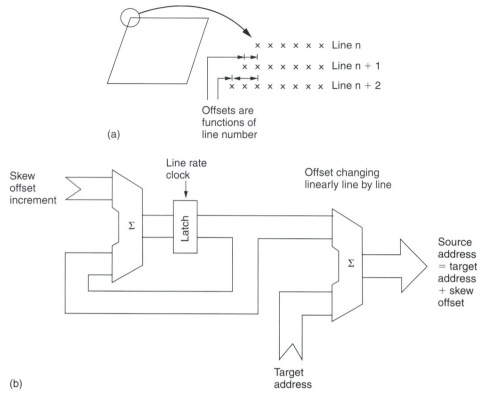

FIGURE 5.17
(a) Skew is achieved by subjecting each line of pixels to a different offset. (b) The hardware necessary to perform a skew in which the left-hand accumulator produces the offset, which increases every line, and the right-hand accumulator adds it to the address.

Unfortunately skew rotations cannot approach 90°, because the skew parameter goes to infinity, and so a skew rotate is generally restricted to rotations of ±45°. This is not a real restriction, because the apparatus already exists to turn a picture on its side. This can be done readily by failing to transpose from rows to columns at some stage so the picture will be turned through 90°.

Figure 5.17d shows how continuous rotation can be obtained. From −45° to +45°, normal skew rotation is used. At 45° during the vertical interval, the memory transpose is turned off, causing the picture to be flipped 90° and laterally inverted. Reversing the source address sequence cancels the lateral inversion, and at the same time the skew parameters are changed from +45° to −45°. In this way the picture passes smoothly through the 45° barrier, and skew parameters continue to change until 135° (90° transpose +45° skew) is reached. At this point, three things happen, again during the vertical interval. The transpose is switched

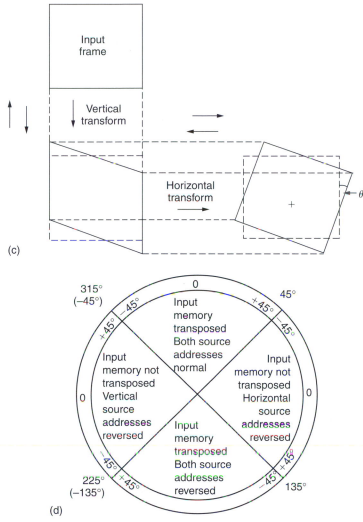

(c)

(d)

FIGURE 5.17
(Continued) (c) A z-axis rotate is performed using a pair of skews in succession. The magnification of each transform must also change from unity to cos θ because horizontal and vertical components of distances on the frame reduce as the frame turns. (d) The four modes necessary for a complete z-axis rotation using skews. Switching between modes at the vertical interval allows a skew range of ±45° (outer ring) to embrace a complete revolution in conjunction with memory transposes, which exchange rows and columns to give 90° changes.

back on, re-orienting the picture; the source addresses are both reversed, which turns the picture upside down; and a skew rotate of 45° is applied, returning the picture to 135° of rotation, from which point motion can continue. The remainder of the rotation takes place along similar lines, which can be followed in the diagram.

The rotation described is in the z axis, i.e., the axis coming out of the source picture at right angles. Rotation about the other axes is rather more difficult, because to perform the effect properly, perspective is needed. In simple machines, there is no perspective, and the effect of rotation is as if viewed from a long way away. These nonperspective pseudo-rotations are achieved by simply changing the magnification in the appropriate axis as a cosine function of the rotation angle.

PERSPECTIVE ROTATION

To follow the operation of a true perspective machine, some knowledge of perspective is necessary. Stated briefly, the phenomenon of perspective is due to the angle subtended to the eye by objects being a function not only of their size but also of their distance. Figure 5.18 shows that the size of an image on the rear wall of a pinhole camera can be increased by either making the object larger or bringing it closer. In the absence of stereoscopic vision, it is not possible to tell which has happened. The pinhole camera is very useful for the study of perspective and has indeed been used by artists for that purpose. The clinically precise perspective of Canaletto paintings was achieved through the use of the camera obscura ("darkened room" in Italian).[3]

It is sometimes claimed that the focal length of the lens used on a camera changes the perspective of a picture. This is not true; perspective is only a function of the relative positions of the camera and the subject. Fitting a wide-angle lens simply allows the camera to come near enough to keep dramatic perspective within the frame, whereas fitting a long-focus lens allows the camera to be far enough away to display a reasonably sized image with flat perspective.[4]

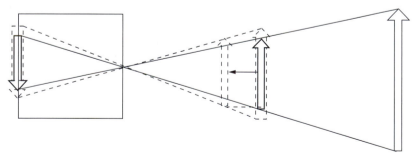

FIGURE 5.18
The image on the rear of the pinhole camera is identical for the two solid objects shown because the size of the object is proportional to distance, and the subtended angle remains the same. The image can be made larger (dotted) by making the object larger or moving it closer.

Because a single eye cannot tell distance unaided, all current effects machines work by simply producing the correct subtended angles, which the brain perceives as a three-dimensional effect. Figure 5.19 shows that to a single eye, there is no difference between a three-dimensional scene and a two-dimensional image formed where rays traced from features to the eye intersect an imaginary plane. This is exactly the reverse of the map projection shown in Figure 5.13 and is the principle of all perspective manipulators.

The case of perspective rotation of a plane source will be discussed first. Figure 5.19 shows that, when a plane input frame is rotated about a horizontal axis, the distance from the top of the picture to the eye is no longer the same as the distance from the bottom of the picture to the eye. The result is that the top and bottom edges of the picture subtend different angles to the eye, and where the rays cross the target plane, the image has become trapezoidal. There is now no such thing as the magnification of the picture. The magnification changes continuously from top to bottom of the picture, and if a uniform grid is input, after a perspective rotation it will appear non-linear as the diagram shows.

Early DVEs (digital video effects generators) performed perspective transforms by separate but co-operative processes in two orthogonal axes, whereas with greater computing power, it is possible to perform the manipulation in one stage using two-dimensional addressing and interpolation. Clearly a significant part of the process must be the calculation of the addresses, magnifications, and interpolation phases.

The address generators for perspective operation are necessarily complex, and a careful approach is necessary to produce the complex calculations at the

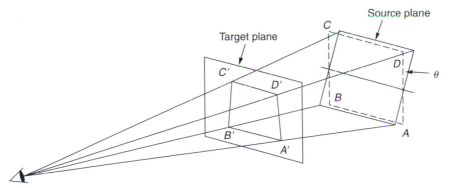

FIGURE 5.19
In a planar rotation effect the source plane *ABCD* is the rectangular input picture. If it is rotated through the angle shown, ray tracing to a single eye at left will produce a trapezoidal image *A′ B′ C′ D′* on the target. Magnification will now vary with position on the picture.

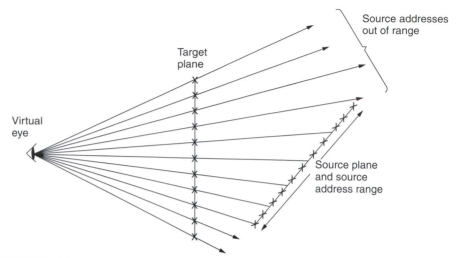

Target plane

Virtual eye

Source addresses out of range

Source plane and source address range

FIGURE 5.20
A rotation of the source plane along with a movement away from the observer is shown here. The system has to produce pixel values at the spacing demanded by the output. Thus a ray from the eye to each target pixel is produced to locate a source pixel. Because the chances of exactly hitting a source pixel are small, the need for interpolation is clear. If the source plane is missed, this will result in an out-of-range source address, and a background value will be substituted.

necessary speed.[5] Figure 5.20 shows a section through a transform in which the source plane has been rotated about an axis perpendicular to the page. The mapping or ray-tracing process must produce a straight line from every target pixel (corresponding to where an output value is needed) to locate a source address (corresponding to where an input value is available). Moving the source value to the target performs the necessary transform.

The derivation of the address generator equations is in highly complex mathematics, which can be found in Newman and Sproull[2] and in the ADO patent.[5] For the purposes of this chapter, an understanding of the result can be had by considering the example of Figure 5.21. In this figure, successive integer values of x have been used in a simple source address calculation equation, which contains a division stage. The addresses produced form a non-linear sequence and will be seen to lie on a rotated source plane.

All perspective machines must work with dynamic changes in magnification throughout the frame. The situation often arises in which at one end of a pixel row the magnification is greater than unity, and the FIR filter has to interpolate between available pixels, whereas at the other end of the row the magnification will be less than unity and the FIR filter has to adopt a low-pass and decimate

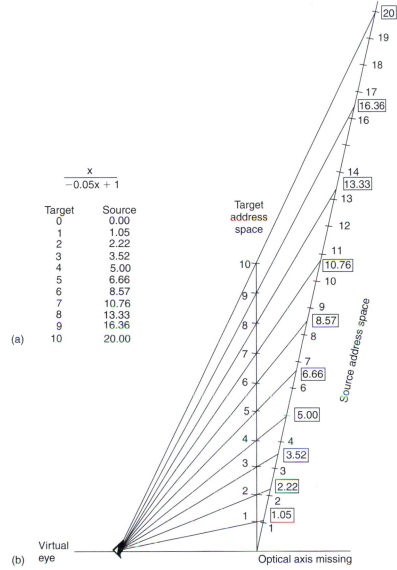

$$\frac{x}{-0.05x + 1}$$

Target	Source
0	0.00
1	1.05
2	2.22
3	3.52
4	5.00
5	6.66
6	8.57
7	10.76
8	13.33
9	16.36
10	20.00

(a)

(b) Virtual eye

Optical axis missing

FIGURE 5.21
(a) The equation at the top calculates the source address for each evenly spaced target address from 0 to 10. All numbers are kept positive for simplicity, so only one side of the picture is represented here. (b) A ray-tracing diagram corresponding to the calculations of (a). Following a ray from the virtual eye through any target pixel address will locate the source addresses calculated.

mode to eliminate excessive pixels without aliasing. The characteristics of the filter are changed at will by selecting different coefficient sets from pages of memory according to the instantaneous magnification at the centre of the filter window. The magnification can be determined by computing the address

slope. This is done by digitally differentiating the output of the address generator, which is to say that the difference between one source address and the next
is computed. This produces the address slope, which is inversely proportional to the magnification and can be used to select the appropriate impulse
response width in the interpolator. The interpolator output is then a transformed image.

NON-PLANAR EFFECTS

The basic approach to perspective rotation of plane pictures has been described,
and this can be extended to embrace transforms that make the source picture
appear non-planar. Effects in this category include rolling the picture onto the
surface of an imaginary solid such as a cylinder or a cone. Figure 5.22 shows
that the ray-tracing principle is still used, but that the relationship between

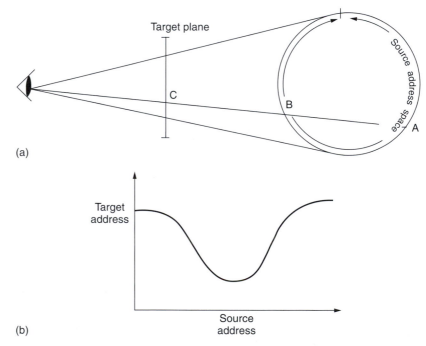

FIGURE 5.22
(a) To produce a rolled-up image for a given target pixel address *C*, there will be two
source addresses *A* and *B*. Pixel data from *A* and *B* must be added with weighting
dependent on the transparency of the nearer pixel to produce the pixel value to be put on
the target plane at *C*. (b) Transfer function for a rolling-up transform. There are two source
addresses for every target address; hence the need for target accumulation.

source and target addresses has become much more complex. The problem is that when a source picture can be curved, it may be put in such an attitude that one part of the source can be seen through another part. This results in two difficulties. First, the source address function needs to be of higher order, and second, the target needs to be able to accept and accumulate pixel data from two different source addresses, with weighting given to the one nearer the viewer according to the transparency allocated to the picture.

CONTROLLING EFFECTS

The basic mechanism of the transform process has been described, but this is only half of the story, because these transforms have to be controlled. There is a lot of complex geometrical calculation necessary to perform even the simplest effect, and the operator cannot be expected to calculate directly the parameters required for the transforms. All effects machines require a computer of some kind, with which the operator communicates using keyboard entry or joystick/trackball movements at high level. These high-level commands will specify such things as the position of the axis of rotation of the picture relative to the viewer, the position of the axis of rotation relative to the source picture, and the angle of rotation in the three axes.

An essential feature of this kind of effects machines is fluid movement of the source picture as the effect proceeds. If the source picture is to be made to move smoothly, then clearly the transform parameters will be different in each field. The operator cannot be expected to input the source position for every field, because this would be an enormous task. Additionally, storing the effect would require a lot of space. The solution is for the operator to specify the picture position at strategic points during the effect, and then digital filters are used to compute the intermediate positions so that every field will have different parameters.

The specified positions are referred to as knots, nodes, or keyframes, the first being the computer graphics term. The operator is free to enter knots anywhere in the effect, and so they will not necessarily be evenly spaced in time, i.e., there may well be different numbers of fields between each knot. In this environment it is not possible to use conventional FIR-type digital filtering, because a fixed-impulse response is inappropriate for irregularly spaced samples.

Interpolation of various orders is used, ranging from zero-order hold for special jerky effects through linear interpolation to cubic interpolation for very smooth motion. The algorithms used to perform the interpolation are known as splines, a term that has come down from shipbuilding via computer graphics.[6] When a ship is designed, the draughtsman produces hull cross sections at intervals along the keel, whereas the shipyard needs to re-create a continuous structure. The solution is a lead-filled bar, known as a spline, which can be formed to join up each cross section in a smooth curve and then used as a template to form the hull plating.

The filter that does not ring cannot be made, and so the use of spline algorithms for smooth motion sometimes results in unintentional overshoots of the picture position. This can be overcome by modifying the filtering algorithm. Spline algorithms usually look ahead beyond the next knot to compute the degree of curvature in the graph of the parameter against time. If a break is put in that parameter at a given knot, the spline algorithm is prevented from looking ahead, and no overshoot will occur. In practice the effect is created and run without breaks, and then breaks are added later where they are subjectively thought necessary.

It will be seen that there are several levels of control in an effects machine. At the highest level, the operator can create, store, and edit knots and specify the times that elapse between them. The next level is for the knots to be interpolated by spline algorithms to produce parameters for every field in the effect. The field frequency parameters are then used as the inputs to the geometrical computation of transform parameters, which the lowest level of the machine will use as microinstructions to act upon the pixel data. Each of these layers will often have a separate processor, not just for speed, but also to allow software to be updated at certain levels without disturbing others.

GRAPHICS

Although there is no easy definition of a video graphics system that distinguishes it from a graphic art system, for the purposes of discussion it can be said that graphics consists of generating alphanumerics on the screen, whereas graphic art is concerned with generating more general images. The simplest form of screen presentation of alphanumerics is the visual display unit (VDU), which was used to control early computer-based systems. The mechanism used for character generation in such devices is very simple and thus makes a good introduction to the subject.

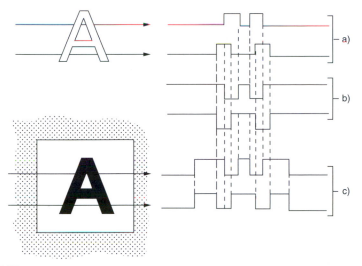

FIGURE 5.23

Elementary character generation. (a) White on black waveform for two raster lines passing through letter A. (b) Black on white is simple inversion. (c) Reverse video highlight waveforms.

In VDUs, there is no grey scale, and the characters are formed by changing the video signal between two levels at the appropriate place in the line. Figure 5.23 shows how a character is built up in this way and also illustrates how easy it is to obtain the reversed video used in some word processor displays to simulate dark characters on white paper. Also shown is the method of highlighting single characters or words by using localized reverse video.

Figure 5.24 is a representative character generator, as might be used in a VDU. The characters to be displayed are stored as ASCII symbols in a RAM, which has one location for each character position on each available text line on the screen. Each character must be used to generate a series of dots on the screen, which will extend over several lines. Typically the characters are formed by an array 5 dots by 9. To convert from the ASCII code to a dot pattern, a table is programmed with a conversion. This will be addressed by the ASCII character, and the column and row addresses in the character array, and will output a high or low (bright or dark) output.

As the VDU screen is a raster-scanned device, the display scan will begin at the lefthand end of the top line. The first character in the ASCII RAM will be selected, and this and the first row and column addresses will be sent to the

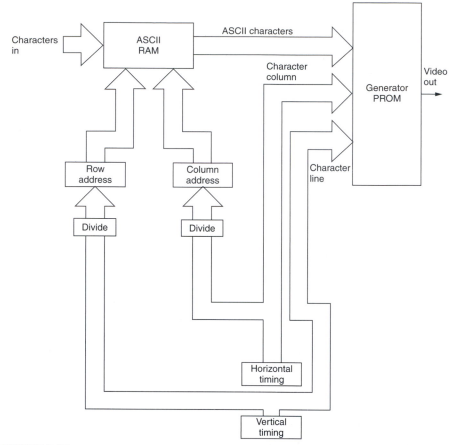

FIGURE 5.24
Simple character generator produces characters as rows and columns of pixels. See text for details.

character generator, which outputs the video level for the first pixel. The next column address will then be selected, and the next pixel will be output. As the scan proceeds, it will pass from the top line of the first character to the top line of the second character, so that the ASCII RAM address will need to be incremented. This process continues until the whole video line is completed. The next line on the screen is generated by repeating the selection of characters from the ASCII RAM, but using the second array line as the address to the character generator. This process will repeat until all the video lines needed to form one row of characters are complete. The next row of characters in the ASCII RAM can then be accessed to create the next line of text on the screen and so on.

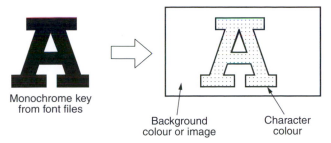

Monochrome key
from font files

Background
colour or image

Character
colour

FIGURE 5.25
Font characters store only the shape of the character. This can be used to key any
coloured character into a background.

High-quality broadcast graphics requires further complexity. The characters will
be needed in colour and in varying sizes. Different fonts will be necessary, and
additional features such as solid lines around characters and drop shadows are
desirable.

To generate a character in a broadcast machine, a font and the character within
that font are selected. The characters are actually stored as key signals, because
the only difference between one character and another in the same font is the
shape. A character is generated by specifying a constant background colour and
luminance, and a constant character colour and luminance, and by using the
key signal to cut a hole in the background and insert the character colour. This
is illustrated in Figure 5.25. The problem of stepped diagonal edges is overcome by giving the key signal a grey scale. The grey scale eliminates the quantizing distortion responsible for the stepped edges. The edge of the character
now takes the form of a ramp, which has the desirable characteristic of limiting the bandwidth of the character generator output. Early character generators
were notorious for producing out-of-band frequencies, which drove equipment
further down the line to distraction and in some cases would interfere with the
sound channel on being broadcast. Figure 5.26 illustrates how, in a system with
grey scale and sloped edges, the edge of a character can be positioned to subpixel resolution, which completely removes the stepped effect on diagonals.

In a powerful system, the number of fonts available will be large, and all the
necessary characters will be stored on disk drives. Some systems allow users to
enter their own fonts using a rostrum camera. A frame grab is performed, but
the system can be told to file the image as a font character key signal rather than
as a still frame. This approach allows infinite flexibility if it is desired to work
in Kanji or Cyrillic and allows European graphics to be done with all necessary umlauts, tildes, and cedillas.

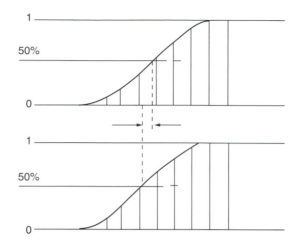

FIGURE 5.26
When a character has a ramped edge, the edge position can be moved in subpixel steps by changing the pixel values in the ramp.

To create a character string on the screen, it is necessary to produce a key signal that has been assembled from all the individual character keys. The keys are usually stored in a large format to give highest quality, and it will be necessary to reduce the size of the characters to fit the available screen area. The size reduction of a key signal in the digital domain is exactly the same as the zoom function of an effects machine, requiring FIR filtering and interpolation, but again, it is not necessary for it to be done in real time, and so less hardware can be used. The key source for the generation of the final video output is a RAM that has one location for every screen pixel. Position of the characters on the screen is controlled by changing the addresses in the key RAM into which the size-reduced character keys are written.

The keying system necessary is shown in Figure 5.27. The character colour and the background colour are produced by latches on the control system bus, which output continuous digital parameters. The grey-scale key signal obtained by scanning the key memory is used to provide coefficients for the digital cross-fader, which cuts between background and character colour to assemble the video signal in real time.

If characters with contrasting edges are required, an extra stage of keying can be used. The steps described above take place, but the background colour is replaced by the desired character edge colour. The size of each character key is then increased slightly, and the new key signal is used to cut the characters and a contrasting border into the final background.

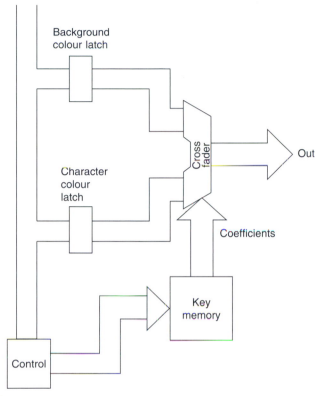

FIGURE 5.27
Simple character generator using keying. See text for details.

Early character generators were based on a frame store, which refreshes the dynamic output video. Recent devices abandon the frame-store approach in favour of real-time synthesis. The symbols that make up a word can move on and turn with respect to the plane in which they reside as a function of time in any way, individually or together. Text can also be mapped onto an arbitrarily shaped line. The angle of the characters can follow a tangent to the line or can remain at a fixed angle regardless of the line angle.

By controlling the size of planes, characters or words can appear to zoom into view from a distance and recede again. Rotation of the character planes off the plane of the screen allows the perspective effects to be seen. Rotating a plane back about a horizontal axis by 90° will reduce it to an edge-on line, but lowering the plane to the bottom of the screen allows the top surface to be seen, receding into the distance like a road. Characters or text strings can then roll off into the distance, getting smaller as they go. In fact the planes do not rotate, but a perspective transform is performed on them.

CONVERTING BETWEEN COMPUTER AND VIDEO FORMATS

Computer terminals have evolved quite rapidly from devices that could display only a few lines of text in monochrome into high-resolution colour graphics displays that outperform conventional television. The domains of computer graphics and television have in common only that images are represented. The degree of incompatibility is such that one could be forgiven for thinking that it was the outcome of a perverse competition. Nevertheless with sufficient care good results can be obtained. Figure 5.28 shows that the number of issues involved is quite large. If only one of these is not correctly addressed, the results will be disappointing. The number of processes also suggests that each must be performed with adequate precision, otherwise there will be a tolerance buildup or generation loss problem.

Figure 5.29 shows a typical graphics card. The pixel values to be displayed are written into a frame store by the CPU and the display mechanism reads the frame store line by line to produce a raster scanned image. Pixel array sizes are described as *x* by *y* pixels and these have been subject to much greater variation than has been the case in television. Figure 5.30 shows some of the array sizes supported in graphics devices. Note that datacine frame sizes eclipse these examples. As computer screens tend to be used in brighter ambient

| Colour primaries |
| Gamma |
| Digital gamut |
| Pixel aspect ratio |
| Interlace/progressive |
| Picture aspect ratio |
| Picture rate |

FIGURE 5.28
The various issues involved in converting between broadcast video and computer graphics formats. The problem is non-trivial but failure to address any one of these aspects will result in impairment.

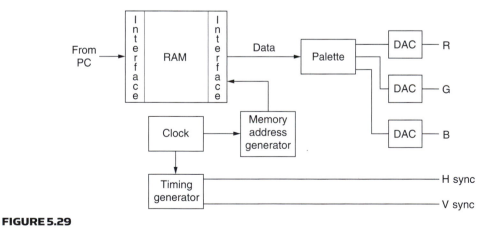

FIGURE 5.29
A typical computer graphics card. See text for details.

light than television screens, the displays have to be brighter and this makes flicker more visible. This can be overcome by running at a frame rate of 75 Hz or more.

A typical graphics card outputs analog RGB, which can drive a CRT or more recent type of display. The analog outputs are provided by 8-bit DACs. Figure 5.31 shows the standard IBM graphics connector. To avoid storing 24 bits per pixel, some systems restrict the number of different colours that can be displayed at once. Between the frame store and the DACs is a device called a palette or Colour Look Up Table (CLUT). This can be preloaded with a range of colours that are appropriate for the image to be displayed. Whilst this is adequate for general-purpose computing, it is unsuitable for quality image portrayal.

Computer graphics takes a somewhat more casual view of gamma than does television. This may be due to the fact that early computer displays had no grey scale and simply produced binary video (black or white),

$$320 \times 200$$
$$320 \times 350$$
$$360 \times 400$$
$$640 \times 200$$
$$720 \times 400$$
$$720 \times 350$$
$$640 \times 350$$
$$640 \times 400$$
$$640 \times 480$$
$$640 \times 473$$
$$800 \times 600$$
$$1056 \times 350$$
$$1056 \times 480$$
$$1056 \times 473$$
$$1118 \times 350$$
$$1118 \times 480$$
$$1118 \times 473$$
$$1024 \times 768$$

FIGURE 5.30
The array sizes that may be found in computer graphics.

Pin

1 Red
2 Green
3 Blue
4 N/C
5 Ground
6 Red return
7 Green return
8 Blue return
9 Key pin
10 Sync return
11 Monitor ID (not used)
12 Ground if monochrome monitor
13 H sync
14 V sync
15 N/C

FIGURE 5.31
The standard IBM graphics connector and its associated signals.

in which linearity has no meaning. As computer graphics became more sophisticated, each pixel became a binary number and a grey scale was possible. The gamma of the CRT display was simply compensated by an inverse gamma lookup table (LUT) prior to the video DAC as shown in Figure 5.32a. This approach means that the pixel data within the computer are in the linear light domain. This in itself is not a problem, but when linear light is represented by only 8-bit pixels, then contouring in dark areas is inevitable. Linear light needs to be expressed by around 14 bits for adequate resolution, as was seen in Chapter 2. To improve the situation, certain manufacturers moved away from the linear light domain, but without going as far as conventional television practice. The solution was that the internal data would be subject to a partial inverse gamma, as shown in Figure 5.32b, followed by a further partial inverse gamma stage in the LUT of the graphics card. The combined effect of the two inverse gammas was correctly to oppose the display gamma.

Unfortunately Silicon Graphics and Macintosh came up with systems in which the two gamma stages were completely incompatible, even though the overall result in both cases is correct. Data from one format cannot be displayed on the other format (or as video) without gamma conversion. In the absence of gamma conversion the grey scale will be non-linear, crushing either dark areas or light areas depending on the direction of data transfer. Gamma conversion is relatively straightforward, as a simple lookup table can be created with 8-bit data. Whatever the direction of conversion, one of the formats involved is likely to be RGB. It is useful if this is made the internal format of the conversion. Figure 5.33 shows that if the input is colour-difference based, conversion should be done early, whereas if the output is to be colour-difference based, the conversion should be done late. It is also worth considering the use of the linear light domain and suitably long word length within the conversion process. This overcomes any quality loss due to failure of constant luminance and distortion due to interpolating gamma-based signals. Figure 5.34 shows the principle. The gamma of the input format is reversed at the input

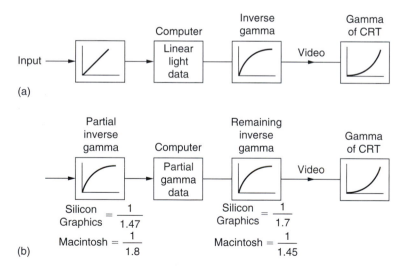

FIGURE 5.32
Computers and gamma: a dog's dinner. (a) A simple system uses linear light-coding internals and an inverse gamma LUT prior to the CRT. With only 8-bit data this suffers excessive quantizing error.
(b) Improved performance is obtained by having partial inverse gamma internal data in tandem with a further partial inverse gamma prior to the CRT. Unfortunately there are two conflicting incompatible standards.

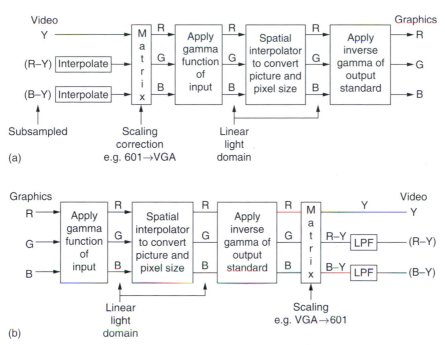

FIGURE 5.33
Possible strategies for video/computer conversion. (a) Video to graphics RGB. (b) Graphics RGB to video.

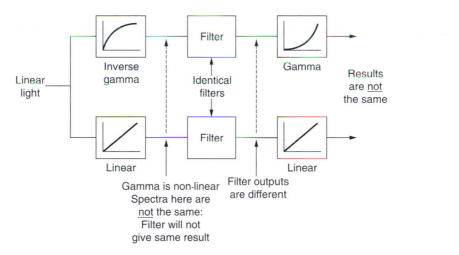

FIGURE 5.34
Gamma is a compression technique and for the finest results it should not be used in any image-manipulation process because the result will be distorted. Accurate work should be done in the linear light domain.

and the gamma of the output format is re-created after all other processing is complete. Gamma in television signals generally follows a single standard, whereas with a computer format it will be necessary to establish exactly what gamma was assumed.

Computer formats tend to use the entire number scale from black to white, such that in 8-bit systems black is 00Hex and white is FF. However, television signals according to ITU-601 have some head room above white and foot room below black. If in gamma head room and foot room conversion is not properly performed, the result will be black crushing, white crushing, lack of contrast, or a distorted grey scale.

Colorimetry may be a problem in conversion. Television signals generally abide by ITU-709 colorimetry, whereas computer graphic files could use almost any set of primaries. It is not unusual for computer screens to run at relatively high colour temperatures to give brighter pictures. If the primaries are known, then it is possible to convert between colour spaces using matrix arithmetic. Figure 5.35 shows that if two triangles are created on the chromaticity diagram, one for each set of primaries, then wherever the triangles overlap, ideal conversion is possible. In the case of colours in which there is no overlap the best that can be done is to produce the correct hue by calculating the correct vector from the white point, even if the saturation is incorrect. When the colorimetry is not known, accurate conversion is impossible. However, in practice acceptable results can be obtained by adjusting the primary gains to achieve an acceptable colour balance on a recognizable part of the image, such as a white area or a flesh tone.

The image size or pixel count will be different and, with the exception of recent formats, the television signal will be interlaced and will not necessarily use square pixels. Spatial interpolation will be needed to move between pixel array sizes and pixel aspect ratios. The frame rate may also be different. The best results will be obtained using motion compensation. If both formats are progressively scanned, resizing and rate conversion are separable, but if interlace is involved the problem is not separable and resizing and rate conversion should be done simultaneously in a three-dimensional filter.

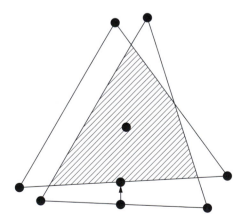

FIGURE 5.35
Conversion between colour spaces works only where the areas enclosed by the primary triangles overlap (shaded). Outside these areas the best that can be done is to keep the hue correct by accepting a saturation error.

GRAPHIC ART/PAINT SYSTEMS

In graphic art systems, there is a requirement for disk storage of the generated images, and some art machines incorporate a still store unit, whereas others can be connected to a separate one by an interface. Disk-based stores are discussed in Chapter 9. The essence of an art system is that an artist can draw images that become a video signal directly with no intermediate paper and paint. Central to the operation of most art systems is a digitizing tablet, which is a flat surface over which the operator draws a stylus. The tablet can establish the position of the stylus in vertical and horizontal axes. One way in which this can be done is to launch ultrasonic pulses down the tablet, which are detected by a transducer in the stylus. The time taken to receive the pulse is proportional to the distance to the stylus. The coordinates of the stylus are converted to addresses in the frame store that correspond to the same physical position on the screen. To make a simple sketch, the operator specifies a background parameter, perhaps white, which would be loaded into every location in the frame store. A different parameter is then written into every location addressed by movement of the stylus, which results in a line drawing on the screen. The art world uses pens and brushes of different shapes and sizes to obtain a variety of effects, one common example being the rectangular pen nib, in which the width of the resulting line depends on the angle at which the pen is moved. This can be simulated on art systems, because the address derived from the tablet is processed to produce a range of addresses within a certain screen distance of the stylus. If all these locations are updated as the stylus moves, a broad stroke results.

If the address range is larger in the horizontal axis than in the vertical axis, for example, the width of the stroke will be a function of the direction of stylus travel. Some systems have a sprung tip on the stylus that connects to a force transducer, so that the system can measure the pressure the operator uses. By making the address range a function of pressure, broader strokes can be obtained simply by pressing harder. To simulate a set of colours available on a palette, the operator can select a mode in which small areas of each colour are displayed in boxes on the monitor screen. The desired colour is selected by moving a screen cursor over the box using the tablet. The parameter to be written into selected locations in the frame RAM now reflects the chosen colour. In more advanced systems, simulation of airbrushing is possible. In this technique, the transparency of the stroke is great at the edge, where the background can be seen showing through, but transparency reduces to the centre of the stroke. A read–modify–write process is necessary in the frame memory, in which background values are read, mixed with paint values with the appropriate transparency, and written back. The position of the stylus effectively determines the centre of a two-dimensional transparency contour, which is convolved with the memory contents as the stylus moves.

LINEAR AND NON-LINEAR EDITING

The term "editing" covers a multitude of possibilities in video production. Simple video editors work in two basic ways, by assembling or by inserting sections of material or clips comprising a whole number of frames to build the finished work. Assembly begins with a blank master recording. The beginning of the work is copied from the source, and new material is successively appended to the end of the previous material. Figure 5.36 shows how a master recording is made up by assembly from source recordings. Insert editing begins with an existing recording in which a section is replaced by the edit process.

At its most general, editing is subdivided into horizontal editing, which refers to any changes with respect to the time axis, and vertical editing,[7] which is the generic term for processes taking place on an imaginary z axis running back into the screen. These include keying, dissolves, wipes, layering, and so on.[8] DVEs may also be used for editing, where a page turn or rotate effect reveals a new scene.

In all types of editing the goal is the appropriate sequence of material at the appropriate time. The first type of picture editing was done physically by cutting and splicing film, to assemble the finished work mechanically. This approach was copied on early quadruplex video recorders, a difficult and

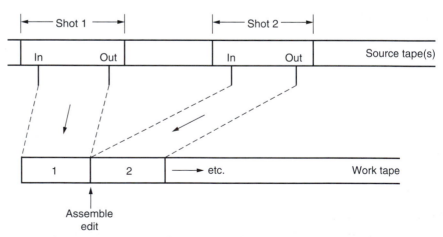

FIGURE 5.36
Assembly is the most basic form of editing, in which source clips are sequentially added to the end of a recording.

laborious process. This gave way to electronic editing on VTRs, in which lengths of source tape were copied to the master. Once the speed and capacity of disk drives became sufficient, it was obvious that they would ultimately take over as editing media as soon as they became economical.

When video tape was the only way of editing, it did not need a qualifying name. Now that video is stored as data, alternative storage media have become available, which allow editors to reach the same goal but using different techniques. Whilst digital VTR formats copy their analog predecessors and support field-accurate editing on the tape itself, in all other digital editing, pixels from various sources are brought from the storage media to various pages of RAM. The edit is previewed by selectively processing two (or more) sample streams retrieved from RAM. Once the edit is satisfactory it may subsequently be written on an output medium. Thus the nature of the storage medium does not affect the form of the edit in any way except for the amount of time needed to execute it.

Tapes allow only serial or linear access to data, whereas disks and RAM allow random access and so can be much faster. Editing using random access storage devices is very powerful as the shuttling of tape reels is avoided. The technique is called non-linear editing. This is not a very helpful name, as all editing is non-linear. In fact it is only the time axis of the storage medium that is non-linear.

ONLINE AND OFFLINE EDITING

In many workstations, compression is employed, and the appropriate coding and decoding logic will be required adjacent to the inputs and outputs. With mild compression, the video quality of the machine may be used directly for some purposes. This is known as online editing and this may be employed for the creation of news programs. Alternatively a high compression factor may be used, and the editor is then used only to create an edit decision list (EDL). This is known as offline editing. The EDL is subsequently used to control automatic editing of the full-bandwidth source material, possibly on tape. The full-bandwidth material is conformed to the edit decisions taken on the compressed material.

One of the advantages of offline editing is that the use of compression in the images seen by the editor reduces the bandwidth/bit rate requirement between the hardware and the control panel. Consequently it becomes possible for editing to be performed remotely. The high-resolution images on a central file server can be conformed locally to an EDL created by viewing compressed images in any location that has Internet access.

DIGITAL FILMMAKING

The power of non-linear editing can be applied to filmmaking as well as to video production. There are various levels at which this can operate. Figure 5.37 shows the simplest level. Here the filming takes place as usual, and after development the uncut film is transferred to video using a telecine or datacine machine. The data are also compressed and stored on a disk-based workstation. The workstation is used to make all the edit decisions and these are stored as an EDL. This will be sent to the film laboratory to control the film cutting.

In Figure 5.38 a more sophisticated process is employed. Here the film camera viewfinder is replaced with a video camera so that a video signal is available

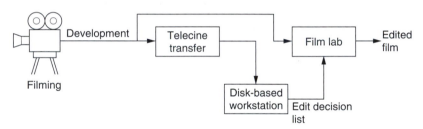

FIGURE 5.37
Films can be edited more quickly by transferring the uncut film to video and then to disk-based storage.

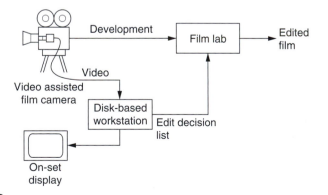

FIGURE 5.38
With a modified film camera that can also output video, the editing can begin before the film is developed.

TIMECODE

Timecode is essential to editing, as many different processes occur during an edit, and each one is programmed beforehand to take place at a given timecode value. Provision of a timecode reference effectively synchronises the processes.

SMPTE standard timecode for 525/60 use is shown in Figure 5.39. EBU timecode is basically similar to SMPTE except that the frame count will reach a lower value in each second. These store hours, minutes, seconds, and frames as binary-coded decimal (BCD) numbers, which are serially encoded along with user bits into an FM channel code (see Chapter 8), which is recorded on one of the linear audio tracks of the tape. The user bits are not specified in the standard, but a common use is to record the take or session number. Disks also use timecode for synchronisation, but the timecode forms part of the file structure so that frames of data may be retrieved by specifying the required timecode.

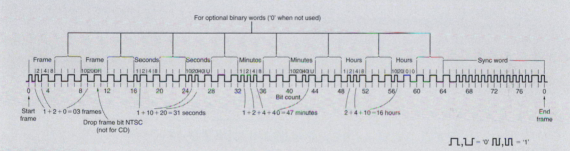

FIGURE 5.39
In SMPTE standard timecode, the frame number and time are stored as eight BCD symbols. There is also space for 32 user-defined bits. The code repeats every frame. Note the asymmetrical sync word, which allows the direction of media movement to be determined.

during filming. This can be recorded on disk so that an immediate replay is available following each take. In the event that a retake is needed, the film need not be developed, reducing costs. Edit decisions can be taken before the film has been developed.

In some cases the disk database can be extended to include the assistant's notes and the film dialog. The editor can search for an edit point by having the system search for a text string. The display would then show a mosaic of all frames in which that dialog was spoken.

The complex special effects seen on modern films can be performed only in the digital domain. In this case the film is converted to data in a datacine and all production is then done by manipulating that data. The extremely high pixel counts used in digital film result in phenomenal amounts of data and it is common to use adapted broadcast DVTR formats to store it economically. After production the digital images are transferred back to release prints.

Ultimately films may be made entirely electronically. When cameras of sufficient resolution and dynamic range become available, the cost of storage will be such that filming will be replaced by a direct camera-to-disk transfer. The production process will consist entirely of digital signal-processing steps, resulting in a movie in the shape of a large data file. One of the present difficulties with electronic film production is the small physical size of CCD sensors in comparison with the traditional film frame, which makes controlled depth of focus difficult to achieve.

Digital films can be distributed to the cinema via copper or fibre-optic link, using encryption to prevent piracy and mild compression for economy. At the cinema the signal would be stored on a file server. Projection would then consist of accessing the data, decrypting, decoding the compression, and delivering the data to a digital projector. This technology will change the nature of the traditional cinema out of recognition.

THE NON-LINEAR WORKSTATION

Figure 5.40 shows the general arrangement of a hard-disk-based workstation. The graphic display in such devices has a screen that is a montage of many different signals, each of which appears in a window. In addition to the video windows there will be a number of alphanumeric and graphic display areas required by the control system. There will also be a cursor, which can be positioned by a trackball or mouse. The screen is refreshed by a frame store, which is read at the screen refresh rate. The frame store can be written by various processes simultaneously to produce a windowed image. In addition to the graphic display, there may be one or more further screens that reproduce full-size images for preview purposes.

A master timing generator provides reference signals to synchronise the internal processes. This also produces an external reference to which source devices such as VTRs can lock. The timing generator may free-run in a standalone system or genlock to station reference to allow playout to air.

Digital inputs and outputs are provided, along with optional convertors to allow working in an analog environment. A compression process will generally be employed to extend the playing time of the disk storage.

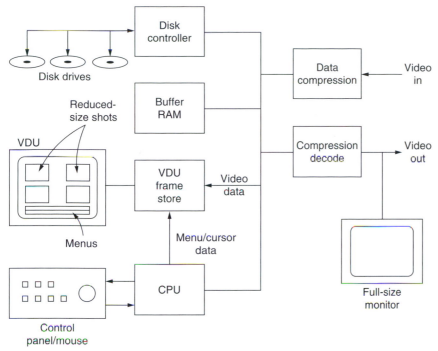

FIGURE 5.40
A hard-disk-based workstation. Note the screen, which can display numerous clips at the same time.

Disk-based workstations fall into several categories depending on the relative emphasis of the vertical or horizontal aspects of the process. High-end postproduction emphasizes the vertical aspect of the editing, as a large number of layers may be used to create the output image. The length of such productions is generally quite short and so disk capacity is not an issue and compression may not be employed. It is unlikely that such a machine would need to play out to air. In contrast, a general-purpose editor used for program production will emphasize the horizontal aspect of the task. Extended recording ability will be needed, and the use of compression is more likely. News-editing systems would emphasize speed and simplicity, such that the editing could be performed by journalists.

A typical machine will be based around a high-data-rate bus, connecting the I/O, RAM, disk server, and processor. If magnetic disks are used, these will be Winchester types, because they offer the largest capacity. Exchangeable magneto-optic disks may also be supported.

Before any editing can be performed, it is necessary to have source material online. If the source material exists on MO disks with the appropriate file structure, these may be used directly. Otherwise it will be necessary to input the material in real time and record it on magnetic disks via the data-reduction system. In addition to recording the data-reduced source video, reduced-size versions of each frame that are suitable for the screen windows may also be recorded.

LOCATING THE EDIT POINT

Digital editors simulate the "rock and roll" process of edit-point location originally used in VTRs, in which the tape is moved to and fro by the action of a jog wheel or joystick. Whilst DVTRs with track-following systems can work in this way, disks cannot. Disk drives transfer data intermittently and not necessarily in real time. The solution is to transfer the recording in the area of the edit point to RAM in the editor. RAM access can take place at any speed or direction and the precise edit point can then conveniently be found by monitoring signals from the RAM. In a window-based display, a source recording is attributed to a particular window and will be reproduced within that window, with time-code displayed adjacently.

Figure 5.41 shows how the area of the edit point is transferred to the memory. The source device is commanded to play, and the operator watches the replay

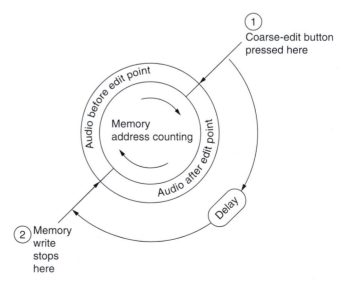

FIGURE 5.41
The use of a ring memory, which overwrites and allows storage of frames before and after the coarse edit point.

in the selected window. The same frames are continuously written into a memory within the editor. This memory is addressed by a counter, which repeatedly overflows to give the memory a ring-like structure rather like that of a time base corrector, but somewhat larger. When the operator sees the rough area in which the edit is required, he or she will press a button. This action stops the memory writing, not immediately, but one-half of the memory contents later. The effect is then that the memory contains an equal number of samples before and after the rough edit point. Once the recording is in the memory, it can be accessed at leisure, and the constraints of the source device play no further part in the edit-point location.

There are a number of ways in which the memory can be read. If the field address in memory is supplied by a counter that is clocked at the appropriate rate, the edit area can be replayed at normal speed, or at some fraction of normal speed, repeatedly. To simulate the analog method of finding an edit point, the operator is provided with a scrub wheel or rotor, and the memory field address will change at a rate proportional to the speed with which the rotor is turned and in the same direction. Thus the recording can be seen forward or backward at any speed, and the effect is exactly that of manually jogging an analog tape. The operation of a jog-wheel encoder was shown in Chapter 3 under Digital Faders and Controls.

If the position of the jog address pointer through the memory is compared with the addresses of the ends of the memory, it will be possible to anticipate that the pointer is about to reach the end of the memory. A disk transfer can be performed to fetch new data farther up the time axis, so that it is possible to jog an indefinite distance along the source recording. The user is never aware of the finite amount of memory between the storage device and the display. Data that will be used to make the master recording need never pass through these processes; they are solely to assist in the location of the edit points.

The act of pressing the coarse edit-point button stores the timecode of the source at that point, which is frame-accurate. As the rotor is turned, the memory address is monitored and used to update the timecode.

Before the edit can be performed, two edit points must be determined, the out-point at the end of the previously recorded signal and the in-point at the beginning of the new signal. The second edit point can be determined by moving the cursor to a different screen window in which video from a different source is displayed. The jog wheel will now roll this material to locate the second edit point whilst the first source video remains frozen in the deselected window.

The editor's microprocessor stores these in an EDL to control the automatic assemble process.

It is also possible to locate a rough edit point by typing in a previously noted timecode, and the image in the window will automatically jump to that time. In some systems, in addition to recording video and audio, there may also be text files locked to timecode that contain the dialog. Using these systems one can allocate a textual dialog display to a further window and scroll down the dialog or search for a key phrase as in a word processor. Unlike a word processor, the timecode pointer from the text access is used to jog the video window. As a result an edit point can be located in the video if the actor's lines at the desired point are known.

PERFORMING THE EDIT

Using one or other of the above methods, an edit list can be made that contains an in-point, an out-point, and a filename for each of the segments of video that need to be assembled to make the final work, along with a time-code-referenced transition command and period for the vision mixer. This edit list will also be stored on the disk. When a preview of the edited work is required, the edit list is used to determine what files will be necessary and when, and this information drives the disk controller.

Figure 5.42 shows the events during an edit between two files. The edit list causes the relevant blocks from the first file to be transferred from disk to memory, and these will be read by the signal processor to produce the preview output. As the edit point approaches, the disk controller will also place blocks from the incoming file into the memory. In different areas of the memory there will simultaneously be the end of the outgoing recording and the beginning of the incoming recording. Before the edit point, only pixels from the outgoing recording are accessed, but as the transition begins, pixels from the incoming recording are also accessed, and for a time both data streams will be input to the vision mixer according to the transition period required.

The output of the signal processor becomes the edited preview material, which can be checked for the required subjective effect. If necessary the in- or out-point can be trimmed, or the cross-fade period changed, simply by modifying the edit-list file. The preview can be repeated as often as needed, until the desired effect is obtained. At this stage the edited work does not exist as a file, but is re-created each time by a further execution of the EDL. Thus a lengthy editing session need not fill up the disks.

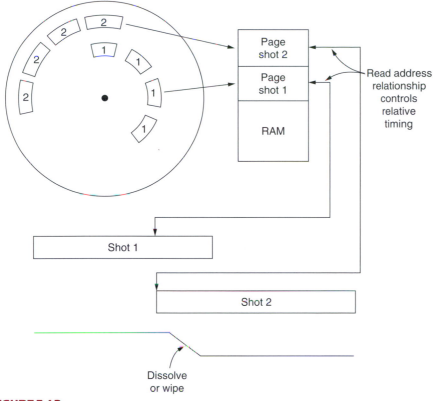

FIGURE 5.42
Sequence of events for a hard-disk edit. See text for details.

It is important to realize that at no time during the edit process were the original files modified in any way. The editing was done solely by reading the files. The power of this approach is that if an edit list is created wrongly, the original recording is not damaged, and the problem can be put right simply by correcting the edit list. The advantage of a disk-based system for such work is that location of edit points, previews, and reviews are all performed almost instantaneously, because of the random access of the disk. This can reduce the time taken to edit a program to a fraction of that needed with a tape machine.

During an edit, the disk controller has to provide data from two different files simultaneously, and so it has to work much harder than for a simple playback. If there are many close-spaced edits, the controller and drives may be hard-pressed to keep ahead of real time, especially if there are long transitions, because during a transition a vertical edit is taking place between two video signals and the source data rate is twice as great as during replay. A large buffer memory helps this situation because the drive can fill the memory with files before the edit actually begins, and thus the instantaneous sample rate can be met by allowing the memory to empty during disk-intensive periods.

Disk formats that handle defects dynamically, such as defect skipping, will also be superior to bad-block files when throughput is important. Some drives rotate the sector addressing from one cylinder to the next so that the drive does not lose a revolution when it moves to the next cylinder. Disk-editor performance is usually specified in terms of peak editing activity that can be achieved, but with a recovery period between edits. If an unusually severe editing task is necessary for which the drive just cannot access files fast enough, it will be necessary to rearrange the files on the disk surface so that the files that will be needed at the same time are on nearby cylinders.[8] An alternative is to spread the material between two or more drives so that overlapped seeks are possible.

Once the editing is finished, it will generally be necessary to transfer the edited material to form a contiguous recording so that the source files can make way for new work. If the source files already exist on tape the disk files can simply be erased. If the disks hold original recordings they will need to be backed up to tape if they will be required again. In large broadcast systems, the edited work can be broadcast directly from the disk file server. In smaller systems it will be necessary to output to some removable medium, because the Winchester drives in the editor have fixed media.

APPLICATIONS OF MOTION COMPENSATION

In Chapter 2, the section Motion Portrayal and Dynamic Resolution introduced the concept of eye tracking and the optic flow axis. The optic flow axis is the locus of some point on a moving object that will be in a different place in successive pictures. Any device that computes with respect to the optic flow axis is said to be motion compensated. Until recently the amount of computation required in motion compensation was too expensive, but now that this is no longer the case the technology has become very important in moving-image portrayal systems.

Figure 5.43a shows an example of a moving object that is in a different place in each of three pictures. The optic flow axis is shown. The object is not moving with respect to the optic flow axis and if this axis can be found some

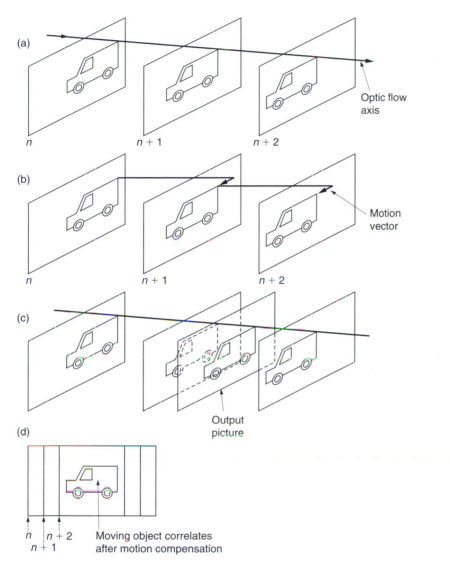

(a)

Optic flow
axis

n $n+1$ $n+2$

(b)

Motion
vector

n $n+1$ $n+2$

(c)

Output
picture

(d)

n $n+2$ Moving object correlates
$n+1$ after motion compensation

FIGURE 5.43

Motion compensation is an important technology. (a) The optic flow axis is found
for a moving object. (b) The object in pictures $(n+1)$ and $(n+2)$ can be re-created
by shifting the object of picture n using motion vectors. MPEG uses this process
for compression. (c) A standards convertor creates a picture on a new time base by
shifting object data along the optic flow axis. (d) With motion compensation a moving
object can still correlate from one picture to the next so that noise reduction is possible.

very useful results are obtained. The process of finding the optic flow axis is called motion estimation. Motion estimation is literally a process that analyses successive pictures and determines how objects move from one to the next. It is an important enabling technology because of the way it parallels the action of the human eye.

Figure 5.43b shows that if the object does not change its appearance as it moves, it can be portrayed in two of the pictures by using data from one picture only, simply by shifting part of the picture to a new location. This can be done using vectors as shown. Instead of transmitting a lot of pixel data, a few vectors are sent instead. This is the basis of motion-compensated compression, which is used extensively in MPEG as will be seen in Chapter 6.

Figure 5.43c shows that if a high-quality standards conversion is required between two different frame rates, the output frames can be synthesized by moving-image data, not through time but along the optic flow axis. This locates objects where they would have been if frames had been sensed at those times, and the result is a judder-free conversion. This process can be extended to drive image displays at a frame rate higher than the input rate so that flicker and background strobing are reduced. This technology is available in certain high-quality consumer television sets.

Attempts to use this approach to eliminate judder from 24 Hz film have not been successful. It appears that at this very low frame rate there is simply insufficient motion information available.

Figure 5.43d shows that noise reduction relies on averaging two or more images so that the images add but the noise cancels. Conventional noise reducers fail in the presence of motion, but if the averaging process takes place along the optic flow axis, noise reduction can continue to operate.

The way in which eye tracking avoids aliasing is fundamental to the perceived quality of television pictures. Many processes need to manipulate moving images in the same way to avoid the obvious difficulty of processing with respect to a fixed frame of reference. Processes of this kind are referred to as motion compensated and rely on a quite separate process that has measured the motion.

Motion compensation is also important when interlaced video needs to be processed as it allows de-interlacing with the smallest number of artifacts.

MOTION-ESTIMATION TECHNIQUES

There are three main methods of motion estimation, which are to be found in various applications: block matching, gradient matching, and phase correlation. Each has its own characteristics, which are quite different from those of the others.

BLOCK MATCHING

This is the simplest technique to follow. In a given picture, a block of pixels is selected and stored as a reference. If the selected block is part of a moving object, a similar block of pixels will exist in the next picture, but not in the same place. As Figure 5.44 shows, block matching simply moves the reference block around over the second picture looking for matching pixel values. When a match is found, the displacement needed to obtain it is used as a basis for a motion vector.

Whilst simple in concept, block matching requires an enormous amount of computation because every possible motion must be tested over the assumed range. Thus if the object is assumed to have moved over a 16-pixel range, then it will be necessary to test 16 different horizontal displacements in each of 16 vertical positions, in excess of 65,000 positions. At each position every pixel in the block must be compared with every pixel in the second picture. In a typical video, displacements of twice the figure quoted here may be found, particularly for sporting events, and the computation then required becomes enormous. If the motion is required to subpixel accuracy, then before any matching can be attempted the picture will need to be interpolated, requiring further computation.

One way of reducing the amount of computation is to perform the matching in stages of which the first stage is inaccurate but covers a large motion range and the last stage is accurate but covers a small range. The first matching stage is performed on a heavily filtered and subsampled picture, which contains far fewer pixels.

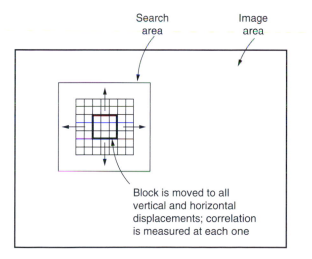

Search area

Image area

Block is moved to all vertical and horizontal displacements; correlation is measured at each one

FIGURE 5.44
In block matching the search block has to be positioned at all possible relative motions within the search area and a correlation measured at each one.

When a match is found, the displacement is used as a basis for a second stage, which is performed with a less heavily filtered picture. Eventually the last stage takes place to any desired accuracy, including subpixel. This hierarchical approach does reduce the computation required, but it suffers from the problem that the filtering of the first stage may make small objects disappear and they can never be found by subsequent stages if they are moving with respect to their background. This is not a problem for compression, because a prediction error will provide the missing detail, but it is an issue for standards convertors, which require more accurate motion than compressors. Many televised sports events contain small, fast-moving objects. As the matching process depends upon finding similar luminance values, this can be confused by objects moving into shade or fades.

GRADIENT MATCHING

At some point in a picture, the function of brightness with respect to distance across the screen will have a certain slope, known as the spatial luminance gradient. If the associated picture area is moving, the slope will traverse a fixed point on the screen and the result will be that the brightness now changes with respect to time. This is a temporal luminance gradient. Figure 5.45 shows the principle. For a given spatial gradient, the temporal gradient becomes steeper as the speed of movement increases. Thus motion speed can be estimated from the ratio of the spatial and temporal gradients.[9]

In practice this is difficult because there are numerous processes that can change the luminance gradient. When an object moves so as to obscure or reveal the background, the spatial gradient will change from field to field even if the motion is constant. Variations in illumination, such as when an object moves into shade, also cause difficulty. The process can be assisted by recursion, in which the motion in a current picture is predicted by extrapolating the optic flow axis from earlier pictures, but this will result in problems at cuts.

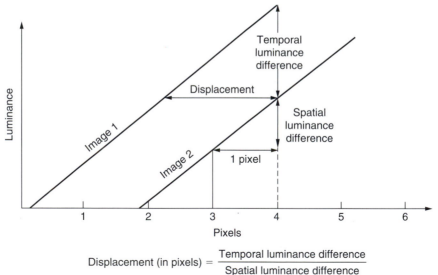

$$\text{Displacement (in pixels)} = \frac{\text{Temporal luminance difference}}{\text{Spatial luminance difference}}$$

FIGURE 5.45
The principle of gradient matching. The luminance gradient across the screen is compared with that through time.

PHASE CORRELATION

Phase correlation works by performing a discrete Fourier transform on two successive fields and then subtracting all the phases of the spectral components. The phase differences are then subject to a reverse transform, which directly reveals peaks whose positions correspond to motions between the fields.[10,11] The nature of the transform domain means that if the distance and direction of the motion is measured accurately, the area of the screen in which it took place is not. Thus in practical systems the phase-correlation stage is followed by a matching stage not dissimilar to the block-matching process. However, the matching process is steered by the motions from the phase correlation, and so there is no need to attempt to match at all possible motions. By attempting matching on measured motion the overall process is made much more efficient.

One way of considering phase correlation is that by using the Fourier transform to break the picture into its constituent spatial frequencies the hierarchical structure of block matching at various resolutions is in fact performed in parallel. In this way small objects are not missed because they will generate high-frequency components in the transform.

Although the matching process is simplified by adopting phase correlation, the Fourier transforms themselves require complex calculations. The high performance of phase correlation would remain academic if it were too complex to put into practice. However, if realistic values are used for the motion speeds that can be handled, the computation required by block matching actually exceeds that required for phase correlation. The elimination of amplitude information from the phase correlation process ensures that motion estimation continues to work in the case of fades, objects moving into shade, or flashguns firing.

The details of the Fourier transform are described in Chapter 3. A one-dimensional example of phase correlation will be given here by way of introduction. A line of luminance, which in the digital domain consists of a series of samples, is a function of brightness with respect to distance across the screen. The Fourier transform converts this function into a spectrum of spatial frequencies (units of cycles per picture width) and phases.

All television signals must be handled in linear-phase systems. A linear-phase system is one in which the delay experienced is the same for all frequencies. If video signals pass through a device that does not exhibit linear phase, the various frequency components of edges become displaced across the screen.

Figure 5.46 shows what phase linearity means. If the left-hand end of the frequency axis (DC) is considered to be firmly anchored, but the right-hand end can be rotated to represent a change of position across the screen, it will be seen that as the axis twists evenly the result is phase shift proportional to frequency. A system having this characteristic is said to display linear phase.

In the spatial domain, a phase shift corresponds to a physical movement. Figure 5.47 shows that if between fields a waveform moves along the line, the lowest frequency in the Fourier transform will suffer a given phase shift, twice that frequency will suffer twice that phase shift, and so on. Thus it is potentially possible to measure movement between two successive fields if the phase differences between the Fourier spectra are analysed. This is the basis of phase correlation.

Figure 5.48 shows how a one-dimensional phase correlator works. The Fourier transforms of two lines from successive fields are computed and expressed in polar (amplitude and phase) notation (see Chapter 3).

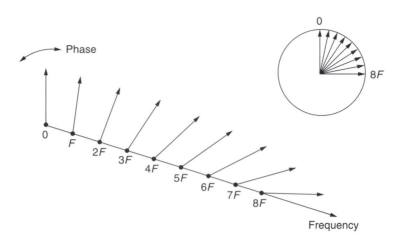

FIGURE 5.46
The definition of phase linearity is that phase shift is proportional to frequency. In phase-linear systems the waveform is preserved and simply moves in time or space.

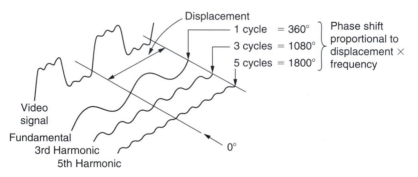

FIGURE 5.47
In a phase-linear system, shifting the video waveform across the screen causes phase shifts in each component proportional to frequency.

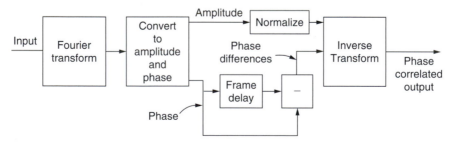

FIGURE 5.48
The basic components of a phase correlator.

The phases of one transform are all subtracted from the phases of the same frequencies in the other transform. Any frequency component having significant amplitude is then normalized, or boosted to full amplitude.

The result is a set of frequency components that all have the same amplitude, but have phases corresponding to the difference between two fields. These coefficients form the input to an inverse transform. Figure 5.49a shows what happens. If the two fields are the same, there are no phase differences between the two, and so all the frequency components are added with zero-degree phase to produce a single peak in the centre of the inverse transform. If, however, there was motion between the two fields, such as a pan, all the components will have phase differences, and this results in a peak shown in Figure 5.49b, which is displaced from the centre of the inverse transform by the distance moved. Phase correlation thus actually measures the movement between fields. In the case in which the line of video in question intersects objects moving at different speeds, Figure 5.49c shows that the inverse transform would contain one peak corresponding to the distance moved by each object.

Whilst this explanation has used one dimension for simplicity, in practice the entire process is two dimensional. A two-dimensional Fourier transform of each field is computed, the phases are subtracted, and an inverse two-dimensional transform is computed, the output of which is a flat plane out of which three-dimensional peaks rise. This is known as a correlation surface.

Figure 5.50 shows some examples of a correlation surface. In Figure 5.50a there has been no motion between fields and so there is a single central peak. In (b) there has been a pan and the peak moves across the surface. In (c) the camera has been depressed and the peak moves upward.

Where more complex motions are involved, perhaps with several objects moving in different directions and/or at different speeds, one peak will appear in the correlation surface for each object.

It is a fundamental strength of phase correlation that it actually measures the direction and speed of moving objects rather than estimating, extrapolating, or searching for them. The motion can be measured to subpixel accuracy. However, it should be understood that according to Heisenberg's uncertainty theorem, accuracy in the transform domain is incompatible with accuracy in the spatial domain. Although phase correlation accurately measures motion speeds and directions, it cannot specify where in the picture these motions are taking place. It is necessary to look for them in a further matching process. The efficiency of this process is dramatically improved by the inputs from the phase-correlation stage.

The input to a motion estimator for most applications consists of interlaced fields. The lines of one field lie between those of the next, making comparisons between them difficult. A further problem is that vertical spatial aliasing may exist in the fields. Preprocessing solves these problems by performing a two-dimensional spatial low-pass filtering operation on input fields. Alternate fields are also interpolated up or down by half a line using the techniques of Chapter 3 under Sampling-Rate Conversion, so that interlace disappears and all fields subsequently have the same sampling grid. The spatial frequency response in 625-line systems is filtered to 72 cycles per picture height. This is half the response possible from the number of lines in a field, but is necessary because subsequent correlation causes a frequency-doubling effect. The spatial filtering also cuts down the amount of computation required.

The computation needed to perform a two-dimensional Fourier transform increases dramatically with the size of the block employed, and so no attempt is made to transform the down-sampled fields directly. Instead the fields are converted into overlapping blocks by the use of window functions as shown in Figure 5.51. The size of the window controls the motion speed that can be handled, and so a window size is chosen that allows motion to be detected up to the limit of human judder visibility.

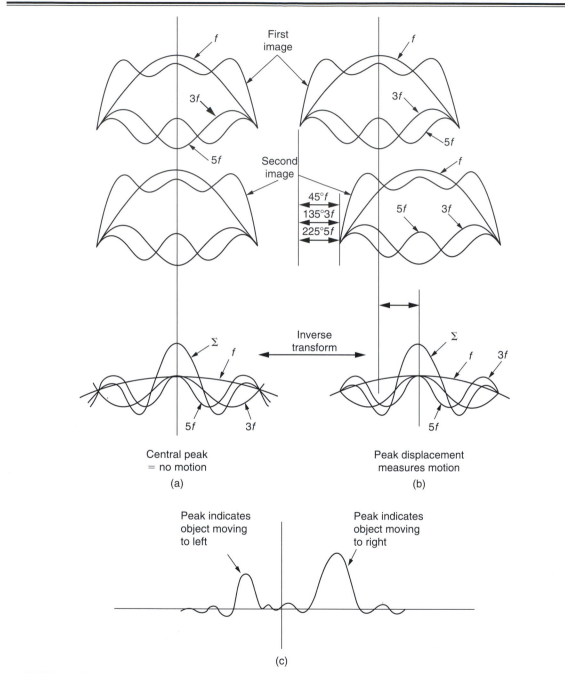

FIGURE 5.49

(a) The peak in the inverse transform is central for no motion. (b) In the case of motion, the peak shifts by the distance moved. (c) If there are several motions, each one results in a peak.

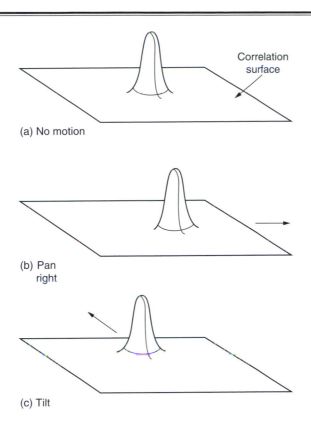

(a) No motion

(b) Pan right

(c) Tilt

FIGURE 5.50
(a) A two-dimensional correlation surface has a central peak when there is no motion. (b) In the case of a pan, the peak moves laterally. (c) A camera tilt moves the peak at right angles to the pan.

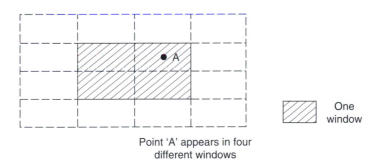

One window

Point 'A' appears in four different windows

FIGURE 5.51
The input fields are converted into overlapping windows. Each window is individually transformed.

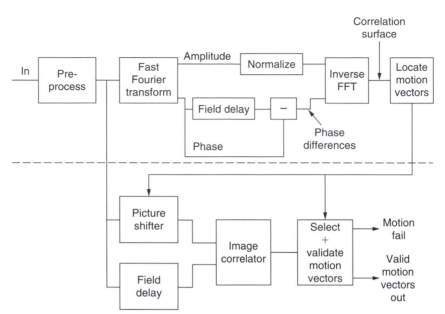

FIGURE 5.52
The block diagram of a phase-correlated motion estimator. See text for details.

Figure 5.52 shows a block diagram of a phase-correlated motion-estimation system. Following the preprocessing, each windowed block is subject to a fast Fourier transform (FFT), and the output spectrum is converted to the amplitude and phase representation. The phases are subtracted from those of the previous field in each window, and the amplitudes are normalized to eliminate any variations in illumination or the effect of fades from the motion sensing. A reverse transform is performed, which results in a correlation surface. The correlation surface contains peaks whose positions actually measure distances and directions moved by some feature in the window.

It is a characteristic of all transforms that the more accurately the spectrum of a signal is known, the less accurately the spatial domain is known. Thus the whereabouts within the window of the moving objects that gave rise to the correlation peaks is not known. Figure 5.53 illustrates the phenomenon. Two windowed blocks are shown in consecutive fields. Both contain the same objects, moving at the same speed, but from different starting points. The correlation surface will be the same in both cases. The phase-correlation process therefore needs to be followed by a further process called image correlation, which identifies the picture areas in which the measured motion took place and establishes a level of confidence in the identification. This stage can also be seen in the block diagram of Figure 5.52.

To employ the terminology of motion estimation, the phase-correlation process produces candidate vectors, and the image-correlation process assigns the vectors to specific areas of the picture. In many ways the vector-assignment process is more difficult than the phase-correlation process, as the latter is a fixed computation, whereas the vector assignment has to respond to infinitely varying picture conditions.

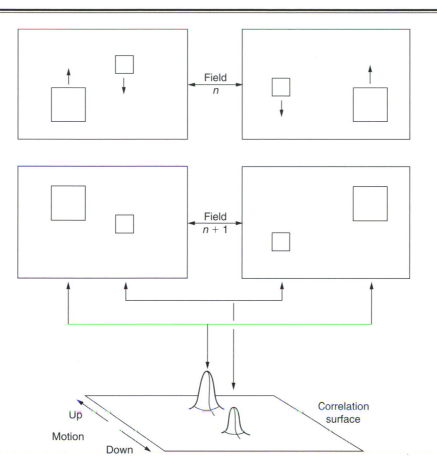

FIGURE 5.53
Phase correlation measures motion, not the location of moving objects. These two examples give the
same correlation surface.

Figure 5.54 shows the image-correlation process, which is used to link the candidate vectors from the phase
correlator to the picture content. In this example, the correlation surface contains three peaks, which define three
possible motions between two successive fields. One down-sampled field is successively shifted by each of the
candidate vectors and compared with the next field a pixel at a time. Similarities or correlations between pixel
values indicate that an area with the measured motion has been found. This happens for two of the candidate
vectors, and these vectors are then assigned to those areas. However, shifting by the third vector does not result
in a meaningful correlation. This is taken to mean that it was a spurious vector, one which was produced in error
because of difficult program material. The ability to eliminate spurious vectors and establish confidence levels in
those that remain is essential to artifact-free conversion.

The phase-correlation process produces candidate vectors in each window. The vectors from all windows must
be combined to obtain an overall view of the motion in the field before attempting to describe the motion of each
pixel individually.

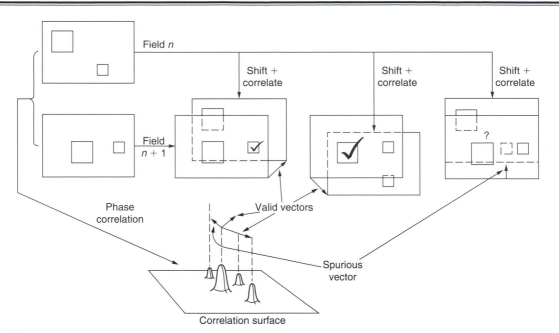

FIGURE 5.54
Image correlation uses candidate vectors to locate picture areas with the corresponding motion. If no image correlation is found the vector was spurious and is discounted.

Figure 5.55a shows that if a zoom is in progress, the vectors in the various windows will form a geometric progression, becoming longer in proportion to the distance from the axis of the zoom. However, if there is a pan, it will be seen from Figure 5.55b that there will be similar vectors in all the windows. In practice both motions may occur simultaneously.

An estimate will be made of the speed of a field-wide zoom or of the speed of picture areas that contain receding or advancing motions, which give a zoom-like effect. If the effect of zooming is removed from each window by shifting the peaks by the local zoom magnitude, but in the opposite direction, the positions of the peaks will reveal any component due to panning. This can be found by summing all the windows to create a histogram. Panning results in a dominant peak in the histogram, where all windows contain peaks in a similar place, which reinforce the dominant peak.

Each window is then processed in turn. Where only a small part of an object overlaps into a window, it will result in a small peak in the correlation surface, which might be missed. The windows are deliberately overlapped so that a given pixel may appear in four windows. Thus a moving object will appear in more than one window. If most of an object lies within one window, a large peak will be produced from the motion in that window. The resulting vector will be added to the candidate vector list of all adjacent windows. When the vector assignment is performed, image correlations will result if a small overlap occurred, and the vector will be validated. If there was no overlap, the vector will be rejected.

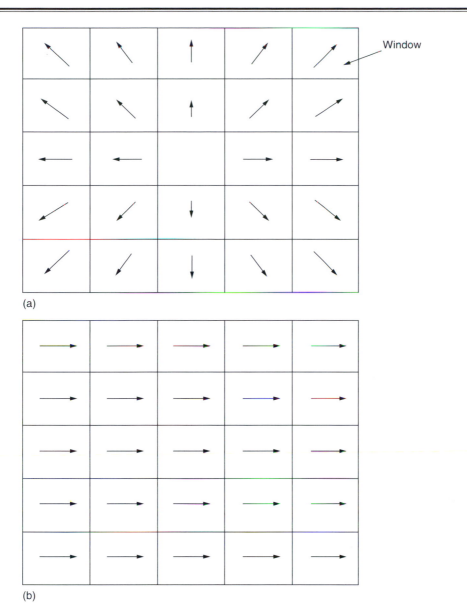

(a)

(b)

FIGURE 5.55
The results of (a) a zoom and (b) a pan on the vectors in various windows in the field.

The peaks in each window reflect the degree of correlation between the two fields for different offsets in two dimensions. The volume of the peak corresponds to the amount of the area of the window (i.e., the number of pixels) having that motion. Thus peaks should be selected starting with the largest. However, periodic structures in the input field, such as grilles and striped shirts, will result in partial correlations at incorrect distances that differ from the correct distance by the period of the structure. The effect is that a large peak on the correlation surface will be flanked by smaller peaks at uniform spacing in a straight line. The characteristic pattern of subsidiary peaks can be identified and the vectors invalidated.

One way in which this can be done is to compare the positions of the peaks in each window with those estimated by the pan/zoom process. The true peak due to motion will be similar; the false subpeaks due to image periodicity will not be and can be rejected.

Correlations with candidate vectors are then performed. The image in one field is shifted in an interpolator by the amount specified by a candidate vector and the degree of correlation is measured. Note that this interpolation is to subpixel accuracy because phase correlation can accurately measure subpixel motion. High correlation results in vector assignment, low correlation results in the vector being rejected as unreliable.

If all the peaks are evaluated in this way, then most of the time valid assignments for which there is acceptable confidence from the correlator will be made. Should it not be possible to obtain any correlation with confidence in a window, then the pan/zoom values will be inserted so that that the window moves in a way similar to the overall field motion.

MOTION-COMPENSATED STANDARDS CONVERSION

A conventional standards convertor is not transparent to motion portrayal, and the effect is judder and loss of resolution. Figure 5.56 shows what happens on the time axis in a conversion between 60 and 50 Hz (in either direction). Fields in the two standards appear in different planes cutting through the spatiotemporal volume, and the job of the standards convertor is to interpolate along the time axis between input planes in one standard to estimate what an intermediate plane in the other standard would look like. With still images, this is easy, because planes can be slid up and down the time axis with no ill effect. If an object is moving, it will be in a different place in successive fields. Interpolating between several fields results in multiple images of the object. The position of the dominant image will not move smoothly, an effect that is perceived as judder. Motion compensation is designed to eliminate this undesirable judder.

A conventional standards convertor interpolates only along the time axis, whereas a motion-compensated standards convertor can swivel its interpolation axis off the time axis. Figure 5.57a shows the input fields in which three objects are moving in a different way. In Figure 5.57b it will be seen that the interpolation axis is aligned with the optic flow axis of each moving object in turn.

Each object is no longer moving with respect to its own optic flow axis, and so on that axis it no longer generates temporal frequencies due to motion, and temporal aliasing due to motion cannot occur.[12] Interpolation along the optic flow axes will then result in a sequence of output fields in which motion is properly portrayed. The process requires a standards convertor that contains filters that are modified to allow the interpolation axis to move dynamically within each output field. The signals that move the interpolation axis are known

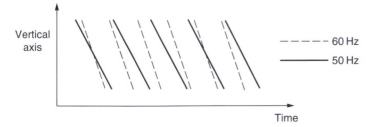

FIGURE 5.56
The different temporal distributions of input and output fields in a 50/60 Hz convertor.

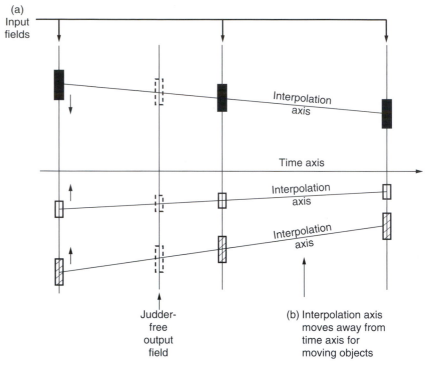

FIGURE 5.57
(a) Input fields with moving objects. (b) Moving the interpolation axes to make them parallel to the trajectory of each object.

as motion vectors. It is the job of the motion-estimation system to provide these motion vectors. The overall performance of the convertor is determined primarily by the accuracy of the motion vectors. An incorrect vector will result in unrelated pixels from several fields being superimposed, and the result is unsatisfactory.

Figure 5.58 shows the sequence of events in a motion-compensated standards convertor. The motion estimator measures movements between successive fields. These motions must then be attributed to objects by creating boundaries around sets of pixels having the same motion. The result of this process is a set of motion vectors, hence the term "vector assignation." The motion vectors are then input to a modified four-field standards convertor to deflect the interfield interpolation axis.

The vectors from the motion estimator actually measure the distance moved by an object from one input field to another. What the standards convertor

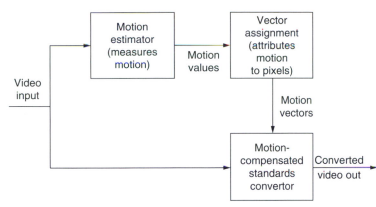

FIGURE 5.58
The essential stages of a motion-compensated standards convertor.

requires is the value of motion vectors at an output field. A vector interpolation stage is required, which computes where between the input fields A and B the current output field lies and uses this to proportion the motion vector into two parts. Figure 5.59a shows that the first part is the motion between field A and the output field; the second is the motion between field B and the output field. Clearly the difference between these two vectors is the motion between input fields. These processed vectors are used to displace parts of the input fields so that the axis of interpolation lies along the optic flow axis. The moving object is stationary with respect to this axis so interpolation between fields along it will not result in any judder.

Whilst a conventional convertor needs to interpolate only vertically and temporally, a motion-compensated convertor also needs to interpolate horizontally to account for lateral movement in images. Figure 5.59b shows that the motion vector from the motion estimator is resolved into two components, vertical and horizontal. The spatial impulse response of the interpolator is shifted in two dimensions by these components. This shift may be different in each of the fields that contribute to the output field.

When an object in the picture moves, it will obscure its background. The vector interpolator in the standards convertor handles this automatically, provided the motion estimation has produced correct vectors. Figure 5.60 shows an example of background handling. The moving object produces a finite vector associated with each pixel, whereas the stationary background produces zero vectors except in the area OX where the background is being obscured. Vectors converge in the area where the background is being obscured and diverge where it is being revealed. Image correlation is poor in these areas so no valid vector is assigned.

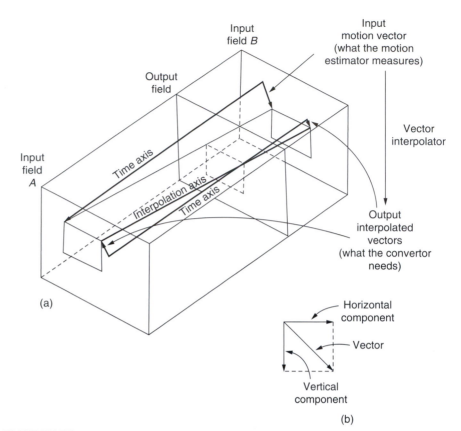

FIGURE 5.59
(a) The motion vectors on the input field structure must be interpolated onto the output field structure. The field to be interpolated is positioned temporally between source fields and the motion vector between them is apportioned according to the location. Motion vectors are two dimensional and can be transmitted as vertical and horizontal components, shown in (b), which control the spatial shifting of input fields.

An output field is located between input fields, and vectors are projected through it to locate the intermediate position of moving objects. These are interpolated along an axis that is parallel to the optic flow axis. This results in address mapping that locates the moving object in the input field RAMs. However, the background is not moving and so the optic flow axis is parallel to the time axis. The pixel immediately below the leading edge of the moving object does not have a valid vector because it is in the area OX where forward image correlation failed.

The solution is for that pixel to assume the motion vector of the background below point X, but only to interpolate in a backward direction, taking pixel data from previous fields. In a similar way, the pixel immediately behind the trailing

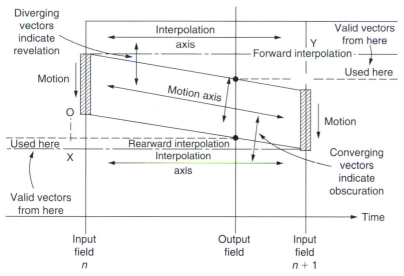

FIGURE 5.60
Background handling. When a vector for an output pixel near a moving object is
not known, the vectors from adjacent background areas are assumed. Converging
vectors imply obscuring is taking place, which requires that interpolation can use only
previous field data. Diverging vectors imply that the background is being revealed and
interpolation can use data only from later fields.

edge takes the motion vector for the background above point Y and interpolates
only in a forward direction, taking pixel data from future fields. The result is
that the moving object is portrayed in the correct place on its trajectory, and the
background around it is filled in only from fields that contain useful data.

The technology of the motion-compensated standards convertor can be used in
other applications. When video recordings are played back in slow motion, the
result is that the same picture is displayed several times, followed by a jump to
the next picture. Figure 5.61 shows that a moving object would remain in the
same place on the screen during picture repeats, but jump to a new position as
a new picture was played. The eye attempts to track the moving object, but, as
Figure 5.61 also shows, the location of the moving object wanders with respect
to the trajectory of the eye, and this is visible as judder.

Motion-compensated slow-motion systems are capable of synthesizing new
images that lie between the original images from a slow-motion source.
Figure 5.62 shows that two successive images in the original recording (using
DVE terminology, these are source fields) are fed into the unit, which then
measures the distance travelled by all moving objects between those images.
Using interpolation, intermediate fields (target fields) are computed in which
moving objects are positioned so that they lie on the eye trajectory. Using the

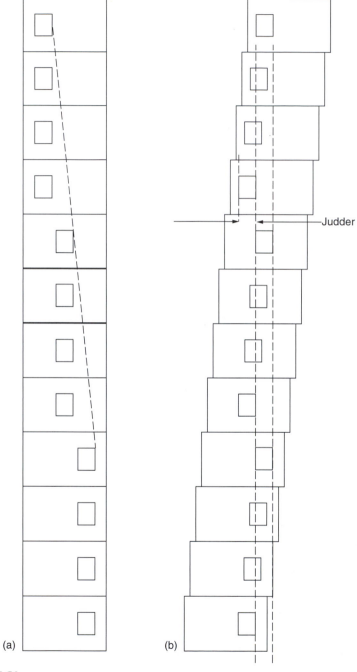

(a) (b)

FIGURE 5.61
(a) Conventional slow motion using field repeating with stationary eye. (b) With a tracking eye the source of judder can be seen.

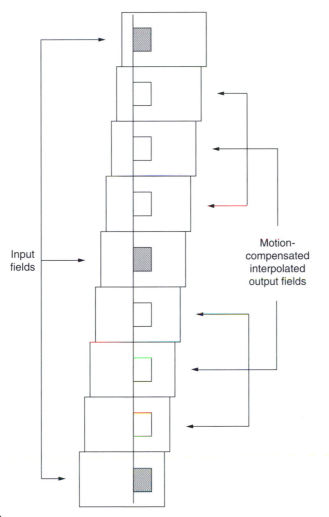

FIGURE 5.62
In motion-compensated slow motion, output fields are interpolated with moving objects displaying judder-free linear motion between input fields.

principles described above, background information is removed as moving objects conceal it and replaced as the rear of an object reveals it. Jitter is thus removed and motion with a fluid quality is obtained.

CAMERA-SHAKE COMPENSATION

As video cameras become smaller and lighter, it becomes increasingly difficult to move them smoothly and the result is camera shake. This is irritating to watch, as well as requiring a higher bit-rate in compression systems. There are

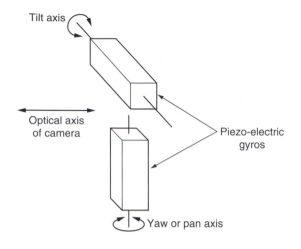

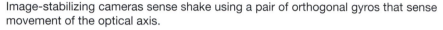

FIGURE 5.63
Image-stabilizing cameras sense shake using a pair of orthogonal gyros that sense movement of the optical axis.

two solutions to the problem, one that is contained within the camera and one that can be used at some later time on the video data.

Figure 5.63 shows that image-stabilizing cameras contain miniature gyroscopes, which produce an electrical output proportional to their rate of turn about a specified axis. A pair of these, mounted orthogonally, can produce vectors describing the camera shake. This can be used to oppose the shake by shifting the image. In one approach, the shifting is done optically. Figure 5.64 shows a pair of glass plates with the intervening spaced filled with transparent liquid. By tilting the plates a variable-angle prism can be obtained and this is fitted in the optical system before the sensor. If the prism plates are suitably driven by servos from the gyroscopic sensors, the optical axis along which the camera is looking can remain constant despite shake.

Alternatively, the camera can contain a DVE by which the vectors from the gyroscopes cause the CCD camera output to be shifted horizontally or vertically so that the image remains stable. This approach is commonly used in consumer camcorders.

A great number of video recordings and films already exist in which there is camera shake. Film also suffers from weave in the telecine machine. In this case the above solutions are inappropriate and a suitable signal processor is required. Figure 5.65 shows that motion compensation can be used. If a motion estimator

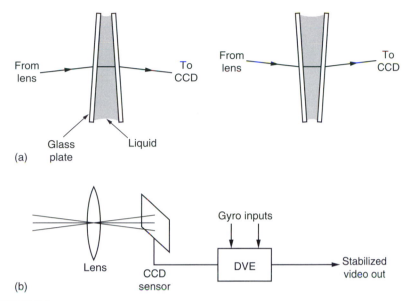

FIGURE 5.64

Image-stabilizing cameras. (a) The image is stabilized optically prior to the CCD sensors. (b) The CCD output contains image shake, but this is opposed by the action of a DVE configured to shift the image under control of the gyro inputs.

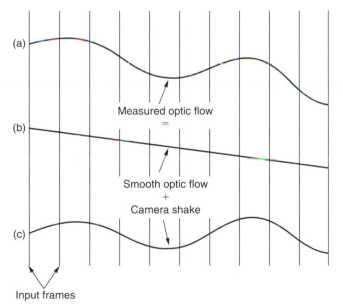

FIGURE 5.65

(a) In digital image stabilising the optic flow axis of objects in the input video is measured. (b) This motion is smoothed to obtain a close approximation to the original motion. (c) If this is subtracted from (a) the result is the camera-shake motion, which is used to drive the image stabiliser.

is arranged to find the motion between a series of pictures, camera shake will add a fixed component in each picture to the genuine object motions. This can be used to compute the optic flow axis of the camera, independent of the objects portrayed.

Operating over several pictures, the trend in camera movement can be separated from the shake by filtering, to produce a position error for each picture. Each picture is then shifted in a DVE to cancel the position error. The result is that the camera shake is gone and the camera movements appear smooth. To prevent the edges of the frame moving visibly, the DVE also performs a slight magnification so that the edge motion is always outside the output frame.

DE-INTERLACING

Interlace is a legacy compression technique that sends only half of the picture lines in each field. Whilst this works reasonably well for transmission, it causes difficulty in any process that requires image manipulation. This includes DVEs, standards convertors, and display convertors. All these devices give better results when working with progressively scanned data, and if the source material is interlaced, a de-interlacing process will be necessary.

Interlace distributes vertical detail information over two fields, and for maximum resolution all that information is necessary. Unfortunately it is not possible to use the information from two different fields directly. Figure 5.66 shows a scene in which an object is moving. When the second field of the scene leaves the camera, the object will have assumed a position different from the one it had in the first field, and the result of combining the two fields to make a de-interlaced frame will be a double image. This effect can easily be demonstrated on any video recorder that offers a choice of still field or still frame. Stationary objects before a stationary camera, however, can be de-interlaced perfectly.

In simple de-interlacers, motion sensing is used so that de-interlacing can be disabled when movement occurs, and interpolation from a single field is used instead. Motion sensing implies comparison of one picture with the next. If interpolation is to be used only in areas where there is movement, it is necessary to test for motion over the entire frame. Motion can be simply detected by comparing the luminance value of a given pixel with the value of the same pixel two fields earlier. As two fields are to be combined, and motion can occur in either, then the comparison must be made between two odd fields and two even fields. Thus four fields of memory are needed to perform motion sensing correctly. The luminance from four fields requires about a megabyte of storage.

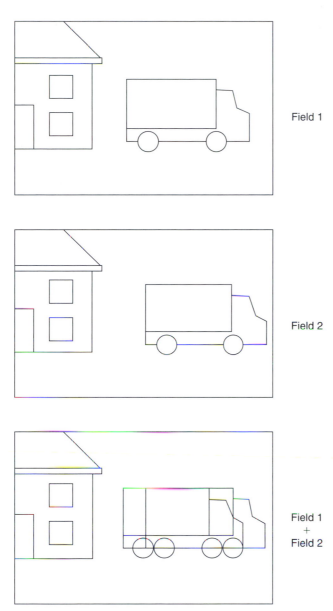

Field 1

Field 2

Field 1
+
Field 2

FIGURE 5.66
A moving object will be in a different place in two successive fields and will produce a double image.

At some point a decision must be made to abandon pixels from the previous field that are in the wrong place due to motion and to interpolate them from adjacent lines in the current field. Switching suddenly in this way is visible, and there is a more sophisticated mechanism that can be used. In Figure 5.67, two fields, separated in time, are shown. Interlace can be seen by following

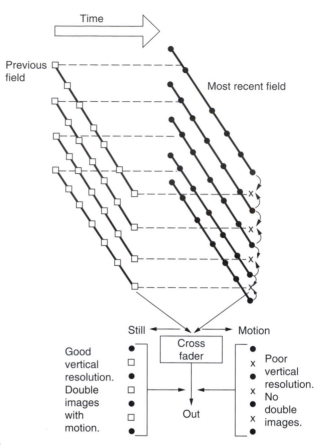

FIGURE 5.67
Pixels from the most recent field are interpolated spatially to form low vertical resolution pixels, which will be used if there is excessive motion; pixels from the previous field will be used to give maximum vertical resolution. The best possible de-interlaced frame results.

lines from pixels in one field, which pass between pixels in the other field. If there is no movement, the fact that the two fields are separated in time is irrelevant, and the two can be superimposed to make a frame array. When there is motion, pixels from above and below the unknown pixels are added together and divided by two, to produce interpolated values. If both of these mechanisms work all the time, a better quality picture results if a cross-fade is made between the two based on the amount of motion. At some motion value, or some magnitude of pixel difference, the loss of resolution due to a double image is equal to the loss of resolution due to interpolation. That amount of motion should result in the cross-fader arriving at a 50/50 setting. Any less motion will result in a fade toward both fields, any more motion will result in a fade toward the interpolated values.

The most efficient way to de-interlace is to use motion compensation. Figure 5.68 shows that when an object moves in an interlaced system, the interlace breaks down with respect to the optic flow axis as was seen in Chapter 2. If the motion is known, two or more fields can be shifted so that a moving object is in the same place in both. Pixels from both fields can then be used to describe the object with better resolution than would be possible from one field alone. It can be seen in Figure 5.69 that the combination of two fields in this way will

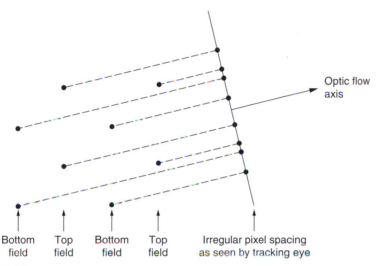

FIGURE 5.68
In the presence of vertical motion or motion having a vertical component, interlace breaks down and the pixel spacing with respect to the tracking eye becomes irregular.

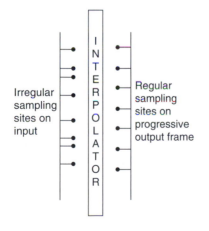

FIGURE 5.69
A de-interlacer needs an interpolator, which can operate with input samples that are positioned arbitrarily rather than regularly.

result in pixels having a highly irregular spacing, and a special type of filter is needed to convert this back to a progressive frame with regular pixel spacing. At some critical vertical speeds there will be alignment between pixels in adjacent fields and no improvement is possible, but at other speeds the process will always give better results.

NOISE REDUCTION

The basic principle of all video noise reducers is that there is a certain amount of correlation between the video content of successive frames, whereas there is no correlation between the noise content.

A basic recursive device is shown in Figure 5.70. There is a frame store, which acts as a delay, and the output of the delay can be fed back to the input through an attenuator, which in the digital domain will be a multiplier. In the case of a still picture, successive frames will be identical, and the recursion will be large. This means that the output video will actually be the average of many frames. If there is movement of the image, it will be necessary to reduce the amount of recursion to prevent the generation of trails or smears. Probably the most famous examples of recursion smear are the television pictures sent back of astronauts walking on the moon. The received pictures were very noisy and needed a lot of averaging to make them viewable. This was fine until the astronaut moved. The technology of the day did not permit motion sensing.

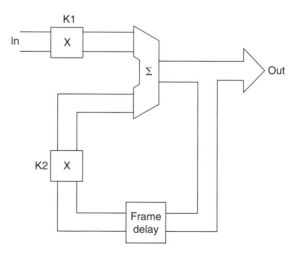

FIGURE 5.70
A basic recursive device feeds back the output to the input via a frame store, which acts as a delay. The characteristics of the device are controlled totally by the values of the two coefficients, K_1 and K_2, which control the multipliers.

The noise reduction increases with the number of frames over which the noise is integrated, but image motion prevents simple combining of frames. If motion estimation is available, the image of a moving object in a particular frame can be integrated from the images in several frames that have been superimposed on the same part of the screen by displacements derived from the motion measurement. The result is that greater reduction of noise becomes possible.[13] In fact a motion-compensated standards convertor performs such a noise-reduction process automatically and can be used as a noise reducer, albeit an expensive one, by setting both input and output to the same standard.

References

1. Aird, B. Three dimensional picture synthesis. Broadcast Syst. Eng., 12 No. 3, 34–40 (1986).
2. Newman, W.M., and Sproull, R.F. *Principles of Interactive Computer Graphics.* Tokyo: McGraw–Hill (1979).
3. Gernsheim, H. *A Concise History of Photography,* p. 915, London: Thames & Hudson (1971).
4. Hedgecoe, J. *The Photographer's Handbook,* pp. 104–105, London: Ebury Press (1977).
5. Bennett, P., et al. Spatial transformation system including key signal generator. U.S. Patent No. 4,463,372 (1984).
6. de Boor, C. *A Practical Guide to Splines.* Berlin: Springer (1978).
7. Rubin, M. The emergence of the desktop: implications to offline editing. Record of 18th ITS (Montreaux), pp. 384–389 (1993).
8. Trottier, L. Digital video compositing on the desktop. Record of 18th ITS (Montreaux), pp. 564–570 (1993).
9. Limb, J.O., and Murphy, J.A. Measuring the speed of moving objects from television signals. IEEE Trans. Commun., 474–478 (1975).
10. Thomas, G.A. Television motion measurement for DATV and other applications. BBC Res. Dept. Rept, RD 1987/11 (1987).
11. Pearson, J.J., et al. Video rate image correlation processor. SPIE, Vol. 119, *Application of Digital Image Processing,* IOCC (1977).
12. Lau, H., and Lyon, D. Motion compensated processing for enhanced slow motion and standards conversion. IEE Conference Publ. No. 358, pp. 62–66 (1992).
13. Weiss, P., and Christensson, J., Real time implementation of sub-pixel motion estimation for broadcast applications. IEE Digest, 128 (1990).

CHAPTER 6
Video Compression and MPEG

INTRODUCTION TO COMPRESSION

Compression, bit rate reduction, and data reduction are all terms that mean basically the same thing in this context. An impression of the original information is expressed using a smaller quantity or rate of data. It should be pointed out that in audio, compression traditionally means a process in which the dynamic range of the sound is reduced. In the context of MPEG the same word means that the bit rate is reduced, ideally leaving the dynamics of the signal unchanged. Provided the context is clear, the two meanings can co-exist without a great deal of confusion.

There are several reasons compression techniques are popular:

1. Compression extends the playing time of a given storage device.
2. Compression allows miniaturization. With fewer data to store, the same playing time is obtained with smaller hardware. This is useful in ENG (electronic news gathering) and consumer devices.
3. Tolerances can be relaxed. With fewer data to record, storage density can be reduced, making equipment that is more resistant to adverse environments and that requires less maintenance.
4. In transmission systems, compression allows a reduction in bandwidth, which will generally result in a reduction in cost, to make possible some process that would be impracticable without it.
5. If a given bandwidth is available to an uncompressed signal, compression allows faster-than-real-time transmission in the same bandwidth.
6. If a given bandwidth is available, compression allows a better quality signal in the same bandwidth.

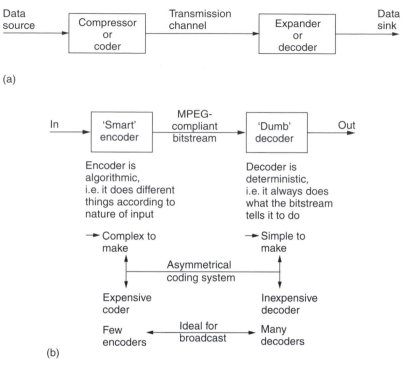

FIGURE 6.1
(a) A compression system consists of a compressor or coder, a transmission channel, and a matching expander or decoder. The combination of coder and decoder is known as a codec. (b) MPEG is asymmetrical because the encoder is much more complex than the decoder.

Compression is summarised in Figure 6.1. It will be seen in Figure 6.1a that the data rate is reduced at the source by the compressor. The compressed data are then passed through a communication channel and returned to the original rate by the expander. The ratio between the source data rate and the channel data rate is called the compression factor. The term "coding gain" is also used. Sometimes a compressor and an expander in series are referred to as a compander. The compressor may equally well be referred to as a coder and the expander a decoder, in which case the tandem pair may be called a codec.

In audio and video compression, when the encoder is more complex than the decoder the system is said to be asymmetrical, as in Figure 6.1b. The encoder needs to be algorithmic or adaptive, whereas the decoder is "dumb" and carries out fixed actions. This is advantageous in applications such as broadcasting in which the number of expensive complex encoders is small but the number of simple inexpensive decoders is large. In point-to-point applications the advantage of asymmetrical coding is not so great.

Although there are many different coding techniques, all of them fall into one of these categories. In lossless coding, the data from the expander are identical bit for bit with the original source data. The so-called "stacker" programs, which increase the apparent capacity of disk drives in personal computers, use lossless codecs. Clearly with computer programs the corruption of a single bit can be catastrophic. Lossless coding is generally restricted to compression factors of around 2:1.

It is important to appreciate that a lossless coder cannot guarantee a particular compression factor and the communications link or recorder used with it must be able to function with the variable output data rate. Source data that result in poor compression factors on a given codec are described as difficult. It should be pointed out that the difficulty is often a function of the codec. In other words, data that one codec finds difficult may not be found difficult by another. Lossless codecs can be included in bit-error-rate testing schemes. It is also possible to cascade or concatenate lossless codecs without any special precautions.

In lossy coding, data from the expander are not identical bit for bit with the source data, and as a result comparing the input with the output is bound to reveal differences. Lossy codecs are not suitable for computer data, but are used in MPEG as they allow greater compression factors than lossless codecs. Successful lossy codecs are those in which the errors are arranged so that a human viewer or listener finds them subjectively difficult to detect. Thus lossy codecs must be based on an understanding of psychoacoustic and psychovisual perception and are often called perceptive codes.

In perceptive coding, the greater the compression factor required, the more accurately the human senses must be modelled. Perceptive coders can be forced to operate at a fixed compression factor. This is convenient for practical transmission applications in which a fixed data rate is easier to handle than a variable rate. The result of a fixed compression factor is that the subjective quality can vary with the "difficulty" of the input material. Perceptive codecs should not be concatenated indiscriminately, especially if they use different algorithms. As the reconstructed signal from a perceptive codec is not bit-for-bit accurate, clearly such a codec cannot be included in any bit-error-rate testing system, as the coding differences would be indistinguishable from real errors.

Although the adoption of digital techniques is recent, compression itself is as old as television. Figure 6.2 shows some of the compression techniques used in traditional television systems.

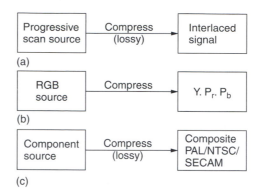

FIGURE 6.2
Compression is as old as television. (a) Interlace is a primitive way of halving the bandwidth. (b) Colour difference working invisibly reduces colour resolution.
(c) Composite video transmits colour in the same bandwidth as monochrome.

One of the oldest techniques is interlace, which has been used in analog television from the very beginning as a primitive way of reducing bandwidth. As seen in Chapter 2, interlace is not without its problems, particularly in motion rendering. MPEG-2 supports interlace simply because legacy interlaced signals exist and there is a requirement to compress them further. This should not be taken to mean that it is an optimal approach.

The generation of colour difference signals from RGB in video represents an application of perceptive coding. The HVS (human visual system) sees no change in quality although the bandwidth of the colour difference signals is reduced. This is because human perception of detail in colour changes is much less than that in brightness changes. This approach is sensibly retained in MPEG.

Composite video systems such as PAL, NTSC, and SECAM are all analog compression schemes that embed a modulated subcarrier in the luminance signal so that colour pictures are available in the same bandwidth as monochrome. In comparison with a progressive-scan RGB picture, interlaced composite video has a compression factor of 6:1.

In a sense MPEG-2 can be considered to be a modern digital equivalent of analog composite video, as it has most of the same attributes. For example, the eight-field sequence of a PAL subcarrier that makes editing difficult has its equivalent in the GOP (group of pictures) of MPEG.[1]

In a PCM digital system the bit rate is the product of the sampling rate and the number of bits in each sample and this is generally constant. Nevertheless the information rate of a real signal varies. In all real signals, part of the signal is obvious from what has gone before or what may come later and a suitable receiver can predict that part so that only the true information actually has to be sent. If the characteristics of a predicting receiver are known, the transmitter can omit parts of the message in the knowledge that the receiver has the ability to re-create it. Thus all encoders must contain a model of the decoder.

One definition of information is that it is the unpredictable or surprising element of data. Newspapers are a good example of information because they mention only items that are surprising. Newspapers never carry items about individuals who have not been involved in an accident, as this is the normal case. Consequently the phrase "no news is good news" is remarkably true because if an information channel exists but nothing has been sent, then it is most likely that nothing remarkable has happened.

The difference between the information rate and the overall bit rate is known as the redundancy. Compression systems are designed to eliminate as much of that redundancy as practicable or perhaps affordable. One way in which this can be done is to exploit statistical predictability in signals. The information content or entropy of a sample is a function of how different it is from the predicted value. Most signals have some degree of predictability. A sine wave is highly predictable, because all cycles look the same. According to Shannon's theory, any signal that is totally predictable carries no information. In the case of the sine wave this is clear because it represents a single frequency and so has no bandwidth.

At the opposite extreme a signal such as noise is completely unpredictable, and as a result all codecs find noise difficult. There are two consequences of this characteristic. First, a codec that is designed using the statistics of real material should not be tested with random noise because it is not a representative test. Second, a codec that performs well with clean source material may perform badly with source material having superimposed noise. Most practical compression units require some form of pre-processing before the compression stage proper and appropriate noise reduction should be incorporated into the pre-processing if noisy signals are anticipated. It will also be necessary to restrict the degree of compression applied to noisy signals.

All real signals fall part way between the extremes of total predictability and total unpredictability or noisiness. If the bandwidth (set by the sampling rate) and the dynamic range (set by the word length) of the transmission system delineate an area, this sets a limit on the information capacity of the system.

Figure 6.3a shows that most real signals occupy only part of that area. The signal may not contain all frequencies, or it may not have full dynamics at certain frequencies.

Entropy can be thought of as a measure of the actual area occupied by the signal. This is the area that must be transmitted if there are to be no subjective differences or artifacts in the received signal. The remaining area is called the redundancy because it adds nothing to the information conveyed. Thus an ideal coder could be imagined that miraculously sorts out the entropy from the redundancy and sends only the former. An ideal decoder would then re-create the original impression of the information quite perfectly.

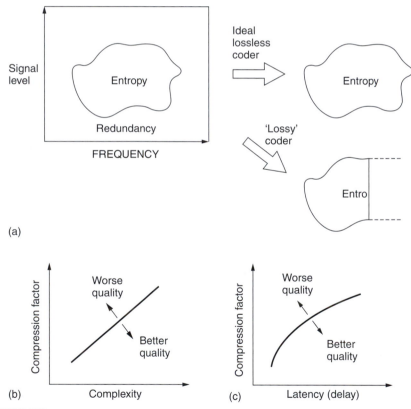

FIGURE 6.3
(a) A perfect coder removes only the redundancy from the input signal and results in subjectively lossless coding. If the remaining entropy is beyond the capacity of the channel some of it must be lost and the codec will then be lossy. An imperfect coder will also be lossy as it fails to keep all entropy. (b) As the compression factor rises, the complexity must also rise to maintain quality. (c) High compression factors also tend to increase latency or delay through the system.

As the ideal is approached, the coder complexity and the latency, or delay, both rise. Figure 6.3b shows how complexity increases with compression factor and (c) shows how increasing the codec latency can improve the compression factor. Obviously we would have to provide a channel that could accept whatever entropy the coder extracts to have transparent quality. As a result moderate coding gains that remove only redundancy need not cause artifacts and result in systems that are described as subjectively lossless.

If the channel capacity is not sufficient for that, then the coder will have to discard some of the entropy and with it useful information. Larger coding gains that remove some of the entropy must result in artifacts. It will also be seen from Figure 6.3 that an imperfect coder will fail to separate the redundancy and may discard entropy instead, resulting in artifacts at a sub-optimal compression factor.

A single variable-rate transmission or recording channel is inconvenient and unpopular with channel providers because it is difficult to police. The requirement can be overcome by combining several compressed channels into one constant rate transmission in a way that flexibly allocates the data rate between the channels. Provided the material is unrelated, the probability of all channels reaching peak entropy at once is very small and so those channels that are at one instant passing easy material will free up transmission capacity for those channels that are handling difficult material. This is the principle of statistical multiplexing.

Where the same type of source material is used consistently, e.g., English text, then it is possible to perform a statistical analysis on the frequency with which particular letters are used. Variable-length coding is used, in which frequently used letters are allocated short codes and letters that occur infrequently are allocated long codes. This results in a lossless code. The well-known Morse code used for telegraphy is an example of this approach. The letter "E" is the most frequent letter in English and is sent with a single dot.

An infrequent letter such as "Z" is allocated a long complex pattern. It should be clear that codes of this kind that rely on a prior knowledge of the statistics of the signal are effective only with signals actually having those statistics. If Morse code is used with another language, the transmission becomes significantly less efficient because the statistics are quite different; the letter "Z", for example, is quite common in Czech.

The Huffman code[2] is one that is designed for use with a data source having known statistics and shares the same principles with the Morse code.

The probability of the different code values to be transmitted is studied, and the most frequent codes are arranged to be transmitted with short word-length symbols. As the probability of a code value falls, it will be allocated a longer word length. The Huffman code is used in conjunction with a number of compression techniques and is shown in Figure 6.4.

The input or source codes are assembled in order of descending probability. The two lowest probabilities are distinguished by a single code bit and their probabilities are combined. The process of combining probabilities is continued until unity is reached and at each stage a bit is used to distinguish the path. The bit will be a 0 for the most probable path and 1 for the least. The compressed output is obtained by reading the bits that describe which path to take going from right to left.

In the case of computer data, there is no control over the data statistics. Data to be recorded could be instructions, images, tables, text files, and so on, each having its own code value distributions. In this case a coder relying on fixed-source statistics will be completely inadequate. Instead a system that can learn the statistics as it goes along is used. The LZW (Lempel-Ziv-Welch) Lempel–Ziv–Welch lossless codes are in this category. These codes build up a conversion table between frequent long-source data strings and short transmitted data

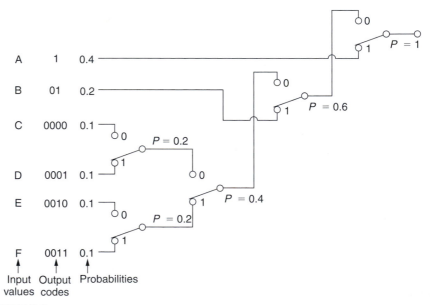

FIGURE 6.4
The Huffman code achieves compression by allocating short codes to frequent values. To aid in de-serializing, the short codes are not prefixes of longer codes.

codes at both coder and decoder, and initially their compression factor is below unity as the contents of the conversion tables are transmitted along with the data. However, once the tables are established, the coding gain more than compensates for the initial loss. In some applications, a continuous analysis of the frequency of code selection is made and if a data string in the table is no longer being used with sufficient frequency it can be deselected and a more common string substituted.

Lossless codes are less common for audio and video coding in which perceptive codes are permissible. The perceptive codes often obtain a coding gain by shortening the word length of the data representing the signal waveform. This must increase the noise level and the trick is to ensure that the resultant noise is placed at frequencies at which human senses are least able to perceive it. As a result, although the received signal is measurably different from the source data, it can appear the same to the human listener or viewer at moderate compression factors. As these codes rely on the characteristics of human sight and hearing, they can be fully tested only subjectively.

The compression factor of such codes can be set at will by choosing the word length of the compressed data. Whilst mild compression will be undetectable, with greater compression factors, artifacts become noticeable. Figure 6.3 shows that this is inevitable from entropy considerations.

WHAT IS MPEG?

MPEG is actually an acronym for the Moving Pictures Experts Group, which was formed by the ISO (International Standards Organization) to set standards for audio and video compression and transmission. The first compression standard for audio and video was MPEG-1,[3,4] but this was of limited application and the subsequent MPEG-2 standard was considerably broader in scope and of wider appeal. For example, MPEG-2 supports interlace, whereas MPEG-1 did not.

The approach of the ISO to standardisation in MPEG is novel because it is not the encoder that is standardised. Instead, the way in which a decoder shall interpret the bitstream, is defined. Figure 6.5a shows that a decoder can successfully interpret the bitstream is said to be compliant. Figure 6.5b shows that the advantage of standardising the decoder is that, over time, encoding algorithms can improve yet compliant decoders will continue to function with them.

Manufacturers can supply encoders using algorithms that are proprietary and their details do not need to be published. A useful result is that there can be

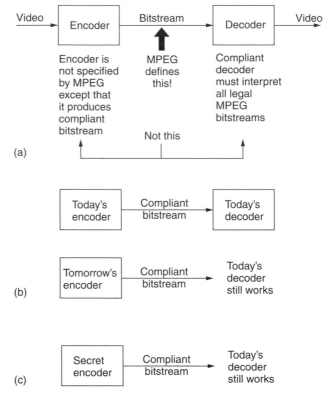

FIGURE 6.5
(a) MPEG defines the protocol of the bitstream between encoder and decoder. The decoder is defined by implication, the encoder is left very much to the designer.
(b) This approach allows future encoders of better performance to remain compatible with existing decoders. (c) This approach also allows an encoder to produce a standard bitstream, whereas its technical operation remains a commercial secret.

competition between different encoder designs, which means that better designs will evolve. The user will have greater choice because different levels of cost and complexity can exist in a range of coders, yet a compliant decoder will operate with them all.

MPEG is, however, much more than a compression scheme, as it also standardises the protocol and syntax under which it is possible to combine or multiplex audio data with video data to produce a digital equivalent of a television program. Many such programs can be combined in a single multiplex and MPEG defines the way in which such multiplexes can be created and transported. The definitions include the metadata that decoders require to demultiplex correctly and that users will need to locate programs of interest.

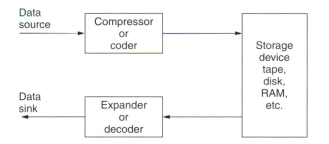

FIGURE 6.6
Compression can be used around a recording medium. The storage capacity may be increased or the access time reduced according to the application.

As with all video systems there is a requirement for synchronising or genlocking and this is particularly complex when a multiplex is assembled from many signals that are not necessarily synchronised with one another.

The applications of audio and video compression are limitless and the ISO has done well to provide standards that are appropriate to the wide range of possible compression products.

MPEG-2 embraces video pictures from the tiny screen of a videophone to the high-definition images needed for electronic cinema. Audio coding stretches from speech-grade mono to multichannel surround sound.

Figure 6.6 shows the use of a codec with a recorder. The playing time of the medium is extended in proportion to the compression factor. In the case of tapes, the access time is improved because the length of tape needed for a given recording is reduced and so it can be rewound more quickly.

In the case of DVD (digital video disc, aka digital versatile disc) the challenge was to store an entire movie on one 12cm disc. The storage density available is such that recording of SD uncompressed video would be out of the question. By the same argument, compression is also required in HD video disks.

In communications, the cost of data links is often roughly proportional to the data rate and so there is simple economic pressure to use a high compression factor. However, it should be borne in mind that implementing the codec also has a cost, which rises with compression factor, and so a degree of compromise will be inevitable.

In the case of video-on-demand, technology exists to convey full bandwidth video to the home, but to do so for a single individual at the moment would be prohibitively expensive. Without compression, HDTV (high-definition television)

MPEG-1, -2, AND -4 AND H.264 CONTRASTED

The first compression standard for audio and video was MPEG-1. Although many applications have been found, MPEG-1 was basically designed to allow moving pictures and sound to be encoded into the bit rate of an audio Compact Disc. The resultant video CD was quite successful but has now been superseded by DVD. To meet the low bit requirement, MPEG-1 down sampled the images heavily as well as using picture rates of only 24–30 Hz, and the resulting quality was moderate.

The subsequent MPEG-2 standard was considerably broader in scope and of wider appeal. For example, MPEG-2 supports interlace and HD, whereas MPEG-1 did not. MPEG-2 has become very important because it has been chosen as the compression scheme for both DVB (digital video broadcasting) and DVD (digital video disc). Developments in standardising scaleable and multiresolution compression that would have become MPEG-3 were ready by the time MPEG-2 was ready to be standardised and so this work was incorporated into MPEG-2, and as a result there is no MPEG-3 standard.

MPEG-4 uses further coding tools with additional complexity to achieve higher compression factors than MPEG-2. In addition to more efficient coding of video, MPEG-4 moves closer to computer graphics applications. In the more complex profiles, the MPEG-4 decoder effectively becomes a rendering processor and the compressed bitstream describes three-dimensional shapes and surface texture. It is to be expected that MPEG-4 will become as important to the Internet and wireless delivery as MPEG-2 has become in DVD and DVB.

The MPEG-4 standard is extremely wide ranging and it is unlikely that a single decoder will ever be made that can handle every possibility. Many of the graphics applications of MPEG-4 are outside telecommunications requirements. In 2001 the International Telecommunications Union (ITU) VCEG (Video Coding Experts Group) joined with ISO MPEG to form the JVT (Joint Video Team). The resulting standard is variously known as AVC (advanced video coding), H.264, or MPEG-4 Part 10. This standard further refines the video coding aspects of MPEG-4, which were themselves refinements of MPEG-2, to produce a coding scheme having the same applications as MPEG-2 but with the higher performance needed to broadcast HDTV.

To avoid tedium, in cases in which the term MPEG is used in this chapter without qualification, it can be taken to mean MPEG-1, -2, or -4 or H.264. Where a specific standard is being contrasted it will be made clear.

requires too much bandwidth. With compression, HDTV can economically be transmitted to the home. Compression does not make video-on-demand or HDTV possible, it makes them economically viable.

In workstations designed for the editing of audio and/or video, the source material is stored on hard disks for rapid access. Whilst top-grade systems may function without compression, many systems use compression to offset the high cost of disk storage. When a workstation is used for offline editing, a high compression factor can be used and artifacts will be visible in the picture.

This is of no consequence, as the picture is seen only by the editor, who uses it to make an EDL (edit decision list), which is no more than a list of actions and the timecodes at which they occur. The original uncompressed material is then conformed to the EDL to obtain a high-quality edited work. When online editing is being performed, the output of the workstation is the finished product and clearly a lower compression factor will have to be used.

Perhaps it is in broadcasting where the use of compression will have its greatest impact. There is only one electromagnetic spectrum and pressure from other services such as cellular telephones makes efficient use of bandwidth mandatory. Analog television broadcasting is an old technology and makes very inefficient use of bandwidth. Its replacement by a compressed digital transmission will be inevitable for the practical reason that the bandwidth is needed elsewhere.

Fortunately in broadcasting there is a mass market for decoders and these can be implemented as low-cost integrated circuits. Fewer encoders are needed and so it is less important if these are expensive. Whilst the cost of digital storage goes down year by year, the cost of electromagnetic spectrum goes up. Consequently in the future the pressure to use compression in recording will ease, whereas the pressure to use it in radio communications will increase.

SPATIAL AND TEMPORAL REDUNDANCY IN MPEG

Video signals exist in four dimensions: the attributes of the sample, the horizontal and vertical spatial axes, and the time axis. Compression can be applied in any or all of those four dimensions. MPEG-2 assumes 8-bit colour difference signals as the input, requiring rounding if the source is 10-bit. The sampling rate of the colour signals is less than that of the luminance. This is done by down sampling the colour samples horizontally and generally vertically as well. Essentially an MPEG-2 system has three parallel simultaneous channels, one for luminance and two for colour difference, which after coding are multiplexed into a single bitstream.

Figure 6.7a shows that when individual pictures are compressed without reference to any other pictures, the time axis does not enter the process, which is therefore described as intra-coded (intra = within) compression. The term spatial coding will also be found. It is an advantage of intra-coded video that there is no restriction to the editing that can be carried out on the picture sequence. As a result compressed VTRs such as Digital Betacam, DVC, and D-9 use spatial coding. Cut editing may take place on the compressed data directly if necessary. As spatial coding treats each picture independently, it can employ certain techniques developed for the compression of still pictures. The ISO JPEG (Joint Photographic Experts

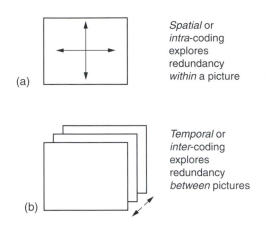

FIGURE 6.7
(a) Spatial or intra-coding works on individual images. (b) Temporal or inter-coding works on successive images.

Group) compression standards[5,6] are in this category. Where a succession of JPEG-coded images is used for television, the term "motion JPEG" will be found.

Greater compression factors can be obtained by taking account of the redundancy from one picture to the next. This involves the time axis, as Figure 6.7b shows, and the process is known as inter-coded (inter = between) or temporal compression.

Temporal coding allows a higher compression factor, but has the disadvantage that an individual picture may exist only in terms of the differences from a previous picture. Clearly editing must be undertaken with caution and arbitrary cuts simply cannot be performed on the MPEG bitstream. If a previous picture is removed by an edit, the difference data will then be insufficient to re-create the current picture.

Intra-coding works in three dimensions: on the horizontal and vertical spatial axes and on the sample values. Analysis of typical television pictures reveals that, whilst there is a high spatial frequency content due to detailed areas of the picture, there is a relatively small amount of energy at such frequencies. Often pictures contain sizeable areas in which the same or similar pixel values exist. This gives rise to low spatial frequencies. The average brightness of the picture results in a substantial zero frequency component. Simply omitting the high-frequency components is unacceptable as this causes an obvious softening of the picture.

A coding gain can be obtained by taking advantage of the fact that the amplitude of the spatial components falls with frequency. It is also possible to take advantage of the eye's reduced sensitivity to noise in high spatial frequencies. If the spatial frequency spectrum is divided into frequency bands the high-frequency bands can be described by fewer bits, not only because their amplitudes are smaller, but also because more noise can be tolerated. The wavelet transform and the discrete cosine transform used in MPEG allow two-dimensional pictures to be described in the frequency domain and these were discussed in Chapter 3. Inter-coding takes further advantage of the similarities between successive pictures in real material. Instead of sending information for each picture separately, inter-coders will send the difference between the previous picture and the current picture in a form of differential coding. Figure 6.8 shows the principle. A picture store is required at the coder to allow comparison to be made between successive pictures and a similar store is required at the decoder to make the previous picture available. The difference data may be treated as a picture itself and subjected to some form of transform-based spatial compression.

The simple system of Figure 6.8a is of limited use, as in the case of a transmission error, every subsequent picture would be affected. Channel switching in a television set would also be impossible. In practical systems a modification is required. One approach is the so-called "leaky predictor" in which the next picture is predicted from a limited number of previous pictures rather than from an indefinite number. As a result errors cannot propagate indefinitely. The approach used in MPEG is that periodically some absolute picture data are transmitted in place of difference data.

Figure 6.8b shows that absolute picture data, known as I or intra pictures, are interleaved with pictures that are created using difference data, known as P or predicted pictures. I pictures require a large amount of data, whereas the P pictures require fewer data. As a result the instantaneous data rate varies dramatically and buffering has to be used to allow a constant transmission rate. The leaky predictor needs less buffering as the compression factor does not change so much from picture to picture.

The I picture and all the P pictures prior to the next I picture are called a group of pictures (GOP). For a high compression factor, a large number of P pictures should be present between I pictures, making a long GOP. However, a long GOP delays recovery from a transmission error. The compressed bitstream can be edited only at I pictures as shown.

In the case of moving objects, although their appearance may not change greatly from picture to picture, the data representing them on a fixed sampling grid will change and so large differences will be generated between successive

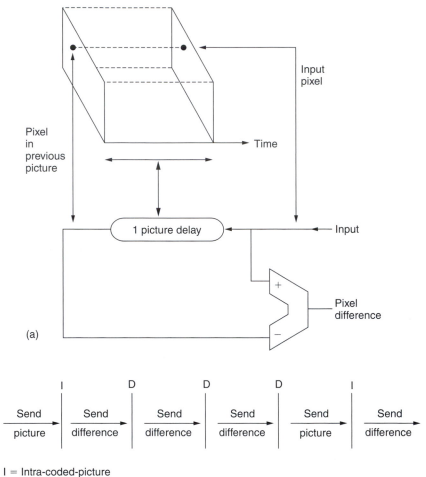

(a)

I = Intra-coded-picture
(b)   D = Differentially coded picture

FIGURE 6.8
(a) An inter-coded system uses a delay to calculate the pixel differences between successive pictures. To prevent error propagation, (b) intra-coded pictures may be used periodically.

pictures. It is a great advantage if the effect of motion can be removed from difference data so that they reflect only the changes in appearance of a moving object because a much greater coding gain can then be obtained. This is the objective of motion compensation.

In real television program material objects move around before a fixed camera or the camera itself moves. Motion compensation is a process that effectively measures motion of objects from one picture to the next so that it can allow for that motion when looking for redundancy between pictures.

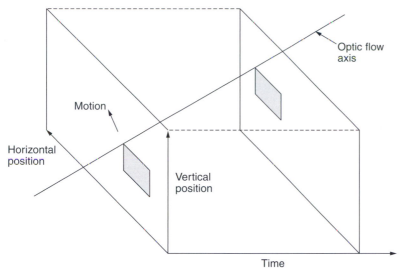

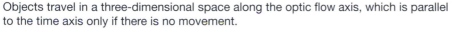

FIGURE 6.9
Objects travel in a three-dimensional space along the optic flow axis, which is parallel to the time axis only if there is no movement.

Figure 6.9 shows that moving pictures can be expressed in a three-dimensional space, which results from the screen area moving along the time axis. In the case of still objects, the only motion is along the time axis. However, when an object moves, it does so along the optic flow axis, which is not parallel to the time axis. The optic flow axis joins the same point on a moving object as it takes on various screen positions.

It will be clear that the data values representing a moving object change with respect to the time axis. However, looking along the optic flow axis, the appearance of an object changes only if it deforms, moves into shadow, or rotates. For simple translational motions the data representing an object are highly redundant with respect to the optic flow axis. Thus if the optic flow axis can be located, coding gain can be obtained in the presence of motion.

A motion-compensated coder works as follows. An I picture is sent, but is also locally stored so that it can be compared with the next input picture to find motion vectors for various areas of the picture. The I picture is then shifted according to these vectors to cancel interpicture motion. The resultant predicted picture is compared with the actual picture to produce a prediction error also called a residual. The prediction error is transmitted with the motion vectors. At the receiver the original I picture is also held in a memory. It is shifted according to the transmitted motion vectors to create the predicted picture and then the prediction error is added to it to re-create the original. When a picture is encoded in this way MPEG calls it a P picture.

Figure 6.10a shows that spatial redundancy is redundancy within a single image, for example, repeated pixel values in a large area of blue sky. Temporal redundancy (Figure 6.10b) exists between successive images.

Where temporal compression is used, the current picture is not sent in its entirety; instead the difference between the current picture and the previous picture is sent. The decoder already has the previous picture, and so it can add the difference to make the current picture. A difference picture is created by subtracting every pixel in one picture from the corresponding pixel in another pixel. This is trivially easy in a progressively scanned system, but MPEG-2 has had to develop greater complexity so that this can also be done with interlaced pictures. The handling of interlace in MPEG will be detailed later.

A difference picture is an image of a kind, although not a viewable one, and so should contain some kind of spatial redundancy. Figure 6.10c shows that

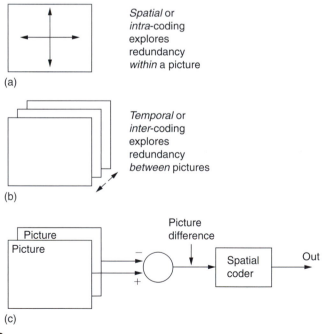

FIGURE 6.10
(a) Spatial or intra-coding works on individual images. (b) Temporal or inter-coding works on successive images. (c) In MPEG inter-coding is used to create difference images. These are then compressed spatially.

MPEG-2 takes advantage of both forms of redundancy. Picture differences are spatially compressed prior to transmission. At the decoder the spatial compression is decoded to re-create the difference picture, and this difference picture is added to the previous picture to complete the decoding process.

Whenever objects move they will be in a different place in successive pictures. This will result in large amounts of difference data. MPEG-2 overcomes the problem using motion compensation. The encoder contains a motion estimator, which measures the direction and distance of motion between pictures and outputs these as vectors, which are sent to the decoder. When the decoder receives the vectors it uses them to shift data in a previous picture to resemble the current picture more closely. Effectively the vectors are describing the optic flow axis of some moving screen area, along which axis the image is highly redundant. Vectors are bipolar codes that determine the amount of horizontal and vertical shift required.

In real images, moving objects do not necessarily maintain their appearance as they move; for example, objects may turn, move into shade or light, or move behind other objects. Consequently motion compensation can never be ideal and it is still necessary to send a picture difference to make up for any shortcomings in the motion compensation.

Figure 6.11 shows how this works. In addition to the motion-encoding system, the coder also contains a motion decoder. When the encoder outputs motion vectors, it also uses them locally in the same way that a real decoder will and is able to produce a predicted picture based solely on the previous picture shifted by motion vectors. This is then subtracted from the actual current picture to produce a prediction error or residual, which is an image of a kind that can be spatially compressed.

The decoder takes the previous picture, shifts it with the vectors to re-create the predicted picture, and then decodes and adds the prediction error to produce the actual picture. Picture data sent as vectors plus prediction error are said to be P coded.

The concept of sending a prediction error is a useful approach because it allows both the motion estimation and the compensation to be imperfect.

A good motion-compensation system will send just the right amount of vector data. With insufficient vector data, the prediction error will be large, but transmission of excess vector data will also cause the bit rate to rise. There will be an

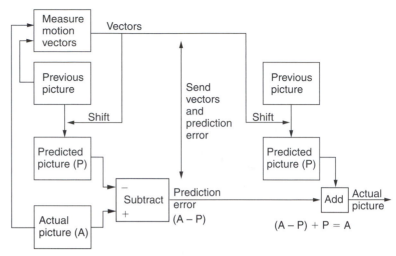

FIGURE 6.11
A motion-compensated compression system. The coder calculates motion vectors, which are transmitted as well as being used locally to create a predicted picture. The difference between the predicted picture and the actual picture is transmitted as a prediction error.

optimum balance, which minimizes the sum of the prediction error data and the vector data.

In MPEG-2 the balance is obtained by dividing the screen into areas called macroblocks, which are 16 luminance pixels square. Each macroblock is steered by a vector. The boundary of a macroblock is fixed and so the vector does not move the macroblock. Instead the vector tells the decoder where to look in another frame to find pixel data to fetch to the macroblock. Figure 6.12a shows this concept. The shifting process is generally done by modifying the read address of a RAM using the vector. This can shift by one-pixel steps. MPEG-2 vectors have half-pixel resolution, so it is necessary to interpolate between pixels from RAM to obtain half-pixel-shifted values.

Real moving objects will not coincide with macroblocks and so the motion compensation will not be ideal but the prediction error makes up for any shortcomings. Figure 6.12b shows the case in which the boundary of a moving object bisects a macroblock. If the system measures the moving part of the macroblock and sends a vector, the decoder will shift the entire block, making the stationary part wrong. If no vector is sent, the moving part will be wrong. Both approaches are legal in MPEG-2, because the prediction error sorts out the incorrect values.

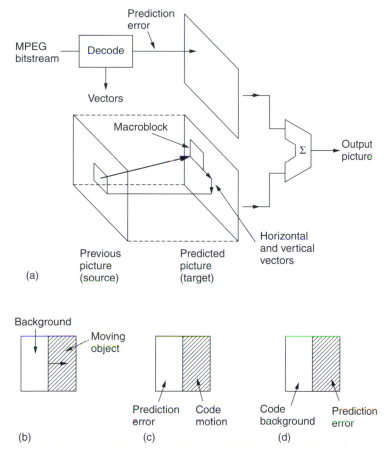

FIGURE 6.12
(a) In motion compensation, pixel data are brought to a fixed macroblock in the target picture from a variety of places in another picture. (b) Where only part of a macroblock is moving, motion compensation is nonideal. The motion can be coded (c), causing a prediction error in the background, or the background can be coded (d), causing a prediction error in the moving object.

An intelligent coder might try both approaches to see which requires the least prediction error data.

The prediction error concept also allows the use of simple but inaccurate motion estimators in low-cost systems. The greater prediction error data are handled using a higher bit rate. On the other hand, if a precision motion estimator is available, a very high compression factor may be achieved because the prediction error data are minimized. MPEG-2 does not specify how motion is to be measured; it simply defines how a decoder will interpret the vectors. Encoder designers are free to use any motion-estimation system provided that the right vector protocol is created. Chapter 5 contrasted a number of motion estimation techniques.

Figure 6.13a shows that a macroblock contains both luminance and colour difference data at different resolutions. Most of the MPEG-2 profiles use a 4:2:0 structure, which means that the colour is down sampled by a factor of 2 in both axes. Thus in a 16×16 pixel block, there are only 8×8 colour difference sampling sites. MPEG-2 is based upon the 8×8 DCT (see The Discrete Cosine Transform in Chapter 3) and so the 16×16 block is the screen area that contains an 8×8 colour difference sampling block. Thus in 4:2:0 in each macroblock there are four luminance DCT blocks, one R–Y DCT block, and one B–Y DCT block, all steered by the same vector.

In the 4:2:2 profile of MPEG-2, shown in Figure 6.13b, the chroma is not down sampled vertically, and so there are twice as many chroma data in each macroblock, which is otherwise substantially the same.

I AND P CODING

Predictive (P) coding cannot be used indefinitely, as it is prone to error propagation. A further problem is that it becomes impossible to decode the transmission

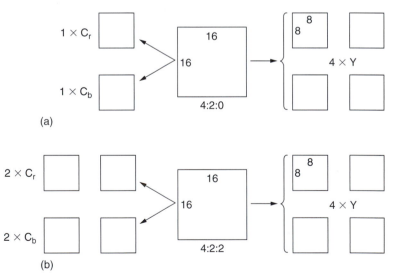

FIGURE 6.13
The structure of a macroblock. (A macroblock is the screen area steered by one vector.) (a) In 4:2:0, there are two chroma DCT blocks per macroblock, whereas (b) in 4:2:2 there are four; 4:2:2 needs 33% more data than 4:2:0.

if reception begins part way through. In real video signals, cuts or edits can be present, across which there is little redundancy and which make motion estimators throw up their hands.

In the absence of redundancy over a cut, there is nothing to be done but to send the new picture information in absolute form. This is called I coding, in which I is an abbreviation of intra-coding. As I coding needs no previous picture for decoding, then decoding can begin at I-coded information.

MPEG-2 is effectively a toolkit and there is no compulsion to use all the tools available. Thus an encoder may choose whether to use I or P coding, either once and for all or dynamically on a macroblock-by-macroblock basis.

For practical reasons, an entire frame may be encoded as I macroblocks periodically. This creates a place where the bitstream might be edited or where decoding could begin.

Figure 6.14 shows a typical application of the Simple Profile of MPEG-2. Periodically an I picture is created. Between I pictures are P pictures, which are based on the previous picture. These P pictures predominantly contain macroblocks having vectors and prediction errors. However, it is perfectly legal for P pictures to contain I macroblocks. This might be useful where, for example, a camera pan introduces new material at the edge of the screen that cannot be created from an earlier picture.

Note that although what is sent is called a P picture, it is not a picture at all. It is a set of instructions to convert the previous picture into the current picture. If the previous picture is lost, decoding is impossible. An I picture together with all the pictures before the next I picture form a GOP.

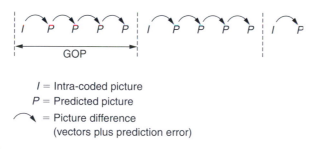

I = Intra-coded picture
P = Predicted picture
= Picture difference
(vectors plus prediction error)

FIGURE 6.14
A Simple Profile MPEG-2 signal may contain periodic I pictures with a number of P pictures between.

BI-DIRECTIONAL CODING

Motion-compensated predictive coding is a useful compression technique, but it does have the drawback that it can take data only from a previous picture. When moving objects reveal a background this is completely unknown in previous pictures and forward prediction fails. However, more of the background is visible in later pictures. Figure 6.15 shows the concept. In the centre of the diagram, a moving object has revealed some background. The previous picture can contribute nothing, whereas the next picture contains all that is required.

Bi-directional coding is shown in Figure 6.16. A bi-directional or B macroblock can be created using a combination of motion compensation and the addition of a prediction error. This can be done by forward prediction from a previous picture or backward prediction from a subsequent picture. It is also possible to use an average of both forward and backward prediction. On noisy material this may result in some reduction in bit rate. The technique is also a useful way of portraying a dissolve.

The averaging process in MPEG-2 is a simple linear interpolation, which works well when only one B picture exists between the reference pictures before and after. A larger number of B pictures would require weighted interpolation but MPEG-2 does not support this.

Typically two B pictures are inserted between P pictures or between I and P pictures. As can be seen, B pictures are never predicted from one another, only from I or P pictures. A typical GOP for broadcasting purposes might have the structure IBBPBBPBBPBB. Note that the last B pictures in the GOP require the I picture in the next GOP for decoding and so the GOPs are not truly independent. Independence can be obtained by creating a closed

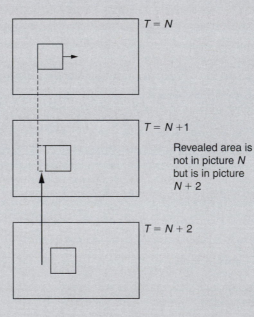

FIGURE 6.15
In bi-directional coding the revealed background can be efficiently coded by bringing data back from a future picture.

GOP that may contain B pictures but that ends with a P picture. It is also legal to have a B picture in which every macroblock is forward predicted, needing no future picture for decoding.

Bi-directional coding is very powerful. Figure 6.17 is a constant quality curve showing how the bit rate changes with the type of coding. On the left, only I or spatial coding is used, whereas on the right an IBBP structure is used. This means that there are two bi-directionally coded pictures in between a spatially coded picture (I) and a forward-predicted picture (P). Note how, for the same quality, the system that uses only spatial coding needs two and a half times the bit rate that the bi-directionally coded system needs.

Clearly information in the future has yet to be transmitted and so is not normally available to the decoder. MPEG-2 gets around the problem by sending pictures in the wrong order. Picture reordering requires a delay in the encoder and a delay in the decoder to put the order right again. Thus the overall codec delay must rise when bi-directional coding is used. This is quite consistent with Figure 6.3, which showed that as the compression factor rises the latency must also rise.

Figure 6.18 shows that although the original picture sequence is IBBPBBPBBIBB…, this is transmitted as IPBBPBBBIBB… so that the future picture is already in the decoder before bi-directional decoding begins. Note that the I picture of the next GOP is actually sent before the last B pictures of the current GOP.

Figure 6.18 also shows that the amount of data required by each picture is dramatically different. I pictures have only spatial redundancy and so need a lot of data to describe them. P pictures need fewer data because they are created by shifting the I picture with vectors and then adding a prediction error picture. B pictures need the fewest data of all because they can be created from I or P.

With pictures requiring a variable length of time to transmit, arriving in the wrong order, the decoder needs some help. This takes the form of picture-type flags and time stamps.

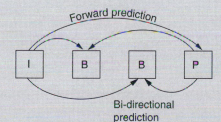

    I = Intra- or spatially coded
         'anchor' picture.
    P = Forward predicted. Coder sends
        difference between I and P decoder.
        Adds difference to create P.

    B = Bi-directionally coded picture can
        be coded from a previous.
        I or P picture or a later I or P picture.
        B pictures are not coded from each other.

FIGURE 6.16
In bi-directional coding, a number of B pictures can be inserted between periodic forward-predicted pictures. See text.

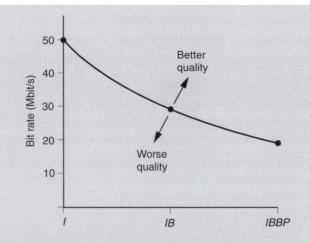

FIGURE 6.17
Bi-directional coding is very powerful as it allows the same quality with only 40 percent of the bit rate of intra-coding. However, the encoding and decoding delays must increase. Coding over a longer time span is more efficient but editing is more difficult.

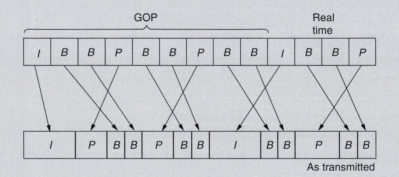

FIGURE 6.18
Comparison of pictures before and after compression showing sequence change and varying amount of data needed by each picture type. I, P, and B pictures use unequal amounts of data.

CODING APPLICATIONS

Figure 6.19 shows a variety of GOP structures. The simplest is the III... sequence in which every picture is intra-coded. Pictures can be fully decoded without reference to any other pictures and so editing is straightforward. However, this approach requires about two and a half times the bit rate of a full bi-directional system. Bi-directional coding is most useful for final delivery of postproduced material either by broadcast or on pre-recorded media, as there is then no editing

I I I I I I ...	I only freely editable, needs high bit rate
I P P P P I P ...	Forward predicted only, needs less decoder memory, used in Simple Profile.
I B B P B B P B ...	Forward and bi-directional, best compression factor, needs large decoder memory, hard to edit.
I B I B I B ...	Lower bit rate than I only, editable with moderate processing.

FIGURE 6.19
Various possible GOP structures used with MPEG. See text for details.

requirement. As a compromise the IBIB... structure can be used, which has some of the bit rate advantage of bi-directional coding but without too much latency. It is possible to edit an IBIB stream by performing some processing. If it is required to remove the video following a B picture, that B picture could not be decoded because it needs I pictures on either side of it for bi-directional decoding. The solution is to decode the B picture first and then reencode it with forward prediction only from the previous I picture. The subsequent I picture can then be replaced by an edit process. Some quality loss is inevitable in this process but this is acceptable in applications such as ENG and industrial video.

SPATIAL COMPRESSION

Spatial compression in MPEG-2 is used in I pictures on actual picture data and in P and B pictures on prediction error data. MPEG-2 uses the discrete cosine transform described in Chapter 3. The DCT works on blocks and in MPEG-2 these are 8×8 pixels. The macroblocks of the motion-compensation structure are designed so they can be broken down into 8×8 DCT blocks. In a 4:2:0 macroblock there will be six DCT blocks, whereas in a 4:2:2 macroblock there will be eight.

Figure 6.20 shows the table of basis functions or wave table for an 8×8 DCT. Adding these two-dimensional waveforms together in different proportions will give any original 8×8-pixel block. The coefficients of the DCT simply control the proportion of each wave that is added in the inverse transform. The top-left wave has no modulation at all because it conveys the DC component of the block. This coefficient will be a unipolar (positive only) value in the case

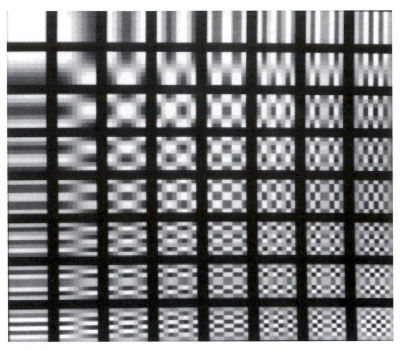

FIGURE 6.20
The discrete cosine transform breaks up an image area into discrete frequencies in two dimensions. The lowest frequency can be seen here at the top-left corner. Horizontal frequency increases to the right and vertical frequency increases downward.

of luminance and will typically be the largest value in the block as the spectrum of typical video signals is dominated by the DC component.

Increasing the DC coefficient adds a constant amount to every pixel. Moving to the right, the coefficients represent increasing horizontal spatial frequencies, and moving downward, the coefficients represent increasing vertical spatial frequencies. The bottom-right coefficient represents the highest diagonal frequencies in the block. All these coefficients are bipolar, where the polarity indicates whether the original spatial waveform at that frequency was inverted.

Figure 6.21 shows a one-dimensional example of an inverse transform. The DC coefficient produces a constant level throughout the pixel block. The remaining waves in the table are AC coefficients. A zero coefficient would result in no modulation, leaving the DC level unchanged. The wave next to the DC component represents the lowest frequency in the transform, which is half a cycle per block. A positive coefficient would make the left side of the block brighter and the right side darker, whereas a negative coefficient would do the opposite. The magnitude

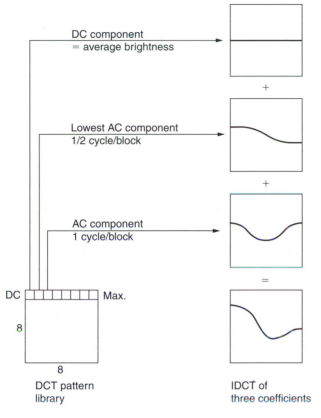

FIGURE 6.21
A one-dimensional inverse transform. See text for details.

of the coefficient determines the amplitude of the wave that is added. Figure 6.21 also shows that the next wave has a frequency of one cycle per block, i.e., the block is made brighter at both sides and darker in the middle.

Consequently an inverse DCT is no more than a process of mixing various pixel patterns from the wave table in which the relative amplitudes and polarity of these patterns are controlled by the coefficients. The original transform is simply a mechanism that finds the coefficient amplitudes from the original pixel block.

The DCT itself achieves no compression at all. Sixty-four pixels are converted to 64 coefficients. However, in typical pictures, not all coefficients will have significant values; there will often be a few dominant coefficients. The coefficients representing the higher two-dimensional spatial frequencies will often be zero or of small value in large areas, due to blurring or simply plain undetailed areas before the camera.

Statistically, the farther from the top-left corner of the wave table the coefficient is, the smaller will be its magnitude. Coding gain (the technical term for reduction in the number of bits needed) is achieved by transmitting the low-valued coefficients with shorter word lengths. The zero-valued coefficients need not be transmitted at all. Thus it is not the DCT that compresses the data, it is the subsequent processing. The DCT simply expresses the data in a form that makes the subsequent processing easier.

Higher compression factors require the coefficient word length to be further reduced using requantizing. Coefficients are divided by some factor that increases the size of the quantizing step. The smaller number of steps that result permits coding with fewer bits, but, of course, with an increased quantizing error. The coefficients will be multiplied by a reciprocal factor in the decoder to return to the correct magnitude.

Inverse transforming a requantized coefficient means that the frequency it represents is reproduced in the output with the wrong amplitude. The difference between original and reconstructed amplitude is regarded as a noise added to the wanted data. Figure 6.22 shows that the visibility of such noise is far from uniform. The maximum sensitivity is found at DC and falls thereafter. As a result the top-left coefficient is often treated as a special case and left unchanged. It may warrant more error protection than other coefficients.

MPEG-2 takes advantage of the falling sensitivity to noise. Prior to requantizing, each coefficient is divided by a different weighting constant as a function

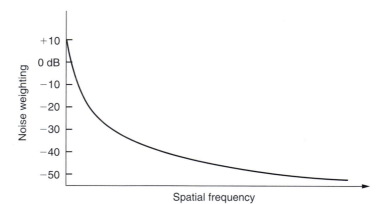

FIGURE 6.22
The sensitivity of the eye to noise is greatest at low frequencies and drops rapidly with increasing frequency. This can be used to mask quantizing noise caused by the compression process.

of its frequency. Figure 6.23 shows a typical weighting process. Naturally the decoder must have a corresponding inverse weighting. This weighting process has the effect of reducing the magnitude of high-frequency coefficients dispro-portionately. Clearly, different weighting will be needed for colour difference data as colour is perceived differently.

P and B pictures are decoded by adding a prediction error image to a refer-ence image. That reference image will contain weighted noise. One purpose of the prediction error is to cancel that noise to prevent tolerance buildup. If the prediction error were also to contain weighted noise, this result would not be obtained. Consequently prediction error coefficients are flat weighted.

When forward prediction fails, such as in the case of new material introduced in a P picture by a pan, P coding would set the vectors to zero and encode the new data entirely as an unweighted prediction error. In this case it is better to encode that material as an I macroblock because then weighting can be used and this will require fewer bits.

Requantizing increases the step size of the coefficients, whereas the inverse weighting in the decoder results in step sizes that increase with frequency. The larger step size increases the quantizing noise at high frequencies where

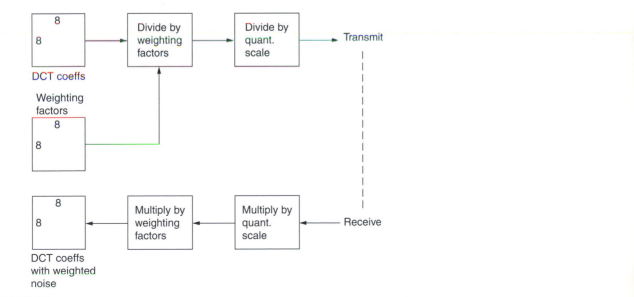

FIGURE 6.23
Weighting is used to make the noise caused by requantizing different at each frequency.

it is less visible. Effectively the noise floor is shaped to match the sensitivity of the eye. The quantizing table in use at the encoder can be transmitted to the decoder periodically in the bitstream.

SCANNING AND RUN-LENGTH/VARIABLE-LENGTH CODING

Study of the signal statistics gained from extensive analysis of real material is used to measure the probability of a given coefficient having a given value. This probability turns out to be highly nonuniform, suggesting the possibility of a variable-length encoding for the coefficient values. On average, the higher the spatial frequency, the lower the value of a coefficient will be. This means that the value of a coefficient falls as a function of its radius from the DC coefficient.

Typical material often has many coefficients that are zero valued, especially after requantizing. The distribution of these also follows a pattern. The non-zero values tend to be found in the top-left corner of the DCT block, but as the radius increases, not only do the coefficient values fall, but it becomes increasingly likely that these small coefficients will be interspersed with zero-valued coefficients. As the radius increases further it is probable that a region where all coefficients are zero will be entered.

MPEG-2 uses all these attributes of DCT coefficients when encoding a coefficient block. By sending the coefficients in an optimum order, by describing their values with Huffman coding, and by using run-length encoding for the zero-valued coefficients it is possible to achieve a significant reduction in coefficient data that remains entirely lossless. Despite the complexity of this process, it does contribute to improved picture quality because for a given bit rate lossless coding of the coefficients must be better than requantizing, which is lossy. Of course, for lower bit rates both will be required.

It is an advantage to scan in a sequence of which the largest coefficient values are scanned first. Then the next coefficient is more likely to be zero than the previous one. With progressively scanned material, a regular zig-zag scan begins in the top-left corner and ends in the bottom-right corner as shown in Figure 6.24. Zig-zag scanning means that significant values are more likely to be transmitted first, followed by the zero values. Instead of coding these zeros, a unique "end of block" (EOB) symbol is transmitted instead.

As the zig-zag scan approaches the last finite coefficient it is increasingly likely that some zero-value coefficients will be scanned. Instead of transmitting the coefficients as zeros, the zero-run-length, i.e., the number of zero-valued coefficients

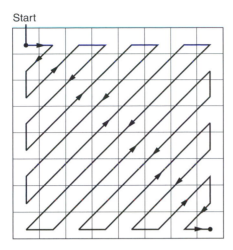

Start

FIGURE 6.24
The zig-zag scan for a progressively scanned image.

in the scan sequence, is encoded into the next nonzero coefficient, which is itself variable-length coded. This combination of run-length and variable-length coding is known as RLC/VLC in MPEG-2.

The DC coefficient is handled separately because it is differentially coded and this discussion relates to the AC coefficients. Three items need to be handled for each coefficient: the zero-run-length prior to this coefficient, the word length, and the coefficient value itself. The word length needs to be known by the decoder so that it can correctly parse the bitstream. The word length of the coefficient is expressed directly as an integer called the size.

Figure 6.25a shows that a two-dimensional run/size table is created. One dimension expresses the zero-run-length, the other the size. A run length of zero is obtained when adjacent coefficients are nonzero, but a code of 0/0 has no meaningful run/size interpretation and so this bit pattern is used for the EOB symbol.

In the case in which the zero-run-length exceeds 14, a code of 15/0 is used, signifying that there are 15 zero-valued coefficients. This is then followed by another run/size parameter whose run-length value is added to the previous 15.

The run/size parameters contain redundancy because some combinations are more common than others. Figure 6.25b shows that each run/size value is converted to a variable-length Huffman code word for transmission. The Huffman codes are designed so that short codes are never a prefix of long codes, so that the decoder can deduce the parsing by testing an increasing number of bits until a match with the lookup table is found. Having parsed and decoded

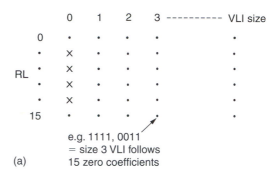

e.g. 1111, 0011
= size 3 VLI follows
15 zero coefficients

(a)

Run \ Size	0	1	2	3	→ etc.
0	1010 (EOB)	00	01	100	
1	–	1100	11011		
2	–	11100	11111001		
3	–	111010	111110111		
4	–	111011	1111111000		
5	–	1111010			

(b)   etc.

FIGURE 6.25
Run-length and variable-length coding simultaneously compresses runs of zero-valued coefficients and describes the word length of a non-zero coefficient.

the Huffman run/size code, the decoder then knows what the coefficient word length will be and can correctly parse that.

The variable-length coefficient code has to describe a bipolar coefficient, i.e., one that can be positive or negative. Figure 6.25c shows that for a particular size, the coding scale has a certain gap in it. For example, all values from −7 to +7 can be sent by a size 3 code, so a size 4 code has to send only the values of −15 to −8 and +8 to +15. The coefficient code is sent as a pure binary number whose value ranges from all zeros to all ones where the maximum value is a function of the size. The number range is divided into two, the lower half of the codes specifying negative values and the upper half specifying positive values.

In the case of positive numbers, the transmitted binary value is the actual coefficient value, whereas in the case of negative numbers a constant must be subtracted that is a function of the size. In the case of a size 4 code, the constant etc.

Coefficient to be transmitted	Coefficient code	Size parameter
15	1 1 1 1	
14	1 1 1 0	
13	1 1 0 1	
12	1 1 0 0	4
11	1 0 1 1	
10	1 0 1 0	
9	1 0 0 1	
8	1 0 0 0	
7	1 1 1	
6	1 1 0	3
5	1 0 1	
4	1 0 0	
3	1 1	2
2	1 0	
1	1	1
−1	0	
−2	0 1	2
−3	0 0	
−4	0 1 1	
−5	0 1 0	3
−6	0 0 1	
−7	0 0 0	
−8	0 1 1 1	
−9	0 1 1 0	
−10	0 1 0 1	
−11	0 1 0 0	4
−12	0 0 1 1	
−13	0 0 1 0	
−14	0 0 0 1	
−15	0 0 0 0	

(c)

etc.

FIGURE 6.25
(Continued)

is 15_{10}. Thus a size 4 parameter of 0111_2 (7_{10}) would be interpreted as $7-15 = -8$. A size of 5 has a constant of 31 so a transmitted code of 01010_2 (10_2) would be interpreted as $10-31 = -21$.

This technique saves a bit because, for example, 63 values from -31 to $+31$ are coded with only 5 bits having only 32 combinations. This is possible because that extra bit is effectively encoded into the run/size parameter.

Figure 6.26 shows the whole spatial coding subsystem. Macroblocks are subdivided into DCT blocks and the DCT is calculated. The resulting coefficients are multiplied by the weighting matrix and then requantized. The coefficients are

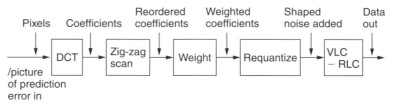

FIGURE 6.26

A complete spatial coding system, which can compress an I picture or the prediction error in P and B pictures. See text for details.

then reordered by the zig-zag scan so that full advantage can be taken of run-length and variable-length coding. The last non-zero coefficient in the scan is followed by the EOB symbol.

In predictive coding, sometimes the motion-compensated prediction is nearly exact and so the prediction error will be almost zero. This can also happen on still parts of the scene. MPEG-2 takes advantage of this by sending a code to tell the decoder there is no prediction error data for the macroblock concerned.

The success of temporal coding depends on the accuracy of the vectors. Trying to reduce the bit rate by reducing the accuracy of the vectors is false economy as this simply increases the prediction error. Consequently for a given GOP structure it is only in the spatial coding that the overall bit rate is determined. The RLC/VLC coding is lossless and so its contribution to the compression cannot be varied. If the bit rate is too high, the only option is to increase the size of the coefficient-requantizing steps. This has the effect of shortening the word length of large coefficients, and rounding small coefficients to zero, so that the bit rate goes down. Clearly if taken too far the picture quality will also suffer because at some point the noise floor will become visible as some form of artifact.

A BI-DIRECTIONAL CODER

MPEG-2 does not specify how an encoder is to be built or what coding decisions it should make. Instead it specifies the protocol of the bitstream at the output. As a result the coder shown in Figure 6.27 is only an example.

Figure 6.27a shows the component parts of the coder. At the input is a chain of picture stores, which can be bypassed for re-ordering purposes. This allows a picture to be encoded ahead of its normal timing when bi-directional coding is employed.

At the centre is a dual motion estimator, which can simultaneously measure motion between the input picture, an earlier picture, and a later picture. These reference pictures are held in frame stores. The vectors from the motion estimator

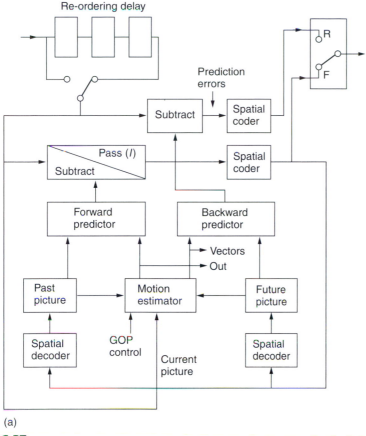

(a)

FIGURE 6.27
A bi-directional coder. (a) The essential components.

are locally used to shift a picture in a frame store to form a predicted picture. This is subtracted from the input picture to produce a prediction error picture, which is then spatially coded.

The bi-directional encoding process will now be described. A GOP begins with an I picture, which is intra-coded. In Figure 6.27b the I picture emerges from the reordering delay. No prediction is possible on an I picture so the motion estimator is inactive. There is no predicted picture and so the prediction error subtractor is set simply to pass the input. The only processing that is active is the forward spatial coder, which describes the picture with DCT coefficients. The output of the forward spatial coder is locally decoded and stored in the past picture frame store.

The reason for the spatial encode/decode is that the past picture frame store now contains exactly what the decoder frame store will contain, including the

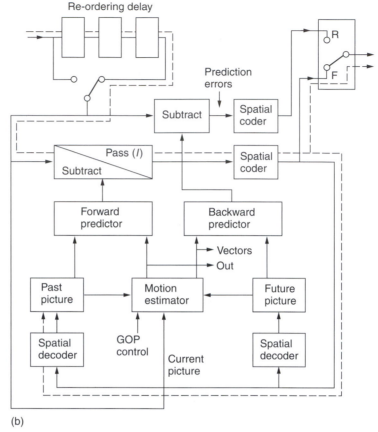

(b)

FIGURE 6.27

(Continued) (b) Signal flow when coding an I picture.

effects of any requantizing errors. When the same picture is used as a reference at both ends of a differential coding system, the errors will cancel out.

Having encoded the I picture, attention turns to the P picture. The input sequence is IBBP, but the transmitted sequence must be IPBB. Figure 6.27c shows that the reordering delay is bypassed to select the P picture. This passes to the motion estimator, which compares it with the I picture and outputs a vector for each macroblock. The forward predictor uses these vectors to shift the I picture so that it more closely resembles the P picture. The predicted picture is then subtracted from the actual picture to produce a forward prediction error. This is then spatially coded. Thus the P picture is transmitted as a set of vectors and a prediction error image.

The P picture is locally decoded in the right-hand decoder. This takes the forward-predicted picture and adds the decoded prediction error to obtain exactly what the decoder will obtain.

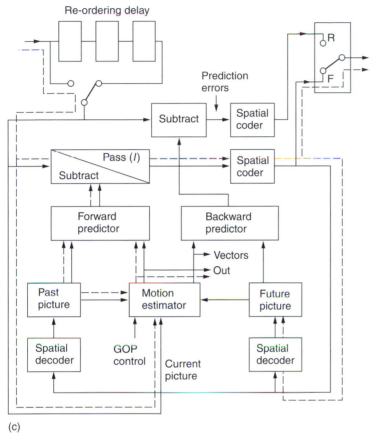

(c)

FIGURE 6.27
(Continued) (c) Signal flow when coding a P picture.

Figure 6.27d shows that the encoder now contains an I picture in the left store and a P picture in the right store. The reordering delay is reselected so that the first B picture can be input. This passes to the motion estimator by which it is compared with both the I and the P pictures to produce forward and backward vectors. The forward vectors go to the forward predictor to make a B prediction from the I picture. The backward vectors go to the backward predictor to make a B prediction from the P picture. These predictions are simultaneously subtracted from the actual B picture to produce a forward prediction error and a backward prediction error. These are then spatially encoded. The encoder can then decide which direction of coding resulted in the best prediction, i.e., the smallest prediction error.

Not shown in the interests of clarity is a third signal path, which creates a predicted B picture from the average of forward and backward predictions. This is subtracted from the input picture to produce a third prediction error. In some

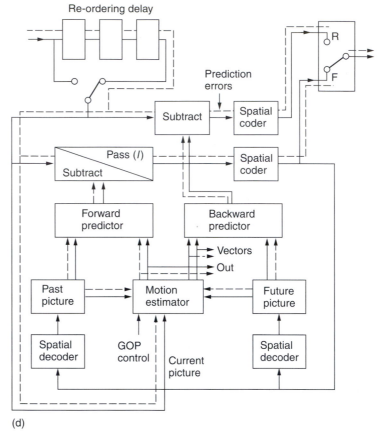

(d)

FIGURE 6.27
(Continued) (d) Signal flow when bi-directional coding.

circumstances this prediction error may use fewer data than either forward or backward prediction alone.

As B pictures are never used to create other pictures, the decoder does not locally decode the B picture. After decoding and displaying the B picture, the decoder will discard it. At the encoder, I and P pictures remain in their frame stores and the second B picture is input from the reordering delay.

Following the encoding of the second B picture, the encoder must reorder again to encode the second P picture in the GOP. This will locally be decoded and will replace the I picture in the left store. The stores and predictors switch designation because the left store is now a future P picture and the right store is now a past P picture. B pictures between them are encoded as before.

SLICES

There is still some redundancy in the output of a bi-directional coder and MPEG-2 is remarkably diligent in finding it. In I pictures, the DC coefficient describes the average brightness of an entire DCT block. In real video the DC component of adjacent blocks will be similar much of the time. A saving in bit rate can be obtained by differentially coding the DC coefficient.

In P and B pictures this is not done because these are prediction errors, not actual images, and the statistics are different. However, P and B pictures send vectors and instead the redundancy in these is explored. In a large moving object, many macroblocks will be moving at the same velocity and their vectors will be the same. Thus differential vector coding will be advantageous.

As has been seen, differential coding cannot be used indiscriminately as it is prone to error propagation. Periodically absolute DC coefficients and vectors must be sent and the slice is the logical structure that supports this mechanism. In I pictures, the first DC coefficient in a slice is sent in absolute form, whereas the subsequent coefficients are sent differentially. In P or B pictures, the first vector in a slice is sent in absolute form, but the subsequent vectors are differential.

Slices are horizontal picture strips that are one macroblock (16 pixels) high and that proceed from left to right across the screen. The sides of the picture must coincide with the beginning or the end of a slice in MPEG-2, but otherwise the encoder is free to decide how big slices should be and where they begin.

In the case of a central dark building silhouetted against a bright sky, there would be two large changes in the DC coefficients, one at each edge of the building. It may be advantageous to the encoder to break the width of the picture into three slices, one each for the left and right areas of sky and one for the building. In the case of a large moving object, different slices may be used for the object and the background.

Each slice contains its own synchronising pattern, so after a transmission error, correct decoding can resume at the next slice. Slice size can also be matched to the characteristics of the transmission channel. For example, in an error-free transmission system the use of a large number of slices in a packet simply wastes data capacity on surplus synchronising patterns. However, in a non-ideal system it might be advantageous to have frequent resynchronising.

HANDLING INTERLACED PICTURES

Spatial coding, predictive coding, and motion compensation can still be performed using interlaced source material at the cost of considerable complexity. Despite that complexity, MPEG-2 cannot be expected to perform as well with interlaced material.

Figure 6.28 shows that in an incoming interlaced frame there are two fields, each of which contains half of the lines in the frame. In MPEG-2 these are known as the top field and the bottom field. In video from a camera, these fields represent the state of the image at two different times. When there is little image motion, this is unimportant and the fields can be combined, obtaining more effective compression. However, in the presence of motion the fields become increasingly decorrelated because of the displacement of moving objects from one field to the next.

This characteristic determines that MPEG-2 must be able to handle fields independently or together. This dual approach permeates all aspects of MPEG-2 and affects the definition of pictures, macroblocks, DCT blocks, and zig-zag scanning.

Figure 6.28 also shows how MPEG-2 designates interlaced fields. In picture types I, P, and B, the two fields can be superimposed to make a frame picture or the two fields can be coded independently as two field pictures. As a third possibility, in I pictures only, the bottom field picture can be predictively coded from the top field picture to make an IP frame picture.

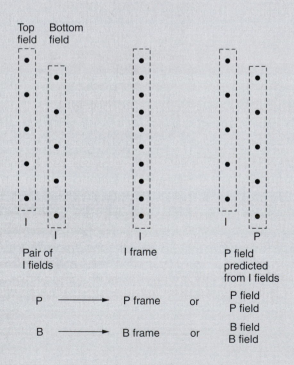

FIGURE 6.28
An interlaced frame consists of top and bottom fields. MPEG-2 can code a frame in the ways shown here.

A frame picture is one in which the macroblocks contain lines from both field types over a picture area 16 scan lines high. Each luminance macroblock contains the usual four DCT blocks but there are two ways in which these can be assembled. Figure 6.29a shows how a frame is divided into frame DCT blocks. This is identical to the progressive scan approach in that each DCT block contains 8 contiguous picture lines. In 4:2:0, the colour difference signals have been down sampled by a factor of 2 and shifted as was shown in Chapter 4. Figure 6.29a also shows how one 4:2:0 DCT block contains the chroma data from 16 lines in two fields.

Even small amounts of motion in any direction can destroy the correlation between odd and even lines and a frame DCT will result in an excessive number of coefficients. Figure 6.29b shows that instead the luminance component of a frame can also be divided into field DCT blocks. In this case one DCT block contains odd lines and the other contains even lines. In this mode the chroma still produces one DCT block from both fields as in Figure 6.29a.

When an input frame is designated as two field pictures, the macroblocks come from a screen area that is 32 lines high. Figure 6.29c shows that the DCT blocks contain the same data as if the input frame had been designated a frame picture but with field DCT. Consequently it is only frame pictures that have the option of field or frame DCT. These may be selected by the encoder on a macroblock-by-macroblock basis and, of course, the resultant bitstream must specify what has been done.

In a frame that contains a small moving area, it may be advantageous to encode as a frame picture with frame DCT except in the moving area where field DCT is used. This approach may result in fewer bits than coding as two field pictures. In a field picture and in a frame picture using field DCT, a DCT block contains lines from one field type only and this must have come from a screen area 16 scan lines high, whereas in progressive scan and frame DCT the area is only 8 scan lines high. A given vertical spatial frequency in the image is sampled at points twice as far apart, which is interpreted by the field DCT as a doubled spatial frequency, whereas there is no change in the horizontal spectrum.

Following the DCT calculation, the coefficient distribution will be different in field pictures and field DCT frame pictures. In these cases, the probability of coefficients is not a constant function of radius from the DC coefficient as it is in progressive scan, but is elliptical, in which the ellipse is twice as high as it is wide.

Using the standard 45° zig-zag scan with this different coefficient distribution would not have the required effect of putting all the significant coefficients at the beginning of the scan. To achieve this requires a different zig-zag scan, which is shown in Figure 6.30. This scan, sometimes known as the Yeltsin walk, attempts to match the elliptical probability of interlaced coefficients with a scan slanted at 67.5° to the vertical. This is clearly sub-optimal and is one of the reasons MPEG-2 does not work so well with interlaced video.

Motion estimation is more difficult in an interlaced system. Vertical detail can result in differences between fields and this reduces the quality of the match. Fields are vertically subsampled without filtering and so contain alias products. This aliasing will mean that the vertical waveform representing a moving object will not be the same in successive pictures and this will also reduce the quality of the match.

Even when the correct vector has been found, the match may be poor, so the estimator fails to recognize it. If it is recognized, a poor match means that the quality of the prediction in P and B pictures will be poor and so a large prediction error or residual has to be transmitted. In an attempt to reduce the residual, MPEG-2 allows field pictures to use motion-compensated prediction from either the adjacent field or the same field type in another frame. In this case the encoder will use the better match. This technique can also be used in areas of frame pictures that use field DCT.

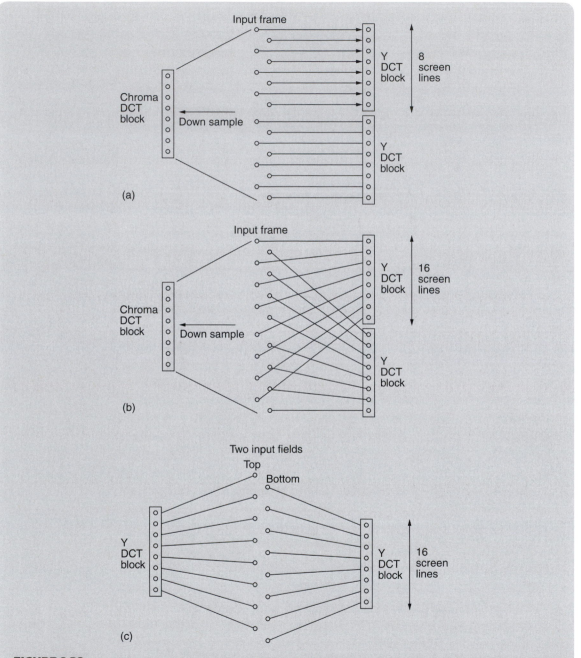

FIGURE 6.29

(a) In frame DCT, a picture is effectively de-interlaced. (b) In field DCT, each DCT block contains lines from only one field, but over twice the screen area. (c) The same DCT content results when field pictures are assembled into blocks.

The motion compensation of MPEG-2 has half-pixel resolution and this is inherently compatible with interlace because an interpolator must be present to handle the half-pixel shifts. Figure 6.31a shows that in an interlaced system, each field contains half of the frame lines and so interpolating halfway between lines of one field type will actually create values lying on the sampling structure of the other field type. Thus it is equally possible for a predictive system to decode a given field type based on pixel data from the other field type or of the same type.

If when using predictive coding from the other field type the vertical motion vector contains a half-pixel component, then no interpolation is needed because the act of transferring pixels from one field to another results in such a shift.

Figure 6.31b shows that a macroblock in a given P field picture can be encoded using a vector that shifts data from the previous field or from the field before that, irrespective of which frames these fields occupy. As noted above, field-picture macroblocks come from an area of screen 32 lines high and this means that the vector density is halved, resulting in larger prediction errors at the boundaries of moving objects.

As an option, field pictures can restore the vector density by using 16×8 motion compensation in which separate vectors are used for the top and bottom halves of the macroblock. Frame-pictures can also use 16×8 motion compensation in conjunction with field DCT. Whilst the 2×2 DCT block luminance structure of a macroblock can easily be divided vertically in two, in 4:2:0 the same screen area is represented by only one chroma macroblock of each component type. As it cannot be divided in half, this chroma is deemed to belong to the luminance DCT blocks of the upper field. In 4:2:2 no such difficulty arises.

MPEG-2 supports interlace simply because interlaced video exists in legacy systems and there is a requirement to compress it. However, when the opportunity arises to define a new system, interlace should be avoided. Legacy interlaced source material should be handled using a motion-compensated de-interlacer prior to compression in the progressive domain.

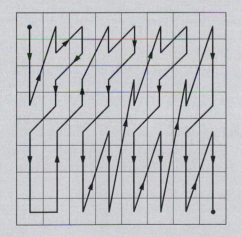

FIGURE 6.30
The zig-zag scan for an interlaced image has to favour vertical frequencies twice as much as horizontal.

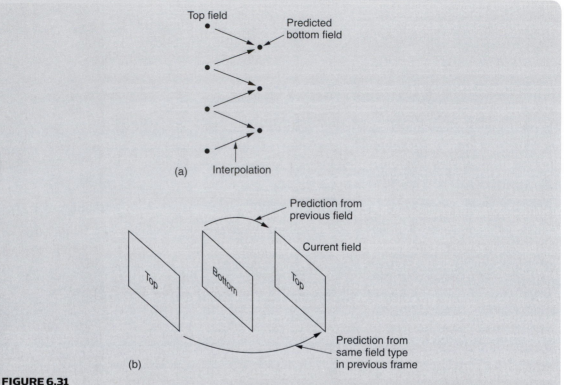

FIGURE 6.31
(a) Each field contains half of the frame lines and so interpolation is needed to create values lying on the sampling structure of the other field type. (b) Prediction can use data from the previous field or the one before that.

AN MPEG-2 CODER

Figure 6.32 shows the complete coder. The bi-directional coder outputs coefficients and vectors and the quantizing table in use. The vectors of P and B pictures and the DC coefficients of I pictures are differentially encoded in slices and the remaining coefficients are RLC/VLC coded. The multiplexer assembles all these data into a single bitstream called an elementary stream. The output of the encoder is a buffer that absorbs the variations in bit rate between different picture types. The buffer output has a constant bit rate determined by the demand clock. This comes from the transmission channel or storage device. If the bit rate is low, the buffer will tend to fill up, whereas if it is high the buffer will tend to empty. The buffer content is used to control the severity of

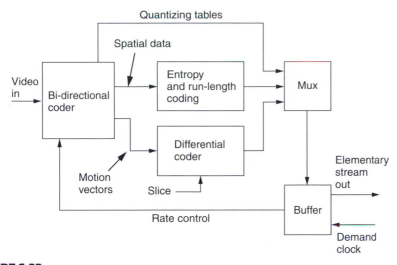

Quantizing tables

Spatial data

Video in → Bi-directional coder

Entropy and run-length coding

Differential coder

Motion vectors

Slice

Mux

Buffer

Elementary stream out

Demand clock

Rate control

FIGURE 6.32
An MPEG-2 coder. See text for details.

the requantizing in the spatial coders. The more the buffer fills, the bigger the requantizing steps get.

The buffer in the decoder has a finite capacity and the encoder must model the occupancy of the decoder's buffer so that it neither overflows nor underflows. An overflow might occur if an I picture is transmitted when the buffer content is already high. The buffer occupancy of the decoder depends somewhat on the memory access strategy of the decoder. Instead of defining a specific buffer size, MPEG-2 defines the size of a particular mathematical model of a hypothetical buffer. The decoder designer can use any strategy that implements the model, and the encoder can use any strategy that does not overflow or underflow the model. The elementary stream has a parameter called the video buffer verifier (VBV), which defines the minimum buffering assumptions of the encoder. Buffering is one way of ensuring constant quality when picture entropy varies. An intelligent coder may run down the buffer contents in anticipation of a difficult picture sequence so that a large amount of data can be sent.

MPEG-2 does not define what a decoder should do if a buffer underflow or overflow occurs, but because both irrecoverably lose data it is obvious that there will be more or less of an interruption in the decoding. Even a small loss of data may cause loss of synchronisation and in the case of a long GOP the lost data may make the rest of the GOP undecodable. A decoder may choose to repeat the last properly decoded picture until it can begin to operate correctly again.

Buffer problems occur if the VBV model is violated. If this happens, more than one underflow or overflow can result from a single violation. Switching an MPEG bitstream can cause a violation because the two encoders concerned may have radically different buffer occupancy at the switch.

THE ELEMENTARY STREAM

Figure 6.33 shows the structure of the elementary stream from an MPEG-2 encoder. The structure begins with a set of coefficients representing a DCT block. Six or eight DCT blocks form the luminance and chroma content of one macroblock. In P and B pictures a macroblock will be associated with a vector for motion compensation. Macroblocks are associated into slices in which DC coefficients of I pictures and vectors in P and B pictures are differentially coded. An arbitrary number of slices forms a picture and this needs I/P/B flags describing the type of picture it is. The picture may also have a global vector that efficiently deals with pans.

Several pictures form a Group of Pictures (GOP). The GOP begins with an I picture and may or may not include P and B pictures in a structure that may vary dynamically.

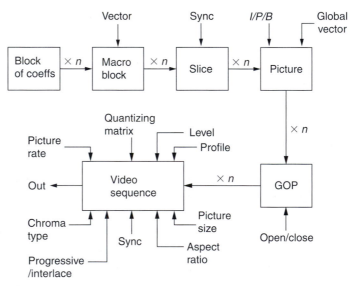

FIGURE 6.33
The structure of an elementary stream. MPEG defines the syntax precisely.

Several GOPs form a sequence, which begins with a sequence header containing important data to help the decoder. It is possible to repeat the header within a sequence, and this helps lock-up in random access applications. The sequence header describes the MPEG-2 profile and level, whether the video is progressive or interlaced, whether the chroma is 4:2:0 or 4:2:2, the size of the picture, and the aspect ratio of the pixels. The quantizing matrix used in the spatial coder can also be sent. The sequence begins with a standardised bit pattern, which is detected by a decoder to synchronise the de-serialization.

AN MPEG-2 DECODER

The decoder is defined only by implication from the definitions of syntax, and any decoder that can correctly interpret all combinations of syntax at a particular profile will be deemed compliant, however it works. The first problem a decoder has is that the input is an endless bitstream that contains a huge range of parameters, many of which have variable length. Unique synchronising patterns must be placed periodically throughout the bitstream so that the decoder can identify a known starting point. The pictures that can be sent under MPEG-2 are so flexible that the decoder must first find a sequence header so that it can establish the size of the picture, the frame rate, the colour coding used, etc.

The decoder must also be supplied with a 27 MHz system clock. In a DVD player, this would come from a crystal, but in a transmission system this would be provided by a numerically locked loop running from the program clock reference parameter in the bitstream (see Chapter 10). Until this loop has achieved lock the decoder cannot function properly.

Figure 6.34 shows a bi-directional decoder. The decoder can begin decoding only with an I picture and as this uses only intra-coding there will be no vectors. An I picture is transmitted as a series of slices. These slices begin with subsidiary synchronising patterns. The first macroblock in the slice contains an absolute DC coefficient, but the remaining macroblocks code the DC coefficient differentially, so the decoder must subtract the differential values from the previous one to obtain the absolute value.

The AC coefficients are sent as Huffman-coded run/size parameters followed by coefficient value codes. The variable-length Huffman codes are decoded by using a lookup table and extending the number of bits considered until a match is obtained. This allows the zero-run-length and the coefficient size to be established. The right number of bits is taken from the bitstream corresponding

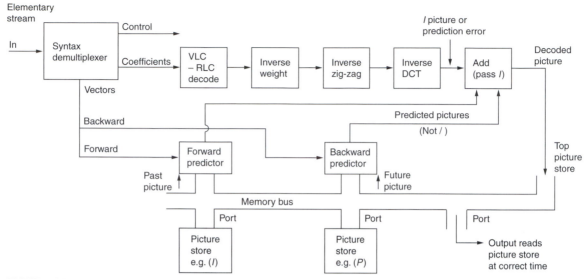

FIGURE 6.34
A bi-directional MPEG-2 decoder. See text for details.

to the coefficient code and this is decoded to the actual coefficient using the size parameter.

If the correct number of bits has been taken from the stream, the next bit must be the beginning of the next run/size code and so on until the EOB symbol is reached. The decoder uses the coefficient values and the zero-run-lengths to populate a DCT coefficient block following the appropriate zig-zag scanning sequence. Following EOB, the bitstream then continues with the next DCT block. Clearly this Huffman decoding will work perfectly or not at all. A single bit slippage in synchronism or a single corrupted data bit can cause a spectacular failure.

Once a complete DCT coefficient block has been received, the coefficients need to be inverse quantized and inverse weighted. Then an inverse DCT can be performed and this will result in an 8 × 8-pixel block. A series of DCT blocks will allow the luminance and colour information for an entire macroblock to be decoded and this can be placed in a frame store. Decoding continues in this way until the end of the slice, when an absolute DC coefficient will once again be sent. Once all the slices have been decoded, an entire picture will be resident in the frame store.

The amount of data needed to decode the picture is variable and the decoder just keeps going until the last macroblock is found. It will obtain data from the input buffer. In a constant bit rate transmission system, the decoder will remove more data to decode an I picture than has been received in one picture period, leaving the buffer emptier than it began. Subsequent P and B pictures need much fewer data and allow the buffer to fill again. The picture will be output when the time stamp sent with the picture matches the state of the decoder's time count.

Following the I picture may be another I picture or a P picture. Assuming a P picture, this will be predictively coded from the I picture. The P picture will be divided into slices as before. The first vector in a slice is absolute, but subsequent vectors are sent differentially. However, the DC coefficients are not differential.

Each macroblock may contain a forward vector. The decoder uses this to shift pixels from the I picture into the correct position for the predicted P picture. The vectors have half-pixel resolution and when a half-pixel shift is required, an interpolator will be used.

The DCT data are sent much as for an I picture; they will require inverse quantizing, but not inverse weighting because P and B coefficients are flat-weighted. When decoded this represents an error-cancelling picture, which is added pixel by pixel to the motion-predicted picture. This results in the output picture.

If bi-directional coding is being used, the P picture may be stored until one or more B pictures have been decoded. The B pictures are sent essentially as a P picture might be, except that the vectors can be forward, backward, or bi-directional. The decoder must take pixels from the I picture, the P picture, or both and shift them according to the vectors to make a predicted picture. The DCT data decode to produce an error-cancelling image as before.

In an interlaced system, the prediction mechanism may alternatively obtain pixel data from the previous field or the field before that. Vectors may relate to macroblocks or to 16×8-pixel areas. DCT blocks after decoding may represent frame lines or field lines. This adds up to a lot of different possibilities for a decoder handling an interlaced input.

MPEG-4 AND ADVANCED VIDEO CODING (AVC)

MPEG-4 advances the coding art in a number of ways. Whereas MPEG-1 and MPEG-2 were directed only to coding the video pictures that resulted after shooting natural scenes or from computer synthesis, MPEG-4 moves farther back in the process of how those scenes are created. For example, the rotation of a detailed three-dimensional object before a video camera produces huge changes in the video from picture to picture, which MPEG-2 would find difficult to code. Instead, if the three-dimensional object is re-created at the decoder, rotation can be portrayed by transmitting a trivially small amount of vector data. If the above object is synthetic, effectively the synthesis or rendering process is completed in the decoder. However, a suitable if complex image processor at the encoder could identify such objects in natural scenes. MPEG-4 objects are defined as a part of a scene that can independently be accessed or manipulated. An object is an entity that exists over a certain time span. The pictures of conventional imaging become *object planes* in MPEG-4. When an object intersects an object plane, it can be described by the coding system using intra-coding, forward prediction, or bi-directional prediction.

Figure 6.35 shows that MPEG-4 has four object types. A video object is an arbitrarily shaped planar pixel array describing the appearance or *texture* of part of a scene. A still texture object or *sprite* is a planar video object in which there is no change with respect to time. A mesh object describes a two- or three-dimensional shape as a set of points. The shape and its position can change with respect to time. Using computer graphics techniques, texture can be mapped onto meshes, a process known as warping, to produce rendered images. Using two-dimensional warping, a still texture object can be made to move. In three-dimensional graphic rendering, mesh coding allows an arbitrary solid shape to be created, which is then covered with texture.

Perspective computation then allows this three-dimensional object to be viewed in correct perspective from any viewpoint. MPEG-4 provides tools to

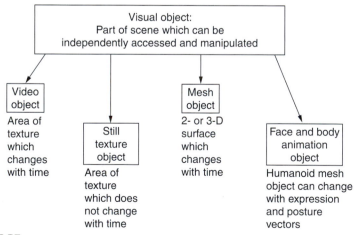

FIGURE 6.35
In MPEG-4 four types of objects are coded.

allow two- or three-dimensional meshes to be created in the decoder and then oriented by vectors. Changing the vectors then allows realistic moving images to be created with an extremely low bit rate.

Face and body animation is a specialized subset of three-dimensional mesh coding in which the mesh represents a human face and/or body. As the subject moves, carefully defined vectors carry changes of expression, which allow rendering of an apparently moving face and/or body that has been almost entirely synthesized from a single still picture.

In addition to object coding, MPEG-4 refines the existing MPEG tools by increasing the efficiency of a number of processes using lossless prediction. AVC extends this concept further still. This improves the performance of both the motion compensation and the coefficient coding, allowing either a lower bit rate or improved quality. MPEG-4 also extends the idea of scalability introduced in MPEG-2. Multiple scalability is supported, in which a low-bit rate base-level picture may optionally be enhanced by adding information from one or more additional bitstreams. This approach is useful in network applications in which the content creator cannot know the bandwidth that a particular user will have available. Scalability allows the best quality in the available bandwidth.

Although most of the spatial compression of MPEG-4 is based on the DCT as in earlier MPEG standards, MPEG-4 also introduces wavelet coding of still objects. Wavelets are advantageous in scalable systems because they naturally decompose the original image into various resolutions.

In contrast to the rest of MPEG-4, AVC is intended for use with entire pictures and as such is more of an extension of MPEG-2. AVC adds refinement to the existing coding tools of MPEG and also introduces some new ones. The emphasis is on lossless coding to obtain performance similar to that of MPEG-2 at around half the bit rate.

TEXTURE CODING

In MPEG-1 and MPEG-2 the only way of representing an image is with pixels and this requires no name. In MPEG-4 there are various types of image description tools and it becomes necessary to give the pixel representation of the earlier standards a name. This is *texture coding*, which is that part of MPEG-4 that operates on pixel-based areas of image. Coming later than MPEG-1 and MPEG-2, the MPEG-4 and AVC texture-coding systems can afford additional complexity in the search for higher performance. Figure 6.36 contrasts MPEG-2, MPEG-4,

MPEG-2	MPEG-4	AVC
DCT	DCT	Small block size integer coefficient transform
DC coefficient prediction in slice	DC coefficient prediction AC coefficient prediction	Spatial prediction with edge direction adaptation
Single coefficient scan	3 × coefficient scans	Multiple coefficient scans
Fixed resolution weighting	Reduced resolution weighting	Reduced resolution weighting
VLC/RLC	VLC/RLC	
Differential vectors in slice one vector/MB	Vector prediction up to 4 vectors/MB	Vector prediction up to 16 vectors/MB
(a)	(b)	(c)

FIGURE 6.36
(a) The texture coding system of MPEG-2. (b) Texture coding in MPEG-4.
(c) Texture coding in AVC.

and AVC. Figure 6.36a shows the texture decoding system of MPEG-2, whereas (b) shows MPEG-4 and (c) shows AVC. The latter two are refinements of the earlier technique. These refinements are lossless in that the reduction in bit rate they allow does not result in a loss of quality. When inter-coding, there is always a compromise needed over the quantity of vector data. Clearly if the area steered by each vector is smaller, the motion compensation is more accurate, but the reduction in residual data is offset by the increase in vector data.

In MPEG-1 and MPEG-2 only a small amount of vector compression is used. In contrast, MPEG-4 and AVC use advanced forms of lossless vector compression, which can, without any bit rate penalty, increase the vector density to one vector per DCT block in MPEG-4 and to one vector per 4 × 4-pixel block in AVC. AVC also allows quarter-pixel-accurate vectors. In inter-coded pictures the prediction of the picture is improved so that the residual to be coded is smaller. When intra-coding, MPEG-4 looks for further redundancy between coefficients using prediction. When a given DCT block is to be intra-coded, certain of its coefficients will be predicted from adjacent blocks.

The choice of the most appropriate block is made by measuring the picture gradient, defined as the rate of change of the DC coefficient. Figure 6.37a shows

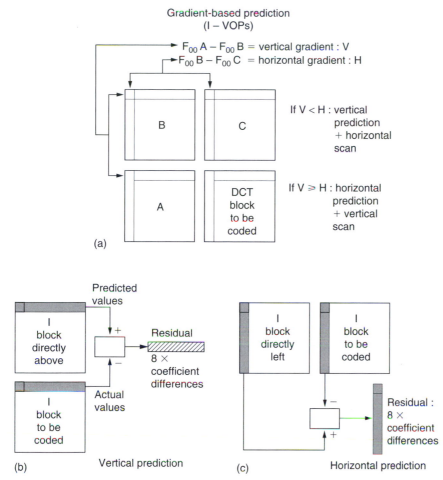

Gradient-based prediction
(I – VOPs)

$F_{00}A - F_{00}B$ = vertical gradient : V
$F_{00}B - F_{00}C$ = horizontal gradient : H

B   C

If V < H : vertical
prediction
+ horizontal
scan

A   DCT
block
to be
coded

If V ⩾ H : horizontal
prediction
+ vertical
scan

(a)

Predicted
values

I
block
directly
above

Residual

+

8 ×
coefficient
differences

−

Actual
values

I
block
to be
coded

(b)   Vertical prediction

I
block
directly
left

I
block
to be
coded

−

Residual :
8 ×
coefficient
differences

+

(c)   Horizontal prediction

FIGURE 6.37
(a) DC coefficients are used to measure the picture gradient. (b) In vertical prediction
the top row of coefficients is predicted using those above as a basis. (c) In horizontal
prediction the left column of coefficients is predicted from those to the left.

that the three adjacent blocks, A, B, and C, are analysed to decide whether to
predict from the DCT block above (vertical prediction) or to the left (horizontal prediction). Figure 6.37b shows that in vertical prediction the top row
of coefficients is predicted from the block above so that only the differences
between them need to be coded.

Figure 6.37c shows that in horizontal prediction the left column of coefficients
is predicted from the block on the left so that again only the differences need
be coded. Choosing the blocks above and to the left is important because these

blocks will already be available in both the encoder and the decoder. By making the same picture gradient measurement, the decoder can establish whether vertical or horizontal prediction has been used and so no flag is needed in the bitstream.

Some extra steps are needed to handle the top row and the left column of a picture or object when true prediction is impossible. In these cases both encoder and decoder assume standardised constant values for the missing prediction coefficients. The picture gradient measurement determines the direction in which there is the least change from block to block. There will generally be fewer DCT coefficients present in this direction. There will be more coefficients in the other axis, where there is more change. Consequently it is advantageous to alter the scanning sequence so that the coefficients that are likely to exist are transmitted earlier in the sequence.

Figure 6.38 shows the two alternate scans for MPEG-4. The alternate horizontal scan concentrates on horizontal coefficients early in the scan and will be used in conjunction with vertical prediction. Conversely the alternate vertical scan concentrates on vertical coefficients early in the scan and will be used in conjunction with horizontal prediction. The decoder can establish which scan has been used in the encoder from the picture gradient.

MPEG-4 coefficient scans

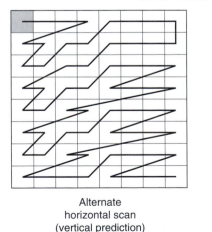 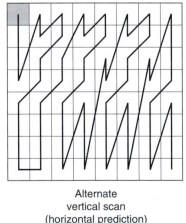

Alternate
horizontal scan
(vertical prediction)

Alternate
vertical scan
(horizontal prediction)

FIGURE 6.38
The alternate zig-zag scans employed with vertical and horizontal prediction.

Coefficient prediction is not employed when inter-coding because the statistics of residual images are different. Instead of attempting to predict residual coefficients, in inter-coded texture, pixel-based prediction may be used to reduce the magnitude of texture residuals. This technique is known as overlapped block motion compensation (OBMC), which is used only in P-VOPs. With only one vector per DCT block, clearly in many cases the vector cannot apply to every pixel in the block. If the vector is considered to describe the motion of the centre of the block, the vector accuracy falls toward the edge of the block. A pixel in the corner of a block is almost equidistant from a vector in the centre of an adjacent block.

OBMC uses vectors from adjacent blocks, known as *remote vectors,* in addition to the vector of the current block for prediction. Figure 6.39 shows that the motion-compensation process of MPEG-1 and MPEG-2, which uses a single vector, is modified by the addition of the pixel prediction system, which considers three

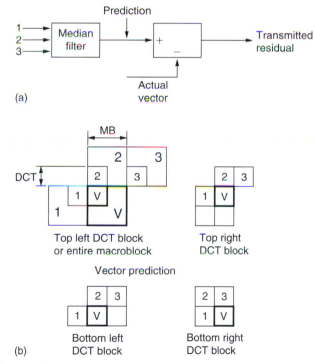

FIGURE 6.39
(a) MPEG-4 inter-coded pixel values may be predicted from three remote vectors as well as the true vector. (b) The three remote vectors are selected according to the macroblock quadrant. Macroblocks may have one or four vectors and the prediction mechanism allows prediction between blocks of either type.

vectors. A given pixel in the block to be coded is predicted from the weighted sum of three motion-compensated pixels taken from the previous I- or P-VOP. One of these pixels is obtained in the normal way by accessing the previous VOP with a shift given by the vector of this block. The other two are obtained by accessing the same VOP pixels using the remote vectors of two adjacent blocks. The remote vectors that are used and the weighting factors are both a function of the pixel position in the block. Figure 6.39 shows that the block to be coded is divided into quadrants. The remote vectors are selected from the blocks closest to the quadrant in which the pixel resides.

For example, a pixel in the bottom-right quadrant would be predicted using remote vectors from the DCT block immediately below and the block immediately to the right. Not all blocks can be coded in this way. In P-VOPs it is permissible to have blocks that are not coded or intrablocks that contain no vector. Remote vectors will not all be available at the boundaries of a VOP. In the normal sequence of macroblock transmission, vectors from macroblocks below the current block are not yet available. Some additional steps are needed to handle these conditions. Adjacent to boundaries where a remote vector is not available it is replaced by a copy of the actual vector.

This is also done when an adjacent block is intra-coded and for blocks at the bottom of a macroblock when the vectors for the macroblocks below will not be available yet. In the case of noncoded blocks the remote vector is set to zero.

Figure 6.40a shows that the weighting factors for pixels near the centre of a block favour that block. In the case of pixels at the corner of the block, the weighting is even between the value obtained from the true vector and the sum

4	5	5	5	5	5	5	4
5	5	5	5	5	5	5	5
5	5	6	6	6	6	5	5
5	5	6	6	6	6	5	5
5	5	6	6	6	6	5	5
5	5	6	6	6	6	5	5
5	5	5	5	5	5	5	5
4	5	5	5	5	5	5	4

(a) Weighting values for use with motion vector of current Y block (true vector)

2	2	2	2	2	2	2	2
1	1	2	2	2	2	1	1
1	1	1	1	1	1	1	1
1	1	1	1	1	1	1	1
1	1	1	1	1	1	1	1
1	1	1	1	1	1	1	1
1	1	2	2	2	2	1	1
2	2	2	2	2	2	2	2

(b) Weighting values for use with motion vector of Y blocks above or below current Y block (remote vector)

2	1	1	1	1	1	1	2
2	2	1	1	1	1	2	2
2	2	1	1	1	1	2	2
2	2	1	1	1	1	2	2
2	2	1	1	1	1	2	2
2	2	1	1	1	1	2	2
2	2	1	1	1	1	2	2
2	1	1	1	1	1	1	2

(c) Weighting values for use with motion vector of Y blocks left or right of current Y block (remote vector)

FIGURE 6.40
Vector prediction.

of the two pixel values obtained from remote vectors. The weighted sum produces a predicted pixel, which is subtracted from the actual pixel in the current VOP to be coded to produce a residual pixel. Blocks of residual pixels are DCT coded as usual. OBMC reduces the magnitude of residual pixels and gives a corresponding reduction in the number or magnitude of DCT coefficients to be coded.

OBMC is lossless because the decoder already has access to all the vectors and knows the weighting tables. Consequently the only overhead is the transmission of a flag that enables or disables the mechanism. MPEG-4 also has the ability to down sample prediction error or residual macroblocks that contain little detail. A 16×16 macroblock is down sampled to 8 by 8 and flagged. The decoder will identify the flag and interpolate back to 16×16.

In vector prediction, each macroblock may have only one or four vectors as the coder decides. Consequently the prediction of a current vector may have to be done from either macroblock or DCT block vectors. In the case of predicting one vector for an entire macroblock, or the top-left DCT block vector, the process shown in Figure 6.40b is used. Three earlier vectors, which may be macroblock or DCT block vectors, as available, are used as the input to the prediction process. In the diagram the large squares show the macroblock vectors to be selected and the small squares show the DCT block vectors to be selected. The three vectors are passed to a median filter, which outputs the vector in the centre of the range unchanged.

A median filter is used because the same process can be performed in the decoder with no additional data transmission. The median vector is used as a prediction, and comparison with the actual vector enables a residual to be computed and coded for transmission. At the decoder the same prediction can be made and the received residual is added to re-create the original vector.

The remaining parts of Figure 6.40b show how the remaining three DCT block vectors are predicted from adjacent DCT block vectors. If the relevant block is only macroblock coded, that vector will be substituted.

ADVANCED VIDEO CODING

AVC, or H.264, is intended to compress moving images that take the form of 8-bit 4:2:0 coded pixel arrays. As in MPEG-2 these may be pixel arrays or fields from an interlaced signal. It does not support object-based coding. Incoming pixel arrays are subdivided into 16×16-macroblocks as in previous MPEG standards. In those previous standards, macroblocks were transmitted only in a raster-scan fashion. Whilst this is fine when the coded data are delivered via a reliable channel, AVC is designed to operate with imperfect channels that are subject to error or packet loss. One mechanism that supports this is known as FMO (flexible macroblock ordering).

When FMO is in use, the picture can be divided into different areas along horizontal or vertical macroblock boundaries. Figure 6.41a shows an approach in which macroblocks are chequerboarded. If the shaded macroblocks are sent in a different packet to the unshaded macroblocks, the loss of a packet will result in a degraded picture rather than no picture. Figure 6.41b shows another approach in which the important elements of the picture are placed in one area and less important elements in another. The important data may be afforded higher priority in a network. Note that when interlaced input is being coded, it may be necessary to constrain the FMO such that the smallest element becomes a macroblock pair in which one macroblock is vertically above the other.

In FMO these areas are known as *slice groups* that contain integer numbers of slices. Within slice groups, macroblocks are always sent in raster-scan fashion with respect to that slice group. The decoder must be able to establish the

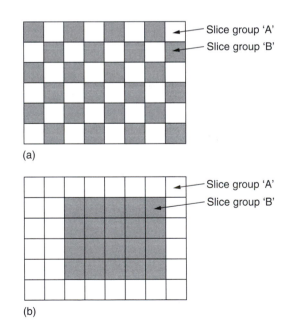

(a)

(b)

FIGURE 6.41
(a) Chequerboarded macroblocks that have come from two different slice groups. Loss of one slice group allows a degraded picture to be seen. (b) Important picture content is placed in one slice, whereas background is in another.

position of every received macroblock in the picture. This is the function of the *macroblock to slice group map*, which can be deduced by the decoder from picture header and slice header data.

Another advantage of AVC is that the bitstream is designed to be transmitted or recorded in a greater variety of ways, having distinct advantages in certain applications. AVC may convert the direct coder output in a NAL (network application layer) that formats the data in an appropriate manner.

In previous MPEG standards, prediction was used primarily between pictures. In MPEG-2 I pictures the only prediction was in DC coefficients, whereas in MPEG-4 some low-frequency coefficients were predicted. In AVC, I pictures are subject to spatial prediction and it is the prediction residual that is transform coded, not pixel data.

In I PCM mode, the prediction and transform stages are both bypassed and actual pixel values enter the remaining stages of the coder. In nontypical images such as noise, PCM may be more efficient. In addition, if the channel bit rate is high enough, a truly lossless coder may be obtained by the use of PCM. Figure 6.42 shows that the encoder contains a spatial predictor that is switched in for I pictures, whereas for P and B pictures the temporal predictor operates. The predictions are subtracted from the input picture and the residual is coded.

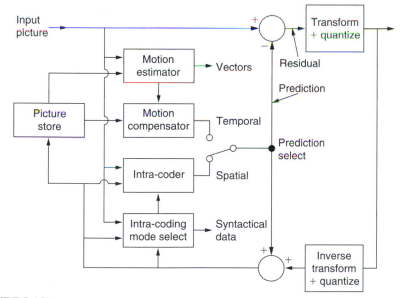

FIGURE 6.42
AVC encoder has a spatial predictor as well as a temporal predictor.

Spatial prediction works in two ways. In featureless parts of the picture, the DC component, or average brightness, is highly redundant. Edges between areas of differing brightness are also redundant. Figure 6.43a shows that in a picture having a strong vertical edge, rows of pixels traversing the edge are highly redundant, whereas (b) shows that in the case of a strong horizontal edge, columns of pixels are redundant. Sloping edges will result in redundancy on diagonals.

According to picture content, spatial prediction can operate on 4×4-pixel blocks or 16×16-pixel blocks. Figure 6.44a shows eight of the nine spatial prediction modes for 4×4 blocks. Mode 2, not shown, is the DC prediction that is directionless. Figure 6.44b shows that in 4×4 prediction, up to 13 pixel values above and to the left of the block will be used. This means that these pixel values are already known by the decoder because of the order in which decoding takes place. Spatial prediction cannot take place between different slices because the error recovery capability of a slice would be compromised if it depended on an earlier one for decoding.

Figure 6.44c shows that in vertical prediction (Mode 0), four pixel values above the block are copied downward so that all four rows of the predicted block are

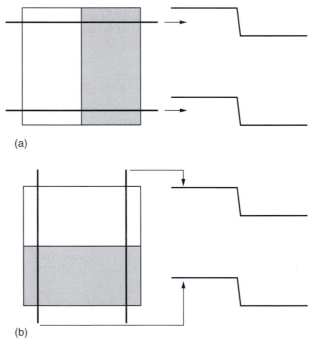

(a)

(b)

FIGURE 6.43
(a) In the case of a strong vertical edge, pixel values in rows tend to be similar.
(b) Horizontal edges result in columns of similar values.

identical. Figure 6.44d shows that in horizontal prediction (Mode 1) four pixel values to the left are copied across so that all four columns of the predicted block are identical. Figure 6.44e shows how in diagonal prediction (Mode 4) seven pixel values are copied diagonally. Figure 6.44f shows that in DC prediction (Mode 2) pixel values above and to the left are averaged and the average value is copied into all 16 predicted pixel locations.

With 16 × 16 blocks, only four modes are available: vertical, horizontal, DC, and plane. The first three of these are identical in principle to Modes 0, 1, and 2 with 4 × 4 blocks. Plane mode is a refinement of DC mode. Instead of setting every predicted pixel in the block to the same value by averaging the reference pixels, the predictor looks for trends in changing horizontal brightness in the top reference row and similar trends in vertical brightness in the left reference column and computes a predicted block whose values lie on a plane that may be tilted in the direction of the trend.

Clearly it is necessary for the encoder to have circuitry or software that identifies edges and their direction (or the lack of them) to select the appropriate mode. The standard does not suggest how this should work, only how its outputs should be encoded. In each case the predicted pixel block is subtracted from the actual pixel block to produce a residual. Spatial prediction is also used on chroma data.

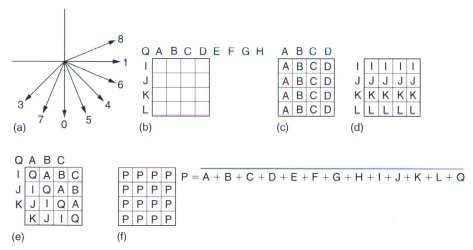

FIGURE 6.44
(a) Spatial prediction works in eight different directions. (b) Adjacent pixels from which predictions will be made. (c) Vertical prediction copies rows of pixels downward. (d) Horizontal prediction copies columns of pixels across. (e) Diagonal prediction. (f) DC prediction copies the average of the reference pixels into every predicted pixel location.

$$H = \begin{bmatrix} 1 & 1 & 1 & 1 \\ 2 & 1 & -1 & -2 \\ 1 & -1 & -1 & 1 \\ 1 & -2 & 2 & -1 \end{bmatrix}$$

FIGURE 6.45
The transform matrix used in AVC. The coefficients are all integers.

When spatial prediction is used, the statistics of the residual will be different from the statistics of the original pixels. When the prediction succeeds, the lower frequencies in the image are largely taken care of and so only higher frequencies remain in the residual. This suggests the use of a smaller transform than the 8×8 transform of previous systems. AVC uses a 4×4 transform. It is not, however, a DCT, but a DCT-like transform, using coefficients that are integers. This gives the advantages that coding and decoding require only shifting and addition and that the transform is perfectly reversible even when limited word length is used. Figure 6.45 shows the transform matrix of AVC.

One of the greatest deficiencies of earlier coders was blocking artifacts at transform block boundaries. AVC incorporates a deblocking filter. In operation, the filter examines sets of pixels across a block boundary. If it finds a step in value, this may or may not indicate a blocking artifact. It could be a genuine transition in the picture. However, the size of pixel value steps can be deduced from the degree of quantizing in use. If the step is bigger than the degree of quantizing would suggest, it is left alone. If the size of the step corresponds to degree of quantizing, it is filtered or smoothed.

The adaptive deblocking algorithm is deterministic and must be the same in all decoders. This is because the encoder must also contain the same deblocking filter to prevent drift when temporal coding is used. This is known as in-loop deblocking. In other words, when, for example, a P picture is being predicted from an I picture, the I picture in both encoder and decoder will have been identically deblocked. Thus any errors due to imperfect deblocking are cancelled out by the P picture residual data.

Deblocking filters are modified when interlace is used because the vertical separation of pixels in a field is twice as great as in a frame. Figure 6.46 shows an in-loop deblocking system. The I picture is encoded and transmitted and is decoded and deblocked identically at both encoder and decoder. At the decoder the deblocked I picture forms the output as well as the reference with which a future P or I picture can be decoded. Thus when the encoder sends a residual, it will send the difference between the actual input picture and the

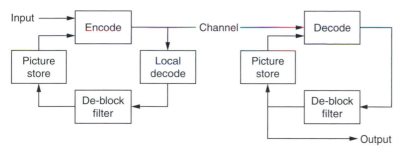

FIGURE 6.46
The in-loop deblocking filter exists at both encoder and decoder to prevent drift.

deblocked I picture. The decoder adds this residual to its own deblocked I picture and recovers the actual picture.

MOTION COMPENSATION (MC) IN AVC

AVC has a more complex motion-compensation system than previous standards. Smaller picture areas are coded using vectors that may have quarter-pixel accuracy. The interpolation filter for subpixel motion compensation is specified so that the same filter is present in all encoders and decoders. The interpolator is then effectively in the loop like the deblocking filter. Figure 6.47 shows that more than one previous reference picture may be used to decode a motion-compensated picture. A larger number of future pictures are not used as this would increase latency. The ability to select a number of previous pictures is advantageous when a single nontypical picture is found inserted in normal material. An example is the white frame that results from a flashgun firing. MPEG-2 deals with this poorly, whereas AVC could deal with it well, simply by decoding the picture after the flash from the picture before the flash. Bi-directional coding is enhanced because the weighting of the contribution from earlier and later pictures can now be coded. Thus a dissolve between two pictures could be coded efficiently by changing the weighting. In previous standards a B picture could not be used as a basis for any further decoding, but in AVC this is allowed.

AVC macroblocks may be coded with between one and 16 vectors. Prediction using 16×16 macroblocks fails when the edge of a moving object intersects the macroblock. In such cases it may be better to divide the macroblock up according to the angle and position of the edge. Figure 6.48a shows the number of ways a 16×16 macroblock may be partitioned in AVC for motion-compensation purposes. There are four high-level partition schemes, one of which is to use four 8×8 blocks. When this mode is selected, these 8×8 blocks may be further

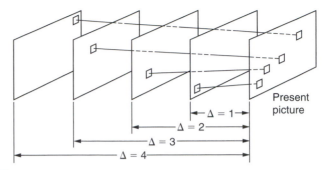

FIGURE 6.47
The motion compensation of AVC allows a picture to be built up from more than one previous picture.

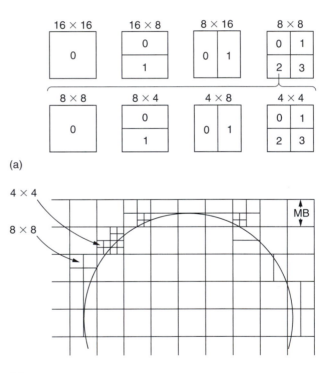

(a)

(b)

FIGURE 6.48
(a) Macroblock partitioning for motion compensation in AVC. (b) How an encoder might partition macroblocks at the boundary of a moving object.

partitioned as shown. This finer subdivision requires additional syntactical data to specify to the decoder what has been done. It will be self-evident that if more vectors have to be transmitted, there must be a greater reduction in the amount of residual data to be transmitted to make it worthwhile. Thus the encoder

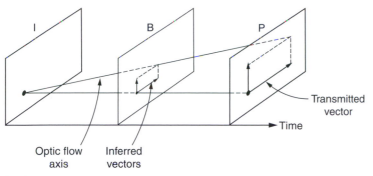

FIGURE 6.49
Vector inference. By assuming the optic flow axis to be straight, the vector for a B block can be computed from the vector for a P block.

needs to intelligently decide the partitioning to be used. Figure 6.48b shows an example. There also needs to be some efficient vector coding scheme.

In P coding, vectors are predicted from those in macroblocks already sent, provided that slice independence is not compromised. The predicted vector is the median of those on the left of, above, and above right of the macroblock to be coded. A different prediction is used if 16×8 or 8×16 partitions are used. Only the prediction error needs to be sent. In fact if nothing is sent, as in the case of a skipped block, the decoder can predict the vector for itself.

In B coding, the vectors are predicted by inference from the previous P vectors. Figure 6.49 shows the principle. To create the P picture from the I picture, a vector must be sent for each moving area. As the B picture is at a known temporal location with respect to these anchor pictures, the vector for the corresponding area of the B picture can be predicted by assuming the optic flow axis is straight and performing a simple linear interpolation.

AN AVC CODEC

Figure 6.50 shows an AVC coder–decoder pair. There is a good deal of general similarity with the previous standards. In the case of an I picture, there is no motion compensation and no previous picture is relevant. However, spatial prediction will be used. The prediction error will be transformed and quantized for transmission, but is also locally inverse quantized and inverse transformed prior to being added to the prediction to produce an unfiltered reconstructed macroblock. Thus the encoder has available exactly what the decoder will have and both use the same data to make predictions to avoid drift. The type of intra prediction used is determined from the characteristics of the input picture.

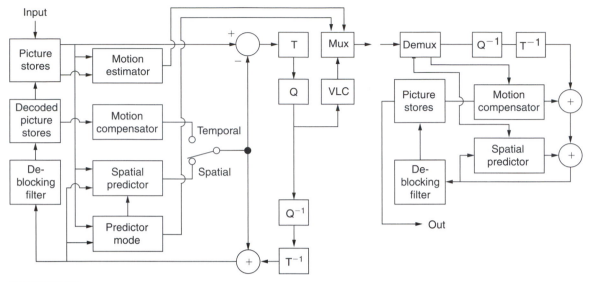

FIGURE 6.50
AVC coder and decoder. See text for details.

The locally reconstructed macroblocks are also input to the deblocking filter. This is identical to the decoder's deblocking filter and so the output will be identical to the output of the decoder. The deblocked, decoded I picture can then be used as a basis for encoding a P picture. Using this architecture the deblocking is in-loop for inter-coding purposes, but does not interfere with the intra prediction. Operation of the decoder should be obvious from what has gone before as the encoder effectively contains a decoder.

Like earlier formats, AVC uses lossless arithmetic coding, or entropy coding, to pack the data more efficiently. However, AVC takes the principle further. Arithmetic coding is used to compress syntax data as well as coefficients. Syntax data take a variety of forms: vectors, slice headers, etc. A common exp-Golomb variable-length arithmetic code is used for all syntax data. The different types of data are mapped appropriately for their statistics before that code. Coefficients are coded using a system called CAVLC (context adaptive variable-length coding).

Optionally, a further technique known as CABAC (context adaptive binary arithmetic coding) may be used in some profiles. This is a system that adjusts the coding dynamically according to the local statistics of the data instead of relying on statistics assumed at the design stage. It is more efficient and allows a coding gain of about 15% with more complexity. CAVLC performs the same function as RLC/VLC in MPEG-2 but it is more efficient. As in MPEG-2 it relies on the probability that coefficient values fall with increasing spatial frequency and that at the higher frequencies coefficients will be spaced apart by zero values.

Trailing 1s (T1s)
Non-zero coefficients (N)
Value of coefficients
Sign
Total number of zero coefficients (TotalZeros)
Distribution of zeros (RunBefore)

FIGURE 6.51
CAVLC parameters used in AVC. See text for details.

The efficient prediction of AVC means that coefficients will typically be smaller than in earlier standards. It becomes useful to have specific means to code coefficients of value ± 1 as well as zero. These are known as trailing ones (T1s). Figure 6.51 shows the parameters used in CAVLC.

The coefficients are encoded in the reverse order of the zig-zag scan. The number of nonzero coefficients N and the number of trailing 1's is encoded into a single VLC symbol. The TotalZeros parameter defines the number of zero coefficients between the last non-zero coefficient and its start. The difference between N and TotalZeros must be the number of zeros within the transmitted coefficient sequence but does not reveal where they are. This is the function of the RunBefore parameter, which is sent prior to any coefficient that is preceded by zeros in the transmission sequence. If N is 16, the TotalZeros must be zero and will not be sent. RunBefore parameters will not occur.

Coefficient values for trailing ones need only a single bit to denote the sign. Values above one embed the polarity into the value input to the VLC.

CAVLC obtains extra coding efficiency because it can select different codes according to circumstances. For example if in a 16-coefficient block N is 7, then TotalZeros must have a value between zero and nine. The encoder selects a VLC table optimized for nine values. The decoder can establish what table has been used by subtracting N from 16 so no extra data need be sent to switch tables. The N and T1s parameter can be coded using one of four tables selected using the values of N and T1 in nearby blocks. Six code tables are available for adaptive coefficient encoding.

CODING ARTIFACTS

This section describes the visible results of imperfect coding. Imperfect coding may be where the coding algorithm is suboptimal, where the coder latency is too short, or where the compression factor in use is simply too great for the material.

In motion-compensated systems such as MPEG, the use of periodic intra fields means that the coding noise varies from picture to picture and this may be visible as noise pumping. Noise pumping may also be visible when the amount of motion changes. If a pan is observed, as the pan speed increases the motion vectors may become less accurate and reduce the quality of the prediction processes. The prediction errors will get larger and will have to be more coarsely quantized. Thus the picture gets noisier as the pan accelerates and the noise reduces as the pan slows down. The same result may be apparent at the edges of a picture during zooming. The problem is worse if the picture contains fine detail. Panning on grass, or trees waving in the wind, taxes most coders severely. Camera shake from a handheld camera also increases the motion vector data and results in more noise, as does film weave.

Input video noise or film grain degrades inter-coding as there is less redundancy between pictures and the difference data become larger, requiring coarse quantizing and adding to the existing noise.

When a codec is really fighting, the quantizing may become very coarse and as a result the video level at the edge of one DCT block may not match that of its neighbour. Therefore the DCT block structure becomes visible as a mosaicing or tiling effect. Coarse quantizing also causes some coefficients to be rounded up and appear larger than they should be. High-frequency coefficients may be eliminated by heavy quantizing and this forces the DCT to act as a steep-cut low-pass filter. This causes fringing or ringing around sharp edges and extra shadowy edges that were not in the original. This is most noticeable on text.

Excess compression may also result in colour bleed where fringing has taken place in the chroma or where high-frequency chroma coefficients have been discarded. Graduated colour areas may reveal banding or posterizing as the colour range is restricted by requantizing. These artifacts are almost impossible to measure with conventional test gear.

Neither noise pumping nor blocking is suffered by analog video recorders, and so it is nonsense to liken the performance of a codec to the quality of a VCR. In fact noise pumping is extremely objectionable because, unlike steady noise, it attracts attention in peripheral vision and may result in viewing fatigue.

In addition to highly detailed pictures with complex motion, certain types of video signal are difficult for MPEG-2 to handle and will usually result in a higher level of artifacts than usual. Noise has already been mentioned as a source of problems. Time base error from, for example, VCRs is undesirable because this puts successive lines in different horizontal positions. A straight vertical line becomes jagged and this results in high spatial frequencies in the DCT process. Spurious coefficients that need to be coded are created.

Much archive video is in composite form and MPEG-2 can handle this only after it has been decoded to components. Unfortunately many general-purpose composite decoders have a high level of residual subcarrier in the outputs. This is normally not a problem because the subcarrier is designed to be invisible to the naked eye. Figure 6.52 shows that in PAL and NTSC the subcarrier frequency is selected so that a phase reversal is achieved between successive lines and frames.

Whilst this makes the subcarrier invisible to the eye, it is not invisible to an MPEG decoder. The subcarrier waveform is interpreted as a horizontal frequency, the vertical phase reversals are interpreted as a vertical spatial frequency, and the picture-to-picture reversals increase the magnitude of the prediction errors. The subcarrier level may be low but it can be present over the whole screen and may require an excess of coefficients to describe it.

Composite video should not in general be used as a source for MPEG-2 encoding, but where this is inevitable the standard of the decoder must be much higher than average, especially in the residual subcarrier specification. Some MPEG pre-processors support high-grade composite decoding options.

Judder from conventional linear standards convertors degrades the performance of MPEG-2. The optic flow axis is corrupted and linear filtering causes multiple images, which confuse motion estimators and result in larger prediction errors. If standards conversion is necessary, the MPEG-2 system must be used to encode the signal in its original format and the standards convertor should be installed after the decoder. If a standards convertor has to be used before the encoder, then it must be a type that has effective motion compensation.

Film weave causes movement of one picture with respect to the next and this results in more vector activity and larger prediction errors. Movement of the

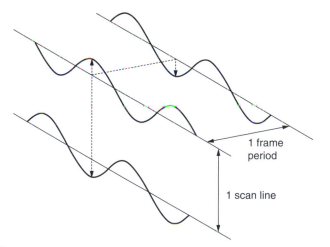

1 frame
period

1 scan line

FIGURE 6.52
In composite video the subcarrier frequency is arranged so that inversions occur between adjacent lines and pictures to help reduce the visibility of the chroma.

centre of the film frame along the optical axis causes magnification changes that also result in excess prediction error data. Film grain has the same effect as noise: it is random and so cannot be compressed.

Perhaps because it is relatively uncommon, MPEG-2 cannot handle image rotation well because the motion-compensation system is designed only for translational motion. When a rotating object is highly detailed, such as in certain fairground rides, the motion-compensation failure requires a significant amount of prediction error data and if a suitable bit rate is not available the level of artifacts will rise.

Flashguns used by still photographers are a serious hazard to MPEG-2, especially when long GOPs are used. At a press conference where a series of flashes may occur, the resultant video contains intermittent white frames, which defeat prediction. A huge prediction error is required to turn the previous picture into a white picture, followed by another huge prediction error to return the white frame to the next picture. The output buffer fills and heavy requantizing is employed. After a few flashes the picture has generally gone to tiles.

PROCESSING MPEG-2 AND CONCATENATION

Concatenation loss occurs when the losses introduced by one codec are compounded by a second codec. All practical compressors, MPEG-2 included, are lossy because what comes out of the decoder is not bit-identical to what went into the encoder. The bit differences are controlled so that they have minimum visibility to a human viewer.

MPEG-2 is a toolbox that allows a variety of manipulations to be performed in both the spatial and the temporal domains. There is a limit to the compression that can be used on a single frame, and if higher compression factors are needed, temporal coding will have to be used. The longer the run of pictures considered, the lower the bit rate needed, but the harder it becomes to edit.

The most editable form of MPEG-2 is to use I pictures only. As there is no temporal coding, pure-cut edits can be made between pictures. The next best thing is to use a repeating IB structure that is locked to the odd/even field structure. Cut edits cannot be made as the B pictures are bi-directionally coded and need data from both adjacent I pictures for decoding. The B picture has to be decoded prior to the edit and re-encoded after the edit. This will cause a small concatenation loss.

Beyond the IB structure processing gets harder. If a long GOP is used for the best compression factor, an IBBPBBP… structure results. Editing this is very difficult because the pictures are sent out of order so that bi-directional decoding can be used. MPEG allows closed GOPs in which the last B picture is coded wholly from the previous pictures and does not need the I picture in the next GOP. The bitstream can be switched at this point but only if the GOP structures in the two source video signals are synchronised (makes colour framing seem easy). Consequently in practice a long GOP bitstream will need to be decoded prior to any production step. Afterward it will need to be re-encoded.

This is known as naive concatenation and an enormous pitfall awaits. Unless the GOP structure of the output is identical to and synchronised with the input the results will be disappointing. The worst case is that in which an I picture is encoded from a picture that was formerly a B picture. It is easy enough to lock the GOP structure of a coder to a single input, but if an edit is made between two inputs, the GOP timings could well be different.

As there are so many structures allowed in MPEG, there will be a need to convert between them. If this has to be done, it should be only in the direction that increases the GOP length and reduces the bit rate. Going the other way is inadvisable. The ideal way of converting from, say, the IB structure of a news system to the IBBP structure of an emission system is to use a re-compressor. This is a kind of standards convertor that will give better results than a decode followed by an encode.

The DCT part of MPEG-2 itself is lossless. If all the coefficients are preserved intact an inverse transform yields the same pixel data. Unfortunately this does not give enough compression for many applications. In practice the coefficients are made less accurate by removing bits, starting at the least significant end and working upward. This process is weighted, or made progressively more aggressive as spatial frequency increases.

Small-value coefficients may be truncated to zero and large-value coefficients are most coarsely truncated at high spatial frequencies, where the effect is least visible.

Figure 6.53 shows what happens in the ideal case in which two identical coders are put in tandem and synchronised. The first coder quantizes the coefficients to finite accuracy and causes a loss on decoding. However, when the second coder performs the DCT calculation, the coefficients obtained will be identical to the quantized coefficients in the first coder and so if the second weighting and requantizing step is identical the same truncated coefficient data will result and there will be no further loss of quality.[7]

In practice this ideal situation is elusive. If the two DCTs become nonidentical for any reason, the second requantizing step will introduce further error in the coefficients and the artifact level goes up. Figure 6.53b shows that non-identical concatenation can result from a large number of real-world effects.

An intermediate processing step such as a fade will change the pixel values and thereby the coefficients. A DVE (digital video effects generator) resize or shift will move pixels from one DCT block to another. Even if there is no processing step, this effect will also occur if the two codecs disagree on where the MPEG picture boundaries are within the picture. If the boundaries are correct there will still be concatenation loss if the two codecs use different weighting.

One problem with MPEG is that the compressor design is unspecified. Whilst this has advantages, it does mean that the chances of finding identical coders is minute because each manufacturer will have his or her own views on the best compression algorithm. In a large system it may be worth obtaining the coders from a single supplier.

It is now increasingly accepted that concatenation of compression techniques is potentially damaging, and results are worse if the codecs are different. Clearly, feeding a digital coder such as MPEG-2 with a signal that has been subject to analog compression comes into the category of worse. Using interlaced video as a source for MPEG coding is suboptimal and using decoded composite video is even worse.

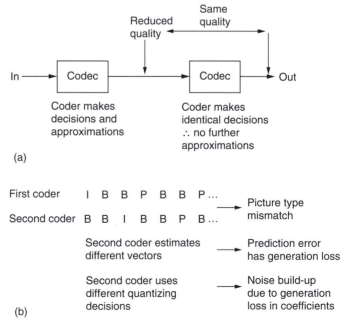

FIGURE 6.53
(a) Two identical coders in tandem that are synchronised make similar coding decisions and cause little loss. (b) There are various ways in which concatenated coders can produce nonideal performance.

One way of avoiding concatenation is to stay in the compressed data domain. If the goal is just to move pictures from one place to another, decoding to traditional video so an existing router can be used is not ideal, although substantially better than going through the analog domain.

Figure 6.54 shows some possibilities for picture transport. Clearly, if the pictures exist as a compressed file on a server, a file transfer is the right way to do it as there is no possibility of loss because there has been no concatenation. File transfer is also quite indifferent to the picture format. It doesn't care whether the pictures are interlaced or not or whether the colour is 4:2:0 or 4:2:2.

Decoding to SDI (serial digital interface) standard is sometimes done so that existing serial digital routing can be used. This is concatenation and has to be done carefully. The compressed video can use interlace only with nonsquare pixels and the colour coding has to be 4:2:2 because SDI allows only that. If a compressed file has 4:2:0 the chroma has to be interpolated up to 4:2:2 for SDI transfer and then subsampled back to 4:2:0 at the second coder, and this will cause generation loss. An SDI transfer also can be performed only in real time, thus negating one of the advantages of compression. In short, traditional SDI is not really at home with compression.

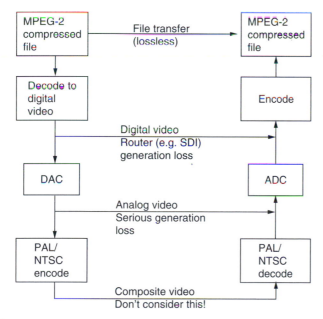

FIGURE 6.54
Compressed picture transport mechanisms contrasted.

As 4:2:0 progressive scan gains popularity and video production moves steadily toward non-format-specific hardware using computers and data networks, use of the serial digital interface will eventually decline. In the short term, if an existing SDI router has to be used, one solution is to produce a bitstream that is sufficiently similar to SDI that a router will pass it. In other words, the signal level, frequency, and impedance are pure SDI, but the data protocol is different so that a bit-accurate file transfer can be performed. This has two advantages over SDI. First, the compressed data format can be anything appropriate and noninterlaced and/ or 4:2:0 can be handled in any picture size, aspect ratio, or frame rate. Second, a faster than real-time transfer can be used depending on the compression factor of the file. Equipment that allows this is becoming available and its use can mean that the full economic life of a SDI-routing installation can be obtained.

An improved way of reducing concatenation loss has emerged from the ATLANTIC research project.[8] Figure 6.55 shows that the second encoder in a concatenated scheme does not make its own decisions from the incoming video, but is instead steered by information from the first bitstream. As the second encoder has less intelligence, it is known as a dim encoder.

The information bus carries all the structure of the original MPEG-2 bitstream, which would be lost in a conventional decoder. The ATLANTIC decoder does more than decode the pictures. It also places on the information bus all parameters needed to make the dim encoder reenact what the initial MPEG-2 encoder did as closely as possible.

The GOP structure is passed on so that pictures are reencoded as the same type. Positions of macroblock boundaries become identical so that DCT blocks contain the same pixels and motion vectors relate to the same screen data. The weighting and quantizing tables are passed so that coefficient truncation is identical. Motion vectors from the original bitstream are passed on so that the dim encoder does not need to perform motion estimation. In this way predicted pictures will be identical to the original prediction and the prediction error data will be the same.

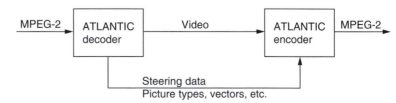

FIGURE 6.55
In an ATLANTIC system, the second encoder is steered by information from the decoder.

One application of this approach is in re-compression, in which an MPEG-2 bit-stream has to have its bit rate reduced. This has to be done by heavier requantizing of coefficients, but if as many other parameters as possible can be kept the same, such as motion vectors, the degradation will be minimized. In a simple recom-pressor just requantizing the coefficients means that the predictive coding will be impaired. In a proper encode, the quantizing error due to coding, say, an I picture is removed from the P picture by the prediction process. The prediction error of P is obtained by subtracting the decoded I picture rather than the original I picture.

In simple re-compression this does not happen and there may be a tolerance buildup known as drift.[9] A more sophisticated re-compressor will need to repeat the prediction process using the decoded output pictures as the prediction reference.

MPEG-2 bitstreams will often be decoded for the purpose of switching. Local insertion of commercial breaks into a centrally originated bitstream is one obvious requirement. If the decoded video signal is switched, the information bus must also be switched. At the switch point identical re-encoding becomes impossible because prior pictures required for predictive coding will have dis-appeared. At this point the dim encoder has to become bright again because it has to create an MPEG-2 bitstream without assistance.

It is possible to encode the information bus into a form that allows it to be invisi-bly carried in the serial digital interface. When a production process such as a vision mixer or DVE performs no manipulation, i.e., becomes bit transparent, the subsequent encoder can extract the bus information and operate in "dim" mode. When a manipulation is performed, the information bus signal will be corrupted and the encoder has to work in "bright" mode. The encoded information signal is known as a "mole"[10] because it burrows through the processing equipment!

There will be a generation loss at the switch point because the re-encode will be making different decisions in bright mode. This may be difficult to detect because the human visual system is slow to react to a vision cut, and defects in the first few pictures after a cut are masked.

In addition to the video computation required to perform a cut, the process has to consider the buffer occupancy of the decoder. A downstream decoder has finite buffer memory, and individual encoders model the decoder buffer occupancy to ensure that it neither overflows nor underflows. At any instant the decoder buffer can be nearly full or nearly empty without a problem, provided there is a subsequent correction. An encoder that is approaching a complex I picture may run down the buffer so it can send a lot of data to describe that picture. Figure 6.56a shows that if a decoder with a nearly full buffer is suddenly switched to an encoder that has been running down its buffer occupancy, the decoder buffer will overflow when the second encoder sends a lot of data.

An MPEG-2 switcher will need to monitor the buffer occupancy of its own output to avoid overflow of downstream decoders. When this is a possibility the second encoder will have to recompress to reduce the output bit rate temporarily. In practice there will be a recovery period in which the buffer occupancy of the newly selected signal is matched to that of the previous signal. This is shown in Figure 6.56b.

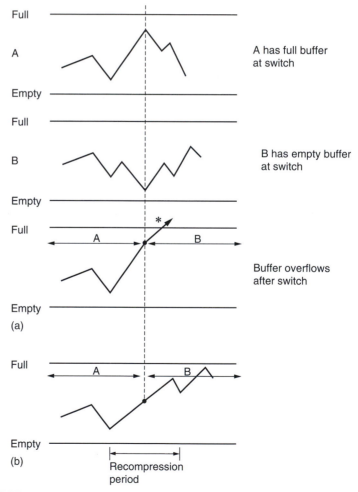

FIGURE 6.56
(a) A bitstream switch at a different level of buffer occupancy can cause a decoder overflow.
(b) Recompression after a switch to return to correct buffer occupancy.

References

1. MPEG Video Standard ISO/IEC 138182: Information technology generic coding of moving pictures and associated audio information. (video) (aka ITU-T Rec. H-262) (1996).

2. Huffman, D.A. A method for the construction of minimum redundancy codes. Proc. IRE, 40, 1098–1101 (1952).

3. LeGall, D. MPEG: a video compression standard for multimedia applications. Commun. ACM, 34, No. 4, 46–58 (1991).

4. ISO/IEC JTC1/SC29/WG11 MPEG. International Standard ISO 11172: Coding of moving pictures and associated audio for digital storage media up to 1.5 Mbits/s. (1992).

5. ISO Joint Photographic Experts Group Standard JPEG-8-R8.

6. Wallace, G.K. Overview of the JPEG (ISO/CCITT) still image compression standard. ISO/JTC1/SC2/WG8 N932 (1989).

7. Stone, J., and Wilkinson, J. Concatenation of video compression systems. Presented at the 137th SMPTE Tech. Conf. (New Orleans) (1995).

8. Wells, N.D. The ATLANTIC project: models for program production and distribution. Proc. Eur. Conf. Multimedia Applications Services and Techniques (ECMAST), 243–253 (1996).

9. Werner, O. Drift analysis and drift reduction for multiresolution hybrid video coding. Image Commun., 8, 387–409 (1996).

10. Knee, M.J., and Wells, N.D. Seamless concatenation: a 21st century dream. Presented at the Int. Television Symp. (Montreux) (1997).

CHAPTER 7
Digital Audio in Video

WHAT IS SOUND?

Physics can tell us the mechanism by which disturbances propagate through the air. If this is our definition of sound, we have the problem that in physics there are no limits to the frequencies and levels that must be considered. Biology can tell us that the ear responds to only a certain range of frequencies provided a threshold level is exceeded. This is a better definition of sound; reproduction is easier because it is necessary only to reproduce that range of levels and frequencies that the ear can detect.

Psycho-acoustics can describe how our hearing has finite resolution in both time and frequency domains such that what we perceive is an inexact impression. Some aspects of the original disturbance are inaudible to us and are said to be masked. If our goal is the highest quality, we can design our imperfect equipment so that the shortcomings are masked. Conversely if our goal is economy we can use compression and hope that masking will disguise the inaccuracies it causes.

By definition, the sound quality of a perceptive coder can be assessed only by human hearing. Equally, a useful perceptive coder can be designed only with a good knowledge of the human hearing mechanism.[1] The acuity of the human ear is astonishing. The frequency range is extremely wide, covering some 10 octaves (an octave is a doubling of pitch or frequency) without interruption. It can detect tiny amounts of distortion and will accept an enormous dynamic range. If the ear detects a different degree of impairment between two codecs having the same bit rate in properly conducted tests, we can say that one of them is superior. Thus quality is completely subjective and can be checked

THE EAR

The sense we call hearing results from acoustic, mechanical, hydraulic, nervous, and mental processes in the ear/brain combination, leading to the term psycho-acoustics. It is possible to introduce the subject here only briefly.[2]

Figure 7.1 shows that the structure of the ear is traditionally divided into the outer, middle, and inner ear. The outer ear works at low impedance, the inner ear works at high impedance, and the middle ear is an impedance-matching device. The visible part of the outer ear is called the pinna, which plays a subtle role in determining the direction of arrival of sound at high frequencies. It is too small to have any effect at low frequencies. Incident sound enters the auditory canal or meatus. The pipe-like meatus causes a small resonance at around 4 kHz. Sound vibrates the eardrum or tympanic membrane, which seals the outer ear from the middle ear. The inner ear or cochlea works by sound travelling though a fluid. Sound enters the cochlea via a membrane called the oval window. If airborne sound were to be incident on the oval window directly, the serious impedance mismatch would cause most of the sound to be reflected. The middle ear remedies that mismatch by providing a mechanical advantage. The tympanic membrane is linked to the oval window by three bones known as ossicles, which act as a lever system such that a large displacement of the tympanic membrane results in a smaller displacement of the oval window but with greater force. Figure 7.2 shows that the malleus applies a tension to the tympanic

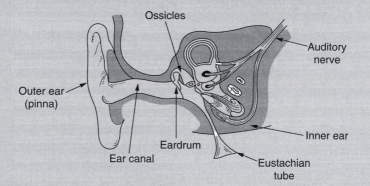

FIGURE 7.1
The structure of the human ear. See text for details.

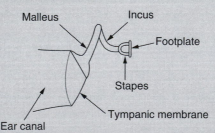

FIGURE 7.2
The malleus tensions the tympanic membrane into a conical shape. The ossicles provide an impedance-transforming lever system between the tympanic membrane and the oval window.

membrane, rendering it conical in shape. The malleus and the incus are firmly joined together to form a lever. The incus acts upon the stapes through a spherical joint. As the area of the tympanic membrane is greater than that of the oval window, there is a further multiplication of the available force. Consequently small pressures over the large area of the tympanic membrane are converted to high pressures over the small area of the oval window.

The middle ear is normally sealed, but ambient pressure changes will cause static pressure on the tympanic membrane, which is painful. The pressure is relieved by the Eustachian tube, which opens involuntarily during swallowing. The Eustachian tubes open into the cavities of the head and must normally be closed to avoid one's own speech seeming deafeningly loud.

The ossicles are located by minute muscles, which are normally relaxed. However, the middle ear reflex is an involuntary tightening of the tensor tympani and stapedius muscles, which heavily damp the ability of the tympanic membrane and the stapes to transmit sound by about 12 dB at frequencies below 1 kHz. The main function of this reflex is to reduce the audibility of one's own speech. However, loud sounds will also trigger this reflex, which takes some 60–120 ms to occur, too late to protect against transients such as gunfire.

The cochlea, shown in Figure 7.3a, is a tapering spiral cavity within bony walls, which is filled with fluid. The widest part, near the oval window, is called the base and the distant end is the apex. Figure 7.3b shows that the cochlea is divided lengthwise into three volumes by Reissner's membrane and the basilar membrane. The scala vestibuli and the scala tympani are connected by a small aperture at the apex of the cochlea known as the helicotrema. Vibrations from the stapes are transferred to the oval window and become fluid pressure variations, which are relieved by the flexing of the round window. Effectively the basilar membrane is in series with the

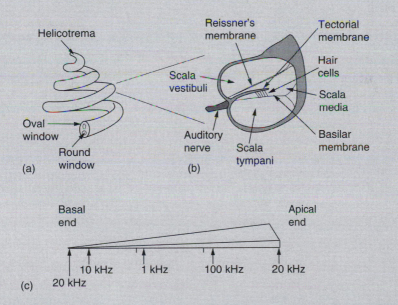

FIGURE 7.3
(a) The cochlea is a tapering spiral cavity. (b) The cross section of the cavity is divided by Reissner's membrane and the basilar membrane. (c) The basilar membrane tapers so its resonant frequency changes along its length.

fluid motion and is driven by it except at very low frequencies, at which the fluid flows through the helicotrema, bypassing the basilar membrane.

Figure 7.3c shows that the basilar membrane is not uniform, but tapers in width and varies in thickness in the opposite sense to the taper of the cochlea. The part of the basilar membrane that resonates as a result of an applied sound works as a function of the frequency. High frequencies cause resonance near to the oval window, whereas low frequencies cause resonance farther away. More precisely, the distance from the apex where the maximum resonance occurs is a logarithmic function of the frequency. Consequently tones spaced apart in octave steps will excite evenly spaced resonances in the basilar membrane. The prediction of resonance at a particular location on the membrane is called *place theory.* Essentially the basilar membrane is a mechanical frequency analyser. A knowledge of the way it operates is essential to an understanding of musical phenomena such as pitch discrimination, timbre, consonance, and dissonance and to auditory phenomena such as critical bands, masking, and the precedence effect.

The vibration of the basilar membrane is sensed by the organ of Corti, which runs along the centre of the cochlea. The organ of Corti is active in that it contains elements that can generate vibration as well as sense it. These are connected in a regenerative fashion so that the Q factor, or frequency selectivity of the ear, is higher than it would otherwise be. The deflection of hair cells in the organ of Corti triggers nerve firings and these signals are conducted to the brain by the auditory nerve.

Nerve firings are not a perfect analog of the basilar membrane motion. A nerve firing appears to occur at a constant phase relationship to the basilar vibration, a phenomenon called phase locking; but firings do not necessarily occur on every cycle. At higher frequencies firings are intermittent, yet each is in the same phase relationship.

The resonant behaviour of the basilar membrane is not observed at the lowest audible frequencies below 50 Hz. The pattern of vibration does not appear to change with frequency and it is possible that the frequency is low enough to be measured directly from the rate of nerve firings.

only by listening tests. However, any characteristic of a signal that can be heard can also be measured by a suitable instrument. The subjective tests can tell us how sensitive the instrument should be. Then the objective readings from the instrument give an indication of how acceptable a signal is in respect to that characteristic. Instruments for assessing the performance of codecs are currently extremely rare and there remains much work to be done.

LEVEL AND LOUDNESS

At its best, the ear can detect a sound pressure variation of only 2×10^{-5} pascals rms and so this figure is used as the reference against which sound pressure level (SPL) is measured. The sensation of loudness is a logarithmic function of SPL and consequently a logarithmic unit, the decibel, is used in audio measurement.

The dynamic range of the ear exceeds 130 dB, but at the extremes of this range, the ear is either straining to hear or in pain. Neither of these cases can be described as pleasurable or entertaining, and it is hardly necessary to produce audio of this dynamic range because, among other things, the consumer is unlikely to have anywhere sufficiently quiet to listen to it. On the other hand, extended listening to music whose dynamic range has been excessively compressed is fatiguing.

The frequency response of the ear is not at all uniform and it also changes with SPL. The subjective response to level is called loudness and is measured in phons. The phon scale and the SPL scale coincide at one kHz, but at other frequencies the phon scale deviates because it displays the actual SPLs judged by a human subject to be equally as loud as a given level at one kHz. Figure 7.4 shows the so-called equal loudness contours, which were originally measured by Fletcher and Munson and subsequently by Robinson and Dadson. Note the irregularities caused by resonances in the meatus at about 4 and 13 kHz.

Usually, people's ears are at their most sensitive between about two and five kHz, and although some people can detect 20 kHz at high level, there is much evidence to suggest that most listeners cannot tell if the upper frequency limit of sound is 20 or 16 kHz.[3,4] For a long time it was thought that frequencies below about 40 Hz were unimportant, but it is now clear that reproduction of frequencies down to 20 Hz improves reality and ambience.[5] The generally accepted frequency range for high-quality audio is 20–20,000 Hz, although for broadcasting an upper limit of 15,000 Hz is often applied. The most dramatic effect of the curves of Figure 7.4 is that the bass content of reproduced sound is disproportionately reduced as the level is turned down.

Loudness is a subjective reaction and is almost impossible to measure. In addition to the level-dependent frequency response problem, the listener uses the sound not for its own sake but to draw some conclusion about the source. For example, most people hearing a distant motorcycle will describe it as being loud. Clearly at the source, it *is* loud, but the listener has compensated for the distance.

The best that can be done is to make some compensation for the level-dependent response using weighting curves. Ideally there should be many, but in practice the A, B, and C weightings were chosen, in which the A curve is based on the 40-phon response. The measured level after such a filter is in units of dBA. The A curve is almost always used because it most nearly relates to the annoyance factor of distant noise sources.

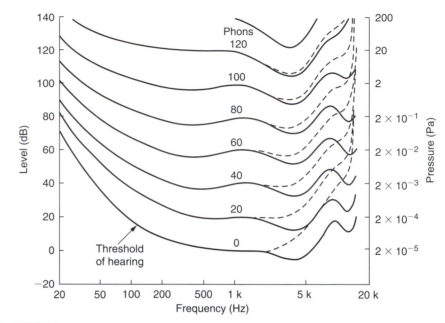

FIGURE 7.4
Contours of equal loudness showing that the frequency response of the ear is highly level-dependent (solid line, age 20; dashed line, age 60).

CRITICAL BANDS

Figure 7.5 shows an uncoiled basilar membrane with the apex on the left so that the usual logarithmic frequency scale can be applied. The envelope of displacement of the basilar membrane is shown for a single frequency in Figure 7.5a. The vibration of the membrane in sympathy with a single frequency cannot be localized to an infinitely small area, and nearby areas are forced to vibrate at the same frequency with an amplitude that decreases with distance. Note that the envelope is asymmetrical because the membrane is tapering and because of frequency-dependent losses in the propagation of vibrational energy down the cochlea. If the frequency is changed, as in Figure 7.5b, the position of maximum displacement will also change. As the basilar membrane is continuous, the position of maximum displacement is infinitely variable, allowing extremely good pitch discrimination of about one-twelfth of a semitone, which is determined by the spacing of hair cells.

In the presence of a complex spectrum, the finite width of the vibration envelope means that the ear fails to register energy in some bands when there is more

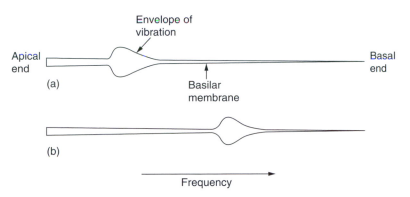

Apical end

Basal end

Envelope of vibration

(a)

Basilar membrane

(b)

Frequency

FIGURE 7.5
The basilar membrane symbolically uncoiled. (a) Single frequency causes the vibration envelope shown. (b) Changing the frequency moves the peak of the envelope.

energy in a nearby band. Within those areas, other frequencies are mechanically excluded because their amplitude is insufficient to dominate the local vibration of the membrane. Thus the Q factor of the membrane is responsible for the degree of auditory masking, defined as the decreased audibility of one sound in the presence of another.

The term used in psycho-acoustics to describe the finite width of the vibration envelope is "critical bandwidth." Critical bands were first described by Fletcher.[6] The envelope of basilar vibration is a complicated function. It is clear from the mechanism that the area of the membrane involved will increase as the sound level rises. Figure 7.6 shows the bandwidth as a function of level.

As was shown in Chapter 3, transform theory teaches that the higher the frequency resolution of a transform, the worse the time accuracy. As the basilar membrane has finite frequency resolution measured in the width of a critical band, it follows that it must have finite time resolution. This also follows from the fact that the membrane is resonant, taking time to start and stop vibrating in response to a stimulus. There are many examples of this. Figure 7.7 shows the impulse response. Figure 7.8 shows that the perceived loudness of a tone burst increases with duration up to about 200 ms due to the finite response time.

The ear has evolved to offer intelligibility in reverberant environments, which it does by averaging all received energy over a period of about 30 ms. Reflected sound that arrives within this time is integrated to produce a louder sensation, whereas reflected sound that arrives after that time can be temporally discriminated and is perceived as an echo. Our simple microphones have no such ability,

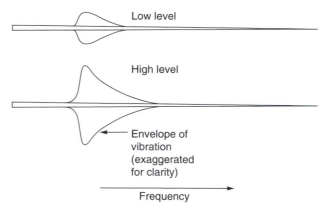

FIGURE 7.6
The critical bandwidth changes with SPL.

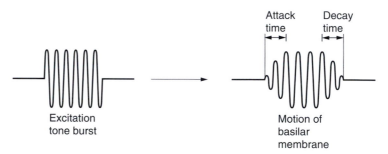

FIGURE 7.7
Impulse response of the ear showing slow attack and decay due to resonant behaviour.

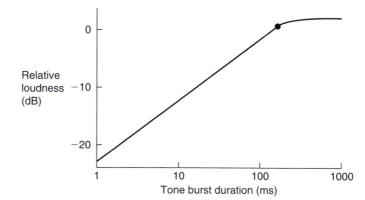

FIGURE 7.8
Perceived level of tone burst rises with duration as resonance builds up.

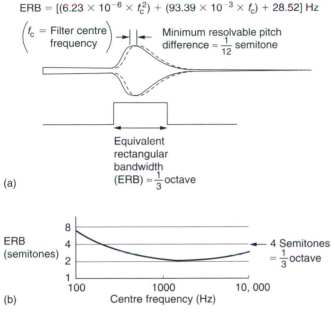

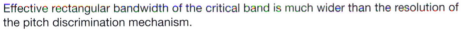

(b)

FIGURE 7.9
Effective rectangular bandwidth of the critical band is much wider than the resolution of the pitch discrimination mechanism.

which is why we often need to have acoustic treatment in areas where microphones are used.

A further example of the finite time discrimination of the ear is the fact that short interruptions to a continuous tone are difficult to detect. Finite time resolution means that masking can take place even when the masking tone begins after and ceases before the masked sound. This is referred to as forward and backward masking.[7]

As the vibration envelope is such a complicated shape, Moore and Glasberg[8] have proposed the concept of equivalent rectangular bandwidth ERB (equivalent rectangular bandwidth) to simplify matters. The ERB is the bandwidth of a rectangular filter that passes the same power as a critical band. Figure 7.9a shows the expression they have derived linking the ERB with frequency. This is plotted in Figure 7.9b, in which it will be seen that one-third of an octave is a good approximation. This is about 30 times broader than the pitch discrimination also shown in Figure 7.9b.

STEREO AND SURROUND SOUND

The human listener can determine reasonably well where a sound is coming from. An understanding of the mechanisms of direction sensing is important for the successful implementation of spatial illusions such as stereophonic sound. As Figure 7.10 shows, having a pair of spaced ears allows a number of mechanisms. In Figure 7.10a a phase shift will be apparent between the two versions of a tone picked up at the two ears unless the source of the tone is dead ahead (or behind). In (b) the distant ear is shaded by the head, resulting in reduced response compared to the nearer ear. In (c) a transient sound arrives later at the more distant ear.

If the phase-shift mechanism (Figure 7.10a) is considered, then it will be clear that there will be considerable variation in this effect with frequency. At a low frequency such as 30 Hz, the wavelength is around 11.5 m. Even if heard from the side, the ear spacing of about 0.2 m will result in a phase shift of only 6° and so this mechanism must be quite weak at low frequencies. At high frequencies such as 10 kHz, the ear spacing is many wavelengths, and variations in the pathlength difference will produce a confusing and complex phase relationship. The problem with tones or single frequencies is that they produce a sinusoidal waveform, one cycle of which looks much like another, leading to ambiguities in the time between two versions. This is shown in Figure 7.11a.

Pure tones are extremely difficult to localize, especially as they will often excite room-standing waves, which give a completely misleading impression of the location of the sound source. Consequently the phase-comparison mechanism must be restricted to frequencies at which the wavelength is short enough to give a reasonable phase shift, but not so short that complete cycles of shift are introduced. This suggests a frequency limit of around 1500 Hz, which has been confirmed by experiment.

The shading mechanism of Figure 7.10b will be a function of the directivity factor, suggesting that at low and middle frequencies sound will diffract round the head sufficiently well that there will be no significant difference between the level at the two ears. Only at high frequencies does sound become directional enough for the head to shade the distant ear, causing what is called an interaural intensity difference. At very high frequencies, the shape of the pinnae must have some effect on the sound that is a function of direction. It is thought that the pinnae allow some discrimination in all axes.

Phase differences are useful only at low frequencies and shading works only at high frequencies. Fortunately real-world sounds are timbral or broadband and often contain transients, especially those sounds that indicate a potential hazard. Timbral, broadband, and transient sounds differ from tones in that they contain many different frequencies. A transient has a unique aperiodic waveform, which Figure 7.11b shows has the advantage that there can be no ambiguity in the interaural delay (IAD) between two versions. Figure 7.12 shows the time difference for different angles of incidence for a typical head.

Note that a 1° change in sound location causes an IAD of around 10 µs. The smallest detectable IAD is a remarkable 6 µs. The basilar membrane is a frequency analysis device, which produces nerve impulses from different physical locations according to which frequencies are present in the incident sound. Clearly when a timbral or transient sound arrives from one side, many frequencies will be excited simultaneously in the nearer ear, resulting in a pattern of nerve firings. This will be closely followed by a similar excitation pattern in the further ear.

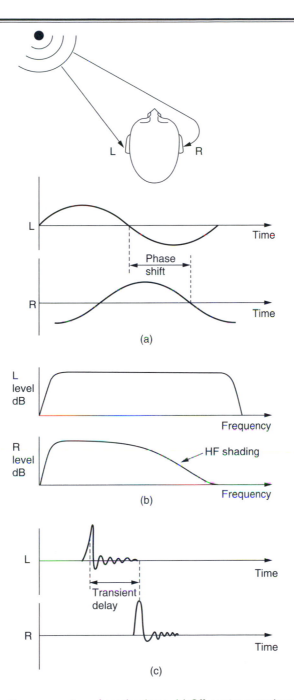

FIGURE 7.10
Having two spaced ears allows a number of mechanisms. (a) Off-centre sounds result in phase difference.
(b) Distant ear is shaded by head, producing loss of high frequencies. (c) Distant ear detects transient later.

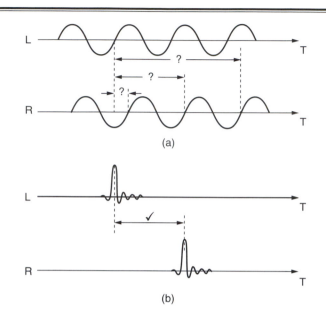

(a)

(b)

FIGURE 7.11
(a) Pure tones cause ambiguity in timing differences. (b) Transients have no ambiguity and are easier to localize.

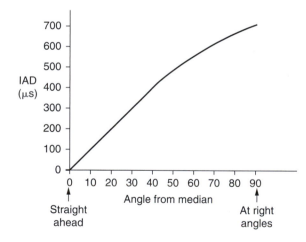

FIGURE 7.12
The IAD for various arrival directions.

Shading may change the relative amplitudes of the higher frequencies, but it will not change the pattern of frequency components present. A timbral waveform is periodic at the fundamental frequency but the presence of harmonics means that a greater number of nerve firings can be compared between the two ears. As the statistical deviation of nerve firings with respect to the incoming waveform is about 100 μs, the only way an IAD of 6 μs can be perceived is if the timing of many nerve firings is correlated in some way.

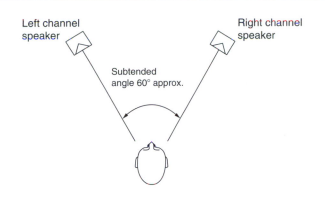

FIGURE 7.13
Configuration used for stereo listening.

The broader the range of frequencies in the sound source, the more effective this process will be. Analysis of the arrival time of transients is a most effective lateral direction-sensing mechanism. This is easily demonstrated by wearing a blindfold and having a helper move around the room making a variety of noises. The helper will be easier to localize when making clicking noises than when humming. It is easy to localize a double bass despite the low fundamental as it is a harmonically rich instrument.

It must be appreciated that human hearing can locate a number of different sound sources simultaneously. The hearing mechanism must be constantly comparing excitation patterns from the two ears with different delays. Strong correlation will be found where the delay corresponds to the interaural delay for a given source. This is apparent in the binaural threshold of hearing, which is 3–6 dB better than monaural at around four kHz. This delay-varying mechanism will take time and it is to be expected that the ear would then be slow to react to changes in source direction. This is indeed the case and experiments have shown that oscillating sources can be tracked only up to 2–3 Hz.

The ability to locate bursts of noise improves with burst duration up to about 700 ms. The interaural phase, delay, and level mechanisms vary in their effectiveness depending on the nature of the sound to be located. A fixed response to each mechanism would be ineffective. For example, on a low-frequency tone, the time-of-arrival mechanism is useless, whereas on a transient it excels. The different mechanisms are quite separate on one level, but at some point in the brain's perception a fuzzy logic or adaptive decision has to be made as to how the outcome of these mechanisms will be weighted to make the final judgment of direction.

The most popular technique for giving an element of spatial realism in sound is stereophony, nowadays abbreviated to stereo, based on two simultaneous audio channels feeding two spaced loudspeakers. Figure 7.13 shows that the optimum listening arrangement for stereo is one in which the speakers and the listener are at different points of a triangle that is almost equilateral. Stereophony works by creating differences of phase and time of arrival of sound at the listener's ears. It was shown above that these are the most powerful hearing mechanisms for determining direction. Figure 7.14a shows that this time-of-arrival difference is achieved by producing the same waveform at each speaker simultaneously, but with a difference in the relative level, rather than phase. Each ear picks up sound from both loudspeakers and sums the waveforms.

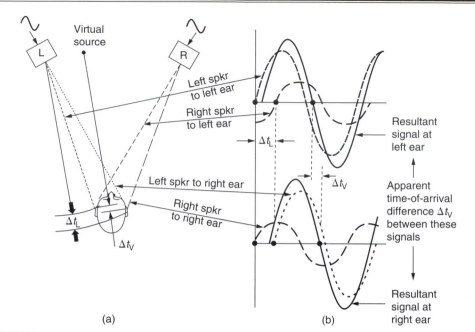

FIGURE 7.14

(a) Stereo illusion is obtained by producing the same waveform at both speakers, but with different amplitudes. (b) As both ears hear both speakers, but at different times, relative level causes apparent time shift at the listener.

The sound picked up by the ear on the same side as the speaker is in advance of the same sound picked up by the opposite ear. When the level emitted by the left loudspeaker is greater than that emitted by the right, it will be seen from Figure 7.14b that the sum of the signals received at the left ear is a waveform that is phase advanced with respect to the sum of the waveforms received at the right ear. If the waveforms concerned are transient the result will be a time-of-arrival difference. These differences are interpreted as being due to a sound source left of centre.

The stereophonic illusion works properly only if the two loudspeakers are producing in-phase signals. In the case of an accidental phase reversal, the spatial characteristic will be ill-defined and lack images. At low frequencies the two loudspeakers are in one another's near field and so anti-phase connection results in bass cancellation. As the apparent position of a sound source between the two speakers can be controlled solely by the relative level of the sound emitted by each one, stereo signals in this format are called intensity stereo. In intensity stereo it is possible to "steer" a monophonic signal from a single microphone into a particular position in a stereo image using a form of differential gain control.

Figure 7.15 shows that this device, known as a panoramic potentiometer, or panpot for short, will produce equal outputs when the control is set to the centre. If the panpot is moved left or right, one output will increase and the other will reduce, moving or panning the stereo image to one side. If the system is perfectly linear, more than one sound source can be panned into a stereo image, with each source heard in a different location. This is done using a stereo mixer, shown in Figure 7.16, in which monophonic inputs pass via panpots to a stereo mix bus.

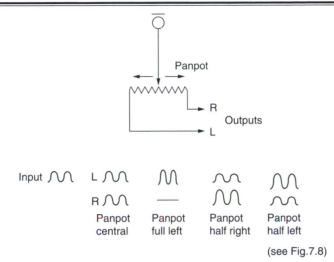

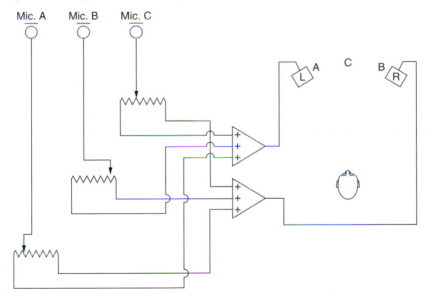

FIGURE 7.15

The panpot distributes a monophonic microphone signal into two stereo channels, allowing the sound source to be positioned anywhere in the image.

FIGURE 7.16

Multichannel mixing technique pans multiple sound sources into one stereo image.

Whilst the stereo illusion is very rewarding when well executed, the development of digital transmission allows an arbitrary number of sound channels to accompany video. In this way surround-sound techniques developed for the cinema can be enjoyed in the home.

Figure 7.17 shows the 5.1 channel system proposed for advanced television sound applications. In addition to the conventional L and R stereo speakers at the front, a centre speaker is used. When normal L–R stereo is heard from off-centre, the image will be pulled toward the nearer speaker. The centre speaker is primarily to pull central images back for the off-centre listener.

In most television applications it is only the dialog that needs to be centralized and consequently the centre speaker need not be capable of the full frequency range. Rear L and R speakers are also provided, making a total of five channels. A narrow bandwidth subwoofer channel is also provided to produce low frequencies for the inevitable earthquakes and explosions. The restricted bandwidth means that six full channels are not required, hence the term 5.1. Such systems require the separate channels to be carried individually to the viewer.

It should be appreciated that surround sound is something of a misnomer. Consider four speakers in a square in which the listener in the middle would face any pair of speakers. Anywhere between the front pair of speakers virtual sound sources can be presented. Anywhere between the rear pair of speakers more virtual sound sources can be located. Unfortunately there isn't a mechanism to put sound sources at the sides between the front and the rear speakers. This is simply because with respect to a pair of speakers to his or her side, the ears of a forward-facing listener are in tandem and the stereo illusion simply cannot function. Thus 4.0 or 5.0 surround sound isn't surround sound at all, but is front and rear stereo. The only way any sound will approach the listener from the side is if the room is reverberant and if the loudspeakers are capable of launching accurate sound in more than just the one direction. In order to mix 4.0 or 5.0 sound, the traditional acoustically dead room approach has to be abandoned and monitoring must be performed in surroundings more representative of the consumer environment. If sound from the sides is essential, a seven-channel system that actually has side speakers will be needed.

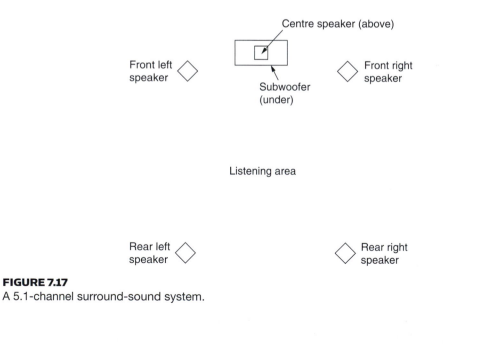

FIGURE 7.17
A 5.1-channel surround-sound system.

CHOICE OF SAMPLING RATE FOR AUDIO

Sampling theory is only the beginning of the process that must be followed to arrive at a suitable sampling rate. The finite slope of realizable filters will compel designers to raise the sampling rate. For consumer products, the lower the sampling rate, the better, because the cost of the medium is directly proportional to the sampling rate; thus sampling rates near to twice 20 kHz are to be expected. For professional products, there is a need to operate at variable speed

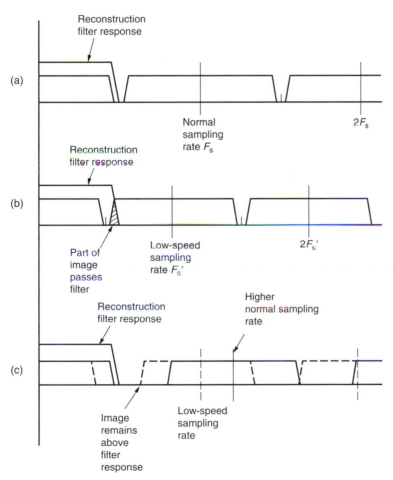

FIGURE 7.18
(a) At normal speed, the reconstruction filter correctly prevents images entering the baseband. (b) When speed is reduced, the sampling rate falls, and a fixed filter will allow part of the lower sideband of the sampling frequency to pass. (c) If the sampling rate of the machine is raised, but the filter characteristic remains the same, the problem can be avoided.

for pitch correction. When the speed of a digital recorder is reduced, the reproduced sampling rate falls, and Figure 7.18 shows that with a minimal sampling rate the first image frequency can become low enough to pass the reconstruction filter. If the sampling frequency is raised without changing the response of the filters, the speed can be reduced without this problem.

In the early days of digital audio research, the necessary bandwidth of about one megabit per second per audio channel was difficult to store. Disk drives then had the bandwidth but not the capacity for long recording time, so attention turned to video recorders. These were adapted to store audio samples by creating a pseudo-video waveform, which could convey binary as black and white levels. The sampling rate of such a system is constrained to relate simply to the field rate and field structure of the television standard used, so that an integer number of samples can be stored on each usable TV line in the field. Such a recording can be made on a monochrome recorder, and these recordings are made in two standards, 525 lines at 60 Hz and 625 lines at 50 Hz. Thus it is possible to find a frequency that is a common multiple of the two and also suitable for use as a sampling rate.

The allowable sampling rates in a pseudo-video system can be deduced by multiplying the field rate by the number of active lines in a field (blanked lines cannot be used) and again by the number of samples in a line. By careful choice of parameters it is possible to use either 525/60 or 625/50 video with a sampling rate of 44.1 kHz.

In 60 Hz video, there are 35 blanked lines, leaving 490 lines per frame, or 245 lines per field for samples. If three samples are stored per line, the sampling rate becomes

$$60 \times 245 \times 3 = 44.1\,\text{kHz}.$$

In 50 Hz video, there are 37 lines of blanking, leaving 588 active lines per frame, or 294 per field, so the same sampling rate is given by

$$50.00 \times 294 \times 3 = 44.1\,\text{kHz}.$$

The sampling rate of 44.1 kHz came to be that of the Compact Disc. Even though a CD has no video circuitry, the equipment used to make CD masters was video based and determined the sampling rate.

For landlines to FM stereo broadcast transmitters having a 15 kHz audio bandwidth, the sampling rate of 32 kHz is more than adequate and has been in use for some time in the United Kingdom and Japan. This frequency is also in use in the NICAM 728 stereo TV sound system and in DVB. It is also used for the Sony NT format minicassette. The professional sampling rate of 48 kHz was proposed as having a simple relationship to 32 kHz, being far enough above 40 kHz for variable-speed operation.

Although in a perfect world the adoption of a single sampling rate might have had virtues, for practical and economic reasons digital audio now has essentially three rates to support: 32 kHz for broadcast, 44.1 kHz for CD and its mastering equipment, and 48 kHz for "professional" use.[9] A rate of 48 kHz is used extensively in television production, in which it can be synchronised to both U.S. and European line standards relatively easily. The currently available DVTR formats offer 48 kHz audio sampling. A number of formats can operate at more than one sampling rate although not all available hardware implements every possibility of the format. Most hard disk recorders will operate at a range of rates. Although higher sampling rates than 48 kHz are available, these appear to be offered because they have become technically possible rather than because there is a demonstrated need. Certainly there is nothing in psychoacoustics to justify their use.

BASIC DIGITAL-TO-ANALOG CONVERSION

This direction of conversion will be discussed first, because ADCs often use embedded DACs in feedback loops. The purpose of a digital-to-analog convertor is to take numerical values and reproduce the continuous waveform that they represent. Figure 7.19 shows the major elements of a conventional conversion subsystem, i.e., one in which oversampling is not employed. The jitter

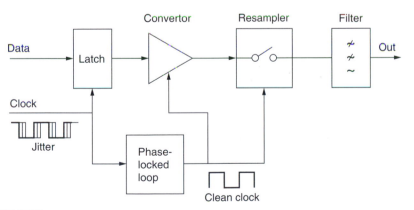

FIGURE 7.19
The components of a conventional convertor. A jitter-free clock drives the voltage conversion, whose output may be resampled prior to reconstruction.

in the clock needs to be removed with a VCO (voltage-controlled oscillator) or VCXO. Sample values are buffered in a latch and fed to the convertor element, which operates on each cycle of the clean clock. The output is then a voltage proportional to the number for at least a part of the sample period. A resampling stage may be found next, to remove switching transients, reduce the aperture ratio, or allow the use of a convertor, which takes a substantial part of the sample period to operate. The resampled waveform is then presented to a reconstruction filter, which rejects frequencies above the audio band.

This section is primarily concerned with the implementation of the convertor element. There are two main ways of obtaining an analog signal from PCM (pulse code modulation) data. One is to control binary-weighted currents and sum them; the other is to control the length of time a fixed current flows into an integrator. The two methods are contrasted in Figure 7.20. They appear simple, but are of no use for audio in these forms because of practical limitations. In Figure 7.20c, the binary code is about to have a major overflow, and all the low-order currents are flowing. In (d), the binary input has increased by one,

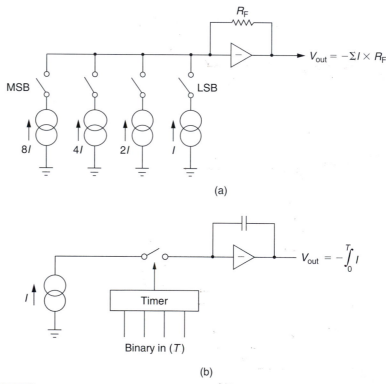

FIGURE 7.20
Elementary conversion: (a) weighted current DAC, (b) timed integrator DAC,

and only the most significant current flows. This current must equal the sum of all the others plus one. The accuracy must be such that the step size is within the required limits. In this simple four-bit example, if the step size needs to be a rather casual 10 percent accurate, the necessary accuracy is only one part in 160, but for a 16-bit system it would become one part in 655,360, or about two ppm. This degree of accuracy is almost impossible to achieve, let alone maintain in the presence of ageing and temperature change.

The integrator-type convertor in this four-bit example is shown in Figure 7.20c; it requires a clock for the counter, which allows it to count up to the maximum in less than one sample period. This will be more than 16 times the sampling rate. However, in a 16-bit system, the clock rate would need to be 65,536 times the sampling rate, or about three GHz. Whilst there may be a market for a CD player that can defrost a chicken, clearly some refinements are necessary to allow either of these convertor types to be used in audio applications.

One method of producing currents of high relative accuracy is *dynamic element matching*.[10,11] Figure 7.21 shows a current source feeding a pair of nominally

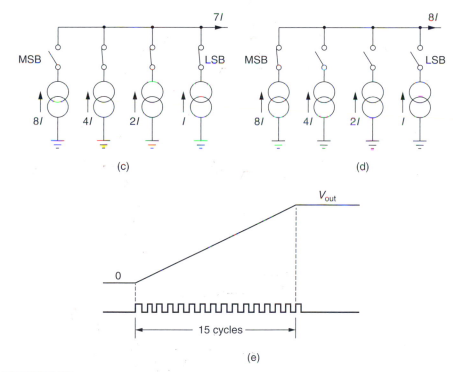

(c)

(d)

(e)

FIGURE 7.20
(Continued) (c) current flow with 0111 input, (d) current flow with 1000 input, (e) integrator ramps up for 15 cycles of clock for input 1111.

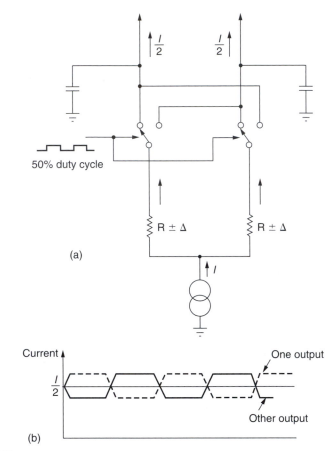

FIGURE 7.21
Dynamic element matching. (a) Each resistor spends half its time in each current path.
(b) Average current of both paths will be identical if duty cycle is 50 percent accurate.

equal resistors. The two will not be the same due to manufacturing tolerances and drift, and thus the current is only approximately divided between them. A pair of change-over switches places each resistor in series with each output. The average current in each output will then be identical, provided that the duty cycle of the switches is exactly 50 percent. This is readily achieved in a divide-by-2 circuit. The accuracy criterion has been transferred from the resistors to the time domain in which accuracy is more readily achieved. Current averaging is performed by a pair of capacitors that do not need to be of any special quality. By cascading these divide-by-2 stages, a binary-weighted series of currents can be obtained, as in Figure 7.22.

In practice, a reduction in the number of stages can be obtained by using a more complex switching arrangement. This generates currents of ratio 1:1:2 by dividing

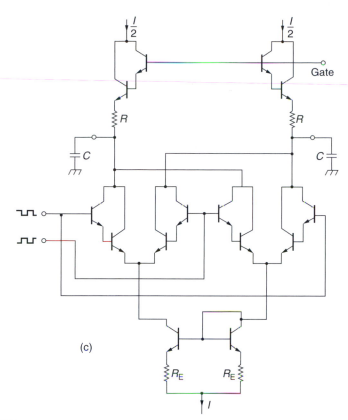

FIGURE 7.21

(Continued) (c) Typical monolithic implementation. Note that clock frequency is arbitrary.

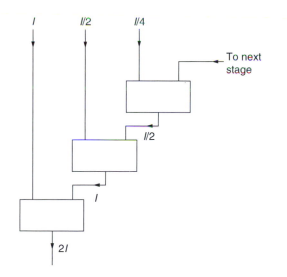

FIGURE 7.22

Cascading the current dividers of Figure 7.21 produces a binary-weighted series of currents.

the current into four paths and feeding two of them to one output, as shown in Figure 7.23. A major advantage of this approach is that no trimming is needed in manufacture, making it attractive for mass production. Freedom from drift is a further advantage.

To prevent interaction between the stages in weighted-current convertors, the currents must be switched to ground or into the virtual earth by change-over

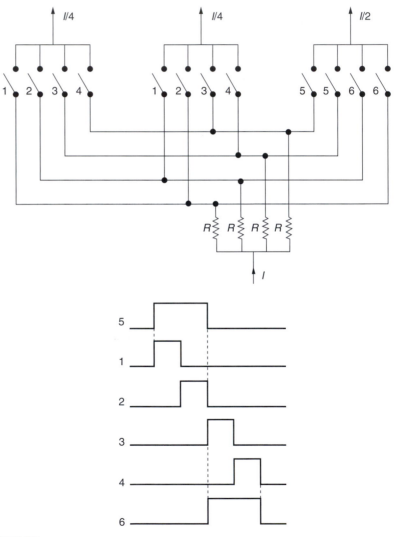

FIGURE 7.23
A more complex dynamic element-matching system. Four drive signals (1, 2, 3, 4) of 25 percent duty cycle close switches of corresponding numbers. Two signals (5, 6) have 50 percent duty cycle, resulting in two current shares going to right-hand output. Division is thus into 1:1:2.

switches. The on-resistance of these switches is a source of error, particularly the MSB, which passes most current. A solution in monolithic convertors is to fabricate switches whose area is proportional to the weighted current, so that the voltage drops of all the switches are the same. The error can then be removed with a suitable offset. The layout of such a device is dominated by the MSB switch because, by definition, it is as big as all the others put together.

The practical approach to the integrator convertor is shown in Figures 7.24 and 7.25, in which two current sources, whose ratio is 256:1, are used; the larger is timed by the high byte of the sample and the smaller is timed by the low byte. The necessary clock frequency is reduced by a factor of 256. Any inaccuracy in the current ratio will cause one quantizing step in every 256 to be of the wrong size, as shown in Figure 7.26, but current tracking is easier to achieve

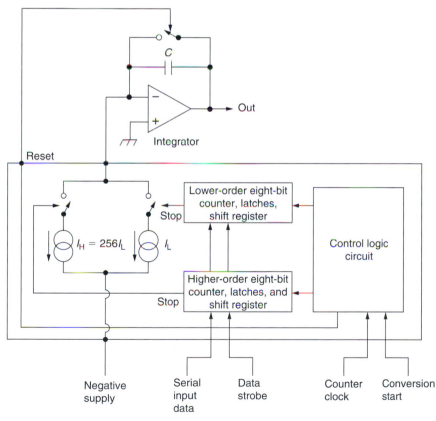

FIGURE 7.24
Simplified diagram of Sony CX-20017. The high-order and low-order current sources (I_H and I_L) and associated timing circuits can be seen. The necessary integrator is external.

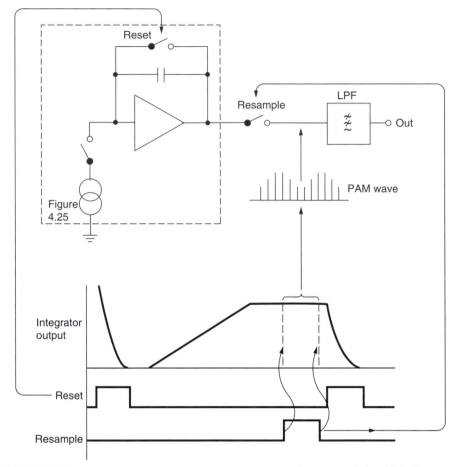

FIGURE 7.25
In an integrator convertor, the output level is stable only when the ramp finishes. An analog switch is necessary to isolate the ramp from subsequent circuits. The switch can also be used to produce a PAM (pulse amplitude-modulated) signal, which has a flatter frequency response than a zero-order hold (staircase) signal.

in a monolithic device. The integrator capacitor must have low dielectric leakage and relaxation, and the operational amplifier must have low bias current as this will have the same effect as leakage.

The output of the integrator will remain constant once the current sources are turned off, and the resampling switch will be closed during the voltage plateau to produce the pulse amplitude-modulated output. Clearly this device cannot produce a zero-order hold output without an additional sample-hold stage, so it is naturally complemented by resampling. Once the output pulse has been gated to the reconstruction filter, the capacitor is discharged with a further switch

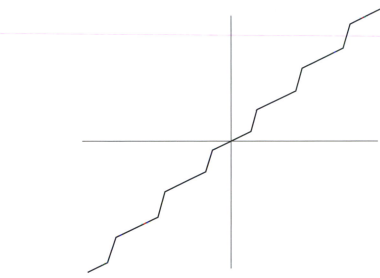

FIGURE 7.26
Imprecise tracking in a dual-slope convertor results in the transfer function shown here.

in preparation for the next conversion. The conversion count must take place in rather less than one sample period to permit the resampling and discharge phases. A clock frequency of about 20 MHz is adequate for a 16-bit 48 kHz unit, which permits the ramp to complete in 12.8 ms, leaving 8 ms for resampling and reset.

BASIC ANALOG-TO-DIGITAL CONVERSION

A conventional analog-to-digital subsystem is shown in Figure 7.27. Following the anti-aliasing filter there will be a sampling process. Many of the ADCs described here will need a finite time to operate, whereas an instantaneous sample must be taken from the input. The solution is to use a track/hold circuit. Following sampling the sample voltage is quantized. The number of the quantized level is then converted into a binary code, typically two's complement. This section is concerned primarily with the implementation of the quantizing step.

The flash convertor is probably the simplest technique available for PCM and DPCM (differential pulse code modulation) conversion. The principle was shown in Chapter 4. Although the device is simple in principle, it contains a lot of circuitry and can be practically implemented only on a chip. A 16-bit device would need a ridiculous 65,535 comparators, and thus these convertors are not practicable for direct audio conversion, although they will be used to advantage

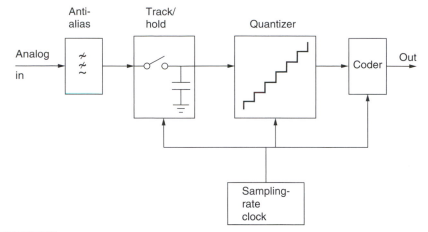

FIGURE 7.27
A conventional analog-to-digital subsystem. Following the anti-aliasing filter there will be a sampling process, which may include a track-hold circuit. Following quantizing, the number of the quantized level is then converted to a binary code, typically two's complement.

in the DPCM and oversampling convertors described later in this chapter. The analog signal has to drive a lot of inputs, which results in a significant parallel capacitance, and a low-impedance driver is essential to avoid restricting the slewing rate of the input. The extreme speed of a flash convertor is a distinct advantage in oversampling. Because computation of all bits is performed simultaneously, no track/hold circuit is required, and droop is eliminated.

Reduction in component complexity can be achieved by quantizing serially. The most primitive method of generating different quantized voltages is to connect a counter to a DAC as in Figure 7.28. The resulting staircase voltage is compared with the input and used to stop the clock to the counter when the DAC output has just exceeded the input. This method is painfully slow, and is not used, as a much faster method that is only slightly more complex exists. Using successive approximation, each bit is tested in turn, starting with the MSB. If the input is greater than half-range, the MSB will be retained and used as a base to test the next bit, which will be retained if the input exceeds three-quarters range, and so on. The number of decisions is equal to the number of bits in the word, in contrast to the number of quantizing intervals, which was the case in the previous example. A drawback of the successive approximation convertor is that the least significant bits are computed last, when droop is at its worst. Figures 7.29 and 7.30 show that droop can cause a successive approximation convertor to make a significant error under certain circumstances.

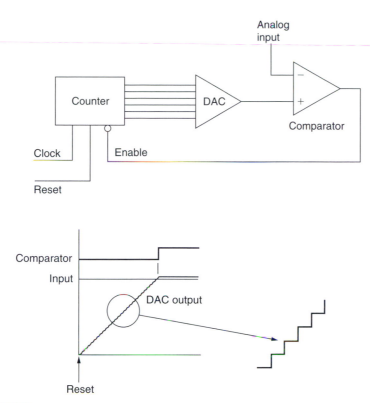

FIGURE 7.28
A simple-ramp ADC compares the output of the DAC with the input. The count is stopped when the DAC output just exceeds the input. This method, although potentially accurate, is much too slow for digital audio.

Analog-to-digital conversion can also be performed using the dual-current-source type DAC principle in a feedback system; the major difference is that the two current sources must work sequentially rather than concurrently. Figure 7.31 shows a 16-bit application in which the capacitor of the track-hold circuit is also used as the ramp integrator. The system operates as follows. When the track-hold FET switches off, the capacitor C will be holding the sample voltage. Two currents of ratio 128:1 are capable of discharging the capacitor. As a result of this ratio, the smaller current will be used to determine the seven least significant bits, and the larger current will determine the nine most significant bits. The currents are provided by current sources of ratio 127:1. When both run together, the current produced is 128 times that from the smaller source alone. This approach means that the current can be changed simply by turning off the larger source, rather than by attempting a change-over.

With both current sources enabled, the high-order counter counts up until the capacitor voltage has fallen below the reference of $-128Q$ supplied to

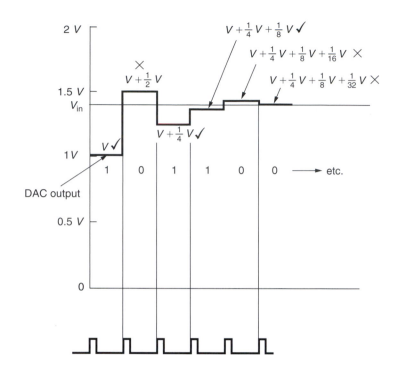

FIGURE 7.29
Successive approximation tests each bit in turn, starting with the most significant. The DAC output is compared with the input. If the DAC output is below the input (✓) the bit is made 1; if the DAC output is above the input (✕) the bit is made 0.

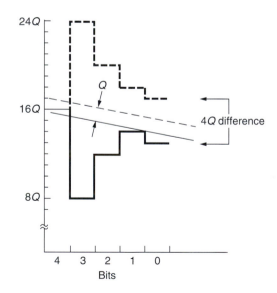

FIGURE 7.30
Two drooping track-hold signals (solid and dashed lines) that differ by one quantizing interval Q are shown here to result in conversions that are 4Q apart. Thus droop can destroy the monotonicity of a convertor. Low-level signals (near the midrange of the number system) are especially vulnerable.

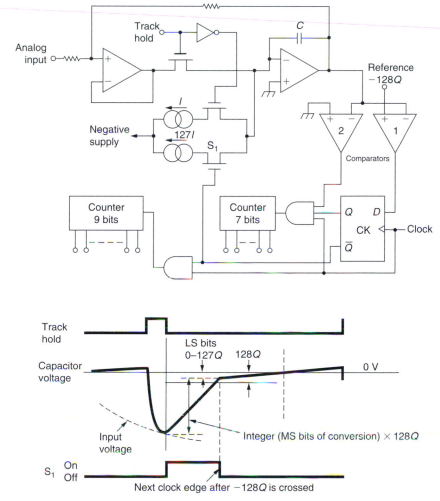

FIGURE 7.31
Dual-ramp ADC using track-hold capacitor as integrator.

comparator 1. At the next clock edge, the larger current source is turned off. Waiting for the next clock edge is important, because it ensures that the larger source can run only for entire clock periods, which will discharge the integrator by integer multiples of 128Q. The integrator voltage will overshoot the 128Q reference, and the remaining voltage on the integrator will be less than 128Q and will be measured by counting the number of clocks for which the smaller current source runs before the integrator voltage reaches zero. This process is termed residual expansion. The break in the slope of the integrator voltage gives rise to the alternative title of gear-change convertor. Following ramping to ground in the conversion process, the track-hold circuit must settle in time for the next conversion. In this 16-bit example, the high-order conversion needs a maximum count of 512, and the low order needs 128: a total of 640. Allowing 25 percent of the sample period for the track-hold circuit to operate, a 48 kHz convertor would need to be clocked at some 40 MHz. This is rather faster than the clock needed for the DAC using the same technology.

ALTERNATIVE CONVERTORS

Although PCM audio is universal because of the ease with which it can be recorded and processed numerically, there are several alternative related methods of converting an analog waveform to a bitstream. The output of these convertor types is not Nyquist rate PCM, but this can be obtained from them by appropriate digital processing. In advanced conversion systems it is possible to adopt an alternative convertor technique specifically to take advantage of a particular characteristic. The output is then digitally converted to Nyquist rate PCM to obtain the advantages of both.

Conventional PCM has already been introduced. In PCM, the amplitude of the signal depends only on the number range of the quantizer and is independent of the frequency of the input. Similarly, the amplitude of the unwanted signals introduced by the quantizing process is also largely independent of input frequency.

Figure 7.32 introduces the alternative convertor structures. The top half of the diagram shows convertors that are differential. In differential coding the value of the output code represents the difference between the current sample voltage and that of the previous sample. The lower half of the diagram shows convertors that are PCM. In addition, the left side of the diagram shows single-bit convertors, whereas the right side shows multibit convertors.

In DPCM, shown at top right, the difference between the previous absolute sample value and the current one is quantized into a multibit binary code. It is possible to produce a DPCM signal from a PCM signal simply by subtracting successive samples; this is digital differentiation. Similarly the reverse process is possible by using an accumulator or digital integrator (see Chapter 3) to compute sample values from the differences received. The problem with this approach is that it is very easy to lose the baseline of the signal if it commences at some arbitrary time. A digital high-pass filter can be used to prevent unwanted offsets.

Differential convertors do not have an absolute amplitude limit. Instead there is a limit to the maximum rate at which the input signal voltage can change.

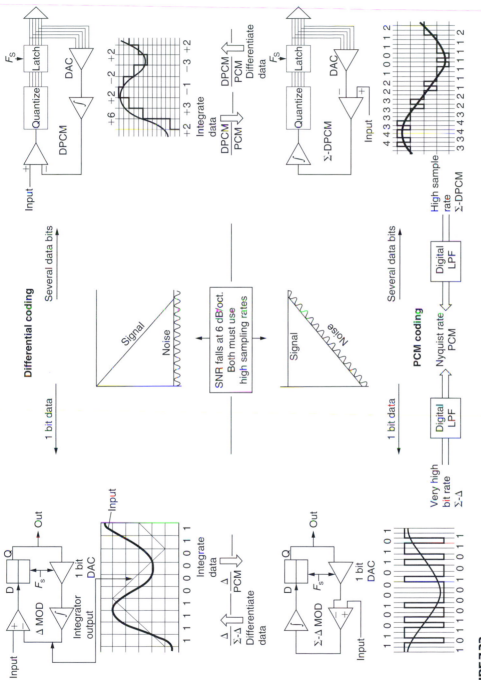

FIGURE 7.32

The four main alternatives to simple PCM conversion are compared here. Delta modulation is a one-bit case of differential PCM and conveys the slope of the signal. The digital output of both can be integrated to give PCM. Σ-Δ (sigma-delta) is a one-bit case of Σ-DPCM. The application of integrator before differentiator makes the output true PCM, but tilts the noise floor; hence these can be referred to as "noise-shaping" convertors.

They are said to be slew rate limited, and thus the permissible signal amplitude falls at six dB per octave. As the quantizing steps are still uniform, the quantizing error amplitude has the same limits as PCM. As input frequency rises, ultimately the signal amplitude available will fall down to it.

If DPCM is taken to the extreme case in which only a binary output signal is available, then the process is described as delta modulation (top left in Figure 7.32). The meaning of the binary output signal is that the current analog input is above or below the accumulation of all previous bits. The characteristics of the system show the same trends as DPCM, except that there is severe limiting of the rate of change of the input signal. A DPCM decoder must accumulate all the difference bits to provide a PCM output for conversion to analog, but with a one-bit signal the function of the accumulator can be performed by an analog integrator.

If an integrator is placed in the input to a delta modulator, the integrator's amplitude response loss of six dB per octave parallels the convertor's amplitude limit of six dB per octave; thus the system amplitude limit becomes independent of frequency. This integration is responsible for the term sigma-delta modulation, because in mathematics sigma (Σ) is used to denote summation. The input integrator can be combined with the integrator already present in a delta modulator by a slight rearrangement of the components (bottom left in Figure 7.32). The transmitted signal is now the amplitude of the input, not the slope; thus the receiving integrator can be dispensed with, and all that is necessary to do after the DAC is a low-pass filter to smooth the bits. The removal of the integration stage at the decoder now means that the quantizing error amplitude rises at six dB per octave, ultimately meeting the level of the wanted signal.

The principle of using an input integrator can also be applied to a true DPCM system and the result should perhaps be called sigma-DPCM (bottom right in Figure 7.32). The dynamic range improvement over delta-sigma modulation is six dB for every extra bit in the code. Because the level of the quantizing error signal rises at six dB per octave in both delta-sigma modulation and sigma-DPCM, these systems are sometimes referred to as "noise-shaping" convertors, although the word "noise" must be used with some caution. The output of a sigma-DPCM system is again PCM, and a DAC will be needed to receive it, because it is a binary code.

As the differential group of systems suffers from a wanted signal that converges with the unwanted signal as frequency rises, all the systems in the group must use very high sampling rates.[12] It is possible to convert from sigma-DPCM to conventional PCM by reducing the sampling rate digitally. When the sampling rate is reduced in this way, the reduction of bandwidth excludes a dispropor-tionate amount of noise because the noise shaping concentrated it at frequencies beyond the audio band. The use of noise shaping and oversampling is the key to the high resolution obtained in advanced convertors.

OVERSAMPLING AND NOISE SHAPING

It was seen in Chapter 4 that oversampling has a number of advantages for video conversion and the same is true for audio. Although it can be used alone, the advantages of oversampling in audio are better realized when it is used in conjunction with noise shaping. Thus in practice the two processes are generally used together and the terms are often seen used in the loose sense as if they were synonymous. For a detailed and quantitative analysis of audio oversampling having exhaustive references the serious reader is referred to Hauser.[13]

Under Basic Analog-to-Digital Conversion, where dynamic element matching was described, it was seen that component accuracy was traded for accuracy in the time domain. Oversampling is another example of the same principle. Oversampling permits the use of a convertor element of shorter word length, making it possible to use a flash convertor for audio conversion. The flash con-vertor is capable of working at very high frequency and so large oversampling factors are easily realized. The flash convertor needs no track-hold system as it works instantaneously. The drawbacks of track-hold set out under Alternative Convertors are thus eliminated.

If the sigma-DPCM convertor structure of Figure 7.32 is realized with a flash convertor element, it can be used with a high oversampling factor. This class of convertor has a rising noise floor. If the highly oversampled output is fed to a digital low-pass filter that has the same frequency response as an analog anti-aliasing filter used for Nyquist rate sampling, the result is a disproportion-ate reduction in noise because the majority of the noise is outside the audio band. A high-resolution convertor can be obtained using this technology with-out requiring unattainable component tolerances.

Noise shaping dates from the work of Cutler[14] in the 1950s. It is a feedback technique applicable to quantizers and requantizers in which the quantizing process of the current sample is modified in some way by the quantizing error of the previous sample.

When used with requantizing, noise shaping is an entirely digital process, which is used, for example, following word extension due to the arithmetic in digital mixers or filters to return to the required word length. It will be found in this form in oversampling DACs. When used with quantizing, part of the noise-shaping circuitry will be analog. As the feedback loop is placed around an ADC it must contain a DAC. When used in convertors, noise shaping is primarily an implementation technology. It allows processes that are conveniently available in integrated circuits to be put to use in audio conversion. Once integrated circuits can be employed, complexity ceases to be a drawback and low-cost mass production is possible.

It has been stressed throughout this chapter that a series of numerical values or samples is just another analog of an audio waveform. Chapter 3 showed that all analog processes such as mixing, attenuation, or integration have exact numerical parallels. It has been demonstrated that digitally dithered requantizing is no more than a digital simulation of analog quantizing. It should be no surprise that in this section noise shaping will be treated in the same way. Noise shaping can be performed by manipulating analog voltages or numbers representing them or both. If the reader is content to make a conceptual switch between the two, many obstacles to understanding fall, not just in this topic, but in digital audio and video in general.

The term "noise shaping" is idiomatic and in some respects unsatisfactory because not all devices that are called noise shapers produce true noise. The caution that was given when treating quantizing error as noise is also relevant in this context. Whilst "quantizing-error-spectrum shaping" is a bit of a mouthful, it is useful to keep in mind that noise shaping means just that in order to avoid some pitfalls. Some noise shaper architectures do not produce a signal-decorrelated quantizing error and need to be dithered.

Figure 7.33a shows a requantizer using a simple form of noise shaping. The low-order bits that are lost in requantizing are the quantizing error. If the value of these bits is added to the next sample before it is requantized, the quantizing error will be reduced. The process is somewhat like the use of negative feedback in an operational amplifier except that it is not instantaneous, but encounters a one-sample delay. With a constant input, the mean or average quantizing error will be brought to zero over a number of samples, achieving one of the goals of additive dither. The more rapidly the input changes, the greater the effect of the delay and the less effective the error feedback will be. Figure 7.33b shows the equivalent circuit seen by the quantizing error, which is created at the requantizer and subtracted from itself one sample period later. As a result the quantizing error spectrum is not uniform, but has the shape of a raised sine wave shown in Figure 7.33c, hence the term noise shaping. The noise is very small at

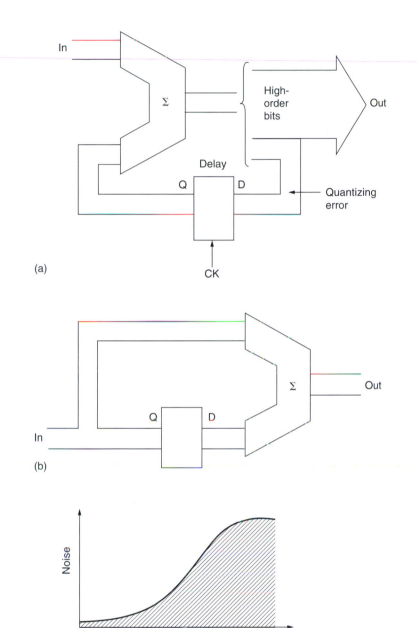

(a)

(b)

(c)

FIGURE 7.33
(a) A simple requantizer that feeds back the quantizing error to reduce the error of
subsequent samples. The one-sample delay causes the quantizing error to see the
equivalent circuit shown in (b), which results in a sinusoidal quantizing error spectrum
shown in (c).

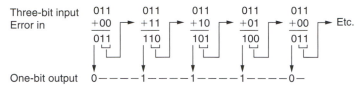

FIGURE 7.34
By adding the error caused by truncation to the next value, the resolution of the lost bits is maintained in the duty cycle of the output. Here, truncation of 011 by two bits would give continuous 0's, but the system repeats 0111, 0111, which, after filtering, will produce a level of three quarters of a bit.

DC and rises with frequency, peaking at the Nyquist frequency at a level determined by the size of the quantizing step. If used with oversampling, the noise peak can be moved outside the audio band.

Figure 7.34 shows a simple example in which 2 low-order bits need to be removed from each sample. The accumulated error is controlled by using the bits that were neglected in the truncation, and adding them to the next sample. In this example, with a steady input, the roundoff mechanism will produce an output of 01110111.… If this is low-pass filtered, the three ones and one zero result in a level of three-quarters of a quantizing interval, which is precisely the level that would have been obtained by direct conversion of the full digital input. Thus the resolution is maintained even though two bits have been removed.

Noise shaping can also be used without oversampling. In this case the noise cannot be pushed outside the audio band. Instead the noise floor is shaped or weighted to complement the unequal spectral sensitivity of the ear to noise.[15–17] Unless we wish to violate Shannon's theory, this psychoacoustically optimal noise shaping can reduce the noise power at certain frequencies only by increasing it at others. Thus the average log PSD (power spectral density) over the audio band remains the same, although it may be raised slightly by noise induced by imperfect processing.

Figure 7.35 shows noise shaping applied to a digitally dithered requantizer. Such a device might be used when, for example, making a CD master from a 20-bit recording format. The input to the dithered requantizer is subtracted from the output to give the error due to requantizing. This error is filtered (and inevitably delayed) before being subtracted from the system input. The filter is not designed to be the exact inverse of the perceptual weighting curve because this would cause extreme noise levels at the ends of the band. Instead the perceptual curve is levelled off[18] such that it cannot fall more than, e.g., 40 dB below the peak.

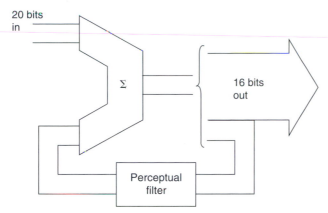

FIGURE 7.35
Perceptual filtering in a requantizer gives a subjectively improved SNR.

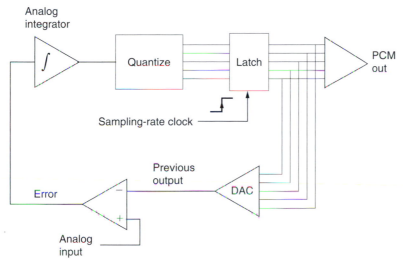

FIGURE 7.36
The Σ-DPCM convertor of Figure 7.32 is shown here in more detail.

Psycho-acoustically optimal noise shaping can offer nearly three bits of increased dynamic range compared with optimal spectrally flat dither. Enhanced Compact Discs recorded using these techniques are now available. The sigma-DPCM convertor introduced in Figure 7.32 has a natural application here and is shown in more detail in Figure 7.36. The current digital sample from the quantizer is converted back to analog in the embedded DAC. The DAC output differs from the ADC input by the quantizing error. It is subtracted from the analog input to produce an error, which is integrated to drive the quantizer in such a way that the error is reduced. With a constant input voltage the average error will be zero because the loop gain is infinite at DC. If the average error is zero, the mean or average of the DAC outputs must be equal to the analog input. The instantaneous output will deviate from the average in what is called an idling pattern. The presence of the integrator in the error feedback loop makes the loop gain fall with rising frequency. With the feedback falling at six dB per octave, the noise floor will rise at the same rate.

Figure 7.37 shows a simple oversampling system using a sigma-DPCM convertor and an oversampling factor of only four. The sampling spectrum shows that the noise is concentrated at frequencies outside the audio part of the over-sampling baseband. Because the scale used here means that noise power is represented by the area under the graph, the area left under the graph after the filter shows the noise-power reduction. Using the relative areas of similar triangles shows that the reduction has been by a factor of 16. The corresponding noise-voltage reduction would be a factor of four or 12 dB, which corresponds to an additional two bits in word length. These bits will be available in the word

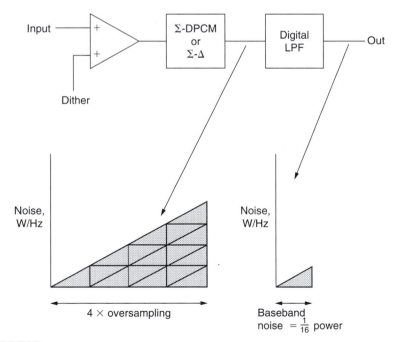

FIGURE 7.37
In a Σ-DPCM or Σ-Δ convertor, noise amplitude increases by 6 dB/octave, noise power by 12 dB/octave. In this 4$\times$ oversampling convertor, the digital filter reduces bandwidth by 4, but noise power is reduced by a factor of 16. Noise voltage falls by a factor of 4 or 12 dB.

length extension that takes place in the decimating filter. Due to the rise of 6 dB per octave in the PSD of the noise, the SNR (signal-to-noise ratio) will be 3 dB worse at the edge of the audio band.

One way in which the operation of the system can be understood is to consider that the coarse DAC in the loop defines fixed points in the audio transfer function. The time averaging that takes place in the decimator then allows the transfer function to be interpolated between the fixed points. True signal-independent noise of sufficient amplitude will allow this to be done to infinite resolution. By making the noise primarily outside the audio band the resolution is maintained, but the audio band signal-to-noise ratio can be extended. A first-order noise-shaping ADC of the kind shown can produce signal-dependent quantizing error and requires analog dither. However, this can be outside the audio band and so need not reduce the SNR achieved.

A greater improvement in dynamic range can be obtained if the integrator is supplanted to realize a higher-order filter.[19] The filter is in the feedback loop and so the noise will have the opposite response to the filter and will therefore rise more steeply to allow a greater SNR enhancement after decimation. Figure 7.38 shows the theoretical SNR enhancement possible for various loop filter orders and oversampling factors. A further advantage of high-order loop filters is that the quantizing noise can be decorrelated from the signal, making dither unnecessary. High-order loop filters were at one time thought to be impossible to stabilize, but

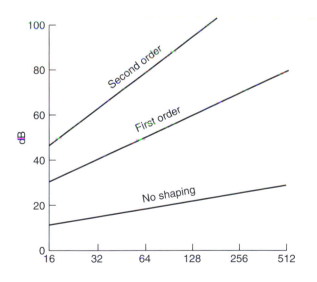

FIGURE 7.38
The enhancement of SNR possible with various filter orders and oversampling factors in noise-shaping convertors.

this is no longer the case, although care is necessary. One technique that may be used is to include some feedforward paths as shown in Figure 7.39.

An ADC with high-order noise shaping was disclosed by Adams[20] and a simplified diagram is shown in Figure 7.40. The comparator outputs of the 128 times oversampled four-bit flash ADC are directly fed to the DAC, which consists of 15 equal resistors fed by CMOS switches. As with all feedback loops, the transfer characteristic cannot be more accurate than the feedback, and in this case the feedback accuracy is determined by the precision of the DAC.[21] Driving the DAC directly from the ADC comparators is more accurate because each input has equal weighting. The stringent MSB tolerance of the conventional binary-weighted DAC is then avoided. The comparators also drive a 16 to 4 priority

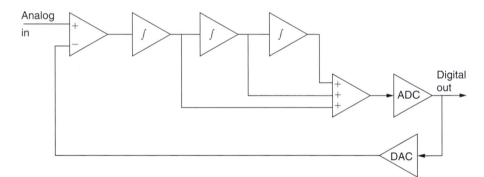

FIGURE 7.39
Stabilizing the loop filter in a noise-shaping convertor can be assisted by the incorporation of feedforward paths as shown here.

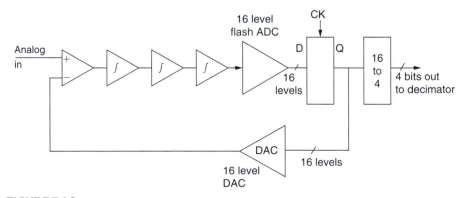

FIGURE 7.40
An example of a high-order noise-shaping ADC. See text for details.

encoder to provide the four-bit PCM output to the decimator. The DAC output is subtracted from the analog input at the integrator. The integrator is followed by a pair of conventional analog operational amplifiers having frequency-dependent feedback and a passive network, which gives the loop a fourth-order response overall. The noise floor is thus shaped to rise at 24 dB per octave beyond the audio band. The time constants of the loop filter are optimized to minimize the amplitude of the idling pattern as this is an indicator of the loop stability. The four-bit PCM output is low-pass filtered and decimated to the Nyquist frequency. The high oversampling factor and high-order noise shaping extend the dynamic range of the four-bit flash ADC to 108 dB at the output.

ONE-BIT CONVERTORS

It might be thought that the waveform from a one-bit DAC is simply the same as the digital input waveform. In practice this is not the case. The input signal is a logic signal that needs only to be above or below a threshold for its binary value to be correctly received. It may have a variety of waveform distortions and a duty cycle offset. The area under the pulses can vary enormously. In the DAC output the amplitude needs to be extremely accurate. A one-bit DAC uses only the binary information from the input, but reclocks to produce accurate timing and uses a reference voltage to produce accurate levels. The area of pulses produced is then constant. One-bit DACs will be found in noise-shaping ADCs as well as in the more obvious application of producing analog audio.

Figure 7.41a shows a one-bit DAC that is implemented with MOS field-effect switches and a pair of capacitors. Quanta of charge are driven into or out of a virtual earth amplifier configured as an integrator by the switched capacitor action. Figure 7.41b shows the associated waveforms. Each data bit period is divided into two equal portions: that for which the clock is high and that for which it is low. During the first half of the bit period, pulse $P+$ is generated if the data bit is a one, or pulse $P-$ is generated if the data bit is a zero. The reference input is a clean voltage corresponding to the gain required.

C1 is *discharged* during the second half of every cycle by the switches driven from the complemented clock. If the next bit is a one, during the next high period of the clock the capacitor will be connected between the reference and the virtual earth. Current will flow into the virtual earth until the capacitor is charged. If the next bit is not a one, the current through C1 will flow to ground.

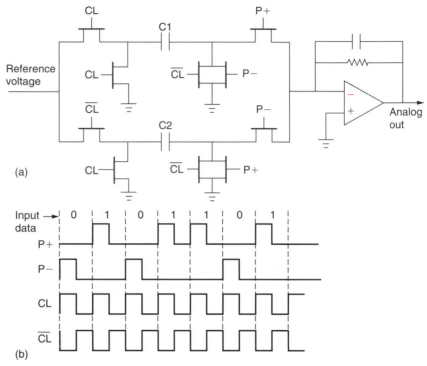

(a)

(b)

FIGURE 7.41
(a) The operation of a one-bit DAC relies on switched capacitors. (b) The switching waveforms are shown.

C2 is *charged* to reference voltage during the second half of every cycle by the switches driven from the complemented clock. On the next high period of the clock, the reference end of C2 will be grounded, and so the op-amp end will assume a negative reference voltage. If the next bit is a zero, this negative reference will be switched into the virtual earth. If not, the capacitor will be discharged.

Thus on every cycle of the clock, a quantum of charge is either pumped into the integrator by C1 or pumped out by C2. The analog output therefore precisely reflects the ratio of ones to zeros.

To overcome the DAC accuracy constraint of the sigma-DPCM convertor, the sigma-delta convertor can be used as it has only one-bit internal resolution. A one-bit DAC cannot be nonlinear by definition, as it defines only two points on a transfer function. It can, however, suffer from other deficiencies such as DC offset and gain error, although these are less offensive in audio. The one-bit ADC is a comparator.

As the sigma-delta convertor is only a one-bit device, clearly it must use a high oversampling factor and high-order noise shaping to have sufficiently good SNR for audio.[22] In practice the oversampling factor is limited not so much by the convertor technology as by the difficulty of computation in the decimator. A sigma-delta convertor has the advantage that the filter input "words" are one bit long and this simplifies the filter design as multiplications can be replaced by selection of constants.

Conventional analysis of loops falls down heavily in the one-bit case. In particular the gain of a comparator is difficult to quantify, and the loop is highly non-linear so that considering the quantizing error as additive white noise to use a linear loop model gives rather optimistic results. In the absence of an accurate mathematical model, progress has been made empirically, with listening tests and by using simulation.

Single-bit sigma-delta convertors are prone to long idling patterns because the low resolution in the voltage domain requires more bits in the time domain to be integrated to cancel the error. Clearly the longer the period of an idling pattern, the more likely it is to enter the audio band as an objectionable whistle or "birdie." They also exhibit threshold effects or deadbands when the output fails to react to an input change at certain levels. The problem is reduced by the order of the filter and the word length of the embedded DAC. Second- and third-order feedback loops are still prone to audible idling patterns and threshold effect.[23] The traditional approach to linearizing sigma-delta convertors is to use dither. Unlike conventional quantizers, the dither used was of a frequency outside the audio band and of considerable level. Square-wave dither has been used and it is advantageous to choose a frequency that is a multiple of the final output sampling rate, as then the harmonics will coincide with the troughs in the stopband ripple of the decimator. Unfortunately the level of dither needed to linearize the convertor is high enough to cause premature clipping of high-level signals, reducing the dynamic range. This problem is overcome by using in-band white-noise dither at low level.[24]

An advantage of the one-bit approach is that in the one-bit DAC, precision components are replaced by precise timing in switched capacitor networks. The same approach can be used to implement the loop filter in an ADC. Figure 7.42 shows a third-order sigma-delta modulator incorporating a DAC based on the principle of Figure 7.41. The loop filter is also implemented with switched capacitors.

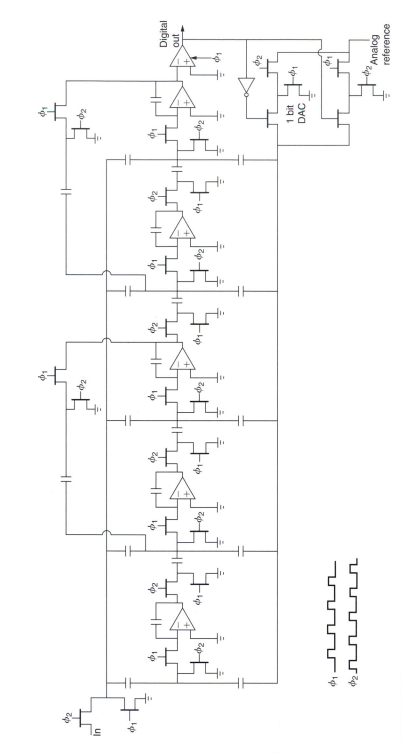

FIGURE 7.42

A third-order Σ-Δ modulator using a switched capacitor loop filter.

OPERATING LEVELS IN DIGITAL AUDIO

Analog tape recorders use operating levels that are some way below saturation. The range between the operating level and saturation is called the headroom. In this range, distortion becomes progressively worse and sustained recording in the headroom is avoided. However, transients may be recorded in the headroom as the ear cannot respond to distortion products unless they are sustained. The PPM level meter has an attack time constant, which simulates the temporal distortion sensitivity of the ear. If a transient is too brief to deflect a PPM into the headroom, it will not be heard, either.

Operating levels are used in two ways. On making a recording from a microphone, the gain is increased until distortion is just avoided, thereby obtaining a recording having the best SNR. In post-production the gain will be set to whatever level is required to obtain the desired subjective effect in the context of the program material. This is particularly important to broadcasters who require the relative loudness of different material to be controlled so that the listener does not need to make continuous adjustments to the volume control.

To maintain level accuracy, analog recordings are traditionally preceded by line-up tones at standard operating level. These are used to adjust the gain in various stages of dubbing and transfer along landlines so that no level changes occur to the program material.

Unlike analog recorders, digital recorders do not have headroom, as there is no progressive onset of distortion until convertor clipping, the equivalent of saturation, occurs at zero dBFs. Accordingly many digital recorders have level meters that read in dBFs. The scales are marked with zero at the clipping level and all operating levels are below that. This causes no difficulty provided the user is aware of the consequences.

In the situation in which a digital copy of an analog tape is to be made, however, it is very easy to set the input gain of the digital recorder so that line-up tone from the analog tape reads zero dB. This lines up digital clipping with the analog operating level. When the tape is dubbed, all signals in the headroom suffer convertor clipping.

To prevent such problems, manufacturers and broadcasters have introduced artificial headroom on digital level meters, simply by calibrating the scale and changing the analog input sensitivity so that zero dB analog is some way below clipping. Unfortunately there has been little agreement on how much artificial

DIGITAL AUDIO AND VIDEO SYNCHRONISATION

Digital audio with video is rather more difficult than in an audio-only environment because the characteristic frame rate of the video must be considered. This first came to be important with the development of digital video recorders, but the development of hard-disk-based workstations and digital transmission using MPEG transport streams has maintained the importance of synchronisation.

In digital VTRs and workstations, the audio data and the video data are both referenced to timecode for access and editing purposes. Broadcast timecode is always locked to the video standard. It follows that to avoid slippage between video and audio there must be a fixed number of audio samples in a timecode frame. This can be achieved only if the audio sampling rate is derived from the video timing system.

In MPEG transport streams, programs, i.e., video and associated sound channels, are carried in a packet-based multiplex. However, for each program there is only one timing system that is video locked. Consequently if the audio sampling rate is not synchronous with video the result will be buffer overflow or underflow in MPEG decoders.

In a practical system the master timing generator for a facility not only will generate video reference signals but also will derive synchronous audio clocks. Alternatively video syncs alone may be distributed and each device must obtain its own synchronous audio sampling rate from the video reference.

headroom should be provided, and machines that have it are seldom labelled with the amount. There is an argument that suggests that the amount of headroom should be a function of the sample word length, but this causes difficulties when transferring from one word length to another. The EBU[25] concluded that a single relationship between analog and digital level was desirable. In 16-bit working, 12 dB of headroom is a useful figure, but now that 18- and 20-bit convertors are available, the later EBU recommendation specifies 18 dB. Some modern equipment allows the user to specify the amount of artificial headroom.

MPEG AUDIO COMPRESSION

The ISO (International Standards Organization) and the IEC (International Electrotechnical Commission) recognized that compression would have an important part to play in future digital video products and in 1988 established the ISO/IEC/MPEG (Moving Picture Experts Group) to compare and assess various coding schemes to arrive at an international standard. The terms of reference were extended the same year to include audio, and the MPEG/Audio group was formed.

As part of the Eureka 147 project, a system known as MUSICAM[26] (masking pattern adapted universal subband integrated coding and multiplexing) was developed jointly by CCETT in France, IRT in Germany, and Philips in The Netherlands. MUSICAM was designed to be suitable for DAB (digital audio broadcasting).

As a parallel development, the ASPEC[27] (adaptive spectral perceptual entropy coding) system was developed from a number of earlier systems as a joint proposal by AT&T Bell Labs, Thomson, the Fraunhofer Society, and CNET. ASPEC was designed for high degrees of compression to allow audio transmission on ISDN.

These two systems were both fully implemented by July 1990, when comprehensive subjective testing took place at the Swedish Broadcasting Corporation.[28,29] As a result of these tests, the MPEG/Audio group combined the attributes of both ASPEC and MUSICAM into a draft standard[30] having three levels of complexity and performance.

These three different levels are needed because of the number of possible applications. Audio coders can be operated at various compression factors with different quality expectations. Stereophonic classical music requires different quality criteria compared to monophonic speech. As was seen in Chapter 6, the complexity of the coder will be reduced with a smaller compression factor. For moderate compression, a simple codec will be more cost-effective. On the other hand, as the compression factor is increased, it will be necessary to employ a more complex coder to maintain quality.

At each level, MPEG coding allows input sampling rates of 32, 44.1, and 48 kHz and supports output bit rates of 32, 48, 56, 64, 96, 112, 128, 192, 256, and 384 kbps. The transmission can be mono, dual channel (e.g., bilingual), stereo, and joint stereo, which is where advantage is taken of redundancy between the two audio channels.

MPEG Layer 1 is a simplified version of MUSICAM that is appropriate for mild compression applications at low cost. It is very similar to PASC. Layer II is identical to MUSICAM and is very likely to be used for DAB. Layer III is a combination of the best features of ASPEC and MUSICAM and is mainly applicable to telecommunications, in which high compression factors are required.

The earlier MPEG-1 standard compresses audio and video into about 1.5 Mbps. The audio content of MPEG-1 may be used on its own to encode one or two channels at bit rates up to 448 kbps. MPEG-2 allows the number of channels to increase to 5: left, right, centre, left surround, right surround, and subwoofer. To retain reverse compatibility with MPEG-1, the MPEG-2 coding converts the five-channel input to a compatible two-channel signal, L_o and R_o, by matrixing.[31] The data from these two channels are encoded in a standard MPEG-1 audio frame, and this is followed in MPEG-2 by an ancillary data frame, which an MPEG-1 decoder will ignore. The ancillary frame contains data for three further audio channels. An MPEG-2 decoder will extract those three channels in addition to the MPEG-1 frame and then recover all five original channels by an inverse matrix.

In various countries, it has been proposed to use an alternative compression technique for the audio content of DVB. This is the AC-3 system developed by Dolby Laboratories. The MPEG transport stream structure has also been standardised to allow it to carry AC-3-coded audio. The digital video disc can also carry AC-3 or MPEG audio coding.

There are many different approaches to audio compression, each having advantages and disadvantages. MPEG audio coding combines these tools in various ways in the three different coding levels. The approach of this section will be to examine the tools separately before seeing how they are used in MPEG and AC-3.

The simplest coding tool is companding, which is a digital parallel of the analog noise reducers used in tape recording. Figure 7.43a shows that in companding the input signal level is monitored. Whenever the input level falls below maximum, it is amplified at the coder. The gain, which was applied at the coder, is added to the data stream so that the decoder can apply an equal attenuation. The advantage of companding is that the signal is kept as far away from the noise floor as possible. In analog noise reduction this is used to maximize the SNR of a tape recorder, whereas in digital compression it is used to keep the signal level as far as possible above the noises and artifacts introduced by various coding steps.

One common way of obtaining coding gain is to shorten the word length of samples so that fewer bits need to be transmitted. Figure 7.43b shows that when this is done, the noise floor will rise by 6 dB for every bit removed. This is because removing a bit halves the number of quantizing intervals, which then must be twice as large, doubling the noise level. Clearly if this step follows the compander in Figure 7.43a, the audibility of the noise will be minimized. As an alternative to shortening the word length, the uniform quantized PCM signal can be converted to a nonuniform format. In nonuniform coding, shown in Figure 7.43c, the size of the quantizing step rises with the magnitude of the sample so that the noise level is greater when higher levels exist.

Companding is a relative of floating-point coding shown in Figure 7.44, in which the sample value is expressed as a mantissa and a binary exponent,

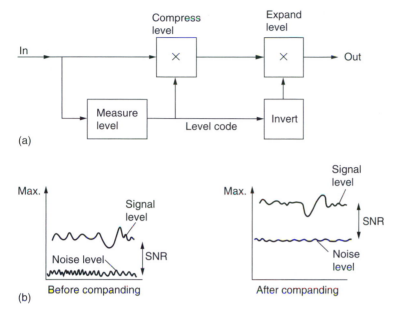

FIGURE 7.43
Digital companding. (a) The encoder amplifies the input to maximum level and the decoder attenuates by the same amount. (b) In a companded system, the signal is kept as far as possible above the noise caused by shortening the sample word length.

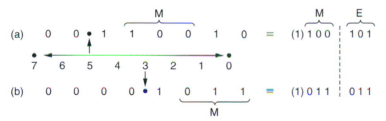

FIGURE 7.44
In this example of floating-point notation, the radix point can have eight positions determined by the exponent E. The point is placed to the left of the first "1", and the next four bits to the right form the mantissa M. As the MSB of the mantissa is always 1, it need not always be stored.

which determines how the mantissa needs to be shifted to have its correct absolute value on a PCM scale. The exponent is the equivalent of the gain setting or scale factor of a compander.

Clearly in floating point the signal-to-noise ratio is defined by the number of bits in the mantissa, and as shown in Figure 7.45, this will vary as a sawtooth function of signal level, as the best value, obtained when the mantissa is near

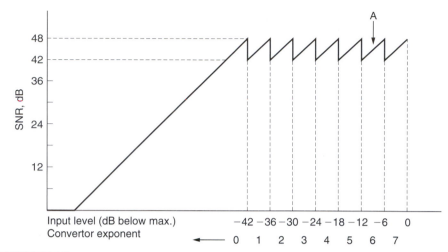

FIGURE 7.45

In this example of an 8-bit mantissa, 3-bit exponent system, the maximum SNR is $6 \times 8 = 48$ dB, with maximum input of 0 dB. As input level falls by 6 dB, the convertor noise remains the same, so the SNR falls to 42 dB. Further reduction in signal level causes the convertor to shift range (point A in the diagram) by increasing the input analog gain by 6 dB. The SNR is restored, and the exponent changes from 7 to 6 to cause the same gain change at the receiver. The noise modulation would be audible in this simple system. A longer mantissa word is needed in practice.

overflow, is replaced by the worst value when the mantissa overflows and the exponent is incremented. Floating-point notation is used within DSP chips as it eases the computational problems involved in handling long word lengths. For example, when multiplying floating-point numbers, only the mantissae need to be multiplied. The exponents are simply added.

A floating-point system requires one exponent to be carried with each mantissa and this is wasteful because in real audio material the level does not change so rapidly and there is redundancy in the exponents. A better alternative is floating-point block coding, also known as near-instantaneous companding, in which the magnitude of the largest sample in a block is used to determine the value of an exponent that is valid for the whole block. Sending one exponent per block requires a lower data rate than in true floating point.[32]

In block coding the requantizing in the coder raises the quantizing noise, but it does so over the entire duration of the block. Figure 7.46 shows that if a transient occurs toward the end of a block, the decoder will reproduce the waveform correctly, but the quantizing noise will start at the beginning of the block and may result in a pre-noise (also called pre-echo), where the noise is audible

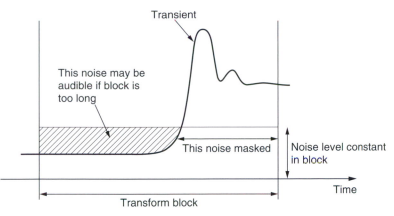

Transient

This noise may be
audible if block is
too long

This noise masked

Noise level constant
in block

Time

Transform block

FIGURE 7.46
If a transient occurs toward the end of a transform block, the quantizing noise will still
be present at the beginning of the block and may result in a pre-echo, in which the
noise is audible before the transient.

before the transient. Temporal masking may be used to make this inaudible.
With a one ms block, the artifacts are too brief to be heard.

Another solution is to use a variable time window according to the transient
content of the audio waveform. When musical transients occur, short blocks
are necessary and the coding gain will be low. At other times the blocks become
longer, allowing a greater coding gain.

Whilst the above systems used alone do allow coding gain, the compression
factor has to be limited because little benefit is obtained from masking. This is
because the techniques above produce noise that spreads equally over the entire
audio band. If the audio input spectrum is narrow, the noise will not be masked.

Subband coding splits the audio spectrum up into many different frequency
bands. Once this has been done, each band can individually be processed.
In real audio signals most bands will contain signals at a lower level than the
loudest one. Individual companding of each band will be more effective than
broadband companding. Subband coding also allows the noise floor to be
raised selectively so that noise is added only at frequencies at which spectral
masking will be effective.

There is little conceptual difference between a subband coder with a large
number of bands and a transform coder. In transform coding, a FFT or DCT of
the waveform is computed periodically. Because the transform of an audio signal changes slowly, it needs to be sent much less often than audio samples.

The receiver performs an inverse transform. Finally the data may be subject to a lossless binary compression using, for example, a Huffman code.

Audio is usually considered to be a time domain waveform as this is what emerges from a microphone. As has been seen in Chapter 3, spectral analysis allows any periodic waveform to be represented by a set of harmonically related components of suitable amplitude and phase. In theory it is perfectly possible to decompose a periodic input waveform into its constituent frequencies and phases and to record or transmit the transform. The transform can then be inverted and the original waveform will be precisely re-created.

Although one can think of exceptions, the transform of a typical audio waveform changes relatively slowly. The slow speech of an organ pipe or a violin string, or the slow decay of most musical sounds, allows the rate at which the transform is sampled to be reduced, and a coding gain results. At some frequencies the level will be below maximum and a shorter word length can be used to describe the coefficient. Further coding gain will be achieved if the coefficients describing frequencies that will experience masking are quantized more coarsely. The transform of an audio signal is computed in the main signal path in a transform coder and has sufficient frequency resolution to drive the masking model directly.

In practice there are some difficulties. Real sounds are not periodic, but contain transients that transformation cannot accurately locate in time. The solution to this difficulty is to cut the waveform into short segments and then to transform each individually. The delay is reduced, as is the computational task, but there is a possibility of artifacts arising because of the truncation of the waveform into rectangular time windows. A solution is to use window functions (see Chapter 3) and to overlap the segments as shown in Figure 7.47. Thus every input sample appears in just two transforms, but with variable weighting depending upon its position along the time axis.

The DFT (discrete frequency transform) does not produce a continuous spectrum, but instead produces coefficients at discrete frequencies. The frequency resolution (i.e., the number of different frequency coefficients) is equal to the

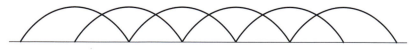

FIGURE 7.47
Transform coding can be practically performed only on short blocks. These are overlapped using window functions to handle continuous waveforms.

number of samples in the window. If overlapped windows are used, twice as many coefficients are produced as are theoretically necessary. In addition, the DFT requires intensive computation, due to the requirement to use complex arithmetic to render the phase of the components as well as the amplitude. An alternative is to use discrete cosine transforms.

Figure 7.48 shows a block diagram of a Layer I coder, which is a simplified version of that used in the MUSICAM system. A polyphase quadrature mirror filter network divides the audio spectrum into 32 equal sub-bands. The output data rate of the filter bank is no higher than the input rate because each band has been heterodyned to a frequency range from DC upward.

Subband compression takes advantage of the fact that real sounds do not have uniform spectral energy. The word length of PCM audio is based on the

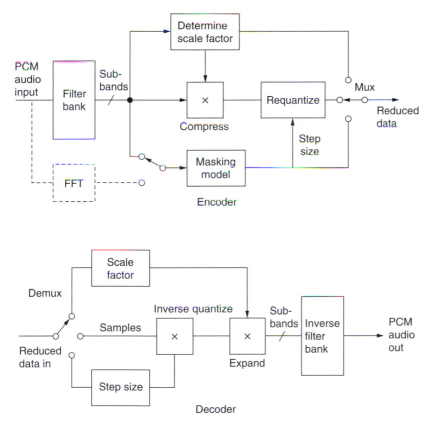

FIGURE 7.48
A simple sub-band coder. The bit allocation may come from analysis of the sub-band energy, or, for greater reduction, from a spectral analysis in a side chain.

dynamic range required and this is generally constant with frequency although any pre-emphasis will affect the situation. When a signal with an uneven spectrum is conveyed by PCM, the whole dynamic range is occupied only by the loudest spectral component, and all the other components are coded with excessive headroom. In its simplest form, sub-band coding[33] works by splitting the audio signal into a number of frequency bands and companding each band according to its own level. Bands in which there is little energy result in small amplitudes, which can be transmitted with short word length. Thus each band results in variable-length samples, but the sum of all the sample word lengths is less than that of PCM and so a coding gain can be obtained.

As MPEG audio coding relies on auditory masking, the subbands should preferably be narrower than the critical bands of the ear, hence the large number required. Figure 7.49 shows the critical condition in which the masking tone is at the top edge of the subband. It will be seen that the narrower the subband, the higher the requantizing noise that can be masked. The use of an excessive number of sub-bands will, however, raise complexity and the coding delay.

Constant-size input blocks containing 384 samples are used. At 48 kHz, 384 samples corresponds to a period of eight ms. After the subband filter each band contains 12 samples per block. The block size was based on the premasking phenomenon of Figure 7.46. The samples in each subband block, or bin, are companded according to the peak value in the bin. A six-bit scale factor is used for each subband, which applies to all 12 samples.

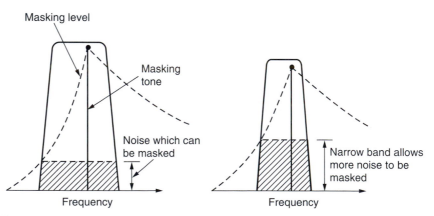

FIGURE 7.49
In sub-band coding the worst case occurs when the masking tone is at the top edge of the sub-band. The narrower the band, the higher the noise level which can be masked.

If a fixed compression factor is employed, the size of the coded output block will be fixed. The word lengths in each bin will have to be such that the sum of the bits from all of the subband equals the size of the coded block. Thus some subbands can have long word-length coding if others have short word-length coding. The process of determining the requantization step size, and hence the word length in each subband, is known as bit allocation.

For simplicity, in Layer I the levels in the 32 subbands themselves are used as a crude spectral analysis of the input to drive the masking model. The masking model uses the input spectrum to determine a new threshold of hearing, which in turn determines how much the noise floor can be raised in each subband. When masking takes place, the signal is quantized more coarsely until the quantizing noise is raised to just below the masking level. The coarse quantization requires shorter word lengths and allows a coding gain. The bit allocation may be iterative as adjustments are made to obtain the best NMR within the allowable data rate.

The samples of differing word length in each bin are then assembled into the output coded block. Unlike a PCM block, which contains samples of fixed word length, a coded block contains many different word lengths, and these can vary from one block to the next. To de-serialize the block into samples of various word lengths and demultiplex the samples into the appropriate frequency bins, the decoder has to be told what bit allocations were used when it was packed, and some synchronising means is needed to allow the beginning of the block to be identified.

The compression factor is determined by the bit-allocation system. It is not difficult to change the output block size parameter to obtain a different compression factor. If a larger block is specified, the bit allocator simply iterates until the new block size is filled. Similarly the decoder need correctly de-serialize only the larger block into coded samples and then the expansion process is identical except for the fact that expanded words contain less noise. Thus codecs with varying degrees of compression are available, which can perform different bandwidth/performance tasks with the same hardware.

Figure 7.50 shows the format of the Layer I data stream. The frame begins with a sync pattern, to reset the phase of de-serialization, and a header, which describes the sampling rate and any use of preemphasis. Following this is a block of 32 four-bit allocation codes. These specify the word length used in each subband and allow the decoder to de-serialize the subband sample block. This is followed by a block of 32 six-bit scale factor indices, which specify the

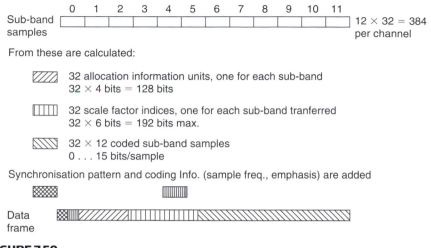

FIGURE 7.50
The Layer I data frame showing the allocation codes, the scale factors and the sub-band samples.

gain given to each band during companding. The last block contains 32 sets of 12 samples. These samples vary in word length from one block to the next and can be from zero to 15 bits long. The de-serializer has to use the 32 allocation information codes to work out how to de-serialize the sample block into individual samples of variable length.

The Layer I MPEG decoder is shown in Figure 7.51. The elementary stream is de-serialized using the sync pattern and the variable-length samples are assembled using the allocation codes. The variable-length samples are returned to 15-bit word length by adding zeros. The scale factor indices are then used to determine multiplication factors used to return the waveform in each sub-band to its original level. The 32 sub-band signals are then merged into one spectrum by the synthesis filter. This is a set of bandpass filters, which returns every sub-band to the correct place in the audio spectrum and then adds them to produce the audio output.

MPEG Layer II audio coding is identical to MUSICAM. The same 32-band filter bank and the same block companding scheme as in Layer I is used. Figure 7.52 shows that using the level in a sub-band to drive the masking model is sub-optimal because it is not known where in the sub-band the energy lies. As the skirts of the masking curve are asymmetrical, the noise floor can be raised higher if the masker is at the low end of the sub-band than if it is at the high end.

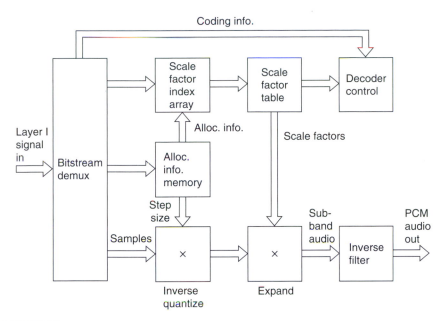

FIGURE 7.51
The Layer I decoder. See text for details.

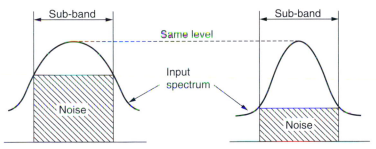

FIGURE 7.52
Accurate knowledge of the spectrum allows the noise floor to be raised higher while remaining masked.

To give better spectral resolution than the filter bank, a side-chain FFT having 1024 points is computed, resulting in an analysis of the audio spectrum eight times better than the subband width. The FFT drives the masking model, which controls the bit allocation. To give the FFT sufficient resolution, the block length is increased to 1152 samples. This is three times the block length of Layer I.

The QMF (quadrature mirror filter) band-splitting technique is restricted to bands of equal width. It might be thought that this is a drawback because the critical bands of the ear are nonuniform. In fact this is only a problem when very low bit rates are required. In all cases it is the masking model of hearing that must have correct critical bands. This model can then be superimposed on bands of any width to determine how much masking and therefore coding gain is possible. Uniform-width sub-bands will not be able to obtain as much masking as bands that are matched to critical bands, but for many applications the additional coding gain is not worth the added filter complexity.

The block-companding scheme of Layer II is the same as in Layer I because the 1152-sample block is divided into three 384-sample blocks. However, not all the scale factors are transmitted, because they contain a degree of redundancy on real program material. The difference between scale factors in successive blocks in the same band exceeds two dB less than 10 percent of the time. Layer II analyses the set of three successive scale factors in each subband. On a stationary program, these will be the same and only one scale factor of three is sent. As the transient content increases in a given subband, two or three scale factors will be sent. A scale factor select code must be sent to allow the decoder to determine what has been sent in each subband. This technique effectively halves the scale factor bit rate. The requantized samples in each subband, bit-allocation data, scale factors, and scale factor select codes are multiplexed into the output bitstream.

The Layer II decoder is not much more complex than the Layer I decoder as the only additional processing is to decode the compressed scale factors to produce one scale factor per 384-sample block. This is the most complex layer of the ISO standard and is really necessary only when the most severe data rate constraints must be met with high quality. It is a transform code based on the ASPEC system with certain modifications to give a degree of commonality with Layer II. The original ASPEC coder used a direct MDCT (modified discrete cosine transform) on the input samples. In Layer III this was modified to use a hybrid transform incorporating the existing polyphase 32-band QMF of Layers I and II. In Layer III, the 32 subbands from the QMF are each processed by a 12-band MDCT to obtain 384 output coefficients. Two window sizes are used to avoid pre-echo on transients. The window switching is performed by the psychoacoustic model. It has been found that preecho is associated with the entropy in the audio rising above the average value.

A highly accurate perceptive model is used to take advantage of the high-frequency resolution available. Nonuniform quantizing is used, along with Huffman coding. This is a technique in which the most common code values are allocated the shortest word length.

DOLBY AC-3

Dolby AC-3 is in fact a family of transform coders based on time domain aliasing cancellation (TDAC), which allow various compromises between coding delay and bit rate to be used. In the MDCT,[34] windows with 50 percent overlap are used. Thus twice as many coefficients as necessary are produced. These are subsampled by a factor of two to give a critically sampled transform, which results in potential aliasing in the frequency domain. However, by making a slight change to the transform, the alias products in the second half of a given window are equal in size but of opposite polarity to the alias products in the first half of the next window and so will be cancelled on reconstruction. This is the principle of TDAC.

Figure 7.53 shows the generic block diagram of the AC-3 coder. Input audio is divided into 50 percent overlapped blocks of 512 samples. These are subject to a TDAC transform, which uses alternate modified sine and cosine transforms. The transforms produce 512 coefficients per block, but these are redundant, and after the redundancy has been removed there are 256 coefficients per block. The input waveform is constantly analysed for the presence of transients and if these are present the block length will be halved to prevent prenoise. This halves the frequency resolution but doubles the temporal resolution.

The coefficients have high frequency resolution and are selectively combined in subbands that approximate the critical bands. Coefficients in each subband are normalized and expressed in floating-point block notation with common exponents. The exponents in fact represent the logarithmic spectral envelope

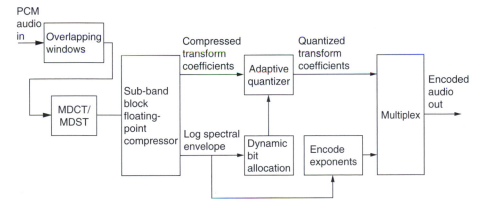

FIGURE 7.53
Block diagram of the Dolby AC-3 coder. See text for details.

of the signal and can be used to drive the perceptive model, which operates the bit allocation. The mantissae of the transform coefficients are then requantized according to the bit allocation.

The output bitstream consists of the requantized coefficients and the log spectral envelope in the shape of the exponents. There is a great deal of redundancy in the exponents. In any block, only the first exponent, corresponding to the lowest frequency, is transmitted absolutely. Remaining coefficients are transmitted differentially. When the input has a smooth spectrum the exponents in several bands will be the same and the differences will then be zero. In this case exponents can be grouped using flags.

Further use is made of temporal redundancy. An AC-3 sync frame contains six blocks. The first block of the frame contains absolute exponent data, but where stationary audio is encountered, successive blocks in the frame can use the same exponents.

The receiver uses the log spectral envelope to de-serialize the mantissae of the coefficients into the correct word lengths. The highly redundant exponents are decoded starting with the lowest frequency coefficient in the first block of the frame and adding differences to create the remainder. The exponents are then used to return the coefficients to fixed-point notation. Inverse transforms are then computed, followed by a weighted overlapping of the windows to obtain PCM data.

References

1. Johnston, J.D. Transform coding of audio signals using perceptual noise criteria. IEEE J. Selected Areas in Communications, JSAC-6, 314–323 (1988).
2. Moore, B.C.J. *An Introduction to the Psychology of Hearing,* London: Academic Press (1989).
3. Muraoka, T., Iwahara, M., and Yamada, Y. Examination of audio bandwidth requirements for optimum sound signal transmission. J. Audio Eng. Soc., 29, 2–9 (1982).
4. Muraoka, T., Yamada, Y., and Yamazaki, M. Sampling frequency considerations in digital audio. J. Audio Eng. Soc., 26, 252–256 (1978).
5. Fincham, L.R. The subjective importance of uniform group delay at low frequencies. Presented at the 74th Audio Engineering Society Convention (New York), Preprint No. 2056 (H-1) (1983).
6. Fletcher, H. Auditory patterns. Rev. Modern Physics, 12, 47–65 (1940).
7. Zwicker, E. Subdivision of the audible frequency range into critical bands. J. Acoust. Soc. Amer., 33, 248 (1961).

8. Moore, B., Glasberg, B., Formulae describing frequency selectivity as a function of frequency and level, and their use in calculating excitation patterns. Hearing Res., 28, 209–225 (1987).

9. Anonymous. AES recommended practice for professional digital audio applications employing pulse code modulation: preferred sampling frequencies. AES5-1984 (ANSI S4.28-1984). J. Audio Eng. Soc., 32, 781–785 (1984).

10. v.d. Plassche, R.J. Dynamic element matching puts trimless convertors on chip. Electronics, 16 June (1983).

11. v.d. Plassche, R.J., and Goedhart, D. A monolithic 14 bit D/A convertor. IEEE J. Solid-State Circuits, SC-14, 552–556 (1979).

12. Adams, R.W. Companded predictive delta modulation: a low-cost technique for digital recording. J. Audio Eng. Soc., 32, 659–672 (1984).

13. Hauser, M.W. Principles of oversampling A/D conversion. J. Audio Eng. Soc., 39, 3–26 (1991).

14. Cutler, C.C. Transmission systems employing quantization. U.S. Patent No. 2.927,962 (1960).

15. Fielder, L.D. Human auditory capabilities and their consequences in digital audio convertor design. In *Audio in Digital Times*, New York: Audio Engineering Society (1989).

16. Gerzon, M., and Craven, P.G. Optimal noise shaping and dither of digital signals. Presented at the 87th Audio Engineering Society Convention (New York), Preprint No. 2822 (J-1) (1989).

17. Wannamaker, R.A. Psychoacoustically optimal noise shaping. J. Audio Eng. Soc., 40, 611–620 (1992).

18. Lipshitz, S.P., Wannamaker, R.A., and Vanderkooy, J. Minimally audible noise shaping. J. Audio Eng. Soc., 39, 836–852 (1991).

19. Adams, R.W. Design and implementation of an audio 18-bit A/D convertor using oversampling techniques. Presented at the 77th Audio Engineering Society Convention (Hamburg), Preprint No. 2182 (1985).

20. Adams, R.W. An IC chip set for 20 bit A/D conversion. In *Audio in Digital Times*, New York: Audio Engineering Society (1989).

21. Richards, M., Improvements in oversampling analogue to digital convertors. Presented at the 84th Audio Engineering Society Convention (Paris), Preprint No. 2588 (D-8) (1988).

22. Inose, H., and Yasuda, Y. A unity bit coding method by negative feedback. Proc. IEEE, 51, 1524–1535 (1963).

23. Naus, P.J., et al. Low signal level distortion in sigma-delta modulators. Presented at the 84th Audio Engineering Society Convention (Paris), Preprint No. 2584 (1988).

24. Stikvoort, E. High order one bit coder for audio applications. Presented at the 84th Audio Engineering Society Convention (Paris), Preprint No. 2583 (D-3) (1988).

25. Moller, L. Signal levels across the EBU/AES digital audio interface. In Proceedings of the 1st NAB Radio Montreux Symposium (Montreux) pp. 16–28 (1992).

26. Wiese, D. MUSICAM: flexible bitrate reduction standard for high quality audio. Presented at the Digital Audio Broadcasting Conference (London) (1992).

27. Brandenburg, K. ASPEC coding. In Proceedings of the 10th Audio Engineering Society International Conference (New York) pp. 81–90 (1991).

28. ISO/IEC JTC1/SC2/WG11 N0030: MPEG/AUDIO test report. Stockholm (1990).

29. ISO/IEC JTC1/SC2/WG11: MPEG 91/010, the SR report on the MPEG/AUDIO subjective listening test. Stockholm (1991).

30. ISO/IEC JTC1/SC2/WG11: Committee draft 11172.

31. Bonicel, P., et al. A real time ISO/MPEG2 multichannel decoder. Presented at the 96th Audio Engineering Society Convention, Preprint No. 3798 (P3.7) (1994).

32. Caine, C.R., English, A.R., and O'Clarey, J.W.H. NICAM-3: near-instantaneous companded digital transmission for high-quality sound programmes. J. IERE, 50, 519–530 (1980).

33. Crochiere, R.E. Sub-band coding. Bell Syst. Tech. J., 60, 1633–1653 (1981).

34. Princen, J.P., Johnson, A., and Bradley, A.B. Sub-band/transform coding using filter bank designs based on time domain aliasing cancellation. Proc. ICASSP, 2161–2164 (1987).

CHAPTER 8
Digital Coding Principles

The reliable storage of data for later use and the reliable transmission of data from one place to another are central to information technology. Whilst they would appear to be different tasks, they actually have a great deal in common. Digital transmission consists of converting data into a waveform suitable for the path along which it is to be sent. Digital recording is basically the process of recording a digital transmission waveform on a suitable medium. In this chapter the fundamentals of digital recording and transmission are introduced along with descriptions of the coding and error-correction techniques used in practical applications.

INTRODUCTION

Data may be recorded on many different media and conveyed using many forms of transmission. The generic term for the path down which the information is sent is the *channel*. In a transmission application, the channel may be a point-to-point cable, a network stage, or a radio link. In a recording application the channel will include the record head, the medium, and the replay head. In solid-state recording media, such as flash memory cards, the data are recorded directly as bits, but the memory can still be regarded as a channel for the purposes of assessing reliability.

In digital circuitry there is a great deal of noise immunity because the signal has only two states, which are widely separated compared with the amplitude of noise. In both digital recording and transmission this is not always the case. In magnetic recording, noise immunity is a function of track width, and reduction of the working SNR (signal-to-noise ratio) of a digital track allows the same information to be carried in a smaller area of the medium, improving economy of operation. In broadcasting, the noise immunity is a function of the transmitter power and reduction of working SNR allows lower power to be used with consequent economy. These reductions also increase the random error rate, but, as was seen in Chapter 1, an error-correction system may already be necessary in a practical system and it is simply made to work harder.

In real channels, the signal may *originate* with discrete states that change at discrete times, but the channel will treat it as an analog waveform and so it will not be *received* in the same form. Various frequency-dependent loss mechanisms will reduce the amplitude of the signal. Noise will be picked up as a result of stray electric fields or magnetic induction and in radio receivers the circuitry will contribute some noise. As a result the received voltage will have an infinitely varying state along with a degree of uncertainty due to the noise. Different frequencies can propagate at different speeds in the channel; this is the phenomenon of group delay. An alternative way of considering group delay is that there will be frequency-dependent phase shifts in the signal and these will result in uncertainty in the timing of pulses.

In digital circuitry, the signals are generally accompanied by a separate clock signal, which re-clocks the data to remove jitter as was shown in Chapter 1. Whilst this technique can be applied to RAM and flash memory, it is generally not feasible to provide a separate clock in applications such as recording on media and transmission. In the transmission case, a separate clock line not only would raise cost, but also is impractical because at high frequency it is virtually impossible to ensure that the clock cable propagates signals at the same speed as the data cable except over short distances. In the recording media case, provision of a separate clock track is impractical at high density because mechanical tolerances cause phase errors between the tracks. The result is the same: timing differences between parallel channels, which are known as skew.

The solution is to use a self-clocking waveform and the generation of this is a further essential function of the coding process. Clearly if data bits are simply clocked serially from a shift register in so-called direct recording or transmission, this characteristic will not be obtained. If all the data bits are the same, for example all zeros, there is no clock when they are serialized.

It is not the channel that is digital; instead the term describes the way in which the received signals are *interpreted*. When the receiver makes discrete decisions from the input waveform it attempts to reject the uncertainties in voltage and time. The technique of channel coding is one in which transmitted waveforms are restricted to those that still allow the receiver to make discrete decisions despite the degradations caused by the analog nature of the channel.

TYPES OF TRANSMISSION CHANNEL

Transmission can be by electrical conductors, radio, or optical fibre. Although these appear to be completely different, they are in fact just different examples of electromagnetic energy travelling from one place to another. If some characteristic of that energy is made time-variant, information can be carried.

Electromagnetic energy propagates in a manner that is a function of frequency, and our partial understanding requires it to be considered as electrons, waves, or photons so that we can predict its behaviour in given circumstances.

At DC and at the low frequencies used for power distribution, electromagnetic energy is called electricity and needs to be transported completely inside conductors. It has to have a complete circuit to flow in, and the resistance to current flow is determined by the cross-sectional area of the conductor. The insulation around the conductor and the spacing between the conductors have no effect on the ability of the conductor to pass current. At DC an inductor appears to be a short circuit, and a capacitor appears to be an open circuit.

As frequency rises, resistance is exchanged for impedance. Inductors display increasing impedance with frequency; capacitors show falling impedance. Electromagnetic energy increasingly tends to leave the conductor. The first symptom is the skin effect: the current flows only in the outside layer of the conductor, effectively causing the resistance to rise.

As the energy starts to leave the conductors, the characteristics of the space between them become important. This determines the impedance. A change in impedance causes reflections in the energy flow and some of it heads back toward the source. Constant-impedance cables with fixed conductor spacing are necessary, and these must be suitably terminated to prevent reflections. The most important characteristic of the insulation is its thickness as this determines the spacing between the conductors.

As frequency rises still further, the energy travels less in the conductors and more in the insulation between them, its composition becomes important and it begins to be called a dielectric. A poor dielectric like PVC absorbs high-frequency energy and attenuates the signal. So-called low-loss dielectrics such as PTFE are used, and one way of achieving low loss is to incorporate as much

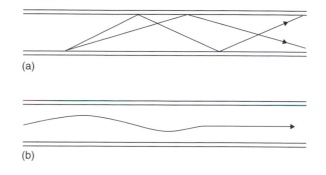

FIGURE 8.1
(a) Early optical fibres operated on internal reflection, and signals could take a variety of paths along the fibre, hence they were multi-mode. (b) Later fibres used graduated refractive index, which meant that light was guided to the centre of the fibre and only one mode was possible.

air into the dielectric as possible by making it in the form of a foam or extruding it with voids.

High-frequency signals can also be propagated without a medium; they are called radio. As frequency rises further the electromagnetic energy is termed light, which can also travel without a medium, but can also be guided through a suitable medium. Figure 8.1a shows an early type of optical fibre in which total internal reflection is used to guide the light. It will be seen that the length of the optical path is a function of the angle at which the light is launched. Thus at the end of a long fibre sharp transitions would be smeared by this effect. The newer optical fibres are made with a radially varying refractive index such that light diverging from the axis is automatically refracted back into the fibre. Figure 8.1b shows that in single-mode fibre light can travel down only one path and so the smearing of transitions is avoided.

TRANSMISSION LINES

Frequency-dependent behaviour is the most important factor in deciding how best to harness electromagnetic energy flow for information transmission. It is obvious that the higher the frequency, the greater the possible information rate, but in general, losses increase with frequency, and flat frequency response is elusive. The best that can be managed is that over a narrow band of frequencies, the response can be made reasonably constant with the help of equalization. Unfortunately raw data when serialized have an unconstrained spectrum. Runs of identical bits can produce frequencies much lower than the bit rate would suggest. One of the essential steps in a transmission system is to modify the spectrum of the data into something more suitable.

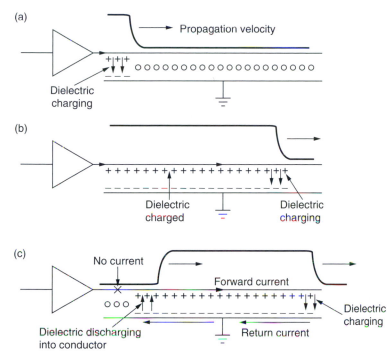

FIGURE 8.2

A transmission line conveys energy packets that appear with respect to the dielectric. In (a) the driver launches a pulse, which charges the dielectric at the beginning of the line. As it propagates the dielectric is charged further along as in (b). (c) When the driver ends the pulse, the charged dielectric discharges into the line. A current loop is formed in which the current in the return loop flows in the opposite direction, to the current in the "hot" wire.

At moderate bit rates of a few megabits per second, and with moderate cable lengths, say a few metres, the dominant effect will be the capacitance of the cable due to the geometry of the space between the conductors and the dielectric between. The capacitance behaves under these conditions as if it were a single capacitor connected across the signal. The effect of the series source resistance and the parallel capacitance is that signal edges or transitions are turned into exponential curves as the capacitance is effectively being charged and discharged through the source impedance.

As cable length increases, the capacitance can no longer be lumped as if it were a single unit; it has to be regarded as being distributed along the cable. With rising frequency, the cable inductance also becomes significant, and it too is distributed.

The cable is now a transmission line, and pulses travel down it as current loops that roll along as shown in Figure 8.2. If the pulse is positive, as it is launched along the line, it will charge the dielectric locally as in Figure 8.2a. As the pulse moves along, it will continue to charge the local dielectric as at (b). When the driver finishes the pulse, the trailing edge of the pulse follows the leading edge along the line. The voltage of the dielectric charged by the leading edge of the pulse is now higher than the voltage on the line, and so the dielectric discharges into the line as at (c). The current flows forward as it is in fact the same current that is flowing into the dielectric at the leading edge. There is thus a loop of current rolling down the line flowing forward in the "hot" wire and backward in the return.

The constant to-ing and fro-ing of charge in the dielectric results in dielectric loss of signal energy. Dielectric loss increases with frequency and so a long transmission line acts as a filter. Thus the term "low-loss" cable refers primarily to the kind of dielectric used.

Transmission lines that transport energy in this way have a characteristic impedance caused by the interplay of the inductance along the conductors with the parallel capacitance. One consequence of that transmission mode is that correct termination or matching is required between the line and both the driver and the receiver. When a line is correctly matched, the rolling energy rolls straight out of the line into the load and the maximum energy is available. If the impedance presented by the load is incorrect, there will be reflections from the mismatch. An open circuit will reflect all the energy back in the same polarity as the original, whereas a short circuit will reflect all the energy back in the opposite polarity. Thus impedances above or below the correct value will have a tendency toward reflections whose magnitude depends upon the degree of mismatch and whose polarity depends upon whether the load is too high or too low. In practice it is the need to avoid reflections that is the most important reason to terminate correctly.

A perfectly square pulse contains an indefinite series of harmonics, but the higher ones suffer progressively more loss. A square pulse at the driver becomes less and less square with distance, as Figure 8.3 shows. The harmonics are progressively lost until in the extreme case all that is left is the fundamental. A transmitted square wave is received as a sine wave. Fortunately data can still be recovered from the fundamental signal component.

Once all the harmonics have been lost, further losses cause the amplitude of the fundamental to fall. The effect worsens with distance and it is necessary to ensure that data recovery is still possible from a signal of unpredictable level.

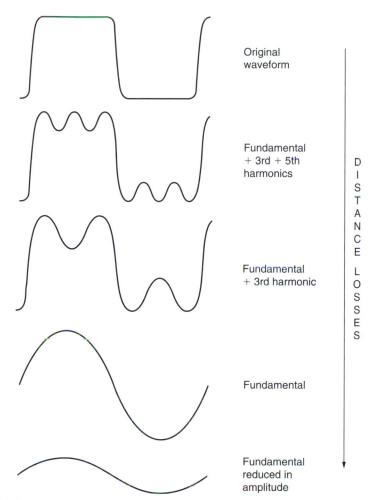

Original
waveform

Fundamental
+ 3rd + 5th
harmonics

Fundamental
+ 3rd harmonic

Fundamental

Fundamental
reduced in
amplitude

D
I
S
T
A
N
C
E

L
O
S
S
E
S

FIGURE 8.3
A signal may be square at the transmitter, but losses increase with frequency, and
as the signal propagates, more of the harmonics are lost until only the fundamental
remains. The amplitude of the fundamental then falls with further distance.

TYPES OF RECORDING MEDIUM

Digital media do not need to have linear transfer functions, nor do they need
to be noise-free or continuous. All they need to do is allow the player to be
able to distinguish the presence or absence of replay events, such as the generation of pulses, with reasonable (rather than perfect) reliability. In a magnetic
medium, the event will be a flux change from one direction of magnetization to
another. In an optical medium, the event must cause the pickup to perceive a

change in the intensity of the light falling on the sensor. This may be obtained through selective absorption of light by dyes or by phase contrast (see Chapter 9). In magneto-optical disks the recording itself is magnetic, but it is made and read using light. In solid-state memory, the data may be stored by the presence or absence of electric charge in ideally insulated wells. Such memories are inherently discrete and the individual bits are located by addressing techniques. In contrast, recording media are continuous and it is necessary to identify the boundaries between stored bits as a conscious step.

MAGNETIC RECORDING

Magnetic recording relies on the hysteresis of certain magnetic materials. After an applied magnetic field is removed, the material remains magnetized in the same direction. By definition the process is non-linear.

Figure 8.4 shows the construction of a typical digital record head. A magnetic circuit carries a coil through which the record current passes and generates flux. A non-magnetic gap forces the flux to leave the magnetic circuit of the head and penetrate the medium. The current through the head must be set to suit the coercivity of the tape and is arranged to almost saturate the track. The amplitude of the current is constant, and recording is performed by reversing the direction of the current with respect to time. As the track passes the head, this is converted to the reversal of the magnetic field left on the tape with respect to distance. The magnetic recording is therefore bipolar. Figure 8.5 shows that the recording is actually made just after the trailing pole of the record head where the flux strength from the gap is falling. As in analog recorders, the width of the gap is generally

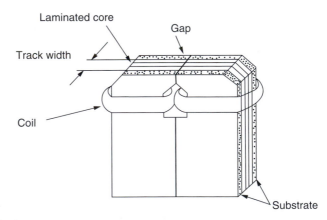

FIGURE 8.4
A digital record head is similar in principle to an analog head but uses much narrower tracks.

made quite large to ensure that the full thickness of the magnetic coating is recorded, although this cannot be done if the same head is intended to replay.

Figure 8.6 shows what happens when a conventional inductive head, i.e., one having a solenoid-like winding, is used to replay the bipolar track made by

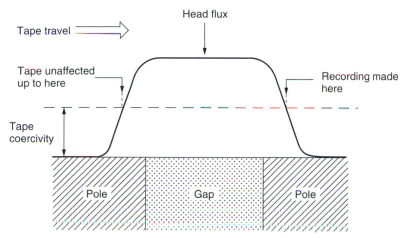

FIGURE 8.5
The recording is actually made near the trailing pole of the head where the head flux falls below the coercivity of the tape.

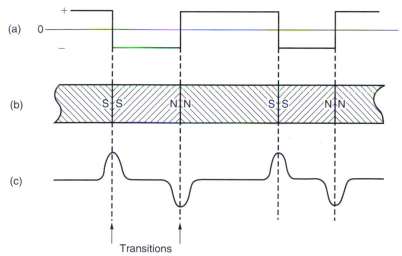

FIGURE 8.6
Basic digital recording. (a) The write current in the head is reversed from time to time, leaving a binary magnetization pattern shown in (b). When replayed, the waveform in (c) results because an output is produced only when flux in the head changes. Changes are referred to as transitions.

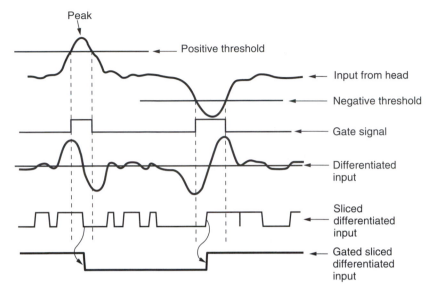

FIGURE 8.7
Gated peak detection rejects noise by disabling the differentiated output between transitions.

reversing the record current. The head output is proportional to the rate of change of flux and so occurs only at flux reversals. In other words, the replay head differentiates the flux on the track. The polarity of the resultant pulses alternates as the flux changes and changes back. A circuit is necessary, which locates the peaks of the pulses and outputs a signal corresponding to the original record current waveform. There are two ways in which this can be done.

The amplitude of the replay signal is of no consequence and often an AGC system is used to keep the replay signal constant in amplitude. What matters is the time at which the write current, and hence the flux stored on the medium, reverses. This can be determined by locating the peaks of the replay impulses, which can conveniently be done by differentiating the signal and looking for zero crossings. Figure 8.7 shows that this results in noise between the peaks. This problem is overcome by the gated peak detector, by which only zero crossings from a pulse that exceeds the threshold will be counted. The AGC system allows the thresholds to be fixed. As an alternative, the record waveform can also be restored by integration, which opposes the differentiation of the head, as in Figure 8.8.[1]

The head shown in Figure 8.4 has a frequency response shown in Figure 8.9. At DC there is no change of flux and no output. As a result inductive heads are at a disadvantage at very low speeds. The output rises with frequency until the rise is halted by the onset of thickness loss. As the frequency rises, the recorded

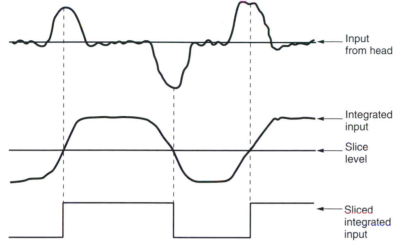

FIGURE 8.8
Integration method for re-creating write-current waveform.

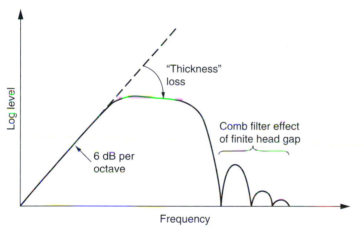

FIGURE 8.9
The major mechanisms defining magnetic channel bandwidth.

wavelength falls and flux from the shorter magnetic patterns cannot be picked up so far away. At some point, the wavelength becomes so short that flux from the back of the tape coating cannot reach the head and a decreasing thickness of tape contributes to the replay signal.[2] In digital recorders using short wavelengths to obtain high density, there is no point in using thick coatings. As wavelength further reduces, the familiar gap loss occurs, in which the head gap is too big to resolve detail on the track. The construction of the head results in the same action as that of a two-point transversal filter, as the two poles of the head see the tape with a small delay interposed due to the finite gap.

As expected, the head response is like a comb filter with the well-known nulls in which flux cancellation takes place across the gap. Clearly the smaller the gap, the shorter the wavelength of the first null. This contradicts the requirement of the record head to have a large gap. In quality analog audio recorders, it is the norm to have different record and replay heads for this reason, and the same will be true in digital machines that have separate record and playback heads. Clearly where the same pair of heads are used for record and play, the head gap size will be determined by the playback requirement.

As can be seen, the frequency response is far from ideal, and steps must be taken to ensure that recorded data waveforms do not contain frequencies that suffer excessive losses. A more recent development is the magnetoresistive (M-R) head. This is a head that measures the flux on the tape rather than using it to generate a signal directly. Flux measurement works down to DC and so offers advantages at low tape speeds. Unfortunately flux-measuring heads are not polarity conscious but sense the modulus of the flux and, if used directly, they respond to positive and negative flux equally, as shown in Figure 8.10. This is overcome by using a small extra winding in the head carrying a constant current. This creates a steady bias field, which adds to the flux from the tape. The flux seen by the head is now unipolar and changes between two levels and a more useful output waveform

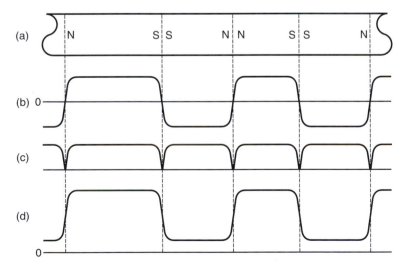

FIGURE 8.10
The sensing element in a magnetoresistive head is not sensitive to the polarity of the flux, only the magnitude. (a) The track magnetization is shown. This causes a bi-directional flux variation in the head (b), resulting in the magnitude output (c). However, if the flux in the head due to the track is biased by an additional field, it can be made unipolar as (d) and the correct waveform is obtained.

results. Magneto-resistive replay has been boosted dramatically by the discovery of GMR (giant magneto-resistivity) in which the variations in resistivity show a much higher sensitivity to magnetism.

Recorders that have low head-to-medium speed use M-R heads, whereas recorders with high bit rates, such as DVTRs, tend to use inductive heads. Heads designed for use with tape work in actual contact with the magnetic coating. The tape is tensioned to pull it against the head. There will be a wear mechanism and a need for periodic cleaning. In the hard disk, the rotational speed is high to reduce access time, and the drive must be capable of staying online for extended periods. In this case the heads do not contact the disk surface, but are supported on a boundary layer of air. The presence of the air film causes spacing loss, which restricts the wavelengths at which the head can replay. This is the penalty of rapid access. Digital media must operate at high density for economic reasons. This implies that shortest possible wavelengths will be used. Figure 8.11 shows that when two flux changes, or transitions, are recorded close together, they affect each other on replay. The amplitude of the composite signal is reduced, and the positions of the peaks are pushed outward. This is known as intersymbol interference, or peak-shift distortion, and it occurs in all magnetic media.

The effect is primarily due to high-frequency loss and it can be reduced by equalization on replay, as is done in most tapes, or by precompensation on record, as is done in hard disks.

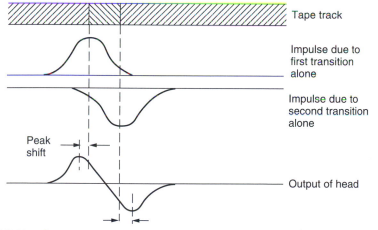

FIGURE 8.11
Readout pulses from two closely recorded transitions are summed in the head and the effect is that the peaks of the waveform are moved outward. This is known as peak-shift distortion and equalization is necessary to reduce the effect.

AZIMUTH RECORDING AND ROTARY HEADS

Figure 8.12a shows that in azimuth recording, the transitions are laid down at an angle to the track by using a head that is tilted. Machines using azimuth recording must always have an even number of heads, so that adjacent tracks can be recorded with opposite azimuth angle. This is easily achieved with a rotary head recorder. The two track types are usually referred to as A and B. Figure 8.12b shows the effect of playing a track with the wrong type of head. The playback process suffers from an enormous azimuth error. The effect of azimuth error can be understood by imagining the tape track to be made from many identical parallel strips. In the presence of azimuth error, the strips at one edge of the track are played back with a phase shift relative to strips at the other side. At some wavelengths, the phase shift will be 180° and there will be no output; at other wavelengths, especially long wavelengths, some output will reappear.

The effect is rather like that of a comb filter and serves to attenuate cross talk due to adjacent tracks so that no guard bands are required. Because no tape is wasted between the tracks, more efficient use is made of the tape. The term "guard-band-less" recording is often used instead of, or in addition to, the term "azimuth recording." The failure of the azimuth effect at long wavelengths is a characteristic of azimuth recording, and it is necessary to ensure that the spectrum of the signal to be recorded has a small low-frequency content. The signal will need to pass through a rotary transformer to reach the heads and cannot therefore contain a DC component.

In some rotary head recorders there is no separate erase process, and erasure is achieved by overwriting with a new waveform. Overwriting is successful only when there are no long wavelengths in the earlier recording, because these penetrate deeper into the tape, and the short wavelengths in a new recording will not be able to erase them. In this case the ratio between the shortest and the longest wavelengths recorded on tape should be limited. Restricting the spectrum of the code to allow erasure by overwrite also eases the design of the rotary transformer.

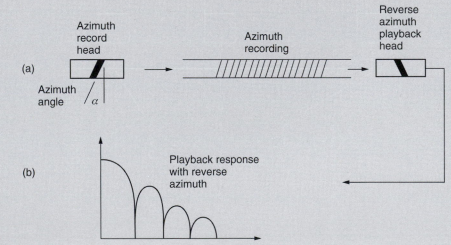

FIGURE 8.12
(a) In azimuth recording, the head gap is tilted. If the track is played with the same head, playback is normal, but the response of the reverse azimuth head (b) is attenuated.

OPTICAL AND MAGNETO-OPTICAL DISKS

Optical recorders have the advantage that light can be focused at a distance, whereas magnetism cannot. This means that there need be no physical contact between the pickup and the medium and no wear mechanism. In the same way that the recorded wavelength of a magnetic recording is limited by the gap in the replay head, the density of optical recording is limited by the size of light spot that can be focused on the medium. This is controlled by the wavelength of the light used and by the aperture of the lens. When the light spot is as small as these limits allow, it is said to be diffraction limited.

The frequency response of an optical disk is shown in Figure 8.13. The response is best at DC and falls steadily to the optical cut-off frequency. Although the optics work down to DC, this cannot be used for the data recording. DC and low frequencies in the data would interfere with the focus and tracking servos and, as will be seen, difficulties arise when attempting to demodulate a unipolar signal. In practice the signal from the pickup is split by a filter. Low frequencies go to the servos, and higher frequencies go to the data circuitry. As a result the optical disk channel has the same inability to handle DC as does a magnetic recorder, and the same techniques are needed to overcome it.

When a magnetic material is heated above its Curie temperature, it becomes demagnetized, and on cooling will assume the magnetization of an applied field, which would be too weak to influence it normally. This is the principle

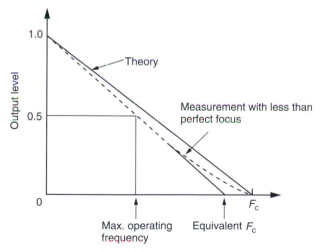

FIGURE 8.13

Frequency response of laser pickup. Maximum operating frequency is about half of cut-off frequency F_c.

of magneto-optical recording. The heat is supplied by a finely focused laser, the field is supplied by a coil, which is much larger. A disadvantage of magneto-optical recording is that all materials having a Curie point low enough to be useful are highly corrodible by air and need to be kept under an effectively sealed protective layer.

Figure 8.14 shows that the medium is initially magnetized in one direction only. To record, the coil is energized with a current in the opposite direction. This is too weak to influence the medium in its normal state, but when it is heated by the recording laser beam the heated area will take on the magnetism from the coil when it cools. Thus a magnetic recording with very small dimensions can be made even though the magnetic circuit involved is quite large in comparison.

Readout is obtained using the Kerr effect or the Faraday effect, which are phenomena whereby the plane of polarization of light can be rotated by a magnetic field. The angle of rotation is very small and needs a sensitive pickup. The pickup contains a polarizing filter before the sensor. Changes in polarization change the ability of the light to get through the polarizing filter and result in an intensity change, which once more produces a unipolar output.

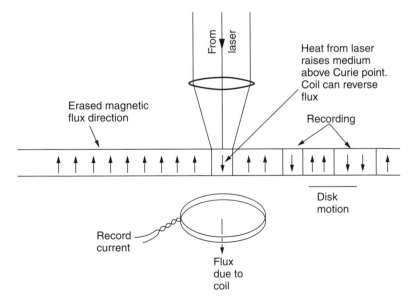

FIGURE 8.14
The thermo-magneto-optical disk uses the heat from a laser to allow a magnetic field to record on the disk.

The magneto-optic recording can be erased by reversing the current in the coil and operating the laser continuously as it passes along the track. A new recording can then be made on the erased track.

EQUALIZATION AND DATA SEPARATION

The characteristics of most channels are that signal loss occurs, which increases with frequency. This has the effect of slowing down rise times and thereby sloping off edges. If a signal with sloping edges is sliced, the time at which the waveform crosses the slicing level will be changed, and this causes jitter. Figure 8.15 shows that slicing a sloping waveform in the presence of baseline wander causes more jitter.

On a long cable, high-frequency roll-off can cause sufficient jitter to move a transition into an adjacent bit period. This is called intersymbol interference and the effect becomes worse in signals that have greater asymmetry, i.e., short pulses alternating with long ones. The effect can be reduced by the application of equalization, which is typically a high-frequency boost, and by choosing a channel code that has restricted asymmetry.

Compensation for peak-shift distortion in recording requires equalization of the channel,[3] and this can be done by a network after the replay head, termed an equalizer or pulse sharpener,[4] as in Figure 8.16a. This technique uses transversal filtering to oppose the inherent transversal effect of the head. As an alternative, pre-compensation in the record stage can be used as shown in Figure 8.16b. Transitions are written in such a way that the anticipated peak shift will move the readout peaks to the desired timing.

The important step of information recovery at the receiver or replay circuit is known as data separation. The data separator is rather like an analog-to-digital convertor because the two processes of sampling and quantizing are both present.

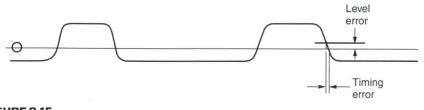

FIGURE 8.15
A DC offset can cause timing errors.

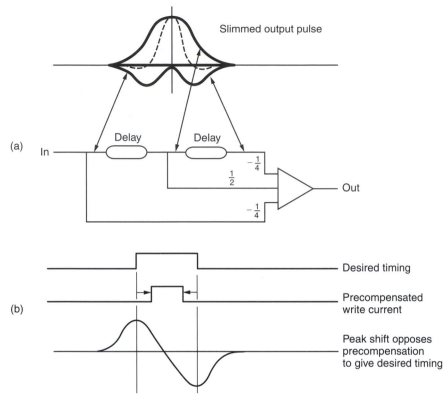

FIGURE 8.16
Peak-shift distortion is due to the finite width of replay pulses. The effect can be reduced by the pulse slimmer shown in (a), which is basically a transversal filter. The use of a linear operational amplifier emphasizes the analog nature of channels. Instead of replay-pulse slimming, transitions can be written with a displacement equal and opposite to the anticipated peak shift (b).

In the time domain, the sampling clock is derived from the clock content of the channel waveform. In the voltage domain, the process of slicing converts the analog waveform from the channel back into a binary representation. The slicer is thus a form of quantizer that has only one-bit resolution. The slicing process makes a discrete decision about the voltage of the incoming signal to reject noise. The sampler makes discrete decisions along the time axis to reject jitter. These two processes will be described in detail.

SLICING AND JITTER REJECTION

The slicer is implemented with a comparator, which has analog inputs but a binary output. In a cable receiver, the input waveform can be sliced directly.

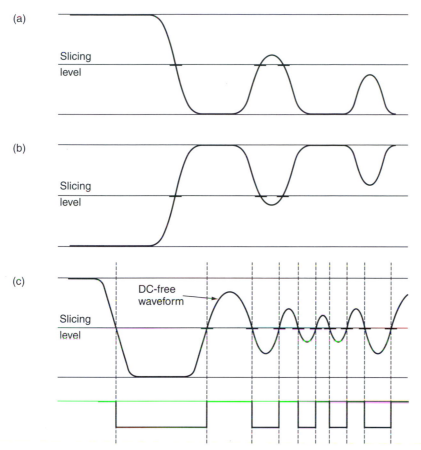

FIGURE 8.17
Slicing a signal that has suffered losses works well if the duty cycle is even. If the duty cycle is uneven, as in (a), timing errors will become worse until slicing fails. With the opposite duty cycle, the slicing falls in the opposite direction as in (b). If, however, the signal is DC free, correct slicing can continue, even in the presence of serious losses, as (c) shows.

In an inductive magnetic replay system, the replay waveform is differentiated and must first pass through a peak detector (Figure 8.7) or an integrator (Figure 8.8). The signal voltage is compared with the midway voltage, known as the threshold, baseline, or slicing level, by the comparator. If the signal voltage is above the threshold, the comparator outputs a high level; if below, a low level results.

Figure 8.17 shows some waveforms associated with a slicer. In Figure 8.17a the transmitted waveform has an uneven duty cycle. The DC component, or average level, of the signal is received with high amplitude, but the pulse amplitude falls as the pulse gets shorter. Eventually the waveform cannot be sliced.

In (b) the opposite duty cycle is shown. The signal level drifts to the opposite polarity and once more slicing is impossible. The phenomenon is called baseline wander and will be observed with any signal whose average voltage is not the same as the slicing level. In (c) it can be seen that if the transmitted waveform has a relatively constant average voltage, slicing remains possible up to high frequencies even in the presence of serious amplitude loss, because the received waveform remains symmetrical about the baseline.

It is clearly not possible simply to serialize data in a shift register for so-called direct transmission, because successful slicing can be obtained only if the number of ones is equal to the number of zeros; there is little chance of this happening consistently with real data. Instead, a modulation code or channel code is necessary. This converts the data into a waveform that is DC-free or nearly so for the purpose of transmission.

The slicing threshold level is naturally zero in a bipolar system such as magnetic inductive replay or a cable. When the amplitude falls it does so symmetrically and slicing continues. The same is not true of M-R heads and optical pickups, which both respond to intensity and therefore produce a unipolar output. If the replay signal is sliced directly, the threshold cannot be zero, but must be some level approximately half the amplitude of the signal as shown in Figure 8.18a. Unfortunately when the signal level falls it falls toward zero and not toward the slicing level. The threshold will no longer be appropriate for the signal as can be seen in (b). This can be overcome by using a DC-free coded waveform. If a series capacitor is connected to the unipolar signal from an optical pickup, the waveform is rendered bipolar because the capacitor blocks any DC component in the signal. The DC-free channel waveform passes through unaltered. If an amplitude loss is suffered, (c) shows that the resultant bipolar signal now reduces in amplitude about the slicing level and slicing can continue.

The binary waveform at the output of the slicer will be a replica of the transmitted waveform, except for the addition of jitter or time uncertainty in the position of the edges due to noise, baseline wander, intersymbol interference, and imperfect equalization.

Binary circuits reject noise by using discrete voltage levels, which are spaced farther apart than the uncertainty due to noise. In a similar manner, digital coding combats time uncertainty by making the time axis discrete using events, known as transitions, spaced apart at integer multiples of some basic time period, called a detent, which is larger than the typical time uncertainty.

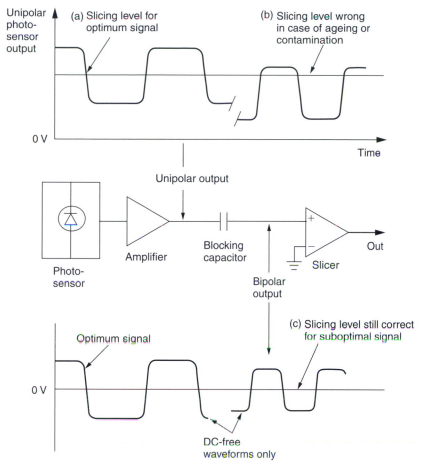

FIGURE 8.18
(a) Slicing a unipolar signal requires a non-zero threshold. (b) If the signal amplitude changes, the threshold will then be incorrect. (c) If a DC-free code is used, a unipolar waveform can be converted to a bipolar waveform using a series capacitor. A zero threshold can be used and slicing continues with amplitude variations.

Figure 8.19 shows how this jitter-rejection mechanism works. All that matters is to identify the detent in which the transition occurred. Exactly where it occurred within the detent is of no consequence.

As ideal transitions occur at multiples of a basic period, an oscilloscope, which is repeatedly triggered on a channel-coded signal carrying random data, will show an eye pattern if connected to the output of the equalizer. Study of the eye pattern reveals how well the coding used suits the channel. In the case of transmission, with a short cable, the losses will be small, and the eye opening will be virtually square except for some edge sloping due to cable capacitance. As cable length

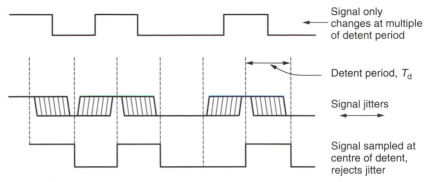

Signal only changes at multiple of detent period

Detent period, T_d

Signal jitters

Signal sampled at centre of detent, rejects jitter

FIGURE 8.19
A certain amount of jitter can be rejected by changing the signal at multiples of the basic detent period T_d.

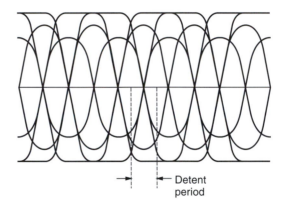

Detent period

FIGURE 8.20
A transmitted waveform will appear like this on an oscilloscope as successive parts of the waveform are superimposed on the tube. When the waveform is rounded off by losses, diamond-shaped eyes are left in the centre, spaced apart by the detent period.

increases, the harmonics are lost and the remaining fundamental gives the eyes a diamond shape. The same eye pattern will be obtained with a recording channel for which it is uneconomic to provide bandwidth much beyond the fundamental.

Noise closes the eyes in a vertical direction, and jitter closes the eyes in a horizontal direction, as in Figure 8.20. If the eyes remain sensibly open, data separation will be possible. Clearly more jitter can be tolerated if there is less noise, and vice versa. If the equalizer is adjustable, the optimum setting will be where the greatest eye opening is obtained.

In the centre of the eyes, the receiver must make binary decisions at the channel bit rate about the state of the signal, high or low, using the slicer output. As stated, the receiver is sampling the output of the slicer, and it needs to have a sampling clock to do that. To give the best rejection of noise and jitter, the clock edges that operate the sampler must be in the centre of the eyes.

As has been stated, a separate clock is not practicable in recording or transmission. A fixed-frequency clock at the receiver is of no use as even if it were sufficiently stable, it would not know what phase to run at. The only way in which the sampling clock can be obtained is to use a PLL (phase-locked loop) to regenerate it from the clock content of the self-clocking channel-coded waveform. In phase-locked loops, the VCO (voltage-controlled oscillator) is driven by a phase error measured between the output and some reference, such that the output eventually has the same frequency as the reference. If a divider is placed between the voltage-controlled oscillator and the phase comparator, the VCO frequency can be made to be a multiple of the reference. This also has the effect of making the loop more heavily damped.

If a channel-coded waveform is used as a reference to a phase-locked loop, the loop will be able to make a phase comparison whenever a transition arrives and will run at the channel bit rate. When there are several detents between transitions, the loop will *flywheel* at the last known frequency and phase until it can rephase at a subsequent transition. Thus a continuous clock is re-created from the clock content of the channel waveform. In a recorder, if the speed of the medium should change, the PLL will change frequency to follow. Once the loop is locked, clock edges will be phased with the average phase of the jittering edges of the input waveform. If, for example, rising edges of the clock are phased to input transitions, then falling edges will be in the centre of the eyes. If these edges are used to clock the sampling process, the maximum jitter and noise can be rejected. The output of the slicer when sampled by the PLL edge at the centre of an eye is the value of a channel bit. Figure 8.21 shows the complete clocking system of a channel code from encoder to data separator.

Clearly data cannot be separated if the PLL is not locked, but it cannot be locked until it has seen transitions for a reasonable period. In recorders that have discontinuous recorded blocks to allow editing, the solution is to precede each data block with a pattern of transitions whose sole purpose is to provide a timing reference for synchronising the phase-locked loop. This pattern is known as a preamble. In interfaces, the transmission can be continuous and there is no difficulty remaining in lock indefinitely. There will simply be a short delay on first applying the signal before the receiver locks to it.

One potential problem area that is frequently overlooked is to ensure that the VCO in the receiving PLL is correctly centred. If it is not, it will be running with

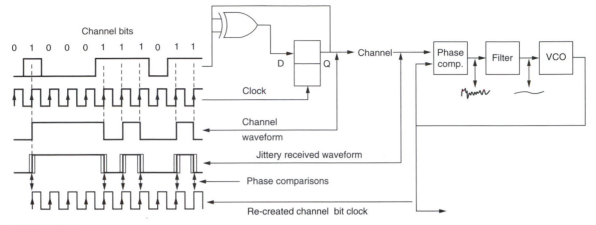

FIGURE 8.21
The clocking system when channel coding is used. The encoder clock runs at the channel bit rate, and any transitions in the channel must coincide with encoder clock edges. The reason for doing this is that, at the data separator, the PLL can lock to the edges of the channel signal, which represent an intermittent clock, and turn it into a continuous clock. The jitter in the edges of the channel signal causes noise in the phase error of the PLL, but the damping acts as a filter and the PLL runs at the average phase of the channel bits, rejecting the jitter.

a static phase error and will not sample the received waveform at the centre of the eyes. The sampled bits will be more prone to noise and jitter errors. VCO centring can be checked simply by displaying the control voltage. This should not change significantly when the input is momentarily interrupted.

CHANNEL CODING

It is not practicable simply to serialize raw data in a shift register for the purpose of recording or for transmission except over relatively short distances. Practical systems require the use of a modulation scheme, known as a channel code, which expresses the data as waveforms that are self-clocking in order to reject jitter, separate the received bits, and avoid skew on separate clock lines. The coded waveforms should further be DC-free or nearly so to enable slicing in the presence of losses and have a narrower spectrum than the raw data both for economy and to make equalization easier.

Jitter causes uncertainty about the time at which a particular event occurred. The frequency response of the channel then places an overall limit on the spacing of events in the channel. Particular emphasis must be placed on the interplay of bandwidth, jitter, and noise, which will be shown here to be the key to the design of a successful channel code.

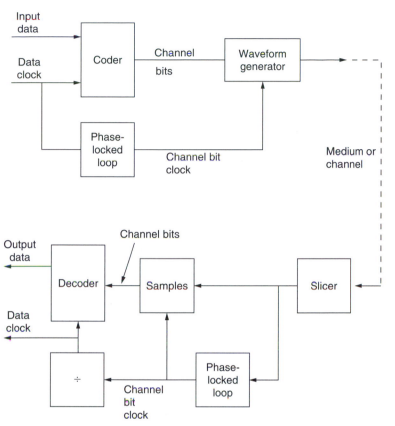

FIGURE 8.22
The major components of a channel coding system. See text for details.

Figure 8.22 shows that a channel coder is necessary prior to the record stage and that a decoder, known as a data separator, is necessary after the replay stage. The output of the channel coder is generally a logic level signal that contains a "high" state when a transition is to be generated. The waveform generator produces the transitions in a signal whose level and impedance are suitable for driving the medium or channel. The signal may be bipolar or unipolar as appropriate.

Some codes eliminate DC entirely, which is advantageous for cable transmission, optical media, and rotary head recording. Some codes can reduce the channel bandwidth needed by lowering the upper spectral limit. This permits higher linear density, usually at the expense of jitter rejection. Other codes narrow the spectrum by raising the lower limit. A code with a narrow spectrum has a number of advantages. The reduction in asymmetry will reduce peak shift and data separators can lock more readily because the range of frequencies in the code is smaller. In theory the narrower the spectrum, the less noise will be suffered, but this is achieved only if filtering is employed. Filters can easily cause phase errors, which will nullify any gain.

A convenient definition of a channel code (for there are certainly others) is: "A method of modulating real data such that they can be reliably received despite the shortcomings of a real channel, whilst making maximum economic use of the channel capacity."

The basic time periods of a channel-coded waveform are called positions or detents, in which the transmitted voltage will be reversed or stay the same. The symbol used for the units of channel time is T_d.

One of the fundamental parameters of a channel code is the density ratio (DR). One definition of density ratio is that it is the worst-case ratio of the number of data bits recorded to the number of transitions in the channel. It can also be thought of as the ratio between the Nyquist rate of the data (one-half the bit rate) and the frequency response required in the channel. The storage density of data recorders has steadily increased due to improvements in medium and transducer technology, but modern storage densities are also a function of improvements in channel coding.

As jitter is such an important issue in digital recording and transmission, a parameter has been introduced to quantify the ability of a channel code to reject time instability. This parameter, the jitter margin, also known as the window margin or phase margin (T_w), is defined as the permitted range of time over which a transition can still be received correctly, divided by the data bit-cell period (T).

Because equalization is often difficult in practice, a code that has a large jitter margin will sometimes be used because it resists the effects of intersymbol interference well. Such a code may achieve a better performance in practice than a code with a higher density ratio but poor jitter performance.

A more realistic comparison of code performance will be obtained by taking into account both density ratio and jitter margin. This is the purpose of the figure of merit (FoM), which is defined as DR $\times$ T_w.

SIMPLE CODES

In the non-return to zero (NRZ) code shown in Figure 8.23a, the record current does not cease between bits, but flows at all times in one direction or the other dependent on the state of the bit to be recorded. This results in a replay pulse only when the data bits change from one state to another. As a result if

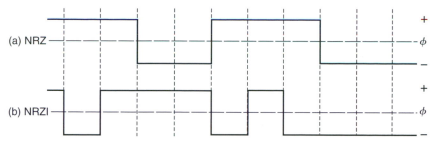

FIGURE 8.23
In the NRZ code (a) a missing replay pulse inverts every following bit. This was overcome in the NRZI code (b), which reverses write current on a data 1.

one pulse is missed, the subsequent bits will be inverted. This was avoided by adapting the coding such that the record current would change state or invert whenever a data one occurred, leading to the term non-return to zero invert or NRZI, shown in Figure 8.23b. In NRZI a replay pulse occurs whenever there is a data one. Clearly neither NRZ nor NRZI is self-clocking, but both require a separate clock track. Skew between tracks can be avoided only by working at low density and so the system cannot be used directly for digital video. However, virtually all the codes used for magnetic recording are based on the principle of reversing the record current to produce a transition.

The FM code, also known as Manchester code or biphase mark code, shown in Figure 8.24a, was the first practical self-clocking binary code and it is suitable for both transmission and recording. It is DC-free and very easy to encode and decode. It is the code specified for the AES/EBU digital audio interconnect standard. In the field of recording it remains in use today only where density is not of prime importance, for example in SMPTE/EBU timecode for professional audio and video recorders.

In FM there is always a transition at the bit-cell boundary, which acts as a clock. For a data 1, there is an additional transition at the bit-cell centre. Figure 8.24a shows that each data bit can be represented by two channel bits. For a data 0, they will be 10, and for a data 1 they will be 11. Because the first bit is always one, it conveys no information and is responsible for the density ratio of only one-half. Because there can be two transitions for each data bit, the jitter margin can be only half a bit, and the resulting FoM is only 0.25. The high clock content of FM does, however, mean that data recovery is possible over a wide range of speeds; hence the use for timecode. The lowest frequency in FM is due to a stream of zeros and is equal to half the bit rate. The highest frequency is due to a stream of ones and is equal to the bit rate. Thus the fundamentals of FM are within a band of

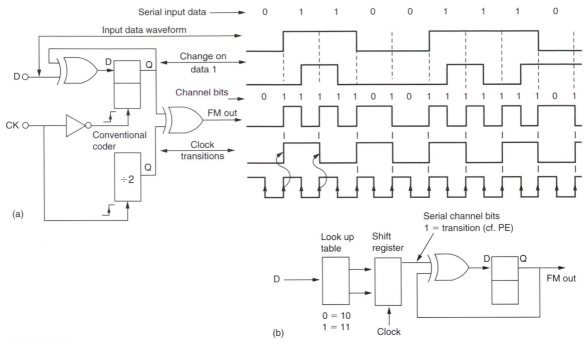

FIGURE 8.24
In (a) are shown the FM waveform from a conventional coder and the channel bits that may be used to describe transitions in it. A coder based on a lookup table is shown in (b).

one octave. Effective equalization is generally possible over such a band. FM is not polarity conscious and can be inverted without changing the data.

Figure 8.24b shows how an FM coder works. Data words are loaded into the input shift register, which is clocked at the data bit rate. Each data bit is converted to two channel bits in the code book or lookup table. These channel bits are loaded into the output register. The output register is clocked twice as fast as the input register because there are twice as many channel bits as data bits. The ratio of the two clocks is called the code rate; in this case it is a rate one-half code. Ones in the serial channel bit output represent transitions, whereas zeros represent no change. The channel bits are fed to the waveform generator, which is a one-bit delay, clocked at the channel bit rate, and an exclusive-OR gate. This changes state when a channel bit one is input. The result is a coded FM waveform in which there is always a transition at the beginning of the data bit period and a second optional transition whose presence indicates a one.

In modified frequency modulation (MFM), also known as Miller code,[5] the highly redundant clock content of FM was reduced by the use of a phase-locked loop in the receiver, which could flywheel over missing clock transitions.

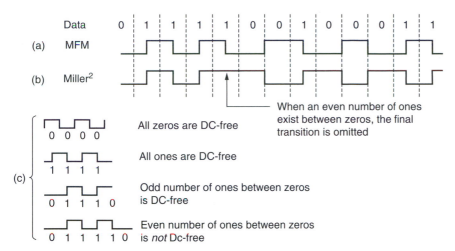

When an even number of ones exist between zeros, the final transition is omitted

All zeros are DC-free

All ones are DC-free

Odd number of ones between zeros is DC-free

Even number of ones between zeros is *not* Dc-free

FIGURE 8.25
MFM or Miller code is generated as shown here. The minimum transition spacing is twice that of FM or PE. MFM is not always DC-free, as shown in (c). This can be overcome by the modification of (b), which results in the Miller^2 code.

This technique is implicit in all the more advanced codes. Figure 8.25a shows that the bit-cell centre transition on a data 1 was retained, but the bit-cell boundary transition is now required only between successive zeros. There are still two channel bits for every data bit, but adjacent channel bits will never be one, doubling the minimum time between transitions, and giving a DR of one. Clearly the coding of the current bit is now influenced by the preceding bit. The maximum number of prior bits that affect the current bit is known as the constraint length, L_c, measured in data-bit periods. For MFM $L_c = T$. Another way of considering the constraint length is that it assesses the number of data bits that may be corrupted if the receiver misplaces one transition. If L_c is long, all errors will be burst errors.

MFM doubled the density ratio compared to FM and PE without changing the jitter performance; thus the FoM also doubles, becoming 0.5. It was adopted for many rigid disks at the time of its development and remains in use on double-density floppy disks. It is not, however, DC-free. Figure 8.25b shows how MFM can have DC content under certain conditions.

The Miller^2 code is derived from MFM, and Figure 8.25c shows that the DC content is eliminated by a slight increase in complexity.[6,7] Wherever an even number of ones occur between zeros, the transition at the last one is omitted. This creates two additional, longer run lengths and increases the T_{max} of the code. The decoder can detect these longer run lengths in order to reinsert the suppressed ones. The FoM of Miller^2 is 0.5, as for MFM.

GROUP CODES

Further improvements in coding rely on converting patterns of real data to patterns of channel bits with more desirable characteristics using a conversion table known as a code book. If a data symbol of m bits is considered, it can have 2^m different combinations. As it is intended to discard undesirable patterns to improve the code, it follows that the number of channel bits n must be greater than m. The number of patterns that can be discarded is

$$2^n - 2^m.$$

One name for the principle is GCR (group code recording), and an important parameter is the code rate, defined as

$$R = \frac{m}{n}$$

It will be evident that the jitter margin T_w is numerically equal to the code rate, and so a code rate near to unity is desirable. The choice of patterns used in the code book will be those that give the desired balance between clock content, bandwidth, and DC content.

Figure 8.26 shows that the upper spectral limit can be made to be some fraction of the channel bit rate according to the minimum distance between ones in the channel bits. This is known as T_{min}, also referred to as the minimum transition parameter M, and in both cases is measured in data bits T. It can be obtained by multiplying the number of channel detent periods between transitions by the code rate. Unfortunately, codes are measured by the number of consecutive zeros in the channel bits, given the symbol d, which is always one less than the number of detent periods. In fact T_{min} is numerically equal to the density ratio,

$$T_{min} = M = DR = \frac{(d+1) \times m}{n}.$$

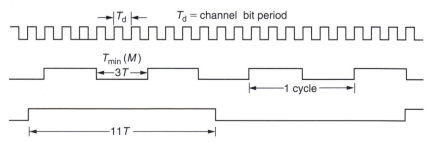

FIGURE 8.26
A channel code can control its spectrum by placing limits on T_{min} (M) and T_{max}, which define upper and lower frequencies. The ratio of T_{max}/T_{min} determines the asymmetry of waveform and predicts DC content and peak shift.

It will be evident that choosing a low code rate could increase the density ratio, but it will impair the jitter margin. The figure of merit is

$$\text{FoM} = \text{DR} \times T_w = \frac{(d+1) \times m^2}{n^2},$$

since $T_w = m/n$.

Figure 8.26 also shows that the lower spectral limit is influenced by the maximum distance between transitions T_{max}. This is also obtained by multiplying the maximum number of detent periods between transitions by the code rate. Again, codes are measured by the maximum number of zeros between channel ones, k, and so

$$T_{max} = \frac{(k+1) \times m}{n},$$

and the maximum/minimum ratio P is

$$P = \frac{(k+1)}{(d+1)}.$$

The length of time between channel transitions is known as the *run length*. Another name for this class is the run-length-limited (RLL) codes.[8] Because m data bits are considered as one symbol, the constraint length L_c will be increased in RLL codes to at least m. It is, however, possible for a code to have run-length limits without it being a group code.

In practice, the junction of two adjacent channel symbols may violate run-length limits, and it may be necessary to create a further code book of symbol size $2n$, which converts violating code pairs to acceptable patterns. This is known as merging and follows the golden rule that the substitute $2n$ symbol must finish with a pattern that eliminates the possibility of a subsequent violation. These patterns must also differ from all other symbols.

Substitution may also be used to different degrees in the same nominal code to allow a choice of maximum run length, e.g., 3PM. The maximum number of symbols involved in a substitution is denoted by r. There are many RLL codes and the parameters $d, k, m, n,$ and r are a way of comparing them.

Group codes are used extensively in recording and transmission. Digital VTRs and magnetic disks use group codes optimized for jitter rejection, whereas optical disks use group codes optimized for density ratio.

SYNCHRONISING

In serial transmission and in recording, multi-bit or multi-channel-bit symbols are sent one after the other with no spaces in between, so that although the designer knows that a data block contains, for example, 128 bytes, the receiver simply finds 1024 bits in a row. If the exact position of the first bit is not known, then it is not possible to put all the bits in the right places in the right bytes; a process known as de-serializing. The effect of sync slippage is devastating, because a one-bit disparity between the bit count and the bitstream will corrupt every symbol in the block.

In a group code, it is essential to know where a group of channel bits begins in order to assemble groups for decoding to data bit groups. In a randomizing system it is equally vital to know at what point in the serial data stream the words or samples commence.

The synchronisation of the data separator and the synchronisation to the block format are two distinct problems, which are often solved by the same sync pattern. De-serializing requires a shift register, which is fed with serial data and read out once per word. The sync detector is simply a set of logic gates that are arranged to recognize a specific pattern in the register. The sync pattern either is identical for every block or has a restricted number of versions and it will be recognized by the replay circuitry and used to reset the bit count through the block. Then by counting channel bits and dividing by the group size, groups can be de-serialized and decoded to data groups. In a randomized system, the pseudo-random sequence generator is also reset. Then counting de-randomized bits from the sync pattern and dividing by the word length enables the replay circuitry to de-serialize the data words.

Even if a specific code were excluded from the recorded data so it could be used for synchronising, this cannot ensure that the same pattern cannot be falsely created at the junction between two allowable data words. Figure 8.27 shows how false synchronising can occur due to concatenation. It is thus not practical to use a bit pattern that is a data code value in a simple synchronising detector. The problem is overcome in some synchronous systems by using the fact that sync patterns occur exactly once per block and therefore contain redundancy. If the pattern is seen by the detector at block rate, a genuine sync condition exists. Sync patterns seen at other times must be false. Such systems take a few milliseconds before sync is achieved, but once achieved it should not be lost unless the transmission is interrupted.

In run-length-limited codes false syncs are not a problem. The sync pattern is no longer a data bit pattern but is a specific waveform. If the sync waveform contains run lengths that violate the normal coding limits, there is no way that these run lengths can occur in encoded data nor any possibility that they will be interpreted as data. They can, however, be readily detected by the replay circuitry.

In a group code there are many more combinations of channel bits than there are combinations of data bits. Thus after all data bit patterns have been allocated group patterns, there are still many unused group patterns that cannot occur in the data. With care, group patterns can be found that cannot occur due to the concatenation of any pair of groups representing data. These are then unique and can be used for synchronising.

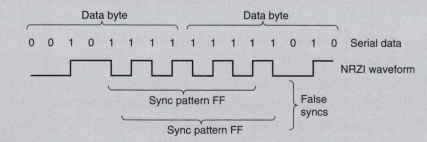

FIGURE 8.27
Concatenation of two data words can result in the accidental generation of a word that is reserved for synchronising.

RANDOMIZING AND ENCRYPTION

Randomizing is not a channel code, but a technique that can be used in conjunction with, or sometimes instead of, a channel code. It is widely used in digital audio and video broadcasting and in a number of recording and transmission formats. The randomizing system is arranged outside any channel coder. Figure 8.28 shows that, at the encoder, a pseudo-random sequence is added modulo-2 to the serial data. This process makes the signal spectrum in the channel more uniform, drastically reduces T_{max}, and reduces DC content. At the receiver the transitions are converted back to a serial bitstream to which the same pseudo-random sequence is again added modulo-2. As a result the random signal cancels itself out to leave only the serial data, provided that the two pseudo-random sequences are synchronised to bit accuracy.

Many channel codes, especially group codes, display pattern sensitivity because some waveforms are more sensitive to peak-shift distortion than others. Pattern sensitivity is a problem only if a sustained series of sensitive symbols needs to be recorded. Randomizing ensures that this cannot happen because it breaks up any regularity or repetition in the data. The data randomizing is performed by using the exclusive-OR function of the data and a pseudo-random sequence as the input to the channel coder. On replay the same sequence is generated, synchronised to bit accuracy, and the exclusive-OR of the replay bitstream and the sequence is the original data.

The generation of randomizing polynomials was described in Chapter 3. Clearly the sync pattern cannot be randomized, because this causes a Catch-22 situation in which it is not possible to synchronise the sequence for replay until the sync

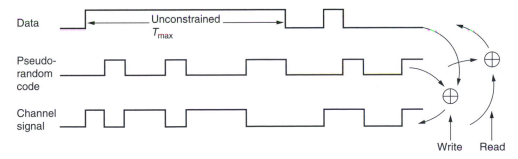

FIGURE 8.28
Modulo-2 addition with a pseudo-random code removes unconstrained runs in real data. An identical process must be provided on replay.

pattern is read, but it is not possible to read the sync pattern until the sequence is synchronised!

In recorders, the randomizing is block based, because this matches the block structure on the medium. Where there is no obvious block structure, convolutional, or endless randomizing can be used. In convolutional randomizing, the signal sent down the channel is the serial data waveform, which has been convolved with the impulse response of a digital filter. On reception the signal is deconvolved to restore the original data.

Convolutional randomizing is used in the serial digital interface (SDI), which carries production digital video. Figure 8.29a shows that the filter is an IIR (infinite impulse response) filter, which has recursive paths from the output back to the input. As it is a one-bit filter its output cannot decay, and once excited, it runs indefinitely. The filter is followed by a transition generator, which consists of a one-bit delay and an exclusive-OR gate. An input one results in an output transition on the next clock edge. An input zero results in no transition.

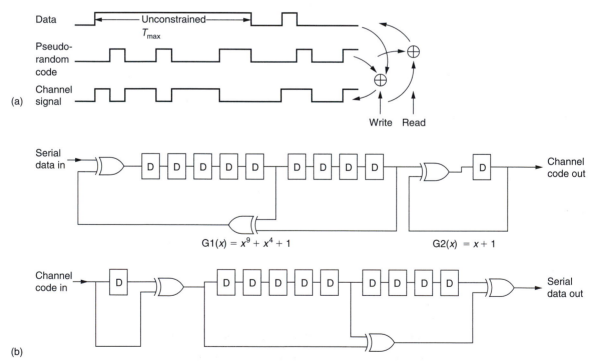

FIGURE 8.29
(a) Convolutional randomizing encoder transmits exclusive-OR of three bits at a fixed spacing in the data. One bit delay, far right, produces channel transitions from data 1's. (b) Decoder has opposing one-bit delay to return from transitions to data levels, followed by an opposing shift register, which exactly reverses the coding process.

A result of the infinite impulse response of the filter is that frequent transitions are generated in the channel, which result in sufficient clock content for the phase-locked loop in the receiver.

Transitions are converted back to ones by a differentiator in the receiver. This consists of a one-bit delay with an exclusive-OR gate comparing the input and the output. When a transition passes through the delay, the input and the output will be different and the gate outputs a one, which enters the deconvolution circuit.

Figure 8.29b shows that in the deconvolution circuit a data bit is simply the exclusive-OR of a number of channel bits at a fixed spacing. The deconvolution is implemented with a shift register having the exclusive-OR gates connected in a pattern that is the reverse of that in the encoder. The same effect as block randomizing is obtained, in that long runs are broken up and the DC content is reduced, but it has the advantage over block randomizing that no synchronising is required to remove the randomizing, although it will still be necessary for de-serialization. Clearly the system will take a few clock periods to produce valid data after commencement of transmission, but this is no problem on a permanent wired connection in which the transmission is continuous.

In a randomized transmission, if the receiver is not able to re-create the pseudo-random sequence, the data cannot be decoded. This can be used as the basis for encryption in which only authorised users can decode transmitted data. In an encryption system, the goal is security, whereas in a channel-coding system the goal is simplicity. Channel coders use pseudo-random sequences because these are economical to create using feedback shift registers. However, there are a limited number of pseudo-random sequences and it would be too easy to try them all until the correct one was found. Encryption systems use the same processes, but the key sequence that is added to the data at the encoder is truly random. This makes it much harder for unauthorised parties to access the data. Only a receiver in possession of the correct sequence can decode the channel signal. If the sequence is made long enough, the probability of stumbling across the sequence by trial and error can be made sufficiently small. Security systems of this kind can be compromised if the delivery of the key to the authorised user is intercepted.

Given sufficient computing power, it is possible to attack encrypted information by trying different keys at random. Consequently there is no such thing as a truly secure encryption system based on randomizing alone. However, for many commercial purposes it is sufficient to keep the number of unauthorised recipients to a very low level.

PARTIAL RESPONSE

It has been stated that a magnetic head acts as a transversal filter, because it has two poles that scan the medium at different times. In addition the output is differentiated, so that the head may be thought of as a $(1 - D)$ impulse response system, where D is the delay, which is a function of the tape speed and gap size. It is this delay that results in inter-symbol interference. Conventional equalizers attempt to oppose this effect and succeed in raising the noise level in the process of making the frequency response linear. Figure 8.30 shows that the frequency response necessary to pass data with insignificant peak shift is a bandwidth of half the bit rate, which is the Nyquist rate. In Class IV partial response, the frequency response of the system is made to have nulls at DC and at the bit rate. Such a frequency response is particularly advantageous for rotary head recorders as it is DC-free and the low-frequency content is minimal, hence the use in Digital Betacam. The required response is achieved by an overall impulse response of $(1 - D^2)$, where D is now the bit period. There are a number of ways in which this can be done.

If the head gap is made equal to one bit, the $(1 - D)$ head response may be converted to the desired response by the use of a $(1 + D)$ filter, as in Figure 8.31a.[9] Alternatively, a head of unspecified gap width may be connected to an integrator and equalized flat to reproduce the record current waveform before being fed to a $(1 - D^2)$ filter as in Figure 8.31b.[10]

The result of both of these techniques is a ternary signal. The eye pattern has two sets of eyes as in Figure 8.31c.[11] When slicing such a signal, a smaller amount of noise than in the binary case will cause an error.

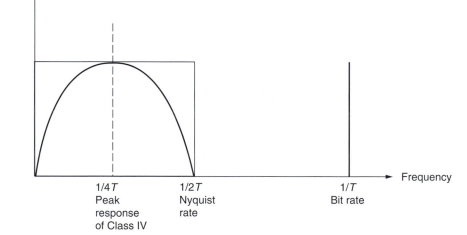

FIGURE 8.30
Class IV response has spectral nulls at DC and the Nyquist rate, giving a noise advantage, because magnetic replay signal is weak at both frequencies in a high-density channel.

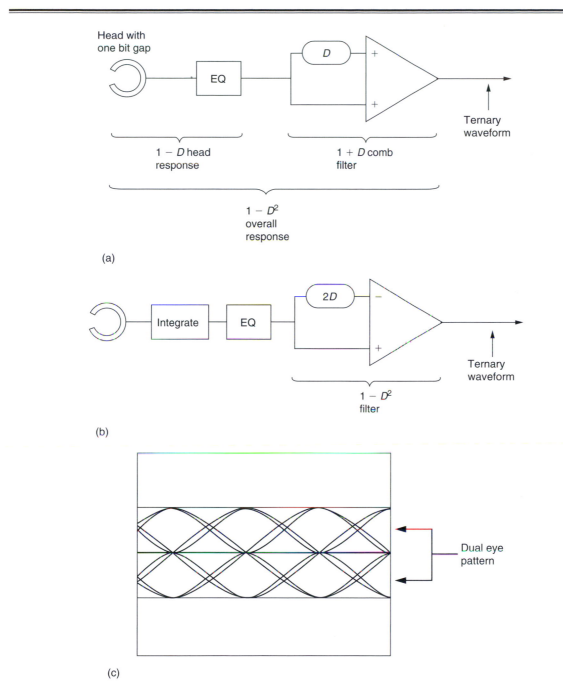

FIGURE 8.31
(a and b) Two ways of obtaining partial response. (c) Characteristic eye pattern of ternary signal.

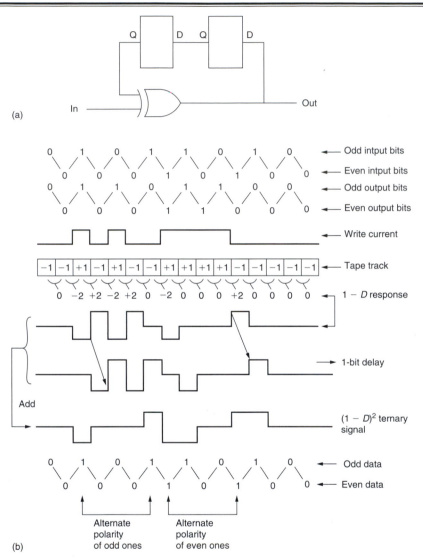

FIGURE 8.32
Class IV precoding (a) causes redundancy in replay signal, as derived in (b).

The treatment of the signal thus far represents an equalization technique, and not a channel code. However, to take full advantage of Class IV partial response, suitable precoding is necessary prior to recording, which does then constitute a channel-coding technique. This pre-coding is shown in Figure 8.32a. Data are added modulo-2 to themselves with a two-bit delay. The effect of this precoding is that the outer levels of the ternary signals, which represent data ones, alternate in polarity on all odd bits and on all even bits. This is because the precoder acts like two interleaved one-bit delay circuits, as in Figure 8.32b. As this alternation of polarity is a form of redundancy, it can be used to recover the three dB SNR loss encountered in slicing a ternary eye pattern.

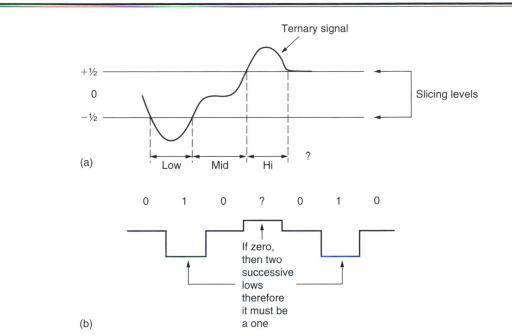

FIGURE 8.33
(a) A ternary signal suffers a noise penalty because there are two slicing levels. (b) The redundancy is used to determine the bit value in the presence of noise. Here the pulse height has been reduced to make it ambiguous 1/0, but only 1 is valid, as 0 violates the redundancy rules.

Viterbi decoding[12] can be used for this purpose. In Viterbi decoding, each channel bit is not sliced individually; the slicing decision is made in the context of adjacent decisions. Figure 8.33 shows a replay waveform that is so noisy that, at the decision point, the signal voltage crosses the centre of the eye, and the slicer alone cannot tell whether the correct decision is an inner or an outer level. In this case, the decoder essentially allows both possibilities to stand, in order to see what happens. A symbol representing indecision is output. It will be seen from the figure that as subsequent bits are received, one of these decisions will result in an absurd situation, which indicates that the other decision was the right one. The decoder can then locate the undecided symbol and set it to the correct value.

Viterbi decoding requires more information about the signal voltage than a simple binary slicer can discern. Figure 8.34 shows that the replay waveform is sampled and quantized so that it can be processed in digital logic. The sampling rate is obtained from the embedded clock content of the replay waveform. The digital Viterbi processing logic must be able to operate at high speed to handle serial signals from a DVTR head. Its application in Digital Betacam is eased somewhat by the adoption of compression, which reduces the data rate at the heads by a factor of two.

Clearly a ternary signal having a dual eye pattern is more sensitive than a binary signal, and it is important to keep the maximum run length T_{max} small to have accurate AGC. The use of pseudo-random coding along with partial response equalization and precoding is a logical combination.[13]

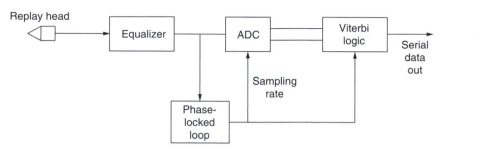

FIGURE 8.34
A Viterbi decoder is implemented in the digital domain by sampling the replay waveform with a clock locked to the embedded clock of the channel code.

There is then considerable overlap between the channel code and the error-correction system. Viterbi decoding is primarily applicable to channels with random errors due to Gaussian statistics, and they cannot cope with burst errors. In a head-noise-limited system, however, the use of a Viterbi detector could increase the power of a separate burst error-correction system by relieving it of the need to correct random errors due to noise. The error-correction system could then concentrate on correcting burst errors unimpaired.

BASIC ERROR CORRECTION

There are many different types of recording and transmission channels and consequently there will be many different mechanisms that may result in errors. Bit errors in video cause "sparkles" in the picture, whose effect depends upon the significance of the affected bit. Errors in compressed data are more serious as they may cause the decoder to lose sync.

In magnetic recording, data may be corrupted by mechanical problems such as media dropout and poor tracking or head contact, or Gaussian thermal noise in replay circuits and heads. In optical recording, contamination of the medium interrupts the light beam. When group codes are used, a single defect in a group changes the group symbol and may cause errors up to the size of the group. Single-bit errors are therefore less common in group-coded channels. Inside equipment, data are conveyed on short wires and the noise environment is under the designer's control. With suitable design techniques, errors may be made effectively negligible, whereas in communication systems, there is considerably less control of the electromagnetic environment.

Irrespective of the cause, all these mechanisms cause one of two effects. There are large isolated corruptions, called error bursts, in which numerous bits are corrupted all together in an area that is otherwise error-free, or there are random errors affecting single bits or symbols. Whatever the mechanism, the result will be that the received data will not be exactly the same as those sent. In binary the discrete bits will each be either right or wrong. If a binary digit is known to be wrong, it is necessary only to invert its state and then it must be right. Thus error correction itself is trivial; the hard part is working out *which* bits need correcting.

There are a number of terms that have idiomatic meanings in error correction. The raw BER (bit error rate) is the error rate of the medium or channel, whereas the residual or uncorrected BER is the rate at which the error-correction system fails to detect or miscorrects errors. In practical digital systems, the residual BER is negligibly small. If the error correction is turned off, the two figures become the same.

Error correction works by adding some bits to the data that are calculated from the data. This creates an entity called a code word, which spans a greater length of time than one bit alone. The statistics of noise means that, whilst one bit may be lost in a code word, the loss of the rest of the code word because of noise is highly improbable. As will be described later in this chapter, code words are designed to be able to correct totally a finite number of corrupted bits.

PARITY

The error-detection and error-correction processes are closely related and will be dealt with together here. The actual correction of an error is simplified tremendously by the adoption of binary. As there are only two symbols, zero and one, it is enough to know that a symbol is wrong, and the correct value is obvious. Figure 8.35 shows a minimal circuit required for correction once the bit in error has been identified. The XOR (exclusive-OR) gate shows up extensively in error correction and the figure also shows the truth table. One way of remembering the characteristics of this useful device is that there will be an output when the inputs are different. Inspection of the truth table will show that there is an even number of ones in each row (zero is an even number) and so the device could also be called an even parity gate. The XOR gate is also an adder in modulo-2.

Parity is a fundamental concept in error detection. In Figure 8.36, an example is given of a four-bit data word that is to be protected. If an extra bit is added to the word, which is calculated in such a way that the total number of ones in the five-bit word is even, this property can be tested on receipt. The generation of the parity bit can be performed by a number of the ubiquitous XOR gates configured into what is known as a parity tree. In the figure, if a bit is corrupted, the received message will be seen no longer to have an even number of ones. If two bits are corrupted, the failure will be undetected.

Truth table
of XOR gate

A	B	C
0	0	0
0	1	1
1	0	1
1	1	0

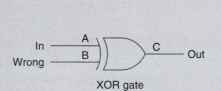

$$A \oplus B = C$$

FIGURE 8.35
Once the position of the error is identified, the correction process in binary is easy.

The greater the time span over which the coding is performed, or, on a recording medium, the greater the area over which the coding is performed, the greater will be the reliability achieved, although this does mean that an encoding delay will be experienced on recording and a similar or greater decoding delay on reproduction.

Shannon[14] disclosed that a message can be sent to any desired degree of accuracy provided that it is spread over a sufficient time span. Engineers have to compromise, because an infinite coding delay in the recovery of an error-free

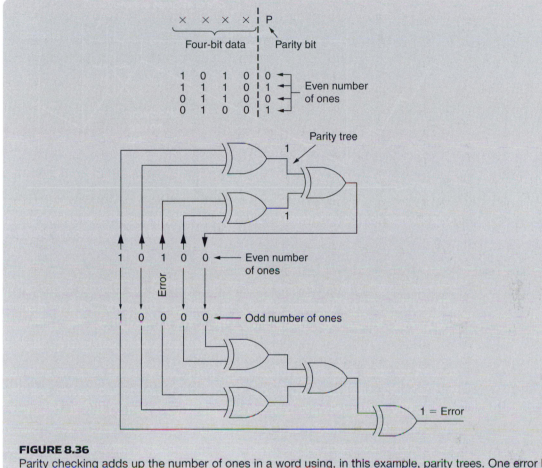

FIGURE 8.36
Parity checking adds up the number of ones in a word using, in this example, parity trees. One error bit and odd numbers of errors are detected. Even numbers of errors cannot be detected.

signal is not acceptable. Digital interfaces such as SDI (see Chapter 10) do not employ error correction because the buildup of coding delays in large production systems is unacceptable.

If error correction is necessary as a practical matter, it is then only a small step to put it to maximum use. All error correction depends on adding bits to the original message, and this, of course, increases the number of bits to be recorded, although it does not increase the information recorded. It might be imagined that error correction is going to reduce storage capacity, because space has to be found for all the extra bits. Nothing could be further from the truth. Once an error-correction system is used, the signal-to-noise ratio of the channel can be reduced, because the raised BER of the channel will be overcome by the error-correction system. Reduction of the SNR by three dB in a magnetic track can be achieved by halving the track width, provided that the system is not dominated by head or preamplifier noise. This doubles the recording density, making the storage of the additional bits needed for error correction a trivial matter. By a similar argument, the power of a digital transmitter can be reduced if error correction is used. In short, error correction is not a nuisance to be tolerated; it is a vital tool needed to maximise the efficiency of storage devices and transmission. Information technology would not be economically viable without it.

Figure 8.37 shows the broad subdivisions of error handling. The first stage might be called error avoidance and includes such measures as creating bad block files on hard disks or using verified media. Properly terminating network cabling is also in this category. Placing the audio blocks near to the centre of the tape in DVTRs is a further example. The data pass through the channel, which causes whatever corruptions it feels like. On receipt of the data the occurrence of errors is first detected, and this process must be extremely reliable, as it does not matter how effective the correction or how good the

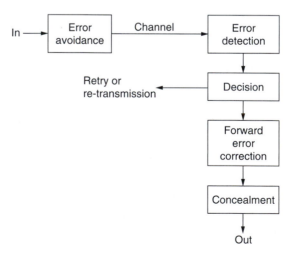

FIGURE 8.37
Error-handling strategies can be divided into avoiding errors, detecting errors, and deciding what to do about them. Some possibilities are shown here. Of all these, detection is the most critical, as nothing can be done if the error is not detected.

concealment algorithm if it is not known that they are necessary! The detection of an error then results in a course of action being decided.

In the case of a file transfer, real-time operation is not required. If a disk drive detects a read error, a retry is easy, as the disk is turning at several thousand rpm and will quickly re-present the data. An error due to a dust particle may not occur on the next revolution. A packet in error in a network will result in a re-transmission. Many magnetic tape systems have *read after write*. During recording, off-tape data are immediately checked for errors. If an error is detected, the tape may abort the recording, reverse to the beginning of the current block, and erase it. The data from that block may then be recorded farther down the tape. This is the recording equivalent of a re-transmission in a communications system.

In many cases of digital video or audio replay a retry or re-transmission is not possible because the data are required in real time. In this case the solution is to encode the message using a system that is sufficiently powerful to correct the errors in real time. These are called forward error-correcting schemes. The term "forward" implies that the transmitter does not need to take any action in the case of an error; the receiver will perform the correction.

Error correction uses its own idiomatic terminology, which will be defined here. The extra bits added to the message carry no information, because they are calculated from the original data. They are therefore called *redundant* bits.

The addition of redundancy gives the message a special property. In the case of parity, that property is that the number of ones is even, although in more advanced codes the property can be described only mathematically. A message having some special property *irrespective of the actual data content* is called a code word. All error correction relies on adding redundancy to real data to form code words for transmission. If any corruption occurs, the intention is that the received message will not have the special property; in other words, if the received message is not a code word there has definitely been an error. The receiver can check for the special property without any prior knowledge of the data content. Thus the same check can be made on all received data. If the received message is a code word, there probably has not been an error. The word "probably" must be used because of the possibility that the error turns one code word into another, which cannot be discerned from an error-free message.

If it is known that generally the only failure mechanism in the channel in question is the loss of a single bit, it is *assumed* that receipt of a code word means

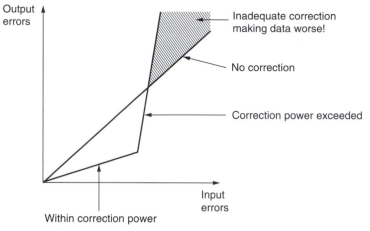
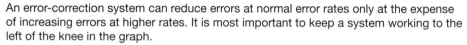

FIGURE 8.38

An error-correction system can reduce errors at normal error rates only at the expense of increasing errors at higher rates. It is most important to keep a system working to the left of the knee in the graph.

that there has been no error. If there is a probability of two error bits, that becomes very nearly the probability of failing to detect an error, because all odd numbers of errors will be detected, and a four-bit error is much less likely. It is paramount in all error-correction systems that the protection used should be appropriate for the probability of errors to be encountered. An inadequate error-correction system is actually worse than not having any correction. Error correction works by trading probabilities. Error-free performance with a certain error rate is achieved at the expense of performance at higher error rates. Figure 8.38 shows the effect of an error-correction system on the residual BER for a given raw BER. It will be seen that there is a characteristic knee in the graph. If the expected raw BER has been misjudged, the consequences can be disastrous. Another result demonstrated by the example is that we can guarantee only to detect the same number of bits in error as there are redundant bits.

CONCEALMENT BY INTERPOLATION

There are some practical differences between data recording for video and the computer data recording application. Although video or audio recorders seldom have time for retries, they have the advantage that there is a certain amount of redundancy in the information conveyed. Thus if an error cannot be corrected, then it can be concealed. If a sample is lost, it is possible to obtain an approximation to it by interpolating between samples in the vicinity of the missing one. Clearly concealment of any kind cannot be used with computer instructions or compressed data, although concealment can be applied after compressed signals have been decoded.

If there is too much corruption for concealment, the only course in video is to repeat the previous field or frame in a freeze as it is unlikely that the corrupt picture is watchable. In audio the equivalent is muting.

In general, if use is to be made of concealment on replay, the data must generally be reordered or shuffled prior to recording. To take a simple example, odd-numbered samples and even-numbered samples are recorded in different areas of the medium. On playback, if a gross error occurs on the medium, depending on its position, the result will be either corrupted odd samples or corrupted even samples, but it is most unlikely that both will be lost. Interpolation is then possible if the power of the correction system is exceeded. In practice the shuffle employed in digital video recorders is two-dimensional and rather more complex. Further details can be found in Chapter 9. The concealment technique described here is suitable only for PCM recording. If compression has been employed, different concealment techniques will be needed.

It should be stressed that corrected data are indistinguishable from the original and thus there can be no visible or audible artifacts. In contrast, concealment is only an approximation to the original information and could be detectable. In practical equipment, concealment occurs infrequently unless there is a defect requiring attention, and its presence is difficult to see.

BLOCK AND CONVOLUTIONAL CODES

Figure 8.39a shows a strategy known as a crossword code, or product code. The data are formed into a two-dimensional array, in which each location can be a single bit or a multibit symbol. Parity is then generated on both rows and columns. If a single bit or symbol fails, one row parity check and one column parity check will fail, and the failure can be located at the intersection of the two failing checks. Although two symbols in error confuse this simple scheme, using more complex coding in a two-dimensional structure is very powerful, and further examples will be given throughout this chapter.

The example of Figure 8.39a assembles the data to be coded into a block of finite size and then each code word is calculated by taking a different set of

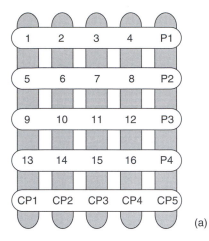

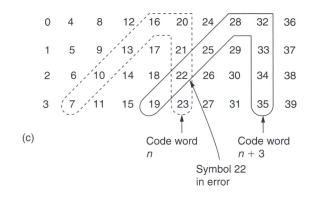

(c)

Code word
n

Code word
n + 3

Symbol 22
in error

(a)

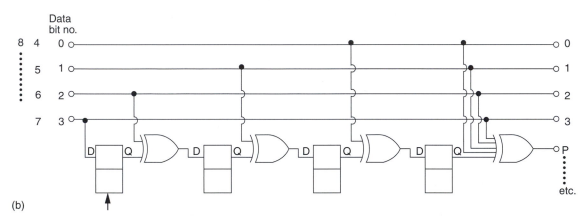

(b)

FIGURE 8.39

(a) A block code. Each location in the block can be a bit or a word. Horizontal parity checks are made by adding P1, P2, etc., and cross-parity or vertical checks are made by adding CP1, CP2, etc. Any symbol in error will be at the intersection of the two failing code words. (b) A convolutional coder. Symbols entering are subject to different delays, which result in the code words in (c) being calculated. These have a vertical part and a diagonal part. A symbol in error will be at the intersection of the diagonal part of one code and the vertical part of another.

symbols. This should be contrasted with the operation of the circuit of (b). Here the data are not in a block, but form an endless stream. A shift register allows four symbols to be available simultaneously to the encoder. The action of the encoder depends upon the delays. When symbol 3 emerges from the first delay, it will be added (modulo-2) to symbol 6. When this sum emerges from the second delay, it will be added to symbol 9 and so on. The code word produced is shown in Figure 8.39c, in which it can be seen to be bent such that it has a vertical section and a diagonal section. Four symbols later the next code word will be created one column farther over in the data.

This is a convolutional code because the coder always takes parity on the same pattern of symbols, which is convolved with the data stream on an endless basis. Figure 8.39c also shows that if an error occurs, it can be located because it will cause parity errors in two code words. The error will be on the diagonal part of one code word and on the vertical part of the other so that it can be located uniquely at the intersection and corrected by parity.

Comparison with the block code of Figure 8.39a will show that the convolutional code needs less redundancy for the same single symbol location and correction performance as only a single redundant symbol is required for every four data symbols. Convolutional codes are computed on an endless basis, which makes them inconvenient in recording applications where editing is anticipated. Here the block code is more appropriate as it allows edit gaps to be created between codes. In the case of uncorrectable errors, the convolutional principle causes the syndromes to be affected for some time afterward and results in miscorrections of symbols that were not actually in error. This is called error propagation and is a characteristic of convolutional codes. Recording media tend to produce somewhat variant error statistics because media defects and mechanical problems cause errors that do not fit the classical additive noise channel. Convolutional codes can easily be taken beyond their correcting power if used with real recording media.

In transmission and broadcasting, the error statistics are more stable and the editing requirement is absent. As a result convolutional codes tend to be used in digital broadcasting as will be seen in Chapter 10.

CYCLIC CODES

In digital recording applications, the data are stored serially on a track, and it is desirable to use relatively large data blocks to reduce the amount of the medium devoted to preambles, addressing, and synchronising. The principle of code words having a special characteristic will still be employed, but they will be generated and checked algorithmically by equations. The syndrome will then be converted to the bit(s) in error by solving equations.

When data can be accessed serially, simple circuitry can be used because the same gate will be used for many XOR operations. The circuit of Figure 8.40 is a kind of shift register, but with a particular feedback arrangement, which leads

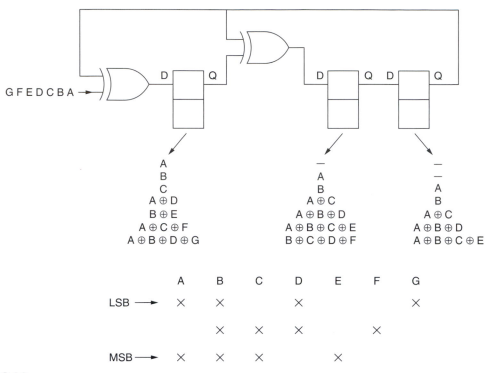

FIGURE 8.40
When seven successive bits A–G are clocked into this circuit, the contents of the three latches are shown for each clock. The final result is a parity-check matrix.

it to be known as a twisted-ring counter. If seven message bits A–G are applied serially to this circuit, and each one of them is clocked, the outcome can be followed in the diagram. As bit A is presented and the system is clocked, bit A will enter the left-hand latch. When bits B and C are presented, A moves across to the right. Both XOR gates will have A on the upper input from the right-hand latch, the left one has D on the lower input, and the right one has B on the lower input. When clocked, the left latch will thus be loaded with the XOR of A and D, and the right one with the XOR of A and B. The remainder of the sequence can be followed, bearing in mind that when the same term appears on both inputs of an XOR gate, it goes out, as the exclusive-OR of something with itself is nothing. At the end of the process, the latches contain three different expressions. Essentially, the circuit makes three parity checks through the message, leaving the result of each in the three stages of the register. In the figure, these expressions have been used to draw up a check matrix. The significance of these steps can now be explained.

The bits A, B, C, and D are four data bits, and the bits E, F, and G are redundancy. When the redundancy is calculated, bit E is chosen so that there are an even number of ones in bits A, B, C, and E; bit F is chosen such that the same applies to bits B, C, D, and F, and similarly for bit G. Thus the four data bits and the three check bits form a seven-bit code word. If there is no error in the code word, when it is fed into the circuit shown, the result of each of the three parity checks will be zero and every stage of the shift register will be cleared. As the register has eight possible states, and one of them is the error-free condition, then there are seven remaining states, hence the seven-bit code word.

If a bit in the code word is corrupted, there will be a non-zero result. For example, if bit D fails, the check on bits A, B, D, and G will fail, and a one will appear in the left-hand latch. The check on bits B, C, D, and F will also fail, and the centre latch will set. The check on bits A, B, C, and E will not fail, because D is not involved in it, making the right-hand bit zero. There will be a syndrome of 110 in the register, and this will be seen from the check matrix to correspond to an error in bit D. Whichever bit fails, there will be a different three-bit syndrome that uniquely identifies the failed bit.

As there are only three latches, there can be eight different syndromes. One of these is zero, which is the error-free condition, and so there are seven remaining error syndromes. The length of the code word cannot exceed seven bits, or there would not be enough syndromes to correct all the bits. This can also be made to tie in with the generation of the check matrix. If 14 bits, A to N, were fed into the circuit shown, the result would be that the check matrix repeated twice, and if a syndrome of 101 were to result, it could not be determined whether bit D or bit K failed. Because the check repeats every seven bits, the code is said to be a cyclic redundancy check (CRC) code.

It has been seen that the circuit shown makes a matrix check on a received word to determine if there has been an error, but the same circuit can also be used to generate the check bits. To visualize how this is done, examine what happens if only the data bits A, B, C, and D are known, and the check bits E, F, and G are set to zero. If this message, ABCD000, is fed into the circuit, the left-hand latch will afterward contain the XOR of A, B, C, and 0, which is, of course what E should be. The centre latch will contain the XOR of B, C, D, and 0, which is what F should be, and so on.

This process is not quite ideal, however, because it is necessary to wait for three clock periods after entering the data before the check bits are available. When

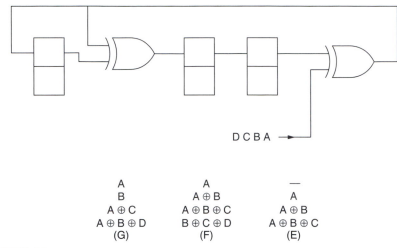

DCBA →

A	A	—
B	A ⊕ B	A
A ⊕ C	A ⊕ B ⊕ C	A ⊕ B
A ⊕ B ⊕ D	B ⊕ C ⊕ D	A ⊕ B ⊕ C
(G)	(F)	(E)

FIGURE 8.41
By moving the insertion point three places to the right, the calculation of the check bits is completed in only four clock periods and they can follow the data immediately. This is equivalent to premultiplying the data by three.

the data are simultaneously being recorded and fed into the encoder, the delay would prevent the check bits being easily added to the end of the data stream. This problem can be overcome by slightly modifying the encoder circuit as shown in Figure 8.41. By moving the position of the input to the right, the operation of the circuit is advanced so that the check bits are ready after only four clocks. The process can be followed in the diagram for the four data bits A, B, C, and D. On the first clock, bit A enters the left two latches, whereas on the second clock, bit B will appear on the upper input of the left XOR gate, with bit A on the lower input, causing the centre latch to load the XOR of A and B, and so on.

The way in which the cyclic codes work has been described in engineering terms, but it can be described mathematically if analysis is contemplated.

Just as the position of a decimal digit in a number determines the power of 10 (whether that digit means 1, 10, or 100), the position of a binary digit determines the power of 2 (whether it means 1, 2, or 4). It is possible to rewrite a binary number so that it is expressed as a list of powers of 2. For example, the binary number 1101 means $8 + 4 + 1$ and can be written

$$2^3 + 2^2 + 2^0.$$

INTERLEAVING

The concept of bit interleaving was introduced in connection with a single-bit correcting code to allow it to correct small bursts. With burst-correcting codes such as Reed–Solomon, bit interleave is unnecessary. In most channels, particularly high-density recording channels used for digital video or audio, the burst size may be many bytes rather than bits, and to rely on a code alone to correct such errors would require a lot of redundancy. The solution in this case is to employ symbol interleaving, as shown in Figure 8.42. Several code words are encoded from input data, but these are not recorded in the order they were input, but are physically reordered in the channel, so that a real burst error is split into smaller bursts in several code words. The size of the burst seen by each code word is now determined primarily by the parameters of the interleave, and Figure 8.43 shows that the probability of occurrence of bursts with respect to the burst length in a given code word is modified. The number of bits in the interleave word can be made equal to the burst-correcting ability of the code in the knowledge that it will be exceeded only very infrequently.

There are a number of different ways in which interleaving can be performed. Figure 8.44 shows that in block interleaving, words are re-ordered within blocks, which are themselves in the correct order. This approach is attractive for rotary-head recorders, because the scanning process naturally divides the tape up into blocks. The block interleave is achieved by writing samples into a memory in sequential address locations from a counter, and reading the memory with nonsequential addresses from a sequencer. The effect is to convert a one-dimensional sequence of samples into a two-dimensional structure having rows and columns.

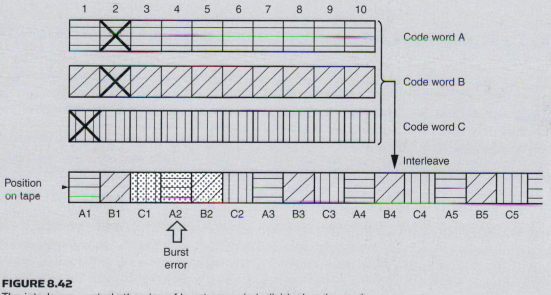

FIGURE 8.42
The interleave controls the size of burst errors in individual code words.

The alternative to block interleaving is convolutional interleaving, in which the interleave process is endless. In Figure 8.45 symbols are assembled into short blocks and then delayed by an amount proportional to the position in the block. It will be seen from the figure that the delays have the effect of shearing the symbols so that columns on the left side of the diagram become diagonals on the right. When the columns on the right are read, the convolutional interleave will be obtained. Convolutional interleave works well in transmission applications such as DVB, in which there is no natural track break. Convolutional interleave has the advantage of requiring less memory to implement than a block code. This is because a block code requires the entire block to be written into the memory before it can be read, whereas a convolutional code requires only enough memory to cause the required delays.

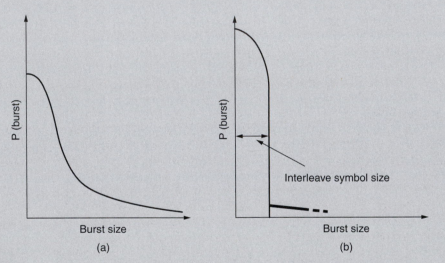

FIGURE 8.43
(a) The distribution of burst sizes might look like this. (b) Following interleave, the burst size within a code word is controlled to that of the interleave symbol size, except for gross errors, which have low probability.

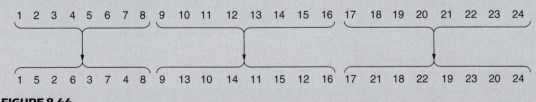

FIGURE 8.44
In block interleaving, data are scrambled within blocks, which are themselves in the correct order.

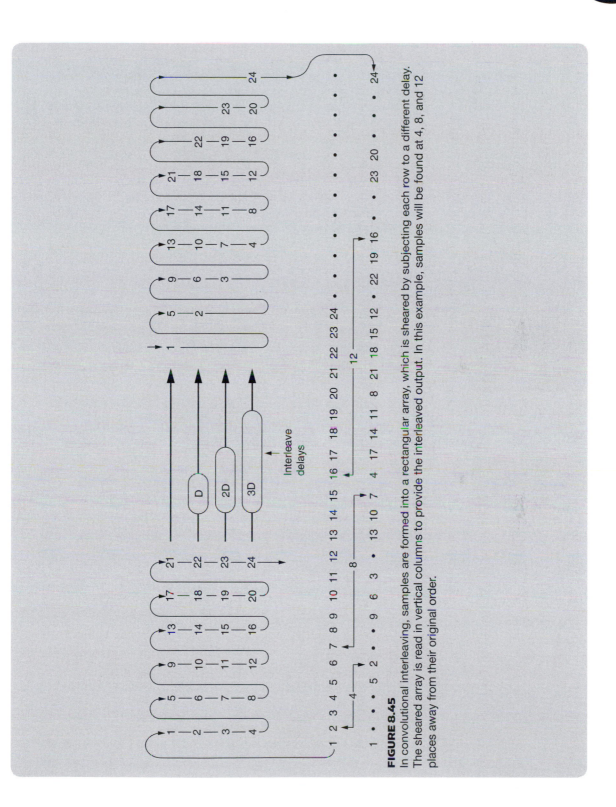

FIGURE 8.45

In convolutional interleaving, samples are formed into a rectangular array, which is sheared by subjecting each row to a different delay. The sheared array is read in vertical columns to provide the interleaved output. In this example, samples will be found at 4, 8, and 12 places away from their original order.

In fact, much of the theory of error correction applies to symbols in number bases other than 2, so that the number can also be written more generally as

$$x^3 + x^2 + 1 \ (x^0 = 1),$$

which also looks much more impressive. This expression, containing as it does various powers, is of course a polynomial, and the circuit of Figure 8.40, which has been seen to construct a parity-check matrix on a code word, can also be described as calculating the remainder due to dividing the input by a polynomial using modulo-2 arithmetic. In modulo-2 there are no borrows or carries, and addition and subtraction are replaced by the XOR function, which makes hardware implementation very easy. In Figure 8.46 it can be seen that the circuit of Figure 8.47 actually divides the code word by a polynomial, which is

$$x^3 + x + 1 \quad \text{or} \quad 1011.$$

This can be deduced from the fact that the righthand bit is fed into two lower-order stages of the register at once. Once all the bits of the message have been clocked in, the circuit contains the remainder. In mathematical terms, the special property of a code word is that it is a polynomial that yields a remainder of 0 when divided by the generating polynomial. The receiver will make this division, and the result should be zero in the error-free case. Thus the code word itself disappears from the division. If an error has occurred it is considered that this is due to an error polynomial that has been added to the code word polynomial. If a code word divided by the check polynomial is zero, a nonzero syndrome must represent the error polynomial divided by the check polynomial. Thus if the syndrome is multiplied by the check polynomial, the latter will be cancelled out and the result will be the error polynomial. If this is added modulo-2 to the received word, it will cancel out the error and leave the corrected data.

Some examples of modulo-2 division are given in Figure 8.46, which can be compared with the parallel computation of parity checks according to the matrix of Figure 8.40.

The process of generating the code word from the original data can also be described mathematically. If a code word has to give zero remainder when divided, it follows that the data can be converted to a code word by adding the remainder when the data are divided. Generally speaking the remainder would have to be subtracted, but in modulo-2 there is no distinction. This process is also illustrated in Figure 8.46. The four data bits have three zeros placed on the right-hand end, to make the word length equal to that of a code word, and this

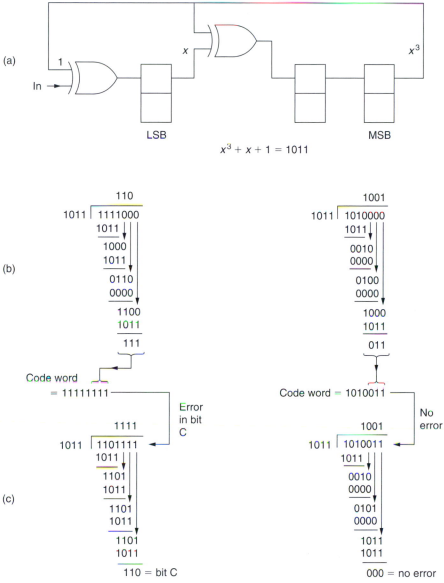

FIGURE 8.46
Circuit of Figure 8.40 divides by $x^3 + x + 1$ to find remainder. In (b) this is used to calculate check bits. In (c) right, zero syndrome, no error.

word is then divided by the polynomial to calculate the remainder. The remainder is added to the zero-extended data to form a code word. The modified circuit of Figure 8.41 can be described as premultiplying the data by x^3 before dividing.

CRC codes are of primary importance for detecting errors, and several have been standardised for use in digital communications. The most common of these are

$$x^{16} + x^{15} + x^2 + 1 \text{ (CRC-16)},$$

$$x^{16} + x^{12} + x^5 + 1 \text{ (CRC-CCITT)}.$$

The 16-bit cyclic codes have code words of length $2^{16} - 1$ or 65,535 bits. This may be too long for the application. Another problem with very long codes is that with a given raw BER, the longer the code, the more errors will occur in it. There may be enough errors to exceed the power of the code. The solution in both cases is to shorten or puncture the code. Figure 8.47 shows that in a punctured code, only the end of the code word is used, and the data and redundancy are preceded by a string of zeros. It is not necessary to record these zeros, and, of course, errors cannot occur in them. Implementing a punctured code is easy. If a CRC generator starts with the register cleared and is fed with serial ones, it will not change its state. Thus it is not necessary to provide the zeros; encoding can begin with the first data bit. In the same way, the leading zeros need not be provided during playback. The only precaution needed is that if a syndrome calculates the location of an error, this will be from the beginning of the code word, not from the beginning of the data. When codes are used for detection only, this is of no consequence.

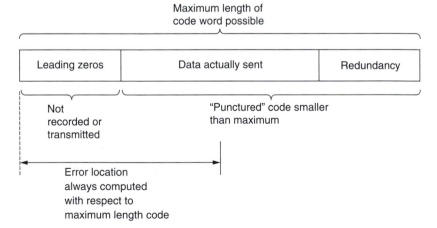

FIGURE 8.47
Code words are often shortened, or punctured, which means that only the end of the code word is actually transmitted. The only precaution to be taken when puncturing codes is that the computed position of an error will be from the beginning of the code word, not from the beginning of the message.

THE REED–SOLOMON CODES

The Reed–Solomon codes (Irving Reed and Gustave Solomon) are inherently burst correcting[15] because they work on multi-bit symbols rather than individual bits. The R-S codes are also extremely flexible in use. One code may be used both to detect and to correct errors and the number of bursts that are correctable can be chosen at the design stage by the amount of redundancy. A further advantage of the R-S codes is that they can be used in conjunction with a separate error-detection mechanism, in which case they perform the correction only by erasure. R-S codes operate at the theoretical limit of correcting efficiency. In other words, no more efficient code can be found.

In the simple CRC system, the effect of the error is detected by ensuring that the code word can be divided by a polynomial. The CRC code word was created by adding a redundant symbol to the data. In the Reed–Solomon codes, several errors can be isolated by ensuring that the code word will divide by a number of polynomials. Clearly if the code word must divide by, say, two polynomials, it must have two redundant symbols. This is the minimum case of an R-S code. On receiving an R-S-coded message there will be two syndromes following the division. In the error-free case, these will both be zero. If both are not zero, there is an error.

The effect of an error is to add an error polynomial to the message polynomial. The number of terms in the error polynomial is the same as the number of errors in the code word. The code word divides to zero and the syndromes are a function of the error only. There are two syndromes and two equations. By solving these simultaneous equations it is possible to obtain two unknowns. One of these is the position of the error, known as the *locator,* and the other is the error bit pattern, known as the *corrector.* As the locator is the same size as the code symbol, the length of the code word is determined by the size of the symbol. A symbol size of eight bits is commonly used because it fits in conveniently with both 16-bit audio samples and byte-oriented computers. An eight-bit syndrome results in a locator of the same word length. Eight bits have 2^8 combinations, but one of these is the error-free condition, and so the locator can specify one of only 255 symbols. As each symbol contains eight bits, the code word will be $255 \times 8 = 2040$ bits long.

As further examples, five-bit symbols could be used to form a code word 31 symbols long, and three-bit symbols would form a code word seven symbols long. The latter size is small enough to permit some worked examples and will be used further here. Figure 8.48 shows that in the seven-symbol code word, five symbols of three bits

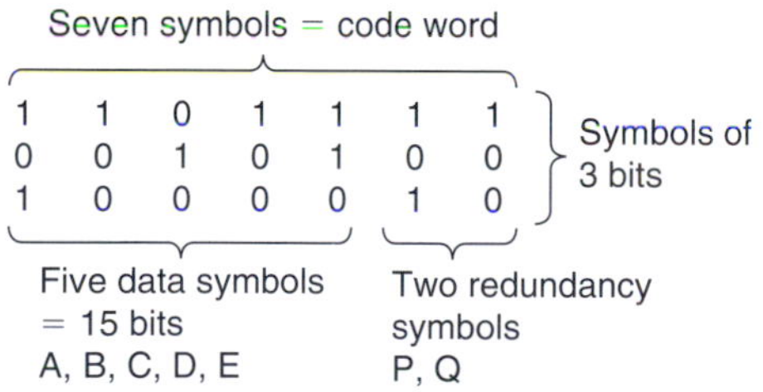

FIGURE 8.48

A Reed–Solomon code word. As the symbols are of three bits, there can only be eight possible syndrome values. One of these is all zeros, the error-free case, and so it is possible only to point to seven errors; hence the code word length of seven symbols. Two of these are redundant, leaving five data symbols.

each, A–E, are the data, and P and Q are the two redundant symbols. This simple example will locate and correct a single symbol in error. It does not matter, however, how many bits in the symbol are in error.

The two check symbols are solutions to the following equations,

$$A \oplus B \oplus C \oplus D \oplus E \oplus P \oplus Q = 0 \ (\oplus = \text{XOR symbol}),$$

$$a^7A \oplus a^6B \oplus a^5C \oplus a^4D \oplus a^3E \oplus a^2P \oplus aQ = 0,$$

where a is a constant. The original data A–E followed by the redundancy P and Q pass through the channel.

The receiver makes two checks on the message to see if it is a code word. This is done by calculating syndromes using the following expressions, where the (') implies the received symbol, which is not necessarily correct:

$$S_0 = A' \oplus B' \oplus C' \oplus D' \oplus E' \oplus P' \oplus Q'$$

(this is in fact a simple parity check)

$$S_1 = a^7A' \oplus a^6B' \oplus a^5C' \oplus a^4D' \oplus a^3E' \oplus a^2P' \oplus aQ'.$$

If two syndromes of all zeros are not obtained, there has been an error. The information carried in the syndromes will be used to correct the error. For the purpose of illustration, let it be considered that D' has been corrupted before moving to the general case. D' can be considered to be the result of adding an error of value E in the original value D such that $D' = D \oplus E$.

$$\text{As } A \oplus B \oplus C \oplus D \oplus E \oplus P \oplus Q = 0,$$

$$\text{then } A \oplus B \oplus C \oplus (D \oplus E) \oplus E \oplus P \oplus Q = E = S_0.$$

$$\text{As } D' = D \oplus E,$$

$$\text{then } D = D' \oplus E = D' \oplus S_0.$$

Thus the value of the corrector is known immediately because it is the same as the parity syndrome S_0. The corrected data symbol is obtained simply by adding S_0 to the incorrect symbol.

At this stage, however, the corrupted symbol has not yet been identified, but this is equally straightforward:

$$\text{As } a^7A \oplus a^6B \oplus a^5C \oplus a^4D \oplus a^3E \oplus a^2P \oplus aQ = 0,$$

then

$$a^7A \oplus a^6B \oplus a^5C \oplus a^4(D \oplus E) \oplus a^3E \oplus a^2P \oplus aQ = a^4E = S_1.$$

Thus the syndrome S_1 is the error bit pattern E, but it has been raised to a power of a that is a function of the position of the error symbol in the block. If the position of the error is in symbol k, then k is the locator value and

$$S_0 \times a^k = S_1.$$

Hence:

$$a^k = S_1/S_0.$$

The value of k can be found by multiplying S_0 by various powers of a until the product is the same as S_1. Then the power of a necessary is equal to k. The use of the descending powers of a in the code-word calculation is now clear because the error is then multiplied by a different power of a dependent upon its position, known as the locator because it gives the position of the error. The process of finding the error position by experiment is known as a Chien search.

Whilst the expressions above show that the values of P and Q are such that the two syndrome expressions sum to 0, it is not yet clear how P and Q are calculated from the data. Expressions for P and Q can be found by solving the two R–S equations simultaneously. For a Reed–Solomon code word over GF (2^3), there will be seven three-bit symbols. For location and correction of one symbol, there must be two redundant symbols, P and Q, leaving A–E for data.

The following expressions must be true, where a is the primitive element of $x^3 \oplus x \oplus 1$ and $\oplus$ is XOR throughout:

$$A \oplus B \oplus C \oplus D \oplus E \oplus P \oplus Q = 0 \tag{8.1}$$

$$a^7A \oplus a^6B \oplus a^5C \oplus a^4D \oplus a^3E \oplus a^2P \oplus aQ = 0 \tag{8.2}$$

Dividing Eq. (8.2) by a:

$$a^6A \oplus a^5B \oplus a^4C \oplus a^3D \oplus a^2E \oplus aP \oplus Q = 0$$

$$= A \oplus B \oplus C \oplus D \oplus E \oplus P \oplus Q.$$

Cancelling Q, and collecting terms:

$$(a^6 \oplus 1)A \oplus (a^5 \oplus 1)B \oplus (a^4 \oplus 1)C \oplus (a^3 \oplus 1)D \oplus (a^2 \oplus 1)E = (a + 1)P.$$

In Chapter 3 the operation of a Galois field was explained. Using that explanation, it is possible to calculate $(a^n + 1)$, e.g., $a^6 + 1 = 101 + 001 = 100 = a^2$. The result is

$$a^2A \oplus a^4B \oplus a^5C \oplus aD \oplus a^6E = a^3P,$$

$$P = a^6A \oplus aB \oplus a^2C \oplus a^5D \oplus a^3E.$$

Multiply Eq. (8.1) by a^2 and equating to Eq. (8.2):

$$a^2A \oplus a^2B \oplus a^2C \oplus a^2D \oplus a^2E \oplus a^2P \oplus a^2Q = 0$$

$$= a^7A \oplus a^6B \oplus a^5C \oplus a^4D \oplus a^3E \oplus a^2P \oplus aQ.$$

Cancelling terms a^2P and collecting terms (remember $a^2 \oplus a^2 = 0$):

$$(a^7 \oplus a^2)A \oplus (a^6 \oplus a^2)B \oplus (a^5 \oplus a^2)C \oplus (a^4 \oplus a^2)D \oplus (a^3 \oplus a^2)E = (a^2 \oplus a)Q.$$

Adding powers according to Chapter 3, e.g.,

$$a^7 \oplus a^2 = 001 \oplus 100 = 101 = a^6:$$

$$a^6A \oplus B \oplus a^3C \oplus aD \oplus a^5E = a^4Q,$$

$$Q = a^2A \oplus a^3B \oplus a^6C \oplus a^4D \oplus aE.$$

The above expressions must be used to calculate P and Q from the data to satisfy the code word equations.

In both the calculation of the redundancy shown here and the calculation of the corrector and the locator it is necessary to perform numerous multiplications and raising to powers. This appears to present a formidable calculation problem at both the encoder and the decoder. This would be the case if the calculations involved were conventionally executed. However, the calculations can be simplified by using logarithms. Instead of multiplying two numbers, their logarithms are added. To find the cube of a number, its logarithm is added three times. Division is performed by subtracting the logarithms. Thus all the manipulations necessary can be achieved with addition or subtraction, which are straightforward in logic circuits.

The success of this approach depends upon simple implementation of log tables. As was seen in Chapter 3, raising a constant, a, known as the *primitive element*, to successively higher powers in modulo-2 gives rise to a Galois field. Each element of the field represents a different power n of a. It is a fundamental of the R-S codes that all the symbols used for data, redundancy, and syndromes are considered to be elements of a Galois field. The number of bits in the symbol determines the size of the Galois field and hence the number of symbols in the code word.

In Figure 8.49, the binary values of the elements are shown alongside the power of a they represent. In the R-S codes, symbols are no longer considered simply as binary numbers, but also as equivalent powers of a. In Reed–Solomon coding and decoding, each symbol will be multiplied by some power of a. Thus if the symbol is

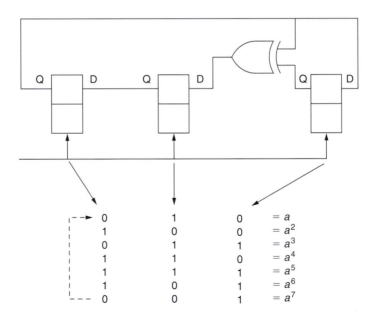

FIGURE 8.49
The bit patterns of a Galois field expressed as powers of the primitive element a. This diagram can be used as a form of log table to multiply binary numbers. Instead of an actual multiplication, the appropriate powers of a are simply added.

also known as a power of a it is necessary only to add the two powers. For example, if it is necessary to multiply the data symbol 100 by a^3, the calculation proceeds as follows, referring to Figure 8.49:

$$100 = a^2 \text{ so } 100 \times a^3 = a^{(2+3)} = a^5 = 111.$$

Note that the results of a Galois multiplication are quite different from binary multiplication. Because all products must be elements of the field, sums of powers that exceed seven wrap around by having seven subtracted. For example:

$$a^5 \times a^6 = a^{11} = a^4 = 110.$$

Figure 8.50 shows some examples of circuits that will perform this kind of multiplication. Note that they require a minimum amount of logic.

Figure 8.51 shows an example of the Reed–Solomon encoding process. The Galois field shown in Figure 8.49 has been used, having the primitive element $a = 010$. At the beginning of the calculation of P, the symbol A is multiplied by a^6. This is done by converting A to a power of a. According to Figure 8.49, $101 = a^6$ and so the product will be $a^{(6+6)} = a^{12} = a^5 = 111$. In the same way, B is multiplied by a, and so on, and the products are added modulo-2. A similar process is used to calculate Q.

Figure 8.52 shows a circuit that can calculate P or Q. The symbols A–E are presented in succession, and the circuit is clocked for each one. On the first clock, a^6A is stored in the left-hand latch. If B is now provided at the

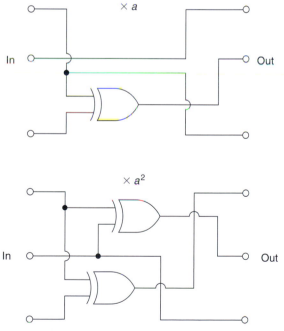

FIGURE 8.50
Some examples of GF multiplier circuits.

$$
\begin{array}{llll}
& A & 101 & a^6A = 111 & a^2A = 010 \\
\text{Input} & B & 100 & a\,B = 011 & a^3B = 111 \\
\text{data} & C & 010 & a^2C = 011 & a^6C = 001 \\
& D & 100 & a^5D = 001 & a^4D = 101 \\
& E & 111 & a^3E = \underline{010} & a\,E = \underline{101} \\
\text{Check} & P & 100 & \quad\quad\ 100 & \quad\quad\ 100 \\
\text{symbols} & Q & 100
\end{array}
$$

$$
\begin{array}{lll}
& A & 101 & a^7A = 101 \\
& B & 100 & a^6B = 010 \\
& C & 010 & a^5C = 101 \\
\text{Code word} & D & 100 & a^4D = 101 \\
& E & 111 & a^3E = 010 \\
& P & 100 & a^2P = 110 \\
& Q & 100 & a\,Q = \underline{011} \\
& S_0 & = \overline{000} & S_1 = \overline{000} \longleftarrow \text{Both syndromes zero}
\end{array}
$$

FIGURE 8.51
Five data symbols A–E are used as terms in the generator polynomials to calculate the two redundant symbols P and Q. An example is shown at the top. Beneath is the result of using the code-word symbols A–Q as terms in the checking polynomials. As there is no error, both syndromes are zero.

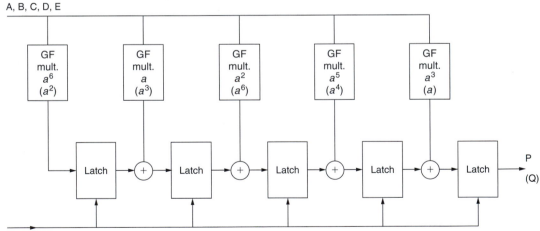

FIGURE 8.52
If the five data symbols of Figure 8.51 are supplied to this circuit in sequence, after five clocks, one of the check symbols will appear at the output. Terms without parentheses will calculate P, terms in parentheses calculate Q.

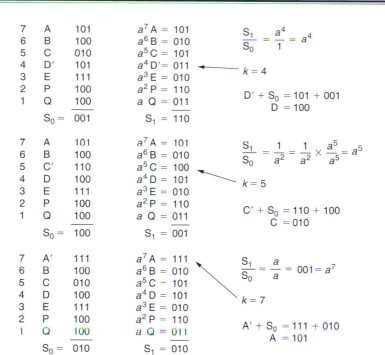

First example:

7	A	101	$a^7 A = 101$	$\dfrac{S_1}{S_0} = \dfrac{a^4}{1} = a^4$
6	B	100	$a^6 B = 010$	
5	C	010	$a^5 C = 101$	
4	D'	101	$a^4 D' = 011$	$k = 4$
3	E	111	$a^3 E = 010$	
2	P	100	$a^2 P = 110$	
1	Q	100	$a\, Q = 011$	$D' + S_0 = 101 + 001$
	$S_0 =$ 001		$S_1 =$ 110	$D = 100$

Second example:

7	A	101	$a^7 A = 101$	$\dfrac{S_1}{S_0} = \dfrac{1}{a^2} = \dfrac{1}{a^2} \times \dfrac{a^5}{a^5} = a^5$
6	B	100	$a^6 B = 010$	
5	C'	110	$a^5 C = 100$	
4	D	100	$a^4 D = 101$	$k = 5$
3	E	111	$a^3 E = 010$	
2	P	100	$a^2 P = 110$	
1	Q	100	$a\, Q = 011$	$C' + S_0 = 110 + 100$
	$S_0 =$ 100		$S_1 =$ 001	$C = 010$

Third example:

7	A'	111	$a^7 A = 111$	$\dfrac{S_1}{S_0} = \dfrac{a}{a} = 001 = a^7$
6	B	100	$a^6 B = 010$	
5	C	010	$a^5 C = 101$	
4	D	100	$a^4 D = 101$	$k = 7$
3	E	111	$a^3 E = 010$	
2	P	100	$a^2 P = 110$	
1	Q	100	$a\, Q = 011$	$A' + S_0 = 111 + 010$
	$S_0 =$ 010		$S_1 =$ 010	$A = 101$

FIGURE 8.53
Three examples of error location and correction. The number of bits in error in a symbol is irrelevant; if all three were wrong, S_0 would be 111, but correction is still possible.

input, the second GF multiplier produces aB and this is added to the output of the first latch and when clocked will be stored in the second latch, which now contains $a^6A + aB$. The process continues in this fashion until the complete expression for P is available in the right-hand latch. The intermediate contents of the right-hand latch are ignored.

The entire code word now exists and can be recorded or transmitted. Figure 8.53 also demonstrates that the code word satisfies the checking equations. The modulo-2 sum of the seven symbols, S_0, is 000 because each column has an even number of ones. The calculation of S_1 requires multiplication by descending powers of a. The modulo-2 sum of the products is again zero. These calculations confirm that the redundancy calculation was properly carried out.

Figure 8.53 gives three examples of error correction based on this code word. The erroneous symbol is marked with a prime. As there has been an error, the syndromes S_0 and S_1 will not be zero.

Figure 8.54 shows circuits suitable for parallel calculation of the two syndromes at the receiver. The S_0 circuit is a simple parity checker, which accumulates the modulo-2 sum of all symbols fed to it. The S_1 circuit is more subtle, because it contains a GF multiplier in a feedback loop, such that early symbols fed in are raised to higher powers than later symbols because they have been recirculated through the GF multiplier more often. It is possible to

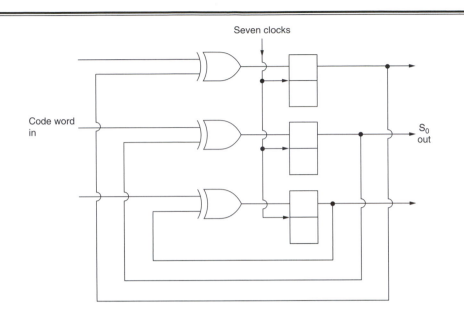

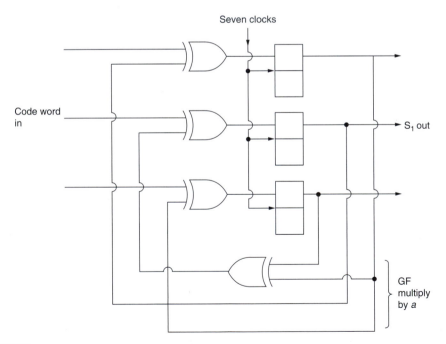

FIGURE 8.54

Circuits for parallel calculation of syndromes S_0 and S_1. S_0 is a simple parity check. S_1 has a GF multiplication by a in the feedback, so that A is multiplied by a^7, B is multiplied by a^6, etc., and all are summed to give S_1.

compare the operation of these circuits with the example of Figure 8.53 and with subsequent examples to confirm that the same results are obtained.

CORRECTION BY ERASURE

In the examples of Figure 8.53, two redundant symbols P and Q have been used to locate and correct one error symbol. If the positions of errors are known by some separate mechanism (see product codes) the locator need not be calculated. The simultaneous equations may instead be solved for two correctors. In this case the number of symbols that can be corrected is equal to the number of redundant symbols. In Figure 8.55a two errors have taken place, and it is known that they are in symbols C and D. Because S_0 is a simple parity check, it will reflect the modulo-2 sum of the two errors. Hence,

$$S_0 = EC \oplus ED.$$

The two errors will have been multiplied by different powers in S_1, such that

$$S_1 = a^5 EC \oplus a^4 ED.$$

These two equations can be solved, as shown in the figure, to find EC and ED, and the correct value of the symbols will be obtained by adding these correctors to the erroneous values. It is, however, easier to set the values of the symbols in error to zero. In this way the nature of the error is rendered irrelevant and it does not enter the calculation. This setting of symbols to zero gives rise to the term erasure. In this case,

$$S_0 = C \oplus D,$$
$$S_1 = a^5 C + a^4 D.$$

Erasing the symbols in error makes the errors equal to the correct symbol values and these are found more simply as shown in Figure 8.55b.

Practical systems will be designed to correct more symbols in error than in the simple examples given here. If it is proposed to correct by erasure an arbitrary number of symbols in error given by t, the code word must be divisible by t different polynomials. Alternatively if the errors must be located and corrected, $2t$ polynomials will be needed. These will be of the form $(x + a^n)$ where n takes all values up to t or $2t$. a is the primitive element of the Galois field discussed in Chapter 3.

Where four symbols are to be corrected by erasure, or two symbols are to be located and corrected, four redundant symbols are necessary, and the code-word polynomial must then be divisible by

$$(x + a^0)(x + a^1)(x + a^2)(x + a^3).$$

Upon receipt of the message, four syndromes must be calculated, and the four correctors or the two error patterns and their positions are determined by solving four simultaneous equations. This generally requires an iterative procedure, and a number of algorithms have been developed for the purpose.[16–18] Modern DVTR formats use eight-bit R-S codes and erasure extensively. The primitive polynomial commonly used with GF(256) is

$$x^8 + x^4 + x^3 + x^2 + 1.$$

$$
\begin{array}{lll}
A & 101 & a^7A = & 101 \\
B & 100 & a^6B = & 010 \\
(C \oplus E_C) & 001 & a^5(C \oplus E_C) & 111 \\
(D \oplus E_D) & 010 & a^4(D \oplus E_D) & 111 \\
E & 111 & a^3E = & 010 \\
P & 100 & a^2P = & 110 \\
Q & \underline{100} & a\,Q = & \underline{011} \\
S_1 & = 101 & S_1 = & 000
\end{array}
$$

$$S_0 = E_C \oplus E_D \qquad S_1 = a^5E_C \oplus a^4E_D$$

$$S_1 = a^5E_C \oplus a^4(S_0 \oplus E_C)$$

$$= a^5E_C \oplus a^4S_0 \oplus a^4E_C$$

$$\therefore E_C = \frac{S_1 \oplus a^4S_0}{a^5 \oplus a^4} = \frac{000 \oplus 011}{001} = 011$$

$$C = (C \oplus E_C) \oplus E_C = 001 \oplus 011 = \underline{010}$$

$$S_1 = a^5(S_0 \oplus E_D) \oplus a^4E_D$$

$$= a^5S_0 \oplus a^5E_D \oplus a^4E_D$$

$$\therefore E_D = \frac{S_1 \oplus a^5S_0}{a^5 \oplus a^4} = \frac{000 \oplus 110}{001} = 110$$

$$D = (D \oplus E_D) \oplus E_D = 010 \oplus 110 = \underline{100} \qquad \text{(a)}$$

$$
\begin{array}{lll}
A & 101 & a^7A = 101 \\
B & 100 & a^6B = 010 \qquad S_0 = C \oplus D \\
C & \underline{000} & a^5C = \underline{000} \qquad S_1 = a^5C \oplus a^4D \\
D & \underline{000} & a^4D = \underline{000} \\
E & 111 & a^3E = 010 \\
P & 100 & a^2P = 110 \\
Q & \underline{100} & a\,Q = \underline{011} \\
S_0 & = 100 & S_1 = 000
\end{array}
$$

$$S_1 = a^5S_0 \oplus a^5D \oplus a^4D = a^5S_0 \oplus D$$

$$\therefore D = S_1 \oplus a^5S_0 = 000 \oplus 100 = \underline{100}$$

$$S_1 = a^5C \oplus a^4C \oplus a^4S_0 = C \oplus a^4S_0$$

$$\therefore C = S_1 \oplus a^4S_0 = 000 \oplus 010 = \underline{010} \qquad \text{(b)}$$

FIGURE 8.55
(a) If the location of errors is known, then the syndromes are a known function of the two errors. (b) It is, however, much simpler to set the incorrect symbols to zero, i.e., to erase them. Then the syndromes are a function of the wanted symbols and correction is easier.

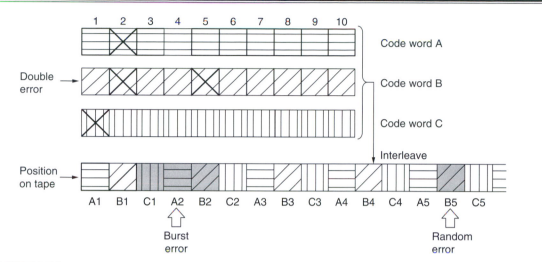

FIGURE 8.56
The interleave system falls down when a random error occurs adjacent to a burst.

The code word will be 255 bytes long but will often be shortened by puncturing. The larger Galois fields require less redundancy, but the computational problem increases. LSI chips have been developed specifically for R-S decoding in many high-volume formats.

PRODUCT CODES

In the presence of burst errors alone, the system of interleaving works very well, but it is known that in most practical channels there are also uncorrelated errors of a few bits due to noise. Figure 8.56 shows an interleaving system in which a dropout-induced burst error that is at the maximum correctable size has occurred. All three code words involved are working at their limit of one symbol. A random error due to noise in the vicinity of a burst error will cause the correction power of the code to be exceeded. Thus a random error of a single bit causes a further entire symbol to fail. This is a weakness of an interleave solely designed to handle dropout-induced bursts. Practical high-density equipment must address the problem of noise-induced or random errors and burst errors occurring at the same time. This is done by forming code words both before and after the interleave process. In block interleaving, this results in a *product code,* whereas in the case of convolutional interleave the result is called *cross-interleaving.*

Figure 8.57 shows that in a product code the redundancy calculated first and checked last is called the outer code, and the redundancy calculated second and checked first is called the inner code. The inner code is formed along tracks on the medium. Random errors due to noise are corrected by the inner code and do not impair the burst-correcting power of the outer code. Burst errors are declared uncorrectable by the inner code, which flags the bad samples on the way into the de-interleave memory. The outer code reads the error flags to correct the flagged symbols by erasure. The error flags are also known as erasure flags. As it does not have to compute the

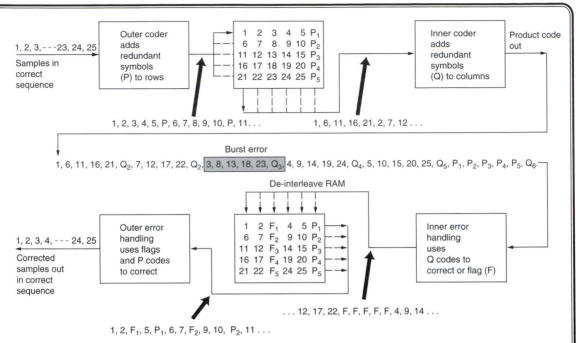

FIGURE 8.57
In addition to the redundancy P on rows, inner redundancy Q is also generated on columns. On replay, the Q code checker will pass on flags F if it finds an error too large to handle itself. The flags pass through the de-interleave process and are used by the outer error correction to identify which symbol in the row needs correcting with P redundancy. The concept of crossing two codes in this way is called a product code.

error locations, the outer code needs half as much redundancy for the same correction power. Thus the inner code redundancy does not raise the code overhead. The combination of code words with interleaving in several dimensions yields an error-protection strategy that is truly synergistic, in that the end result is more powerful than the sum of the parts. Needless to say, the technique is used extensively in modern storage formats.

References

1. Deeley, E.M. Integrating and differentiating channels in digital tape recording. Radio Electron. Eng., 56, 169–173 (1986).
2. Mee, C.D. *The Physics of Magnetic Recording*, Amsterdam/New York: Elsevier–North Holland (1978).
3. Jacoby, G.V. Signal equalization in digital magnetic recording. IEEE Trans. Magnetics, MAG-11, 302–305 (1975).
4. Schneider, R.C. An improved pulse-slimming method for magnetic recording. IEEE Trans. Magnetics, MAG-11, 1240–1241 (1975).
5. Miller, A. U.S. Patent. No. 3 108 261.
6. Mallinson, J.C., and Miller, J.W. Optimum codes for digital magnetic recording. Radio Electron. Eng., 47, 172–176 (1977).
7. Miller, J.W. DC-free encoding for data transmission system. U.S. Patent No. 4 027 335 (1977).
8. Tang, D.T. Run-length-limited codes. Presented at the IEEE International Symposium on Information Theory (1969).
9. Yokoyama, K. Digital video tape recorder. NHK Technical Monograph No. 31 (1982).
10. Coleman, C.H., et al., High data rate magnetic recording in a single channel. J. IERE, 55, 229–236 (1985).
11. Kobayashi, H. Application of partial response channel coding to magnetic recording systems. IBM J. Res. Dev., 14, 368–375 (1970).
12. Forney, G.D., Jr. The Viterbi algorithm. Proc. IEEE, 61, 268–278 (1973).
13. Wood, R.W., and Petersen, D.A. Viterbi detection of Class IV partial response on a magnetic recording channel. IEEE Trans. Communications, 34, 454–461 (1968).
14. Shannon, C.E. A mathematical theory of communication. Bell Syst. Tech. J., 27, 379 (1948).
15. Reed, I.S., and Solomon, G. Polynomial codes over certain finite fields. J. Soc. Indust. Appl. Math., 8, 300–304 (1960).
16. Berlekamp, E.R. *Algebraic Coding Theory*, New York: McGraw–Hill (1967). [Reprint edition: Laguna Hills, CA: Aegean Park Press (1983)]
17. Sugiyama, Y., et al. An erasures and errors decoding algorithm for Goppa codes. IEEE Trans. Information Theory, IT-22 (1976).
18. Peterson, W.W., and Weldon, E.J. *Error Correcting Codes*, second edition, Cambridge, MA: MIT Press (1972).

CHAPTER 9
Storage Technology

INTRODUCTION

Digital technology depends heavily on reliable storage devices. A number of storage technologies co-exist because there is as yet no one ideal solution. Given the use of error correction to allow arbitrary reliability, the main ways of comparing storage devices are cost per bit and access time. These attributes are usually incompatible. The hard disk drive evolved to provide rapid access, whereas the rotary head tape evolved to provide low-cost bulk storage. Technology will continue to advance, and as a result recording densities of all media will continue to increase, along with improvements in transfer rate. The large market for disk drives in PCs has meant that tape has received less development of late than it might have.

A disk controller automatically divides files up into blocks of the appropriate size for recording. If any partial blocks are left over, these will be zero stuffed. Consequently disk stores are not constrained to files of a particular size. This means that disks are not standards dependent. A disk system can mix 4:4:4, 4:2:2, and 4:2:0 files and it does not care whether the video is interlaced or not or compressed or not. It can mix 525- and 625-line files and it can mix 4:3 and 16:9 aspect ratios. This an advantage in news systems in which compression is used. If a given compression scheme is used at the time of recording, e.g., DVCPRO, the video can remain in the compressed data domain when it is loaded onto the disk system for editing. This avoids concatenation of codecs, which is generally bad news in compressed systems.

One of the happy consequences of the move to disk drives in production is that the actual picture format used need no longer be fixed. With computer graphics and broadcast video visibly merging, interlace may well be doomed. In the near future it will be possible to use non-interlaced HD cameras and down-convert to a non-interlaced intermediate resolution production format.

As production units such as mixers, character generators, paint systems, and DVEs become increasingly software driven, such a format is much easier to adopt than in the days of analog in which the functionality was frozen into the circuitry. Following production the intermediate format can be converted to any present or future emission standard.

In a network-based system it is useful to have tape and disk drives that can transfer faster than real time to speed up the process. The density of tape recording has a great bearing on the cost per bit. One limiting factor is the track width. In current DVTR formats, the track width is much greater than theoretically necessary because of the difficulty of mechanically tracking with the heads. This is compounded by the current insistence on editing to picture accuracy on the tape itself. This is a convention inherited from analog VTRs, and it is unnecessary in digital machines. Digital VTRs employ read–modify–write, and this makes the edit precision in the data independent of the block size on tape. Future DVTRs may be able to edit only once per second, by employing edit gaps. This allows the tracks to be much narrower and the recording density can rise. Picture-accurate editing requires the block to be read intact, edited elsewhere, and written back whole. The obvious way to do this is on a disk. Thus a future for hybrid storage systems is to integrate the DVTR with the disk system and give it a format that it could not use as a standalone unit. This brings the DVTR very close in functionality to the streaming tape recorder, which has evolved in the computer industry.

DISK STORAGE

Disk drives came into being as random-access file-storage devices for digital computers. The explosion in personal computers has fuelled demand for low-cost high-density disk drives and the rapid access offered has revolutionized video production. Optical disks are represented by DVD and its HD successor.

Figure 9.1 shows that, in a disk drive, the data are recorded on a circular track. In hard-disk drives, the disk rotates at several thousand revolutions per minute so that the head-to-disk speed is on the order of 100 miles per hour. At this speed no contact can be tolerated, and the head flies on a boundary layer of air turning with the disk at a height measured in microinches. The longest time it is

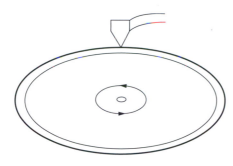

FIGURE 9.1
The rotating store concept. Data on the rotating circular track are repeatedly presented on the head.

necessary to wait to access a given data block is a few milliseconds. To increase the storage capacity of the drive without a proportional increase in cost, many concentric tracks are recorded on the disk surface, and the head is mounted on a positioner that can rapidly bring the head to any desired track. Such a machine is termed a moving-head disk drive. An increase in capacity could be obtained by assembling many disks on a common spindle to make a disk pack. The small size of magnetic heads allows the disks to placed close together. If the positioner is designed so that it can remove the heads away from the disk completely, it can be exchanged. The exchangeable pack moving-head disk drive became the standard for mainframe and minicomputers for a long time.

Later came the so-called Winchester technology disks, in which the disk and positioner formed a compact sealed unit that allowed increased storage capacity but precluded exchange of the disk pack alone. Disk drive development has been phenomenally rapid. The first flying head disks were about 3 feet across. Subsequently disk sizes of 14, 8, 5¼, 3½, and 1⅞ inches were developed. Despite the reduction in size, the storage capacity is not compromised because the recording density has increased and continues to increase. In fact there is an advantage in making a drive smaller because the moving parts are then lighter and travel a shorter distance, improving access time. There are numerous types of optical disks, which have different characteristics:

1. The Compact Disc, its data derivative CD-ROM, and the later DVD are examples of a read-only laser disk, which is designed for mass duplication by stamping. They cannot be recorded.
2. Some laser disks can be recorded, but once recorded they cannot be edited or erased because some permanent mechanical or chemical change has been made. These are usually referred to as write-once–read-many (WORM) disks.

3. Erasable optical disks have essentially the same characteristic as magnetic disks, in that new and different recordings can be made in the same track indefinitely, but there is usually a separate erase cycle needed before a new recording can be made because overwrite is not always possible.

Figure 9.2 introduces the essential subsystems of a disk drive, which will be discussed here. Magnetic drives and optical drives are similar in that both have a spindle drive mechanism to revolve the disk, and a positioner to give radial access across the disk surface. In the optical drive, the positioner has to carry a collection of lasers, lenses, prisms, gratings, and so on and will be rather larger than a magnetic head. The heavier pickup cannot be accelerated as fast as a magnetic-drive positioner, and access time is slower. A large number of pickups on one positioner makes matters worse. For this reason and because of the larger spacing needed between the disks, multiplatter optical disks are uncommon. Instead "juke box" mechanisms have been developed to allow a large library of optical disks to be mechanically accessed by one or more drives. Access time is sometimes reduced by having more than one positioner per disk, a technique adopted rarely in magnetic drives. A penalty of the very small track pitch possible in laser disks, which gives the enormous storage capacity, is that very accurate track following is needed, and it takes some time to lock onto a track. For this reason tracks on laser disks are usually made as a continuous spiral, rather than the concentric rings of magnetic disks. In this way, a continuous data transfer involves no more than track following once the beginning of the file is located.

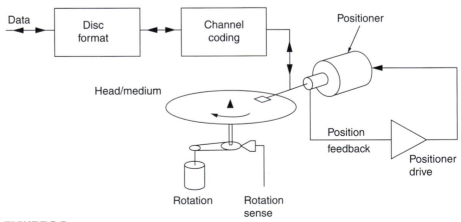

FIGURE 9.2
The main subsystems of a typical disk drive.

Rigid disks are made from aluminium alloy. Magnetic-oxide types use an aluminium oxide substrate, or undercoat, giving a flat surface to which the oxide binder can adhere. Later metallic disks having higher coercivity are electroplated with the magnetic medium. In both cases the surface finish must be extremely good owing to the very small flying height of the head. As the head-to-disk speed and recording density are functions of track radius, the data are confined to the outer areas of the disks to minimize the change in these parameters. As a result, the centre of the pack is often an empty well. In fixed (i.e., noninterchangeable) disks the drive motor is often installed in the centre well.

The information layer of optical disks may be made of a variety of substances, depending on the working principle. This layer is invariably protected beneath a thick transparent layer of glass or polycarbonate. Exchangeable optical and magnetic disks are usually fitted in protective cartridges. These have various shutters, which retract on insertion into the drive to allow access by the drive spindle and heads. Removable packs usually sit on a taper to ensure concentricity and are held to the spindle by a permanent magnet. A lever mechanism may be incorporated into the cartridge to assist their removal.

MAGNETIC DISKS

In all technologies there are specialist terms, and those relating to magnetic disks will be explained here. Figure 9.3 shows a typical multiplatter magnetic disk pack in conceptual form. Given a particular set of coordinates (cylinder, head, sector), known as a disk physical address, one unique data block is defined. A common block capacity is 512 bytes. The subdivision into sectors is sometimes omitted for special applications. A disk drive can be randomly accessed, because any block address can follow any other, but unlike a RAM, at each address a large block of data is stored, rather than a single word.

Magnetic disk drives permanently sacrifice storage density to offer rapid access. The use of a flying head with a deliberate air gap between it and the medium is necessary because of the high medium speed, but this causes a severe separation loss, which restricts the linear density available. The air gap must be accurately maintained, and consequently the head is of low mass and is mounted flexibly.

The aerodynamic part of the head is known as the slipper; it is designed to provide lift from the boundary layer, which changes rapidly with changes in flying height. It is not initially obvious that the difficulty with disk heads is not making them fly, but making them fly close enough to the disk surface.

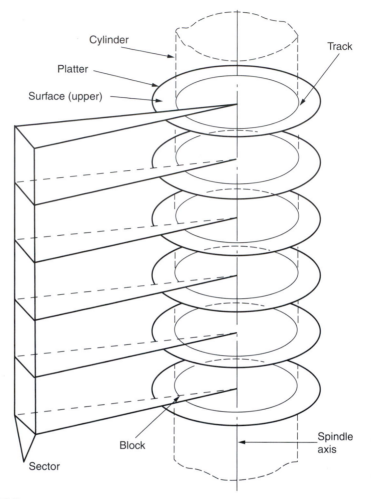

FIGURE 9.3
Disk terminology. Surface: one side of a platter. Track: path described on a surface by a fixed head. Cylinder: imaginary shape intersecting all surfaces at tracks of the same radius. Sector: angular subdivision of pack. Block: that part of a track within one sector. Each block has a unique cylinder, head, and sector address.

The boundary layer travelling at the disk surface has the same speed as the disk, but as height increases, it slows down due to drag from the surrounding air. As the lift is a function of relative air speed, the closer the slipper comes to the disk, the greater the lift will be. The slipper is therefore mounted at the end of a rigid cantilever sprung toward the medium. The force with which the head is pressed toward the disk by the spring is equal to the lift at the designed flying height. Because of the spring, the head may rise and fall over small warps in the disk. It would be virtually impossible to manufacture disks flat enough to dispense with this feature. As the slipper negotiates a warp it will pitch and roll in addition to rising and falling, but it must be prevented from yawing, as this would cause an azimuth error. Downthrust is applied to the aerodynamic centre by a spherical thrust button, and the required degrees of freedom are supplied by a thin flexible gimbal. The slipper has to bleed away surplus air to approach close enough to the disk, and holes or grooves are usually provided for this purpose.

In exchangeable-pack drives, there will be a ramp on the side of the cantilever that engages a fixed block when the heads are retracted in order to lift them away from the disk surface.

Figure 9.4 shows how disk heads are made. The magnetic circuit of disk heads was originally assembled from discrete magnetic elements. As the gap and flying height became smaller to increase linear recording density, the slipper was made from ferrite and became part of the magnetic circuit. This was completed by a small C-shaped ferrite piece, which carried the coil. Ferrite heads were restricted in the coercivity of disk they could write without saturating. In thin-film heads, the magnetic circuit and coil are both formed by deposition on a substrate, which becomes the rear of the slipper.

In a moving-head device it is not practicable to position separate erase, record, and playback heads accurately. Erase is by overwriting, and reading and writing are carried out by the same head. The presence of the air film causes severe separation loss, and peak-shift distortion is a major problem. The flying height of the head varies with the radius of the disk track, and it is difficult to provide accurate equalization of the replay channel because of this. The write current is often controlled as a function of track radius so that the changing reluctance of the air gap does not change the resulting record flux. Automatic gain control (AGC) is used on replay to compensate for changes in signal amplitude from the head. Equalization may be used on recording in the form of precompensation, which moves recorded transitions in such a way as to oppose the effects of peak shift in addition to any replay equalization used. Early disks used FM coding, which was easy to decode, but had a poor density ratio. The invention of MFM (modified frequency modulation) revolutionized hard disks, and further progress led to run-length-limited codes such as 2/3 and 2/7, which had a high density ratio without sacrificing the large jitter window necessary to reject peak shift distortion. Partial response is also suited to disks.

Typical drives have several heads, but with the exception of special-purpose parallel-transfer machines, only one head will be active at any one time, which

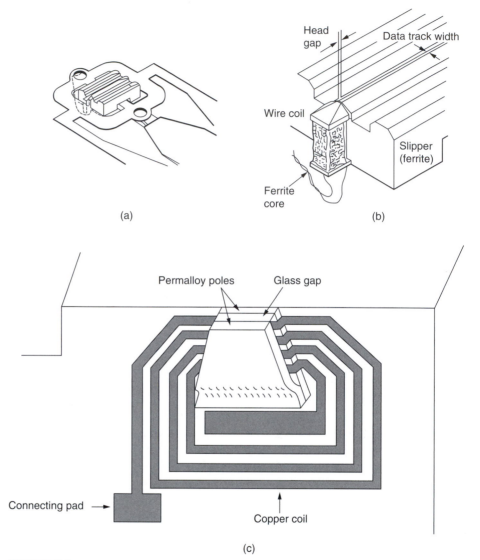

(a)

(b)

(c)

FIGURE 9.4
(a) Winchester head construction showing large air-bleed grooves. (b) Close-up of slipper showing magnetic circuit on trailing edge. (c) The thin-film head is fabricated on the end of the slipper using microcircuit technology.

means that the read and write circuitry can be shared between the heads. The read channel usually incorporates AGC, which will be overridden by the control logic between data blocks to search for address marks, which are short unmodulated areas of track. As a block preamble is entered, the AGC will be enabled to allow a rapid gain adjustment.

ACCESSING THE BLOCKS

The servo system required to move the heads rapidly between tracks, and yet hold them in place accurately for data transfer, is a fascinating and complex piece of engineering. In exchangeable pack drives, the disk positioner moves on a straight axis, which passes through the spindle. Motive power is generally by moving-coil drive, because of the small moving mass that this technique permits.

When a drive is track-following, it is said to be detented, in fine mode or in linear mode depending on the manufacturer. When a drive is seeking from one track to another, it can be described as being in coarse mode or velocity mode. These are the two major operating modes of the servo.

Moving-coil actuators do not naturally detent and require power to stay on-track. The servo system needs positional feedback of some kind. The purpose of the feedback will be one or more of the following:

1. To count the number of cylinders crossed during a seek
2. To generate a signal proportional to carriage velocity
3. To generate a position error proportional to the distance from the centre of the desired track

Magnetic and optical drives obtain these feedback signals in different ways. Many positioners incorporate a tacho, which may be a magnetic moving-coil type or its complementary equivalent, the moving-magnet type. Both generate a voltage proportional to velocity and can give no positional information.

A seek is a process in which the positioner moves from one cylinder to another. The speed with which a seek can be completed is a major factor in determining the access time of the drive. The main parameter controlling the carriage during a seek is the cylinder difference, which is obtained by subtracting the current cylinder address from the desired cylinder address. The cylinder difference will be a signed binary number representing the number of cylinders to be crossed to reach the target, direction being indicated by the sign. The cylinder difference is loaded into a counter, which is decremented each time a cylinder is crossed. The counter drives a DAC, which generates an analog voltage proportional to the cylinder difference. As Figure 9.5 shows, this voltage, known as the scheduled velocity, is compared with the output of the carriage-velocity tacho. Any difference between the two results in a velocity error, which drives the carriage to cancel the error. As the carriage approaches the target cylinder, the cylinder difference becomes smaller, with the result that the run-in to the target is critically damped to eliminate overshoot.

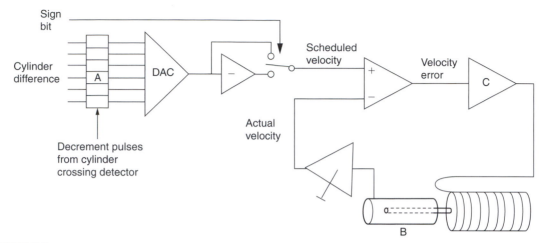

FIGURE 9.5
Control of carriage velocity by cylinder difference. The cylinder difference is loaded into the difference counter A. A digital-to-analog convertor generates an analog voltage from the cylinder difference, known as the scheduled velocity. This is compared with the actual velocity from the transducer B to generate the velocity error, which drives the servo amplifier C.

Figure 9.6a shows graphs of scheduled velocity, actual velocity, and motor current with respect to cylinder difference during a seek. In the first half of the seek, the actual velocity is less than the scheduled velocity, causing a large velocity error, which saturates the amplifier and provides maximum carriage acceleration. In the second half of the graphs, the scheduled velocity is falling below the actual velocity, generating a negative velocity error, which drives a reverse current through the motor to slow the carriage down. The scheduled deceleration slope can clearly not be steeper than the saturated acceleration slope. Areas A and B on the graphs will be about equal, as the kinetic energy put into the carriage has to be taken out. The current through the motor is continuous and would result in a heating problem, so to counter this, the DAC is made nonlinear so that above a certain cylinder difference no increase in scheduled velocity will occur. This results in the graph of Figure 9.6b. The actual velocity graph is called a velocity profile. It consists of three regions: acceleration, in which the system is saturated; a constant velocity plateau, in which the only power needed is to overcome friction; and the scheduled run-in to the desired cylinder. Dissipation is significant only in the first and last regions.

The track-following accuracy of a drive positioner will be impaired if there is bearing runout, and so the spindle bearings are made to a high degree of precision.

To control reading and writing, the drive control circuitry needs to know which cylinder the heads are on and which sector is currently under the head. Sector

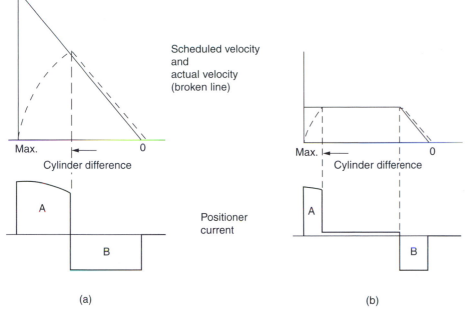

Scheduled velocity
and
actual velocity
(broken line)

Positioner
current

(a)   (b)

FIGURE 9.6
In the simple arrangement in (a) the dissipation in the positioner is continuous, causing
a heating problem. The effect of limiting the scheduled velocity above a certain
cylinder difference is apparent in (b), where heavy positioner current flows only during
acceleration and deceleration. During the plateau of the velocity profile, only enough
current to overcome friction is necessary. The curvature of the acceleration slope is due
to the back EMF of the positioner motor.

information used to be obtained from a sensor that detected holes or slots cut in
the hub of the disk. Modern drives obtain this information from the disk surface,
as will be seen. The result is that a sector counter in the control logic remains in
step with the physical rotation of the disk. The desired sector address is loaded
into a register, which is compared with the sector counter. When the two match,
the desired sector has been found. This process is referred to as a search and usually takes place after a seek. Having found the correct physical place on the disk,
the next step is to read the header associated with the data block to confirm that
the disk address contained there is the same as the desired address.

SERVO-SURFACE DISKS

One of the major problems to be overcome in the development of high-density
disk drives was that of keeping the heads on track despite changes in temperature. The very narrow tracks used in digital recording have similar dimensions

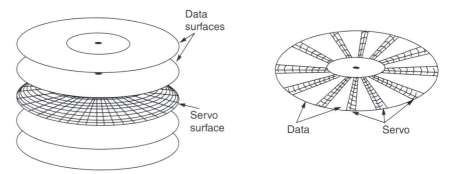

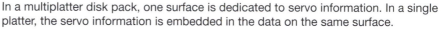

FIGURE 9.7
In a multiplatter disk pack, one surface is dedicated to servo information. In a single platter, the servo information is embedded in the data on the same surface.

to the amount a disk will expand as it warms up. The cantilevers and the drive base all expand and contract, conspiring with thermal drift in the cylinder transducer to limit track pitch. The breakthrough in disk density came with the introduction of the servo-surface drive. The position error in a servo-surface drive is derived from a head reading the disk itself. This virtually eliminates thermal effects on head positioning and allows great increases in storage density. In a multiplatter drive, one surface of the pack holds servo information, which is read by the servo head. In a 10-platter pack this means that five percent of the medium area is lost, but this is unimportant because the increase in density allowed is enormous. Using one side of a single-platter cartridge for servo information would be unacceptable as it represents 50 percent of the medium area, so in this case the servo information can be interleaved with sectors on the data surfaces. This is known as an embedded-servo technique. These two approaches are contrasted in Figure 9.7.

The servo surface is written at the time of disk pack manufacture, and the disk drive can only read it. Writing the servo surface has nothing to do with disk formatting, which affects the data storage areas only. As there is exactly the same number of pulses on every track on the servo surface, it is possible to describe the rotational position of the disk simply by counting them. All that is needed is a unique pattern of missing pulses once per revolution to act as an index point, and the sector transducer can also be eliminated. The advantage of deriving the sector count from the servo surface is that the number of sectors on the disk can be varied. Any number of sectors can be accommodated by feeding the pulse signal through a programmable divider, so the same disk and drive can be used in numerous different applications.

THE DISK CONTROLLER

A disk controller is a unit that is interposed between the drives and the rest of the system. It consists of two main parts: that which issues control signals to and obtains status from the drives and that which handles the data to be stored and retrieved. Both parts are synchronised by the control sequencer. The essentials of a disk controller are determined by the characteristics of drives and the functions needed, and so they do not vary greatly. It is desirable for economic reasons to use a commercially available disk controller intended for computers. Such controllers are adequate for still store applications, but cannot support the data rate required for real-time moving video unless data reduction is employed. Disk drives are generally built to interface to a standard controller interface. The disk controller will then be a unit that interfaces the drive bus to the host computer system. The execution of a function by a disk subsystem requires a complex series of steps, and decisions must be made between the steps to decide what the next will be. There is a parallel with computation, in that the function is the equivalent of an instruction, and the sequencer steps needed are the equivalent of the microinstructions needed to execute the instruction. The major failing in this analogy is that the sequence in a disk drive must be accurately synchronised to the rotation of the disk.

Most disk controllers use direct memory access, which means that they have the ability to transfer disk data in and out of the associated memory without the assistance of the processor. To cause a file transfer, the disk controller must be told the physical disk address (cylinder, sector, track), the physical memory address where the file begins, the size of the file, and the direction of transfer (read or write). The controller will then position the disk heads, address the memory, and transfer the samples.

One disk transfer may consist of many contiguous disk blocks, and the controller will automatically increment the disk-address registers as each block is completed. As the disk turns, the sector address increases until the end of the track is reached. The track or head address will then be incremented and the sector address reset so that transfer continues at the beginning of the next track. This process continues until all the heads have been used in turn. In this case both the head address and the sector address will be reset, and the cylinder address will be incremented, which causes a seek. A seek that takes place because of a data transfer is called an implied seek, because it is not necessary formally to instruct the system to perform it. As disk drives are block-structured devices, and the error correction is code-word-based, the controller will always complete a

WINCHESTER TECHNOLOGY

To offer extremely high capacity per spindle, which reduces the cost per bit, a disk drive must have very narrow tracks placed close together and must use very short recorded wavelengths, which implies that the flying height of the heads must be small. The so-called Winchester technology is one approach to high storage density. The technology was developed by IBM, and the name came about because the model number of the development drive was the same as that of the famous rifle.

Reduction in flying height magnifies the problem of providing a contaminant-free environment. A conventional disk is well protected whilst inside the drive, but outside the drive the effects of contamination become intolerable.

In exchangeable-pack drives, there is a real limit to the track pitch that can be achieved because of the difficulty or cost of engineering head alignment mechanisms to make the necessary minute adjustments to give interchange compatibility.

The essence of Winchester technology is that each disk pack has its own set of read/write and servo heads, with an integral positioner. The whole is protected by a dust-free enclosure, and the unit is referred to as a head disk assembly, or HDA.

As the HDA contains its own heads, compatibility problems do not exist, and no head alignment is necessary or provided for. It is thus possible to reduce track pitch considerably compared with exchangeable-pack drives. The sealed environment ensures complete cleanliness, which permits a reduction in flying height without loss of reliability and hence leads to an increased linear density. If the rotational speed is maintained, this can also result in an increase in data transfer rate. The HDA is completely sealed, but some have a small filtered port to equalize pressure.

An exchangeable-pack drive must retract the heads to facilitate pack removal. With Winchester technology this is not necessary. An area of the disk surface is reserved as a landing strip for the heads. The disk surface is lubricated, and the heads are designed to withstand landing and takeoff without damage. Winchester heads have very large air-bleed grooves to allow low flying height with a much smaller downthrust from the cantilever, and so they exert less force on the disk surface during contact. When the term "parking" is used in the context of Winchester technology, it refers to the positioning of the heads over the landing area.

Disk rotation must be started and stopped quickly to minimize the length of time the heads slide over the medium. This is conveniently achieved with a servo-controlled brushless motor, which has dynamic braking ability. A major advantage of contact start/stop is that more than one head can be used on each surface if retraction is not needed. This leads to two gains: first, the travel of the positioner is reduced in proportion to the number of heads per surface, reducing access time, and second, more data can be transferred at a given detented carriage position before a seek to the next cylinder becomes necessary. This increases the speed of long transfers. Figure 9.8 illustrates the relationships of the heads in such a system.

Figure 9.9 shows that rotary positioners are feasible in Winchester drives; they cannot be used in exchangeable-pack drives because of interchange problems. There are some advantages to a rotary positioner. It can be placed in the corner of a compact HDA, allowing smaller overall size. The manufacturing cost will be less than a linear positioner because fewer bearings and precision bars are needed. Significantly, a rotary positioner can be made faster because its inertia is smaller. With a linear positioner all parts move at the same speed. In a

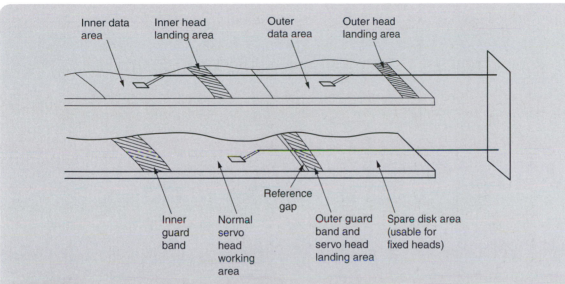

Inner data area

Inner head landing area

Outer data area

Outer head landing area

Reference gap

Inner guard band

Normal servo head working area

Outer guard band and servo head landing area

Spare disk area (usable for fixed heads)

FIGURE 9.8
When more than one head is used per surface, the positioner still requires only one servo head. This is often arranged to be equidistant from the read/write heads for thermal stability.

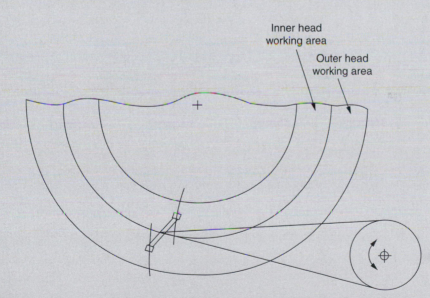

Inner head working area

Outer head working area

FIGURE 9.9
A rotary positioner with two heads per surface. The tolerances involved in the spacing between the heads and the axis of rotation mean that each arm records data in a unique position. Those data can be read back only by the same heads, which rules out the use of a rotary positioner in exchangeable-pack drives. In a head disk assembly the problem of compatibility does not arise.

rotary positioner, only the heads move at full speed, as the parts closer to the shaft must move more slowly. The principle of many rotary positioners is exactly that of a moving-coil ammeter, in which current is converted directly into torque.

One characteristic of rotary positioners is that there is a component of windage on the heads, which tends to pull the positioner in toward the spindle. Windage can be overcome in rotary positioners by feeding the current cylinder address to a table that outputs a code to a DAC. This produces an offset voltage, which is fed to the positioner driver to generate a torque, which balances the windage whatever the position of the heads.

When extremely small track spacing is contemplated, it cannot be assumed that all the heads will track the servo head due to temperature gradients. In this case the embedded-servo approach must be used, in which each head has its own alignment patterns. The servo surface is often retained in such drives to allow coarse positioning, velocity feedback, and index and write-clock generation, in addition to locating the guard bands for landing the heads.

Winchester drives have been made with massive capacity, but the problem of backup is then magnified, and the general trend has been for the physical size of the drive to come down as the storage density increases, to improve access time and to facilitate the construction of storage arrays. Very small Winchester disk drives are now available, which plug into standard integrated circuit sockets. These are competing with RAM for memory applications when nonvolatility is important.

block even if the size of the file is less than a whole number of blocks. This is done by packing the last block with zeros.

The status system allows the controller to find out about the operation of the drive, both as a feedback mechanism for the control process and to handle any errors. Upon completion of a function, it is the status system that interrupts the control processor to tell it that another function can be undertaken.

In a system in which there are several drives connected to the controller via a common bus, it is possible for non-data-transfer functions such as seeks to take place in some drives simultaneous with a data transfer in another.

Before a data transfer can take place, the selected drive must physically access the desired block and confirm this by reading the block header. Following a seek to the required cylinder, the positioner will confirm that the heads are on track and settled. The desired head will be selected, and then a search for the correct sector will begin. This is done by comparing the desired sector with the current sector register, which is typically incremented by dividing down servo-surface pulses. When the two counts are equal, the head is about to enter the desired block. Figure 9.10 shows the structure of a typical magnetic disk track.

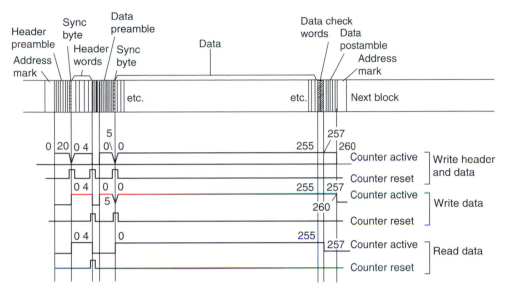

FIGURE 9.10
The format of a typical disk block related to the count process used to establish where in the block the head is at any time. During a read the count is derived from the actual data read, but during a write, the count is derived from the write clock.

In between blocks are placed address marks, which are areas without transitions that the read circuits can detect. Following detection of the address mark, the sequencer is roughly synchronised to begin handling the block. As the block is entered, the data separator locks to the preamble, and in due course the sync pattern will be found. This sets to zero a counter that divides the data bit rate by eight, allowing the serial recording to be correctly assembled into bytes and also allowing the sequencer to count the position of the head through the block in order to perform all the necessary steps at the right time.

The first header word is usually the cylinder address, and this is compared with the contents of the desired cylinder register. The second header word will contain the sector and track address of the block, and these will also be compared with the desired addresses. There may also be bad-block flags and/or defect-skipping information. At the end of the header is a CRCC, which will be used to ensure that the header was read correctly. Figure 9.11 shows a flowchart of the position verification, after which a data transfer can proceed. The header reading is completely automatic. The only time it is necessary formally to command a header to be read is when checking that a disk has been formatted correctly.

During the read of a data block, the sequencer is employed again. The sync pattern at the beginning of the data is detected as before, following which

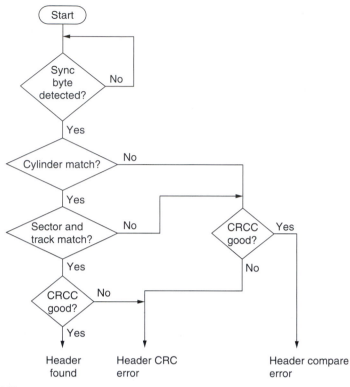

FIGURE 9.11
The vital process of position confirmation is carried out in accordance with the
flowchart shown. The appropriate words from the header are compared in turn with
the contents of the disk-address registers in the subsystem. Only if the correct header
has been found and read properly will the data transfer take place.

the actual data arrive. These bits are converted to byte or sample parallel and
sent to the memory by DMA (direct memory access). When the sequencer has
counted the last data byte off the track, the redundancy for the error-correction
system will be following.

During a write function, the header-check function will also take place, as it is
perhaps even more important not to write in the wrong place on a disk. Once
the header has been checked and found to be correct, the write process for
the associated data block can begin. The preambles, sync pattern, data block,
redundancy, and postamble all have to be written contiguously. This is taken
care of by the sequencer, which is obtaining timing information from the
servo surface to lock the block structure to the angular position of the disk.
This should be contrasted with the read function, for which the timing comes
directly from the data.

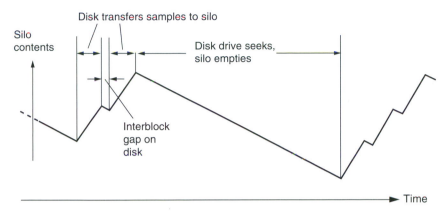

FIGURE 9.12
During a video replay sequence, the silo is constantly emptied to provide samples and is refilled in blocks by the drive.

When video samples are fed into a disk-based system, from a digital interface, or from an ADC, they will be placed in a buffer memory, from which the disk controller will read them by DMA. The continuous-input sample stream will be split up into disk blocks for disk storage.

The disk transfers must by definition be intermittent, because there are headers between contiguous sectors. Once all the sectors on a particular cylinder have been used, it will be necessary to seek to the next cylinder, which will cause a further interruption in the data transfer. If a bad block is encountered, the sequence will be interrupted until it has passed. The instantaneous data rate of a parallel transfer drive is made higher than the continuous video data rate, so that there is time for the positioner to move whilst the video output is supplied from the FIFO (First In First Out) memory. In replay, the drive controller attempts to keep the FIFO as full as possible by issuing a read command as soon as one block space appears in the FIFO. This allows the maximum time for a seek to take place before reading must resume. Figure 9.12 shows the action of the FIFO. Whilst recording, the drive controller attempts to keep the FIFO as empty as possible by issuing write commands as soon as a block of data is present. In this way the amount of time available to seek is maximised in the presence of a continuous video sample input.

DEFECT HANDLING

The protection of data recorded on disks differs considerably from the approach used on other media in digital video. This has much to do with the intolerance

RAID ARRAYS

Whilst the MTBF of a disk drive is very high, it is a simple matter of statistics that when a large number of drives is assembled in a system the time between failures becomes shorter. Disk drives are sealed units and the disks cannot be removed if there is an electronic failure. Even if this were possible the system cannot usually afford down time whilst such a data recovery takes place.

Consequently any system in which the data are valuable must take steps to ensure data integrity. This is commonly done using RAID (redundant array of inexpensive disks) technology. Figure 9.13 shows that in a RAID array data blocks are spread across a number of drives. An error-correcting check symbol (typically Reed–Solomon) is stored on a redundant drive. The error correction is powerful enough to correct fully any error in the block due to a single failed drive. In RAID arrays the drives are designed to be hot-plugged (replaced without removing power) so if a drive fails it is simply physically replaced with a new one. The error-correction system will rewrite the drive with the data that were lost with the failed unit.

When a large number of disk drives are arrayed together, it is necessary and desirable to spread files across all the drives in a RAID array. Whilst this ensures data integrity, it also means that the data transfer rate is multiplied by the number of drives sharing the data. This means that the data transfer rate can be extremely high and new approaches are necessary to move the data in and out of the disk system.

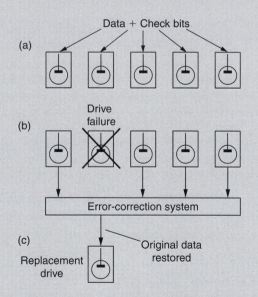

FIGURE 9.13
(a) In RAID technology, data and redundancy are spread over a number of drives. (b) In the case of a drive failure the error-correction system can correct for the loss and continue operation. (c) When the drive is replaced the data can be rewritten so that the system can then survive a further failure.

of data processors to errors compared with video data. In particular, it is not possible to interpolate to conceal errors in a computer program or a data file.

In the same way that magnetic tape is subject to dropouts, magnetic disks suffer from surface defects whose effect is to corrupt data. The shorter wavelengths employed as disk densities increase are affected more by a given size of defect. Attempting to make a perfect disk is subject to a law of diminishing returns, and eventually a state is reached at which it becomes more cost-effective to invest in a defect-handling system.

In the construction of bad-block files, a brand new disk is tested by the operating system. Known patterns are written everywhere on the disk, and these are read back and verified. Following this the system gives the disk a volume name and creates on it a directory structure that keeps records of the position and size of every file subsequently written. The physical disk address of every block that fails to verify is allocated to a file that has an entry in the disk directory. In this way, when genuine data files come to be written, the bad blocks appear to the system to be in use storing a fictitious file, and no attempt will be made to write there. Some disks have dedicated tracks where defect information can be written during manufacture or by subsequent verification programs, and these permit a speedy construction of the system bad-block file.

DISK SERVERS

A disk server is a subsystem using disks as a storage medium that is intended to store and retrieve data for a number of different users. Consequently servers have a network interface over which users communicate with them. Such networks may be of any size according to purpose. A local network may be suitable within a post-production suite, whereas if a broadcaster wishes to make material available to the public the server will be interfaced to the Internet.

Servers need to be reliable and to store large quantities of data, requirements readily met by adopting RAID technology. Frequently the design is such that failing drives can be hot-swapped. The data storage itself is straightforward. More difficult aspects of server design include security, such that only those authorised get access to data, and matters such as priority. This determines which users will be served first in the event that requests for transfers exceed the server's throughput. The priority protocol may be linked to quality of service parameters of the network, as there is no point in guaranteeing network bandwidth if the server is busy.

OPTICAL DISK PRINCIPLES

To record MO (magneto-optic) disks or replay any optical disk, a source of monochromatic light is required. The light source must have low noise, otherwise the variations in intensity due to the noise of the source will mask the variations due to reading the disk. The requirement for a low-noise monochromatic light source is economically met using a semiconductor laser.

In the LED, the light produced is incoherent or noisy. In the laser, the ends of the semiconductor are optically flat mirrors, which produce an optically resonant cavity. One photon can bounce to and fro, exciting others in synchronism, to produce coherent light. This is known as light amplification by stimulated emission of radiation, mercifully abbreviated to LASER, and can result in a runaway condition, in which all available energy is used up in one flash. In injection lasers, an equilibrium is reached between energy input and light output, allowing continuous operation with a clean output. The equilibrium is delicate, and such devices are usually fed from a current source. To avoid runaway when temperature change disturbs the equilibrium, a photosensor is often fed back to the current source. Such lasers have a finite life and become steadily less efficient. The feedback will maintain output, and it is possible to anticipate the failure of the laser by monitoring the drive voltage needed to give the correct output.

Many re-recordable or erasable optical disks rely on magneto-optics. The storage medium is magnetic, but the writing mechanism is the heat produced by light from a laser, hence the term "thermomagneto-optics." The advantage of this writing mechanism is that there is no physical contact between the writing head and the medium. The distance can be several millimetres, some of which is taken up by a protective layer to prevent corrosion. Originally, this layer was glass, but engineering plastics have now taken over.

The laser beam will supply a relatively high power for writing, because it is supplying heat energy. For reading, the laser power is reduced, such that it cannot heat the medium past the Curie temperature, and it is left on continuously.

Whatever the type of disk being read, it must be illuminated by the laser beam. Some of the light reflected back from the disk re-enters the aperture of the objective lens. The pickup must be capable of separating the reflected light from the incident light. When pre-recorded disks such as CDs or DVDs are being played, the phase-contrast readout process results in a variation of the intensity of the light returning to the pickup. When MO disks are being played, the intensity does not change, but the magnetic recording on the disk rotates the plane of polarization one way or the other depending on the direction of the vertical magnetization.

Figure 9.14a shows that a polarizing prism is required to linearly polarize the light from the laser on its way to the disk. Light returning from the disk has had its plane of polarization rotated by approximately $\pm 1°$. This is an extremely small rotation. Figure 9.14b shows that the returning rotated light can be considered to be composed of two orthogonal components. R_x is the component that is in the same plane as the illumination and is called the ordinary component, and R_y is the component due to the Kerr effect rotation and is known as the magneto-optic component. A polarizing beam splitter mounted squarely would reflect the magneto-optic component R_y very well because it is at right angles to the transmission plane of the prism, but the ordinary component would pass straight on in the direction of the laser. By rotating the prism slightly a small amount of the ordinary component is also reflected. Figure 9.14c shows that when combined with the magneto-optic component, the angle of rotation has increased. Detecting this rotation requires a further polarizing prism or analyser as shown. The prism is twisted such that the transmission plane is 45° to the planes of R_x and R_y. Thus with an unmagnetized disk, half of the light is transmitted by the prism and half is reflected. If the magnetic field of the disk turns the plane of polarization toward the transmission plane of the prism, more light is transmitted and less is reflected. Conversely, if the plane of polarization is rotated away from the transmission plane, less light is transmitted and more is reflected. If two sensors are used, one for transmitted light and one for reflected light, the difference between the two sensor outputs will be a waveform representing the angle of polarization and thus the recording on the disk. This differential analyser eliminates common-mode noise in the reflected beam.

High-density recording implies short wavelengths. Using a laser focused on the disk from a distance allows short wavelength recordings to be played back without physical contact, whereas conventional magnetic recording requires intimate contact and implies a wear mechanism, the need for periodic cleaning, and susceptibility to contamination.

The information layer is read through the thickness of the disk; this approach causes the readout beam to enter and leave the disk surface through the largest possible area. Despite the minute spot size of about one μm diameter, light enters and leaves through a one μm diameter circle. As a result, surface debris has to be three orders of magnitude larger than the readout spot before the beam is

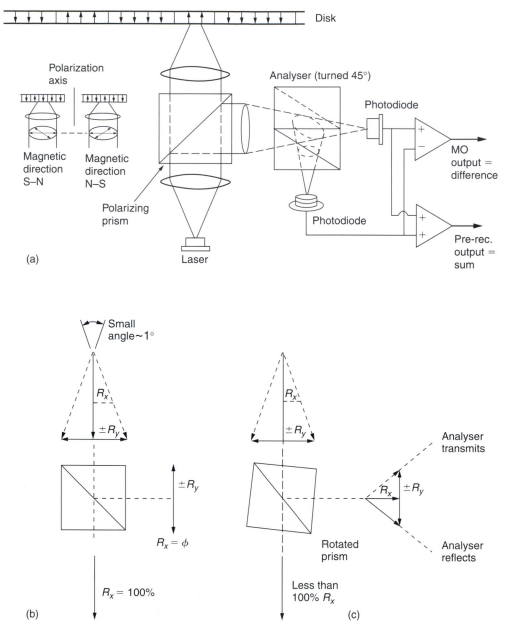

FIGURE 9.14

A pickup suitable for the replay of magneto-optic disks must respond to very small rotations of the plane of polarization.

obscured. This approach has the further advantage in MO drives that the magnetic head, on the opposite side to the laser pickup, is then closer to the magnetic layer in the disk.

FOCUS AND TRACKING SYSTEMS

The frequency response of the laser pickup and the amount of cross talk are both functions of the spot size and care must be taken to keep the beam focused on the information layer. If the spot on the disk becomes too large, it will be unable to discern the smaller features of the track and can also be affected by the adjacent track. Disk warp and thickness irregularities will cause focal-plane movement beyond the depth of focus of the optical system, and a focus servo system will be needed. The depth of field is related to the numerical aperture, which is defined, and the accuracy of the servo must be sufficient to keep the focal plane within that depth, which is typically $\pm 1\,\mu m$.

The track pitch of a typical optical disk is on the order of a micrometre, and this is much smaller than the accuracy to which the player chuck or the disk centre hole can be made; on a typical player, runout will swing several tracks past a fixed pickup. The non-contact readout means that there is no inherent mechanical guidance of the pickup and a suitable servo system must be provided.

The focus servo moves a lens along the optical axis to keep the spot in focus. Because dynamic focus changes are largely due to warps, the focus system must have a frequency response in excess of the rotational speed. A moving-coil actuator is often used owing to the small moving mass that this permits. Figure 9.15 shows that a cylindrical magnet assembly almost identical to that of a loudspeaker can be used, coaxial with the light beam. Alternatively a moving magnet design can be used. A rare-earth magnet allows a sufficiently strong magnetic field without excessive weight.

A focus-error system is necessary to drive the lens. There are a number of ways in which this can be derived, the most common of which will be described here. In Figure 9.16 a cylindrical lens is installed between the beam splitter and the photosensor. The effect of this lens is that the beam has no focal point on the sensor. In one plane, the cylindrical lens appears parallel sided and has negligible effect on the focal length of the main system, whereas in the other plane, the lens shortens the focal length. The image will be an ellipse whose aspect ratio changes as a function of the state of focus. Between the two foci, the image will be circular. The aspect ratio of the ellipse, and hence the focus error, can be found

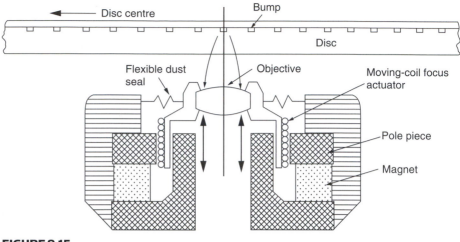

FIGURE 9.15
Moving-coil-focus servo can be coaxial with the light beam as shown.

by dividing the sensor into quadrants. When these are connected as shown, the focus-error signal is generated. The data-readout signal is the sum of the quadrant outputs.

Figure 9.17 shows the knife-edge method of determining focus. A split sensor is also required. In Figure 9.17a the focal point is coincident with the knife edge, so it has little effect on the beam. In (b) the focal point is to the right of the knife edge, and rising rays are interrupted, reducing the output of the upper sensor. In (c) the focal point is to the left of the knife edge, and descending rays are interrupted, reducing the output of the lower sensor. The focus error is derived by comparing the outputs of the two halves of the sensor. A drawback of the knife-edge system is that the lateral position of the knife edge is critical, and adjustment is necessary. To overcome this problem, the knife edge can be replaced by a pair of prisms, as shown in Figures 9.17d–9.17f. Mechanical tolerances then affect only the sensitivity, without causing a focus offset.

The cylindrical lens method is compared with the knife-edge/prism method in Figure 9.18, which shows that the cylindrical lens method has a much smaller capture range. A focus-search mechanism will be required, which moves the focus servo over its entire travel, looking for a zero crossing. At this time the feedback loop will be completed, and the sensor will remain on the linear part of its characteristic. The spiral tracks of DVD, CD, and MiniDisc start at the inside and work outward. This was deliberately arranged because there is less vertical runout near the hub, and initial focusing will be easier.

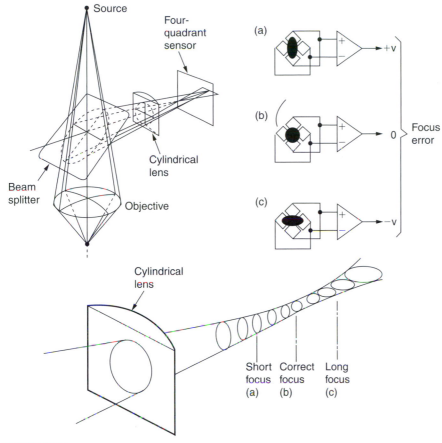

FIGURE 9.16
The cylindrical lens focus method produces an elliptical spot on the sensor, whose aspect ratio is detected by a four-quadrant sensor to produce a focus error.

In addition to the track runout mentioned above, there are further mechanisms that cause tracking error. A warped disk will not present its surface at 90° to the beam, but will constantly change the angle of incidence during two whole cycles per revolution. Owing to the change in refractive index at the disk surface, the tilt will change the apparent position of the track to the pickup, and Figure 9.19 shows that this makes it appear wavy. Warp also results in coma of the readout spot. The disk format specifies a maximum warp amplitude to keep these effects under control. Finally, vibrations induced in the player from outside, particularly in portable and automotive players, will tend to disturb tracking. A track-following servo is necessary to keep the spot centralized on the track in the presence of these difficulties. There are several ways in which a tracking error can be derived.

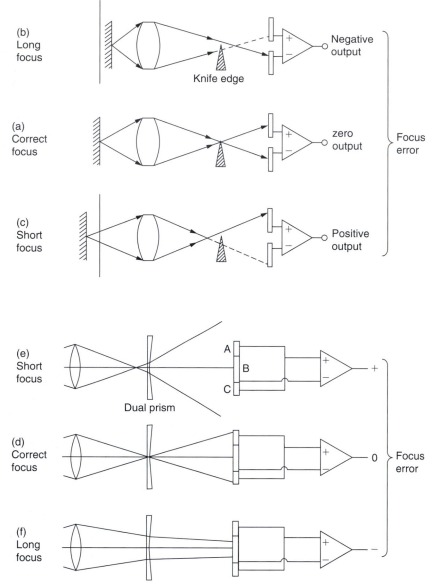

FIGURE 9.17
(a–c) Knife-edge focus method requires only two sensors, but is critically dependent on knife-edge position. (d–f) Twin-prism method requires three sensors (A, B, C), where focus error is $(A + C) - B$. Prism alignment reduces sensitivity without causing focus error.

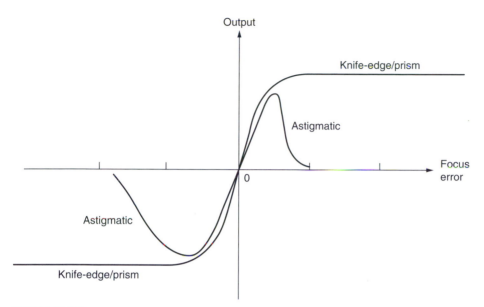

FIGURE 9.18
Comparison of capture range of knife-edge/prism method and astigmatic (cylindrical lens) system. Knife edge may have range of 1 mm, whereas astigmatic may have a range of only 40 μm, requiring a focus-search mechanism.

In the three-spot method, two additional light beams are focused on the disk track, one offset to each side of the track centre line. Figure 9.20 shows that, as one side spot moves away from the track into the mirror area, there is less destructive interference and more reflection. This causes the average amplitude of the side spots to change differentially with tracking error. The laser head contains a diffraction grating, which produces the side spots, and two extra photosensors onto which the reflections of the side spots will fall. The side spots feed a differential amplifier, which has a low-pass filter to reject the channel-code information and retain the average brightness difference. Some players use a delay line in one of the side-spot signals whose period is equal to the time taken for the disk to travel between the side spots. This helps the differential amplifier cancel the channel code.

The side spots are generated as follows. When a wavefront reaches an aperture that is small compared to the wavelength, the aperture acts as a point source, and the process of diffraction can be observed as a spherical wavefront leaving the aperture, as in Figure 9.21. Where the wavefront passes through a regular structure, known as a diffraction grating, light on the far side will form new wavefronts wherever radiation is in phase, and Figure 9.22 shows that these

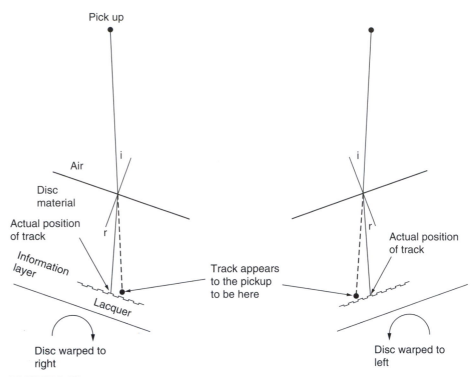

FIGURE 9.19
Owing to refraction, the angle of incidence (*i*) is greater than the angle of refraction (*r*). Disk warp causes the apparent position of the track (dashed line) to move, requiring the tracking servo to correct.

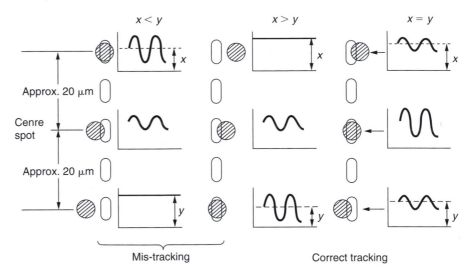

FIGURE 9.20
Three-spot method of detecting tracking error compares average level of side-spot signals. Side spots are produced by a diffraction grating and require their own sensors.

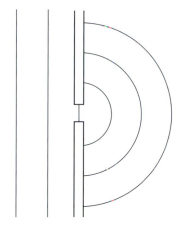

FIGURE 9.21
Diffraction as a plane wave reaches a small aperture.

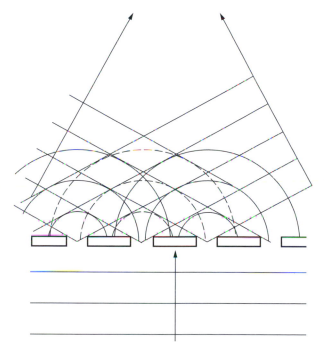

FIGURE 9.22
In a diffraction grating, constructive interference can take place at more than one angle
for a single wavelength.

will be at an angle to the normal depending on the spacing of the structure
and the wavelength of the light. A diffraction grating illuminated by white light
will produce a dispersed spectrum at each side of the normal. To obtain a fixed
angle of diffraction, monochromatic light is necessary.

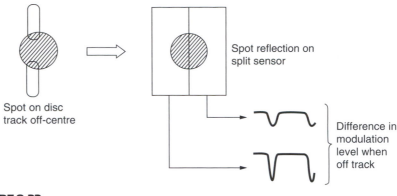

Spot on disc
track off-centre

Spot reflection on
split sensor

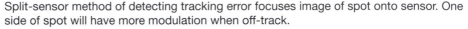

Difference in
modulation
level when
off track

FIGURE 9.23
Split-sensor method of detecting tracking error focuses image of spot onto sensor. One
side of spot will have more modulation when off-track.

The alternative approach to tracking-error detection is to analyse the diffraction
pattern of the reflected beam. The effect of an off-centre spot is to rotate the
radial diffraction pattern about an axis along the track. Figure 9.23 shows that, if
a split sensor is used, one half will see greater modulation than the other when
off-track. Such a system may be prone to develop an offset due either to drift or
to contamination of the optics, although the capture range is large. A further
tracking mechanism is often added to obviate the need for periodic adjustment.
Figure 9.24 shows that in this dither-based system, a sinusoidal drive is fed to
the tracking servo, causing a radial oscillation of spot position of about ±50 nm.
This results in modulation of the envelope of the readout signal, which can be
synchronously detected to obtain the sense of the error. The dither can be produced by vibrating a mirror in the light path, which enables a high frequency to
be used, or by oscillating the whole pickup at a lower frequency.

In pre-recorded disks there is obviously a track to follow, but in recordable
disks provision has to be made for track-following during the first recording of
a blank disk. This is typically done by pressing the tracks in the form of continuous grooves. The grooves may be produced with a lateral wobble so that
the wobble frequency can be used to measure the speed of the track during
recording.

STRUCTURE OF A DVD PLAYER

Figure 9.25 shows the block diagram of a typical DVD player and illustrates the
essential components. The most natural division within the block diagram is into

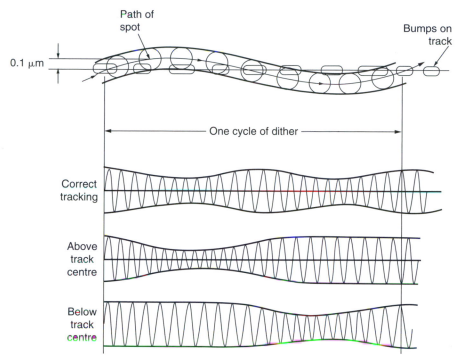

FIGURE 9.24
Dither applied to readout spot modulates the readout envelope. A tracking error can be derived.

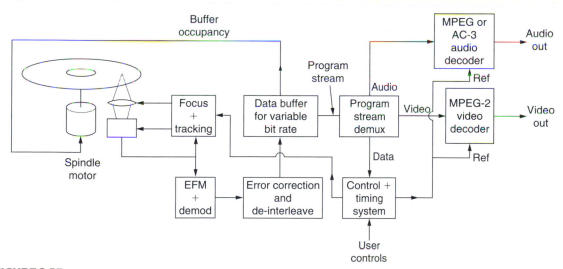

FIGURE 9.25
A DVD player's essential parts. See text for details.

the control/servo system and the data path. The control system provides the interface between the user and the servo mechanisms and performs the logical interlocking required for safety and the correct sequence of operation.

The servo systems include any power-operated loading drawer and chucking mechanism, the spindle-drive servo, and the focus and tracking servos already described.

Power loading is usually implemented on players in which the disk is placed in a drawer. Once the drawer has been pulled into the machine, the disk is lowered onto the drive spindle and clamped at the centre, a process known as chucking. In the simpler top-loading machines, the disk is placed on the spindle by hand, and the clamp is attached to the lid so that it operates as the lid is closed.

The lid or drawer mechanisms have a safety switch, which prevents the laser operating if the machine is open. This is to ensure that there can be no conceivable hazard to the user. In actuality there is very little hazard in a DVD pickup. This is because the beam is focused a few millimetres away from the objective lens, and beyond the focal point the beam diverges and the intensity falls rapidly. It is almost impossible to position the eye at the focal point when the pickup is mounted in the player, but it would be foolhardy to attempt to disprove this.

The data path consists of the data separator and the de-interleaving and error-correction process, followed by a RAM buffer, which supplies the MPEG decoder. The data separator converts the EFMplus readout waveform into data. Following data separation the error-correction and de-interleaving processes take place.

Because of the interleave system, there are two opportunities for correction: first, using the inner code prior to de-interleaving and second, using the outer code after de-interleaving. In Chapter 8 it was shown that interleaving is designed to spread the effects of burst errors among many different code words, so that the errors in each are reduced. However, the process can be impaired if a small random error, due perhaps to an imperfection in manufacture, occurs close to a burst error caused by surface contamination. The function of the inner redundancy is to correct single-symbol errors, so that the power of interleaving to handle bursts is undiminished, and to generate error flags for the outer system when a gross error is encountered.

The EFMplus coding is a group code, which means that a small defect that changes one channel pattern into another could have corrupted up to 8 data bits. In the worst case, if the small defect is on the boundary between two channel patterns, two successive bytes could be corrupted. However, the final odd/even interleave on encoding ensures that the two bytes damaged will be in different inner code words; thus a random error can never corrupt two bytes in one inner code word, and random errors are therefore always correctable.

The de-interleave process is achieved by writing sequentially into a memory and reading out using a sequencer. The outer decoder will then correct any burst errors in the data. As MPEG data are very sensitive to error, the error-correction performance has to be extremely good. Following the de-interleave and outer error-correction process an MPEG program stream (see Chapter 6) emerges. Some of the program stream data will be video, some will be audio, and this will be routed to the appropriate decoder. It is a fundamental concept of DVD that the bit rate of this program stream is not fixed, but can vary with the difficulty of the program material to maintain consistent image quality. The bit rate is changed by changing the speed of the disk. However, there is a complication because the disk uses constant linear velocity rather than constant angular velocity. It is not possible to obtain a particular bit rate with a fixed spindle speed.

The solution is to use a RAM buffer between the transport and the MPEG decoders. The RAM is addressed by counters, which are arranged to overflow, giving the memory a ring structure. Writing into the memory is done using clocks derived from the disk whose frequency rises and falls with runout, whereas reading is done by the decoder, which, for each picture, will take as much data as are required from the buffer.

The buffer will function properly only if the two addresses are kept apart. This implies that the amount of data read from the disk over the long term must equal the amount of data used by the MPEG decoders. This is done by analysing the address relationship of the buffer. If the disk is turning too fast, the write address will move toward the read address; if the disk is turning too slowly, the write address moves away from the read address. Subtraction of the two addresses produces an error signal, which can be fed to the spindle motor.

The speed of the motor is unimportant. The important factor is that the data rate needed by the decoder is correct, and the system will drive the spindle at whatever speed is necessary so that the buffer neither underflows nor overflows. An alternative approach is that the disk drive always delivers data at a rate that is slightly too high and the rate is reduced by causing it to skip back one or more tracks from time to time such that the same length of track is traced again.

The MPEG decoder will convert the compressed elementary streams into PCM video and audio and place the pictures and audio blocks into RAM. These will be read out of RAM whenever the time-stamps recorded with each picture or audio block match the state of a time-stamp counter. If bi-directional coding is used, the RAM readout sequence will convert the recorded picture sequence back to the real-time sequence. The time-stamp counter is derived from a crystal oscillator in the player, which is divided down to provide the 90 kHz time stamp clock.

As a result the frame rate at which the disk was mastered will be replicated as the pictures are read from RAM. Once a picture buffer is read out, this will trigger the decoder to decode another picture. It will read data from the buffer until this has been completed and thus indirectly influence the disk speed. Owing to the use of constant linear velocity, the disk speed will be wrong if the pickup is suddenly made to jump to a different radius using manual search controls. This may force the data separator out of lock, or cause a buffer overflow and the decoder may freeze briefly until this has been remedied.

The control system of a DVD player is inevitably microprocessor-based, and as such it does not differ greatly in hardware terms from any other microprocessor-controlled device. Operator controls will simply interface to processor input ports and the various servo systems will be enabled or overridden by output ports. Software, or more correctly firmware, connects the two. The necessary controls are Play and Eject, with the addition in most players of at least Pause and some buttons that allow rapid skipping through the program material.

Although machines vary in detail, the flowchart of Figure 9.26 shows the logic flow of a simple player, from Start being pressed to pictures and sound emerging. At the beginning, the emphasis is on bringing the various servos into operation. Toward the end, the disk subcode is read to locate the beginning of the first section of the program material. When track-following, the tracking-error feedback loop is closed, but for track-crossing, to locate a piece of music, the loop is opened, and a microprocessor signal forces the laser head to move. The tracking error becomes an approximate sinusoid as tracks are crossed. The cycles of tracking error can be counted as feedback to determine when the correct number of tracks have been crossed. The "mirror" signal obtained when the readout spot is half a track away from target is used to brake pickup motion and re-enable the track-following feedback.

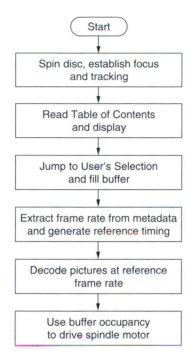

FIGURE 9.26
Simple processes required for a DVD player to operate.

DIGITAL VIDEOTAPE

Whilst numerous experimental machines were built previously, the first production DVTR, launched in 1987, used the D-1 format, which recorded colour-difference data according to CCIR-601 on ¾-inch tape. Whilst it represented a tremendous achievement, the D-1 format was too early to take advantage of high-coercivity tapes and its recording density was quite low, leading to large cassettes and high running costs. The majority of broadcasters then used composite signals, and a component recorder could not easily be used in such an environment. Where component applications existed, the D-1 format could not compete economically with Betacam SP and M-II analog formats. As a result D-1 found application only in high-end post-production suites.

The D-2 format came next, but this was a composite digital format, handling conventional PAL and NTSC signals in digital form and derived from a format developed by Ampex for a robotic cart machine. The choice of composite recording was intended to allow broadcasters directly to replace analog recorders with a digital machine. D-2 retained the cassette shell of D-1 but employed higher-coercivity tape and azimuth recording (see Chapter 8) to improve recording density and playing time. Early D-2 machines had no flying erase heads, and difficulties arose with audio edits. D-2 was also hampered by the imminent arrival of the D-3 format.

D-3 was designed by NHK and put into production by Panasonic. It had twice the recording density of D-2, three times that of D-1. This permitted the use of ½-inch tape, making a digital camcorder a possibility. D-3 used the same sampling structure as D-2 for its composite recordings. Coming later, D-3 had learned from earlier formats and had a more powerful error-correction strategy than earlier formats, particularly in audio recording.

By this time the economics of VLSI chips had made compression in VTRs viable, and the first application was the Ampex DCT format, which used approximately 2:1 data compression so that component video could be recorded on an updated version of the ¾-inch cassettes and transports designed for D-2.

When Sony was developing the Digital Betacam format, compatibility with the existing analog Betacam format was a priority. Digital Betacam uses the same cassette shells as the analog format, and certain models of the digital recorder can play existing analog tapes. Sony also adopted data compression, but this was to allow the construction of a digital component VTR that offered sufficient playing time within the existing cassette dimensions.

The D-5 component format is backward-compatible with D-3. The same cassettes are used and D-5 machines can play D-3 tapes. However, in standard definition, compression is not used; the tape speed is doubled in the component format to increase the bit rate. With mild compression D-5 recorders can handle high-definition video. During the development of the DVTR, hard disk storage was developing rapidly and as costs fell, the advantages of disk-based video storage began to erode the DVTR market. In this environment the most successful tape-based solution recently has been the DV format and its production relative DVCPRO and subsequent HD developments. DV has used compression to allow a highly miniaturized mechanism, which is ideal for port-able use and which outperforms disk-based technology in that application. In the future recording technology will continue to advance and further formats are inevitable as manufacturers perceive an advantage over their competition. This does not mean that the user need slavishly change to every new format, as the cost of format change is high. Astute users retain their current format for long enough to allow a number of new formats to be introduced. They will then make a quantum leap to a format that is much better than the present one, missing out those between and minimizing the change-over costs.

THE ROTARY HEAD TAPE TRANSPORT

The high bit rate of digital video could be accommodated by a conventional tape deck having many parallel tracks, but each would need its own read/write electronics and the cost would be high. However, the main problem with such an approach is that the data rate is proportional to the tape speed. The provision of stunt modes such as still frame or picture in shuttle is difficult or impossible. The rotary head recorder has the advantage that the spinning heads create a high head-to-tape speed, offering a high bit rate recording with a small number of heads and without high tape speed. The head-to-tape speed is dominated by the rotational speed, and the linear tape speed can vary enormously without changing the frequencies produced by the head by very much. Whilst mechanically complex, the rotary head transport has been raised to a high degree of refinement and potentially offers the highest recording density and thus lowest cost per bit of all digital recorders.

Figure 9.27 shows that the tape is led around a rotating drum in a helix such that the entrance and exit heights are different. As a result the rotating heads cross the tape at an angle and record a series of slanting tracks. The rotating heads turn at a speed that is locked to the video field rate so that a whole number of tracks results in each input field. Time compression can be used so that the switch from one track to the next falls within a gap between data blocks. Clearly the slant tracks can be played back properly only if linear tape motion is controlled in some way. This is the job of the linear control track, which carries a pulse corresponding to every slant track. The control track is played back to control the capstan. The breaking up of fields into several tracks is called segmentation and it is used to keep the tracks reasonably short. The segments are invisibly reassembled in memory on replay to restore the original fields.

Figure 9.28 shows the important components of a rotary head helical-scan tape transport. There are four servo systems, which must correctly interact to obtain all modes of operation: two reel servos, the drum servo, and the capstan servo. There are two approaches to capstan drive, those that use a pinch roller and those that do not. In a pinch roller drive, the tape is held against the capstan by pressure from a resilient roller, which is normally pulled toward the capstan by a solenoid. The capstan drives the tape over only a narrow speed range, generally the range in which broadcastable pictures are required. Outside this range,

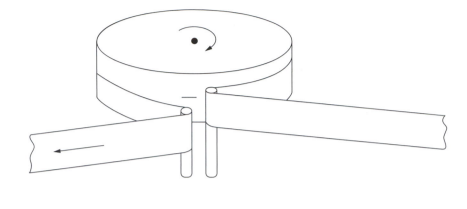

FIGURE 9.27
A rotary head recorder. A helical scan records long diagonal tracks. The capstan and reel servos together move and tension the tape, and the drum servo moves the heads. For variable-speed operation a further servo system will be necessary to deflect the heads.

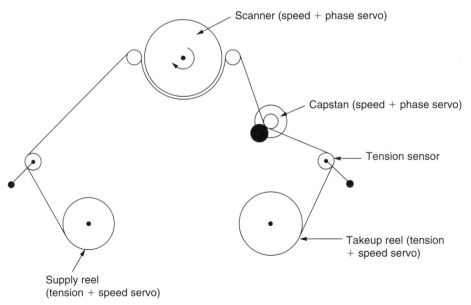

FIGURE 9.28
The four servos essential for proper operation of a helical-scan DVTR. Cassette-based units will also require loading and threading servos, and for variable speed a track-following servo will be necessary.

the pinch roller retracts, the tape will be driven by reel motors alone, and the reel motors will need to change their operating mode; one becomes a velocity servo, whilst the other remains a tension servo.

In a pinch-roller-less transport, the tape is wrapped some way around a relatively large capstan, to give a good area of contact. The tape is always in contact with the capstan, irrespective of operating mode, and so the reel servos never need to change mode. A large capstan has to be used to give sufficient contact area and to permit high shuttle speed without excessive motor rpm. This means that at play speed it will be turning slowly and must be accurately controlled and free from cogging. A multipole ironless rotor pancake-type brush motor is often used, or a sinusoidal drive brushless motor.

The simplest operating mode to consider is the first recording on a blank tape. In this mode, the capstan will rotate at constant speed and drive the tape at the linear speed specified for the format. The drum must rotate at a precisely determined speed, so that the correct number of tracks per unit distance will be laid down on the tape. Because in a segmented recording each track will be a constant fraction of a television field, the drum speed must ultimately be determined by the incoming video signal to be recorded. The phase of the drum rotation with respect to input video timing depends upon the time delay necessary to shuffle and interleave the video samples. This time will vary from a minimum of about one segment to more than a field depending on the format. To obtain accurate tracking on replay, a phase comparison will be made between off-tape control track pulses and pulses generated by the rotation of the drum. If the phase error between these is used to modify the capstan drive, the error can be eliminated, because the capstan drives the tape that produces the control track segment pulses. Eliminating this timing error results in the rotating heads following the tape tracks properly. Artificially delaying or advancing the reference pulses from the drum will result in a tracking adjustment. Alternatively, the capstan phase can be controlled by analysing tracking signals embedded in the slant tracks. This approach is more accurate and allows a finer track pitch, leading to higher recording density. The fixed head is also eliminated.

DIGITAL VIDEO CASSETTES

The main advantages of a cassette are that the medium is better protected from contamination whilst out of the transport and that an unskilled operator or a mechanical elevator can load the tape. The digital cassette contains two fully flanged reels side by side. The centre of each hub is fitted with a thrust pad and when the cassette is not in the drive a spring acts on this pad and presses the lower flange of each reel firmly against the body of the cassette to exclude dust. When the cassette is in the machine the relative heights of the reel turntables and the cassette supports are such that the reels sit on the turntables before the cassette comes to rest. This opens a clearance space between the reel flanges and the cassette body by compressing the springs.

The use of a cassette means that it is not as easy to provide a range of sizes as it is with open reels. Simply putting smaller reels in a cassette with the same hub spacing does not produce a significantly smaller cassette. The only solution is to specify different hub spacings for different sizes of cassette. This gives the best volumetric efficiency for storage, but it does mean that the transport must be able to reposition the reel drive motors if it is to play more than one size of cassette. Cassettes typically have hinged doors to protect the tape when not in a transport and a reel-locking mechanism to prevent the tape from forming a slack loop in storage. There is also typically a write-protect tab. Most cassettes have provision for a barcode for use in automated handling systems. Some contain the equivalent of a smart card that carries metadata describing the recording. This can be read quickly without lacing the tape and independently of how far the tape has been wound.

DIGITAL VTR BLOCK DIAGRAM

Figure 9.29a shows a representative block diagram of a PCM (i.e., un-compressed) DVTR. Following the convertors is the distribution of odd and even samples and a shuffle process for concealment purposes. An interleaved product code will be formed prior to the channel coding stage, which produces the recorded wave-form. On replay the data separator decodes the channel code and the inner and outer codes perform correction as in Chapter 8. Following the deshuffle the data channels are recombined and any necessary concealment will take place. Figure 9.29b shows the block diagram of a DVTR using compression.

Data from the convertors are re-arranged from the normal raster scan to the DCT blocks upon which the compression system works. A common size is eight pixels horizontally by four or eight vertically. The blocks are then shuffled spatially. This has two functions: first, it aids concealment purposes and second, it makes the entropy of the picture more uniform. The shuffled blocks are passed through the compression process. The output of this is distributed and then assembled into product codes and channel coded as for a conventional recorder. On replay

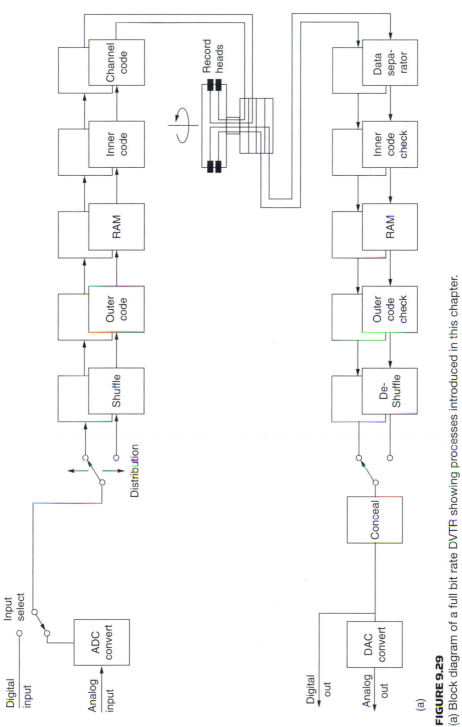

FIGURE 9.29

(a) Block diagram of a full bit rate DVTR showing processes introduced in this chapter.

(a)

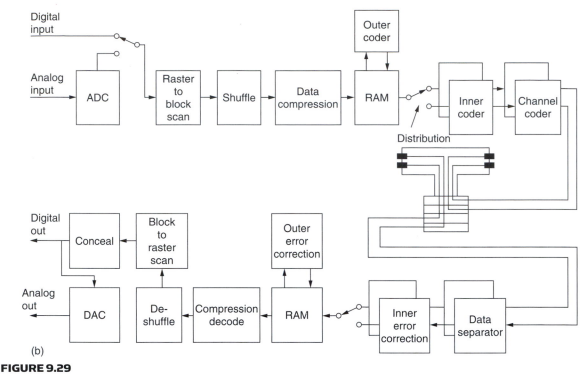

(b)

FIGURE 9.29
(b) A digital VTR using compression.

data separation and error correction take place as before, but there is now a matching decoder, which outputs DCT blocks. These are then de-shuffled prior to the error-concealment stage. As concealment is more difficult with pixel blocks, data from another field may be employed for concealment as well as data within the field.

The various DVTR formats largely employ the same processing stages, but there are considerable differences in the order in which these are applied. Distribution is shown in Figure 9.30a. This is a process of sharing the input bit rate over two or more signal paths so that the bit rate recorded in each is reduced. The data are subsequently re-combined on playback. Each signal path requires its own tape track and head. The parallel tracks that result form a *segment*.

Segmentation is shown in Figure 9.30b. This is the process of sharing the data resulting from one video field over several segments. The replay system must have some means to ensure that associated segments are re-assembled into the original field. This is generally a function of the control track.

Figure 9.30c shows a product code. Data to be recorded are protected by two error-correcting code-word systems at right angles: the inner code and the outer code (see Chapter 8). When it is working within its capacity the error-correction system returns corrupt data to their original value and its operation is undetectable.

If errors are too great for the correction system, concealment will be employed. Concealment is the *estimation* of missing data values from surviving data nearby. Nearby means data on vertical, horizontal, or time axes as shown in Figure 9.30d. Concealment relies upon distribution, as all tracks of a segment are unlikely to be simultaneously lost, and upon the *shuffle* shown in Figure 9.30e. Shuffling re-orders the pixels prior to recording and is reversed on replay. The result is that uncorrectable errors due to dropouts are not concentrated, but are

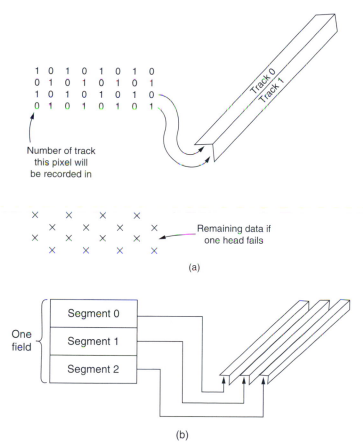

(a)

(b)

FIGURE 9.30
The fundamental stages of DVTR processing. In (a), distribution spreads data over more than one track to make concealment easier and to reduce the data rate per head. In (b) segmentation breaks video fields into manageable track lengths.

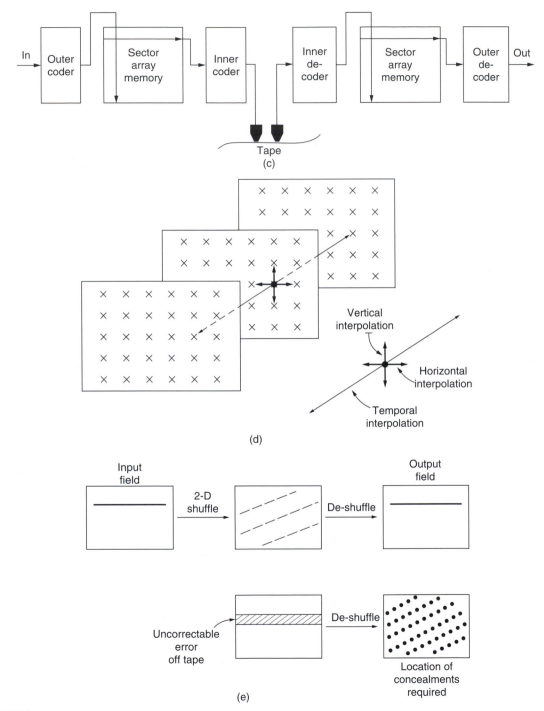

FIGURE 9.30

continued (c) Product codes correct mixture of random and burst errors. In (d) correction failure requires concealment, which may be in three dimensions. Irregular shuffle (e) makes concealments less visible.

spread out by the de-shuffle, making concealment easier. A different approach is required when compression is used because the data recorded are not pixels representing a point, but coefficients representing a DCT block, and it is these that must be shuffled.

There are two approaches to error correction in segmented recordings. In D-1 and D-2 the approach shown in Figure 9.31a is used. Here, following distribution the input field is segmented first, then each segment becomes an independently shuffled product code. This requires less RAM to implement, but it means that from an error-correction standpoint each tape track is self-contained and must deal alone with any errors encountered.

Later formats, beginning with D-3, use the approach shown in Figure 9.31b. Here, following distribution, the entire field is used to produce one large shuffled product code in each channel. The product code is then segmented for recording on tape. Although more RAM is required to assemble the large product code, the

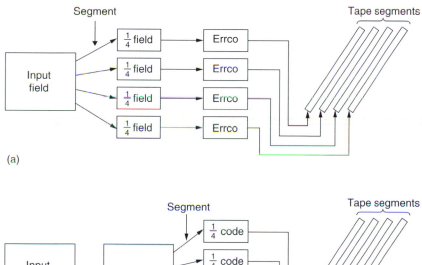

(a)

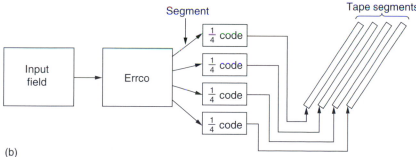

(b)

FIGURE 9.31
(a) Early formats would segment data before producing product codes. (b) Later formats perform product coding first and then segment for recording. This gives more robust performance.

PICTURE-IN-SHUTTLE

A rotary head recorder cannot follow the tape tracks properly when the tape is shuttled. Instead the heads cross the tracks at an angle and intermittently pick up short data blocks. Each of these blocks is an inner error-correcting code word and this can be checked to see if the block was properly recovered. If this is the case, the data can be used to update a frame store that displays the shuttle picture. Clearly the shuttle picture is a mosaic of parts of many fields. In addition to helping the concealment of errors, the shuffle process is beneficial to obtaining picture-in-shuttle. Owing to shuffle, a block recovered from the tape contains data from many places in the picture, and this gives a better result than if many pixels were available from one place in the picture. The twinkling effect seen in shuttle is due to the updating of individual pixels following deshuffle. When compression is used, the picture is processed in blocks, and these will be visible as mosaicing in the shuttle picture as the frame store is updated by the blocks.

result is that outer code words on tape spread across several tracks and redundancy in one track can compensate for errors in another. The result is that the size of a single burst error that can be fully corrected is increased. As RAM is now cheaper than when the first formats were designed, this approach is becoming more common.

DV AND DVCPRO

This component format uses quarter-inch wide ME (metal evaporated) tape, which is only seven µm thick, in conjunction with compression to allow realistic playing times in miniaturized equipment. The format has jointly been developed by all the leading VCR manufacturers. Whilst DV was originally intended as a consumer format, it was clear that such a format is ideal for professional applications such as news gathering and simple production because of the low cost and small size. This led to the development of the DVCPRO format.

In addition to component video there are also two channels of 16-bit uniformly quantized digital audio at 32, 44.1, or 48 kHz, with an option of four audio channels using 12-bit nonuniform quantizing at 32 kHz.

Figure 9.32 shows that two cassette sizes are supported. The standard size cassette offers 4½ hours of recording time and yet is only a little larger than an audio compact cassette. The small cassette is even smaller than a DAT cassette yet plays for one hour. Machines designed to play both tape sizes are equipped with moving-reel motors. Both cassettes are equipped with fixed identification tabs and a moveable write-protect tab. These tabs are sensed by switches in the transport.

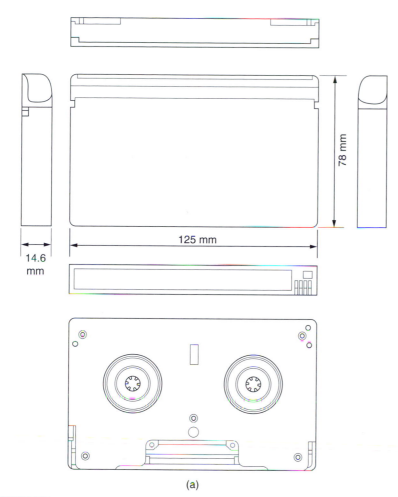

(a)

FIGURE 9.32
The cassettes developed for the ¼-inch DVC format. (a) The standard cassette, which holds 4.5 hours of program material.

DV has adopted many of the features first seen in small formats such as the DAT recorder and the 8 mm analog videotape format. Of these the most significant is the elimination of the control track permitted by recording tracking signals in the slant tracks themselves. The adoption of metal evaporated tape and embedded tracking allows extremely high recording density. Tracks recorded with slant azimuth are only 10 μm wide and the minimum wavelength is only 0.49 μm, resulting in a superficial density of over 0.4 Mbits per square milli-metre. Segmentation is used in DVC in such a way that as much commonality as possible exists between 50 and 60 Hz versions. The transport runs at 300 tape tracks

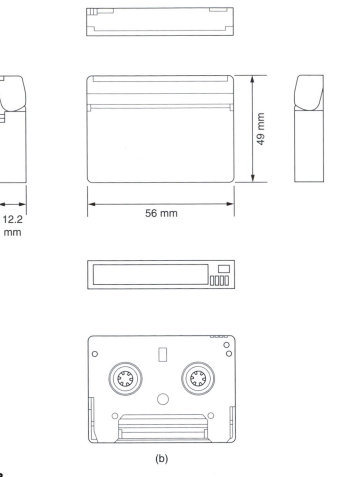

(b)

FIGURE 9.32
continued (b) The small cassette is intended for miniature equipment and plays for
one hour.

per second; Figure 9.33 shows that 50 Hz frames contain 12 tracks and 60 Hz
frames contain 10 tracks.

The tracking mechanism relies upon buried tones in the slant tracks. From a
tracking standpoint there are three types of track, shown in Figure 9.34: F0, F1,
and F2. F1 contains a low-frequency pilot and F2 a high-frequency pilot. F0
contains no pilot tone, but the recorded data spectrum contains notches at the
frequencies of the two tones. Figure 9.34 also shows that every other track will
contain F0 following a four-track sequence.

The embedded tracking tones are recorded throughout the track by inserting
a low frequency into the channel-coded data. Every 24 data bits an extra bit

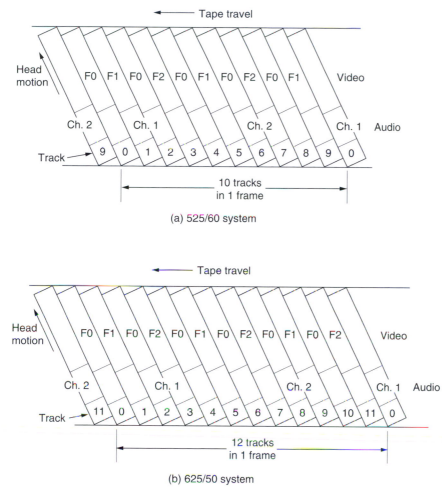

(a) 525/60 system

(b) 625/50 system

FIGURE 9.33
To use a common transport for 50 and 60 Hz standards the segmentation shown here is used. The segment rate is constant but 10 or 12 segments can be used in a frame.

is added whose value has no data meaning but whose polarity affects the average voltage of the waveform. By controlling the average voltage with this bit, low frequencies can be introduced into the channel-coded spectrum to act as tracking tones. The tracking tones have sufficiently long wavelength that they are not affected by head azimuth and can be picked up by the "wrong" head. When a head is following an F0-type track, one edge of the head will detect F1 and the other edge will detect F2. If the head is centralized on the track, the amplitudes of the two tones will be identical. Any tracking error will result in the relative amplitudes of the F1 and F2 tones changing. This can be used to

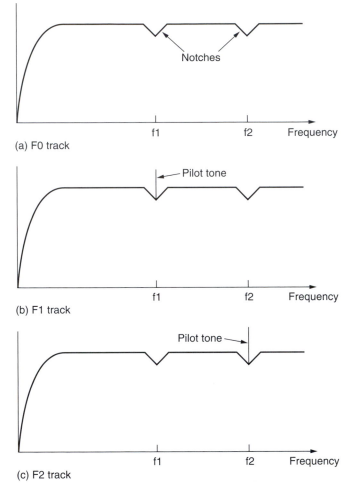

FIGURE 9.34
The tracks are of three types shown here. (a) The F0 track contains spectral notches at two selected frequencies. The other two track types (b and c) place a pilot tone in one or other of the notches.

modify the capstan phase to correct the tracking error. As azimuth recording is used, requiring a minimum of two heads, one head of the pair will always be able to play a type F0 track. In simple machines only one set of heads will be fitted and these will record or play as required. In more advanced machines, separate record and replay heads will be fitted. In this case the replay head will read the tracking tones during normal replay, but in editing modes, the record head would read the tracking tones during the pre-roll to align itself with the existing track structure.

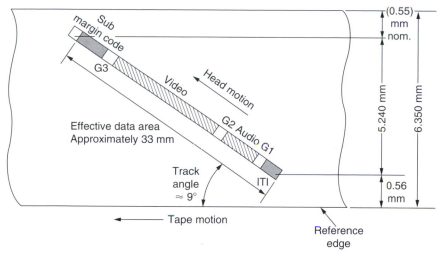

FIGURE 9.35
The dimensions of the DVC track. Audio, video, and subcode can be edited independently. The insert and track information (ITI) block aligns the heads during insert recording.

Figure 9.35 shows the track dimensions. The tracks are approximately 33 mm long and lie at approximately 9° to the tape edge. A transport with a 180° wrap would need a drum of only 21 mm diameter. For camcorder applications with the small cassette this would allow a transport no larger than an audio "Walkman." With the larger cassette it would be advantageous to use time compression to allow a larger drum with partial wrap to be used. This would simplify threading and make room for additional heads in the drum for editing functions.

The audio, video, and subcode data are recorded in three separate sectors with edit gaps between so that they can be independently edited in insert mode. In the case in which all three data areas are being recorded in insert mode, there must be some mechanism to keep the new tracks synchronous with those that are being overwritten. In a conventional VTR this would be the job of the control track.

CHAPTER 10

Communication Systems

INTRODUCTION

The approach taken here must necessarily be broad and must include in principle any system that can deliver data over distance. There appears to be an unwritten rule that anything to do with communications has to be described entirely using acronyms, a rule which this chapter intends to break in the interests of clarity. Figure 10.1 shows some of the classifications of communications systems. The simplest is a uni-directional point-to-point signal path shown in Figure 10.1a. This is common in digital production equipment and includes the AES/EBU (Audio Engineering Society/European Broadcast Union) digital audio interface and the SDI (serial digital interface) for digital video. Bi-directional point-to-point signals include the RS-232 and RS-422 duplex systems. Bi-directional signal paths may be symmetrical, i.e., have the same capacity in both directions (b), or asymmetrical, having more capacity in one direction than the other (c). In this case the low-capacity direction may be known as a back channel.

Back channels are useful in a number of applications. Video-on-demand and interactive video are both systems in which the inputs from the viewer are relatively small, but result in extensive data delivery to the viewer. Archives and databases have similar characteristics.

When more than two devices can be interconnected in such a way that any one can communicate at will with any other, the result is a network as in Figure 10.1d. The traditional telephone system is a network, and although the original

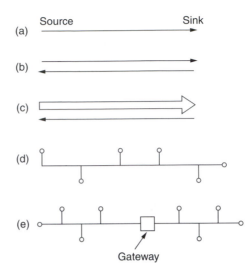

FIGURE 10.1
Classes of communication systems. (a) The uni-directional point-to-point connection used in many digital audio and video interconnects. (b) Symmetrical bi-directional point-to-point system. (c) Asymmetrical point-to-point system. (d) A network must have some switching or addressing ability in addition to delivering data. (e) Networks can be connected by gateways.

infrastructure assumed analog speech transmission, subsequent developments in modems have allowed data transmission.

The computer industry has developed its own network technology, a long-serving example being the Ethernet. Computer networks can work over various distances, giving rise to LANs (local area networks), MANs (metropolitan area networks), and WANs (wide area networks). Such networks can be connected together to form internetworks or internets for short, including the Internet. A private network, linking all employees of a given company, for example, may be referred to as an intranet.

Figure 10.1e shows that networks are connected together by gateways. In this example a private network (typically a local area network within an office block) is interfaced to an access network (typically a metropolitan area network with a radius on the order of a few kilometres), which in turn connects to the transport network. The access networks and the transport network together form a public network.

The different requirements of networks of different sizes have led to different protocols being developed. Where a gateway exists between two such networks, the gateway will often be required to perform protocol conversion. Such a device may be referred to as network termination equipment. Protocol conversion

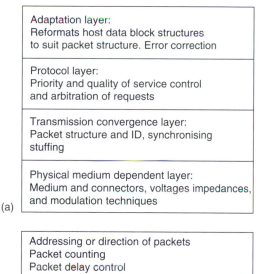

Adaptation layer:
Reformats host data block structures
to suit packet structure. Error correction

Protocol layer:
Priority and quality of service control
and arbitration of requests

Transmission convergence layer:
Packet structure and ID, synchronising
stuffing

Physical medium dependent layer:
Medium and connectors, voltages impedances,
and modulation techniques

(a)

Addressing or direction of packets
Packet counting
Packet delay control
Arbitration between requests

(b)

FIGURE 10.2
(a) Layers are important in communications because they have a degree of independence such that one can be replaced by another, leaving the remainder undisturbed. (b) The functions of a network protocol. See text.

represents unnecessary cost and delay, and recent protocols such as ATM (Asynchronous Transfer Mode) are sufficiently flexible that they can be adopted in any type of network to avoid conversion.

Networks that are optimized for storage devices also exist. These range from the standard buses linking hard drives with their controllers to SANs (storage area networks) in which distributed storage devices behave as one large store.

Communication must also include broadcasting, which initially was analog, but has also adopted digital techniques so that transmitters effectively radiate data. Traditional analog broadcasting was uni-directional, but with the advent of digital techniques, various means for providing a back channel have been developed.

To have an understanding of communications it is important to appreciate the concept of layers shown in Figure 10.2a. The lowest layer is the physical medium-dependent layer. In the case of a cabled interface, this layer would specify the dimensions of the plugs and sockets, so that a connection could be made, and the use of a particular type of conductor such as coaxial, STP (screened twisted pair), or UTP (unscreened twisted pair). The impedance of the cable may also be specified. The medium may also be optical fibre, which will need standardisation of the terminations and the wavelength(s) in use.

Once a connection is made, the physical medium-dependent layer standardises the voltage of the transmitted signal and the frequency at which the voltage changes (the channel bit rate). This may be fixed at a single value, chosen from a set of fixed values, or, rarely, variable. Practical interfaces need some form of channel coding (see Chapter 8) to embed a bit clock in the data transmission.

The physical medium-dependent layer allows binary transmission, but this needs to be structured or formatted. The transmission convergence layer takes the binary signalling of the physical medium-dependent layer and builds a packet or cell structure. This consists at least of some form of synchronisation system, so that the start and end of serialized messages can be recognized, and an addressing or labelling scheme, so that packets can reliably be routed and recognized. Most real cables and optical fibres run at fixed bit rates and a further function of the transmission convergence layer is the insertion of null or stuffing packets, in which insufficient user data exist or to allow that data to be asynchronous with the cable bit rate.

In broadcasting, the physical medium-dependent layer may be one that contains some form of radio signal and a modulation scheme. The modulation scheme will be a function of the kind of service. For example, a satellite modulation scheme would be quite different from one used in a terrestrial service.

In all real networks requests for transmission will arise randomly. Network resources need to be applied to these requests in a structured way to prevent chaos, data loss, or lack of throughput. This raises the requirement for a protocol layer. TCP (Transmission Control Protocol) and ATM are protocols. A protocol is an agreed set of actions in given circumstances. In a point-to-point interface the protocol is trivial, but in a network it is complex. Figure 10.2b shows some of the functions of a network protocol. There must be an addressing mechanism, so that the sender can direct the data to the desired location, and a mechanism by which the receiving device confirms that all the data have been correctly received. In more advanced systems the protocol may allow variations in quality of service whereby the user can select (and pay for) various criteria such as packet delay and delay variation and the packet error rate. This allows the system to deliver isochronous (near-real-time) MPEG data alongside asynchronous (non-time-critical) data such as email by appropriately prioritising packets.

The protocol layer arbit rates between demands on the network and delivers packets at the required quality of service. The user data will not necessarily have

> 1 No correction or checking
> 2 Detection only
> 3 Error detection and re-transmit request
> 4 Error detection and FEC to handle random errors
> 5 FEC and interleaving to handle packet loss
> 6 Automatic re-routing following channel failure

FIGURE 10.3
Different approaches to error checking used in various communications systems.

been packetised or, if it was, the packet size may be different from those used in the network. This situation arises, for example, when MPEG transport packets are to be sent via ATM. The solution is to use an adaptation layer. Adaptation layers re-format the original data into the packet structure needed by the network at the sending device and reverse the process at the destination device. Practical networks must have error checking/correction. Figure 10.3 shows some of the possibilities. In short interfaces, no errors are expected and a simple parity check or checksum with an error indication is adequate. In bi-directional applications a checksum failure would result in a re-transmission request or cause the receiver to fail to acknowledge the transmission so that the sender would try again.

In real-time systems, there may not be time for a re-transmission, and an FEC (forward error correction) system will be needed in which enough redundancy is included with every data block to permit on-the-fly correction at the receiver. The sensitivity to error is a function of the type of data, and so it is a further function of the adaptation layer to take steps such as interleaving and the addition of FEC codes.

PRODUCTION-RELATED INTERFACES

As audio and video production equipment first made the transition from analog to digital technology, computers and networks were still another world and the potential of the digital domain was largely neglected because the digital video interfaces that were developed simply copied analog practice, but transmitted parallel binary numbers in real time instead of the original video waveform. These simple uni-directional interfaces had no addressing or handshaking ability. Creating a network required switching devices called routers controlled independent of the signals themselves.

The AES/EBU interface was developed to provide a short distance point-to-point connection for PCM digital audio. Using serial transmission, the signals could be passed over existing balanced analog audio cabling. Subsequently the standard evolved to handle compressed and surround-sound audio data.

Parallel interfaces using 25-pin D-connectors were not really practical for routers. The SDI was initially developed for interlaced standard definition only, to allow up to 10-bit samples of component or PAL/NTSC composite digital video to be communicated serially on coaxial cable.[1] The 16:9 format component signals with 18 MHz sampling rate can also be handled. As if to emphasize the gulf that then existed between television and computing, the SDI as first standardised had no error-detection ability at all. This was remedied by a later option known as EDH (error detection and handling). The interface allows ancillary data including transparent conveyance of embedded AES/EBU digital audio channels during video blanking periods.

Subsequently the electrical and channel coding layer of SDI was used to create SDTI (serial data transport interface), which is used for transmitting, among other things, elementary streams from video compressors. ASI (asynchronous serial interface) uses only the electrical interface of SDI, with a different channel code and protocol, and is used for transmitting MPEG transport streams through SDI-based equipment.

The SDI format was later supplanted by HD-SDI, which uses a fixed bit rate of 1.485 Gbps independent of the video standard carried. Later came the 2.97 Gbps version, which allowed the larger frame-size progressively scanned formats to be carried, as well as the very large format images required for digital cinema at 24 Hz frame rate.

SERIAL DIGITAL VIDEO INTERFACES

The serial interfaces described here have a great deal of commonality. Any differences will be noted subsequently. All of the SD standards allow up to 10-bit samples to be communicated serially,[1] whereas the HD standards allow a 12-bit option. If the input word length is less than the interface capacity, the missing bits are forced to zero for transmission except for the all-ones condition during synchronising. The interfaces are transparent to ancillary data in the parallel domain, including conveyance of AES/EBU digital audio channels.

The video signals to be carried over serial interfaces must be sampled and quantized in carefully standardised ways as was seen in Chapter 4. Serial transmission uses concepts that were introduced in Chapter 8. At the high bit rates of digital video, the cable is a true transmission line in which a significant number of bits are actually in the cable at any one time, having been sent but not yet received. Under these conditions cable loss is significant. These interfaces operate with cable losses up to 30dB. The losses increase with frequency and so the bit rate in use and the grade of cable employed both affect the maximum distance the signal will safely travel. Figure 10.4 gives some examples of cable lengths that can be used in SD. In HD there are only two bit rates. Using Belden 1649A or equivalent, a distance of 140 m can be achieved with the lower one.

Serial transmission uses a waveform that is symmetrical about ground and has an initial amplitude of 800 mV pk–pk across a 75-Ohm load. This signal can be fed down 75-Ohm coaxial cable having BNC connectors. Serial interfaces are restricted to point-to-point links. Unlike analog video practice, serial digital receivers contain correct termination that is permanently present, and passive loop through is not possible. In permanent installations, no attempt should be made to drive more than one load using T-pieces, as this will result in signal reflections that seriously compromise the data integrity. On the test bench with very short cables, however, systems with all manner of compromises may still function.

The range of waveforms that can be received without gross distortion is quite small and raw data produce waveforms outside this range. The solution is the use of scrambling, or pseudo-random coding. The serial interfaces use convolutional scrambling, as was described in Chapter 8. This is simpler to implement in a cable installation because no separate synchronising of the randomizing is needed. The scrambling process at the transmitter spreads the signal spectrum and makes that spectrum reasonably constant and independent of the picture

System	Clock	Fundamental	Crash knee length	Practical length
NTSC Composite	143 MHz	71.5 MHz	400 m	320 m
PAL Composite	177 MHz	88.5 MHz	360 m	290 m
Component 601	270 MHz	135 MHz	290 m	230 m
Component 16:9	360 MHz	180 MHz	210 m	170 m
CABLE: BICC TM3205, PSF1/2, BELDEN 8281 or any cable with a loss of 8.7 dB/100 m at 100 MHz				

FIGURE 10.4
Suggested maximum cable lengths as a function of cable type and data rate to give a loss of no more than 30dB. It is unwise to exceed these lengths due to the "crash knee" characteristic of SDI.

content. It is possible to assess the degree of equalization necessary by comparing the energy in a low-frequency band with that in higher frequencies. The greater the disparity, the more equalization is needed. Thus fully automatic cable equalization at the receiver is easily achieved.

The essential parts of a serial link are shown in Figure 10.5. Parallel data are fed to a 10-bit shift register, which is clocked at 10 times the input word rate: 2.97 GHz, 1.485 GHz, 360 MHz, or 270 MHz (composite interfaces use 40 × F_{sc}). The serial data emerge from the shift register LSB first and are then passed through the scrambler, in which a given bit is converted to the exclusive-OR of itself and two bits that are five and nine clocks ahead. This is followed by another stage, which converts channel ones into transitions. The transition encoder ensures that the signal is polarity independent. The resulting logic level signal is converted to a 75-Ohm source impedance signal at the cable driver.

The receiver must regenerate a bit clock at 2.97 GHz, 1.485 GHz, 360 MHz, or 270 MHz or from the input signal, and this clock drives the input sampler and slicer, which converts the cable waveform back to serial binary. The local bit clock also drives a circuit that simply reverses the scrambling at the transmitter. The first stage returns transitions to ones. The second stage is a mirror image of the encoder and reverses the exclusive-OR calculation to output the original data. Such descrambling results in error extension, but this is not a practical problem because link error rates must be near zero.

SYNCHRONISING

As with all serial transmissions it is necessary to identify the position of word boundaries so that correct de-serialization can take place at the receiver. The component interfaces carry a multiplex of luminance and colour difference samples and it is also necessary to synchronise the demultiplexing process so that the components are not inadvertently transposed. Only the active line data are sent, so horizontal and vertical synchronising must also be provided. These functions are performed by special bit patterns known as timing reference and identification signals (TRS-ID) sent with each line. TRS-ID differs only slightly between formats. Figure 10.6 shows the location of TRS-ID. Immediately before the digital active line location is the SAV (start of active video) TRS-ID pattern, and immediately after is the EAV (end of active video) TRS-ID pattern. These unique patterns occur on every line and continue throughout the vertical interval.

Each TRS-ID pattern consists of four symbols: the same length as the component multiplex repeating structure. In this way the presence of a TRS-ID does

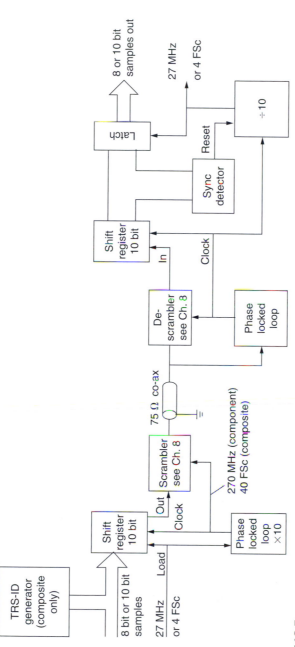

FIGURE 10.5

Major components of a serial scrambled link. Input samples are converted to serial form in a shift register clocked at 10 times the sample rate. The serial data are then scrambled for transmission. On reception, a phase-locked loop re-creates the bit rate clock and drives the descrambler and serial-to-parallel conversion. On detection of the sync pattern, the divide-by-10 counter is re-phased to load parallel samples correctly into the latch. For composite working the bit rate will be 40 times subcarrier, and a sync pattern generator (top left) is needed to inject TRS-ID into the composite data stream.

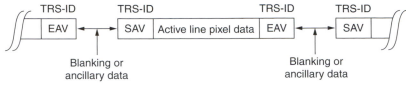

FIGURE 10.6
The active line data are bracketed by TRS-ID codes called SAV and EAV.

not alter the phase of the multiplex. Three of the symbols form a sync pattern for de-serializing and demultiplexing (TRS) and one is an identification symbol (ID) that replaces the analog sync signals. The first symbol contains all ones and the next two contain all zeros. This bit sequence cannot occur in active video, even due to concatenation of successive pixel values, so its detection is reliable. As the transition from a string of ones to a string of zeros occurs at a symbol boundary, it is sufficient to enable unambiguous de-serialization, location of the ID symbol, and demultiplexing of the components. Whatever the word length of the system, all bits should be either ones or zeros during TRS.

The fourth symbol is the ID, which contains three data bits, H, F, and V. These bits are protected by four redundancy bits and together form a seven-bit Hamming code word.

Figure 10.7a shows how the Hamming code is generated. Single-bit errors can be corrected and double-bit errors can be detected according to the decoding table in Figure 10.7b.

Figure 10.8a shows the structure of the TRS-ID. The data bits have the following meanings:

- H is used to distinguish between SAV, where it is set to 0, and EAV, where it is set to 1.
- F defines the state of interlace (if used) and is 0 during the first field and 1 during the second field. F is allowed to change only at EAV. In interlaced systems, one field begins at the centre of a line, but there is no sync pattern at that location so the field bit changes at the end of the line in which the change took place.
- V is 1 during vertical blanking and 0 during the active part of the field. It can change only at EAV.

Figure 10.8b, at the top, shows the relationship between the sync pattern bits and 625-line analog timing, whilst at the bottom is the relationship for 525 lines.

Bit	9	8 F	7 V	6 H	5 P3	4 P2	3 P1	2 P0	1	0
	1	0	0	0	0	0	0	0	0	0
	1	0	0	1	1	1	0	1	0	0
	1	0	1	0	1	0	1	1	0	0
	1	0	1	1	0	1	1	0	0	0
	1	1	0	0	0	1	1	1	0	0
	1	1	0	1	1	0	1	0	0	0
	1	1	1	0	1	1	0	0	0	0
	1	1	1	1	0	0	0	1	0	0

(a) Data Check bits

Received P3–P0	Received bits 8, 7, and 6 (F, V, and H)							
	000	001	010	011	100	101	110	111
0000	000	000	000	*	000	*	*	111
0001	000	*	*	111	*	111	111	111
0010	000	*	*	011	*	101	*	*
0011	*	*	010	*	100	*	*	111
0100	000	*	*	011	*	*	110	*
0101	*	001	*	*	100	*	*	111
0110	*	011	011	011	100	*	*	011
0111	100	*	*	011	100	100	100	*
1000	000	*	*	*	*	101	110	*
1001	*	001	010	*	*	*	*	111
1010	*	001	010	*	101	101	*	101
1011	010	*	010	010	*	101	010	*
1100	*	001	110	*	110	*	110	110
1101	001	001	*	001	*	001	010	*
1110	*	*	*	011	*	101	110	*
1111	*	001	010	*	100	*	*	*

(b)

FIGURE 10.7
The data bits in the TRS are protected with a Hamming code, which is calculated according to the table in (a). Received errors are corrected according to the table in (b), in which a dot shows an error that is detected but not correctable.

Figure 10.9 shows a decode table for SD TRS, which is useful when interpreting logic analyser displays.

The same TRS-ID structure is used in SMPTE 274M and 296M HD. It differs in that the HD formats can support progressive scan in which the F bit is always set to zero.

SD-SDI

This interface supports 525/59.94 2:1 and 625/50 2:1 scanning standards in component and composite. The component interfaces use a common bit rate of 270 MHz for 4:3 pictures with an option of 360 MHz for 16:9. In component, the TRS codes are already present in the parallel domain and SDI does no more than serialize the parallel signal protocol unchanged.

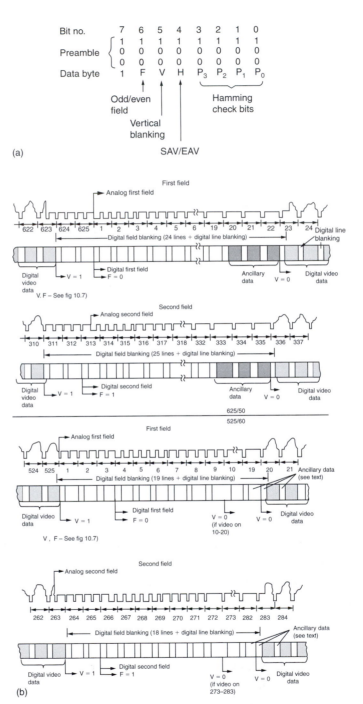

FIGURE 10.8

(a) The four-byte synchronising pattern, which precedes and follows every active line sample block, has this structure. (b) The relationships between analog video timing and the information in the digital timing reference signals for 625/50 (top) and 525/60 (bottom).

TRS (EAV/SAV)- format

| 3FF | 000 | 000 | PQR |

ID

F = 1 = Field 2, F = 0 = Field 1
V = 1 = Vertical blanking
H = 1 = EAV, H = 0 = SAV

Check bits

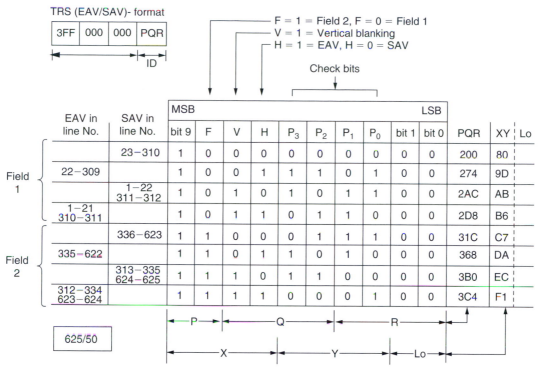

	EAV in line No.	SAV in line No.	MSB bit 9	F	V	H	P₃	P₂	P₁	P₀	bit 1	bit 0 LSB	PQR	XY	Lo
Field 1		23−310	1	0	0	0	0	0	0	0	0	0	200	80	
	22−309		1	0	0	1	1	1	0	1	0	0	274	9D	
		1−22 311−312	1	0	1	0	1	0	1	1	0	0	2AC	AB	
	1−21 310−311		1	0	1	1	0	1	1	0	0	0	2D8	B6	
Field 2		336−623	1	1	0	0	0	1	1	1	0	0	31C	C7	
	335−622		1	1	0	1	1	0	1	0	0	0	368	DA	
		313−335 624−625	1	1	1	0	1	1	0	0	0	0	3B0	EC	
	312−334 623−624		1	1	1	1	0	0	0	1	0	0	3C4	F1	

| 625/50 |

P — Q — R
X — Y — Lo

FIGURE 10.9
Decode table for component TRS.

Composite digital samples at four times the subcarrier frequency and so the bit rate is different between the PAL and the NTSC variants. The composite parallel interface signal is not a multiplex and also carries digitized analog syncs. Consequently there is no need for TRS codes. For serial transmission it is necessary to insert TRS at the serializer and subsequently to strip it out at the serial-to-parallel convertor. The TRS-ID is inserted during blanking, and the serial receiver can detect the patterns it contains. Composite TRS-ID is different from the one used in component signals and consists of five words inserted just after the leading edge of analog video sync. Figure 10.10a shows the location of TRS-ID at samples 967–971 in PAL and Figure 10.10b shows the location at samples 790–794 in NTSC.

Of the five words in TRS-ID, the first four are for synchronising and consist of a single word of all ones, followed by three words of all zeros. Note that the composite TRS contains an extra word of zeros compared with the component TRS, and this could be used for signal identification in multi-standard devices. The fifth word is for identification and carries the line and field numbering information shown in Figure 10.11. The field numbering is colour-framing information useful for editing. In PAL the field numbering will go from 0 to 7, whereas in NTSC it will only reach 3.

On detection of the synchronising symbols, a divide-by-10 circuit is reset, and the output of this will clock words out of the shift register at the correct times. This circuit will also provide the output word clock.

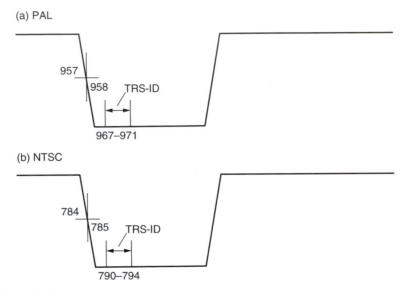

FIGURE 10.10
In composite digital it is necessary to insert a sync pattern during analog sync tip to ensure correct de-serialization. The location of TRS-ID is shown in (a) for PAL and in (b) for NTSC.

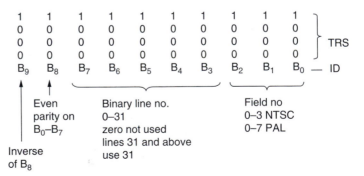

FIGURE 10.11
The contents of the TRS-ID pattern, which is added to the transmission during the horizontal sync pulse just after the leading edge. The field number conveys the composite colour framing field count, and the line number carries a restricted line count intended to give vertical positioning information during the vertical interval. This count saturates at 31 for lines of that number and above.

HD-SDI

The SD serial interface runs at a variety of bit rates according to the television standard being sent. At the high bit rates of HD, variable speed causes too many difficulties, so the HD serial interface[2] runs at only two bit rates: 2.97 and 1.485 Gbps, although it is possible to reduce this by 0.1 percent so that it can lock to traditional 59.94 Hz equipment. Apart from the bit rate, the HD serial interface has as much in common with the SDI standard as possible. Although the impedance, signal level, and channel coding are the same, the HD serial interface has a number of detail differences in the protocol.

The original parallel HD interface had two channels, one for luma and one for multiplexed colour-difference data. Each of these had a symbol rate of 74.25 MHz and its own TRS-ID structure. Essentially the HD serial interface is transparent to these data, as it simply multiplexes between the two channels at symbol rate. As far as the active line is concerned, the result is the same as for SD: a sequence of C_B, Y, C_R, Y, etc. However, in HD, the TRS-IDs of the two channels are also multiplexed. A further difference is that the HD interface has a line number and a CRC (cyclic redundancy check) for each active line inserted immediately after EAV. Figure 10.12a shows the EAV and SAV structure of each channel, with the line count and CRC, whereas Figure 10.12b shows the resultant multiplex.

To keep the interface bit rate constant, variable amounts of packing are placed between the active lines but the result is that the interface no longer works in

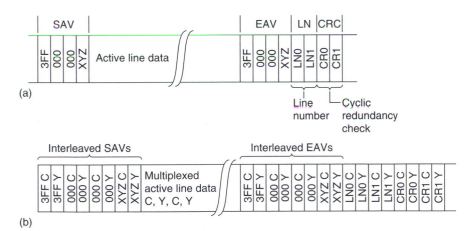

FIGURE 10.12
The HD parallel data are in two channels, each having their own TRS, shown in (a). The EAV is extended by line number and CRC. (b) When the two channels are multiplexed, the TRS codes are interleaved.

real time at all frame rates and requires buffering at source and destination. The interface symbol rate has been chosen to be a common multiple of 24, 25, and 30 times 1125 Hz, so that there can always be an integer number of interface symbol periods in a line period.

A receiver can work out which format is being sent by counting the number of blanking periods between the active lines.

For example, if used at 30 Hz frame rate interlaced, there would be 1125 × 30 = 33,750 lines per second. Figure 10.13a shows that the luma sampling rate is 74.25 MHz and there are 2200 cycles of this clock in one line period. From these, 1920 cycles correspond to the active line and 280 remain for blanking and TRS. The colour difference sampling rate is one-half that of luma at 37.125 MHz and 960 cycles cover to the active line. As there are two colour difference signals, when multiplexed together the symbol rate will be 74.25 + 37.125 + 37.125 = 148.5 MHz. The standard erroneously calls this the interface sampling rate, which is not a sampling rate at all, but a word rate or symbol rate.

The original HD parallel interface had a clock rate of 148.5 MHz. When 10-bit symbols are serialized, the bit rate becomes 1.485 GHz, the lower bit rate of serial HD. If the frame rate is reduced to 25 Hz, as in Figure 10.13b, the line rate falls to 1125 × 25 = 28,125 Hz and the luma sampling rate falls to 2200 × 28,125 = 61.875 MHz. The interface symbol rate does not change, but remains

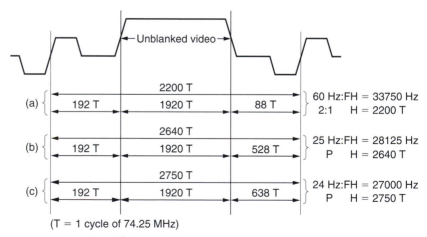

(T = 1 cycle of 74.25 MHz)

FIGURE 10.13
In HD interfaces it is the data rate that is standardised, not the sampling rate. In (a) an 1125/30 picture requires a luma sampling rate of 74.25 MHz to have 1920 square pixels per active line. The data rate of the chroma is the same, thus the interface symbol rate is 148.5 MHz. (b) With 25 Hz pictures, the symbol rate does not change. Instead the blanking area is extended so the data rate is maintained by sending more blanking. (c) An extension of this process allows 24 Hz material to be sent.

at 148.5 MHz. To carry 50 Hz pictures, time compression is used. At 28,125 lines per second, there will be 2640 cycles of 74.25 MHz, the luma interface rate, per line, rather than the 2200 cycles obtained at 60 Hz. Thus the line still contains 1920 active luma samples, but for transmission, the number of blanking/TRS cycles has been increased to 720.

Although the luma is sampled at 61.875 MHz, for transmission luma samples are placed in a buffer and read out at 74.25 MHz. This means that the active line is sent in rather less than an active line period.

Figure 10.13c shows that a similar approach is taken with 24 Hz material in which the number of blanking cycles is further increased.

ANCILLARY DATA

In component standards, only the active line is transmitted and this leaves a good deal of spare capacity. The two line standards differ on how this capacity is used. In 625 lines, only the active line period may be used on lines 20 to 22 and 333 to 335.[3] Lines 20 and 333 are reserved for equipment self-testing.

In 525 lines there is considerably more freedom and ancillary data may be inserted anywhere there is no active video, during either horizontal blanking, where it is known as HANC, or vertical blanking, where it is known as VANC, or both.[4] The spare capacity allows many channels of digital audio and considerably simplifies switching.

The all zeros and all ones codes are reserved for synchronising and cannot be allowed to appear in ancillary data. In practice only seven bits of the eight-bit word can be used as data; the 8th bit is redundant and gives the byte odd parity. As all ones and all zeros are even parity, the sync pattern cannot then be generated accidentally.

Ancillary data are always prefaced by a different four-symbol TRS, which is the inverse of the video TRS in that it starts with all zeros and then has two symbols of all ones followed by the information symbol.

SDTI

SDI is closely specified and is suitable only for transmitting 2:1 interlaced 4:2:2 digital video in 525/60 or 625/50 systems. Since the development of SDI, it has become possible economically to compress digital video and the SDI standard cannot handle this. SDTI (serial data transport interface) is designed to overcome that problem by converting SDI into an interface that can carry a variety of data types whilst retaining compatibility with existing SDI router infrastructures. SDTI[5] sources produce a signal that is electrically identical to an SDI signal and that has the same timing structure. However, the digital active line of SDI becomes a data packet or item in SDTI.

Figure 10.14 shows how SDTI fits into the existing SDI timing. Between EAV and SAV (horizontal blanking in SDI) an ancillary data block is incorporated. The structure of this meets the SDI standard, and the data within describe the contents of the following digital active line. The data capacity of SDTI is about 200 Mbps because some of the 270 Mbps is lost due to the retention of the SDI timing structure. Each digital active line finishes with a CRCC (cyclic redundancy check character) to check for correct transmission.

SDTI raises a number of opportunities, including the transmission of compressed data at faster than real time. If a video signal is compressed at 4:1, then one-quarter as much data would result. If sent in real time the bandwidth required would be one-quarter of that needed by un-compressed video. However, if the same bandwidth is available, the compressed data could be sent in one-quarter of the usual time. This is particularly advantageous for data transfer between compressed camcorders and non-linear editing workstations. Alternatively, four different 50 Mbps signals could be conveyed simultaneously.

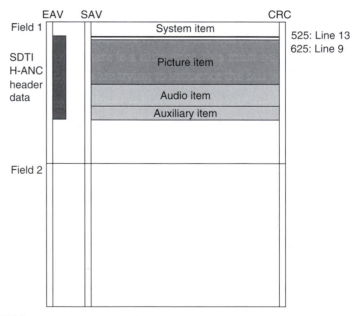

FIGURE 10.14
SDTI is a variation of SDI that allows transmission of generic data. This can include compressed video and non-real-time transfer.

Thus an SDTI transmitter takes the form of a multiplexer that assembles packets for transmission from input buffers. The transmitted data can be encoded according to MPEG, Motion JPEG, Digital Betacam, or DVC formats and all that is necessary is that compatible devices exist at each end of the interface. In this case the data are transferred with bit accuracy and so there is no generation loss associated with the transfer. If the source and destination are different, i.e., having different formats or, in MPEG, different group structures, then a conversion process with attendant generation loss would be needed.

ASI

The asynchronous serial interface is designed to allow MPEG transport streams to be transmitted over standard SDI cabling and routers. ASI offers higher performance than SDTI because it does not adhere to the SDI timing structure. Transport stream data do not have the same statistics as PCM video and so the scrambling technique of SDI cannot be used. Instead ASI uses an 8/10 group code to eliminate DC components and ensure adequate clock content.

SDI equipment is designed to run at a closely defined bit rate of 270 Mbps and has phase-locked loops in receiving and repeating devices, which are intended to remove jitter. These will lose lock if the channel bit rate changes. Transport streams are fundamentally variable in bit rate, and to retain compatibility with SDI routing equipment ASI uses stuffing bits to keep the transmitted bit rate constant.

The use of an 8/10 code means that although the channel bit rate is 270 Mbps, the data bit rate is only 80 percent of that, i.e., 216 Mbps. A small amount of this is lost to overheads.

AES/EBU

The AES/EBU digital audio interface, originally published in 1985, was proposed to embrace all the functions of existing formats in one standard. The goal was to ensure interconnection of professional digital audio equipment irrespective of origin. The EBU ratified the AES proposal with the proviso that the optional transformer coupling was made mandatory and led to the term AES/EBU interface, also called EBU/AES by some Europeans and standardised as IEC-958.

The interface has to be self-clocking and self-synchronising, i.e., the single signal must carry enough information to allow the boundaries between individual bits, words, and blocks to be detected reliably. To fulfil these requirements, the FM channel code is used (see Chapter 8), which is DC-free, strongly self-clocking,

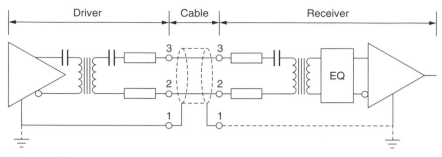

FIGURE 10.15
Recommended electrical circuit for use with the standard two-channel interface.

and capable of working with a changing sampling rate. Synchronisation of de-serialization is achieved by violating the usual encoding rules.

The use of FM means that the channel frequency is the same as the bit rate when sending data ones. Tests showed that in typical analog audio cabling installations, sufficient bandwidth was available to convey two digital audio channels in one twisted pair. The standard driver and receiver chips for RS-422A[6] data communication (or the equivalent CCITT-V.11) are employed for professional use, but work by the BBC[7] suggested that equalization and transformer coupling were desirable for longer cable runs, particularly if several twisted pairs occupy a common shield. Successful transmission up to 350 m has been achieved with these techniques.[8]

Figure 10.15 shows the standard configuration. The output impedance of the drivers will be about 110 Ohms, and the impedance of the cable and receiver should be similar at the frequencies of interest. The driver was specified in AES-3-1985 to produce between 3 and 10 V pk–pk into such an impedance but this was changed to between 2 and 7 V in AES-3-1992 to reflect better the characteristics of actual RS-422 driver chips.

In Figure 10.16, the specification of the receiver is shown in terms of the minimum eye pattern that can be detected without error. It will be noted that the voltage of 200 mV specifies the height of the eye opening at a width of half a channel bit period. The actual signal amplitude will need to be larger than this, and even larger if the signal contains noise. Figure 10.17 shows the recommended equalization characteristic that can be applied to signals received over long lines.

The purpose of the standard is to allow the use of existing analog cabling, and as an adequate connector in the shape of the XLR is already in wide service, the connector made to IEC-268 Part 12 has been adopted for digital audio use.

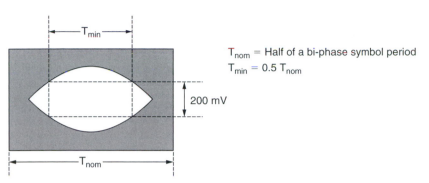

T_{nom} = Half of a bi-phase symbol period
T_{min} = 0.5 T_{nom}

200 mV

FIGURE 10.16
The minimum eye pattern acceptable for correct decoding of standard two-channel data.

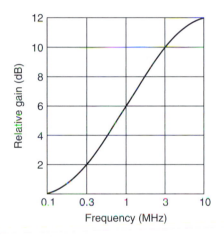

FIGURE 10.17
Equalization characteristic recommended by the AES to improve reception in the case of long lines.

Effectively, existing analog audio cables having XLR connectors can be used without alteration for digital connections.

There is a separate standard[9] for a professional interface using coaxial cable for distances of around 1000 m. This is simply the AES/EBU protocol but with a 75-Ohm coaxial cable carrying a 1 V signal so that it can be handled by analog video distribution amplifiers. Impedance-converting transformers allow balanced 110 Ohm to unbalanced 75 Ohm matching.

In Figure 10.18 the basic structure of the professional and consumer formats can be seen. One subframe consists of 32-bit cells, of which four will be used by a synchronising pattern. Subframes from the two audio channels, A and B, alternate on a time-division basis, with the least significant bit sent first. Up

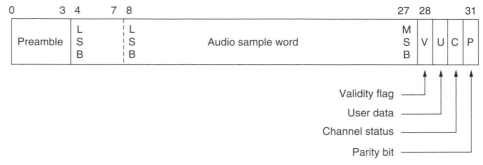

FIGURE 10.18
The basic subframe structure of the AES/EBU format. Sample can be 20 bits, with four auxiliary bits, or 24 bits. LSB is transmitted first.

to 24-bit sample word length can be used, which should cater to all conceivable future developments, but normally 20-bit maximum length samples will be available with four auxiliary data bits, which can be used for a voice-grade channel in a professional application.

The format specifies that audio data must be in two's complement coding. If different word lengths are used, the MSBs must always be in the same bit position, otherwise the polarity will be misinterpreted. Thus the MSB has to be in bit 27 irrespective of word length. Shorter words are leading-zero-filled up to the 20-bit capacity. The channel-status data included from AES-3-1992 signalling of the actual audio word length used, so that receiving devices could adjust the digital dithering level needed to shorten a received word that is too long or pack samples onto a storage device more efficiently.

Four status bits accompany each subframe. The validity flag will be reset if the associated sample is reliable. Whilst there have been many aspirations regarding what the V bit could be used for, in practice a single bit cannot specify much, and if combined with other V bits to make a word, the time resolution is lost. AES-3-1992 described the V bit as indicating that the information in the associated subframe is "suitable for conversion to an analog signal." Thus it might be reset if the interface was being used for non-PCM audio data such as the output of an audio compressor.

The parity bit produces even parity over the subframe, such that the total number of ones in the subframe is even. This allows for simple detection of an odd number of bits in error, but its main purpose is that it makes successive sync patterns have the same polarity, which can be used to improve the probability of detection of sync. The user and channel-status bits are discussed later. Two of the

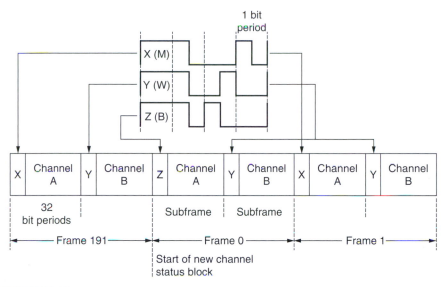

FIGURE 10.19
Three different preambles (X, Y, and Z) are used to synchronise a receiver at the start of subframes.

subframes described above make one frame, which repeats at the sampling rate in use. The first subframe will contain the sample from channel A, or from the left channel in stereo working. The second subframe will contain the sample from channel B, or the right channel in stereo. At 48 kHz, the bit rate will be 3.072 MHz, but as the sampling rate can vary, the clock rate will vary in proportion.

To separate the audio channels on receipt the synchronising patterns for the two subframes are different, as Figure 10.19 shows. These sync patterns begin with a run length of 1.5 bits, which violates the FM channel coding rules and so cannot occur due to any data combination.

The type of sync pattern is denoted by the position of the second transition, which can be 0.5, 1.0, or 1.5 bits away from the first. The third transition is designed to make the sync patterns DC-free. The channel-status and user bits in each subframe form serial data streams with one bit of each per audio channel per frame. The channel-status bits are given a block structure and synchronised every 192 frames, which at 48 kHz gives a block rate of 250 Hz, corresponding to a period of 4 ms. To synchronise the channel-status blocks, the channel A sync pattern is replaced for one frame only by a third sync pattern, which is also shown in Figure 10.19. The AES standard refers to these as X, Y, and Z, whereas IEC-958 calls them M, W, and B. As stated, there is a parity bit in each subframe, which means that the binary level at the end of a subframe will always be the same as at the beginning. Because the sync patterns have the same characteristic, the effect is that sync patterns always have the same polarity and the receiver can use that information to reject noise. The polarity of transmission is not specified, and indeed an accidental inversion in a twisted pair is of no consequence, because it is only the transition that is of importance, not the direction.

In both the professional and the consumer formats, the sequence of channel-status bits over 192 subframes builds up a 24-byte channel-status block. However, the contents of the channel-status data are completely different between the two applications. The professional channel-status structure is shown in Figure 10.20. Byte 0 determines the use of emphasis and the sampling rate. Byte 1 determines the channel usage mode, i.e., whether the data

Byte	
0	Basic control data
1	Mode and user bit management
2	Audio wordlength
3	Vectored target from byte1 (reserved for multichannel applications)
4	AES11 sync ref. identification (bits 0–1), otherwise reserved
5	Reserved
6	Source identification (4 bytes of 7 bit ASCII, no parity)
7	
8	
9	
10	Destination identification (4 bytes of 7 bit ASCII, no parity)
11	
12	
13	
14	Local sample address code (32 bit binary)
15	
16	
17	
18	Time-of-day sample address code (32 bit binary)
19	
20	
21	
22	Channel status reliability flags
23	CRCC

FIGURE 10.20
Overall format of the professional channel-status block.

transmitted are a stereo pair, two unrelated mono signals, or a single mono signal, and details the user bit handling, and byte 2 determines word length. Byte 3 is applicable only to multichannel applications. Byte 4 indicates the suitability of the signal as a sampling rate reference.

There are two slots of four bytes each, which are used for alphanumeric source and destination codes. These can be used for routing. The bytes contain seven-bit ASCII characters (printable characters only) sent LSB first, with the 8th bit set to 0 according to AES-3-1992. The destination code can be used to operate an automatic router.

Bytes 14–17 convey a 32-bit sample address, which increments every channel status frame. It effectively numbers the samples in a relative manner from an arbitrary starting point. Bytes 18–21 convey a similar number, but this is a time-of-day count, which starts from zero at midnight. As many digital audio devices do not have real-time clocks built in, this cannot be relied upon. AES-3-92 specified that the time-of-day bytes should convey the real time at which a recording was made, making it rather like timecode. There are enough combinations in 32 bits to allow a sample count over 24 hours at 48 kHz. The sample count has the advantage that it is universal and independent of local supply frequency.

In theory, if the sampling rate is known, conventional hours, minutes, seconds, frames timecode can be calculated from the sample count, but in practice it is a lengthy computation and users have proposed alternative formats in which the data from the EBU or SMPTE timecode are transmitted directly in these bytes. Some of these proposals are in service as de facto standards.

The penultimate byte contains four flags, which indicate that certain sections of the channel-status information are unreliable. This allows the transmission of an incomplete channel-status block for which the entire structure is not needed or the information is not available. The final byte in the message is a CRCC, which converts the entire channel-status block into a code word. The channel-status message takes 4 ms at 48 kHz and in this time a router could have switched to another signal source. This would damage the transmission, but will also result in a CRCC failure, so the corrupt block is not used.

TELEPHONE-BASED SYSTEMS

The success of the telephone has led to a vast number of subscribers being connected with copper wires and this is a valuable network infrastructure. As technology has developed, the telephone has become part of a global telecommunications industry. Simple economics suggests that in many cases improving the existing telephone cabling with modern modulation schemes is a good way of providing new communications services.

The development of electronics revolutionized telephone exchanges. Whilst the loop current, AC ringing, and hook switch sensing remained for compatibility, the electro-mechanical exchange gave way to electronic exchanges in which the dial pulses were interpreted by digital counters, which then drove crosspoint switches to route the call. The communication remained analog.

The next advance permitted by electronic exchanges was touch-tone dialling, also called DTMF. Touch-tone dialling is based on seven discrete frequencies. The telephone contains tone generators and tuned filters in the exchange can detect each frequency individually. The numbers 0 through 9 and two non-numerical symbols, asterisk and hash, can be transmitted using 12 unique tone pairs. A tone pair can be reliably detected in about 100 ms and this makes dialling much faster than the pulse system.

The first electronic exchanges simply used digital logic to perform the routing function. The next step was to use a fully digital system in which the copper wires from each subscriber terminate in an interface or line card containing ADCs and DACs. The sampling rate of 8 kHz retains the traditional analog bandwidth, and eight-bit quantizing is used. This is not linear, but uses logarithmically sized quantizing steps so that the quantizing error is greater on larger signals. The result is a 64 kbps data rate in each direction.

Packets of data can be time-division multiplexed into high bit rate data buses that can carry many calls simultaneously. The routing function becomes simply one of watching the bus until the right packet comes along for the selected destination. Sixty-four kilobits per second data switching came to be known as IDN (integrated digital network). As a data bus does not care whether it carries 64 kbps of speech or 64 kbps of something else, communications systems based on IDN tend to be based on multiples of that rate. Such a system is called ISDN (integrated services digital network), which is basically a use of the telephone system that allows dial-up data transfer between subscribers in much the same way as a conventional phone call is made.

As it is based on IDN, ISDN works on units of 64 kbps, known as "B channels," so that the communications channel carries the ISDN data just as easily as a voice call. However, for many applications, this bit rate is not enough and ISDN joins together more than one B channel to raise the bit rate. In the lowest cost option, known as Basic Rate ISDN, two B channels are available, allowing 128 kbps communication. Physically, the ISDN connection between the subscriber and the exchange consists of two twisted pairs; one for transmit and one for receive. The existing telephone wiring cannot be used. The signalling data, known as the D channel and running at 16 kbps, is multiplexed into the bitstream. A Basic Rate ISDN link has two B channels and one D channel multiplexed into the twisted pair. The B channels can be used for separate calls or ganged together.

Each twisted pair carries 2×64 plus 1×16 kbps of data, plus synchronising patterns that allow the B and D information to be de-serialized and separated. This results in a total rate of 192 kbps. The network echoes the D bits sent by the terminal. This is used to prove the connection exists in both directions and to detect if more than one terminal has tried to get on the lines at the same time. Figure 10.21 shows what the signalling waveform of ISDN looks like.

A three-level channel code called AMI (alternate mark inversion) is used. The outer two levels (positive or negative voltage) both represent data 0, whereas the centre level (0 V) represents a data 1. Successive zeros must use alternating polarity. Whatever the data bit pattern, AMI coding means that the transmitted waveform is always DC-free because ones cause no offset and any 0 is always balanced by the next 0, which has opposite polarity.

For wider bandwidth, the Primary Rate ISDN system allows, in many parts of the world, up to 30 B channels in a system called E1, whereas in North America a system called T1 is used, which offers 23 or 24 B channels. Naturally the more bit rate that is used, the more the call costs.

For compatibility with IDN, E1 and T1 still use individual 64-kbit channels and the provision of wider bandwidth depends upon units called inverse multiplexers (I-MUXes), which distribute the source data over several B channels. The set of B channels used in an ISDN call do not necessarily all pass down the same route. Depending on how busy lines are, some B channels may pass down a physically different path between subscribers. The data arrive unchanged, but the time axis will be disrupted because the different paths may introduce different delays.

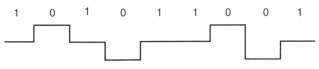

FIGURE 10.21
ISDN uses a modulation scheme known as AMI to deliver data over telephone-type twisted pairs.

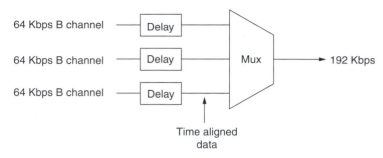

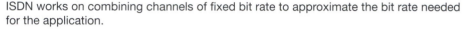

FIGURE 10.22
ISDN works on combining channels of fixed bit rate to approximate the bit rate needed for the application.

Figure 10.22 shows that the multiplexer at the receiving end has to combine the data from a number of B channels and apply suitable delays to each so that the final result is the original bitstream. The I-MUX has to put special time-variant codes in each B channel signal so that the multiplexer can time-align them. An alternative is when a telco has made full use of the synchronising means within the networks. Where suitable control systems are implemented, once a single B channel call has been connected, the remaining B channels are logically attached so that they must follow the same routing, avoiding differential delays. With the subsequent development of broadband networks (B-ISDN), the original ISDN is now known as N-ISDN, in which the N stands for narrowband. B-ISDN is the ultimate convergent network, able to carry any type of data, and uses the well-known ATM protocol. Broadband and ATM are considered in a later section.

One of the difficulties of the AMI coding used in N-ISDN is that the data rate is limited and new cabling to the exchange is needed. ADSL (asymmetric digital subscriber line) is an advanced coding scheme that obtains high bit rate delivery and a back channel down existing subscriber telephone wiring. ADSL works on frequency-division multiplexing using 4 kHz-wide channels, and 249 of these provide the delivery or downstream channel and another 25 provide the back channel. Figure 10.23a shows that the existing bandwidth used by the traditional analog telephone is retained. The back channel occupies the lowest-frequency channels, with the downstream channels above. Figure 10.23b shows that at each end of the existing telephone wiring a device called a splitter is needed. This is basically a high-pass/low-pass filter that directs audio-frequency signals to the telephones and high-frequency signals to the modems.

Telephone wiring was never designed to support high-frequency signalling and is non-ideal. There will be reflections due to impedance mismatches, which will cause an irregular frequency response in addition to high-frequency losses and

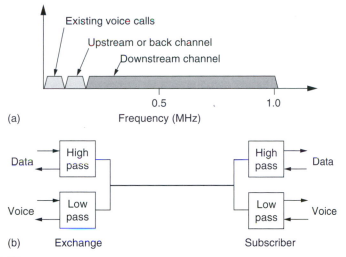

FIGURE 10.23
(a) ADSL allows the existing analog telephone to be retained, but adds delivery and back channels at higher frequencies. (b) A splitter is needed at each end of the subscriber's line.

noise, which will all vary with cable length. ADSL can operate under these circumstances because it constantly monitors the conditions in each channel. If a given channel has adequate signal level and low noise, the full bit rate can be used, but in another channel there may be attenuation and the bit rate will have to be reduced. By independently coding the channels, the optimum data throughput for a given cable is obtained.

Each channel is modulated using DMT (discrete multitone technique), in which combinations of discrete frequencies are used. Within one channel symbol, there are 15 combinations of tones and so the coding achieves 15 bps/Hz. With a symbol rate of 4 kHz, each channel can deliver 60 kbps, resulting in 14.9 Mbps for the downstream channel and 1.5 Mbps for the back channel. It should be stressed that these figures are theoretical maxima, which are not reached in real cables. Practical ADSL systems deliver multiples of the ISDN channel rate up to about 6 Mbps, enough to deliver MPEG-2 coded video.

Over shorter distances, VDSL can reach up to 50 Mbps. Where ADSL and VDSL are being referred to as a common technology, the term xDSL will be found.

DIGITAL TELEVISION BROADCASTING

Digital television broadcasting relies on the combination of a number of fundamental technologies. These are MPEG-2 compression to reduce the bit rate, multiplexing to combine picture and sound data into a common bitstream, digital modulation schemes to reduce the RF bandwidth needed by a given bit rate, and error correction to reduce the error statistics of the channel down to a value acceptable to MPEG data. MPEG compressed video is highly sensitive to bit errors, primarily because they confuse the recognition of variable-length codes so that the decoder loses synchronisation. However, MPEG is a compression and multiplexing standard and does not specify how error correction should be performed. Consequently a transmission standard must define a system that has to correct essentially all errors such that the delivery mechanism is transparent.

Essentially a transmission standard specifies all the additional steps needed to deliver an MPEG transport stream from one place to another. This transport stream will consist of a number of elementary streams of video and audio, in which the audio may be coded according to MPEG audio standards or AC-3. In a system working within its capabilities, the picture and sound quality will be determined only by the performance of the compression system and not by the RF transmission channel. This is the fundamental difference between analog and digital broadcasting. In analog television broadcasting, the picture quality may be limited by composite video encoding artifacts as well as transmission artifacts such as noise and ghosting. In digital television broadcasting the picture quality is determined instead by the compression artifacts and interlace artifacts if interlace has been retained.

If the received error rate increases for any reason, once the correcting power is used up, the system will degrade rapidly as uncorrected errors enter the MPEG decoder. In practice, decoders will be programd to recognize the condition and mute or freeze to avoid outputting garbage. As a result digital receivers tend either to work well or not to work at all. It is important to realise that the signal strength in a digital system does not translate directly to picture quality. A poor signal will increase the number of bit errors. Provided that this is within the capability of the error-correction system, there is no visible loss of quality. In contrast, a very powerful signal may be unusable because of similarly powerful reflections due to multipath propagation.

Whilst in one sense an MPEG transport stream is only data, it differs from generic data in that it must be presented to the viewer with a particular time base. Generic data are usually asynchronous, whereas baseband video and audio are synchronous. However, after compression and multiplexing audio and video are no longer precisely synchronous and so the term isochronous is used. This refers to a signal that was at one time synchronous and will be displayed synchronously, but which uses buffering at transmitter and receiver to accommodate moderate timing errors in the transmission.

Clearly another mechanism is needed so that the time axis of the original signal can be re-created on reception. The time stamp and program clock reference system of MPEG does this.

Figure 10.24 shows that the concepts involved in digital television broadcasting exist at various levels that have an independence not found in analog technology. In a given configuration a transmitter can radiate a given payload data bit rate. This represents the useful bit rate and does not include the necessary overheads needed by error correction, multiplexing, or synchronising. It is fundamental that the transmission system does not care what this payload bit rate is used for. The entire capacity may be used up by one high-definition channel, or a large number of heavily compressed channels may be carried. The details of this data usage are the domain of the transport stream. The multiplexing of transport streams is defined by the MPEG standards, but these do not define any error-correction or transmission technique.

At the lowest level in Figure 10.25, the source coding scheme, in this case MPEG compression, results in one or more elementary streams, each of which

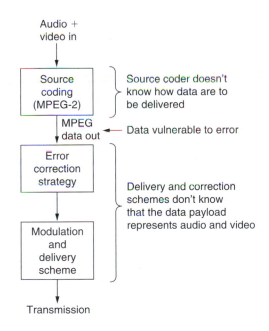

FIGURE 10.24
Source coder does not know delivery mechanism and delivery does not need to know what the data mean.

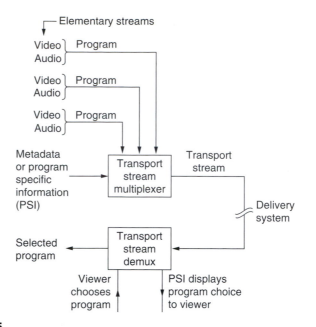

FIGURE 10.25
Program-specific information helps the demultiplexer to select the required program.

carries a video or audio channel. Elementary streams are multiplexed into a transport stream. The viewer then selects the desired elementary stream from the transport stream. Metadata in the transport stream ensure that when a video elementary stream is chosen, the appropriate audio elementary stream will automatically be selected.

MPEG PACKETS AND TIME STAMPS

The video elementary stream is an endless bitstream representing pictures that take variable lengths of time to transmit. Bi-directional coding means that pictures are not necessarily in the correct order. Storage and transmission systems prefer discrete blocks of data and so elementary streams are packetised to form a PES (packetised elementary stream). Audio elementary streams are also packetised. A packet is shown in Figure 10.26. It begins with a header containing a unique packet start code and a code that identifies the type of data stream.

Optionally the packet header also may contain one or more time stamps, which are used for synchronising the video decoder to real time and for obtaining lip-sync. Figure 10.27 shows that a time stamp is a sample of the state of a counter, which is driven by a 90 kHz clock. This is obtained by dividing down the master 27 MHz clock of MPEG-2. This 27 MHz clock must be locked to the

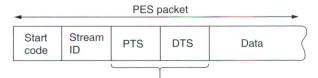

PTS/DTS need not be in every PES packet.
Can be up to 700 milliseconds apart in program
streams or 100 milliseconds apart in transport streams.
Decoder interpolates stamps

FIGURE 10.26
A PES packet structure is used to break up the continuous elementary stream.

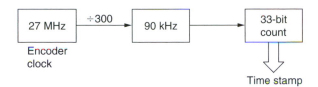

FIGURE 10.27
Time stamps are the result of sampling a counter driven by the encoder clock.

video frame rate and the audio sampling rate of the program concerned. There are two types of time stamp: PTS and DTS. These are abbreviations for presentation time stamp and decode time stamp. A presentation time stamp determines when the associated picture should be displayed on the screen, whereas a decode time stamp determines when it should be decoded. In bi-directional coding these times can be quite different.

Audio packets are not reordered and have only presentation time stamps. Clearly if lip-sync is to be obtained, the audio sampling rate of a given program must have been locked to the same master 27 MHz clock as the video and the time stamps must have come from the same counter driven by that clock. In practice the time between input pictures is constant and so there is a certain amount of redundancy in the time stamps. Consequently PTS/DTS need not appear in every PES packet. Time stamps can be up to 100 ms apart in transport streams. As each picture type (I, P, or B) is flagged in the bitstream, the decoder can infer the PTS/DTS for every picture from the ones actually transmitted.

The MPEG-2 transport stream is intended to be a multiplex of many TV programs with their associated sound and data channels, although a single program transport stream (SPTS) is possible. The transport stream is based upon packets of constant size so that multiplexing, adding error-correction codes, and interleaving in a higher layer are eased. Figure 10.28 shows that these are always 188 bytes long.

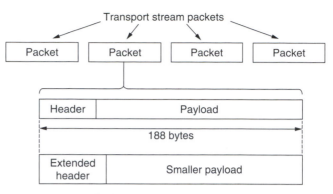

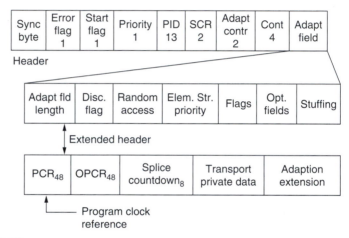

FIGURE 10.28
Transport stream packets are always 188 bytes long to facilitate multiplexing and error correction.

Transport stream packets always begin with a header. The remainder of the packet carries data known as the payload. For efficiency, the normal header is relatively small, but for special purposes the header may be extended. In this case the payload gets smaller so that the overall size of the packet is unchanged. Transport stream packets should not be confused with PES packets, which are larger and which vary in size. PES packets are broken up to form the payload of the transport stream packets.

The header begins with a sync byte, which is a unique pattern detected by a demultiplexer. A transport stream may contain many different elementary streams and these are identified by giving each a unique 13-bit packet identification code or PID, which is included in the header. A multiplexer seeking a particular elementary stream simply checks the PID of every packet and accepts only those that match.

In a multiplex there may be many packets from other programs in between packets of a given PID. To help the demultiplexer, the packet header contains a continuity count. This is a four-bit value that increments at each new packet having a given PID. This approach allows statistical multiplexing, as it does matter how many or how few packets have a given PID; the demux will still find them. Statistical multiplexing has the problem that it is virtually impossible to make the sum of the input bit rates constant. Instead the multiplexer aims to make the average data bit rate slightly less than the maximum and the overall bit rate is kept constant by adding "stuffing" or null packets. These packets have no meaning, but simply keep the bit rate constant. Null packets always have a PID of 8191 (all ones) and the demultiplexer discards them.

PROGRAM-SPECIFIC INFORMATION (PSI)

In a real transport stream, each elementary stream has a different PID, but the demultiplexer has to be told what these PIDs are and what audio belongs with what video before it can operate. This is the function of PSI, which is a form of metadata. Figure 10.30 shows the structure of PSI.

When a decoder powers up, it knows nothing about the incoming transport stream except that it must search for all packets with a PID of 0. PID 0 is reserved for the program association table (PAT) packets. The PAT is transmitted at regular intervals and contains a list of all the programs in this transport stream. Each program is further described by its own program map table (PMT) and the PIDs of the PMTs are contained in the PAT.

Figure 10.30 also shows that the PMTs fully describe each program. The PID of the video elementary stream is defined, along with the PID(s) of the associated audio and data streams. Consequently when the viewer selects a particular program, the demultiplexer looks up the program number in the PAT, finds the right PMT, and reads the audio, video, and data PIDs. It then selects elementary streams having these PIDs from the transport stream and routes them to the decoders.

Program 0 of the PAT contains the PID of the network information table (NIT). This contains information about what other transport streams are available. For example, in the case of a satellite broadcast, the NIT would detail the orbital position, polarization, carrier frequency, and modulation scheme. Using the NIT a set-top box could automatically switch between transport streams.

Apart from 0 and 8191, a PID of 1 is also reserved for the conditional access table. This is part of the access control mechanism needed to support pay-per-view or subscription viewing.

PROGRAM CLOCK REFERENCE

A transport stream is a multiplex of several TV programs and these may have originated from widely different locations. It is impractical to expect all the programs in a transport stream to be genlocked and so the stream is designed from the outset to allow unlocked programs. A decoder running from a transport stream has to genlock to the encoder and the transport stream has to have a mechanism to allow this to be done independently for each program. The synchronising mechanism is called program clock reference (PCR).

Figure 10.29 shows how the PCR system works. The goal is to re-create at the decoder a 27 MHz clock that is synchronous with that at the encoder. The encoder clock drives a 48-bit counter, which continuously counts up to the maximum value before overflowing and beginning again.

A transport stream multiplexer will periodically sample the counter and place the state of the count in an extended packet header as a PCR (see Figure 10.26). The demultiplexer selects only the PIDs of the required program, and it will extract the PCRs from the packets in which they were inserted. The PCR codes are used to control a numerically locked loop (NLL) described in Chapter 4. The NLL contains a 27 MHz VCXO (voltage-controlled crystal oscillator), a variable-frequency oscillator based on a crystal, which has a relatively small frequency range.

The VCXO drives a 48-bit counter in the same way as in the encoder. The state of the counter is compared with the contents of the PCR and the difference is used to modify the VCXO frequency. When the loop reached lock, the decoder counter would arrive at the same value as is contained in the PCR and no change in the VCXO would

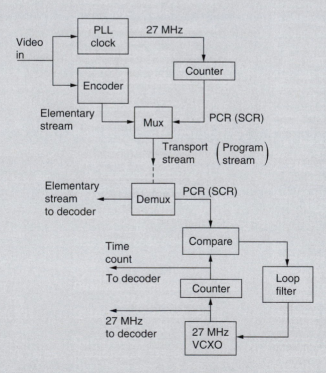

FIGURE 10.29
Program or system clock reference codes regenerate a clock at the decoder. See text for details.

then occur. In practice the transport stream packets will suffer from transmission jitter and this will create phase noise in the loop. This is removed by the loop filter so that the VCXO effectively averages a large number of phase errors.

A heavily damped loop will reject jitter well, but will take a long time to lock. Lockup time can be reduced when switching to a new program if the decoder counter is jammed to the value of the first PCR received in the new program. The loop filter may also use shorter time constants during lockup.

Once a synchronous 27 MHz clock is available at the decoder, this can be divided down to provide the 90 kHz clock, which drives the time stamp mechanism. The entire time-base stability of the decoder is no better than the stability of the clock derived from PCR. MPEG-2 sets standards for the maximum amount of jitter that can be present in PCRs in a real transport stream.

Clearly if the 27 MHz clock in the receiver is locked to one encoder it can receive only elementary streams encoded with that clock. If it is attempted to decode, for example, an audio stream generated from a different clock, the result will be periodic buffer overflows or underflows in the decoder. Thus MPEG defines a program in a manner that relates to timing. A program is a set of elementary streams that have been encoded with the same master clock.

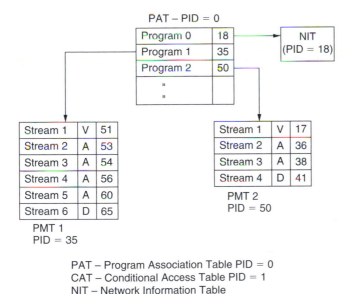

PAT – Program Association Table PID = 0
CAT – Conditional Access Table PID = 1
NIT – Network Information Table
Null packets – PID = 8191

FIGURE 10.30
MPEG-2 PSI is used to tell a de-multiplexer what the transport stream contains.

TRANSPORT STREAM MULTIPLEXING

A transport stream multiplexer is a complex device because of the number of functions it must perform. A fixed multiplexer will be considered first. In a fixed multiplexer, the bit rate of each of the programs must be specified so that the sum does not exceed the payload bit rate of the transport stream. The payload bit rate is the overall bit rate less the packet headers and PSI rate. In practice the programs will not be synchronous to one another, but the transport stream must produce a constant packet rate given by the bit rate divided by 188 bytes, the packet length. Figure 10.31 shows how this is handled. Each elementary stream entering the multiplexer passes through a buffer that is divided into payload-sized areas. Note that periodically the payload area is made smaller because of the requirement to insert PCR.

MPEG-2 decoders also have a quantity of buffer memory. The challenge to the multiplexer is to take packets from each program in such a way that neither its own buffers nor the buffers in any decoder either overflow or underflow. This requirement is met by sending packets from all programs as evenly as possible rather than bunching together a lot of packets from one program. When the bit rates of the programs are different, the only way this can be handled is to use the buffer contents indicators. The fuller a buffer is, the more likely it should be that a packet will be read from it. Thus a buffer content arbitrator can decide which program should have a packet allocated next.

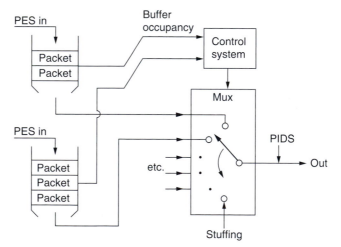

FIGURE 10.31
A transport stream multiplexer can handle several programs that are asynchronous to one another and to the transport stream clock. See text for details.

If the sum of the input bit rates is correct, the buffers should all slowly empty because the overall input bit rate has to be less than the payload bit rate. This allows for the insertion of program-specific information. Whilst PATs and PMTs are being transmitted, the program buffers will fill up again. The multiplexer can also fill the buffers by sending more PCRs as this reduces the payload of each packet. In the event that the multiplexer has sent enough of everything but still cannot fill a packet, it will send a null packet with a PID of 8191. Decoders will discard null packets and, as they convey no useful data, the multiplexer buffers will all fill whilst null packets are being transmitted.

The use of null packets means that the bit rates of the elementary streams do not need to be synchronous with one another or with the transport stream bit rate. As each elementary stream can have its own PCR, it is not necessary for the different programs in a transport stream to be genlocked to one another; in fact they do not even need to have the same frame rate. This approach allows the transport stream bit rate to be accurately defined and independent of the timing of the data carried. This is important because the transport stream bit rate determines the spectrum of the transmitter and this must not vary.

In a statistical multiplexer or STATMUX, the bit rate allocated to each program can vary dynamically. Figure 10.32 shows that there must be a tight connection between the STATMUX and the associated compressors. Each compressor has a buffer memory, which is emptied by a demand clock from the STATMUX. In a normal, fixed bit rate coder, the buffer content feeds back and controls the requantizer. In statmuxing this process is less severe and takes place only if the buffer is very close to full, because the degree of coding difficulty is also fed to the STATMUX.

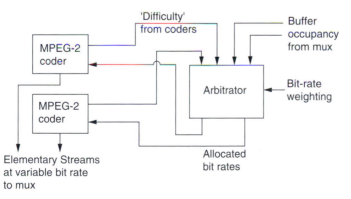

FIGURE 10.32
A statistical multiplexer contains an arbitrator, which allocates bit rate to each program as a function of program difficulty.

REMULTIPLEXING

In real life a program creator may produce a transport stream that carries all its programs simultaneously. A service provider may take in several such streams and create its own transport stream by selecting different programs from different sources. In an MPEG-2 environment this requires a remultiplexer, also known as a transmultiplexer. Figure 10.33 shows what a remultiplexer does. Remultiplexing is easier when all the incoming programs have the same bit rate. If a suitable combination of programs is selected it is obvious that the output transport stream will always have sufficient bit rate. When statistical multiplexing has been used, there is a possibility that the sum of the bit rates of the selected programs will exceed the bit rate of the output transport stream. To avoid this, the remultiplexer will have to employ recompression.

Recompression requires a partial decode of the bitstream to identify the DCT (discrete cosine transform) coefficients. These will then be requantized to reduce the bit rate until it is low enough to fit the output transport stream. Remultiplexers have to edit the PSI (Program Specific Information) such that the PAT (Program Association Tables) and the PMTs (Program Map Tables) correctly reflect the new transport stream content. It may also be necessary to change the PIDs (packet identification codes) because the incoming transport streams could inadvertently have used the same values.

When PCR (Program Clock Reference) data are included in an extended packet header, they represent a real-time clock count, and if the associated packet is moved in time the PCR value will be wrong. Remultiplexers have to re-create a new multiplex from a number of other multiplexes and it is inevitable that this process will result in packets being placed in locations in the output transport stream that are different from those they had in the input. In this case the remultiplexer must edit the PCR values so that they reflect the value the clock counter would have had at the location at which the packet now resides.

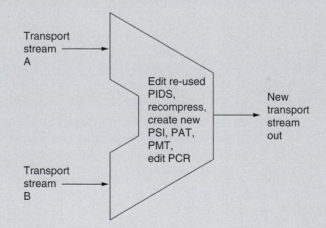

FIGURE 10.33
A remultiplexer creates a new transport stream from selected programs in other transport streams.

The STATMUX contains an arbitrator, which allocates more packets to the program with the greatest coding difficulty. Thus if a particular program encounters difficult material it will produce large prediction errors and begin to fill its output buffer. As the STATMUX has allocated more packets to that program, more data will be read out of that buffer, preventing overflow. Of course this is possible only if the other programs in the transport stream are handling typical video.

In the event that several programs encounter difficult material at once, clearly the buffer contents will rise and the requantizing mechanism will have to operate.

BROADCAST MODULATION TECHNIQUES

A key difference between analog and digital transmission is that the transmitter output is switched between a number of discrete states rather than continuously varying. The process is called channel coding, which is the digital equivalent of modulation. A good code minimizes the channel bandwidth needed for a given bit rate. This quality of the code is measured in bits per second per hertz (bps/Hz) and is roughly the equivalent of the density ratio in recording. Figure 10.34 shows, not surprisingly, that the less bandwidth required, the better the signal-to-noise ratio has to be. The figure shows the theoretical limit as well as the performance of a number of codes that offer different balances of bandwidth/noise performance.

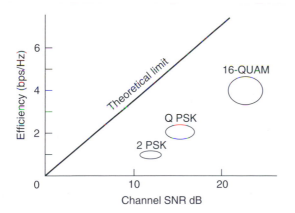

FIGURE 10.34
Where a better SNR exists, more data can be sent down a given bandwidth channel.

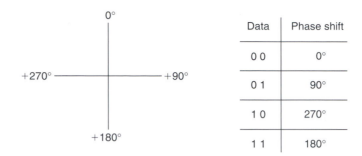

Data	Phase shift
0 0	0°
0 1	90°
1 0	270°
1 1	180°

FIGURE 10.35
Differential quadrature phase-shift keying (DQPSK).

Where the SNR is poor, as in satellite broadcasting, the amplitude of the signal will be unstable, and phase modulation is used. Figure 10.35 shows that phase-shift keying (PSK) can use two or more phases. When four phases in quadrature are used, the result is quadrature phase-shift keying or QPSK. Each period of the transmitted waveform can have one of four phases and therefore conveys the value of two data bits. Eight-PSK uses eight phases and can carry three bits per symbol where the SNR is adequate. PSK is generally encoded in such a way that a knowledge of absolute phase is not needed at the receiver. Instead of encoding the signal phase directly, the data determine the magnitude of the phase shift between symbols. A QPSK coder is shown in Figure 10.36.

In terrestrial transmission more power is available than, for example, from a satellite, and so a stronger signal can be delivered to the receiver. Where a better SNR exists, an increase in data rate can be had using multilevel signalling or *m*-ary coding instead of binary. Figure 10.37 shows that the ATSC system uses an eight-level signal (8-VSB), allowing three bits to be sent per symbol. Four of the levels exist with normal carrier phase and four exist with inverted phase so that a phase-sensitive rectifier is needed in the receiver. Clearly the data separator must have a three-bit ADC, which can resolve the eight signal levels. The gain and offset of the signal must be precisely set so that the quantizing levels register precisely with the centres of the eyes. The transmitted signal contains sync pulses that are encoded using specified code levels so that the data separator can set its gain and offset.

Multilevel signalling systems have the characteristic that the bits in the symbol have different error probability. Figure 10.38 shows that a small noise level will corrupt the low-order bit, whereas twice as much noise will be needed to corrupt the middle bit and four times as much will be needed to corrupt the high-order bit. In ATSC the solution is that the lower two bits are encoded

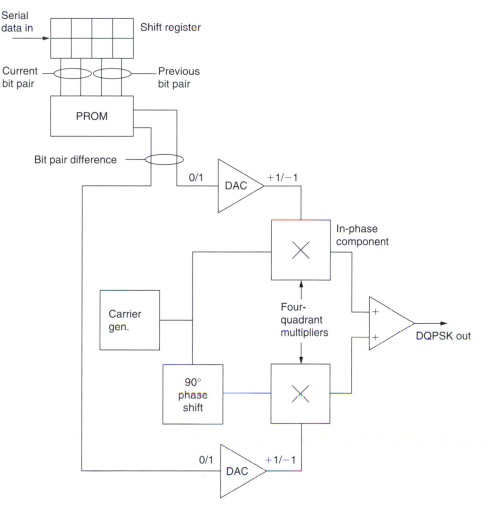

FIGURE 10.36

A QPSK coder conveys two bits for each modulation period. See text for details.

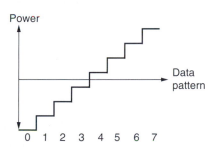

FIGURE 10.37

In eight-VSB the transmitter operates in eight different states enabling three bits to be sent per symbol.

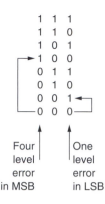

```
1  1  1
1  1  0
1  0  1
1  0  0
0  1  1
0  1  0
0  0  1
0  0  0
```

Four level error in MSB   One level error in LSB

FIGURE 10.38
In multi-level signalling the error probability is not the same for each bit.

together in an inner error-correcting scheme so that they represent only one bit with reliability similar to that of the top bit. As a result the 8-VSB system actually delivers two data bits per symbol even though eight-level signalling is used.

The modulation of the carrier results in a double-sideband spectrum, but following analog TV practice most of the lower sideband is filtered off, leaving a vestigial sideband only, hence the term 8-VSB. A small DC offset is injected into the modulator signal so that the four in-phase levels are slightly higher than the four out-of-phase levels. This has the effect of creating a small pilot at the carrier frequency to help receiver locking.

Multilevel signalling can be combined with PSK to obtain multilevel quadrature amplitude modulation (QUAM). Figure 10.39 shows the example of 64-QUAM. Incoming six-bit data words are split into two three-bit words and each is used to amplitude modulate a pair of sinusoidal carriers that are generated in quadrature. The modulators are four-quadrant devices such that 2^3 amplitudes are available, four of which are in phase with the carrier and four in antiphase. The two AM carriers are linearly added and the result is a signal that has 2^6 or 64 combinations of amplitude and phase. There is a great deal of similarity between QUAM and the colour subcarrier used in analog television in which the two colour difference signals are encoded into one amplitude- and phase-modulated waveform. On reception, the waveform is sampled twice per cycle in phase with the two original carriers and the result is a pair of eight-level signals. Sixteen-QUAM is also possible, delivering only four bits per symbol but requiring a lower SNR.

The data bit patterns to be transmitted can have any combination whatsoever, and if nothing were done, the transmitted spectrum would be non-uniform. This is undesirable because peaks cause interference with other services,

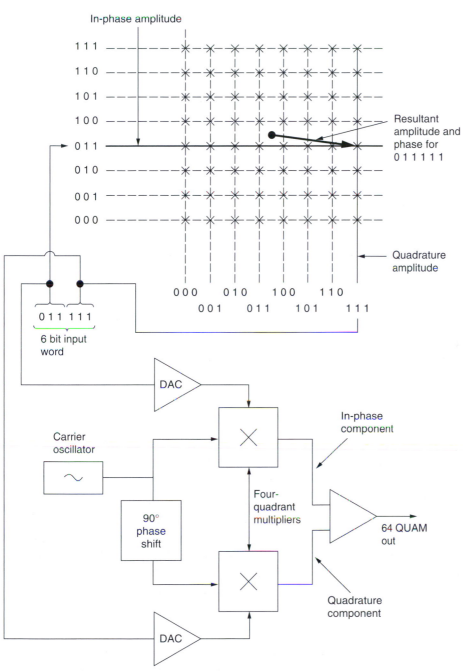

FIGURE 10.39
In 64-QUAM, two carriers are generated with a quadrature relationship. These are independently amplitude modulated to eight discrete levels in four quadrant multipliers. Adding the signals produces a QUAM signal having 64 unique combinations of amplitude and phase. Decoding requires the waveform to be sampled in quadrature like a colour TV subcarrier.

whereas energy troughs allow external interference in. The randomizing technique of Chapter 8 is used to overcome the problem. The process is known as energy dispersal. The signal energy is spread uniformly throughout the allowable channel bandwidth so that it has less energy at a given frequency.

A pseudo-random sequence generator is used to generate the randomizing sequence. Figure 10.40 shows the randomizer used in DVB. This 16-bit device has a maximum sequence length of 65,535 bits and is preset to a standard value at the beginning of each set of eight transport stream packets. The serialized data are XORed with the LSB of the Galois field, which randomizes the output, which then goes to the modulator. The spectrum of the transmission is now more uniform.

On reception, the de-randomizer must contain the identical ring counter, which must also be set to the starting condition to bit accuracy. Its output is then added to the data stream from the demodulator. The randomizing will effectively then have been added twice to the data in modulo-2 and, as a result, is cancelled out, leaving the original serial data.

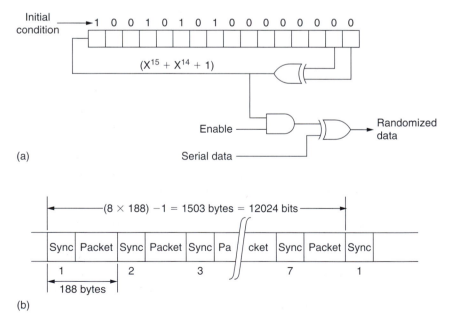

(a)

(b)

FIGURE 10.40
The randomizer of DVB is pre-set to the initial condition once every eight transport stream packets. The maximum length of the sequence is 65535 bits, but only the first 12024 bits are used before resetting again (b).

OFDM

The way that radio signals interact with obstacles is a function of the relative magnitude of the wavelength and the size of the object. AM sound radio transmissions, with a wavelength of several hundred metres, can easily diffract around large objects. The shorter the wavelength of a transmission, the larger objects in the environment appear to it, and these objects can then become reflectors. Reflecting objects produce a delayed signal at the receiver in addition to the direct signal. In analog television transmissions this causes the familiar ghosting. In digital transmissions, the symbol rate may be so high that the reflected signal may be one or more symbols behind the direct signal, causing intersymbol interference. As the reflection may be continuous, the result may be that almost every symbol is corrupted. No error-correction system can handle this.

Raising the transmitter power is no help at all as it simply raises the power of the reflection in proportion. The only solution is to change the characteristics of the RF channel in some way to either prevent the multi-path reception or prevent it being a problem. The RF channel includes the modulator, transmitter, antennae, receiver, and demodulator.

As with analog UHF TV transmissions, a directional antenna is useful with digital transmission as it can reject reflections. However, directional antennae tend to be large and they require a skilled permanent installation. Mobile use on a vehicle or vessel is simply impractical. Another possibility is to incorporate a ghost canceller into the receiver. The transmitter periodically sends a standardised known waveform called a training sequence. The receiver knows what this waveform looks like and compares it with the received signal. In theory it is possible for the receiver to compute the delay and relative level of a reflection and so insert an opposing one. In practice if the reflection is strong it may prevent the receiver from finding the training sequence.

The most elegant approach is to use a system in which multi-path reception conditions cause only a small increase in error rate, which the error-correction system can manage. This approach is used in DVB. Figure 10.41a shows that when one carrier with a high bit rate is used, reflections can easily be delayed by one or more bit periods, causing interference between the bits. Figure 10.41b shows that, instead, OFDM sends many carriers, each having a low bit rate. When a low bit rate is used, the energy in the reflection will arrive during the same bit period as the direct signal. Not only is the system immune to multi-path reflections, but also the energy in the reflections can actually be used. This characteristic can be enhanced by using guard intervals, shown in Figure 10.41c. These reduce multi-path bit overlap even more.

Note that OFDM is not a modulation scheme, and each of the carriers used in an OFDM system still needs to be modulated using any of the digital coding schemes described above. What OFDM does is provide an efficient way of packing many carriers close together without mutual interference. A serial data waveform basically contains a train of rectangular pulses. The transform of a rectangle is the function $\sin x/x$ and so the baseband pulse train has a $\sin x/x$ spectrum. When this waveform is used to modulate a carrier the result is a symmetrical $\sin x/x$ spectrum centred on the carrier frequency.

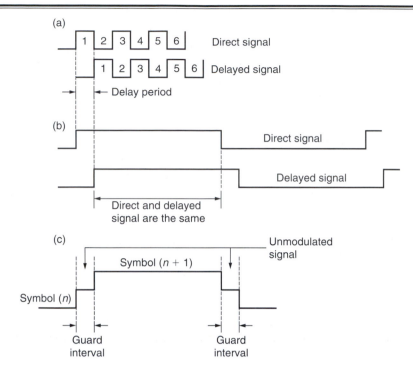

FIGURE 10.41
(a) High-bit rate transmissions are prone to corruption due to reflections. (b) If the bit rate is reduced the effect of reflections is eliminated; in fact, reflected energy can be used. (c) Guard intervals may be inserted between symbols.

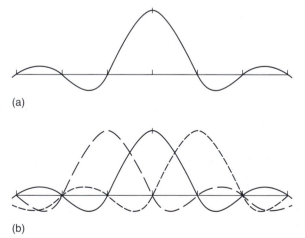

FIGURE 10.42
In OFDM the carrier spacing is critical, but when it is correct the carriers become independent and the most efficient use is made of the spectrum. (a) Spectrum of bitstream has regular nulls. (b) Peak of one carrier occurs at null of another.

Figure 10.42a shows that nulls in the spectrum appear spaced at multiples of the bit rate away from the carrier. Further carriers can be placed at spacings such that each is centred at the null of the another as is shown in (b). The distance between the carriers is equal to 90° or one quadrant of sin$x$. Owing to the quadrant spacing, these carriers are mutually orthogonal, hence the term orthogonal frequency division. A large number of such carriers (in practice several thousand) will be interleaved to produce an overall spectrum that is almost rectangular and that fills the available transmission channel.

When guard intervals are used, the carrier returns to an unmodulated state between bits for a period greater than the period of the reflections. Then the reflections from one transmitted bit decay during the guard interval before the next bit is transmitted. The use of guard intervals reduces the bit rate of the carrier because for some of the time it is radiating carrier not data. A typical reduction is to around 80 percent of the capacity without guard intervals.

This capacity reduction does, however, improve the error statistics dramatically, such that much less redundancy is required in the error correction system. Thus the effective transmission rate is improved. The use of guard intervals also moves more energy from the sidebands back to the carrier. The frequency spectrum of a set of carriers is no longer perfectly flat but contains a small peak at the centre of each carrier.

The ability to work in the presence of multi-path cancellation is one of the great strengths of OFDM. In DVB, more than 2000 carriers are used in single transmitter systems. Provided there is exact synchronism, several transmitters can radiate exactly the same signal so that a SFN (single-frequency network) can be created throughout a whole country. SFNs require a variation on OFDM that uses over 8000 carriers.

With OFDM, directional antennae are not needed and, given sufficient field strength, mobile reception is perfectly feasible. Of course, directional antennae may still be used to boost the received signal outside normal service areas or to enable the use of low-powered transmitters.

An OFDM receiver must perform fast Fourier transforms (FFTs) on the whole band at the symbol rate of one of the carriers. The amplitude and/or phase of the carrier at a given frequency effectively reflects the state of the transmitted symbol at that time slot and so the FFT partially demodulates as well. To assist with tuning in, the OFDM spectrum contains pilot signals. These are individual carriers that are transmitted with slightly more power than the remainder. The pilot carriers are spaced apart through the whole channel at agreed frequencies, which form part of the transmission standard.

Practical reception conditions, including multi-path reception, will cause a significant variation in the received spectrum and some equalization will be needed. Figure 10.43 shows what the possible spectrum looks like in the presence of a powerful reflection. The signal has almost been cancelled at certain frequencies. However, the FFT performed in the receiver is effectively a spectral analysis of the signal and so the receiver computes for free the received spectrum.

As in a flat spectrum the peak magnitude of all the coefficients would be the same (apart from the pilots), equalization is easily performed by multiplying the coefficients by suitable constants until this characteristic is obtained.

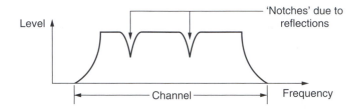

FIGURE 10.43
Multi-path reception can place notches in the channel spectrum. This will require equalization at the receiver.

Although the use of transform-based receivers appears complex, when it is considered that such an approach simultaneously allows effective equalization, the complexity is not significantly higher than that of a conventional receiver, which needs a separate spectral analysis system just for equalization purposes.

The only drawback of OFDM is that the transmitter must be highly linear to prevent intermodulation between the carriers. This is readily achieved in terrestrial transmitters by derating the transmitter so that it runs at a lower power than it would in analog service. This is not practicable in satellite transmitters, which are optimized for efficiency, so OFDM is not really suitable for satellite use.

ERROR CORRECTION IN DIGITAL TELEVISION BROADCASTING

As in recording, broadcast data suffer from both random and burst errors and the error-correction strategies of digital television broadcasting have to reflect that. Figure 10.44 shows a typical system in which inner and outer codes are employed. The Reed–Solomon codes are universally used for burst-correcting outer codes, along with an interleave, which will be convolutional rather than the block-based interleave used in recording media. The inner codes will not be R-S, as more suitable codes exist for the statistical conditions prevalent in broadcasting. DVB uses a parity-based variable-rate system in which the amount of redundancy can be adjusted according to reception conditions. ATSC uses a fixed-rate parity-based system along with trellis coding to overcome cochannel interference from analog NTSC transmitters.

DVB

The DVB system is subdivided into systems optimized for satellite, cable, and terrestrial delivery. This section concentrates on the terrestrial delivery system. Figure 10.45 shows a block diagram of a terrestrial (DVB-T) transmitter. Incoming transport stream packets of 188 bytes each are first subject to R-S outer coding. This adds 16 bytes of redundancy to each packet, resulting in 204 bytes. Outer coding is followed by interleaving. The interleave mechanism is shown in Figure 10.46. Outer code blocks are commutated on a byte basis

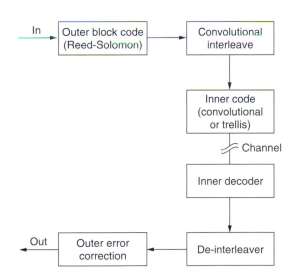

FIGURE 10.44
Error-correcting strategy of digital television broadcasting systems.

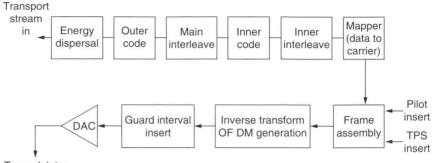

FIGURE 10.45
DVB-T transmitter block diagram. See text for details.

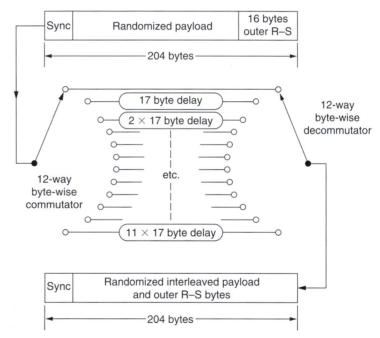

FIGURE 10.46
The interleaver of DVB uses 12 incrementing delay channels to re-order the data. The sync byte passes through the undelayed channel and so is still at the head of the packet after interleave. However, the packet now contains non-adjacent bytes from 12 different packets.

into 12 parallel channels. Each channel contains a different amount of delay, typically achieved by a ring-buffer RAM. The delays are integer multiples of 17 bytes, designed to skew the data by one outer block ($12 \times 17 = 204$). Following the delays, a commutator re-assembles interleaved outer blocks.

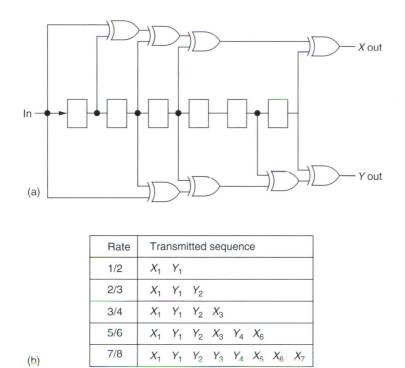

(a)

Rate	Transmitted sequence
1/2	X_1 Y_1
2/3	X_1 Y_1 Y_2
3/4	X_1 Y_1 Y_2 X_3
5/6	X_1 Y_1 Y_2 X_3 Y_4 X_6
7/8	X_1 Y_1 Y_2 Y_3 Y_4 X_5 X_6 X_7

(b)

FIGURE 10.47
(a) The mother inner coder of DVB produces 100 percent redundancy, but this can be punctured by subsampling the X and Y data to give five different code rates, as (b) shows.

These have 204 bytes as before, but the effect of the interleave is that adjacent bytes in the input are 17 bytes apart in the output. Each output block contains data from 12 input blocks, making the data resistant to burst errors.

Following the interleave, the energy-dispersal process takes place. The pseudo-random sequence runs over eight outer blocks and is synchronised by inverting the transport stream packet sync symbol in every eighth block. The packet sync symbols are not randomized. The inner coding process of DVB is shown in Figure 10.47. Input data are serialized and pass down a shift register. Exclusive-OR gates produce convolutional parity symbols X and Y, such that the output bit rate is twice the input bit rate. Under the worst reception conditions, this 100 percent redundancy offers the most powerful correction, with the penalty that a low data rate is delivered. However, Figure 10.47 also shows that a variety of inner redundancy factors can be used from 1/2 down to 1/8 of the transmitted bit rate. The X, Y data from the inner coder are subsampled, such that the coding is punctured.

The DVB standard allows the use of QPSK, 16-QUAM, or 64-QUAM coding in an OFDM system. There are five possible inner code rates, and four different guard intervals, which can be used with each modulation scheme. Thus for each modulation scheme there are 20 possible transport stream bit rates in the standard DVB channel, each of which requires a different receiver SNR. The broadcaster can select any suitable balance between transport stream bit rate and coverage area. For a given transmitter location and power, reception over a larger area may require a channel code with a smaller number of bits per second per hertz, and this reduces the bit rate that can be delivered in a standard channel. Alternatively, a higher amount of inner redundancy means that the proportion of the transmitted bit rate that is data goes down. Thus for wider coverage the broadcaster will have to send fewer programs in the multiplex or use higher compression factors.

THE DVB RECEIVER

Figure 10.48 shows a block diagram of a DVB receiver. The off-air RF signal is fed to a mixer driven by the local oscillator. The IF output of the mixer is band-pass filtered and supplied to the ADC, which outputs a digital IF signal for the FFT stage. The FFT is initially analysed to find the higher-level pilot signals. If these are not in the correct channels the local oscillator frequency is incorrect and it will be changed until the pilots emerge from the FFT in the right channels.

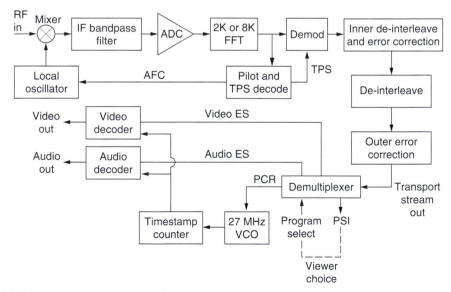

FIGURE 10.48
DVB receiver block diagram. See text for details.

The data in the pilots will be decoded to tell the receiver how many carriers and what inner redundancy rate, guard band rate, and modulation scheme are in use in the remaining carriers. The FFT magnitude information is also a measure of the equalization required.

The FFT outputs are demodulated into 2 K or 8 K bitstreams and these are multiplexed to produce a serial signal. This is subject to inner error correction, which corrects random errors. The data are then de-interleaved to break up burst errors and then the outer R-S error correction operates.

The output of the R-S correction will then be derandomized to become an MPEG transport stream once more. The derandomizing is synchronised by the transmission of inverted sync patterns. The receiver must select a PID of 0 and wait until a PAT (Program Associate Table) is transmitted. This will describe the available programs by listing the PIDs of the PMTs (Program Map Table). By looking for these packets the receiver can determine what PIDs to select to receive any video and audio elementary streams. When an elementary stream is selected, some of the packets will have extended headers containing a PCR (program clock reference). These codes are used to synchronise the 27 MHz clock in the receiver to the one in the MPEG encoder of the desired program.

The 27 MHz clock is divided down to drive the time stamp counter so that audio and video emerge from the decoder at the correct rate and with lip sync. It should be appreciated that time stamps are relative, not absolute. The time stamp count advances by a fixed amount each picture, but the exact count is meaningless. Thus the decoder can establish the frame rate of the video only from time stamps, but not the precise timing. In practice the receiver has finite buffering memory between the demultiplexer and the MPEG decoder. If the displayed video timing is too late, the buffer will tend to overflow, whereas if the displayed video timing is too early the decoding may not be completed.

The receiver can advance or retard the time stamp counter during lockup so that it places the output timing midway between these extremes.

ATSC

The ATSC system is an alternative way of delivering a transport stream, but it is considerably cruder than DVB and supports only one transport stream bit rate of 19.28 Mbps. If any change in the service area is needed, this will require a change in transmitter power. Figure 10.49 shows a block diagram of an ATSC transmitter. Incoming transport stream packets are randomized, except for the sync pattern, for energy dispersal. Figure 10.50 shows the randomizer.

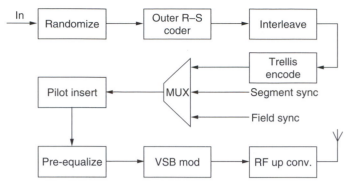

FIGURE 10.49
Block diagram of ATSC transmitter. See text for details.

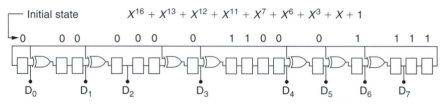

FIGURE 10.50
The randomizer of ATSC. The twisted ring counter is preset to the initial state shown for each data field. It is then clocked once per byte and the eight outputs D0–D7 are X-ORed with the data byte.

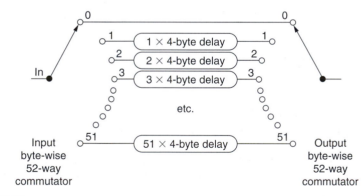

FIGURE 10.51
The ATSC convolutional interleaver spreads adjacent bytes over a period of about 4 ms.

The outer correction code includes the whole packet except for the sync byte. Thus there are 187 bytes of data in each code word, and 20 bytes of R-S redundancy are added to make a 207-byte code word. After outer coding, a convolutional interleave shown in Figure 10.51 is used. This re-orders data over a time

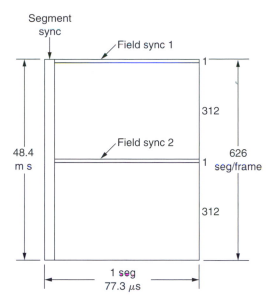

FIGURE 10.52
The ATSC data frame is transmitted one segment at a time. Segment sync denotes the beginning of each segment and the segments are counted from the field sync signals.

span of about 4 ms. Interleave simply exchanges content between packets, but without changing the packet structure.

Figure 10.52 shows that the result of outer coding and interleave is a data frame that is divided into two fields of 313 segments each. The frame is transmitted by scanning it horizontally a segment at a time. There is some similarity with a traditional analog video signal here, because there is a sync pulse at the beginning of each segment and a field sync that occupies two segments of the frame. Data segment sync repeats every 77.3 ms, a segment rate of 12,933 Hz, whereas a frame has a period of 48.4 ms. The field sync segments contain a training sequence to drive the adaptive equalizer in the receiver.

The data content of the frame is subject to trellis coding, which converts each pair of data bits into three channel bits inside an inner interleave. The trellis coder is shown in Figure 10.53 and the interleave in Figure 10.54. Figure 10.53 also shows how the three channel bits map to the eight signal levels in the 8-VSB modulator. Figure 10.55 shows the data segment after eight-level coding. The sync pattern of the transport stream packet, which was not included in the error-correction code, has been replaced by a segment sync waveform.

This acts as a timing reference to allow de-serialized of the segment, but as the two levels of the sync pulse are standardised, it also acts as an amplitude reference

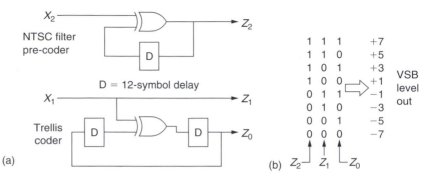

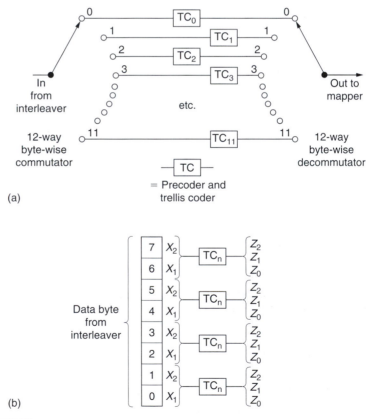

FIGURE 10.53
(a) The precoder and trellis coder of ATSC converts 2 data bits, X_1 and X_2, to 3 output bits, Z_0, Z_1, and Z_2. (b) The Z_0, Z_1, and Z_2 output bits map to the eight-level code as shown.

FIGURE 10.54
The inner interleave (a) of ATSC makes the trellis coding operate as 12 parallel channels working on every 12th byte to improve error resistance. The interleave is byte-wise, and, as (b) shows, each byte is divided into four di-bits for coding into the tri-bits Z_0, Z_1, and Z_2.

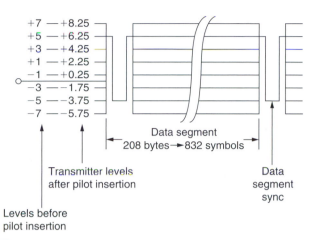

FIGURE 10.55
ATSC data segment. Note the sync pattern, which acts as a timing and amplitude reference. The eight levels are shifted up by 1.25 to create a DC component resulting in a pilot at the carrier frequency.

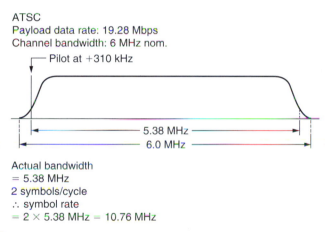

FIGURE 10.56
The spectrum of ATSC and its associated bit and symbol rates. Note pilot at carrier frequency created by DC offset in multi-level coder.

for the eight-level slicer in the receiver. The eight-level signal is subject to a DC offset so that some transmitter energy appears at the carrier frequency to act as a pilot. Each eight-level symbol carries 2 data bits and so there are 832 symbols in each segment. As the segment rate is 12,933 Hz, the symbol rate is 10.76 MHz and so this will require 5.38 MHz of bandwidth in a single sideband. Figure 10.56 shows the transmitter spectrum. The lower sideband is vestigial and an overall channel width of 6 MHz results.

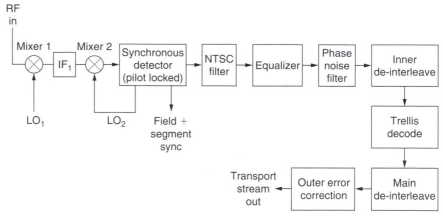

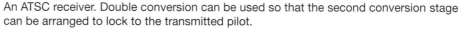

FIGURE 10.57

An ATSC receiver. Double conversion can be used so that the second conversion stage can be arranged to lock to the transmitted pilot.

Figure 10.57 shows an ATSC receiver. The first stages of the receiver are designed to lock to the pilot in the transmitted signal. This then allows the eight-level signal to be sampled at the right times. This process will allow location of the segment sync and then the field sync signals. Once the receiver is synchronised, the symbols in each segment can be decoded. The inner or trellis coder corrects for random errors and then, following de-interleave, the R-S coder corrects burst errors. After de-randomizing, standard transport stream sync patterns are added to the output data.

In practice ATSC transmissions will experience co-channel interference from NTSC transmitters and the ATSC scheme allows the use of an NTSC rejection filter. Figure 10.58 shows that most of the energy of NTSC is at the carrier, sub-carrier, and sound carrier frequencies. A comb filter with a suitable delay can produce nulls or notches at these frequencies. However, the delay-and-add process in the comb filter also causes another effect. When two eight-level signals are added together, the result is a 16-level signal. This will be corrupted by noise of half the level that would corrupt an eight-level signal. However, the 16-level signal contains redundancy because it corresponds to the combinations of four bits, whereas only two bits are being transmitted. This allows a form of error correction to be used.

The ATSC inner precoder results in a known relationship existing between symbols independent of the data. The time delays in the inner interleave are designed to be compatible with the delay in the NTSC rejection comb filter.

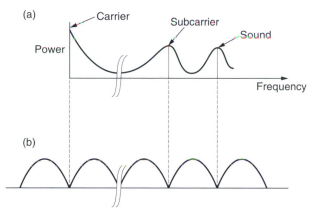

FIGURE 10.58
(a) Spectrum of typical analog transmitter showing maximum power at carrier, subcarrier, and audio carrier. (b) A comb filter with a suitable delay can notch out NTSC interference. The precoding of ATSC is designed to work with the necessary receiver delay.

This limits the number of paths the received waveform can take through a time/voltage graph called a trellis. Where a signal is in error it takes a path sufficiently near to the correct one that the correct one can be implied. ATSC uses a training sequence sent once every data field, but is otherwise helpless against multipath reception, as tests have shown. In urban areas, ATSC must have a correctly oriented directional antenna to reject reflections. Unfortunately the American viewer has been brought up to believe that television reception is possible with a pair of "rabbit ears" on top of the TV set and ATSC will not work like this. Mobile reception is not practicable. As a result the majority of the world's broadcasters appear to be favouring an OFDM-based system.

NETWORKS

A network is basically a communication resource that is shared for economic reasons. Like any shared resource, decisions have to be made somewhere and somehow about how the resource is to be used. In the absence of such decisions the resultant chaos would be such that the resource might as well not exist. In communications networks the resource is the ability to convey data from any node or port to any other. On a particular cable, clearly only one transaction of this kind can take place at any one instant, even though in practice many nodes will simultaneously want to transmit data. Arbitration is needed to determine which node is allowed to transmit.

There are a number of different arbitration protocols and these have evolved to support the needs of different types of networks. In small networks, such as LANs, a single point failure that halts the entire network may be acceptable, whereas in a public transport network owned by a telecommunications company, the network will be redundant so that if a particular link fails data may be sent via an alternative route. A link that has reached its maximum capacity may also be supplanted by transmission over alternative routes. In physically small networks, arbitration may be carried out in a single location. This is fast and efficient, but if the arbitrator fails it leaves the system completely crippled. The processor buses in computers work in this way. In centrally arbit rated systems the arbitrator needs to know the structure of the system and the status of all the nodes. Following a configuration change, due perhaps to the installation of new equipment, the arbitrator needs to be told what the new configuration is or to have a mechanism that allows it to explore the network and learn the configuration. Central arbitration is suitable only for small networks that change their configuration infrequently.

In other networks the arbitration is distributed so that some decision-making ability exists in every node. This is less efficient but is does allow at least some of the network to continue operating after a component failure. Distributed arbitration also means that each node is self-sufficient and so no changes need to be made if the network is reconfigured by adding or deleting a node. This is the only possible approach in wide area networks in which the structure may be very complex and change dynamically in the event of failures or overload.

Ethernet uses distributed arbitration. FireWire is capable of using both types of arbitration. A small amount of decision-making ability is built into every node so that distributed arbitration is possible. However, if one of the nodes happens to be a computer, it can run a centralized arbitration algorithm.

The physical structure of a network is subject to some variation, as Figure 10.59 shows. In radial networks (Figure 10.59a), each port has a unique cable connection to a device called a hub. The hub must have one connection for every port and this limits the number of ports. However, a cable failure will result in the loss of only one port. In a ring system (b) the nodes are connected like a daisy chain, with each node acting as a feedthrough. In this case the arbitration requirement must be distributed. With some protocols, a single cable break does not stop the network operating.

Depending on the protocol, simultaneous transactions may be possible provided they do not require the same cable. For example, in a storage network a

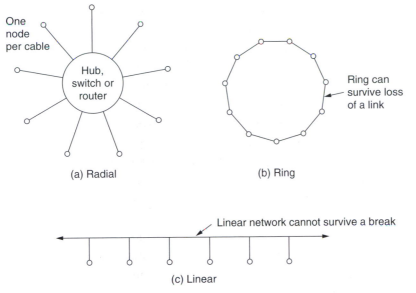

FIGURE 10.59
Network configurations. (a) The radial system uses one cable to each node. (b) The ring system uses less cable than radial. (c) The linear system is simple but has no redundancy.

disk drive may be outputting data to an editor whilst another drive is backing up data to a tape streamer. For the lowest cost, all nodes are physically connected in parallel to the same cable. Figure 10.59c shows that a cable break would divide the network into two halves, but it is possible that the impedance mismatch at the break could stop both halves working.

NETWORK ARBITRATION

One of the concepts involved in arbitration is priority, which is fundamental to providing an appropriate quality of service. If two processes both want to use a network, the one with the highest priority would normally go first. Attributing priority must be done carefully because some of the results are non-intuitive. For example, it may be beneficial to give a high priority to a humble device that has a low data rate for the simple reason that if it is given use of the network it will not need it for long. In a television environment transactions concerned with on-air processes would have priority over file transfers concerning production and editing.

When a device gains access to the network to perform a transaction, generally no other transaction can take place until it has finished. Consequently it is important to limit the amount of time that a given port can stay on the bus.

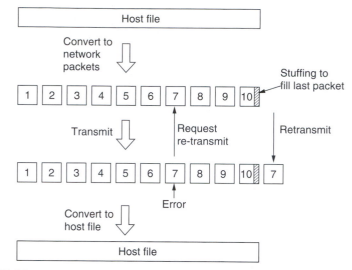

FIGURE 10.60
Receiving a file that has been divided into packets allows for the re-transmission of just the packet in error.

In this way when the time limit expires, a further arbitration must take place. The result is that the network resource rotates between transactions rather than one transfer hogging the resource and shutting out everyone else.

It follows from the presence of a time (or data quantity) limit that ports must have the means to break large files up into frames or cells and reassemble them on reception. This process is sometimes called *adaptation*. If the data to be sent originally exist at a fixed bit rate, some buffering will be needed so that the data can be time-compressed into the available frames. Each frame must be contiguously numbered and the system must transmit a file size or word count so that the receiving node knows when it has received every frame in the file.

The error-detection system interacts with this process because if any frame is in error on reception, the receiving node can ask for a re-transmission of the frame. This is more efficient than re-transmitting the whole file. Figure 10.60 shows the flowchart for a receiving node.

Breaking files into frames helps to keep down the delay experienced by each process using the network. Figure 10.61 shows that each frame may be stored ready for transmission in a silo memory. It is possible to make the priority a function of the number of frames in the silo, as this is a direct measure of how long a process has been kept waiting. Isochronous systems must do this to meet maximum delay specifications. Once frame transmission has completed, the arbitrator

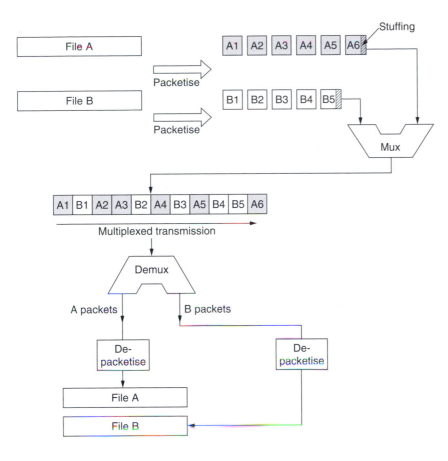

FIGURE 10.61
Files are broken into frames or packets for multiplexing with packets from other users.
Short packets minimize the time between the arrival of successive packets. The priority
of the multiplexing must favour isochronous data over asynchronous data.

will determine which process sends a frame next by examining the depth of all
the frame buffers. MPEG transport stream multiplexers and networks delivering
MPEG data must work in this way because the transfer is isochronous and the
amount of buffering in a decoder is limited for economic reasons.

A central arbitrator is relatively simple to implement because when all decisions are taken centrally there can be no timing difficulty (assuming a well-
engineered system). In a distributed system, there is an extra difficulty due to
the finite time taken for signals to travel down the data paths between nodes.

Figure 10.62 shows the structure of Ethernet, which uses a protocol called
CSMA/CD (carrier sense multiple access with collision detect) developed by

DEC and Xerox. This is a distributed arbitration network in which each node follows some simple rules. The first of these is not to transmit if an existing bus signal is detected. The second is not to transmit more than a certain quantity of data before releasing the bus. Devices wanting to use the bus will see bus signals and so will wait until the present bus transaction finishes. This must happen at some point because of the frame size limit. When the frame is completed, signalling should cease. The first device to sense the bus becoming free and to assert its own signal will prevent any other nodes transmitting according to the first rule. Where numerous devices are present it is possible to give them a priority structure by providing a delay between sensing the bus coming free and beginning a transaction. High-priority devices will have a short delay so they get in first. Lower-priority devices will be able to start a transaction only if the high-priority devices do not need to transfer.

It might be thought that these rules would be enough and everything would be fine. Unfortunately the finite signal speed means that there is a flaw in the system. Figure 10.62 shows why. Device A is transmitting and devices B and C both want to transmit and have equal priority. At the end of A's transaction, devices B and C see the bus become free at the same instant and start a transaction. With two devices driving the bus, the resultant waveform is meaningless. This is known as a collision and all nodes must have means to recover from it. First, each node will read the bus signal at all times. When a node drives the bus, it will also read back the bus signal and compare it with what was sent. Clearly if the two are the same all is well, but if there is a difference, this must be because a collision has occurred and two devices are trying to influence the bus voltage at once.

If a collision is detected, both colliding devices will sense the disparity between the transmitted and readback signals, and both will release the bus to terminate

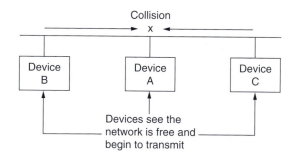

FIGURE 10.62
In Ethernet collisions can occur because of the finite speed of the signals. A "back-off" algorithm handles collisions, but they do reduce the network throughput.

the collision. However, there is no point is adhering to the simple protocol to reconnect because this will simply result in another collision. Instead each device has a built-in delay, which must expire before another attempt is made to transmit. This delay is not fixed, but is controlled by a random-number generator and so changes from transaction to transaction.

The probability of two node devices arriving at the same delay is infinitesimally small.

Consequently, if a collision does occur, both devices will drop the bus, and they will start their back-off timers. When the first timer expires, that device will transmit and the other will see the transmission and remain silent. In this way the collision is not only handled, but also prevented from happening again. The performance of Ethernet is usually specified in terms of the bit rate at which the cabling runs. However, this rate is academic because it is not available all the time. In a real network bit rate is lost by the need to send headers and error-correction codes and by the loss of time due to interframe spaces and collision handling. As the demand goes up, the number of collisions increases and throughput goes down. Collision-based arbitrators do not handle congestion well.

An alternative method of arbitration developed by IBM is shown in Figure 10.63. This is known as a *token ring* system. All the nodes have an input and an output and are connected in a ring that must be complete for the system to work. Data circulate in one direction only. If data are not addressed to a node that receives them, the data will be passed on. When the data arrive at

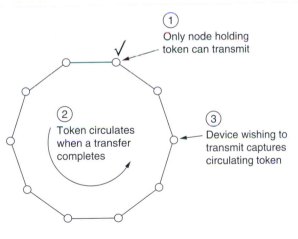

FIGURE 10.63
In a token ring system only the node in possession of the token can transmit, so collisions are impossible. In very large rings the token circulation time causes loss of throughput.

the addressed node, that node will capture the data as well as passing them on with an acknowledge symbol added. Thus the data packet travels right around the ring back to the sending node. When the sending node receives the acknowledge, it will transmit a token packet. This token packet passes to the next node, which will pass it on if it does not wish to transmit.

If no device wishes to transmit, the token will circulate endlessly. However, if a device has data to send, it simply waits until the token arrives again and captures it. This node can now transmit data in the knowledge that there cannot be a collision because no other node has the token. In simple token ring systems, the transmitting node transmits idle characters after the data packet has been sent in order to maintain synchronisation. The idle character transmission will continue until the acknowledge arrives. In the case of long packets the acknowledge will arrive before the packet has all been sent and no idle characters are necessary. However, with short packets idle characters will be generated. These idle characters use up ring bandwidth.

Later token ring systems use ETR (early token release). After the packet has been transmitted, the sending node sends a token straight away. Another node wishing to transmit can do so as soon as the current packet has passed.

It might be thought that the nodes on the ring would transmit in their physical order, but this is not the case because a priority system exists. Each node can have a different priority if necessary. If a high-priority node wishes to transmit, when a packet from elsewhere passes through that node, the node will set *reservation bits* with its own priority level. When the sending node finishes and transmits a token, it will copy that priority level into the token. In this way nodes with a lower priority level will pass the token on instead of capturing it. The token will ultimately arrive at the high-priority node.

The token ring system has the advantage that it does not waste throughput with collisions and so the full capacity is always available. However, if the ring is broken the entire network fails.

In Ethernet the performance is degraded by the number of transactions, not the number of nodes, whereas in token ring the performance is degraded by the number of nodes.

FIREWIRE

FireWire[10] is actually an Apple Computers, Inc., trade name for the interface that is formally known as IEEE 1394-1995. It was originally intended as a digital

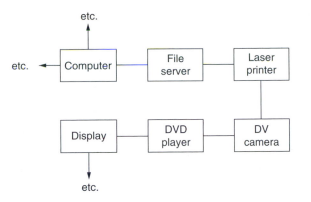

FIGURE 10.64
FireWire supports radial (star) or daisy-chain connection. Two-port devices pass on signals destined for a more distant device—they can do this even when powered down.

audio network, but grew out of recognition. FireWire is more than just an interface as it can be used to form networks and if used with a computer effectively extends the computer's data bus. Figure 10.64 shows that devices are simply connected together as any combination of daisy-chain or star network.

Any pair of devices can communicate in either direction, and arbitration ensures that only one device transmits at a time. Intermediate devices simply pass on transmissions. This can continue even if the intermediate device is powered down, as the FireWire carries power to keep repeater functions active. Communications are divided into cycles, which have a period of 125μs. During a cycle, there are 64 time slots. During each time slot, any one node can communicate with any other, but in the next slot, a different pair of nodes may communicate. Thus FireWire is best described as a TDM (time-division multiplexed) system. There will be a new arbitration between the nodes for each cycle.

FireWire is eminently suitable for video/computer convergent applications because it can simultaneously support asynchronous transfers of non-real-time computer data and isochronous transfers of real-time audio/video data. It can do this because the arbitration process allocates a fixed proportion of slots for isochronous data (about 80 percent) and these have a higher priority in the arbitration than the asynchronous data. The higher the data rate a given node needs, the more time slots it will be allocated. Thus a given bit rate can be guaranteed throughout a transaction; a prerequisite of real-time A/V data transfer.

It is the sophistication of the arbitration system that makes FireWire remarkable. Some of the arbitration is in hardware at each node, but some is in software that only needs to be at one node. The full functionality requires a computer, somewhere in the system, which runs the isochronous bus management arbitration. Without this only asynchronous transfers are possible. It is possible to add or remove devices whilst the system is working. When a device is added the system will recognize it through a periodic learning process. Essentially every node on the system transmits in turn so that the structure becomes clear.

The electrical interface of FireWire is shown in Figure 10.65. It consists of two twisted pairs for signalling and a pair of power conductors. The twisted pairs carry differential signals of about 220 mV swinging around a common mode voltage of about 1.9 V with an impedance of 112 Ohms.

Figure 10.66 shows how the data are transmitted. The host data are simply serialized and used to modulate twisted pair A. The other twisted pair (B) carries a signal called a strobe, which is the exclusive-OR of the data and the clock. Thus whenever a run of identical bits results in no transitions in the data, the strobe signal will carry transitions. At the receiver another exclusive-OR gate adds data and strobe to re-create the clock.

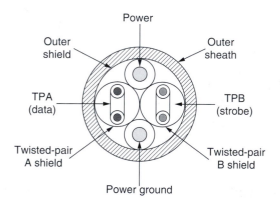

FIGURE 10.65
FireWire uses twin twisted pairs and a power pair.

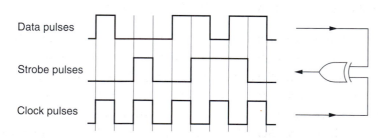

FIGURE 10.66
The strobe signal is the X-OR of the data and the bit clock. The data and strobe signals together form a self-clocking system.

This signalling technique is subject to skew between the two twisted pairs and this limits cable lengths to about 10 m between nodes. Thus FireWire is not a long-distance interface technique; instead it is very useful for interconnecting a large number of devices in close proximity. Using a copper interconnect, FireWire can run at 100, 200, or 400 Mbps, depending on the specific hardware.

BROADBAND NETWORKS AND ATM

Broadband ISDN (B-ISDN) is the successor to N-ISDN, and in addition to offering more bandwidth, it gives practical solutions to the delivery of any conceivable type of data. The flexibility with which ATM operates means that intermittent, or one-off, data transactions that require only asynchronous delivery can take place alongside isochronous MPEG video delivery. This is known as *application independence*, whereby the sophistication of isochronous delivery does not raise the cost of asynchronous data. In this way, generic data, video, speech, and combinations thereof can co-exist.

ATM is multiplexed, but it is not time-division multiplexed. TDM is inefficient because if a transaction does not fill its allotted bandwidth, the capacity is wasted. ATM does not offer fixed blocks of bandwidth, but allows infinitely variable bandwidth to each transaction. This is done by converting all host data into small fixed-size cells at the adaptation layer. The greater the bandwidth needed by a transaction, the more cells per second are allocated to that transaction. This approach is superior to the fixed-bandwidth approach, because if the bit rate of a particular transaction falls, the cells released can be used for other transactions so that the full bandwidth is always available.

As all cells are identical in size, a multiplexer can assemble cells from many transactions in an arbitrary order. The exact order is determined by the quality of service required, where the time positioning of isochronous data would be determined first, with asynchronous data filling the gaps.

Figure 10.67 shows how a broadband system might be implemented. The transport network would typically be optical-fibre based, using SONET (synchronous optical network) or SDH (synchronous digital hierarchy). These standards differ in minor respects. Figure 10.68 shows the bit rates available in each. Lower bit rates will be used in the access networks, which will use different technology such as xDSL. SONET and SDH assemble ATM cells into a structure, known as a container, in the interests of efficiency. Containers are passed intact between exchanges in the transport network. The cells in a container need not

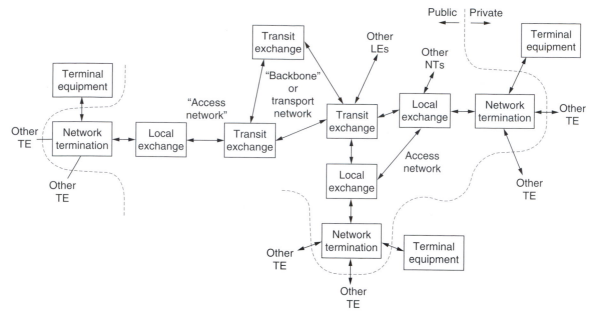

FIGURE 10.67
Structure and terminology of a broadband network. See text.

End user	Access network	Transport network	Access network	End user
		155 or 622 Mbps typical (no actual limit)	50 Mbps (subject to variation)	2–45 Mbps (lower rate typical)

FIGURE 10.68
Bit rates available in SONET and SDH.

belong to the same transaction, they simply need to be going the same way for at least one transport network leg.

The cell-routing mechanism of ATM is unusual and deserves explanation. In conventional networks, a packet must carry the complete destination address so that at every exchange it can be routed closer to its destination. The exact route by which the packet travels cannot be anticipated and successive packets in the same transaction may take different routes. This is known as a *connection-less* protocol. In contrast, ATM is a *connection-oriented* protocol. Before data can be transferred, the network must set up an end-to-end route. Once this is done, the ATM cells do not need to carry a complete destination address. Instead they need only to carry enough addressing so that an exchange or switch can

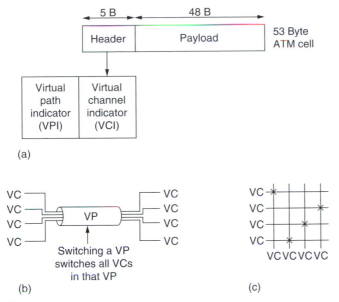

FIGURE 10.69
(a) The ATM cell carries routing information in the header. (b) ATM paths carrying a group of channels can be switched in a virtual path switch. (c) Individual channel switching requires a virtual channel switch, which is more complex and causes more delay.

distinguish between all the expected transactions. This is effectively an application of compression applied to address space.

The end-to-end route is known as a *virtual channel,* which consists of a series of *virtual links* between switches. The term "virtual channel" is used because the system acts like a dedicated channel even though physically it is not. When the transaction is completed the route can be dismantled so that the bandwidth is freed for other users. In some cases, such as delivery of a TV station's output to a transmitter, or as a replacement for analog cable TV, the route can be set up continuously to form what is known as a *permanent virtual channel.*

The addressing in the cells ensures that all cells with the same address take the same path, but owing to the multiplexed nature of ATM, at other times and with other cells a completely different routing scheme may exist. Thus the routing structure for a particular transaction always passes cells by the same route, but the next cell may belong to another transaction and will have a different address causing it to be routed in another way.

The addressing structure is hierarchical. Figure 10.69a shows the ATM cell and its header. The cell address is divided into two fields, the virtual channel identifier and the virtual path identifier. Virtual paths are logical groups of virtual channels that happen to be going the same way. An example would be the output of a video-on-demand server travelling to the first switch. The virtual path concept is useful because all cells in the same virtual path can share the same container in a transport network. A virtual path switch, shown in Figure 10.69b, can operate at the container level, whereas a virtual channel switch (c) would need to dismantle and reassemble containers.

When a route is set up, at each switch a table is created. When a cell is received at a switch the VPI (virtual path indicator) and/or VCI (virtual channel indicator) codes are looked up in the table and used for two purposes. First, the configuration of the switch is obtained, so that this switch will correctly route the cell; second, the VPI and/or VCI codes may be updated so that they correctly control the next switch. This process repeats until the cell arrives at its destination. To set up a path, the initiating device will initially send cells containing an ATM destination address, the bandwidth, and the quality of service required. The first switch will reply with a message containing the VPI/VCI codes, which are to be used for this channel. The message from the initiator will propagate to the destination, creating lookup tables in each switch. At each switch the logic will add the requested bandwidth to the existing bandwidth in use to check that the requested quality of service can be met. If this succeeds for the whole channel, the destination will reply with a connect message, which propagates back to the initiating device as confirmation that the channel has been set up.

The connect message contains a unique call reference value, which identifies this transaction. This is necessary because an initiator such as a file server may be initiating many channels and the connect messages will not necessarily return in the same order as the set-up messages were sent. The last switch will confirm receipt of the connect message to the destination and the initiating device will confirm receipt of the connect message to the first switch.

ATM AALs

ATM works by dividing all real data messages into cells of 48 bytes each. At the receiving end, the original message must be re-created. This can take many forms. Figure 10.70 shows some possibilities. The message may be a generic data file having no implied timing structure or a serial bitstream with a fixed clock frequency, known as UTD (unstructured data transfer). It may be a burst of data bytes from a TDM system.

Generic data file having no timebase		
Constant bit rate serial data stream		
Audio/video data requiring a timebase		
Compressed A/V data with fixed bit rate		
Compressed A/V data with variable bit rate		

FIGURE 10.70
Types of data that may need adapting to ATM.

ATM Application Layer	Convergence sublayer	Recovers timing of original data
	Segmentation and reassembly	Divides data into cells for transport Reassembles original data format

FIGURE 10.71
ATM adaptation layer has two sublayers, segmentation and convergence.

The application layer in ATM has two sublayers, shown in Figure 10.71. The first is the SAR (segmentation and reassembly) sublayer, which must divide the message into cells and rebuild it to get the binary data right. The second is the CS (convergence sublayer), which recovers the timing structure of the original message. It is this feature that makes ATM so appropriate for delivery of audio/visual material. Conventional networks such as the Internet do not have this ability.

To deliver a particular quality of service, the adaptation layer and the ATM layer work together. Effectively the adaptation layer will place constraints on the ATM layer, such as cell delay, and the ATM layer will meet those constraints without needing to know why. Provided the constraints are met, the adaptation layer can rebuild the message. The variety of message types and timing constraints leads to the adaptation layer having a variety of forms.

The adaptation layers that are most relevant to MPEG applications are AAL-1 and AAL-5. AAL-1 is suitable for transmitting MPEG-2 multiprogram transport streams at constant bit rate and is standardised for this purpose in ETS 300814 for DVB application. AAL-1 has an integral FEC (forward error correction) scheme. AAL-5 is optimized for SPTS (single-program transport streams) at a variable bit rate and has no FEC.

AAL-1 takes as an input the 188-byte transport stream packets that are created by a standard MPEG-2 multiplexer. The transport stream bit rate must be constant

AES 47

AES 47 is a standard designed to facilitate transmission of digital audio over ATM. It supports multiple channels of uncompressed AES/EBU digital audio and transparently carries the entire AES/EBU bitstream. Using the networking techniques explained in this chapter to the full, it exploits the bandwidth reservation technology of the ATM Quality of Service mechanism to ensure synchronous audio sample delivery with low latency.

Multiple AES/EBU channels can be carried, but they do not need to have the same sampling rate. AES 53 describes how time stamps (see MPEG Packets and Time Stamps) can be used to ensure isochronous reception.

The isochronous capability of AES 47 means that the master audio sampling clock used at the data source is re-created at the destination. For real-time use, the destination master sampling clock must be synchronous with the source clock. This may be achieved using a common reference available to both sites, such as GPS. Alternatively a sampling rate convertor may be employed so the source and destination remain unlocked. This will, however, destroy the transparency of the link. Accordingly, some equipment will drop or repeat samples during silent or very quiet passages to avoid rate conversion.

but it does not matter if statistical multiplexing has been used within the transport stream.

The Reed–Solomon FEC of AAL-1 uses a code word of size 128 so that the code words consist of 124 bytes of data and four bytes of redundancy, making 128 bytes in all. Thirty-one 188-byte packets are restructured into this format. The 256-byte code words are then subject to a block interleave. Figure 10.72 shows that 47 such code words are assembled in rows in RAM and then columns are read out. These columns are 47 bytes long and, with the addition of an AAL header byte, make up a 48-byte ATM packet payload. In this way the interleave block is transmitted in 128 ATM cells. The result of the FEC and interleave is that the loss of up to four cells in 128 can be corrected, or a random error of up to two bytes can be corrected in each cell. This FEC system allows most errors in the ATM layer to be corrected so that no retransmissions are needed. This is important for isochronous operation.

The AAL header has a number of functions. One of these is to identify the first ATM cell in the interleave block of 128 cells. Another function is to run a modulo-8 cell counter to detect missing or out-of-sequence ATM cells. If a cell simply fails to arrive, the sequence jump can be detected and used to flag the FEC system so that it can correct the missing cell by erasure (see Chapter 8). In a manner similar to the use of program clock reference in MPEG, AAL-1 embeds a timing code in ATM cell headers. This is called the synchronous residual time stamp (SRTS) and in conjunction with the ATM network clock allows the receiving AAL device to reconstruct the original data bit rate. This is

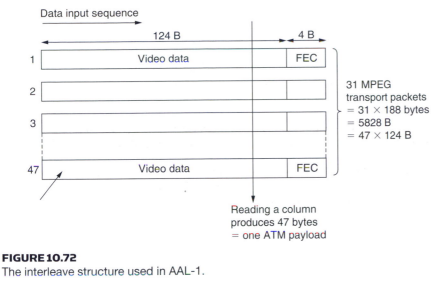

FIGURE 10.72
The interleave structure used in AAL-1.

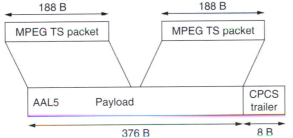

FIGURE 10.73
The AAL-5 adaptation layer can pack MPEG transport packets in this way.

important because in MPEG applications it prevents the PCR jitter specification being exceeded.

In AAL-5 there is no error correction and the adaptation layer simply reformats MPEG transport stream blocks into ATM cells. Figure 10.73 shows one way in which this can be done. Two transport stream blocks of 188 bytes are associated with an eight-byte trailer known as CPCS (common part convergence sublayer). The presence of the trailer makes a total of 384 bytes that can be carried in eight ATM cells. AAL-5 does not offer constant delay, and external buffering will be required, controlled by reading the MPEG PCRs to reconstruct the original time axis.

References

1. SMPTE 259M, 10-bit 4:2:2 Component and $4F_{sc}$ NTSC Composite Digital Signals—Serial Digital Interface.

2. SMPTE 292M, Bit-Serial Digital Interface for High Definition Television Systems.

3. EBU Doc. Tech. 3246.

4. SMPTE 125M, Television—Bit Parallel Digital Interface—Component Video Signal 4:2:2.

5. SMPTE 305M, Serial Data Transport Interface.

6. EIA RS-422A. Electronic Industries Association, 2001 Eye Street NW, Washington, DC 20006, USA.

7. Smart, D.L. Transmission performance of digital audio serial interface on audio tie lines. BBC Designs Department Technical Memorandum 3.296/84.

8. European Broadcasting Union. Specification of the digital audio interface. EBU Doc. Tech. 3250.

9. Rorden, B., and Graham, M. A proposal for integrating digital audio distribution into TV production. J. SMPTE, 606–608 (1992).

10. Wicklegren, I.J. The facts about FireWire. IEEE Spectrum, 19–25 (1997).

Index

665